BETTING AGAINST AMERICA

BETTING AGAINST AMERICA

AMERICA

The Axis Powers' Views of the United States

HARRY YEIDE

CASEMATE
Pennsylvania & Yorkshire

Published in the United States of America and Great Britain in 2024 by
CASEMATE PUBLISHERS
1950 Lawrence Road, Havertown, PA 19083, USA
and
47 Church Street, Barnsley, S70 2AS, UK

Copyright 2024 © Harry Yeide

Hardback Edition: ISBN 978-1-63624-411-2
Digital Edition: ISBN 978-1-63624-412-9

A CIP record for this book is available from the British Library

All rights reserved. No part of this book may be reproduced or transmitted in any form or by any means, electronic or mechanical including photocopying, recording or by any information storage and retrieval system, without permission from the publisher in writing.

Printed and bound in the United Kingdom by CPI Group (UK) Ltd, Croydon, CR0 4YY

Typeset in India by Lapiz Digital Services, Chennai.

For a complete list of Casemate titles, please contact:

CASEMATE PUBLISHERS (US)
Telephone (610) 853-9131
Fax (610) 853-9146
Email: casemate@casematepublishers.com
www.casematepublishers.com

CASEMATE PUBLISHERS (UK)
Telephone (0)1226 734350
Email: casemate@casemateuk.com
www.casemateuk.com

Contents

Preface vi
Acknowledgements xii

1	Fateful Decisions Amidst Global Decay	1
2	1937: The First Pre-World War Year	34
3	1938: America the Afterthought	47
4	1939: War Goes Global	58
5	1940: Japan Opts for War	78
6	1940: Germany Dismisses America—Until It Beats France	100
7	Early 1941: Axis Resolution of the America Problem	114
8	Late 1941: War!	166
9	Early 1942: The Era of Axis Optimism	189
10	Late 1942: The Shock of Reality	216
11	Early 1943: Months of Foreboding	243
12	Late 1943: America Becomes a Rising Priority	260
13	Early 1944: The End Becomes Visible	287
14	Late 1944: Strategic Defeat	304
15	1945: Annihilation	350
16	Taking Stock	384

Appendices 389
Endnotes 407
Glossary 465
Bibliography 467
Index 475

Preface

This book is a red team exercise, looking at the events and decisions that led to the Axis powers going to war against America, and those during the war itself, from the enemy's perspective. During the Cold War, the Western powers traditionally identified the friendly force in military exercises as the blue force, and the enemy as the red force. The participants in an exercise faced a scenario, such as, should we go to war? When playing the red team, the participants emulate the roles of important decision-makers on the opposing side. They attempt to make decisions within the logic of that side's circumstances, known past behavior, known characteristics of the individuals themselves, and actions of the blue team. If the event involves multiple players, a team of session managers may introduce unexpected events into the scenario, just like what happens in the real world.

Why did I write this book? One editor said what would be interesting was the enemy's views of America that underpinned their decision to go to war. Given America's industrial base, why did that make sense? During my time in the intelligence community, I was always a contrarian and spent more than two wonderful years doing red cell analysis. The more I thought about his question, the more it intrigued me. I also wanted to watch the war through their eyes, hoping in part to find that moment when they realized the American enemy was going to contribute greatly to their demise.

An earlier generation of historians did excellent work examining German thinking about the United States before the war, though their books are long out of print. Chief among them are two works published in 1967. James V. Compton produced *The Swastika and the Eagle*, which was nicely summarized on the book cover with, "Germany's myopic view of America in the fatal years before World War II." Saul Friedländer's *Prelude to Downfall: Hitler and the United States, 1939–1941* drew on a thorough review of documents and memoirs to show how dismissiveness of America's potential role in the war gave way to an almost fatalistic assumption of inevitability about American intervention. Neither work captured how thoroughly unprepared the German military was to assess the United States' capabilities and intentions, and both books ended at Germany's declaration of war.

The price of allowing time to pass took form in the release in 2021 of Klaus H. Schmider's *Hitler's Fatal Miscalculation: Why Germany Declared War on the United States* (Cambridge: Cambridge University, 2021). Russell A. Hart's review of the book in the *Journal of Military History* enthused that "it will probably become the definitive, authoritative explanation of a long-neglected and inadequately studied dimension of the Second World War: Why Hitler declared war on the United States."[1]

But on page 2 of the book, Schmider establishes the premise of his work by discussing a meeting between Hitler and his leading industrialists on 29 November 1941, at which they told him Germany could not match its enemies' ability to produce war materiel. Armaments Minister and trusted Nazi comrade Franz Todt suggested he should sue for peace (a meeting this work will also address). The logical conclusion facing Hitler, Schmider suggests, was that he should not expand the war further, at the very least. "At the time of Todt's warning, no commitment had yet been made to Tokyo, so reasons of prestige are unlikely to have played a role in deciding the dictator's mind for him, when on 11 December he went on to declare war on the United States."[2]

This is incorrect. As we shall see, Hitler had promised Japanese Foreign Minister Yosuke Matsuoka on 4 April 1941 that Germany would promptly take part in a Japanese-American war. On 28 November, the day before the meeting, German Foreign Minister Joachim Ribbentrop told Japanese Ambassador Baron Hiroshi Oshima that Hitler was determined that if Japan went to war against America, Germany would join the war immediately. Schmider acknowledges these events but evidently dismisses them as commitments.

Schmider concludes that Hitler's "fundamental decision to join Japan in a war against the USA almost certainly took place around 21–23 November."[3] This work argues that Hitler revealed the fundamental decision in April, subject to the condition that Japan go to war.

Shmider's methodology—to "examine the information that reached the dictator over the course of 1941 in all fields of military strategy as well as foreign and economic policy with a direct or indirect bearing on relations with Japan and the USA"—treats as a rational actor a man who made momentous decisions at times based on his intuition. It also does not reflect the reality of the busy policymaker.[4] American intelligence analysts learn that they have to convey the key message in the first paragraph because that may be all a leader with hundreds of balls in the air will read. Shmider is aware of this problem and takes pains to offer evidence, for example, that Hitler was reading some diplomatic and military cables from the embassy in Washington. The test is in what Hitler internalized and drew upon in discussing policy and issuing instructions. The focus on 1941 also misses the picture of Hitler's views of America when he was deciding on aggressive action from the remilitarization of the Rhineland onward.

Pearl Harbor, of course, is a cottage industry all to its own, and there are many excellent treatments of the subject. But books generally focus on the crucial year of 1941. This work goes back through a more extensive period to unravel the trends in Japan that created a momentum for war well before the fateful decisions of 1941; it argues that Japan crossed the line to war by mid-1940. The book will also devote considerable attention to Japan's war in China, a war in which America was not a participant. Japan went to war with America because of China, and the conflict shaped how Japanese civilian and military leaders thought about America before Pearl Harbor. Moreover, irony of ironies, the decision to go to war with America by 1943 led to Japan feeling compelled to organize ground offensives in China that burned resources and men—not to defeat the Nationalists per se, but to keep American bombers threatening the home islands at a distance.

It may not be apparent to the casual reader, but it is darn hard to tell exactly what happened so many years ago. Indeed, historians sometimes say that the past is gone, never to be recovered; a "history" is merely a story we tell about that vanished past. This book exemplifies that principle. Contemporary reports written by separate participants in any given incident are likely to differ, sometimes substantially. This is true in any field of human endeavor, but it is particularly true in the intrinsically confusing domain of warfare. On top of this, later accounts introduce additional flaws of memory or self-justification.

I do not read Japanese and have chosen to rely as much as possible on reports derived first-hand from participants in the events, including diaries, postwar interrogation reports, and intercepted communications. For example, I have used Prince Konoye's recollection of what Admiral Yamamoto told him about prospects for war rather than the version in wide circulation, which is, at best, a second-hand quotation. Might those individuals have shaped their statements to interrogators to their own advantage? Of course, but so did Allied leaders and generals recounting their actions (see my comments below on the Foreign Military Studies series).

Many quotes derive from MAGIC intercepts of Japanese diplomatic communications and German diplomatic cables reporting conversations with Japanese leaders. The intercepts are as accurate as their translators were skilled.

I treat other sources of Japanese quotes with caution. Eri Hotta's *Japan 1941: Countdown to Infamy* contains numerous purported conversations among senior Japanese officers and civilian officials during the fall of 1941, most sourced to *Gozen Kaigi*, a book by Japanese novelist Junpei Gomikawa. It seems to me that only the two people involved in those talks knew what was said, and I have used only materials that other sources confirm have a basis in *Senshi Sosho*, the postwar official history in 102 volumes by the National Institute for Defense Studies' Military Archives, also published commercially by Shiro Hara.

I have relied heavily for the inside military story on Takushiro Hattori's *The Complete History of the Greater East Asia War*, published by Tenkishi Masukagi, 1953, translated by SIA, G-2, Hqs 500th Military Intelligence Service Group, located in the Gordon W. Prange Papers, Special Collections, University of Maryland Libraries, Series IV, G-2 Historical Division, Box 4. Hattori was chief of operations in the Kwangtung Army in 1939. He served as chief of the Imperial General Headquarters Army Operations Section, 1941–1942. From December 1942 to July 1944, he worked as Hideki Tojo's private secretary and protégé. He again headed the operations section from July 1944 to April 1945. He was transferred to command a regiment in China after crossing swords with a senior officer and remained there until the end of the war.[5] After the war, as related in his history, he served in the Historical Section of the General Headquarters and concurrently compiled historical documents for the Historical Facts Section of the Demobilization Bureau. Though many documents were burned after Japan's surrender, he was able to gather many others saved by responsible individuals and had access to minutes of imperial conferences, liaison conferences, and Supreme War Direction Council meeting records, and the Imperial Japanese Army's Secret War Diary. He also interviewed many army and navy officers.

The key German sources include the reconstructed *Oberkommando der Wehrmacht* (OKW, the High Command) war diary, captured military and Foreign Ministry records, and postwar accounts written for the U.S. Army's History Division by German officers. I did not use the ULTRA intercepts, except index card records in U.S. Navy records. Naval Enigma decrypts are available digitally at the UK National Archives but they represent a dense collection of every intercept translated, organized by date of transmission. Hitler did not need to communicate electronically with an empire scattered across thousands of miles as did Japan, and the Enigma intercepts do not generally reveal thinking within Hitler's inner circle. The MAGIC intercepts of Japanese diplomatic communications, on the other hand, lay bare many of Hitler's views as expressed to his Axis allies.

The key sources for Italian leadership thinking are the German records on Mussolini's exchanges with Hitler and the diary of Foreign Minister Count Galeazzo Ciano de Cortelazzo, kindly translated by the Nazis into German after its capture. The U.S. National Archives has Mussolini's papers on microfilm, but they are an uncatalogued jumble of generally hand-written papers.

For those obsessed with defining the pool of people whose views are worthy of consideration, I will use those of people who had something interesting to say and a plausible claim to access, authority, and credibility. To the extent possible, they are the topmost political leaders and military commanders, but they include others in the civilian and military chains of command with access to decision-makers and information about the course of the war. They include well-informed diplomats and journalists. Occasionally, they are fighting soldiers who were eyewitnesses to crucial events. The definition is flexible. In the intelligence business, one often gets the best information from people observing the senior leaders and unfolding events. Don't get hung up on somebody's position. Did the assessment of a German corps commander in Normandy regarding the effectiveness of George Patton as an army commander deserve consideration, even though he was fighting other corps? Would we dismiss the views of an American division commander in the Gulf wars about Saddam Hussein's competence as a commander? If we would, we are fools.

A few historians have criticized my use of the U.S. Army History Division's Foreign Military Studies (FMS) series, which consists of reports written by captured German officers and some other officials after the war. Robert Citino characterized these reports as "much maligned among scholarly historians. After all, they were often written by men who were facing war crimes charges, who feared for their futures, and who were seeking friends in the west."[6] It is bizarre that historians would dismiss a treasure trove of primary sources written by the officers who commanded the German armed forces. These are first-person accounts of the events!

I am a former intelligence officer. We use vetting of source information to evaluate its credibility. It is often possible to cross-check the FMS accounts against German military records, and many of the reports stand up well to the documentary evidence. Few of the authors faced war crimes charges, and the senior figures who did—such as Hermann Göring, Alfred Jodl, and Wilhelm Keitel—doubtless had a pretty good idea of their fates and had no incentive to win friends in the West. As to modern presumptions about how their circumstances influenced their accounts, it depended. The Americans who dealt with Keitel and Jodl, for example, noted that Keitel appeared to weigh his answers with his looming trial in mind, whereas Jodl applied himself conscientiously to providing detailed answers to questions (see the introduction to *Generalfeldmarschall* Wilhelm Keitel, "*Beantwortung des Fragebogens fuer Feldmarschall Keitel v. 24.7.45.*" A-912, 24 July 1945, National Archives). Walter Warlimont, who stood accused of war crimes in the High Command trial and was found guilty, provided some of the best FMS reports written. From mid-1948, all former German officers and officials writing the FMS reports were willing participants (see "History of the Koenigstein Phase of the German Historical Project, First Report," Jun 1948–Apr 1949, P-029A, May 1949, National Archives). That these authors had personal agendas makes their recollections no more useless than the memoirs of American officers such as Dwight Eisenhower and Omar Bradley, who had plenty of issues they chose to spin in particular ways to make themselves look good.

So, let us stipulate: All the figures in this tale who survived the war probably preferred to portray themselves in the best possible light. To help "FMS maligners" gain a better appreciation for the material, I will address the reliability of key recollections drawn from the FMS series as we go.

I have relied heavily on Eric Hammel's marvelous *How America Saved the World: The Untold Story of U.S. Preparedness Between the Wars* (Minneapolis, MN: Zenith Press, 2009) for many of the brief vignettes of what war-shaping mobilization, weapon, and political developments were occurring in America while the Axis leaders went about their mayhem. His work serves as the tango partner for this appraisal of the Axis.

I do not waste space recapitulating battles well known to the casual reader, such as the battle of Midway or D-Day. In such cases, I provide a synopsis from an authoritative source to remind the reader of the basics. These synopses are accurate enough for the purpose.

I have taken small liberties with texts drawn from the military records and personal accounts to correct grammatical errors and spelling mistakes, and to introduce consistency in references to unit designators, equipment, dates, and so on. I have used the familiar World War II-era names for cities in China and provided their current names in parentheses. Oddly, in the time the book evolved, everyone on the planet learned about Wuhan!

Finally, this is a work of determination to finish the job. I started the project in 2012. The incapacitation and death of first my father and then my mother completely derailed my work for years. I finished most of the archival research in 2018, which is the part I most enjoy. I confess that going through the secondary sources on a war this big did not keep the fire hot in my belly. I had almost completed that task early in 2020 when a data disaster cost me months of work. There were good breaks, too. I visit John Sandoe's bookstore every time I'm in London, and two visits turned up UK imprints of two key sources. Enrik Eberle and Matthias Uhl, ed., *The Hitler Book*, is a translation of a report prepared for Stalin based on interrogations of prisoners of war, including adjutants close to Hitler; it provided the answer to the question of whether Hitler ever admitted defeat. The second was Adam Tooze's *The Wages of Destruction*, a detailed analysis of Germany's war economy. I might have found neither if not for browsing.

Harry Yeide
April 2023

Acknowledgements

I thank my wonderful wife, Nancy, for putting up with the side effects of her husband writing another book, plus for being wonderful more generally. Bob Sprinkle pointed me toward a particularly useful resource on codebreaking in the Pacific. I would also like to thank the cheerful and efficient public servants at the National Archives and Records Administration's (NARA) document and still photo reading rooms in College Park, Maryland. Mark Reardon offered sound critical thoughts on the draft and suggested helpful references after I completed the archival research and was engaging in secondary research. Mark Stout provided me with a fascinating report on Germany's appraisal of American military capabilities in World War I. My particular thanks to Greg Bradsher, NARA, who shared his deep knowledge of records related to both Japan and Germany.

CHAPTER I

Fateful Decisions Amidst Global Decay

One has to start somewhere, and this work assumes that the reader is broadly familiar with the outcome of World War II and the malevolent influence the Treaty of Versailles exerted on European affairs. In this chapter, we will examine the pre-war era through 1936. First, we briefly review the conclusions of Western historians and the International War Crimes Tribunal regarding the Japanese decision to go to war; the strategic thinking regarding national defense, East Asia, and the United States; political-military developments inside Japan related to war-making; and economic forces that shaped the Japanese decision for war. A shorter section follows covering Germany, Hitler's devolution from respecting American power to dismissing it, and Germany's near absence of strategic thinking regarding America. The chapter closes with the formation of the Anti-Comintern Pact between Germany and Japan. Italy will join the story in 1937, the year it adhered to that pact.

The 1930s were not a good time for the human race. The decade began two months after the Wall Street crash of 29 October 1929 set the world on course for the Great Depression. On 18 September 1931, Japanese soldiers staged a bombing in Mukden (Shenyang), China, that led to Japanese occupation of Manchuria. The pointless Chaco War over a wasteland raged between Bolivia and Peru 1932–1935 and claimed 100,000 lives. Adolf Hitler became German Chancellor on 30 January 1933 and announced a relentless war of purification against every force undermining German culture. In October 1934, the communist Red Army in China began its "long march" into an armed struggle that would eventually topple "free China." Italy invaded Abyssinia in October 1935. Joseph Stalin launched his two-year Great Terror in 1936. In the midst of the Spanish Civil War, German bombers of the Condor Legion bombed Guernica on 4 March 1937, the first in a long line of city bombings by many nations over the next eight years. Two years later, Francisco Franco's fascists captured Madrid.[1]

The world has experienced many horrendous decades. One thing that set this decade apart was that leaders in Germany, Italy, and Japan made decisions that would lead them into war against the United States in the next decade. The main conclusions of this work are these.

Japan and Germany went to war against America betting that they could win before the United States could do very much about it.

Japan, after viewing the United States as a future enemy since 1907, reached its decision through a sophisticated process of open internal debate and a strategic assessment. The assessment included analysis of American intentions and capabilities, Japan's ongoing war in China, the expected military outcome in Europe, and careful consideration of Japanese access to strategic raw materials. Given what the Japanese knew, could reasonably have guessed, and could not have known about the United States, the decision was a calculated risk, but one more like a high-end financial gambit than gambling with the dice at the craps table.[2] This is not the first work to argue the case for calculated risk rather than national suicide, but it will establish that the decision for war occurred by late 1940 and will document to the extent possible Japanese thinking leading up to the decision at that time. The key point is that Japan went to war with America over China. It had a plan that it thought would stalemate America and leave it in possession of its conquests.

Germany, which is to say Adolf Hitler, considered the United States until 1941 as an afterthought, a naval power to be sure, but one unlikely to play any role in Europe beyond supplying France and Great Britain with raw materials and weapons. Hitler in April 1941 crossed the psychological line of saying Germany would enter a Japanese-American war. He and his henchmen made a bet like drunks at the racetrack. The German High Command had conducted no appraisal of American military intentions and capabilities as of April, nor by the day Hitler declared war on 11 December. Hitler had no plan and admitted in early January 1942 that he had no idea how to defeat America.

Italian leaders had a fairly accurate view of the implications for the Axis of war against America—all bad—though it seems to have been based more on reasoning than any deep assessment of factual information. They had little choice, though, but to bet on Hitler's horse.

These vastly different ways of thinking about the United States led to the same gravely mistaken decision to go to war against America.

None of the Axis leaders anticipated Allied intelligence breakthroughs that gave their enemy nearly complete insight into their military, foreign policy, economies, resources, and vulnerabilities. Nobody seriously considered their enemies introducing a technological revolution like the atomic bomb.

The Axis leaders' views of the United States naturally evolved during the war. Many key Japanese naval officers said they decided war was lost with defeats at Midway (June 1942) and Guadalcanal (second half of 1942). Japanese diplomats grasped that the mainly American landings in northwest Africa in November 1942 were a decisive inflection point that could lead to Japan being left to fight on alone, though the national leadership did not show signs of prioritizing the American enemy over China until late 1943. The Japanese experienced a growing sense of anxiety as they began to realize what the Empire had unleashed, militarily and in terms of resources. Losses in the Pacific in 1944 and the growing air war against Japanese cities changed the leadership's view of American might.

Likewise, Hitler did not prioritize the Anglo-American over the Soviet threat until early 1944. Germany and Italy got an earlier exposure than Japan to strategic bombings against cities. In Germany that hardened support for the regime, but attacks on military industry from 1943 gradually exacted an enormous cost, destroyed weapons before they reached the troops, and forced Germany to dedicate vast resources to air defense and damage repair.[3] U.S. and Royal Navy successes against the U-boat fleet smashed Hitler's baseline strategic assumptions in the West by mid-1943, and a sense of resignation about the overwhelming Allied superiority in (largely American-supplied) material resources began to creep in as early as the 1943 campaign in North Africa. Benito Mussolini's worst expectations about American involvement in the conflict also bore fruit at that time. The Italian Fascist Council ousted Mussolini on 25 July 1943 as Sicily fell to the Allied armies. Italy switched sides in September.

The first sign that Hitler might desperately consider a peace bid emerged as the U.S. First Army pushed toward Saint-Lô in Normandy in July 1944. Asked by interrogators when he had concluded the war was lost, Jodl replied, "The war was already lost in the West at the time of the [American] breakthrough at Avranches [on 31 July] and the beginning of the war of movement in France."[4]

The last year of the war is the least interesting in terms of Axis attitudes toward America. The German and Japanese leaders' decision in 1945 to accept annihilation of their economies without making peace overtures appears to have been detached from any calculus of what America, Britain, the Soviet Union, and other Allies intended other than fierce rejection of the Allied doctrine of unconditional surrender. The course of military affairs was obvious.

This work will devote more attention to Japan than to Germany or Italy because Japanese decision-makers thought longer and more extensively about America as an enemy and more strategically about the global conflict than did those in Berlin and Rome. The narrative will proceed chronologically, and because there was constant interplay among the key members of the Axis, the accounts of relevant events in Asia and Europe will, except for 1940, be mixed within chapters rather than separated for neatness' sake.

Japan: A War Foreordained?

Japan thought about fighting the United States as early as 1907 and decided on a course to war by 1940 at the latest, when the odds of victory—in the strategic sense of forcing, in cooperation with its Axis allies, ultimate American acquiescence to Japanese dominance in East Asia—looked fairly high, and the decision-making process in 1941 merely ratified what had gone before. Indeed, momentum alone favored the decision to fight. The situation was analogous to that of President George W. Bush, who, according to Bob Woodward's account, began planning to go to war against Iraq in December 2001 but did not make his final decision until January 2003. Although Bush at first considered war his last option, according to Woodward, momentum for military action built within the administration.[5] Judging whether the administration's assumptions about its ability to conquer and then hold Iraq with a relatively small force were more or less irrational than Japan's calculus will require more historical distance from the Iraq war.

Most historians focus on 1940–1941 in searching for explanations of Japan's attack.[6] Eminent British historian B. H. Liddell Hart, for example, begins his narrative of Japan's conflict with America in 1940 with Japan's seizure of southern Indochina and the subsequent American oil embargo.[7] Gordon Prange begins his Pearl Harbor classic *At Dawn We Slept* with a passing reference to the Japanese invasion of northern China in 1937 and then jumps to the same point in time as Liddell Hart.[8] Eri Hotta's *Japan 1941*, which is a fascinating red team account of Japan's march to war, sets its central timeframe in the title. Dr. Raymond O'Conner, in his introduction to *The Japanese Navy in World War II: In the Words of Former Japanese Naval Officers*, starts the chain of decisions at the time of growing American economic pressure in 1941.

Richard Franks, in *Tower of Skulls*, starts his narrative of the initial phase of the Sino-Japanese War at the Marco Polo bridge in 1937 after a brief review of the events that led to the stationing of foreign troops in Beijing and elsewhere in China. He does offer an observation regarding the war with America: Without the occupation of Manchuria in 1931 and its subsequent industrialization, Japan would have lacked the resources to even attempt such a war.[9]

Jeffrey Record in his well-argued monograph for the U.S. Army War College's Strategic Studies Institute, *Japan's Decision for War in 1941: Some Enduring Lessons*, summarizes neatly a widely held view that Japan's decision in 1941 was an act of stupidity or irrationality because Japan should have known it would lose:

> The Japanese attack on Pearl Harbor, Hawaii, continues to perplex. American naval historian Samuel Eliot Morison called Tokyo's decision for war against the United States "a strategic imbecility." How, in mid-1941, could Japan, militarily mired in China and seriously considering an opportunity for war with the Soviet Union, even think about yet another war, this one against a distant country with a 10-fold industrial superiority? The United States was not only stronger; it lay beyond Japan's military reach. The United States could out-produce Japan in every category of armaments as well as build weapons, such as long-range bombers, that Japan could not; and though Japan could fight a war in East Asia and the Western Pacific, it could not threaten the American homeland....
>
> Given the scope of Japan's ambitions, which included the expulsion of Western power and influence from Southeast Asia and given Japan's alliance with Nazi Germany (against whom the United States was tacitly allied with Great Britain), war with the United States was probably inevitable by the end of 1941 even though Japanese prospects for winning a war with the United States were minimal.

> The presumption of Japanese irrationality is natural given Japan's acute imperial overstretch in 1941 and the huge disparity between Japan's industrial base and military power and America's industrial base and latent military power.[10]

Record poses the question of whether the Japanese thought hard about their chances in a war or embarked on national suicide. He does not answer that question directly but concludes that the empire's quest for glory and economic independence from America was bound to collide with America's opposition to expansion by force and expectation that it could manipulate Japan's economic dependence to achieve American goals. Record's central conclusion was that the Japanese decision for war against the United States in 1941 was dictated by Japanese pride and the threatened economic destruction of Japan by the United States.[11] This may well be true, but when Japanese leaders took the first steps toward conflict, they expected to win.

Ambassador Joseph Grew in Tokyo in September and October 1941 anticipated the theme of Japan "risking national hara-kiri" to become impervious to economic embargos from abroad rather than yield to foreign pressure. He sought to dash any misconceptions in Washington about Japan's capacity to rush headlong into a suicidal struggle against the United States. Yet, he conceded, Japanese sanity could not be measured by American standards.[12]

James B. Wood, in his admirable assault on conventional wisdom, *Japanese Military Strategy in the Pacific War: Was Defeat Inevitable?*, is a rare voice arguing that

> Japan's quest for empire and world power status failed, but it need not have. At the very least, the war's endgame might have been different and more complicated, that is to say more problematic for the Allies than it was. Could Japan have escaped utter ruin and total defeat? Perhaps.... [T]he war against the Allies was the right war at the right time for Japan.... The final decision for war ... rested on a realistic appraisal of the international situation, national and imperial interests, and Japan's level of military preparedness.[13]

Wood's work, however, skims the surface of pre-war Japanese thinking about the United States.

Rising Sun, Glinting Bayonets

The postwar Military Tribunal for the Far East judged that in Japan, the outstanding feature in the years from 1928 onward was

> the gradual rise of the military and their supporters to such a predominance in the Government of Japan that no other organ of government, neither the elected representatives of the people, nor the civilian ministers of the Cabinet, nor the civilian advisers of the Emperor in the Privy Council and in his entourage, latterly imposed any effective check on the ambitions of the military.[14]

This conclusion understates the leading role civilian ministers played in escalating military conflict in China, joing the Axis, and formulating the strategy for southern expansion that made war with America nearly inevitable. Nor does it acknowledge the fact that civilian leaders did not really even try to stop the military from going to war against the United States, but rather expressed mere anxieties about the outcome.

Despite the aforesaid, the Imperial Japanese Army (IJA) did exert its power to topple governments, and a school of thought exists that during the buildup to war, civilian leaders had no choice but to accept the military's diktat. The civilian leaders at the time made no such claim during that period or after the war, even as an excuse for their decisions. Even the military was unenthusiastic about going to war against America. Nevertheless, we will briefly examine the events that give rise to the notion that the military imposed its policy through fear.

In 1927, an officer's clique rooted in the Kwantung Army in Manchuria (see below for more detail) forced retired General and Prime Minister Giichi Tanaka to resign to prevent a public investigation into its assassination of a Chinese warlord against express orders not to interfere in his affairs. In early 1932, after the Mukden incident (see below), authorities broke up a coup plot that again involved the clique. The prime minister subsequently resigned, in part because he could not restrain the IJA's unilateral actions in Manchuria. In May, military academy cadets led by radical junior naval officers assassinated Prime Minister Tsuyoshi Inukai in a failed coup attempt.

Radicalized junior officers, some 1,400 strong, on 26 February 1932 seized key ministries in Tokyo and murdered the finance minister and two other men. Emperor Hirohito, appalled by the killings, refused to grant any concessions, and the coup collapsed after four days. The IJA courtmartialed some of the mutineers secretly, without defense counsel, and executed them. A sweeping purge replaced many suspect senior officers with men who favored innovation, modernization, and renovation of the IJA.

The coup plots had aimed at establishing a military government, but few senior officers participated in them, and none acted when the coup attempts launched. The actors were junior officers and enlisted men.

This was hardly a terrifying set of precedents that would cow civilian leaders later during the leadup to war with America. Moreover, while civilian leaders had little sway over what the IJA did in China, they held the budget leash. Control of the budget constrained the military's capabilities and forced the military to gain civilian acquiescence for armaments programs to sustain its ambitions. In 1933, for example, with hardliners dominating the senior ranks, War Minister General Sadao Araki failed to convince the civilian Cabinet members to significantly boost the IJA budget for immediate rearmament and establish wartime controls over the economy. The civilians preferred to underwrite a massive public works program of infrastructure improvement and construction.[15]

As we shall see, some senior Japanese sporadically expressed worry about violence against them if they defied the IJA's wishes. Opponents of the Tripartite Pact *suspected* they would have been assassinated had they still been in their jobs, but they were not, and their successors supported the pact. (Japanese historian Agawa's description of a file containing threats received by Yamamoto and Yonai indicate they came from nationalist kooks, though he personally *suspected* the army had a hand in the matter.)[16] Moreover, at that time, a civilian—Foreign Minister Yosuke Matsuoka—was to be more belligerent and pro-war than the military itself, and not because he feared being murdered.

In another case, Japanese historian Sadao Asada asserts that Navy Chief of Staff Osami Nagano feared an army coup if the IJN did not support war in the months before the final decision (though to what aim that coup would have had is not clear, seeing as the IJA could not fight the U.S. Navy). Konoye told Ambassador Grew in spring 1941 that he wanted to meet President Roosevelt in person as he could not make concessions using diplomatic communications because his pro-Axis foreign minister would tell the military, and he would be assassinated (total bunk: he had no power to make unilateral concessions). Hirohito would claim he feared a coup if he had tried to stop the *final* decision to go to war against America. But he is not known to have expressed such fears in the leadup to that fateful decision, and General Hideki Tojo did not act like a man who would have toppled the emperor. During the closing days of the war, Prime Minister Teiichi Suzuki feared assassination if he moved quickly to secure the negotiated surrender Hirohito wanted. Otherwise, the civilian leaders were voluntary full participants in formulating the path to war.

The lengthy investigations of the war crimes tribunal concluded that the roots of Japanese militarism were to be found in the soil of the very foundation of the Japanese imperial system in 600 BC, when the first emperor, Jimmu Tenno, issued a rescript that established the principle of *Hakko Ichiu*. This meant bringing together all corners of the world under a single ruler in a united "family," a seemingly benign universal force in human development that would eventually permeate the world. The rescript also established the principle of *Kodo*, or loyalty to the emperor—the means to reach *Hakko Ichiu*. The Meiji Restoration reestablished these values as the foundation for modern Japan when Emperor Meiji issued a rescript to that effect in 1871.[17]

While the tribunal looked to historical roots of Japanese militarism, it ignored a tradition of forward defense dating from the late 1800s that in many ways resembled post-World War II American strategic policy—albeit the American one based on alliances rather than conquest.

Yamagata Aritomo was a samurai from Choshu who served as a staff officer during the civil war (1867–1868) that accomplished the Meiji Restoration. The new government sent him to Prussia in 1869 to study European military systems. Upon his return, the Emperor asked him to form a national army, and in 1873, he became the war minister. He modeled the new Imperial Japanese Army on that of Prussia and established the Imperial Japanese Army General Staff, which he headed three times. His modernization program also followed the Prussian example.

While Chief of Staff in 1880, Yamagata warned the Emperor that Russia's advances into East Asia and China's military modernization left Japan, with its long coastlines, vulnerable to attack from multiple directions or to naval blockade and isolation. Yamagata wanted to fortify offshore islands and launch construction of fortifications around Tokyo Bay. Without a strong military, he argued, Japan could not protect its sovereignty against European powers.

Anti-Japanese violence in Korea in 1882 led to a small Japanese military intervention that provoked China to send 5,000 troops to the peninsula and install a pro-Chinese government. The Japanese government believed control of Korea by anyone but Japan posed a threat to the home islands, but the military was too weak to respond.

In 1888, the army adopted a division structure along Prussian lines. As late as 1891, the army's grand maneuvers involved defending against a Russian amphibious invasion.[18]

In 1890, however, now Prime Minister Yamagata warned the Diet that once Russia completed the Trans-Siberian Railroad, Korea would fall under its sway. National security could no longer depend on defending the shoreline—Japan had to give its military the ability to protect a forward line of Japanese interests, chiefly in Korea.[19]

Emperor Meiji in 1893 approved the establishment of an independent Navy General Staff. The two staffs would report directly to him in peacetime. When Japan was at war, an Imperial General Headquarters (IGHQ) under an army officer would unify the services.[20]

In June 1894, China again intervened in Korea to suppress peasant unrest, but this time Japan responded by sending combat troops to Korea and declared war against China on 1 August. The military had studied the Chinese army and industrial base and concluded it could win a war because the Chinese army lacked systems for mobilization and logistics. The Imperial Japanese Navy (IJN) defeated the Chinese fleet in the battle of the Yalu on 17 September, thereby assuring there would be no attack on the home islands and guaranteeing security to troops shipping to Korea. Japan anticipated a quick victory on land, but despite substantial initial successes, winter forced a second year of campaigning. Yamagata, now commanding First Army in northern Korea, was unwilling to wait; he unilaterally ordered his troops into Manchuria on 1 December. They bested the Chinese, and Beijing accepted a peace on 17 April. Japan acquired Formosa (Taiwan), while China acknowledged Japan's special interests in Korea and granted railroad concessions in Manchuria.

China's defeat and obvious weakness touched off a competition among Western imperial powers to carve up the Chinese Empire and East Asia. And not just the Europeans. In 1897, the United States annexed Hawaii and the following year moved into the Philippines.[21]

The Japanese army in the nineteenth century had considered Russia its natural enemy, and in 1900 it created its first operational plan for war. This anticipated capturing Port Arthur in Manchuria, waging a decisive battle near Mukden, and conducting secondary amphibious operations against Russia's maritime provinces. In 1902, the plan changed to anticipate ground operations in Manchuria only if the IJN could control the Yellow Sea. Otherwise, the IJA would land in Korea and defend Japanese interests there.[22]

On 4 February 1904, an imperial conference decided to go to war with Russia because of its meddling in Korea. Japan broke diplomatic ties on the 6th and on the 8th staged a surprise attack on the Russian Pacific fleet squadron anchored at Port Arthur. The attack badly damaged three capital ships but left the squadron intact and the port open. More than a year of bloody but indecisive fighting ensued in Manchuria and Korea; Japanese troops finally captured Port Arthur in November after repeated failure. But on 27 May 1905, Japanese fortunes shifted dramatically when Admiral Heihachiro Togo's Combined Fleet destroyed the Russian Baltic Fleet in Tsushima Strait. The latter had sailed 10,000 miles over eight months, and the Japanese sank a dozen first-line ships and captured four more. Future Foreign Minister Yosuke Matsuoka, then a diplomat in Shanghai, reportedly provided the intelligence on Russian fleet movements that made the stunning victory possible.

The Japanese induced President Theodore Roosevelt to mediate a peace, and the resulting Portsmouth Treaty granted Japan southern Sakhalin Island, exclusive rights in Korea, and possession of a Russian railroad in Manchuria.[23] The railroad would serve as the pretext for Japanese aggression in Manchuria in the 1930s, which would lead to war with America.

Despite America's help in ending the Russo-Japanese War, Japan's formulation of a strategic framework, approved by the Emperor in April 1907, portrayed Russia and the United States as Japan's most likely future enemies.[24] This marks the start of a gradual buildup of momentum toward war.

Japan's conquest of Formosa, Korea, Port Arthur, Sakalin, and the assumption after World War I of the League of Nations mandate over the former German possessions Palau, the northern Marianas, Micronesia, and the Marshall Islands, all aimed at creating a powerful forward defensive wall for the home islands.[25]

Subsequent Japanese thinking about controlling China, based on timing, appears to have fit into the forward defense concept. Japan revealed its aspirations on 18 January 1915, when it took advantage of joining Britain and France in the World War to issue China a secret ultimatum called the Twenty-One Demands, which it backed with the threat of war. Japan cloaked its compulsion in the desire for regional peace and bilateral amity. These required China to stop leasing territory along the coast of China to foreign powers and to grant Japan de facto control of Manchuria and the Shantung peninsula and permit Japanese settlement there. China was to permit Japanese nationals to buy property in southern Manchuria and Inner Mongolia, including mines. China was to extend Japan's rights to Port Arthur and Dairen for 99 years. China had to accept Japanese "advisers" in government bodies.

The Chinese government, knowing it could not fight, conceded on 8 May. Once Britain and the United States learned of the act, they annulled the placement of

Japanese officials in the Chinese government. The Washington Conference in 1921–1922 annulled the rest of the demands, and Japan withdrew its troops from Shantung.[26]

By 1930, Japan was just one of many powers with a piece of the imperialist action in China.

Early Pre-War Japanese Views of the United States

The IJN selected the United States in 1907 as its notional enemy for budgeting purposes and from 1909 as its sole imaginary enemy. The IJN decided it needed to equal 70 percent of American naval strength to guarantee the nation's security, and this aim defined Japanese policy up to the signing of the Washington Arms Limitation Treaty of 1922, though Tokyo had to settle for 60 percent of the strength of each the United States and Great Britain (a ratio of 5:5:3) in exchange for a ban on fortifying islands in the Pacific. During the Washington talks, American codebreakers deciphered Japan's diplomatic communications and knew Tokyo's fallback positions, which conveyed a huge advantage that the Japanese were unable to factor into their own assessments.[27] Behind the scenes, the United States persuaded Britain to use the arms control agreement to let lapse a 1911 defense agreement with Japan.[28]

On 2 November 1917, a note from the U.S. government—what became known as Lansing–Ishii Agreement—said, "Both the United States and the Japanese Government recognize the territorial propinquity created by a special relationship between countries. Therefore, the United States Government recognizes that Japan possesses special interests in China, in general, and in regions adjacent to Japanese possessions, in particular." This was a concession that the Japanese would remember and use to justify future policies.[29]

A revision of Japan's 1907 strategic framework in 1918 posited war against a coalition of America, China, and Russia. The IJA would deploy troops to China and seize strategic locations. The army and navy would jointly conquer Luzon, the Philippines, and the American bases there. The fleet would destroy American vessels in Asian waters and then crush the enemy main fleet in a decisive battle when the Americans tried to retake the Philippines.[30]

The Japanese revised their strategic framework again in 1922. With the demise of Imperial Russia and China looking like it might come apart, America was the only plausible enemy. Japan would ensure that it had sufficient resources on hand to defeat America in a short war before the enemy's industrial resources could affect the outcome. The IJA planned on 21 modern divisions and a substantial air arm, while the IJN requested nine battleships, three aircraft carriers, and 40 cruisers. The IJN was to engage the American fleet in decisive battle, while the IJA captured Guam and the Philippines.[31]

Advocates of military expansion in the 1920s justified their arguments on the grounds of *Hakko Ichiu* and *Kodo*. Dr. Shumei Okawa, for example, was a frequent lecturer at the Army General Staff. In 1924, Okawa argued that Japan was the first state to be created and therefore had a divine mission to rule all nations. He called for occupation of Siberia and the South Seas islands. In 1925, he prophesied a war between East and West in which Japan would champion the East.[32]

With the beginning of militarization in 1928, voices emerged among nationalist Japanese commentators who anticipated conflict with America. The U.S. military attaché reported retrospectively in 1932 that, starting in 1928, a spate of publications had appeared in Japan aimed at convincing the public that the country one day would have to fight the United States.[33]

Japanese military thinkers during the 1920s and 1930s argued over whether to plan for a short war or protracted total war.[34] A book by Kosei Oshima, *The Threat of Military Reduction*, published in 1931, examined that issue in the context of America, primarily the slow military mobilization the United States had conducted in World War I, and he used the case to argue that Japan should not reduce the size of its army. He characterized the American approach to preparing for war as one depending on "special conditions obtaining in America." Conditions in Japan would not permit the same slow buildup, and the nation had to pursue a "quick war-quick decision" strategy of national power. "When the enemy takes a policy of long, continued staying power, then what is to be done, you will probably ask. The answer is that when the enemy adopts the endurance policy, he will be especially embarrassed by the Quick War-Quick Decision Policy," argued Oshima. Japan would

> [c]apture the important points and places which control the fate of the war and influence the trend of events before the enemy is ready. In this way we would be able to take the initiative to our own advantage, and in addition improve the strategical situation of our own by capturing the places containing the important resources in other countries. In that way, we would remove the great threat to our country. Therefore, if we do not carry out the policy of Quick War-Quick Decision to the utmost, I want to assert that we can never expect to get a favorable decision.[35]

Japan was to implement this strategic framework. The thinking reflected here influenced two great Japanese miscalculations: the invasion of China, and the attack on Pearl Harbor.

Collective Leadership: Who Made the Decisions?

Japan was not a dictatorship when it started down the path to war against America, and in fact until 1941 encompassed both democracy and militarism. A U.S. G-2 "political estimate" of Japan, published on 20 August 1941, said:

> Japan is a constitutional monarchy, the imperial constitution having been voluntarily promulgated by the Emperor, Mutsuhito (Meiji), in 1889.... The franchise has been extended twice since the 1889 Constitution and since 1925 embraces all men over 25 who have a permanent residence. But the ordinary man attaches little value to his vote and can be easily persuaded to sell it to a politician more adept at such matters....
>
> The Japanese Government is one of the most stable in the world. This is due to the belief that all Japanese are related by blood to the Emperor who is their father and the representative of the Supreme Being on earth who reigns over his people as spiritual leader....

> Because of Japan's adherence to the "Imperial Way," a national revolution scarcely seems imminent. Nor will it adopt complete fascism, any form of communism, or even entire totalitarianism....
>
> Although the Japanese constitution invests the Emperor with all executive, legislative, and judicial powers, he does not rule in the actual sense of the word. He is the façade for the civil government and reigns in the spiritual sense over his children. In practice he dispenses power to the various organs of the government on the advice of the Premier, the Lord Keeper of the Privy Seal, and the Minister of the Imperial Household, and makes appointments in the same fashion. Because an audience with the Emperor and his official seal are necessary for the enactment of important business, the last two men wield considerable influence; the Minister of the Imperial Household may prevent or delay audiences with the Emperor, and the Lord Privy Seal can refuse the seal. Therefore, one source of influence on the government extends from the Imperial Household. Another is from the Premier and the Cabinet, which, in turn, used to be the façade for the power of the *Genro*, who were a group of older statesmen on an extra-legal consultative basis. A third source of power is the Privy Council, which often in the past acted as a check on the *Genro*.[36]

The G-2 then specifically addressed the role of the military in the system:

> Besides these advisory institutions, there are the army and the navy who are independent of the bureaucrats and responsible only to the Emperor. They automatically have the right to place two men in the Cabinet. They can refuse to place their men so that the formation of the Cabinet is impossible and it is necessary to form the Cabinet again and again until its composition meets with the approval of both the army and the navy. United, the latter also form a consultative body to the Emperor which can influence the Imperial household in the name of the Emperor. In brief, the influence that an organ can assume lies with the men and their adroitness in each case rather than in the legal power of the organ of government with which they are associated.
>
> Because of the various bodies of government which are able to assume power, dissension can hardly be avoided. Since the beginning of the China Incident the army and navy, which may jointly be referred to as the military group, have overshadowed the other organs. Inasmuch as there is no legal means to rid the country of unwanted politicians and councilors and power lies largely with influence, assassinations have been the order of the day and the military have ridden into power via the "clean up" method. Since the Governmental structure of the Japanese State does not permit any single body to become powerful enough to transcend the others, the attempts of the military to reconstruct Japan along fascist lines only increases the complexity of an already complex governing machine.
>
> The press in Japan exerts considerable power around commercial districts such as Tokyo, Osaka, or Kobe, but agrarian Japan is indifferent to politics.[37]

China: The Backdoor Entry to War with America

One senior naval officer told interrogators after the war that in his opinion, the path to war with the United States began with aggression in Manchuria. Admiral Soemu Toyoda, who served as commander of the Combined Fleet and then Chief of the Naval General Staff during the last 15 months of the war, said, "There is great doubt in my mind as to whether the Government that was in power at the beginning of the war should alone be held responsible for the fact that the war started. I wonder whether we should not go back farther, even to the Manchurian Incident ..." because it took the situation in Japan out of the Emperor's hands and made the army a decisive player in domestic politics.[38] Likewise, a month before

Pearl Harbor, Navy Chief of Staff Admiral Osami Nagano told Combined Fleet Chief of Staff Matome Ugaki that Japan was on the brink of war with America because of the Manchuria Incident.[39]

Japan maintained the Kwantung Army in Manchuria under the Portsmouth Treaty to protect Japanese interests. The army was so named because it occupied the leased territory of Kwangtung with 10,000 men. Its dual mission was to protect the territory and the South Manchurian Railway. That enterprise was not just a transportation system but also a parastatal commercial organization modeled in part on the British East India Company.[40]

Egged on by the nationalist intellectual Dr. Okawa, the Army in 1930 launched a propaganda campaign to convince the public that Manchuria was Japan's lifeline, and that Japan should expand into it, develop it industrially, and defend it against the Soviet Union. The Kwantung Army wanted to establish a separate Manchurian state through force of arms. In Japan, a faction that came to be known as *Kodo* emerged within the army that hoped to accomplish a "national reorganization," by force, if necessary, to establish a dictatorship under the titular authority of the Emperor.

The Kwantung Army in September 1931 staged the Mukden Incident, also known as the Manchurian Incident, in which an operative emplaced an explosive charge

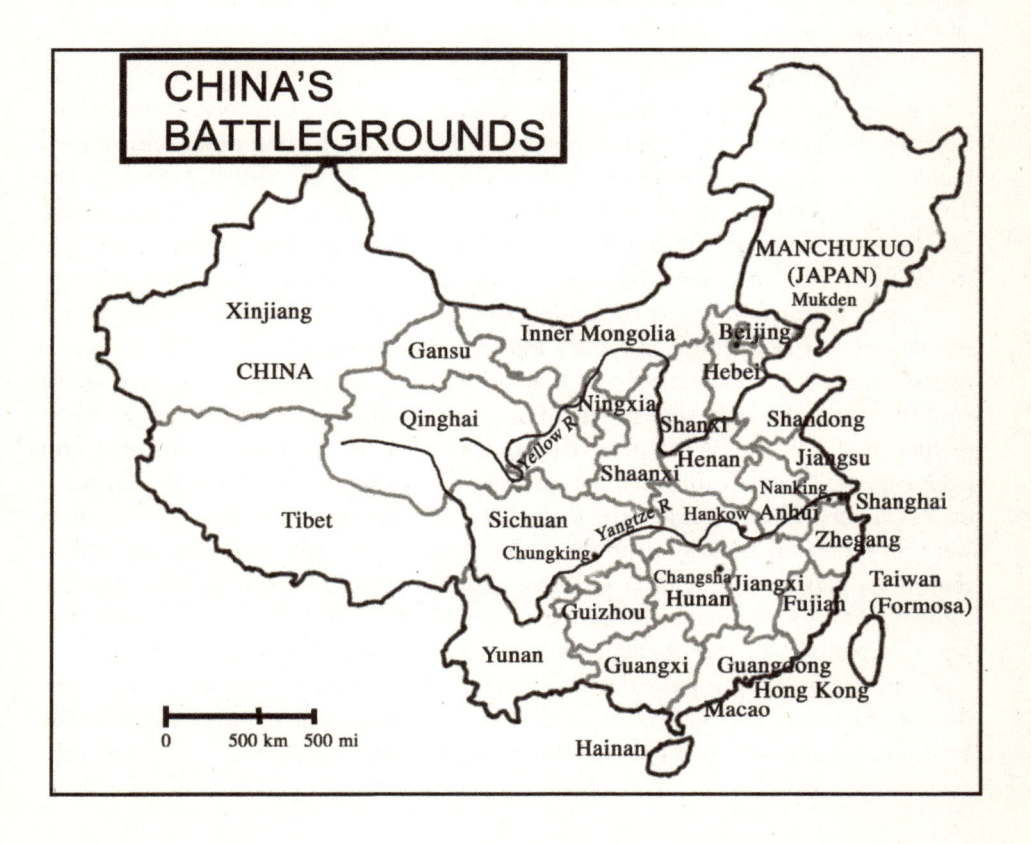

Japanese troops occupy Manchuria after the Mukden Incident in September 1931. Some Japanese military leaders viewed this as the start of the slide toward war against America. (Alchetron.com)

on the South Manchurian Railroad at Mukden. The IJN's view was that tensions between the Japanese and Chinese peoples had boiled to the point that some armed incident was inevitable. About a million Japanese citizens resided in Manchuria. The Chinese Northeaster Army numbered 448,000, by Japanese count, of whom 268,000 were regulars. Outnumbered, the Kwantung Army's "emergency plan" was to occupy the railroad zone, by attacking the Chinese army.[41]

Despite repeated attempts by moderates in Tokyo to stop the Kwangtung Army, troops invaded Manchuria. An army representative informed civilian figures close to the throne on 11 January 1932 that the Kwangtung Army was organizing the establishment of a new state, Manchukuo, intended to appoint the last emperor of the Qing Dynasty as the president, and would place Japanese in all important positions after they became dual nationals. Following a presentation to the Emperor on 21 January, Hirohito asked the senior Japanese diplomat in China whether there were prospects for friendly relations with China, as he hoped. The general replied that as long as the Manchuria problem existed, friendship with China would be difficult. On 18 February, the "independent" state of Manchukuo was declared.[42] Japan recognized an independent state on 15 September 1932.[43]

From the onset, the joint defense protocol considered the Soviet Union as its imagined enemy. The Soviets responded by increasing their troop strength in the Far East and building fortifications along the entire frontier in 1933. The next year, it boosted its air power and deployed bombers to the southern maritime provinces.[44] Thus, the Manchukuo occupation expanded the Japanese forward defense perimeter against a perceived threat, but also increased the menace.

Jonathan Grew, U.S. ambassador to Japan 1932–1942, joined Admiral Toyoda in discerning the role the Manchurian Incident was to play in the events of 1941. Writing in his diary on the train carrying him to San Francisco for his journey to Tokyo, Grew mused:

> Will Japan be content with safeguarding her present rights in Manchuria or, as some would have it, does her program include ideas of far-flung empire throughout Asia, with Korea the first step and Manchuria the second. Can she avoid a clash with Soviet Russia, with America? The big issue is whether the irresistible Japanese impulse is eventually going to come up against the immovable object in world opposition and, if so, what form the resultant conflagration will take, whether internal revolution or external war....
>
> I have a great deal of sympathy for Japan's legitimate aspirations in Manchuria, but no sympathy at all with the illegitimate way in which Japan has been carrying them out.[45]

The invasion of Manchuria created a key group of army officers and civilian associates that saw the world in the context of the Asian mainland and of competition against China and the Soviet Union, a world in which the United States would nevertheless have peripheral importance. From this period, General Seishiro Itagaki and his Kwantung clique, which viewed themselves as an elite, dominated the IJA. Itagaki was a soldier's soldier who spoke little and had been called, perhaps for that reason, the most intelligent soldier in Japan. Of five full general officers in 1939, three were Kwantung men.[46]

Grew, upon his arrival in Japan, quickly concluded, "[O]ne thing is certain and that is that the military are distinctly running the Government and that no step can be taken without their approval."[47]

The occupation of Manchuria also enabled Japan to create a substantial military force on China's border. By 1933, the Kwantung Army had grown from 10,000 to 114,000 men.[48]

In terms of military mindset, the IJA was devoted to the offensive, movement, and surprise. The U.S. military attaché observed in 1932, "The offensive, more offensive, and again the offensive is the fundamental theory of combat.... The enemy is seldom given credit for having good judgment."[49]

Japanese expansionism and the militarization of its politics appear to have reinforced one another during the 1930s to create a momentum toward the specific decision to expand southward that led directly to war with America.

Japanese military men knew the intervention in Manchuria could well lead to conflict with China and the Soviet Union, yet they also spared a thought for faraway America. In July 1932, the Japanese military attaché in Moscow reported that he saw war with the Soviet Union and China as inevitable. The attitude of the United States toward Japanese action in Manchuria suggested a war with that country was a "possibility" for which Japan must be ready.[50]

Ambassador Grew observed in his diary on 1 September 1932,

> The Foreign Office spokesman, Mr. T. Shiatori, released to the Japanese press on August 9 an entirely uncalled-for and provocative interpretation of the speech of the Secretary of State before the Council for Foreign Relations. This was obviously released for the purpose of arousing nationalistic and anti-American feeling.... The people throughout Japan (even the school children) are being urged to subscribe to funds for purchasing and presenting to the army "patriotism" airplanes, tanks, passenger motorcars, armored motorcars and antiaircraft equipment. This is partly for the purpose of conserving army funds and partly to encourage war fever.[51]

On 3 September, Grew recorded his message to Washington in a cable that day.

> [T]he Japanese Government firmly intends to carry out its Manchuria program unless prevented by superior force; furthermore, [the] elements who now control the Government believe that their cause is just [and] this gives added strength to their determination. Liberal statesmen carry little or no weight; the military preparations [against Chinese forces who opposed Manchuria's Japanese-imposed "self-determination"] are going forward steadily. They expect an unfavorable report from the League of Nations but regard America as their greatest stumbling block.[52]

Lieutenant General Shinji Hatta in 1932 published an article entitled "The National Defense of Japan," in which he assessed the possibility of conflict with the Soviet Union, China, and the United States. Hatta portrayed American policy as being to interfere with Japan's expansion in the Orient and depicted America as Japan's most serious enemy.

Hatta judged that America had learned from its woeful lack of preparedness before the Great War and had maintained a system to allow mobilization of reserves far more rapidly to quickly establish a homeland defense force of nine regular and 15 National Guard divisions. While this army guarded the frontiers, the Americans would organize an expeditionary force. Based on America's ability to mobilize 3.7 million men over 18 months in World War I and dispatch 2 million to Europe, one would have to count on a similar force being available for use in the Pacific if circumstances demanded. Hatta was aware that the United States had adopted laws that granted the President the power to conscript industry in wartime and had established a national industrial university under the War Department to train experts to supervise industrial mobilization.

Hatta pointed to the German use of poison gas and the British use of tanks in the Great War and warned that wars of the future would result in similar surprising technological developments; they would be "wars of science." War would hinge on whether the nation could harness the entire scientific knowledge at its command. The demand for ordnance would be huge, the costs astronomical, and the logistical challenges unprecedented. National mobilization would be total.[53]

We can reasonably conclude from this article that the Japanese military had a general grasp of America's ability to mobilize industry and manpower and train, arm, and deploy a large army overseas, though the model of World War I paled by comparison to that that of actual performance in World War II insofar as industry was concerned. Japan also understood that technological developments could have a decisive impact on a war.

Anticipation of a Great War-style mobilization was an accurate interpretation of broad American policy. Congress passed the National Defense Act in 1920 that authorized the War Department to plan for procurement and economic mobilization. Army Chief of Staff John Pershing established a board headed by Major Gen. James Harbord to examine how best to organize the system. The Harbord Board in 1921 created a strong general staff with a War Plans Division to generate requirements for procurement and gave responsibility for production, procurement, and economic mobilization planning to the assistant secretary of war. In principle, all war plans would be based on the ability of the economy to support them. The War Department followed the pattern of the World War I War Industries Board. It established relationships with all key industrial and financial groups, established commodity committees, and during the 1930s created four Industrial Mobilization Plans that greatly resembled the World War I model.[54] The War Department in 1924 established the Army Industrial College to train a corps of experts in procurement and guiding industrial mobilization for war.[55]

Moreover, the U.S. Army up until late 1941 expected that a General Headquarters commanded by the chief of staff or a general appointed by the President would organize and deploy overseas a single, large expeditionary force, as had occurred in World War I. Hatta's estimate of 2 million combat troops sent overseas (the actual number was 1.7 million) in World War I fell only about 10 percent short of the number of U.S. Army troops to be sent abroad in World War II.[56]

These preparations well before the war meant that efficiency was going to be far higher than the mobilization for the Great War, which had started slowly and been such a muddle that it never produced many of the weapons the American Expeditionary Forces (AEF) needed to fight. Indeed, the whole system had nearly come to a screeching halt in the winter of 1917 because the military refused to acknowledge economic realities.[57]

Blue Team: What America Was Thinking

Although this work focuses on the Axis parties, the United States, for its part, also thought about Japan as a potential enemy after its great showing in the Russo-Japanese War. A 1906–1907 war scare with Japan led to a major change in the U.S. Army's strategic thinking. Planners were cognizant of Japan's tendency to strike without a declaration of war and its demonstrated ability to move thousands of troops by sea. Its ground forces had proved adept at mobile and siege warfare. This put American possessions in Hawaii and the Philippines in peril unless the U.S. Navy could protect them, and the navy insisted that the fleet be free to pursue its opponent on the high seas. Maneuvers in Hawaii and the Philippines demonstrated that even if the fortresses there held out, enemy land-based artillery could control access by sea. A war game in 1908 saw those territories fall to Japan in a month. War games in 1909 and 1910 suggested that Japanese expeditionary landings on the northwestern coast of the United States were plausible. The U.S. Army concluded that its role in the Pacific would be defensive for many years.[58]

In 1920, Secretary of the Navy Josephus Daniels established three fleets, of which the Pacific Fleet (called the United States Fleet until 1 February 1941) was the strongest and equipped with all the most modern battleships. He viewed Japan as the dominant emerging anti-American power in the world. The Atlantic Fleet had six old battleships, and the Asiatic Fleet none.[59]

In the post-World War I era, the U.S. Army considered the spectrum of foreign threats to include a two-ocean war against an Anglo–Japanese coalition, a Pacific war against Japan, and trouble on the Mexican border. By 1922, it completed war plans against Great Britain, an Anglo-Japanese alliance, Japan, and Mexico.[60]

More broadly, Japanese–American relations had gradually deteriorated from warm friendship in the late 19th century to mutual suspicion in the 1920s because of Japan's repeated displays of military expansionism and the American entry into the Asian imperial game in the Philippines. By the 1920s, commentators in America also speculated about a possible war with Japan.[61]

The American plan for the defense of the Philippines was called Orange-3 and had existed for many years before the war. But "war plans," until efforts became serious with a real war looming, amounted to little more than staff studies, according to the official U.S. Army history.[62] A 1938 version was completely out of date by early 1941, when planners wrote a new one. That version assumed that the Japanese would attack without a declaration of war and with at most 48 hours warning. American forces, buttressed by Filipino units, would defend only central Luzon and the mouth of Manila Bay. The defenders would try to delay the enemy while withdrawing to the Bataan peninsula, which they were expected to hold for six months. The plan said nothing about what was to happen then.[63]

The U.S. Navy adjusted its part of Orange in 1934 after a thorough review of intercepted messages during the IJN's grand maneuvers in 1933. Instead of sending the Pacific fleet charging into the IJN's arms, the American fleet would capture intermediate objectives, islands to sustain bases to support the final push.[64]

The Americans devoted no consideration to Germany or Italy as enemies and so mirrored the amount of attention the German military was devoting to them. Prior to World War I, Germany had appeared menacing enough that the U.S. Army and Navy created Plan Black for a war against the Reich in 1913. This was primarily a naval plan to defeat an invasion fleet aimed at French colonial possessions in the Caribbean in the waters off Puerto Rico.[65]

Japan Appraises Its Strategic Position Vis-à-Vis America

Pestered by the League of Nations' Lytton Commission, established to investigate Japan's actions in Manchuria, and a subsequent League condemnation, Tokyo on 24 February 1933 withdrew from the organization.[66] The break from the League of Nations caused the Japanese government to conduct a sweeping appraisal of its global position. The study observed:

> While avoiding entanglement in war in the Far East, [the United States], by means of moral pressure, had appeared to be trying to restrain Japan's actions. However, with the outbreak of the Shanghai Incident (1932), the American attitude toward Japan took a sudden turn for the worst. Influential scholars, statesmen, and politicians advocated economic rupture with Japan; some feared the possibility of a clash between American and Japanese warships in Shanghai. To prepare for eventualities, the United States concentrated its entire fleet in the Pacific....
>
> The new Democratic administration is confronted with unprecedented domestic crisis caused by the world economic depression.... In consequence of this situation, it can be observed that with regard to Far Eastern problems the United States is trying as much as possible to take a temperate attitude. [Yet] the fact remains that relations between the United States and Japan have steadily deteriorated since the outbreak of the Manchurian Incident.... At no time have Japanese–American relations been as tense as they are now.[67]

The study directly addressed the issue of war with America:

> With regard to the prospects of a war between the United States and Japan, which is much talked about, there is a faction in Japan that urges that if war were to be fought with the United States, the present would offer the best chance, because as a result of the London Naval Treaty the ratio of naval strength between the two countries will become unfavorable to Japan after 1936. If, however, such a war broke out and Japan succeeded in her operations and captured the Philippines and destroyed the American fleet after drawing it into Japanese home waters, it is clear enough that this alone would not mean that a fatal blow had been dealt to the United States such as would force it to surrender; it is hardly possible to capture Hawaii and the American mainland. Japan, at any rate, might win local battles in the Far East, but little if anything could be expected in the way of victory and advantage outside the Far East. The possibility is great that as an inevitable consequence we would be involved in a protracted war that would be unfavorable to Japan. Furthermore, it is difficult to expect, in the present state of international relations, that the United States would be our only antagonist; the attitude of Great Britain and France in such case is unpredictable, and they might act together against Japan. Therefore, from our viewpoint a Japanese–American war should by all means be avoided.
>
> From the viewpoint of the United States, she does not gain much either in such a war.... [Nevertheless,] it is to be expected as a matter of course that the United States would not countenance the establishment of a Japanese hegemony over all of the Far East.[68]

This marks a crucial baseline in assessing Japanese views of the United States and interpreting the thinking behind decisions Tokyo was to take from this point onward. The Japanese leadership understood the consequences of the actions their government was in fact going to take over the next four years. Any effort to establish Japanese hegemony in East Asia would be, as a "matter of course," intolerable to the United States. The United States had little to *gain* from a war against Japan, but Japanese

Emperor Hirohito inspects the combined maneuvers of all services in 1934. (Military Intelligence Division, NARA)

strategists evidently grasped she would fight, nonetheless. For now, domestic politics were compelling President Franklin Roosevelt to eschew military confrontation in the Far East. There was already a pro-war faction in Japan arguing that it was better to go to war before the balance of naval strength shifted against Japan. If Japan went to war, she would be unable to deliver a deathblow, and any conflict was likely to be protracted and to Japan's disadvantage. Here was a counterargument to the Quick War-Quick Decision Policy, and it represented official thinking in 1933.

On the other hand, the analysis invoked two arguments against war that by 1941 would seem to have taken care of themselves. By then, Britain and France were in no position to make a major contribution to a war against Japan in alliance with America. And Japan's own alliance appeared to guarantee victories beneficial to Japanese interests outside the Far East that she could not achieve on her own.

In far-off Germany, Adolf Hitler took serious notice of Japan for the first time. He admired the bold invasion and annexation of Manchuria. He also was thrilled that Japan had told the established order to stuff it before walking out of the League.[69]

Ambassador Grew offered his view of how Japanese leaders at this time thought about what the country was doing in China; this is not necessarily an unbiased viewpoint, but it represents an outsider's perspective that seems to have predictive power regarding Japanese behavior:

> I doubt if one Japanese in a hundred really believes they have actually broken the Kellogg Pact, the Nine-Power Treaty, and the Covenant of the League. A comparatively few thinking men are capable of frankly facing the facts, and one Japanese said to me, "Yes, we've broken every one of

those instruments; we've waged open war; the argument of 'self-defense' and 'self-determination for Manchuria' are rot; but we needed Manchuria, and that's that." But such men are in the minority. The great majority of Japanese are astonishingly capable of really fooling themselves; they really believe that everything they have done is right....

> Their mental processes and methods of reaching conclusions are radically different from ours; the more one associates with them the more one realizes it; this is one of the great cleavages between the East and West. Westerners believe because the Japanese has adopted Western dress, language, and customs he must think like a Westerner. No greater error can be made. This is one of the reasons why treaty commitments between the West and the East will always be open to misinterpretation and subject to controversy. It isn't that the Japanese has his tongue in his cheek when he signs the obligation. It merely means that when that obligation runs counter to his own interests, as he conceives them, he will interpret the obligations to serve his own interests.[70]

Now, the Western country of Germany would soon exhibit these same allegedly Eastern characteristics—as has America on occasion, such as its treaties with Native American nations—but that does not mean that Grew's description is an inaccurate reflection of Japan at the time.

Japan announced in 1934 that it would withdraw in 1936 from the naval armaments structure, which meant it could engage in unconstrained naval construction and fortify the outer ring of islands it had acquired from Germany.[71]

Despite government policy, the IJN, drawing on its destruction of the Russian fleet in 1905, in the late 1920s and 1930s (prior to the outbreak of the war in China in 1937) created a doctrine for and trained to fight a so-called "decisive battle" against an encroaching American fleet. War plans foresaw the Japanese navy and army cooperating to capture the Philippines and deny the U.S. Navy bases there, and to seize Guam, the midway point for a fleet approaching from Hawaii. The Marianas and Carolines would host submarines and aircraft that would claim a toll on the enemy fleet. As the enemy approached the home islands, cruisers and destroyers would launch a surprise torpedo attack. The next day, the main battle fleet would engage and finish off the weakened and disorganized foe.

Japanese fleets exercised for this clash in large-scale maneuvers in 1930, 1931, 1932, 1934, and 1935. The enemy behaved according to plan. Japanese battlewagons of the main fleet dropped their rain of steel. Aircraft carrier-based bombers also "sank" enemy battleships in these simulated encounters.[72] Pre-war American war plans did, in fact, anticipate sending the fleet across the Pacific to destroy the Japanese fleet and then to blockade and bombard the home islands, just as the Japanese hoped.[73]

IJA preparations on the continent, meanwhile, developed with an eye toward conflict with the USSR.[74] The perceived Soviet menace was to loom large in Japanese strategic thinking into the 1940s, even though, several border clashes aside, the Soviet military would prove nearly irrelevant to Japan's fate until the very end of the war in 1945. Indeed, the ultimate absence of threat from the north following a bilateral neutrality pact was to be far more important in shaping Japan's actions vis-à-vis America.

In 1934, the IJA published a pamphlet entitled, *Principles of National Defense and Suggestions of how to Strengthen the Same*, which offered a critique of the social and economic system that left most of the population, particularly agricultural and fishing families, poor. The pamphlet argued that the concept of defense had evolved from mobilization and the conduct of actual battles into a complex combination of state organization of the economy and politics to sustain war and a system of competing international blocs. National defense depended on the "vitality and motive power" of national life. The Empire, asserted the IJA, was under growing pressure from foreign powers and faced an "extraordinary situation," and Japan needed to strengthen its national defense more than at any time in its history. The Empire needed to change its policies on finance, economics, diplomacy, education, and so on, to tap its latent spiritual and material powers to the utmost.

Following the Manchurian Incident in 1931, the IJA asserted, Japanese naval power deflected U.S. Secretary of State Stimson's attempts at intimidation, which demonstrated the importance of a strong national defense. The equipment of the army, navy, and air arm nevertheless was inadequate. The United States was eager to acquire a naval force superior to Japan's, and Soviet Russia was bent on organizing an invincible army. The United States would use its powerful navy to defend the Monroe Doctrine but also to impose its open-door and equal-opportunity policy in China. Just as it was imperative for America to have a navy "sufficient to overpower the Japanese navy," it was "absolutely necessary for Japan to have a powerful navy sufficient to defeat any state that will attempt to prevent Japan's noble object to make the Far East a paradise of peace and prosperity." Japan should soon abrogate the Washington and London naval treaties, which were disadvantageous to the Empire. Likewise, Japan had to build an army powerful enough to stop the Soviet efforts to encroach upon and Bolshevize the Far East.

The IJA pitched its argument in terms of deterrence: Failure to accomplish these goals would encourage other powers to challenge Japan to fight. Strategically, the IJA argued that Japan's position on the eastern edge of the Far East made it Japan's natural area of dominance, described as its "mission as a guardian of peace in the Far East from a military and political standpoint." China, India, and the South Sea islands represented the "granaries of the world" with a population of 1.1 billion. The second great strategic consideration was the existence of the Soviet Union on one side and the United States on the other.

Modern bombers allowed other states to attack Japan from the Aleutian Islands, the Philippines, Shanghai, or Vladivostok. Bombs would be dropped on non-combatants the minute war was declared. Therefore, Japan needed a powerful air force.

Technology would be a field of national competition in war. The last war was one of tanks and poison gas. "At the present time, the use of a death ray apparatus and the like is not an idle dream."

The IJA pamphlet addressed creating "unity of sentiment" by extirpating "internationalism, individualism, and liberalism" with the aim of rousing the populace to fight for the sake of the Empire in preference to their individual interests.

The IJA said that Japan's population of 65 million, or 92 million with its overseas territories added, together with the population of Manchuria totaled 120 million—sufficient to compete with the United States and Soviet Russia.[75]

The IJA pamphlet raised racial divisions in other states in the context of using a "war of thoughts" to turn minorities against competing states to fracture them internally. The Soviet Union incorporated 150 different nationalities, including 30 million Ukrainians "looking for an opportunity to declare independence." Similarly, "the existence of 12 million black men in the United States is an eternal cancer."[76]

The issue of alleged (by the War Crimes Tribunal, among others) Japanese racism as a factor in decision-making at the time of the war appears to be misleading. The Japanese wanted to drive the Western colonial powers out of the Far East, and arguments for this policy often referred to the "white man."[77] The fact is the colonial powers were embodied in white men. The charge against Japan makes as much sense as alleging that the United States, which displayed extreme racism against the Japanese by interning citizens based on race, in popular wartime culture, and on the battlefield, fought the war for racist reasons.

On the whole, available diaries and records give no indication that racism became a factor in high-level decision-making. Likewise, this author's review of writings by nationalist thinkers who portrayed Japan as the natural center of an East Asian order because of its moral superiority and Heaven-granted role through *Hakko Ichiu* did not denigrate other peoples as inferior in a racial sense.[78] Moreover, Japan had no significant domestic minority to declare an enemy. No racial purges occurred along the lines of removing all non-Aryan personnel from government jobs, as in Germany.[79]

*

The army and navy managed to agree on a new strategic framework in 1936. Both services were already thinking about an "advance to the south" to take control of natural resources. Kanji Ishiwari, head of the Army General Staff Operations Section, wanted to eliminate the Soviet threat and then move south. Captain Shigeru Fukudome, head of the Navy General Staff Operations Section, wanted to defend the northern flank and advance south. The IJA saw the USSR as the main enemy, while the IJN argued it was America. The two staffs worked on a draft, and only one civilian—the prime minister—received a general outline of the new policy. The two chiefs of staff presented the draft to the Emperor in mid-May. The Emperor questioned the huge expenses implied but approved the document on 3 June after the military persuaded the prime minister to endorse it.

The new strategy gave equal priority to likely enemies, the USSR and America, and added as secondary foes Great Britain and China. It did not resolve the axis of advance to the north or south. The IJA was authorized 50 divisions supported by 140 army air force squadrons. The IJN was to receive two new battleships (12 total), seven new carriers (10 total), and 20 new air squadrons (65 total).

The strategy aimed to control the Asian continent and the Western Pacific and anticipated rapid capture of strategic objectives in a short war. Regarding a war against America, it declared,

> The primary objective will be to annihilate the enemy in the Orient, destroy his operational bases and annihilate the main body of the enemy fleet operating from bases on the American mainland. For this purpose, the navy will take control of Oriental waters by destroying the enemy's Far Eastern Fleet at the outset of the operations. Furthermore, in cooperation with the army, it will occupy the key points on Luzon Island and its vicinity and the enemy naval base on Guam. Then it will destroy the main body of the enemy fleet operating in the Far Eastern waters by launching timely attacks.[80]

There was no guidance on how to fight a protracted war, though it acknowledged that one was possible. Subsequent discussion in July involving the foreign minister to craft a unified foreign policy stipulated that the advance to the south was to be peaceful.[81]

Japan had a plan in 1936 for fighting America. The situation was much different in the Third Reich.

Germany: An Offhand Decision

Germany drifted into war with the United States. The German navy had its first skirmish against its American counterpart on 10 April 1941, when an American destroyer attacked a German U-boat that had just sunk a Dutch ship, well before war officially broke out. The German Army, however, considered the possibility of fighting the Americans such a remote prospect that on the day Adolf Hitler declared war, the General Staff did not even have data gathered to make an initial assessment of U.S. intentions and capabilities.

There is no analogous debate among historians to that on Japan as to whether Germany's—effectively Hitler's—decision to declare war on the United States was rational or suicidal. This is probably in part because the Germans put so little thought into the act beforehand, and because it was already at war with so many countries. It probably also derives from the fact that had Japan not attacked the United States—"suicide" focused in a single act—the war in China alone would not have destroyed Japan, whereas Germany might well have eventually succumbed to the combined weight of Soviet and British power backed only by American military and economic aid. Moreover, Japan would not have become the only country ever to be nuked.

Schmider offers a survey of the extremely limited discussion by historians of Hitler's motivations and observes that most historians simply avoid the subject and attribute it to irrationality. In brief, the theories have included that the setbacks on the Eastern Front convinced him he couldn't triumph by Blitzkrieg, and he declared war on America to distract others from that conclusion. Related to this idea, Hitler saw he would lose the war and wanted to go down in world-shaking fashion. Another notion is that he was counting on Japan to tie down American and British naval strength.[82]

Initial Views of the United States: Getting Stupider

In 1930, Hitler was the unquestioned leader of the National Socialist German Workers' Party (NSDAP, Nazi Party), had gained political rehabilitation after being convicted of treason for his attempted putsch in 1923, and was on the cusp of grabbing power. The Nazi party had grown to 210,000 members, and in the general elections of 14 September, Hitler garnered more than 6 million votes, which boosted the Nazi presence in the Reichstag from 12 to 107 deputies.[83]

Hitler had intellectually fit America into his worldview of Jewish-plutocratic (big business) conspiracies that focused on Great Britain and France. In a 1923 speech, he claimed,

> What cause finally had America to enter the war against Germany? With the outbreak of the World War, which Judah had desired so passionately and so long, all the large Jewish firms of the United States began supplying ammunitions.... Yet nothing satisfied the insatiable greed of the Jew. And so the venal press began an unparalleled propaganda campaign.... [T]he Jewish-democratic press of America had to accomplish its masterpiece—that is to say, it had to drive into the most horrible of all wars a great peace-loving people which was as little concerned in European struggles as it was in the north pole: America was to intervene "in defense of civilization."[84]

Hitler at that time held a rather high opinion of the power of the United States, one based in part on misinformation. He spoke admiringly to comrades in 1924 of American mass-production innovations and skyscrapers.[85] In 1925, he wrote in *Mein Kampf* that the United States possessed an "incomparable inner strength" because it was based in North America and had little contact with the outside world, whereas European powers had tiny landmasses, and most of their possessions were in colonies abroad. Germany, he argued, had to likewise obtain large land holdings in Europe. He believed the American population to be primarily Teutonic, mingled with "inferior races" to only a small degree. He credited North American Aryans with enormous scientific and technical achievements alongside their brothers in Europe. He praised American education of the lower classes, which produced people in increasing numbers to make important scientific discoveries. The United States in the Great War, he believed, had established its equality with Britain on the seas. Still, Hitler was convinced the Jews controlled both the stock exchange and the labor movement.[86]

Even as late as a speech in 1932, Hitler acknowledged American economic power, describing it as the globe's "whole-sale" exporter that "perhaps today is not yet all powerful in all spheres, but certainly in individual cases." Europe, he said, could not overcome its production advantages.[87] At times, he described American economic might as a great threat to Europe.[88]

Adam Tooze, in his marvelous history of Germany's war economy, cites Hitler's statements at this time to argue that his grand strategic vision was to prepare Germany for a future struggle with an American economic superpower. This, he suggests, is why Hitler thought he needed to grab vast lands and resources to the east. "America should provide the pivot for our understanding of the Third Reich."[89]

That is a cool red team assertion. But, as we shall see, Hitler went on to at first ignore and then dismiss America's economic potential as more or less irrelevant to his schemes for European conquest. We cannot know what he really thought, but he never invoked a future struggle with American economic power in explaining his policies to subordinates.

Hitler's knowledge of the United States formed the basis for his later fundamental misjudgments about America's power and willingness to thwart his plans of conquest. It appears that for most of his adult life, Hitler enjoyed the Wild West novels of Karl May, a man who had never visited the New World. During the 1920s and early 1930s, Hitler had turned to two comrades who filled him with their views of America. Kurt Ludecke was a Nazi party comrade, who lived in the States off and on as a fundraiser and party publicist. Hitler once commented that Ludecke knew more about America than the entire foreign ministry. What Ludecke "knew" was that the United States until the Civil War had been a largely Nordic country, and then had come a wave of Latin, Jewish, and other immigration that diluted the blood lines. He thought there was little cultural tradition in the United States but was astute enough to observe that Americans had no real experience with military defeat. Once Franklin Roosevelt and Hitler took power nearly at the same time, Ludecke came to believe that a social revolution would be possible if Roosevelt's New Deal failed. Nevertheless, he urged Hitler to pursue good relations with the United States.[90]

The second influential figure was the Harvard-educated art dealer, historian, and bon vivant Dr. Ernest "Putzi" Hanfstaengl, who was acquainted with Roosevelt. Hanfstaengl for some reason had developed a strategic view of the world, and that centered on the importance of the great maritime powers. He advised Hitler that he needed good relations with them. He also extracted from Hitler a statement in 1922, when Hitler was inclined to see the United States as a major player, that the Allies had won the Great War because the Americans joined in. The next war, Hanfstaengl told him, would be won by the side the Americans supported. "Yes, yes. You must be right," Hitler had replied.[91]

Yet when he took power on 30 January 1933, Hitler had little concern for distant America as he set about remaking Germany. Hitler immediately made clear during meetings with government officials that his top priority was to rearm the Wehrmacht (armed forces) and seize *Lebensraum* (living space), territory for the German people. Reconstruction of the economy, employment programs, and the rescue of Germany's peasants were means to that end. With only a third of the vote, Hitler pulled off a masterstroke by convincing a two-thirds majority to pass the Enabling Law of 23 March that allowed his government to rule by decree.[92]

Let us here propose a red team hypothesis: Hitler's preoccupation with rearmament would convince him that he was the world's most insightful observer on the subject. He would one day view America's rearmament through the lens of his own experiences, including all the trade-offs and bottlenecks he was to confront. His expectations would pan out to some degree and are in that sense rational expectations. Others would not, because the American economy was not that of Nazi Germany. It was capable of so much more. The evidence for this hypothesis will be circumstantial. This researcher has found no hard evidence to prove the case.

One can never make a second first impression, and the one flowing from America to Hitler as he grabbed the reins of German leadership was unimpressive. Just as Hitler took power, Roosevelt became president. A financial panic swept the country, and Roosevelt had to close banks and restrict the export of capital. The United States abandoned the gold standard, and the dollar depreciated by 30 percent over four months.[93]

When Hitler withdrew from the League of Nations on 10 October 1933 (he also quit talks in Geneva on armaments ceilings), Berlin conducted no appraisal of its relations with America, as Tokyo had done in January. The Berlin correspondent for the Associated Press, Louis Lochner, interviewed Hitler in 1934 and asked about the importance of German–American relations. Lochner recalled, "For a moment he blushed like a school boy, hemmed and hawed, then stammered an embarrassed something about having so many other problems to ponder that he had not yet had time to take up America."[94]

*

We will examine Germany's rearmament in some depth because, as suggested above, Hitler's experience probably shaped his expectations for American rearmament, and hence why he thought going to war made sense, and because it establishes a basis for comparison for American output of war material. Germany's production of all categories of weapons was relevant to war with America, whereas in Japan, only naval and aircraft output mattered much until 1943.

Exploiting international financial turmoil, including France defaulting on its American war debts and Anglo-American feuding over currency rates, Germany imposed a moratorium on foreign debt payments as of 30 June 1933. The same day the Cabinet reached that decision, 8 June, it agreed to a massive 35 billion Reichsmark (RM, roughly 4 RM equaled one dollar) rearmament program over eight years, or 4.4 billion RM per year. The Reichswehr's preceding armaments plan from December 1931 amounted to 480 million marks spread over five years. The new level amounted to 5–10 percent of GDP. The first big credit-financed employment program launched in May, in comparison, had a price tag of 1 billion marks. Both the employment and rearmament programs were handled off budget through special accounts.[95]

Hermann Göring and his new Reich Air Ministry in September 1933 boosted a 1932 target for a secret air force (Luftwaffe) from 200 planes to 2,000 planes by 1935, which implied a huge increase in production capacity. The Wehrmacht completed its plan in December, which foresaw two phases. The Wehrmacht (in this context amounting essentially to the army) was to have 21 standing divisions with 300,000 men by 1937, capable of expanding to 63 divisions in wartime. It would be able to defend against French or Polish attack. Germany would have to reintroduce conscription, a violation of the Versailles Treaty, and reestablish control over the Rhineland. The second phase would build offensive capabilities between 1938 and 1941. The navy (*Kriegsmarine*) was to join the game in spring 1934, seeking to build eight battleships, three aircraft carriers, and assorted other warships.[96]

The German airplane industry in 1932 employed 2,000 workers and built about 100 units per year. A month after setting the new target in September 1933, Göring had Hugo Junkers, owner of Germany's largest aircraft builder, arrested on 17 October 1943 and held him until he agreed to sign the firm over to the state. Three days later, Göring told the heads of all other companies with a stake in aircraft technology that they were compulsory participants in Hitler's plan to make Germany a great air power. Marks poured in, and by 1935, 54,000 workers were building planes and aircraft engines. German trade agreements with Hungary and Yugoslavia guaranteed adequate supplies of bauxite for aluminum.

A second phase of expansion after 1935 saw Junkers, Dornier, and Heinkel take the lead in building two-engine bombers, while Messerschmidt took the reins on fighters. By 1938, 154,000 workers were making planes, 48,000 producing engines, and 70,000 more equipment and repairing aircraft. Firms competed fiercely against one another to advance the technology. German industry could crank out 10,000 airplanes per year with these resources. It was the Third Reich's greatest success in state-directed arms production.[97]

By 1935, Germany had recovered its GDP of 1928, as had the United States and some other countries, but a radical reallocation of resources into rearmament had boosted the share of military-related spending from 1 to 10 percent of GDP in Germany. About 25 percent of industry was related to non-market items.[98]

Hitler declared in March 1935 that Germany needed a peacetime army of 36 divisions and announced the return of conscription. In autumn 1935, General Ludwig Beck, the new Wehrmacht chief of staff, decided the army could not wait until 1938 to establish an offensive capability and in December added 48 tank battalions to the rearmament plan. The army demanded a doubling of imports of metal ore, rubber, and oil in 1936 for the expansion.[99]

But wait! There was more. The army in June 1936 increased its planned structure to 41 divisions, including three panzer, three "light," and four motorized infantry divisions, plus seven independent tank brigades. The panzer divisions would need 500 tanks each, and the light divisions two hundred. The tank brigades were to be the foundations of future panzer divisions. The backbone was to consist of 1,812 medium tanks that were in development and scheduled for production in 1938, with delivery of 807 by 1939. By 1940, the infrastructure and equipment for 102 divisions and 3.6 million men was to be ready. The Luftwaffe, meanwhile, moved its 2,000-plane target from 1938 to 1937.[100]

Germany, however, lacked the foreign exchange inflows to pay for all the imports needed for the expansion. Hitler in October issued a "Four Year Plan" that directed German industry to make the country self-sufficient in oil, rubber, and iron ore. This led to huge investments in the technology and production facilities for synthetic oil and rubber. Hermann Göring took charge. A secret policy stipulated that German be ready for war within four years.[101]

The plan, however, was going to take two years to produce major results. Production of weapons like tanks, artillery, and ammunition required vast amounts of steel, and that was becoming a major bottleneck. The regime had to cut steel output by 15 percent in November to extend the sufficiency of iron ore and scrap. Rationing ensued.[102]

*

Hitler during the mid-1930s displayed a certain sympathy for Roosevelt and what he was trying to accomplish with his New Deal, which bore some similarity to aspects of Hitler's own economic revitalization program. Hitler even characterized Roosevelt as a man with whom he could ultimately strike a bargain.[103]

Nevertheless, Hitler's aggressive racism and increasing assaults on the Jews between 1933 and 1939 created an atmosphere of German–American hostility that existed between Germany and none of its European neighbors. Racial persecution repelled many Americans, despite the institutionalized racism in their own society. The Nazis, who defined their own nation strictly in terms of race, looked down on the racial mix in America. Berlin hoped that its admirers and the active German American Bund organization would stymie the Jews in the halls of power.[104]

The first German strategic appraisal of its position vis-à-vis the United States occurred in 1939, but then only in passing, which will be covered in a following chapter. What the military was hearing from Washington gave it little reason to expend the effort. The German military attaché, Major General Friedrich Boetticher, reported confidently in May 1934,

> In many cases, vehicles are still in use that long ago disappeared in Germany. Of the 8,309 trucks available as of 1 January 1934, 5,894 were from the [World] War, and 596 more were at least five years old.... With the exception of a dozen vehicles built in the last few years, every tank in the American Army is from the World War. These vehicles are completely obsolete and worthless in battle against armies with modern equipment.[105]

While the U.S. Army could quickly obtain modern trucks in a war situation, the attaché estimated that it would take a year for the United States to begin mass production of tanks. The Americans were hoping to mechanize no more than a cavalry brigade and two infantry regiments, while Germany was building panzer divisions.[106]

Boetticher, who performed his function from 1933 through the closure of the German Embassy after Hitler declared war on 11 December 1941, engaged solely in overt intelligence collection, which foreshadowed a gap the size of the Grand Canyon between the Allies' ability to discern hidden enemy intentions and capabilities through intelligence and the Axis Powers' stunted insight in the opposite direction. Boetticher declared, "It was so easy, the Americans are so broad-minded, they print everything in their papers. You don't need any intelligence service. You only have to be industrious, to see the papers and what they print!" The general refused to handle spies himself and quashed any attempt by the military intelligence service, the *Abwehr* (Defense), to recruit any agents. He feared they would be exposed and disrupt his overt contacts to the Americans.[107]

The German Embassy in Washington, in a mid-1936 overview of U.S. foreign policy—seemingly informed by few contacts with actual American leaders—reported that worry was growing in the United States that a new war would erupt in Europe, and that Germany would be the aggressor. For the moment, though, Washington was more concerned with Japanese and Italian expeditions against peoples without modern weapons, such as the Italian campaign in Ethiopia, and Secretary of State Cordell Hull had told the ambassador privately that he judged the chance of war in Europe at one in ten.[108] The embassy took Roosevelt at his public word that, despite his criticism of "treaty breakers" pursuing imperialist policies based on "racial hatred mixed with fanaticism," the President was committed to neutrality, though he would defend the Western hemisphere.[109] And, despite Hull's public warnings that a new world war would threaten the survival of Western civilization, the embassy reassured Berlin that nobody in the country was thinking about eventual participation in a European conflict.[110]

Had Germany considered its relative economic power to America at this time, it might not have appeared too daunting. In 1870, when Germany unified, the populations of the two countries were roughly equal, and despite America's resources and lands, its output was only a third larger. At the outbreak of World War I, America's economy had grown to about twice the size of Germany's. By 1943, as mobilization was just hitting its stride, the ratio was to be about 4:1.[111]

Totalitarian Rule: One Decider

Two days after Hitler became Chancellor on 30 January 1933, he met informally with Defense Minister General Werner von Blomberg—handpicked by President Paul Hindenburg to keep the military out of politics, but a Nazi sympathizer—and other senior military officers. Hitler told him that he planned to strengthen the army, reintroduce conscription, prepare the youth for war using his party tools, and conquer living space for Germans to the east. He delicately hinted that the non-German populations would be removed. He said that if France were smart, it would launch a preemptive attack with its allies to the east before Germany was militarily strong again. We'll see, he told them. This sounded acceptable to the generals.[112]

When Hitler became Chancellor, Nazis constituted a minority in the Cabinet, which the Weimar Republic and the Third Reich termed the *Reichsregierung* (Reich government). This grouping included ordinary Cabinet members, members of the Council of Ministers for Defense of the Reich, and members of the Secret Cabinet Council. By January 1937, all Cabinet members were Nazis, and the government existed as a tool to implement Nazi Party policies.

Although the *Reichstag* (legislature) existed, by the Act of 24 March 1933, the Cabinet gained the power to legislate on all matters by decree, including deviating from the constitution. In 1935, after the death of President von Hindenburg, Hitler consolidated the positions of Chancellor and President in his own person. By that year, Hitler created the Reich Defense Council—a war planning body—with himself as chairman. He transformed that back into the Council of Ministers for Defense of the Reich in 1939, which was empowered to issue decrees with the force of law.[113]

The Nazi Party's *Führerprinzip* (leader principle) consolidated all power in the Führer, Adolf Hitler. Party documents explained:

> The Führer Principle requires a pyramidal organization structure in its details as well as in its entirety....
> The Führer is at the top.
> He nominates the necessary leaders for the various spheres of work of the Reich's direction, the Party apparatus, and the State administration....
> He shapes the collective will of the people within himself, and he enjoys the political unity and entirety of the people in opposition to individual interests.
> The Führer unites in himself all the sovereign authority of the Reich; all public authority in the state as well as in the movement is derived from the authority of the Führer. We must speak

not of the state's authority but of the Führer's authority if we wish to designate the character of the political authority within the Reich correctly. The state does not hold political authority as an impersonal unit but receives it from the Führer as the executor of the national will. The authority of the Führer is complete and all-embracing; it unites in itself all the means of political direction; it extends into all fields of national life; it embraces the entire people, which is bound to the Führer in loyalty and obedience. The authority of the Führer is not limited by checks and controls, by special autonomous bodies or individual rights, but it is free and independent, all-inclusive and unlimited.[114]

The Nazi Party's aims in the 1930s were: 1) To abrogate and overthrow the Treaty of Versailles and its restrictions upon the military armament and activity of Germany; 2) To acquire the territories lost by Germany as the result of the World War of 1914–1918, and other territories in Europe asserted to be occupied by so-called "racial Germans"; and 3) To acquire further territories in Europe and elsewhere claimed to be required by "racial Germans" as "*Lebensraum*" or living space, at the expense of neighboring and other countries.[115]

Nazi doctrine was overtly racist. Persons of so-called "German blood" were a master race and were accordingly entitled to subjugate, dominate, or exterminate other "races" and "peoples." The Nazi doctrine of racial supremacy was incorporated as Point 4 in the Party Program of 24 February 1930.[116]

Grasping Gauntlets Across the Water

The first step toward the formation of the Axis took place in 1936, after Japan withdrew from the Washington Naval Limitation Treaty of 1922. On 25 November 1936, Japan and Germany concluded the Anti-Comintern Pact, to which Italy adhered in 1937, which included a secret deal. Tokyo and Berlin agreed that "in case one of the signatory powers is attacked or threatened with attack by the Soviet Union without provocation, the other signatory party shall refrain from taking any measure likely to result in any diminution of the burden of the Soviet Union's position, and the two signatories shall immediately discuss measures to be taken for the protection of their mutual interests."[117]

The Emperor's Privy Council considered the pact in Tokyo on 29 November. The Privy Council dated to 1888 and became part of the constitution in 1889; it consisted of a president, a vice president, 24 councilors, a secretary general, and a secretariat. The Emperor appointed the councilors on the advice of the Premier. The council had the authority to consider draft laws, approve declarations of martial law and penal codes, decide the constitutionality of international agreements, and dispose of other matters submitted to it. In practice, the Premier was bound to accept decisions of the Privy Council or resign. President of the Privy Council Baron Kiichiro Hiranuma announced that the draft was unanimously approved.[118]

Hiranuma was to play a central role in leading Japan to war against the United States. Postwar military tribunal prosecutors described him in these terms: "He was not a militarist in the sense that he fought with guns and bombs; he was the sophist fighting with ideas and the skill of his intellect."[119] Hiranuma was a lawyer by training and had served as a public prosecutor in Tokyo. He later became head of a hardline nationalist organization called the *Kokuhon-sha* that supported the "best aspects" of fascism and communism.[120]

CHAPTER 2

1937: The First Pre-World War Year

Japan Mounts the Tiger

The Japanese at least thought about the possibility of American interference when they started what became a global war in earnest in 1937. But first, a great deal of war preparation occurred.

The Japanese Diet in March 1937 adopted the National General Mobilization Bill giving the government new powers. Technical and professional men were compelled to register, and factory owners were asked to plan production.[1]

The IJN was about to launch a shipbuilding program that would give it a reasonable expectation of technological superiority over the United States and Great Britain. Japan on 30 March refused to accept the 14-inch naval gun limitation agreed to by the United States, Britain, and France in London.[2] The key reason was that Navy Minister Admiral Mitsumasa Yonai that same month approved the final plans for building the Yamato-class of battleships, which would be the largest in the world. Displacing 62,000 tons, the behemoths would carry nine 18-inch guns and be able to reach 27 knots.[3]

One year earlier, the IJA had launched a 12-year expansion plan that reflected a rather sober and self-critical assessment of the IJA's capabilities as compared to potential enemies. Its budget proposal indicated that beginning in 1936–1937, the lion's share of a special budget allocation was to go toward expanding the air force and improving air defenses. It noted, "We have at present only two tank units, while the Soviet Army has over a dozen independent motorized units, 20 independent tank battalions, and one half of their cavalry and infantry troops are motorized.... [Regarding equipment], our troops are still far behind the troops of any Occidental power." The proposal blamed losses in China in part on poor equipment.[4] By 1941, the IJA was to double from 24 to 51 divisions and triple from 54 to 150 air companies.[5]

With an initial eye toward strengthening military capabilities vis-à-vis the USSR, the government in May established the Bureau for Planning (reorganized into the Board of Planning in October 1938). The bureau was to spur growth of key industries. The Board produced its first plan for the expansion of production covering 1938–1941, starting in April 1938. At the same time, a five-year plan for building up industry in Manchukuo kicked off in April 1937.[6]

A Mitsubishi reconnaissance test plane called the *Kamikaze* (Divine Wind) flew from Tokyo to London via southwest Asia and landed on 9 April. The nation followed the affair with fascination and pride. The aircrew debarked to the cheers of a crowd of 4,000, including cries of "Banzai! [Long live the Emperor!]"[7]

In June 1937, Prince Fumimaro Konoye became Prime Minister. He had initially refused the honor—and is said to have been the first man ever to do so—and upon taking office had proclaimed that he was not capable of holding it. He was 46 years old and the second-youngest premier in Japanese history. Konoye was a member of one of Japan's greatest and most ancient houses that, like the imperial family, claimed descent from the gods. Born in Tokyo in October 1891, Konoye studied at the universities of Tokyo and Kyoto, when he briefly flirted with an interest in Marxism. Konoye knew quite a bit about the wider world. A friend of his father had taken him to Paris as part of the Japanese delegation to the peace talks in 1919, and he had visited Washington, D.C. In the mid-1930s, he sent one of his sons to Princeton. Konoye loomed almost six feet tall, possessed a subtle and complex mind, and wore his humility like a mask. Konoye had several advantages entering the premiership: the Emperor favored him, the army respected him, and no political party or faction controlled him.[8]

Konoye's travel to Europe and America had left him with a critical attitude toward Anglo-Saxons in particular, whom he judged to be racists regarding what would nowadays be called people of color. Yet, oddly, he would make common cause with the racist Nazis and in 1937 appeared at a costume party dressed as Hitler.[9]

Konoye's election followed months of political maneuvering by the IJA to select a premier to its satisfaction, according to a British analysis in OSS files. The military could force dissolution of the government and Diet by withdrawing their ministers from the Cabinet. In February 1936, army rebels in Tokyo had tried to murder the premier, Admiral Keisuke Okada (who resigned), and months of failed efforts to select a replacement resulted in dissolution of the Diet. After an election, stalemate resumed until the IJA's nominee, Konoye, won acceptance.[10]

In his history of the Sino-Japanese War, Rana Mitter describes the conditions Konoye encountered: "Unlike in Nazi Germany or fascist Italy, there was no single figure in Japan, no Duce or Führer, whose personal megalomania lay at the heart of foreign policy. Japan had ended up in a toxic situation where most of its politicians, military, and public had become infected with 'war fever.'"[11]

Japanese historian Hiroyuki Agawa cites one of the journalists who covered the IJN in 1935–1936 as relating that Yonai, in a rare expression of pessimism about the direction Japan was headed, said, "The Japanese people, you see, have never been defeated in war."[12] Never having lost probably left decision-makers unprepared to even consider the possibility. Herein lies one similarity to the American historical experience.

On 7 July 1937, Japanese troops provoked confrontations with Chinese forces near Beijing at a bridge known to Westerners as Marco Polo Bridge, because the great explorer had mentioned it out of admiration for its decoration with lion heads. The Japanese had become concerned that Chiang Kai-Shek's Nationalist government would succeed in unifying China and incline toward cooperation with the Soviet Union. Chiang had avoided military confrontation over Manchuria, which was outside the historical heart of China, but he knew public reaction would be fierce if he meekly surrendered northeast China. He also recognized that he was going to have to fight Japan at some point, and he and his senior advisers had been planning for an eventual clash since the early 1930s. This incident seemed as good a time as any. Chiang dispatched reinforcements for the still warlord-controlled troops in the area.[13]

Japanese military historian Takushiro Hattori asserts in his history of the war, "The [Manchuria] Incident came as a complete surprise to Japan. In those days, Japan was fully occupied with the construction of Manchukuo, bolstering military preparations against the USSR, and expanding key industries; and made no plans or preparations for an all-out Sino-Japanese war."[14]

In Japan, some in the military wanted to escalate and seize the opportunity to destroy the Chiang regime, but others and the civilian leadership initially adopted a non-expansionist policy and hoped for a local resolution. Matching Chiang's decision to reinforce his troops, Konoye announced on 11 July that Japan was mobilizing in north China. One contemporary observer called Konoye "the man who ordered the nation to cross the Rubicon when the first shots were fired."[15] The reader should keep in mind that this decision ultimately led to war with America.

When Japan started World War II, the IJA intended to deliver a short, sharp lesson to Chiang that would bring him to heel. Nobody expected a years-long quagmire.

As Prime Minister, Fumimaro Konoye escalated the China Incident in 1937 into a full-blown war. In 1940, he pressed to make the advance to the south state policy, which he recognized at the time could lead to war with America. He got cold feet and resigned two months before Pearl Harbor. (Wikimedia Commons)

Hugh Byas, a British editor and expert on Japan, told the Council on Foreign Relations after departing Tokyo in late 1941,

> In the early years of the present war, Japanese generals were fond of quoting the Austro-German war of 1866 as the pattern they wanted to follow. They would teach the Chinese a short, sharp lesson to show them who was master and then make a generous peace, as Bismarck made with Austria, which would tie the two nations together much as the old Austro-Hungarian Empire was tied to the German Empire. The generals who used to talk like that are still in high positions.[16]

Hattori, who served as the Kwangtung Army's chief of operations in 1939 and would know the background, likewise described the Japanese rationale as follows: "In order to bring about an early settlement of the incident, its objective was to deliver a powerful blow against the anti-Japanese troops of China and chastise them for their hostile actions and faithless conduct."[17]

In Tokyo, hawks calling for escalation and a short, decisive, campaign gained the upper hand. Hattori asserts that as a result of Chinese armed provocations on 25 and 26 September (*sic*, almost certainly July), "we were finally compelled to enter into a phase of armed hostilities." Japan struck on 27 July. The High Command and government endorsed the decision. By the end of the month, troops had driven the Chinese from Beijing and Tianjin and by August had expanded well into central China.[18]

The Emperor later confided privately that he had seen the "China Incident," as Japan called it, coming and had urged War Minister Hajime Sugiyama to find a compromise with China. The minister replied that that there was no danger of Soviet intervention, and that China could be settled within a few months. It was a miscalculation on the scale of Hitler's later expectation that he would crush the Soviet Union over the same span of time. Tokyo issued no declaration of war. The League of Nations on 6 October whined that Japan had no legal basis for its invasion. Tokyo declared that it was acting in self-defense in the face of China's violent and anti-Japanese policy.[19]

General Hajime Sugiyama as War Minister assured Hirohito when Japan invaded China in 1937 that the war would last a month. As Army Chief of Staff, he told the Emperor before Pearl Harbor that war with America would require six months. (Wikimedia Commons)

The invasion did not point directly to war with America, but it created conditions in which the United States, though neutral, would become a key patron for Japan's enemy in a long, bloody, and frustrating conflict—like the role China would later play in supporting North Vietnam against its American enemy. The Nationalist Chinese sought to encourage American engagement from the start of the war. As fighting raged around Shanghai, Chiang recorded in his diary that he hoped foreign powers would be angry with Japan and that he would try to induce the United States, Britain, and the USSR to join the war. On 13 September, Song Meiling, Chiang's wife, made a broadcast to the United States that lambasted the West for refusing to back the Chinese cause.[20]

Admiral Fukudome told interrogators after the war,

> Beginning with the Manchurian Incident and continuing through the China Incident, the fleet felt that by getting into these two troubles, our forces were getting their feet deeper and deeper into the mire and if continued long enough, it would lead eventually to war with the United States.... The navy did not have confidence in the event of war with the United States and for that reason, all top-level naval officers, both in Tokyo and with the fleet, feared any trend of event that might eventually lead to war with the United States, and that the China Incident was just such an event.[21]

Some of the fleet, however—the Third Fleet off the coast of China—enthusiastically backed the policy of "punishing" China and were prepared for an all-out war there. This sentiment down range undermined Navy Minister Yonai's initial opposition to sending troops into China at meetings in Tokyo. After Chinese troops shot two Japanese sailors and the situation in Shanghai teetered toward armed conflict, Yonai reversed course and pursued naval mobilization.[22]

To jump ahead, the United States eventually responded by giving military, political, and economic support to Chiang Kai-shek and his Nationalist government. Loans began to flow in February 1939. Arms shipments were to total $35.6 million through June 1941, and American volunteers were to form the core of the Chinese air force—the famous Flying Tigers.

The Soviets acted even before America to buttress Chiang and signed a non-aggression pact on 21 August. Moreover, Soviet loans started to flow before America's or Britain's, the first being signed on 1 March 1938.[23]

Chiang in early November realized he could not hold Shanghai and decided to pull out rather than sacrifice more of his best troops. He would instead defeat the enemy's plan of rapid decision in a quick war by carrying out a war of attrition to wear out the enemy.[24]

Thus, the conflict became an unwinnable war for Japan, although the Japanese did not know that at the time.

The Nationalist military commander and strategist Jiang Baili had introduced the idea of waging a long war against Japan in 1928. The Nationalist government had planned as early as 1932 to withdraw itself and key industrial production to central China if an enemy seized the eastern seaboard. The Nationalists revealed on 21 November that the government would move to Chungking (Chongqing) in southwestern China while the military command moved to Wuhan (Hankow). With the fall of Shanghai, no defense of Nanking (Nanjing) remained possible.[25]

The Japanese command initially intended only to occupy northern China, not to capture the capital of Nanking, but Chiang's decision to fight in the Yangtze valley forced a change of plans. The Japanese on 26 August hurriedly established the Central China Area Army (CCAA), combining the Tenth and Shanghai Expeditionary Armies. The hope for a quick knockout blow evaporated.

Japanese military and civilian leaders gave a thought to America on the outbreak of war, but only as a risk factor. The thought does not appear to have had any influence on decision-making. General Matsui Iwane, commanding the Shanghai Expeditionary Army, announced:

> Unless the Nanking Government reconsiders its attitude and ceases its resistance, Japanese troops will continue to advance to Nanking, Hankow, and even Chungking, China's new capital.... The first point is to make the Nanking Government abandon its policy of depending on the European countries and America.... The second point is to make the Chinese people recognize that Japanese troops are the real friends of China.[26]

This statement at least recognized that America would be part of Japan's China problem.[27]

The Imperial General Headquarters (IGHQ) activated on 24 November to control operations in China. This put Emperor Hirohito in the policy loop, though not in control of it. The first "liaison conference" between the IGHQ and the civilian government occurred that afternoon in the Prime Minister's office. The participants discussed whether Japan should limit its operations because of the Soviet threat and risk of American or British intervention. The military was unwilling to share any details of its operations.[28]

Japan declared a naval blockade of China, and after several incidents of Japanese search and seizure of their national commercial vessels, the U.S. and Royal Navies began escorting merchantmen flying their respective flags into Chinese harbors. On 14 December, during the Japanese offensive to seize Nanking, Japanese naval aircraft accidentally sank the American gunboat *Panay* on the Yangtze River. Japan acknowledged it was in the wrong and apologized, formally and through numerous personal contacts. Tokyo immediately paid reparations. Admiral Kichisaburo Nomura, best known as the last pre-war ambassador to the United States, later wrote that the incident proved to be a "stepping stone to war."[29]

Roosevelt delivered a speech in Chicago on 5 October that garnered attention in Japan. He labeled Japan and Italy "aggressor nations" over their wars in China and Abyssinia. The next day, the State Department accused Japan of violating the Nine Powers Treaty, which guaranteed China's sovereignty, and the Kellogg–Briand Pact that outlawed war. From the Japanese perspective, this set the baseline for American foreign policy until Pearl Harbor. On the other hand, that same day, Mussolini publicly expressed his absolute support for Japan's expansion in China.[30]

In Washington, Roosevelt asked Congress for $1.1 billion ($16.3 billion today) to expand the fleet by 20 percent. Despite having passed the Neutrality Acts in the preceding three years, which forbade participation in a European war and imposed an arms embargo on belligerents (amended to permit sales on a cash-and-carry basis), Congress approved the request. The funding would cover two aircraft carriers, three battleships, 23 destroyers, 9 submarines, and 950 naval aircraft.[31]

Chinese troops, meanwhile, abandoned Nanking on 12 December and set most of the city ablaze to deny the Japanese use of the buildings. The Japanese army entered the city the next day, and witnesses reported the outbreak of additional fires. Over the next six weeks, the Japanese soldiers engaged in widespread murder, looting, and sexual assault across the city, a period that came to be known as the Rape of Nanking.[32]

Germany: The Gambles Begin

There is no indication that strategists in Germany were devoting any time to considering a possible war with the United States. Hitler had only just remilitarized the Rhineland on 7 September 1936 and did not move to incorporate Austria into the Reich until 1938. Hitler's personal assistant, Heinz Linge, told Soviet interrogators that the General Staff reported to Hitler that the American military attaché, Major Truman Smith, approved of the occupation of the Rhineland and even congratulated his contact at the General Staff. Linge also reported that as Hitler and Hermann Göring listened to radio reports of troops marching across the Rhine bridges, Hitler slapped the other man on the shoulder and said, "Göring, we are really complete chancers [gamblers]."[33] Hitler later claimed that "the first forty-eight hours after the march into the Rhineland were the most nerve-wracking in my life."[34]

Hitler's interests in 1937 were parochial and related to consolidating power. Had he chosen to think about the United States, he was receiving perceptive observations from German diplomats.

In April, the German Embassy in Washington observed that Britain's decision to rearm had made a deep impression in the United States that could set the direction of American policy toward the situation in Europe. As debate swirled in Congress over the draft Neutrality Act, the embassy warned that as worded, it would give all advantages in the supply of war materials to Britain because of its command of the sea. The embassy expressed skepticism that Washington would remain neutral in the Pacific region. It observed that America had played an active great-power role in the Far East unlike anything in Europe, that it still had defense commitments in the Philippines that could come into play if Japanese expansionism turned in that direction, and that failure to act in such a case would render it an international "non-power." Should Japan and Britain go to war, American foreign policy circles were clear that the country could not allow a British collapse and total Japanese dominance of the region.[35]

The embassy gave Berlin a clear message on the direction of American opinion in a report on the 20th anniversary in April 1937 of the country's entry into World War I, an event typically ignored but, because of war fears, the cause for policy speeches and press commentaries in 1937. The prevailing view was that America must stay out of any new conflict, but that the country must support the rearmament of the "peaceable countries," Britain and France.[36] Nevertheless, the embassy kept close tabs on the political balance between isolationist and "activist" opinion, because isolationism served Germany's interests given that under no circumstances would the United States enter a war in support of Germany.[37]

Rearmament Sputters

The rationing of steel beginning in December 1936 caused huge disruptions to the schedule for preparation for war within four years. The steel available to the Wehrmacht remained almost the same as in 1936. In May, the chief of staff warned the War Ministry that the fighting strength foreseen for 1940 would not be available for years to come. Manpower would be available, divisions would organize, but equipment would fall short. The army would not be ready for war.

Similarly, the Luftwaffe cut the industrial workforce 10 percent, output 25 percent, and plant expansion 66 percent. Aircraft production slid from April 1937 to summer 1938. It accomplished its program to refit the fighting force with modern planes only by virtually eliminating production of non-fighters, especially trainers.[38]

Necessity drove a solution. Germany had huge reserves of low-grade iron ore at Salzgitter, but the Ruhr industrial oligopolists preferred to import high-grade ore from Scandinavia. The steel shortage persuaded the steel barons to agree to increase production capacity from 19 million to 24 million tons using domestic ore. The Nazi apparatchiks wanted to keep the new blast furnaces out of the barons' hands, and thus was born in July the Reich Works Hermann Göring that was to rival the Ruhr in production. Göring met with the barons and told them the state was seizing all their ore fields because they had failed for four years to meet Germany's steel requirements.

The Reich Works started production in 1939 and absorbed steel mills as Germany occupied other countries.[39]

Hitler Reveals His Plans for Conquest

Hitler only unveiled his initial plans for foreign conquest to his senior leadership in November 1937. In a meeting on the 5th in the Chancellery, which included navy chief Erich Raeder, Foreign Minister Konstantin von Neurath, and Luftwaffe commander and Nazi comrade Göring, he stated that Austria and Czechoslovakia would be acquired by force if necessary to provide added *Lebensraum*—living space—for the 85 million Germans. "The German question," he said, "can only be solved by way of force, and this is never without risk." Germany's military was almost fully prepared, and after 1943–1945, she would have to expect the international balance of forces to produce her relative decline. He discussed the likely reactions of Great Britain, France, Italy, Poland, and Russia should Germany conquer Czechoslovakia, but gave no thought to America. Hitler had already consulted with Field Marshal Werner von Blomberg, the Minister of War and commander of the German army, and Colonel General Werner von Fritsch, about such operations. Fritsch had launched a study to examine how to overcome fortifications on the Czechoslovak side of the border.[40]

It is interesting that Hitler's thinking resembled Japan's regarding an eventual emergence of an unfavorable balance of forces with the United States. Indeed, Hitler was to return to this argument frequently. Given that inevitability, Germany had nothing to lose by acting while it had the most capable armed forces in Europe, and everything to lose as time passed if not. Tooze points out that Hitler made this argument fully cognizant of the stumbling rearmaments in 1939, and that one cannot wave the argument off as a mere rationalization for quick war.[41]

Following this meeting, Hitler authorized cranking up steel output using new domestic sources of iron ore and imports as needed. The year-long slowdown in rearmament was to ease in early 1938.[42]

Again, we will speculate in the absence of hard evidence that Hitler's experience with a year of constrained defense production because of resource constraints predisposed him to be skeptical about American claims on industrial mobilization.

Italy Enters the Axis

Italy joined the Anti-Comintern Pact on 6 November 1937.

Italian military attention in 1937 was on empire building and appeared to reflect a naïve expectation that the next war would not be as long and grueling as the Great War. Italian Under Secretary of War General Alberto Pariani introduced the "war budget" for 1938 to the Chamber of Deputies on 4 May 1937. Pariani said the military was adapting its organization to the "new situation and new exigencies."

> The Italian Army war doctrine is well known: "A rapid war with a rapid conclusion." This doctrine is open to discussion, but it responds to the Italian character, geographical and economic situation, to the Fascist spirit of the Nation.... [I]f a war must be won rapidly, we must have a moral, technical, and material preparation permitting us to do so. This preparation is particularly taken care of by the Ministry for War with the dual purpose of insuring the territorial integrity of the Empire and organizing an adequate rapid mass of maneuver to be thrown into the battle at the right moment and at the right place.[43]

Italy was building frontier fortifications and a Frontier Guard, behind which mobilization would safely take place. A coast militia would guard Italy's shores in cooperation with the navy. Listening posts and air defense centers were under construction. Metropolitan army units were permanently transferred to the colonies to protect them.[44]

What Might They Have Thought About America?

If only they had known how much war material America was to make!

The 1937 Japanese analysis and Hitler's statements once he actually started thinking about the United States as an adversary show that future enemies in 1937 probably thought about America almost solely in terms of a major (for Japan dangerous) naval power capable of providing raw materials, oil, and eventually manpower to its potential allies, as the nation had in the Great War. Nobody had any historical reason to think of the United States as the future Arsenal of Democracy. In fact, the Great War suggested the opposite. The Americans had fought in France using French-supplied tanks and British- and French-made fighter aircraft, artillery, and machine guns.[45]

Up until 1915 in America, the relationship between the military and industry ranged from occasional close cooperation to hostile tolerance. That year, with the war already raging in Europe, the War Department established the principle that it would obtain all but exclusively military items such as munitions and artillery from the private sector and would train military personnel as experts to work with industry. The Naval Consulting Board established the Industrial Committee, which surveyed 18,000 industrial plants to establish their capabilities to produce war materials.[46]

When General John Pershing estimated in 1915 that the army would have to expand to 30 divisions, or about a million men, the Ordnance Bureau reported that it would need a year simply to supply a sufficient number of rifles and small-arms ammunition for such a force—assuming it did not have to compete with the Allies for production from the same sources. There was practically no aircraft industry in the country, and almost no aircraft in the military inventory.

Congress passed the National Defense Act in 1916 that created the Council of National Defense, consisting of the Secretaries of War, Navy, Agriculture, Interior, Commerce, and Labor, and an advisory committee that handled day-to-day affairs. These bodies defined the scope of mobilization and sorted out government–industry relations. In July 1917, the War Industries Board (WIB) was created to centrally procure supplies for the army and navy, which greatly improved efficiency, and to bring leaders of industries directly into decision-making. The WIB had the authority to convert facilities to war production and build new ones if necessary. A substructure of 157 commodity committees and more than 300 materiel committees brought together civilian and military experts.[47]

Although few American-made combat aircraft reached the airmen in Europe, by late 1918 the United States aircraft industry employed 200,000 people and was producing 12,000 planes a year. American factories were producing French-designed tanks.[48] These facts were publicly available.

The anticipation of a quick war with a quick decision, which also lay at the heart of Prussian military tradition, may have blinded Axis decision-makers to the American industrial might that reality handed them. This seems a poor excuse given the recent experience with a long, resource-intensive, industrial world war, even if America had not overawed them during its relatively short involvement in the conflict.

German leaders' later refusal to believe American production statistics shows that this enemy, at least, did not truly grasp the pace and scale of war industry mobilization that the country could ramp up, probably because they had not seen its effects on the weapons they faced in the Great War. In the case of Germany, we shall see, Hitler probably assumed, mistakenly, that America would face the same difficulties Germany had during its rapid industrial mobilization for war. Although there is no evidence that the Japanese disbelieved American industrial output statistics, we will see below that they later acknowledged underestimating the potential.

There was another fateful American capability about which Axis powers had information but they did not take into account: air power. Germany and Japan knew in 1937 that the United States had begun producing a self-protecting strategic bomber, the B-17. Japan and Italy did not plan their military expansion or wage their wars in ways to prepare to battle vast fleets of their like. Nor did any Axis power create its own capabilities to wage strategic bombing. Germany did launch a program in 1937 to build the He 177 four-engine bomber, but the design tended to explode and Hitler eventually wrote it off as "garbage."[49] The Me 264 was a second four-engine bomber that was designed to just reach the American east coast from the Azores that was an expensive design failure.[50]

Phillips O'Brien, in *How the War Was Won*, makes the provocative assertion, "There were no decisive battles in World War II." The decisive war occurred on sea and in the air, he suggests, and he demonstrates that all major combatants except the USSR devoted at least two-thirds of their war production to the wars in the air and at sea. In every year of the war, at least half of Germany's output was aircraft, while Japan's production skewed heavily toward aircraft and warships. Famous individual land battles, such as El Alamein and Kursk, devoured equipment easily replaced by current production. Japan's loss of four carriers at Midway, in contrast, took years to replace. Moreover, Japan's and Germany's growing losses of aircraft to non-combat reasons exceeded the toll in battle. Ultimately, the Axis couldn't beat the Allies' capacity to build, transport, and employ more lethal items, especially America's.[51]

Without accepting the premise that land battles did not matter on grounds that war cannot be won without warriors fighting battles, we will see that worsening material inferiority was to be much on the minds of Axis leaders as the war progressed.

What Could They Not Have Anticipated?

When the Axis leaders launched and planned wars that would ultimately lead to war against America, they had no reason to anticipate three developments that would contribute significantly to their defeat. The first was the adversaries' ability to identify their intentions and capabilities; the Western Allies would achieve information dominance. And that started before hostilities even erupted.

In 1921, the U.S. Navy's Office of Naval Intelligence (ONI) broke into the apartment of the Japanese naval attaché and photographed the 1918 naval code, called "Red" after the binders in which the decrypts were placed; the Japanese fleet used that code until 1931. A small group of analysts in OP-20-G, responsible for codebreaking, including Agnes Driscoll, slowly unraveled the more complex "Blue" code (yep, the binders!) using what they knew about how the Japanese structured codes and cracked it by 1935. The Japanese fleet used Blue until 1938. In 1939, the IJN split its vastly more complex codes into what ONI called the fleet code and, for most sensitive communications, the Admirals' code. Agnes Driscoll led the attack and made so much progress by October 1940 that ONI directed one analyst move over to the German navy communications. A new variant of the code in 1940 was called JN-25, because it was the 25th one ONI had tackled, and its variants over the war were to be tagged by an extension of JN-25, like today would be JN-25.1. As the war spun up, OP-20-G exploded in size and resources.[52]

American analysts gradually cracked Japan's Purple diplomatic code between August 1940 and early 1941. ONI knew it needed help against the new code and teamed up with the U.S. Army's Signal Intelligence Service. The code was machine-based using a device more complex than Germany's Enigma machine. Purple decrypts began to flow in September 1940.[53] This traffic was to receive the code name MAGIC.

President Roosevelt in the first half of 1940 had defined responsibilities for intelligence and counterintelligence to focus efforts efficiently. ONI and the army's Military Intelligence Division (MID) were to collect worldwide except in Latin America, which went to the Federal Bureau of Investigation (FBI). He also created the office of the Coordinator of Information, which was supposed to be a clearing house for intelligence. Under William Donovan, the OCI transformed into the Office of Strategic Services (OSS), the predecessor of the Central Intelligence Agency.

The army's SIS already had the communications intelligence (COMINT) lead on German, Italian, Japanese (in full cooperation with ONI), and Mexican/Latin American diplomatic traffic. The U.S. Coast Guard and Federal Communications Commission developed expertise in detecting and reading secret radio transmissions from German and Italian agents in the United States and Latin America.[54]

American military intelligence leaders, despite ONI reluctance, agreed internally in December to pursue a full exchange with the British on COMINT against the Axis powers, including giving the UK a copy of the machines used to decrypt Purple.

An American delegation secretly visited the UK in February 1941, handed over the Purple machine, and received the first briefings on the UK's success against German Enigma, though no technical information. In the Far East, the British and Americans began a full exchange of COMINT information and Japanese codes. These pre-war moves (for the Americans) launched an amazing relationship between the Allies that Axis leaders could never have imagined.[55]

OP-20-G began a formal COMINT exchange with the British organization the Government Code and Cypher School (GC&CS) in June 1941, first through the British Embassy in Washington, and then through British Security Coordination in New York City (an arm of MI6, the British Secret Service). The documents moved by air. GC&CS reached a similar deal with the U.S. Army's SIS in August.[56]

The MAGIC program was reading nearly every Japanese diplomatic code by mid-1942. It was also decrypting diplomatic messages from the Vichy French, who had posts across Asia, and the Portuguese, who like the French had an embassy in Tokyo. Daily MAGIC summaries were buttressed by military supplements with other SIGINT decrypts. Reviewing the declassified documents at the National Archives in College Park is mind blowing.

Most pertinent to Japan, albeit only at a time when the leadership had already resolved to end the war on more or less Allied terms, the Japanese did not anticipate the appearance of a weapon that could destroy one city apiece. Hisatsune Sakomizu, who served on the War Planning Board under Tojo and as *chef de cabinet* for Prime Minister Teiichi Suzuki at the end of the war, told interrogators that Japanese scientists had assured officials that no country would be able to create an atomic bomb during the war.[57]

Finally, the Japanese never anticipated that they could not defeat China. The Germans had the same issue regarding Britain and the USSR.

CHAPTER 3

1938: America the Afterthought

America in 1938 offered Axis leaders some reason to think about the country, though the signals were largely ignored. Roosevelt was struggling to overcome the Great Depression with his New Deal, and isolationism still had legs. Yet, the President warned publicly about the possibility of a two-front war and urged increased military preparedness and industrial mobilization. And behind the scenes, America was taking steps to ready itself for war.

Japan Sinks into the China Mire with Few Thoughts of America

The diary of then Minister of Education Koichi Kido reveals the issues that engaged the attentions of the most senior officials in Tokyo in early 1938. Kido spoke frequently with Prime Minister Fumimaro Konoye and other key figures, attended Cabinet meetings, and gathered a constant stream of information. In 1938, Japan grappled with many complicated problems, foremost among them trying to find a peaceful way to end the war in China, military tensions with the Soviet Union, negotiations with Germany to join the Axis, and discussion about reorganizing the political system into a single party. What is interesting is that, despite intimations of war with the United States the previous year, relations with the United States were not high on the policy agenda. There was even a faction that still favored establishment of a military alliance with Britain and France.[1]

By the beginning of 1938, the Japanese controlled all the major cities of northern China—though Communist guerrillas in rural areas were active—and were threatening central China.[2] An imperial conference on 11 January established the basic principles for resolving the China Incident. Japan's purported goal was to establish a new and cordial relationship among Japan, Manchukuo, and China, letting bygones be bygones. The conference addressed what to do if the Chinese accepted—or if they refused. Receiving no reply by 15 January, the government, despite strong objections from the Army Supreme Command, declared, "We no longer have any intention of carrying on negotiations with Chiang Kai-shek's government."[3] This is one example of Konoye taking a more belligerent position than the IJA.

The war in China was not moving in the right direction in early 1938. The Soviets on 1 March provided the Nationalist government a loan of $50 million.[4] Chinese forces in Xuzhou (Hsuchow) commanded by Li Zongren handed the Japanese their first defeat at the walled city of Taierzhuang in early April. The urban fighting neutralized the usual Japanese advantage in artillery, and the Nationalists did a better job of supplying their forces than did the invaders. The victory was a huge morale boost for the Chinese. An American military observer reported that it was the Japanese army's first defeat in the field in modern times.[5] (Source note: Hattori's history of the war devotes no attention to the ground conflict in China from this point until 1943, thus leaving us without an insider view of Japanese actions. All of the following derives from secondary sources.)

In response to the setback, the Imperial General Headquarters on 7 April ordered a massive encirclement campaign to destroy the Nationalist field armies. The North China Area Army struck from the north, and the Central China Expeditionary Army from the south. The operation involved seven divisions and 200,000 troops. The pincers were to meet at Xuzhou and trap 50 Chinese divisions.[6]

Chiang on 15 May ordered his forces to withdraw from Xuzhou to avoid encirclement. Having suffered constant Japanese bombing during the battle, much of the civilian population fled the ruined city.[7]

This pattern repeated itself throughout the war. The Japanese rarely had enough manpower to destroy encircled troops, who managed to slip away to fight again. The Germans, by contrast, repeatedly destroyed large Soviet armies trapped in what they called *Kessels* (cauldrons). After this failure, the Japanese switched strategies from seeking decisive engagements to occupying strategic points. The next target would be Wuhan, the military command's location.[8]

Saburo Sakai, an enlisted naval fighter pilot who was to become the highest-ranked Japanese ace to survive the war, arrived in Kiukiang, southeastern China, in May. Equipped with Mitsubishi Type 96 fighters—with open cockpits and fixed landing gear—his unit battled Chinese fighters and bombers—both Soviet-made—piloted by what they suspected were mostly seasoned international volunteers. In the section of his memoir covering this period, he retrospectively anticipated the fate he and Japanese naval aviation were to endure: "The long and difficult air war, so much to our advantage in the early days, degenerated into a vicious nightmare in which we struggled hopelessly against a rising enemy tide impossible to overcome."[9]

China was clearly going to be a long war. Japan adopted the National General Mobilization Law in May 1938, which provided for the total mobilization of the personal and material resources of the nation. By Imperial decree, if war demanded, the government could take control over the economy, education, research, publishing, mass media, public assembly, and strikes.[10]

Ambassador Grew recorded in his diary on 31 March that the Japanese leadership expected continuous trouble with Great Britain as it sought to supplant her influence in China and wanted to avoid provoking America to the point that she made common cause with Britain. The Japanese believed America would not become involved because of the strength of pacifist and isolationist sentiment.[11]

On 3 June, Lieutenant General Seishiro Itagaki, head of the Kwantung clique, became Minister of War. His deputy was Hideki Tojo, another former chief of staff of the Kwantung Army.[12] The proponents of the China conflict now had a powerful voice in the Cabinet.

Chiang, to delay the Japanese advance on Wuhan and give the command time to pull back to Chungking, ordered the army to breach the dikes holding the Yellow River in check. Chinese workers holed the dike at Huayuankou on 8 June, which unleashed a massive flood that quickly covered 500 square miles and caused enormous civilian suffering, but it blocked a Japanese ground thrust to Wuhan for four and a half months. China had literally become a quagmire. Figures released by the Nationalists in 1948 indicated that about 850,000 people died in Henan, Anhui, and Jiangsu provinces because of the flood, and that 4.8 million people became refugees.[13]

The United States imposed a "moral embargo" on Japan on 1 July 1938. From the Japanese perspective, this was the starting point for escalating American economic pressure over China.[14]

Regimental-sized fighting between Japan and the USSR broke out on the Soviet-Korean border in July and August at Lake Khasan and Mount Zozernaya. The Soviets portrayed it as a Japanese attack. The Japanese, however, were uncertain as to whether the Soviets were signaling they would enter the China war or were probing Japanese defenses. IGHQ halted offensive operations around Wuhan until the situation stabilized. The situation instead escalated, and on 20 August, a double-envelopment attack by Soviet armored and mechanized forces destroyed the Japanese 23d Infantry Division.[15]

On 12 October, Japanese forces landed at Bias Bay and captured the key port of Canton only ten days later. The Nationalists abandoned Wuhan on 24 October as the Japanese closed in there. Chungking, the provisional capital, now controlled only Sichuan (Szechuan), Hunan, and Henan provinces, and parts of two others. Chiang labeled the area "Free China," which stood every chance of resonating in America, Britain, and France.[16]

The IJA was burned out and overextended across the vastness of China. The military command decided to halt offensive operations and keep the Nationalists contained. They optimistically expected to reduce their force requirements from

800,000 to 400,000.[17] IGHQ had conceded that it could not defeat China through purely military means.[18]

Having overrun most of China's territory, Japan on 3 November issued a statement concerning the future of East Asia. Tokyo declared its intention to establish a "New Order in East Asia," in pursuit of which the government was to renovate internal systems and develop the total power of the nation. The Japanese Government on 16 December created the China Affairs Board to oversee implementation of the New Order in East Asia.

Japan took its first steps toward alliance with Nazi Germany. On 23 November, the Privy Council agreed to conclude a cultural pact with Germany based on "the characteristic spirit of Japan" and the "racial and national life of Germany." One councilor opined that this "agreement may bring about some kind of influence politically."[19]

With the military drive burned out, the Japanese now tried to undercut the Nationalists using political means and took advantage of a stratagem by one of Chiang's rivals. Wang Jingwei, head of Chiang's National Defense Council, and his circle of followers defected on 19 December by flying to Hanoi, and from there to Japanese-occupied China. They had been negotiating with the Japanese since November. Wang had once been viewed as the natural successor to Sun Yat-sen, founder of the Nationalist movement, and playing second fiddle to Chiang did not suit him. He had concluded that a long war would destroy China, and he viewed an alliance with Japan as a lesser evil than aligning with the United States and Great Britain, Western imperial powers whose behavior in China before the war had not been much better than Japan's. Under the deal with Japan, Wang was to set up an independent Chinese government that would cooperate with Tokyo.[20]

With a puppet now to hand, the Japanese Government launched a transparent and ham-fisted bid to end the war through political means. Konoye on 22 December issued a proposal to resolve the China incident that foreign observers viewed as entailing the de facto annexation of China. Konoye claimed to interrogators after the war that his intention was to leave China sovereign under Japanese leadership and include both the Wang Jingwei and Chiang Kai-shek regimes in the system. "However, the military used [my statement] and interpreted it for their own policies and furthermore, as a result, it was completely misunderstood by China, as well."[21]

Germany: More Guns, America's Soft as Butter

After Hitler's annexation of Austria in March and a war scare in May, Western powers, including America, accelerated their rearmament programs. Hitler ordered his own to speed up dramatically, casting aside any concern for the civilian economy. He wanted the Wehrmacht at wartime establishment by April 1939. The army got all the steel it needed. Between April and October, it spent 5 percent of GDP. Göring ordered 7,000 Ju 88 medium bombers for the Luftwaffe. Hitler told the navy to work faster on the battleships *Bismarck* and *Tirpitz* and expand U-boat construction. Industry redoubled its efforts to increase synthetic fuel and rubber output.[22]

Germany historically had assumed that in wartime, its foes would outnumber its own armies. It had to wage quick wars of annihilation. Therefore, advantages in skillful leadership and top-notch training, and adept maneuvering, had to compensate for material inferiority. This was true of Hitler's day, too.[23]

This confidence in military intangibles closely parallels the Japanese expectation that the same advantages would give them victory over the Americans. Both countries also initially enjoyed qualitative superiority in important weapon systems, notably Germany's radio-rich, combined arms mobile forces and Japan's fighter aircraft and innovative thinking in naval aviation that allowed Pearl Harbor. The approach is not irrational. The modern state of Israel successfully applied similar advantages to win repeated wars against far more numerous enemies.

On 8 July 1938, Göring told a group of industrialists that Germany faced a world war, and that Britain, France, Russia, and America would be the foes.[24]

So far as one can tell, key German leaders as of summer 1938 believed that the United States would support Britain in war, but that was it. Still, the idea of America as an arsenal began to surface. General Ludwig Beck, the army chief of staff, sent Hitler a memo in May that noted America was Britain's main arms supplier and offered his opinion that if it came to war, the United States would provide armaments on a vast scale, as well as proffer political and propaganda help. The finance minister provided a similar warning.[25]

Berlin (and Tokyo) certainly had forewarning that the giant was awakening because the signs were entirely public. In January 1938, the German Embassy reported that Roosevelt spoke to Congress about the serious international situation and warned of the danger of war, indeed of a two-front war. The President urged greater spiritual and military war readiness of the entire nation, said the embassy. Having earlier emphasized improving air defenses, Roosevelt called for strengthening the ground forces. He called for the establishment of a trained reserve, filling out the regular army, and preparation for mobilization. He urged expansion of the navy—three battleships, two aircraft carriers, eight cruisers, 25 destroyers, nine submarines, and thousands of planes. He wanted to accelerate industrial mobilization for war production and increase ammunition output.[26]

German diplomats in Washington were getting the feeling that U.S. involvement might well go beyond supplying arms. In August, they portrayed Roosevelt after a speech at Queen's University in Kingston, Ontario, where he pledged to defend Canada if she were attacked, as determined to break the isolationists. The administration, the embassy argued, was psychologically preparing the public for a two-front war and trying to rally public opinion against Germany, Italy, and Japan: "The speech here is understood as a warning to totalitarian states that America in a future world conflict will to be found on the side of the European democracies."[27]

The text of the speech did not go so far as a warning beyond the defense of Canada, but the German Embassy was fundamentally correct in its assessment of the direction of Roosevelt's policies.[28] The German diplomats also grasped his ability to gradually shift public opinion. In September, the embassy reported, "The isolationists in recent times have steadily lost ground. It would be false to assume their influence is already completely disappeared." A public suggestion by a senator that he would consider a preventive war against fascist nations, for example, had still sparked an uproar in the Midwest.[29]

Still, the mission admitted to Berlin,

> As the embassy has reported, no American preparations have been observed 'til now for its own active participation in a European war either in the military industrial or purely military fields. The American government doubtless does not believe at present that an active deployment of American armed forces will be necessary to help the democratic powers gain victory. They believe the opposite much more strongly, that American moral and economic assistance will suffice to ensure the victory of the democratic powers.[30]

Yet the embassy offered an appraisal of America's strategic motivations that strongly suggested if that belief proved false, U.S. national interests might compel Washington to enter the war:

> The current American foreign policy cannot be explained only by rejection of the totalitarian states or bitterness over allegedly violated human rights. It has deeper reasons.... When one in Germany with good reason asks over and over what the hostile American attitude goes back to, given that we have not wounded American interests, the answer becomes clear by rational consideration of things more or less as follows.
>
> The ideological chasm between America and the totalitarian states is ... far deeper today than the one in 1917 between the United States and Germany. Nevertheless, this plays a secondary role, even though it may have given some observers the impression that it is decisive. What is decisive in truth is the position and role of the United States is a great power that feels itself part of a community of fate with the other democratic powers that are pressured, if not threatened, by the possibility of a hegemony of totalitarian states in Europe and Asia. The bequest of Washington and Jefferson to the American people of the maxim to stay clear of European conflicts lasted as long as the waves from European conflicts did not push against America. By 1812, America already had to take part in a global conflict. Its participation in the world war of our times happened to prevent a threatening shift in the European balance of power that would have sensitively affected America's political and economic world standing.
>
> The relationship between America and England is far clearer today than in 1914, after which America consciously renounced the right to neutrality and England established unconstrained command of the seas. Therewith came clearly to light the English–American community of interests. The history of English–American relations since 1914 teaches that in normal times they are occasionally burdened by tensions, but in critical periods they immediately follow the doctrine of solidarity.... If England becomes embroiled in a war of life or death, then America—as in 1917—will seek to prevent a defeat of England with all means, because it would

as a consequence lead to a shift of power relations in Europe and Asia that would directly affect America. Herein lies the vital American interest that it holds is threatened by the expansion and lust for power of the totalitarian states. America ... will do everything possible to prevent and hinder the growth of totalitarian states' power....[31]

The Embassy shrewdly observed America's penchant for using its economic clout to pressure other countries, also a core irritant to Japan:

> It is not surprising that Secretary of State Hull believes the doctrine that all political problems can be solved from the economic side. The preponderance of the economic over the political arises from the entanglement of American trade with the entire world. The welfare of the United States, despite extensive abilities at self-supply, rests essentially on the economic ties to other powers. Therefore, the isolation of America from the rest of global events is not possible; every change in the political and with it economic field disturbs American interests.... The interests of America are the widest possible advancement of international trade and the maintenance of peace. It holds both interests to be threatened by the totalitarian powers. Therefore, American policy is forced to aim at stopping the advance of the totalitarian states to a position of power, which could have decisive meaning. In the view of realpolitik-inclined Americans, there are only the alternatives of buying peace through submission or resistance with all means, including war-fighting if necessary.... The actual entry of America into a new world war will hang on whether and when prospects for victory favor the totalitarian states.[32]

*

Hitler manipulated British Prime Minister Neville Chamberlain and French Premier Edouard Daladier—both of whom wanted to avoid war at nearly any price—into agreeing to allow him to annex the German-majority Sudetenland region of western Czechoslovakia. The three leaders signed the Munich Agreement on 30 September and therewith established modern history's benchmark for ineffective appeasement. Hitler got to occupy the German-majority Sudetenland along Czechoslovakia's western border without firing a shot. The area included Czechoslovakia's frontier fortifications against attack by Germany. The deal was wildly popular in Britain and France, where the public had no desire for war, either. Though America was a mere bystander, Foreign Minister Joachim von Ribbentrop, according to the Führer's personal assistant, told Hitler that when Daladier returned to a jubilant welcome in Paris, U.S. ambassador to France William Bullitt was at the airport and asked to smoke a cigarette with the German chargé d'affaires as a "peace pipe."[33]

Göring on 14 October announced a massive new program to improve Germany's railroads, highways, and canals. The Luftwaffe was to increase fivefold. The army was to accelerate acquisition of heavy artillery and heavy tanks. The navy was to increase ship production. The Luftwaffe plan for 21,750 aircraft included the 7,000 Ju 88 medium bombers Göring had ordered, plus 800 He 177 four-engine heavy bombers with long-range fighter escorts. This was a close as Germany ever got to having a strategic airpower capability. If wishes were airplanes...

Hitler demanded that armaments production increase by three times. Göring told the newly formed Reich Defense Council in November that virtually all civilian

The European Axis leaders who took Germany and Italy to war. From left: Luftwaffe chief Hermann Göring, Italian dictator Benito Mussolini, Adolf Hitler, and Foreign Minister Count Galeazzo Ciano, in Munich in 1938. (Wikimedia Commons)

construction had to end to free resources for arms and exports. Central control would rationalize activity in firms. Workers would be placed on a national index so they could be assigned where needed. Göring admitted that the budget situation was dire, inflation threatened, and foreign exchange reserves were nonexistent. But Hitler had spoken, and it would be so.

These goals, however, were utterly unrealistic. The Luftwaffe, for example, peaked at 5,000 planes in late 1944.[34] Once again, Hitler's later refusal to accept America's war production announcements may well derive from his own failure to achieve grandiose targets.

Mussolini Ignores America

Italian Prime Minister Benito Mussolini's disinterest in the United States became extremely clear when in February 1938 he began refusing to meet any Americans. He held to this policy until Under Secretary Sumner Welles' peace mediation mission in February and March 1940. Foreign Minister Count Galeazzo Ciano de Cortelazzo continued to meet with the American ambassador, but the American never saw any sign that his views had been shared with *il Duce*, and Ciano never undertook to explain Mussolini's views to the ambassador.[35]

The Italian parliamentary budget committee's report in April 1938 for financial year 1939—which the U.S. military attaché cabled home—observed, "The Chamber ... this year discusses the War Budget during a period that is one of the most crucial in European history, when the political atmosphere permits no negligence in matters of national security." Italy could not stand by while other countries armed. The Italian Army, tempered by the World War—Italy was on the winning side—and the Ethiopian War, was now in the forefront of the world's leading military powers. "Fascist Italy has interests all over the world, and she must be represented everywhere with the weight of her strength and military power." The committee proudly asserted, "The new 'Roman Parade Step' has been adopted in keeping with the vigorous strength of the Army of today, heir to the indomitable power of the legions of Rome."

Under Secretary of War General Pariani reported that since Italy had adopted the principle of "war of rapid decision," it had developed steadily along those lines. The Celeri (Fast) Division and a motorized division had reached wartime strength and opposed each other in the Veneto maneuvers.[36]

Germany + Italy: We'll Be at War in the West Soon

German leaders interpreted Washington's aloof stance during the Sudetenland crisis and what the Germany Embassy claimed was the government's relief over the Munich Agreement as signs that it need not be concerned with the United States. At a meeting on 28 October, Hitler told Mussolini and Ciano that he was convinced their countries would be at war against the Western democracies within a few years—perhaps three or four. Germany and Italy were in an excellent position following the Munich Conference. Germany had such a lead in rearmament that nothing could hold it back. Just before Hitler began speaking, Ribbentrop had proposed that Germany, Italy, and Japan form a military alliance, and Hitler now said this would be a useful and smart step. The Anglo-French alliance still existed, if weakened, and a French-Russian pact was still in force. As for America, Hitler asserted, the country would isolate itself ever more. The Czechoslovak crisis had proved America was "the land of the most complete and rapid withdrawal." The Japanese, he said, shared this view. "The United States will not want to get involved in any conflict, even less so if Japan is involved," said Hitler.

Hitler expected Japan would soon establish complete control in China and that its next target would be Great Britain. He opined that establishing a defense alliance with Japan would strengthen the imperialist faction against moneyed interests that favored accommodation with the democracies. Russia was weak, he claimed, and would be for years. Germany and Italy could concentrate all their efforts against the Western democracies.

Mussolini agreed that war with Britain and France would occur within several years because of a historical dynamic. A chasm had emerged between the two worlds. He offered no comment regarding America. Mussolini assured Hitler that Italy would display military solidarity with Germany but added that the middle and senior ranks of the army and the public were not yet prepared to support a formal military alliance. Conditions had to ripen a bit. Mussolini added that when a formal alliance occurred, it could not be a defensive one because the democracies had no intention of attacking; he wanted one "that would change the world map." Ribbentrop agreed and said Germany would back Italy making the Mediterranean an Italian sea.[37]

In November, Washington responded to two days of attacks on Jewish shops and synagogues by withdrawing Ambassador Hugh Wilson. The German ambassador left Washington and was never replaced. The returning German ambassador told Ribbentrop that "even well-balanced and respectable circles" were adopting a hostile attitude toward Germany in the wake of the violence. Berlin worried that the United States might expel German nationals, break diplomatic ties, and impose economic and financial sanctions. Hitler, meanwhile, delivered a speech in which he described the United States as a conglomeration of races, less than half of them being Anglo-Saxons, and the remainder Negroes, Jews, Mongolians, and other inferior races.[38]

When a Foreign Ministry official suggested during a meeting that Germany consider the growing American anti-German public sentiment in formulating its Jewish policies, Göring dismissively retorted, "That country of scoundrels ... That gangster state!"[39]

The Giant Stops Snoring

On 12 January 1938, an informal U.S. Navy emissary dispatched by the Chief of Naval Operations at Roosevelt's behest returned from London with an informal agreement with the Admiralty: The two navies would permit one another to operate in their respective waters if war came with Japan. The agreement sketched out means of communication and sharing intelligence.[40]

The U.S. Army and Navy on 19 January 1938 began working on a new version of a Plan Orange, the war plan against Japan, which had received its last update in 1928. The service secretaries approved the plan in late February. The army needed navy support to transport troops and provide fire support, and the navy lacked the resources to do those jobs. So, the services requested that the navy's tonnage be boosted by 20 percent, which required $1.1 billion ($77.7 billion today) to build three battleships, two aircraft carriers, nine light cruisers, 23 destroyers, nine submarines, and 950 naval aircraft. Congress agreed, and Roosevelt approved the expansion on 7 May.[41]

Roosevelt on 14 November summoned a group of military and political figures to a meeting that military historian Eric Hammel characterized as the "magic moment" that led to America becoming the arsenal of democracy and saving the world. At the time, the U.S. Army Air Corps had 13 strategic bombers and several hundred tactical bombers. It had no ability to attack Germany, Italy, or Japan and return. The two best pursuit planes (fighters) were obsolete. The ground forces were unready to fight even a major skirmish with an enemy army, had no armored or antitank force, and lacked enough rifles to equip the standing army and National Guard. Roosevelt told the men that in light of the crushing use of air power by Germany in the Spanish Civil War, America needed to build a strong air corps. He authorized the War Department representative to draw up a plan and a budget request to build 10,000 planes within two years, 8,000 at existing factories and 2,000 at newly built government plants.

The army took the opportunity to propose a plan and budget to meet all the needs of a modern balanced army, with all the personnel and equipment, a vastly more expensive proposition. When Roosevelt received the draft, he was shocked, having only asked for airplanes. But he became a believer and used his State of the Union address on 12 January 1939 to begin building political support for rearmament.[42]

CHAPTER 4

1939: War Goes Global

Leaders in Japan, Germany, and Italy in early 1939 expected America to do nothing but wring its hands over their actions. Nevertheless, perhaps due to reports about American plans to expand defense production, German officials began to think about the likelihood of material support for Britain if war broke out in Europe in the next few years (or, as Hitler knew, that year). At least in Berlin, however, the self-evident small size and un-readiness of the U.S. Army let planners set the country aside.

The Japanese, with no apparent reference to events in the United States, in 1939 accelerated their efforts to build a self-sustaining war economy. Italy, far behind Germany, tried to do the same, but even its leaders were skeptical that there was much meat on the bone.

Japan Tries to Awaken Its Own Inner Giant

Japan's view of the United States in 1939, according to the U.S. naval attaché in Tokyo, was that whatever the bilateral differences over China, Washington would restrict its activities to "note writing." Japanese officials watched with some anxiety the growing anti-Japanese feeling in the United States. But they reassured the public that Washington would pursue a "realistic policy." The government censored news of Japanese bombing of American properties in China, mistreatment of American citizens there by Japanese soldiers, and restrictions on American trading rights.[1]

The Japanese Government received a note on 14 January, in which America, Britain, and France jointly notified Tokyo that they did not recognize any new order in East Asia.[2]

Having stoked the escalating war in China, Konoye resigned, purportedly unhappy with the IJA's unwillingness to share information or act on his opinions.[3] This was not to be the last time Konoye quit a conflict he helped create. President of the Privy Council Hiranuma replaced him as premier on 5 January 1939. Hiranuma asked Lieutenant General Seishiro Itagaki to remain as War Minister, and the general agreed after Hiranuma accepted a list of conditions. This included resolution of the China Incident; establishment of a plan for national defense aimed at expanding armaments production; strengthening relations among Japan, Germany, and Italy; reinforcement of the system of total mobilization and its planning board; increased economic production; stimulation of national morale; and expanded trade. The Cabinet, in essence, had cut a deal with the IJA senior chiefs.[4] Admiral Mitsumasa Yonai, an unusually tall and striking figure, former commander of the fleet, and a man with a reputation for moderation, became Navy Minister.[5] Koichi Kido became Home Minister, responsible for internal security, at Hiranuma's request.[6]

The Cabinet on the 17th approved the "Plan for the Expansion of Productive Power," which constituted the implementation of three plans drafted by the War Ministry in May and June 1937. The goal was to develop strategic industries sufficiently that Japan would be self-sufficient in important resources and products, such as munitions, by 1941.[7]

The government's new budget for the IJA substantially expanded spending on the China Incident and, according to the U.S. defense attaché, devoted "large sums" to reorganization and acquisition of materiel. The attaché observed that the war in China had already cost roughly three times more than the Sino-Japanese, Russo-Japanese, and First World Wars combined.[8]

Hiranuma addressed the Diet on 21 January and explained that Japan would ensure "prosperity and progress" in East Asia through the cooperation of Japan, Manchukuo, and China in the political, cultural, and economic spheres. A new order was replacing the old, he said. He trusted that the Chinese would understand correctly and cooperate, but there was no alternative but to exterminate those who persisted in opposing Japan.

War crimes prosecutors deemed this the turning point that set Japan on the road to Pearl Harbor.[9] This is a matter of judgment, but we can add it to the list of explanations involving Japanese actions in 1931 and 1937 that well-informed observers concluded built momentum toward war with America.

The Diet held the power of the purse, but it exercised little authority over the executive branch's conduct of foreign policy or the Emperor's power to issue ordinances, though ordinances expired if not approved by the Diet at its next session. Under the constitution, it had to be in session at least three months out of the year and convened at the Emperor's pleasure. The legislature had done little since 1937 but approve budgets submitted by the IJA and IJN through the Cabinet.[10]

Yonai, despite his reputed moderation, told the Diet in February 1939 that the IJN's policy was "to assure control of the seas and air in the Pacific and to become the propellant force for the enforcement of our national policies. The Navy's present armament is sufficient for the establishment of a new order in East Asia." He would soon submit a supplementary budget for new naval construction to be completed by 1941.[11] The Japanese evinced a sense of naval invincibility, the American naval attaché reported. He submitted one illustrative Japanese analysis that argued the Japanese fleet possessed "superior gun power and technique and unrivaled spiritual strength." No American fleet could approach Japan without suffering constant attack by submarines and aircraft, including its supply ships. There would be no contest of main forces, and the worst Japan would suffer would be some air raids that would little harm industry.[12]

Despite Japanese efforts to hide the fleet's shipbuilding and torpedo developments, the naval attaché in 1939 reported a fairly accurate picture on both topics. U.S. Navy recipients in Washington paid little heed to much of it. The Japanese also concealed their rapid progress in naval aviation, but the American attachés produced accurate estimates of naval air strength in the late 1930s. The assistant attaché for air even managed to sit in the cockpit of the secret new A6M Zero fighter at an IJA air show and reported the technical specifications to Washington straight from the information plate in English. Washington did not believe such a light and powerful aircraft could exist. The main American blind spot was grossly underestimating the quality of Japanese training, in part out of racist biases they shared with other Western observers.[13]

*

Japan officially established the Wang Jingwei puppet regime, called the "Reformed Government of the Republic of China," in Nanking on 28 March.[14]

After a few trial raids over the winter, the Japanese began bombing Chungking in earnest on 3–4 May, and nearly daily bombing continued for years thereafter. Those raids in early May killed 5,000 people.[15]

A woman took the first step in a process that eventually created a strategic air threat to the Japanese homeland. Chiang's wife, Song Meiling, responded to the air attacks by recruiting retired U.S. Army Air Corps Major General Claire Lee Chennault to train China's air force.[16]

Fighting broke out again between Japanese and Soviet forces, this time along the Mongolian border, from May to August. The Japanese command again halted even the modest operations—generally counterstrokes—against Chinese activity.[17]

In August 1939, Vice Admiral Isoruku Yamamoto rose to command the Combined Fleet and First Fleet. Yamamoto had commanded the aircraft carrier *Akagi* and been quoted as early as 1915, arguing that carriers would be the most important ships of the future.[18] That farsighted assessment emerged a year before the dreadnought battle at Jutland. The admiral since 1936 had served as Vice Navy Minister, and he had taken on the additional task of Director of Naval Aviation in 1938. He had personally spurred the development of a new generation of carrier-based planes, including a fighter, a dive-bomber, and a torpedo bomber, as well as a land-based medium bomber. He had popularized naval aviation to such an extent that the American naval attaché estimated in 1938 and 1939 that private donations to the Japanese Naval Air Force were large enough to purchase a hundred new aircraft each year. An exceptionally able, forceful, and quick-thinking officer, Yamamoto was credited with building the naval aviation force into a creditable arm. He was already deemed an excellent tactician. The naval attaché in Tokyo observed, "[He] would as Commander in Chief of the Japanese Fleet in wartime adopt a bold, positive course of action."[19]

Yamamoto had attended Harvard, where he studied the oil industry, and had come to like Americans. He was a baseball fan and played a sharp hand of poker. He had served at the Japanese Embassy in Washington from 1925 to 1927. He did not want to go to war against the United States.[20]

Yamamoto represented the next generation of naval warriors. He climbed aboard his flagship *Nagato* on 1 September 1939. That very day, he learned that Germany had invaded Poland, and that Britain and France had declared war. In a letter to Shigataro Shimada on the 4th, Yamamoto wrote, "The great upheaval now occurring in Europe makes me feel terrified when I think of our relationship with Germany and Italy." On 5 September, in a message to the Combined Fleet, he said, "The situation in Europe shows clear signs of developing into another worldwide conflict. The task facing the Imperial Navy in the days to come will be greater than ever."[21]

As of late 1939, Japan had eight capital ships under construction in its naval yards. Four 40,000-ton vessels were scheduled for completion in 1943, and four more of 43,000 tons in 1944. All were armed with 12 16-inch guns. Construction of a large aircraft carrier and two cruisers was underway at privately owned yards.[22] The number of cadets at naval academies had doubled since 1936.[23]

As of March 1939, however, the Japanese commercial fleet possessed only 35 oil tankers totaling 350,000 tons, with eight more under construction, which the IJN viewed as wholly inadequate.[24]

Japan, pushed by the armed forces, set about with purpose building the economic base it would need to support a major war, or converting Japan from a "land of silk and cotton to a land of iron and steel." The government during early 1939 established national monopolies to control production and distribution of electricity and rice, as well as the mining industry. The IJA and IJN were given authority to compel private businesses to produce what they needed. Of a total national budget of 9 billion yen, 6.4 billion went to military spending. Military manpower increased from 1,130,000 to 1,240,000, and the conscription law was expanded to include previously exempt categories of manpower.[25]

Japanese forces seized Hainan Island off the coast of China in a surprise attack on 10 February. The French-owned Spratley Islands off Indochina fell in March.

The proto-Axis, the Anti-Comintern Pact, appeared to become stronger when Hungary, Manchukuo, and Spain joined the pact during February and March. Japan in March concluded a cultural agreement with Italy like the one it had reached with Germany the preceding year. In Japan, debate simmered between War Minister Itagaki, supported by the finance ministry, who favored establishing a formal military alliance with Germany, and the Navy and Foreign Ministers, who opposed the idea.[26]

In the Netherlands East Indies, government-backed Japanese development corporations had begun to invest heavily in projects ranging from sugar to phosphate production, supplementing extensive private Japanese investment in rubber and mining.[27]

Hitler Nods to and Dismisses America

In a speech to the Reichstag on 30 January 1939, Hitler said,

> Our relations with the United States are suffering from a campaign of defamation. This is carried out to serve obvious political and financial interests, which, under the pretense that Germany threatens American independence and freedom, is endeavoring to stir up an entire continent against the European states that are nationally governed. We all believe, however, that this does not reflect the will of the millions of American citizens. We believe, despite all said to the contrary by a gigantic Jewish-capitalistic propaganda through the press, the radio, and the films, that they cannot fail to realize there is not a word of truth in all these assertions. Germany wishes to live in peace and on friendly terms with all countries, including America.[28]

A review of State Department reporting in the Department's historical series *Foreign Relations of the United States* during the period 1939–1940 indicates that the U.S. Embassy in Berlin had no access to or real insight into German leadership intentions or views of the United States. Indeed, the chargé reported to Washington on 24 February 1939,

> As I have stated in a somewhat different manner earlier in this dispatch, one cannot but be conscious of an underlying uncertainty in reporting from Berlin where one is confronted with an unknown, and unknowable factor which is unqualifiedly dominant in all German policy. I refer to the attitude of Hitler and such decisions as he may reach. In reporting from Berlin one naturally follows the normal tendency of building up an estimate of German policy on the outward aspects of the scene presented, combined with such information from private sources and expressions of competent opinion as may be available. All this may be done and yet the possibility remains that what is reported is far from the mark. At the cost of appearing to labor the point I cannot too strongly emphasize that it must not be lost sight of that all decisions rest in the final analysis in the hands of one man and one man alone.[29]

As if to underscore the point, the U.S. military attaché reported about the same time,

> On February 26th there appears to be practically no chance of German aggression in Europe for the balance of 1939, unless some at present unpredictable development should occur. The Military Attaché has had the opportunity to talk with at least five important officers of the German Army who have heard Hitler discussing foreign political issues within the past week. All of these officers are agreed that Hitler foresaw no immediate complications for the time being.[30]

Rome in March proposed that the Italian and German General Staffs establish immediate contact, with the chiefs to meet forthwith. Ribbentrop informed Ciano on the 10th that Germany agreed and proposed Innsbruck as the meeting site.[31]

The German occupation of Czechoslovakia on 15 March provoked Washington to refuse to recognize the Third Reich's incorporation of Bohemia and Moravia and to impose sanctions that Berlin estimated would cost 85 million marks per year in foreign currency.[32] It also inspired Mussolini to consider occupying Albania, despite a warning from Hitler that he should wait two more years before conducting large foreign operations when 100 "Prussian" divisions would be available to support him. The Duce told Ciano that "Prussia" had now established hegemony, and that a coalition of all the other powers, including Italy, could check German expansion, but not hurl it back. He therefore strongly favored alliance with Germany, even though it would be unpopular with the public.[33]

Less than a month later, on 7 April, Italy attacked and occupied Albania. Roosevelt, in a speech on the 15th, issued a thinly veiled warning that the United States would not remain aloof if further acts of aggression occurred. He sent Hitler and Mussolini a message imploring them to publicly foreswear attacks on a list of 31 countries in Europe and the Middle East—including Poland, the Baltic states, Russia, Denmark, the Netherlands, Belgium, France, and Britain—and offered to participate in efforts to reduce armaments and expand trade.

Mussolini at first refused to read the letter and then dismissed it as "a result of progressive paralysis." Göring was in Rome, and he and Mussolini agreed that the President's message was a sign of "incipient mental disease." On the 21st, Hitler told the Hungarian Premier that "the Americans were mixing up the situation with that of 1914," and, "Roosevelt is fighting for his re-election." Hitler nevertheless evidently found it embarrassing enough that he wanted to reply, but in the form of a speech to the Reichstag at a special session on 28 April.

Hitler told off Roosevelt in a speech that set the deputies to laughing repeatedly. Then journalist William Shirer recalled,

> It was, I believe, the longest major public speech he ever made, taking more than two hours to deliver, in many ways, especially in the power of its appeal to Germans and to the friends of Nazi Germany abroad, it was probably the most brilliant oration he ever gave, certainly the greatest this writer ever heard from him. For sheer eloquence, craftiness, irony, sarcasm, and hypocrisy, it reached a new level that he was never to approach again. It was broadcast not only on all German radio stations but on hundreds of others throughout the world; in the United States it was carried by the major networks. Never before or afterward was there such a worldwide audience as he had that day.[34]

Hitler read off the list of countries, omitting only Poland, and proclaimed peaceful intentions. Near the end, Hitler dismissed Washington's meddling. "Mr. Roosevelt! I fully understand that the vastness of your nation and the immense wealth of your country allow you to feel responsible for the history of the whole world and for the history of all nations. I sir, am placed in a much more modest and smaller sphere."[35]

Meanwhile, in America, famous airman Charles Lindberg met with Lieutenant General Henry "Hap" Arnold, the new chief of the Air Corps, and related everything the enthusiastic Luftwaffe had shown him during a recent visit to Germany. Lindberg believed war was about to engulf Europe, and Arnold now had a clear understanding of the force he would need to build to defeat the German air fleet. Lindberg participated in an advisory panel chaired by Colonel Carl Spaatz, which among other things recommended that the Air Corps commence immediately designing a heavy bomber that could fly twice as far as the B-17. From this beginning came the design specifications of what was to be the B-29.[36] The B-29 program was to cost more than $3 billion ($56 billion today), more than the Manhattan Project.[37]

*

What was Hitler really up to? On 23 May, he met with his senior military officers to discuss attacking Poland and the Western Powers if they went to war over Poland. His inclination to gamble all is evident. Hitler said Germany had dropped from the ranks of the Great Powers, and it was time to remedy the situation. Moreover,

> Living space, in proportion to the magnitude of the state, is the basis of all power.
> The Pole is no "supplementary enemy." Poland will always be on the side of our adversaries.... Danzig is not the subject of the dispute at all. It is a question of expanding our living space in the East and securing our food supplies.... The Polish Problem is inseparable from the conflict with the West.
> We are left with the decision: To attack Poland at the first suitable opportunity. We cannot expect a repetition of the Czech affair. There will be war.... Conflict with Poland—beginning with an attack on Poland—will only be successful if the Western Powers keep out of it.... If there were an alliance of France, England, and Russia against Germany, Italy, and Japan, I would be constrained to attack England and France with a few annihilating blows....
> [I]f England intends to intervene in the Polish war, we must occupy Holland with lightning speed.... The war with England and France will be a life or death struggle. The idea that we can get off cheaply is dangerous; there is no such possibility. We must burn our boats, and it is no longer a question of justice or injustice, but of life or death for 80 million human beings....
> Every country's armed forces or government must aim for a short war. The government, however, must be prepared for a war of 10–15 years duration....
> If Holland and Belgium are successfully occupied and held, and if France is also defeated, the fundamental conditions for a successful war against England will have been secured.[38]

German military procurement, however, had to slash its arms programs dramatically in early 1939 because a foreign exchange crisis threatened necessary imports, and Berlin had to reallocate nearly half the steel the army expected to receive to exports. The army had to slash ammunition orders. Instead of 61,000 new MG 34 machine guns, it would get 13,000; 460 instead of 840 105mm howitzers; and 600 of the expected 1,200 medium tanks and command vehicles. Thirty-four wartime divisions would be seriously short of equipment. The Luftwaffe faced a reduction of one-third in airplanes and had to focus on only the highest priority types. Production of the Ju 87 Stuka dive bomber, for example, ceased.[39]

A few months later, copper became a serious bottleneck. Germany relied entirely on imported copper ore, and the lack of foreign exchange led to anticipated reductions in ammunition output that the army warned would undermine the entire rearmament program.[40]

One bright spot was that Germany in March struck a trade deal with Romania that established a degree of energy independence from British- and American-controlled sources of oil. Military planners, however, warned that Germany would have to occupy Romania to be certain of reliable supplies.[41] Nevertheless, between Romania and its synthetic fuel program, Germany was not to face the same pressing issue of fuel supplies that was to drive Japanese decision-making.

Mussolini and the Council of Ministers on 29 April announced extraordinary appropriations for the War Ministry to boost the army's manpower and equipment. According to the U.S. military attaché, Mussolini asserted, "Whenever either Italy or Germany carry out some slight act of justice or proceed to execute the most natural and logical rectification of dangerous, historical-political mistakes, [some] countries take steps to make a more or less vast military mobilization." Yet, he said, "Italy knows how to wait."

Under Secretary of War Pariani, meanwhile, told the Grand Council of Fascism in May that Italy had organized two experimental armored divisions. The army would soon boast 51 infantry, three fast, three armored, two motorized, and five Alpine divisions.[42] Mussolini, though, was skeptical. Ciano recorded,

> He has the feeling—and he is right—that behind the façade, more or less carefully kept up, there is very little.... I have no precise information concerning the army, but the many rumors that I hear are definitely pessimistic, and also certain impressions gained on the occasion of the mobilization for the Albanian undertaking—a small mobilization at that—have increased my skepticism. The number of divisions is multiplied, while in reality these are so few as to have little more than the strength of a regiment. The artillery is old. Anti-aircraft and anti-tank weapons are completely lacking.[43]

German Foreign Ministry records provide the first inklings that the Germans were thinking about America as a remotely possible enemy emerged about this time. Ribbentrop told the Hungarian Premier on 29 April that the United States would send military equipment but no troops to Europe in a European war. Unlike the Great War, when Japan was part of the Entente, Tokyo was part of the Axis. The American fleet outweighed the Japanese fleet by 10:7.5, but because the quality and spirit of Japanese sailors was twice as high, the ratio was effectively 15:10 in Japan's favor. And about half the American fleet had to remain in the Atlantic, so the ratio, he supposed, was more like 3:1.

The German Embassy in Washington that month estimated that the United States could expand its 400,000-man defensive army into 50 divisions in about seven months. It would need that long to expand industrial production to support mobilization. The dispatch of ground or air units abroad before that time was extremely unlikely. The uncertain position of Japan would force America to divide her fleet. Further, asserted the embassy, American operational plans anticipated a strategic defense in the Atlantic and Pacific, and not the dispatch of expeditionary forces.

The German military attaché in August reported that his observation of army exercises confirmed the lack of modern equipment and trained personnel. Neither the ground nor air forces would be capable of sending units overseas for operations in less than a year.[44] Boetticher shared the embassy's view that the Americans' highest military priority would be the Pacific.[45] (Boetticher pointed out to interrogators after the war that he had warned Berlin about America's ability to mobilize on a massive basis and claimed that German leaders were "living in a fantasy."[46])

These views may explain why the military command was paying little attention to America. Chief of the General Staff Field Marshal Wilhelm Keitel told interrogators after the war that in the period 1939–1940, the High Command (*Oberkommando der Wehrmacht*, or OKW) believed that the United States had learned some lessons during World War I and would be able to mobilize more rapidly for a new war. OKW was aware that America possessed a modern industrial base that could convert fairly rapidly to war production and could equip a wartime army quite quickly. America already had a powerful navy, and its aircraft industry was capable of supplying warplanes capable of combating a modern enemy air force. Nevertheless, OKW judged that the United States would need time to train a large army, particularly its leaders. Key equipment would demand lengthy production processes.

Despite obvious hostility toward Germany, OKW did not expect America to enter a European war, said Keitel. Germany would take care to avoid providing any cause through provocation. Keitel said the High Command was aware that it would need to achieve victory too quickly to allow outside forces to intervene.[47] (Even though, as mentioned in the foreword, interrogators assessed that Keitel kept his looming war crimes trial in mind when he responded to questions, nothing he said regarding OKW views of America at that time rings false or appears to be aimed at undercutting the prosecution. The stated views are consistent with other sources.)

As for Hitler, Boetticher told interrogators that when he visited Germany in 1939, Hitler during his audience was more interested in hearing about the Roosevelt's alleged Jewish ancestry than in current developments.[48] Hans Dieckhoff, the German ambassador from 1937 to 1939, when he was recalled for "consultations," said that neither Hitler nor Ribbentrop really understood the United States and thought the country's mixed races would prevent unity.[49] General Ferdinand Heim recalled in 1944 that Hitler's propaganda chief Josef Goebbels told an audience of soldiers at Rheydt in late 1939, "[The Americans] are business people who want to make money, and now see a favorable opportunity of getting as much as they can out of this war. They would not dream of entering on a war."[50]

The German assessments from Washington of initial American capabilities, at least, were not all that inaccurate. Even with two and a half more years of mobilization ahead of it from this point, the United States was first able to send ground troops into combat on Guadalcanal in August and in North Africa in November 1942, eight and 11 months after Pearl Harbor, respectively.

The Germans repeated many of the analytic mistakes their predecessors made prior to America's entry into the Great War. German military analysts argued then that given the time it took to train an army, America could not intervene in the ground war until 1918 (the 1st Infantry Division entered the line in October 1917). The Allies lacked the shipping to transport even three infantry divisions and a cavalry division to Europe and maintain logistic support. (The Americans seized German and neutral ships and delivered manpower much faster than expected because the UK and France provided the heavy weapons.) The unrestricted U-boat war was sinking hundreds of thousands of tons every month. American help would arrive too late to save the Entente. It came as a shock that the AEF performed credibly along the Marne in the summer of 1918. The Germans soon rated the 2d Infantry Division and a few others as formidable foes.

Postwar German assessments of the AEF's fighting abilities were often critical, however. The men were insufficiently trained and suffered confusion and unnecessary casualties. The war did not reveal how the Americans would do in mobile warfare, only trench combat.[51]

As of summer 1939, moreover, Roosevelt had to abandon an effort to modify the Neutrality Acts of 1937 to permit belligerents to buy arms on a cash-and-carry basis. His intent derived from the shock of Germany's occupation of Czechoslovakia. The isolationist factions in both the House and Senate were big enough to block the amendments, although they supported the President's moves to increase America's military wherewithal. German discussions of America at this time assumed it would take months, if not years, before America could start shipping arms if Germany became embroiled in war with Britain and France.[52]

Mussolini, meanwhile, instructed Ciano on 4 May to persuade Ribbentrop at their next meeting that Germany and Italy needed a period of not less than three years of peace, and the inevitable war against the democracies should wait until 1943. Italy needed time to establish complete control over Albania and Libya and complete its military modernization. He also thought Japan would have settled matters in China by then.[53] He irritated the U.S. ambassador at a reception by telling him in a rare conversation that America was in the hands of the Jews. The ambassador told Ciano that the American people, as descendants of Europeans, all took an interest in European affairs and that it would be madness to think they could remain aloof in case of a conflict.[54]

At their meeting on 7 May, Ribbentrop assured Ciano that Germany also wanted a period of peace lasting four or five years. Yet he said the Führer was willing to grant Poland no concessions and that its desire for peace did not mean Germany was not prepared to go to war before that. If Germany had no choice, Hitler would execute the operations quickly, but he was preparing to wage a multi-year war if necessary.[55]

Toying with an Axis

Germany and Italy signed what became known as the "Pact of Steel" on 22 May. Article 3 obliged each party to provide full military support for the other should it go to war. Ciano recorded in his diary,

> The decision to consummate the alliance was made by Mussolini suddenly, while I was in Milan with Ribbentrop. Some American papers had stated that the Lombard metropolis had given the German minister a hostile reception and that this was proof of a decline in Mussolini's personal prestige. Result: fury. I received strict and preemptory orders by telephone to agree to the German requests for an alliance, requests that I had left in suspension for more than a year and which I was planning to keep pending for a long time to come.[56]

Initially at the behest of the IJA, Tokyo and Berlin had since 1937 been fitfully engaged in discussing a full-blown military alliance. Other Japanese civilian leaders were squeamish, however. Any agreement aimed specifically against Great Britain, they argued, would draw the United States into an eventual war, confronting Japan with a combined Anglo-American naval force. The Germans, however, argued that the display of isolationism over Czechoslovakia meant Washington was safely off the international stage.[57]

Premier Hiranuma secured a compromise in Tokyo after more than 70 meetings—the principle of "an unlimited alliance with certain reservations." This took the form of a declaration Hiranuma sent to Hitler on 4 May. In it, Hiranuma asserted,

> I can affirm that Japan is firmly and steadfastly resolved to stand at the side of Germany and Italy even if one of those two powers were attacked by one or several powers without the participation of the Soviet Union and to afford them political and economic and, to the extent possible to her power, military assistance.... [H]owever, Japan is, in view of the situation in which it now finds itself, neither presently nor in the near future able to extend to them in a practical manner any effective military aid. However, it goes without saying that Japan would gladly grant this support if it should become possible through a change in the circumstances.[58]

The Japanese Cabinet on 5 June reached a final decision that Japan would join a German war against Britain and France, with the reservation that Japan wished to secure the right to choose a favorable time for entering the war. In diplomatic discussions with the Germans and Italians, however, Japan insisted on an exchange of notes underscoring its limited military capabilities and freedom to stay out of a war if circumstances demanded, which Germany countered would cause other powers to conclude the agreement was meaningless. The Japanese ambassador to Italy at one point suggested that Japan should commit to automatic entry into a war only if the Soviet Union or United States were involved. While Japan dithered, Hitler acted to secure his eastern interests, and on 23 August Germany and Russia concluded a non-aggression pact.[59]

Hiranuma's government resigned on 28 August because of its failure to conclude an alliance with Germany, the first time in Japanese history that a government had stepped down citing as the reason a foreign policy issue. The perceived failure rested in the fact that Germany, Japan's greatest friend, had struck a bargain with the Soviet Union, seen at this time as Japan's greatest enemy in continental Asia.[60] The government that replaced it, headed by retired General Nobuyuki Abe, on 4 September pledged not to become involved in the European war that had just broken out and to concentrate on concluding affairs in China.[61]

Germany Lights the Fire

The British Secret Intelligence Service (SIS, MI6) received information from a German source codenamed Esmond in mid-July indicating that all preparations for possible action against Poland would be complete by 15 August. A memorandum on Esmond's reporting record showed that he provided generally reliable information on German strategic intentions—including for the attack in the West—through at least the invasion of Greece in 1941.[62] Of course, having a good idea what was coming in no way enabled the British to defeat the Germans at this stage in the war.

Mussolini by the beginning of August had grasped that Hitler would not wait until 1943 to go to war, as the Duce had proposed, but he still did not want the Pact of Steel members to strike until 1940, when he would have five new battleships ready for action in the Mediterranean. He believed that if Germany attacked Poland, France and England would surely join the conflict. Italy, though, would be able to offer Germany nothing more than sympathetic neutrality. Far better, he argued, if the Pact retained its solidarity and called an international conference of European powers to discuss its demands. Russia, as a transcontinental power, the United States, and Japan would be excluded. Representatives of the democracies would doubtless respond to public opinion and scuttle the conference, and the blame for war would fall firmly on them.[63]

The Duce told Ciano on 9 August that it would be madness to start a war now. Preparation, he said, is not such to ensure victory. He felt Italy had a 50-percent chance, whereas in three more years the chance would be 80 percent. Before Ciano departed the next day for Berlin to meet Ribbentrop, Mussolini told him that war with Poland must be avoided. It would be impossible to localize it, and a general war would be disastrous for everyone. "The Duce has never spoken of the need for peace with such fervor and such lack of reserve as he did today," Ciano recorded.[64] Mussolini was so in the dark on German-Soviet negotiations that he was worried an entente between the Western democracies and the Soviets was a real danger.[65]

Ribbentrop met Ciano on 11 August and left him with little doubt that Germany would go to war with Poland soon. The Germans dismissed his arguments against a war—primarily that intervention by Britain and France, backed by many other countries, was "unavoidable." Ribbentrop assured Ciano that the war would remain localized. The Allies lacked the military capability to intervene, and Belgium and the Netherlands were committed to neutrality. Russia would not intervene; he conveyed in confidence that Berlin and Moscow were negotiating this question. American public opinion, said Ribbentrop, inclined ever more toward neutrality and isolation.[66]

In his diary, Ciano wrote, "I am certain that even if the Germans were given everything they demanded, they would attack just the same because they are possessed by the demon of destruction."[67]

The next day, Hitler explained to Ciano that his defenses in the West were impregnable and described in general terms the plan for operations in Poland, if it came to that. He urged Italy to attack Yugoslavia when the time was ripe and occupy Croatia and Dalmatia. Hitler also assured Ciano the conflict would remain localized because Britain and France were too weak to intervene. They could only engage in theatrical anti-German gestures. At worst, they could blockade the North Sea and launch some air attacks on Germany, but the latter seemed unlikely because of German revenge. German talks with Moscow on a friendship pact, he assured, were advancing well.[68]

The Italian leadership was convinced that a German attack on Poland would lead to a European-wide conflict for which Italy was not prepared. The Italians interpreted the "absolute equality" between the signatories of the Pact of Steel to mean that one party could not launch a war without the agreement of the other, a view the Germans clearly did not share. Messages flew between Rome and the embassy in Berlin as Mussolini, Ciano, and diplomats sought to concoct a formula that would justify avoiding providing full military support as stipulated by Article 3.[69]

Ciano wrote after a second meeting with Hitler on 13 August:

> I return to Rome disgusted with Germany, her leaders, and her methods. They have deceived us and lied to us. And today they are about to set forth on an adventure that we didn't want, and which may critically endanger the Regime and the country. The Italian people will burn with rage when they learn of the attack on Poland and might even want to take up arms against the Germans. I do not know whether to wish for a victory for Italy or a defeat for Germany. However, considering the German attitude, I maintain that our hands are free, and I suggest acting accordingly, that is, to declare that we do not intend to participate in a conflict which we neither wanted nor provoked.
>
> The Duce's reactions are mixed. At first, he agrees with me. Then he says that honor forces him to march with Germany. Finally, he admits that he wants his share of the spoils in Croatia and Dalmatia.[70]

At a meeting at the Berghof in Berchtesgaden on 20 August 1939 with all senior ground force commanders down to army commanding generals and their chiefs of staff, Hitler told them that England and France were unlikely to join the war because their Far Eastern interests were more important, and they were inadequately armed. Colonel Walter Warlimont, deputy to then Brigadier General Alfred Jodl, the operations chief at OKW, recalled at the end of the war that Hitler did not mention the United States at all. The Führer, he opined in retrospect, wanted to avoid inciting the United States into entering a war.[71] (Warlimont's recollection in the FMS report is consistent with the impeccably documented conversations in the preceding days involving Hitler and Ribbentrop and with equally authoritative confirmation later in this book that Hitler wanted to avoid provoking American entry into the war. The story reflects no self-evident attempt to curry favor with the West or to rescue Warlimont from prosecution for war crimes.)

Adam Tooze hypothesizes that Hitler attacked Poland not just because of Germany's relative peak power in a global armaments race, but because of America. Hitler, he argues, truly believed that Roosevelt was the leader of an international Jewish conspiracy that would eventually line up the Western democracies to annihilate Germany. He had to strike first.[72] As noted above, Tooze also argues that Hitler anticipated a global superpower economic struggle with America, which meant Germany had to acquire more land and resources. We mention this line of analysis for the sake of completeness because it relates directly to the question of what Axis leaders were thinking before going to war with America, and its author spent vast amounts of time going through German records. That said, as we shall see, these considerations do not emerge in the records directly related to the future war against America.

On the 21st, Mussolini wrote to Hitler what Italy's policy would be, depending on the course of events. If Germany attacked Poland and the conflict remained localized, Italy would provide any assistance Germany requested. If Poland and the Allies attacked Germany, Italy would intervene in support of Germany. If Germany attacked Poland, and Britain and France attacked Germany, Italy would undertake no initiatives because of the already explained inadequate military preparations. If Germany agreed to negotiate its issues and intransigence on the other side caused failure and Germany decided to take up arms, Italy would intervene on Germany's side.[73]

Ribbentrop on 21 August informed Ciano that he would be going to Moscow to sign a political pact with the Soviets. Ciano recorded in his diary,

> Long telephone conversation with the Duce. There is no doubt that the Germans have affected a master stroke. The situation in Europe has turned upside down. Will France and England, who have made their whole anti-Axis policy on alliance with the Soviets, be able to count on the unconditional support of the extremist masses? And will the system of encirclement by means of the small states still hold now that Moscow has collapsed?[74]

German Ambassador Hans Georg von Mackensen reported from Rome on 23 August that Mussolini believed that if Germany attacked Poland, Britain and France would intervene—"and the United States, too, after a few months."[75]

Hitler on 25 August officially informed Mussolini that he had sent Ribbentrop to Moscow to sign a non-aggression pact, which would be publicly revealed soon. The agreement would create a new global political situation that would greatly benefit the Axis.[76] Mussolini replied that Italy was not ready for war because its industrialization and modernization plans had been based on a target of 1942 and told Hitler that Italy would need considerable supplies of raw materials and German antiaircraft guns to defend its defense industry against French air attack.[77] Hitler replied that he could send batteries immediately with more to come, but that organizing raw material shipments would take time. He expressed understanding that Italy could not immediately engage in military operations and asked Mussolini to tie down British and French forces in the Mediterranean using propaganda and military demonstrations.[78] The German ambassador in Rome requested a list of Italy's needs and—personally opposed to the venture in Poland—suggested the list be extensive, as that might constrain his government in Berlin.[79]

Hitler's assurances that a war in Poland would remain localized were really beside the point because he was already gearing up for war against France and Britain. With his eastern flank protected and a back door created through the USSR to get around any Franco–British naval blockade, Hitler by late August 1939 was already planning to attack the Western democracies. He wrote to Mussolini on the 26th that he would strike in the West in early 1940 with forces at least equal to those of Britain and France.[80]

The German-Soviet non-aggression pact violated the spirit and letter of the Anti-Comintern pact, and Japan recalled Ambassador Oshima from Berlin.[81]

Göring, at least, also acted like he expected to be at war with the Western Allies. As a benchmark for discussion later in this book of strategic air warfare, Göring on 28 August declared publicly that Germany was unconcerned about the threat of strategic bombing by the Allies. "If a single British bomber reaches the Ruhr, I want to be called Hermann Meyer instead of Hermann Göring!" At that time, Germany possessed the most extensive and capable ground-based air defense system in the world. It also had grossly inflated projections of the lethality of *Flugabwehrkanone* (air defense cannons, flak) ordnance.[82]

That said, the RAF in 1936–1938, with inferior radar technology, through exercises and trial and error, had built a functional early warning system that could direct fighters against encroaching aircraft. Military experts and their scientific and engineering partners worked side by side throughout so that each partner understood the needs and limitations of the other. They had not, however, done anything about figuring out how to connect newly developed antiaircraft gun-laying radars to actual guns.[83]

*

The Wehrmacht swept across the border into Poland on 1 September, which officially launched the global war that was already well under way in Asia. Britain and France declared war on the 3rd.

Ciano recorded in his diary,

> The German advance in Poland is tremendously powerful. The predictions that this is to be a blitzkrieg are now credible. How will France and Great Britain be able to extend help to Poland? And when the Germans have liquidated the Poles, will France and Britain wish to continue a conflict the reason for which will have been eliminated? The Duce does not believe they will.

He predicts an early peace and does not think it will come to a battle waged in the field, a thing which he considers impossible from a military standpoint. I, on the other hand, believe this will happen: I do not know how the war will develop, but it will develop, and it will be long, uncertain, inexorable. Great Britain's participation makes me certain of this. London has declared war on Hitler; the end of the war will be determined either by Hitler's disappearance or Great Britain's destruction.[84]

On the 15th, he added, "I predict a hard, fierce, long conflict. Very long—and victorious for Great Britain."[85]

Hitler wrote to Mussolini on 3 September, "Whatever comes, I will wage this battle with all the fanaticism of which I and the German people are capable."[86] For the next 18 months, the record of Hitler's exchanges with Mussolini, other foreign contacts, and experts on the United States within his own party and government reveal intense interest in many things related to the war—but only passing reference to the United States.[87] Ciano's diary likewise reveals no consideration in the Italian leadership of America's possible role in events.

Shortly after the invasion of Poland, Hitler urged his generals to complete the conquest of Warsaw before the U.S. Congress returned from recess on 21 September.[88] The dictator had not even mentioned America at the command meeting in August. But he had also erroneously said Britain and France would not enter the war. They had, and suddenly the prospect of America arming Germany's enemies was relevant. Congress might change the Neutrality Act to permit it.

And, indeed, Congress passed a new Neutrality Act in November that restored a "cash-and-carry" clause axed from its more stringent predecessor. Only the Allies, who controlled the seas, could benefit. Moreover, it removed clauses restricting U.S.-flag vessels from entering belligerent ports, and it allowed the arming of merchantmen.[89]

The German High Command assessed that the cash terms, demands of expanding American forces, and the underdeveloped state of American war industries would result in the Allies receiving no substantial supplies for a long time to come.[90] Hitler on 29 November told military commanders at a conference that the neutrality laws were still constraining enough that "America is still not dangerous to us." America's ability to strengthen Germany's enemies was insignificant; though, he conceded, that might not be true in another six months.[91]

Göring told interrogators after the war that the "decisive factor" in German thinking about the United States at this time was that America would require several years to prepare itself for war. Göring claimed that opinions in the leadership were divided as to whether America would greatly expand its army. In any event, Göring also asserted that as early as the campaign in Poland, he urged Hitler to avoid dragging the United States into the war.

Göring added that in 1939, Hitler thought that American isolationists who termed Roosevelt a "war monger" wielded great influence. He based these views on "some observers" in the United States and on American press reports.[92] (Göring's claim that the leadership believed the United States would need several years to prepare for war is consistent with other evidence and was, in fact, an accurate judgment. He may have been playing to his audience in claiming he urged Hitler to avoid war with America.)

Hitler told generals Brauchitsch, commander of the army, and his chief of staff Halder on 27 September that over the long term, Britain and France had greater economic potential than did Germany. They would soon be able to obtain "cash-and-carry" war material from America. On 9 October, Hitler emphasized that a quick military decision against the West was critical because in a protracted war, America could intervene. A few weeks later, Hitler said that because of the neutrality laws, America was not yet dangerous to Germany, nor the reinforcement of the Allies yet significant.[93]

Despite his confidence that isolationists would keep America at peace, the SIS source Esmond reported on 10 October that Hitler was very preoccupied over the American attitude, which he regarded as one of "pre-belligerency."[94] The Führer issued orders to the navy that its submarines were not to attack U.S.-flagged vessels in order to avoid a pretext for entry into the war, a ban that was to endure until 1941. After 28 Americans died when the steamer *Athenia* was sunk on 3 September, Hitler further barred torpedoing passenger steamers, even if they travelled in a convoy. Grand Admiral Erich Raeder argued that American entry into the war appeared "certain" if the war continued, and that a ruthless blockade of England was necessary to shorten the war, even if it risked provoking America's entry. Raeder offered no appraisal of what war against the United States would demand of Germany—the first example of the cavalier, ill-considered ruminations about conflict with America that would lead to war. This time, Hitler rejected Raeder's advice.[95]

Grand Admiral Karl Dönitz, who commanded the submarine force in 1939, in 1965 sent a letter to Dr. Percy Schramm, the compiler of the reconstructed OWK *Kriegstagebuch* (War Diary), in which he said that Hitler had issued a "think piece" on 9 October 1939 in which he established as a long-term war aim waging a successful war at sea against Britain. Submarines, of course, were Germany's only means of cutting Britain's lines of supply. Hitler, however, did not order a crash U-boat construction program that might have made his aim a reality.[96]

Moreover, Hitler viewed the UK as his real Western enemy, holding the French army in distain. Yet he planned a campaign in the west with no plausible means of defeating Britain.[97] His subsequent statements suggest he hoped the British would tire of the effort, accept the status quo, and make peace, which resembles what passed for a strategic endgame in Japan regarding America. It also, as a precedent, makes Hitler's rather offhand declaration of war against the Unites States seem part of a pattern.

Hitler wanted to attack France immediately with massed tank forces assisted by 88mm guns in the antitank role. He conceived of the notion of flipping the World

War I Schlieffen Plan to overrun the low countries and wheel south to Paris. Instead, the main effort would be to the south and wheel north to the coast to cut off the British and French armies expected to advance into Belgium. His initial idea had limited objectives, but it was the concept that Major General Erich von Manstein would turn into a lethal operational masterpiece.

Hitler needed a quick victory to avoid a long war that would inevitably favor the Allies. Moreover, he argued that Germany could only continue the war if the Ruhr industrial basin were secure from easy air attack. The army leadership argued that the many flaws that surfaced in Poland required remedy through improved training and reequipment before an attack on France. Ultimately, bad weather that grounded the Luftwaffe caused repeated delays of an offensive, which by November was shelved for the year.[98]

The initial skirmishes in the air war looked promising for Germany. The RAF launched three daylight bombing attacks on German ships near ports in late 1939, two of them at low level, and ran into coordinated flak and fighter defenses. High losses convinced the British to bomb only from 10,000 feet or higher. The French had few modern bombers and conducted nothing but reconnaissance flights at night.[99]

In Rome, the view of the probable course of events was more alarmist. This conflict was to see American and British Commonwealth forces invade the Italian mainland four years to the month after the invasion of Poland, and some inkling was already emerging in Rome of a conflagration so large as to make such a day possible. Mussolini still believed a negotiated settlement was possible and offered to mediate between Germany and the Western Allies, a notion spurned immediately by Britain. But Ciano argued that no peaceful outcome could emerge, and he viewed a "general conflagration" as unavoidable.[100] Ciano told the German ambassador the day Germany invaded Poland that he expected France and Britain to engage quickly and decisively, with active participation by the United States in the near future.[101] On 2 October, after talking to Hitler in Berlin, Ciano cabled Mussolini and included the warning, "America's entry into the war on the side of the democracies is becoming practically unavoidable, albeit not an immediate development."[102] Italy for now remained neutral and would do so until June 1940, when she pounced on her share of crippled France.

Reverberations in Asia

On 6 September, Germany's ambassador in Tokyo cabled Berlin that the speech given that day by outgoing War Minister Itagaki and incoming minister Shunroku Hata to German military and air attachés had been most friendly. Itagaki had underscored his personal efforts on behalf of a close relationship with Germany that had been stalled by developments in Europe and emphasized that his successor shared his views.[103]

The outbreak of war in Europe had a major strategic impact on the Pacific region. As the U.S. naval attaché in Tokyo observed:

> Japan will probably be cut off from her major sources of supply of essential war and peacetime materials—*except for the United States* [emphasis in the original].... [T]his new situation may have far-reaching effects on the future of Japan's relations with the United States. The United States must necessarily become Japan's only certain source of raw cotton, wood pulp, iron and steel, oil, machinery and other industrial equipment, non-ferrous metals and those chemicals that have been imported from Germany and Great Britain in the past.

Even though the attaché grasped that Japan's crash development program aimed to replace these very materials by early 1942 with sources in Japan, Manchukuo, and northern China, the attaché told Washington the end result was unclear. One report contained a flawed assumption that was to underlie American policy toward Japan for the next two years:

> If the United States refuses to ratify a new Treaty of Commerce and Navigation, or if, due to Japan's refusal to modify her policies in China the United States were to place an embargo on exports to Japan, the Japanese industrial expansion program for the yen bloc would break down, and even the present productive capacity would be seriously curtailed. Japan must make certain definite and drastic changes in her foreign policy.[104]

A second report, however, conceded,

> On the other hand, it is possible that the Japanese Government—guided by the army—will continue to disregard [its] interests in the future as it has in the past. The United States can be certain of one thing, and that is that if the Japanese decide on [this] course, moral embargoes and threats to use force will not be sufficient to make them change. Forceful measures ... will be necessary.[105]

In China, victory looked no closer to hand after two years of fighting. The IJA launched its first major offensive of the year in September to capture the city of Changsha, which would establish control of Henan Province and open the door both to Sichuan and to an attack on Chungking. A new China Expeditionary Command now controlled all operations in the theater. Under the Cantonese general Xue Yue, the Nationalists stopped the Japanese using a combination of regular field operations and guerrilla warfare that sharply hindered the enemy's ability to resupply.

The Chinese launched a counteroffensive along much of the front and regained considerable ground, but a Japanese advance into Guangxi Province surprised the Nationalists, and they had to shift back to a defensive war.[106] On 3 October, a surprise attack by a dozen Soviet-made Chinese bombers destroyed almost 200 IJN and IJA fighters and bombers parked wingtip to wingtip along the runways at Kiukiang, pilot Sakai's base. The military covered up the disaster and forbade personnel returning to Japan from talking about it.[107]

Sakai recalled this period of the war in his memoirs:

> The conflict in China was an incredible war. Among our forces it was never referred to as a "war," but rather as the Sino-Japanese incident....
>
> Opposing the Japanese land and air forces in China were vast enemy armies of millions of men, hopelessly outnumbering our own troops. This disparity in numbers, however, rarely worked to the Chinese advantage, for their troops were poorly trained and ill equipped. Time after time, hordes of enemy troops would advance against our well-armed forces, only to be thrown back with shattering losses. Even the flood of Allied assistance to China, in the form of supplies rushed through Burma, Mongolia, and Sinkiang, failed to offset our qualitative superiority....
>
> This does not mean, however, that Japan ever conquered—or tried to conquer—the vast Chinese population, or to occupy its tremendous land area. This would have been absolutely impossible. Instead, our troops occupied key walled towns at strategic areas, cutting enemy communications, and then exacted tolls and taxes from the millions of Chinese peasants within the authority of the occupying Japanese forces.
>
> But outside the protection of these major walled towns, violent death awaited all but the most powerful Japanese forces. Chiang's guerrillas, as well as those of the Chinese Communists, waited in savage ambush.[108]

America took its first small step toward alliance with China in September, when the Export-Import Bank provided two loans totaling $45 million ($990 million in today's currency). The money could be used to purchase only civilian goods.[109]

CHAPTER 5

1940: Japan Opts for War

Japanese leaders during 1940 made many decisions they knew would probably lead to war with the United States—which crossed the line to accepting war, if not outright declaring it—and their thinking about America during this period explains the ultimate course of events more than decisions in 1941. By then, Japan would have had to offer massive concessions and adopt a staggering shift in strategic policy adopted in 1940 to avoid conflict.

The main body of the U.S. fleet moved from San Diego to Hawaii during January 1940. The commanding admiral of the Pacific Fleet queried Chief of Naval Operations Admiral Stark, "Why are we here?"

Stark replied, "You are there because of the deterrent effect your presence may have on the Japs going into the East Indies."[1]

And so it came to pass that the U.S. Navy's rebasing of the Pacific Fleet to deter Japanese invasion of the East Indies would force Japanese planners to mount an attack to cripple that fleet when it invaded the East Indies.

Indeed, according to Fukudome, this move to Hawaii started Admiral Isoroku Yamamoto, commanding the Combined Fleet, thinking about attacking the fleet at Pearl Harbor. He and Fukudome, his chief of staff, agreed that the American move was not only a political gesture but a measure of America's war preparations and her determination to fight. To Yamamoto, this put America ahead of Japanese war readiness in the Pacific, and the U.S. Navy might be setting up a sortie to attack his fleet.[2]

Yamamoto, who had taken command the previous September, overhauled the fleet's training program to emphasize air warfare. He strongly asserted that air power would decide the next war. He also took the drastic step of pushing the IJN's baseline defensive perimeter from the Bonin and Mariana line to East Carolines and Marshalls.[3]

Indeed, Japan's perception of America as a potential threat was changing from that of mere "note writers." On 22 February, the IJN spokesman told journalists that the construction by the United States of 45,000-ton battleships was the start of a naval arms race.[4] The IJN's annual Navy Day survey of global affairs opined,

> With progress of Japan's strategical and other operations, [the United States] gradually has been hardening its attitude against Japan. It showed one threat to Japan by announcing its decision to renounce the Treaty of Trade and Navigation last July. Japan had undertaken diplomatic negotiations in all sincerity to save the situation, but, ignoring these, the United States caused the treaty to be nullified after 26 January of this year.... On the other hand, America, since the Manchurian affair, has been carrying on a heavy armament expansion program with Japan as the country in mind.[5]

The survey reviewed American military expansion at length but then noted that Washington had chosen the road of economic pressure. The analysis of American intentions was,

> With its armament as it is, America is not confident of its ability to beat Japan in war. Though there are not a small number of advocates of war with Japan in the ranks of the American navy, the American people in general, let alone pacifists, are against war. America is imbued with the very simple thought that should it put an embargo on export of requisites for war to Japan, it would be depriving the latter of its power to carry on its military actions in China. It thus lacks recognition of Japan's firm resolution to see the China incident to a complete settlement. America has thought that its embargo against Japan would be telling on the latter, as since the outbreak of the European war, the exports to the latter from European countries, including Britain and Germany, have markedly decreased.[6]

Yet Japan was confident of its strength. Masanori Ito, the best-known Japanese naval writer who had excellent connections to the IJN, that same month published two analyses of the global naval arms race. In the first, he concluded, "Closer investigation, however, reveals that although in tonnage the ratio of the US Navy to Japan's is 5 to 3, in real strength it is 4 to 5, in my estimate. This is because obsolescent ships with poor performance are listed in the first fighting units in its lineup. In real battle, these old vessels will prove an impediment rather than help."

In the second, Ito opined,

> [O]ur navy should be able to meet the US Navy and retain control of the west Pacific. From the American standpoint, her navy is not strong enough to insure victory 5,000 nautical miles away. In short, the Japanese Navy in an aggressive campaign will necessarily be defeated, but on the defensive, it will have a chance to win. The US Navy will always be victorious against Japan if it remains on the defensive but may be defeated if it undertakes an overseas campaign. Japan desires to add to the margin of safety in her defensive strategy and eventually to establish a margin which will secure her position for an aggressive campaign.[7]

Japan in 1940 did not publish details of expenditures for the IJA's budget. Nevertheless, the U.S. Army Attaché concluded that large sums continued to flow into the air force and for replacement and improvement of armaments.[8]

*

According to Nobuyuki Abe's account, he decided to resign as prime minister on 15 January 1940 because he opposed any pact with Germany and Italy. Both the IJA and IJN opposed him on nearly every issue.[9]

Admiral Mitsumasa Yonai, a man of dominating personality and complete confidence, became prime minister and formed a new government. Significantly, General Shunroku Hata remained Minister of War, indicating policy continuity. Yonai had been the Navy Minister from 1937 to 1939, who less than a year earlier had told the Diet that Japan's goal was to control the seas and skies of the Pacific. Yonai nevertheless was credited with blocking a proposal to form an alliance with the European Axis powers in April 1939, and he had managed to convince Ambassador Grew that he would pursue Japan's past priorities but progressively moderate them in "scope and methods." His appointment was rumored to be a compromise of sorts between the IJA and the Emperor, who had wanted to appoint a general so the IJA would have to accept responsibility for the conditions it was creating.[10]

There was little sign of moderation, however. The Combined Fleet made a celebratory visit to Osaka Bay on 15 February, and Vice Admiral Yamamoto announced, "We are always prepared to strike a blow at any power in the world any time the state orders us to do so."[11] An IJN publication extolling national characteristics for submarine warfare observed, "The Samurai of former times were accustomed to lie in wait for the enemy and delighted in surprise attacks."[12]

Yamamoto first discussed his idea of attacking Pearl Harbor in March or April 1940, according to Vice Admiral Fukudome after the war. The key idea was that Japan had to deal a fatal blow to America at the very start of a war. For the first time, the naval air arm was sufficiently developed to conduct such an operation, an impossibility during the long years when the IJN planned for a defensive decisive battle. The new Combined Fleet training program demonstrated that the aerial torpedo could play a dominant role in a decisive battle. Yamamoto murmured to Fukudome, "I wonder if an aerial attack can't be made on Pearl Harbor."

Fukudome credited Yamamoto with being the first naval officer to conceive of a naval aerial attack on Pearl Harbor at the outset of a war. The two officers discussed the outlines from time to time through the rest of the year.[13]

Prince Konoye, now President of the Privy Council, anticipated that he would soon receive an imperial mandate to form a new single political party. At a dinner with Home Minister Kido on 26 May, the two decided to abolish all other parties when that day arrived and to establish a cabinet system that appears configured for little but preparing for war. The Cabinet was to be composed of only the Premier and the War and Navy ministers, who would also fill other posts. Two or three other men would be handpicked immediately for a few positions, including Foreign Minister. Eventually, other members of the new party would fill additional ministerial positions. The Supreme National Defense Council was to be established including the Chiefs of the General Staffs of the IJA and the IJN, the Premier, and the Ministers of War and of the Navy. The military's desires concerning foreign policy and finance would carry influence.

Only five days later, Kido received word that he would succeed the ailing Lord Keeper of the Privy Seal, which placed a man planning what looked like a pre-war Cabinet at the Emperor's right hand. The Lord Keeper controlled access to the Emperor, the issuance of imperial rescripts, and liaison with the government. He was the first official the Emperor would consult on the formation of a new Cabinet or when other important decisions loomed. The position held ministerial rank but was not part of the Cabinet, appointments being the province of the Emperor alone. Kido called on the Emperor at his private residence the next day and was asked to accept the assignment. Kido replied that he was not fit for the position, but the Emperor assured him that he had been the unanimous recommendation of the upper class, including Prince Konoye. After begging leave to consult the prince, Kido met Konoye for a "free" exchange of opinions and then telephoned the residence to accept the honor.

If Konoye thought Kido would move the Emperor to his hardline way of thinking, the new Lord Keeper found himself serving a moderate and measured master. Kido's first to-do list included obtaining the Emperor's views on whether there should be a change of government and on "the European problem, as well as our future national policy," Kido wrote in his diary, adding that the global conflict was too important for the government to manage by itself. The Emperor opposed a government change, thought the new political party movement had gone too far, and said he would like a plan drawn up for a compromise with China, where the Army just wanted to send more troops. He did not address events in Europe or national policy other than China.[14]

Meanwhile, the United States announced on 7 May that the fleet would remain based in Hawaii indefinitely.[15]

Admiral Sankichi Takahashi, Supreme War Councilor and former Commander-in-Chief of the Japanese Grand Fleet, on 27 May delivered a speech on the occasion of Navy Day to an audience at the Osaka Public Hall. Takahashi advocated the inclusion of the Netherlands East Indies and South Seas area in the "New Order in East Asia." He accused the United States of putting military and economic pressure on Japan to block the new order. He continued, "One-third of the world must have Japan as a leader. Only then will a new order in the world be born."[16]

This very idea was being staffed for leadership discussion in a few months.

The Navy and War ministers stopped providing the Diet with meaningful information during open sessions. Discussions of defense matters moved to secret sessions.[17]

Japan had every reason to believe that Washington was inclined to enter the European war at some point. Ambassador Kichisaburo Nomura met with Secretary of State Hull on 7 June and recorded in his diary (and apparently sent to the Foreign Minister, given the reference to "your instructions"),

> As to the European war, [Hull] repeated several times the self defense argument *characteristic of the U.S.A.* [emphasis in the original], saying that Hitler was thinking of conquering the world. If Britain should give in, the Atlantic Ocean would be at his mercy, and South America would turn out to be his supply base of materials. This would endanger the U.S.A. Fifteen countries have been destroyed because they had sat with folded arms till their borders were invaded. The United States cannot follow their steps, he declared. (I have tried hard to correct this conception along the lines of your instructions, but for the present there is no hope for success. The U.S.A., however, is not likely to enter the war soon. Holding the United States in restraint is the main point of our future diplomatic policy toward the U.S.A.)[18]

On 8 June 1940, the semi-official *Keijo Nippo* newspaper in Chosen published two editorials that appeared to reflect the Japanese assessment at the time. The first argued that Great Britain was in imminent danger of being defeated, and that Japan must be prepared to take its share of the spoils in the Far East if the British Empire were broken up. This would require that Japan take into account "American interference." The second opined that American entry into the war on the side of Britain and France was only a matter of time. "Of course, Germany must have started the war after considering the possibility of American participation," judged the author, giving Hitler too much credit. American entry would probably prove decisive, he argued, and Germany's one chance was to force a decision before American aid became effective.[19] This, by the way, is one illustration of an ability in Japan to see the war in global terms and draw well-founded conclusions, insofar as other parties were concerned; sadly, this did not apply to their own actions.

The militarized Cabinet was straining at the leash to broaden the war, having consciously in mind that this would affect relations with the United States in some way. Foreign Minister Hachiro Arita on 19 June met the Emperor and informed him of the discussion at the so-called "four ministers' conference" the preceding day. The ministers had adopted two options. 1) Give French Indochina an ultimatum that it stop providing assistance to Chiang Kai-shek and, should that be refused, apply force. 2) Use force without negotiations. The military favored the first option, with a decision on force to remain open for later consideration, which met with agreement from the Premier and Foreign Minister. There is no indication that the subject came up directly, but all of them were doubtless taking into account that Germany just then was wrapping up the invasion and occupation of metropolitan France. Japan was to consult with Germany and Italy on the handling of French Indochina and deal with Britain and the United States according to their responses.

The Emperor told Kido, however, that he did not want to handle French Indochina in the manner of Frederick the Great or Napoleon. He wished to keep in mind the true spirit of *Hakko Ichiu*, "which is our principle since the Age of the Gods." Kido recorded, "I was struck with awe."[20]

Arita reappeared on 27 June to report that American Ambassador Grew had proposed a treaty to maintain the status quo in the Pacific and avoid any forceful changes. Kido recorded in his diary that the question was "quite delicate" and that "*Japan would not accept if its operations in the Netherlands East Indies were restricted in any way* [emphasis added]." The proposal smacked of the Nine Powers Treaty and was hard to swallow in any case, wrote Kido. It might be possible to consider it if the treaty were limited to the islands of Japan and to American possessions in the Pacific.[21]

Ambassador Grew, for his part, recorded in his diary on 2 July that the stunning German victories in Europe had sent Japanese–American relations into a tailspin. The population was increasingly anti-British and anti-American.

> [W]e ourselves take the position that there are three main obstacles to an improvement in our relations, namely (1) Japan's use of force as an instrument of national policy, (2) Japan's failure to respect treaty commitments, and (3) Japan's multifarious interferences with American rights and interests in China. On the other hand, Japan takes the position that these various obstacles cannot be removed as long as hostilities in China are in progress, and that even after the termination of hostilities only some but not all of our grounds for complaint can be removed.

He observed that the military was demanding the cutoff of war materiels flowing to China from Indochina, Hong Kong, and Burma. Japan also demanded that the Netherlands East Indies guarantee the free flow of commodities to Japan, even at the expense of quotas promised to other countries, as well as "cooperation" on matters of immigration and industrial exploitation. The implication, he judged, was "or else."[22]

Chiang Kai-shek's emissary T. V. Soong, meanwhile, visited Washington in June and requested arms and more loans. Despite a sympathetic hearing, he came away disappointed. America was only beginning to mobilize and had minimal stocks, and Britain clearly had first dibs on anything she could spare. Washington also worried that providing arms would solidify Japan's alliance with Germany.[23]

Elsewhere, Kido told the Emperor on 28 June that there were rumors that Lieutenant General Hideki Tojo would be put forth as the next Minister of War. The man had not even held a divisional command! Such a position should go to a general with experience at the head of an army, at least, Kido thought.[24]

The Emperor could see that Japan was already on the threshold of war with Britain. On 11 July, he confided to Kido that he expected Britain to reject Japan's demand that it stop its support to Chiang Kai-shek. This could lead to Japanese occupation of Hong Kong, which would lead to a declaration of war. Kido replied that Japan should summon a firm resolution and be prepared for any possible outcome. Kido urged the Emperor to summon a Supreme Command Liaison Conference and a Council in the Imperial Presence to study all options carefully. A liaison conference, a civilian–military coordination mechanism established in 1937, brought together the

Prime Minister; the Foreign, Navy, and War Ministers; occasionally other Cabinet members such as the Finance Minister; and the IJA and IJN Chiefs and Vice Chiefs of Staff. An Imperial council included these same officials, the President of the Privy Council, and the Emperor, and would typically ratify decisions reached at the liaison conference. The Emperor agreed, but, reflecting on the balance of political power, he said that it would be useless if the IJA opposed the idea.[25]

Disagreements between the IJA, often expressed through the person of War Minister Shunroku Hata, and the IJN in the person of Yonai, over whether to pursue a close alignment with Germany and Italy—the IJA favored it—finally split the Cabinet and brought it down on 17 July. Yonai reminded interrogators after the war,

> I felt from the very first that Germany had no chance. I believed so firmly from the very outset that Germany had no chance that I was one of those who strongly opposed a tie-up with Germany; and because that feeling of mine was known in certain quarters, I was forced, more or less, to resign from my position as Prime Minister, because the feeling in those quarters was that with Admiral Yonai as Prime Minister there was little chance of the tie-up with Germany materializing.[26]

Hata had commanded Japanese Central Army in China in 1938, and from March 1941 through November 1944 was to be the Commander-in-Chief of all Japanese armies in China. He would open the door of power to the man the postwar criminal tribunal called the "arch-criminal of the Pacific area," Hideki Tojo.[27] Ironically, the very day the government resigned, Japan appeared to accomplish a major coup when Great Britain, despite the Emperor's pessimism, closed the Burma Road used to supply Chinese Nationalist forces.

Prince Konoye, who had just stepped down as President of the Privy Council, again became Prime Minister on 22 July. He had urged the selection of someone else who enjoyed the support of the military, to which Kido responded that the military appeared to overwhelmingly support him. Konoye proposed to ask the War Minister to select a successor who could work with the IJN and the Navy Minister to pick a man who could work with the IJA. He would select his own foreign minister and then solicit approval for his Cabinet choices from the Supreme Command.

Thanks to political maneuvering by Hata and others, Lieutenant General Hideki Tojo became the new War Minister. Admiral Zengo Yoshida, said to be popular in the fleet because of his abilities but reticent by nature, remained in place as Navy Minister, though he was replaced in September by Admiral Koshiro Oikawa due to ill health. Yosuke Matsuoka was soon named Foreign Minister. Japanese press commentaries speculated that the new Cabinet would share many views with the IJA.[28]

This group of key ministers held views that may go a long way to explaining the Japanese leadership's collective assessment of the United States as an adversary.

Hideki Tojo was, in the words of a not unflattering profile by *Life* magazine, a "tough and crafty samurai general." Tojo was born in 1884. He entered the Military

Academy in 1904. Japan's victory over a first-class foreign power in 1905 and the subsequent euphoria in Japan was the heady mix in which Tojo formed his first adult opinions about Japan's military standing in the world.[29]

Tojo in 1909 married Katsuko Ito, with whom he would father three sons and four daughters.[30] After Tojo became War Minister, Katsuko would visit bereaved war widows to give them incense to burn before the family shrine.[31]

Tojo graduated from the Military Staff College in 1915, and during 1919–1922 he served as a military attaché in Berlin.[32] Tojo was not a combat soldier. He served as head of the military police of the Kwantung Army in Manchuria from October 1935 to March 1937, when he was promoted to Chief of Staff of the Kwantung Army. In May 1938, he jumped to the position of Vice War Minister in the second Konoye Cabinet and participated in the formulation of the program to create the Greater East Asian Co-Prosperity Sphere.[33]

Tojo's next assignment was as chief of the army air force.[34] It is possible that his familiarity with air power as practiced by Japan led him at the crucial moment of deciding for war to under-appreciate the American potential to use strategic bombing to devastate the Japanese homeland. The Japanese air force, like its German counterpart, was modern and effective but designed primarily to support ground operations. Japan had no vision for strategic bombing.

Tojo is said to have hated the trappings of democracy and wanted a return to the totalitarian traditions of the Shogunate. He is reputed to have been an active member of the Black Dragon Society, a fascist-leaning political organization that in the 1930s pressed for close relations with Germany and Italy.[35]

Tojo was no ascetic like Hitler. Once he had risen to positions in Tokyo, he smoked cigars and enjoyed parties in the backrooms of exclusive restaurants on the bank of the Sumida River, stripping off his military tunic to swap stories with chums over sake. He enjoyed riding horses and drinking with young officers. Tojo frequently attended Kabuki theater. His hobbies included photography, poetry, and sword collecting.[36]

Tojo knew little about America.

Matsuoka was born in 1880 and sent to the United States at the age of 12 where he bussed tables at a hotel in Seattle. Going by "Frank," he lived with American families in Portland, Oregon, and Oakland, California. Matsuoka took odd jobs as a farmhand, janitor, and railroad hand and worked his way through the University of Oregon, where he graduated from the law school second in his class. He was a good poker player. He came to love America but was offended by the blatant racism he encountered.

Matsuoka returned to Japan and joined the diplomatic service, with which he served in China. He was chief delegate to the League of Nations, where he defended the invasion of Manchuria and brought about Japan's withdrawal from the organization. One American journalist who dealt with him in Geneva described him as both slippery as an eel and a realist who could be exceptionally concrete in conversation. Matsuoka compared Japan's expansion in Asia to the expansion of the United States in North America, and China to the Native Americans and Mexico, who violently lost lands to the expanding America. Back in Japan, Matsuoka briefly entered politics, had a rocky career, but landed on his feet when he was appointed head of the South Manchurian Railway from 1933 to 1939, one of the biggest jobs in Japan.[37]

Matsuoka was a Japanese fascist believer. As early as 1933, he became an advocate for abolition of the political parties and launching a "Showa Revolution."[38]

On 21 July 1940, now Foreign Minister, Matsuoka gave an off-the-record background interview to an American journalist, who passed the details to the U.S. Embassy. Matsuoka told him that, in the struggle between democracy and totalitarianism, the latter would surely win and control the world. The era of democracy was finished and the democratic system bankrupt. There was no room in the world for two different systems or economies. Totalitarianism would dominate the world for centuries. The public, he claimed, was demanding a single political party. Konoye was to gradually create one, and the Japanese system with the Emperor at its head was uniquely hospitable to fascism. The journalist concluded that Matsuoka was more pro-Axis than any other Japanese he had met.[39]

Ambassador Grew met privately with Matsuoka on the 26th. Matsuoka told him that he would at times be undiplomatically blunt but believed that much could be gained by frank and direct speech. He mentioned an article he had recently written in which he said that if the United States and Japan ever had to fight each other, they should know precisely the causes and reason for which they were fighting. If war came, it should not be because of misunderstanding, as had often happened historically.

Matsuoka said he had visited Roosevelt in the White House during a trip to Washington in an unofficial capacity and asked Grew to pass a message to the President. He said he shared an interest in preserving world peace, but that peace could not be safeguarded by adhering to the status quo. A new world order must come into being, and peace would have to depend on adapting to that order.[40]

As Foreign Minister 1940–1941, Yosuke Matsuoka was far more pro-war than the senior military officers. He played a key role in setting Japan on the road to war with America. (Wikimedia Commons)

Following Germany's defeat of France, the Japanese learned on 19 July about the Stark Plan to build a two-ocean navy capable of simultaneous combat operations in two theaters. The U.S. fleet would expand by 70 percent and by 1,500 aircraft. The plan anticipated building 2 million tons of shipping, twice Japan's last two expansions combined. Japan doubled its own most recent naval expansion for 1941, but the Navy General Staff estimated that its strength ratio to the United States would drop to 50 percent by 1943 and 30 percent by 1944.[41]

Crossing the Line Toward War

A liaison conference on 27 July adopted a sweeping revision of Japanese foreign policy in light of changes in the world situation. The conference adopted three main goals: 1) To strive for the speedy conclusion of the China Incident by cutting off all assistance to Chungking from outside powers through French Indochina, Burma, and Hong Kong; 2) To maintain a firm stand toward the United States on one front, while strengthening political ties with Germany and Italy and ensuring more cordial diplomatic relations with Russia; and 3) To use diplomatic means to acquire vital resources from the Dutch East Indies.[42]

The draft document submitted by the IJA and the IJN, but also vetted by Konoye and Matsuoka, included several alarming clauses, and Hattori's account suggests that they remained in the final conclusions:

- Use of force was provisionally authorized to establish a military presence in French Indochina and cut off the flow of support through Burma.
- [A] deterioration in relations with the United States is inevitable, as a consequence of our pursuit of essential policies.... No measure shall be taken militarily, on our part, to increase friction in our relations with the United States.
- Diplomatic measures shall be employed toward the Dutch East Indies, for the time being, to acquire vital resources.
- Regarding the use of force, one clause read, "In case the China Incident still remains unsettled, our policies shall be pushed within the limits of not coming into open hostilities with a third power; but in case of particularly favorable developments of the situations at home and abroad, force of arms may be employed in order to solve the Southern Area problems."
- Utmost effort shall be made to employ force of arms against Britain only; and since involvement in a war with the United States may become unavoidable in such an event, all possible preparations shall be made there for.[43]

The military's justification was that Japan now faced a protracted war in China and had to exert heavy pressure to cut off outside support for Chiang.

> It is also urgent for Japan to sever herself from economic dependence on Britain and the United States, and to establish a structure of self-sufficiency based on a nucleus composed of Japan, Manchukuo, and China, with the incorporation of the Southern Area east of India and north of Australia and New Zealand. It would be exceedingly difficult to find another opportunity, like today, to accomplish the above defined objective.[44]

Northern and Southern Areas

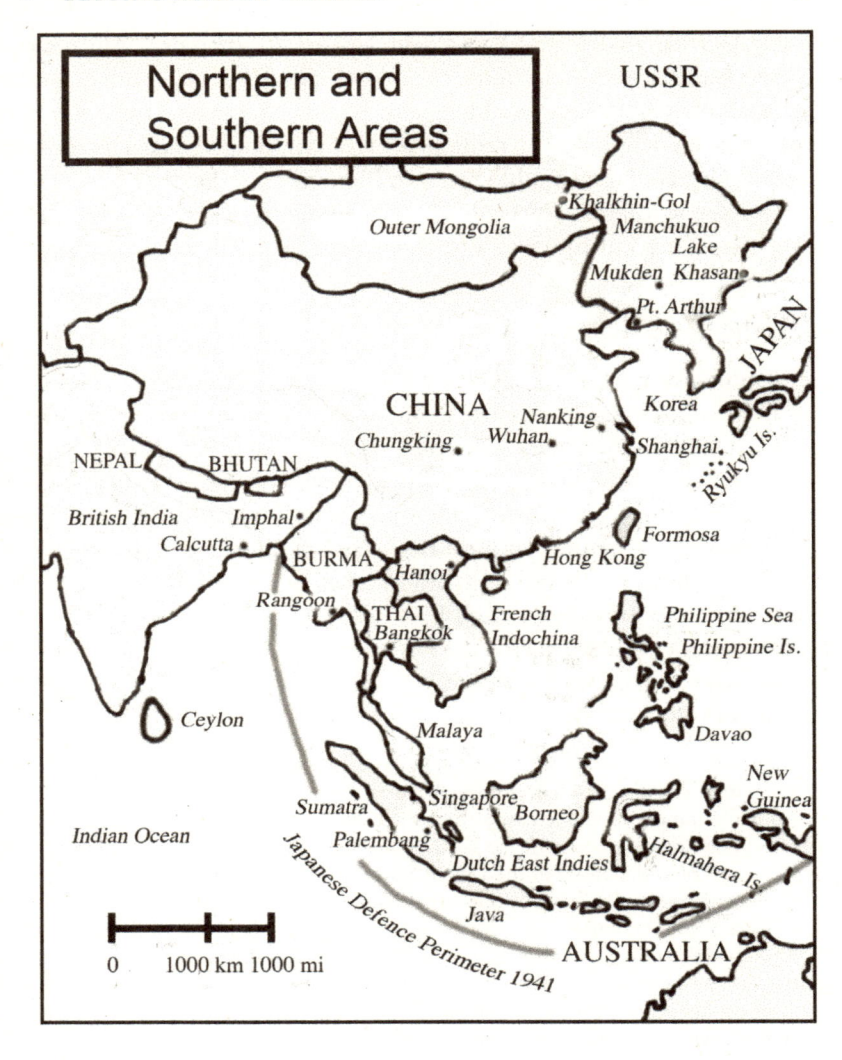

[Map showing East and Southeast Asia with labels: USSR, Outer Mongolia, Khalkhin-Gol, Manchukuo, Lake Khasan, Mukden, Pt. Arthur, JAPAN, China, Chungking, Wuhan, Nanking, Korea, Shanghai, Ryukyu Is., Nepal, Bhutan, British India, Calcutta, Imphal, Burma, Rangoon, Hanoi, Thai, Bangkok, French Indochina, Formosa, Hong Kong, Philippine Sea, Philippine Is., Ceylon, Malaya, Davao, Indian Ocean, Sumatra, Singapore, Palembang, Borneo, New Guinea, Halmahera Is., Dutch East Indies, Java, Australia, Japanese Defence Perimeter 1941; scale 0–1000 km / 1000 mi]

And so, by late July, Japan had decided to make "preparations" for war against America. Japanese military historian Hattori marveled that a policy that fundamentally shaped Japan's actions from this point on came into force after a single liaison conference, with little discussion.[45]

The Emperor on 29 July shared with Kido his impressions of a just-completed imperial conference, which as usual had approved the results of the liaison conference and which appears to have marked the turning point toward inevitable war with the United States. The government, army, and navy cliques held different ideas entirely, said Hirohito. Prince Konoye was convinced that the China Incident could not be resolved quickly, and he wanted to reduce the amount of occupied territory in

China and proceed with "southern operations." The IJA agreed with the southern advance but wanted to leave the China front as it was. The IJN, however, did not appear to want to make a southern advance.[46]

But the IJN had signed off on the policy proposal, and there was public backing for the new strategic axis of advance in naval ranks, as well. Rear Admiral Gumpei Sekine, in a lecture in Osaka on 8 August, argued, "We cannot wait for the German Blitzkrieg on Britain." A clash of interests with Britain was inevitable if Japan were to grow and gain security. Now was the time for quick, decisive action to secure Japan's position in the Netherlands East Indies and Indochina. He denounced rumors that Japan would lose a war because of lack of materials as being the "malicious propaganda of spies." Japan, he said, was not lacking materials, and as long as she remained pro-Axis and Axis-aided, there was nothing to fear even from the combined British and American navies.[47]

Even the IJN command appeared to accept that Japan was about to opt for war. Prince Fushimi, Chief of the Naval General Staff, spoke with the Emperor on 10 August. He explained why the IJN opposed using armed force against the Netherlands East Indies and Singapore. It would take at least eight months for preparation after the decision for war, and it therefore would be better to postpone that decision as long as possible.[48] In other words, for him it was a question of timing. Indeed, the IJN had been the advocate of the southern advance in preference to the IJA's preference for the northern.[49]

The Supreme Command began planning for southern operations once the policy was adopted. At first, neither the IJA nor the IJN seriously contemplated a war against America. In August, the navy staff told the army staff that it needed to give careful consideration to the use of arms.[50] An internal report prepared by the Naval General Staff on 1 August concluded that Japan would march into Indochina to acquire raw materials and to strengthen its strategic position in a war with the United States; America would retaliate by imposing a trade embargo; the oil embargo would compel Japan to seize the Netherlands East Indies; and that this step would require initiating hostilities against the United States.[51]

Let us emphasize this point. The Naval General Staff in July 1940 accurately expected a series of dominoes to fall, ending in an American oil embargo, which would trigger occupation of the East Indies and war with the United States. It expected war. That was the mindset at the time. However, we shall see that when the Japanese actually decided to occupy Indochina, the oil embargo caught them by surprise. They had forgotten or ignored this moment of insight.

Then Rear Admiral Fukudome, at that time assigned as chief of staff to the Combined Fleet under Fleet Admiral Yamamoto, wrote after the war,

> Even though the United States could be kept out of the war for a while, it was absolutely certain that she would not remain an idle spectator forever.... Because the Japanese realized that there was no means of isolating the United States from operations in Southeast Asia, the

main target of the Japanese navy from the outset was to be the US fleet, and all other objectives were to be treated as secondary. How to accomplish the destruction of the US fleet was the grave responsibility entrusted to Admiral Yamamoto.

According to Fukudome, the Combined Fleet concluded that the U.S. fleet posed a much greater threat based in Hawaii than it had when on the west coast:

> Every Japanese naval officer realized that a crushing blow would be inflicted if a successful attack were launched on distant Hawaii, depriving the enemy of the initiative and ensuring us of an impregnable position. The Navy General Staff believed that the IJN, because of the operational limitations of its warships, could not attack Hawaii. But Yamamoto, the "father of naval aviation," had long believed that future wars would be decided by airpower, and he had improved and developed the Japanese navy's air arm to that end. In consequence, he alone originated the idea of aerial surprise attack—and thus made the impossible possible.[52]

According to Fukudome, Yamamoto regarded Pearl Harbor as

> Absolutely necessary for the success of the Southern operations; it was like day preceding the night. He often stressed that if the Pearl Harbor operation could not be carried out, the war should not be started. The [Navy General Staff] did not agree; they were afraid of the Pearl Harbor plan leaking out beforehand and, in this case, it would have to be given up, and if the task force should be spotted, it would have to return. Whereas the Southern operations no matter what would have to be carried out.[53]

In a memorandum from the U.S. War Department G-2 to Chief of Staff Marshall entitled "Japanese Potentialities with Respect to Hawaii" and dated 17 December 1941, the G-2 concurred in substance with Fukudome's explanation of why Japan attacked Pearl Harbor:

> From the general outline of Japanese strategy as developed by their operations to date, it appears that the initial attack on Hawaii was a raid designed to strike an immobilizing blow at the United States Pacific Fleet. The objective was to prevent the fleet from interfering with Japanese offensives in the Western Pacific and Southeast Asia. In this raid, they accomplished their objective, psychologically no less than physically.

Copies of the document went to the President and other senior American leaders.[54]

The direction was set by summer 1940, but the Japanese leadership was as yet uncertain how to address the inevitable American problem. The Emperor spoke with Matsuoka on 9 August and told Kido afterward that the foreign minister was trying to unify Japan's foreign policy and trying to avoid diplomatic isolation. It was regrettable, His Majesty observed, that Matsuoka did not seem to have established a policy regarding the United States.[55]

By mid-August, Konoye had abolished political parties and declared the creation of a "new national structure," soon renamed the Imperial Rule Assistance Association. The War Department G-2 commented that:

> It bore a rather weak resemblance to the totalitarian political system of Germany and Italy, but retained, fundamentally, a Japanese basis. At no time, however, was there any indication that Prince Konoye aspired to become the supreme leader of a dictatorship, and, in fact, he publicly

stated that any one-party system which regarded the State and the party as the same thing was not acceptable in Japan because it would be contrary to the basic principle of "One Sovereign over all." The army [and navy] remained outside the new structure.[56]

The IJA had now fully displaced the evaporated parties as the center of political power, the U.S. Embassy reported, albeit not becoming the master of unchecked power. Virulent nationalists dominated the civilian commission designed to fill out the details of the new system. Konoye's stated goal was classically fascist: "To unite the total energies of the State and the People."[57]

Coincident with Japan's first steps on the path to war with America, the first in a series of intelligence breakthroughs that would expose Tokyo's intentions to the enemy occurred. In August 1940, cryptologic analysts in the U.S. Army's Signals Intelligence Service finished a masterwork: they completed construction of eight machines capable of cracking Japan's most sensitive code, used for transmission of diplomatic messages. Over the coming months, the codebreakers would figure out how to decipher the keys needed to allow the traffic to be read. By early 1941, the President and a handful of other senior officials would be privy to Japan's most secret diplomatic and military attaché communications.[58]

By late 1940, the policy framework for Japan's thinking about America was militarizing, and Japan made its decisions knowing full well that war with America could be the result. The Emperor on 6 September told Kido that it was necessary that the IJA and IJN cooperate in carrying out the policy toward the United States. The Germans, meanwhile, in early September proposed signing a formal military alliance, what would become the Tripartite Pact. The IJA had immediately agreed, but the IJN had called for further study and discussion at a liaison conference.[59] Indeed, Navy Minister Admiral Zengo Yoshida opposed the alliance because signing it could lead to war with America, for which Japan was as yet unprepared. Rather than continue to resist the IJA and suffering from exhaustion, he resigned. Admiral Koshiro Oikawa, his successor, was known for working well with the IJA.[60]

Admiral Matome Ugaki, then head of Section One (Operations), Naval General Staff, also wrote in his diary that he expected joining the pact would lead to the brink of armed confrontation with America, but that most voices in the navy leadership pushed to accept the agreement—and that was the IJN's final position. The IJN leadership, moreover, agreed to immediately launch preparations for employing the fleet against the U.S. Navy instead of waiting for the treaty to be signed and to emphasize the urgency of naval preparations at the coming imperial conference. The shift to war footing, recorded Ugaki, thereafter made fair progress.[61] So, we can date actual gearing up for war against America from September 1940.

The imperial conference occurred on 19 September, and Japanese leaders clearly recognized that approving the pact would probably lead to an economic break with the United States and quite possibly to war. Navy Chief of Staff Prince Fushimi argued, "I foresee that as a result of this alliance, our trade with Great Britain and the United States will undergo a change and that if worse comes to worst, it will become increasingly difficult to import vital materials. Moreover, it is quite likely that a Japanese–American war will be a protracted one."[62]

The Cabinet planning board director offered that steel and copper output would suffer but capacity expansion underway could meet military needs. Oil product stocks were fairly large and "should be alright." In no event would an American embargo leave Japan unable to prosecute the war in China. Eventually, however, fresh oil supplies from the Netherlands East Indies, Sakhalin, or elsewhere would be needed. Fushimi was skeptical that Japan could obtain additional oil, and pointed out that the IJN would be on the front line and need greater supplies.

Prince Konoye agreed that trade would suffer, and Japan would have difficulties obtaining war materials, but, according to the meeting record, he countered,

> We have been aware of this problem, and we have increased our domestic production and added to our stockpiles. Hence, if we tighten controls over consumption by the military ... we should be able to meet military needs for an extended period; and in the event of a war with the United States, we would be able to supply the military and thus withstand a rather prolonged war.[63]

Matsuoka made plain that the pact would oblige Japan to enter the war if the United States joined the conflict in Europe. Japan would itself decide whether that step had actually occurred.

President of the Privy Council Yoshimichi Hara pointed out that the pact was aimed against the United States to prevent American entry into the European war. If the United States did not declare war on Germany or Italy, it would use its economic pressure against Japan in retaliation against the pact to wear Japan down over time to the point she would be unable to endure a conflict.

Matsuoka retorted that Japan would have to abandon half or all of China to reach an accommodation with Washington, but American pressure would not end even then. Roosevelt faced re-election, and he was likely to attract support with Japan-bashing or might even go to war against Japan. A minor clash with the Americans in China could easily lead to war. "Only a firm stand on our part will prevent a war," he concluded.[64]

Tojo reminded the group that under the last government, the council had already adopted a policy of ending the war in China as quickly as possible and resolving the "southern question." Japan would obtain vital materials from the Netherlands East Indies peacefully if possible but could use force if not.

Hara asked whether, if the United States encircled Japan by leasing bases in Australia and New Zealand, would the government consider that an act of war? Matsuoka and Tojo agreed it would depend on the circumstances.

Hara observed, "The United States is a self-confident nation. Accordingly, I wonder if our taking a firm stand might not have a result quite contrary to the one we expect." Matsuoka replied that she might adopt a stern attitude at first but would consider her interests and arrive at a reasonable attitude. He put the odds of America bringing about a critical situation or reacting in a "level-headed" way at fifty-fifty.

In the end, both the IJA and IJN supported signing the pact. Fushimi, however, added three conditions: every step must be taken to avoid war with the United States, the southward advance would be peaceful "as far as possible," and the government would keep the press from spewing anti-British and anti-American rhetoric.[65]

Japanese military historian Asada cites a single source to relate that the Emperor had deep misgivings about the pact. On 30 September, he told Konoye that he could understand why in current circumstances an alliance with German was necessary, but he worried that Japan would lose a naval war against America with unforeseeable consequences. He asked whether Konoye would share his travails. This supposedly brought tears to Konoye's eyes.[66] Konoye himself evidently never recorded this event.

Elsewhere, Japan managed to persuade the Vichy government administration to accept a "Joint Defense Agreement," under which Japan would deploy troops into northern Indochina to plug that supply route to Chiang's forces—the Hanoi–Yunnan railroad. This would leave the Burma Road—which Britain closed for three months under Japanese pressure but reopened in October—as China's only remaining outlet to the Western world. The deal provoked the United States to make a $25 million ($300 million in today's currency) loan to Chiang. Tokyo ordered ships bearing the Japanese ground troops to depart for Indochina on the 23rd.[67]

Matsuoka confirmed to Ambassador Grew on 20 September that Japan had issued an ultimatum to the French Indochina Governor General to permit entry of Japanese troops under a confidential agreement signed with the Vichy representative in Tokyo on 30 August. Matsuoka said that the purpose of the measures was to permit Japanese troops to attack Chiang Kai-shek and bring peace to China. As soon as hostilities ceased, Japan would withdraw her troops.[68]

Kido advised the Emperor on 21 September that Japan would have to oppose both Britain and the United States if it signed a pact with Germany and Italy. Therefore, he urged, Japan must adjust its relationship with China as quickly as possible. Ironically, given what was to come, the Emperor was also concerned at this time with the destruction of civilization in the wake of press reports about German air raids that had struck British museums.[69]

The Privy Council met on 26 September to discuss the proposed military pact and approved it. Before the meeting, Konoye told imperial advisers, "It is necessary to act defiantly with the United States so that it would not underestimate Japan.... But if the worst-case scenario happens, my government is resolved to deal with it."[70]

As the most senior Japanese civilian leaders talked, the 5th Division landed on the coast of French Indochina at 0000 hours on 23 September and attacked, contrary to instructions. Hattori claims that lead elements on both sides opened fire, unaware of the political deal reached between the Japanese and Vichy authorities. The Imperial

General Staff, surprised by the violence, ordered a halt to forward movement at 0300 hours, and fighting generally ended by the 24th.[71]

Ace pilot Sakai participated in the air operation, marked by the first use of the new A6M Zero fighter that was to establish itself as one of the great dogfighters of the war. The Zero had twice the speed of the Mitsubishi Type 96 the pilots had been flying and the range to fly from China to Indochina.[72]

Kido, upon learning about the assault, recorded that this was a great mistake by a single commander who did not grasp the bigger picture. It was an appropriate omen.[73] War Minister Tojo disciplined Major General Kyoji Tominaga, chief of the IGHQ army operations section, who had been given command of the operation.[74]

Installing the Global Axis

The Tripartite Pact, signed in Berlin on 27 September, rhetorically committed the partners to

> stand together and cooperate with one another in their efforts in Greater East Asia and in the regions of Europe, wherein it is their prime purpose to establish a new order of things calculated to promote the prosperity and welfare of the peoples there.... Japan recognizes and respects the leadership of Germany and Italy in the establishment of the new order in Europe.... Germany and Italy recognize and respect the leadership of Japan in the establishment of the new order in Greater East Asia.... Germany, Italy, and Japan agree to cooperate in their efforts on the aforesaid basis. They further undertake to assist one another with all political, economic, and military means, if one of the Contracting Parties is attacked by a Power at present not involved in the European war or the Chinese–Japanese conflict.[75]

Matsuoka's deputy minister admitted bluntly to some foreign diplomats that the pact was aimed against America. Ever since the Immigration Act of 1924 and the Manchuria Incident, the United States had hampered Japan's necessary expansion. World totalitarianism would supplant Anglo-Saxonism, which was bankrupt and would be wiped out. Japan had to ally with the powers that were not intransigently set on maintaining the status quo.

Matsuoka in a written message to the U.S. Embassy denied that the agreement was aimed at the United States and assured Ambassador Grew that there need be no problems between the two countries so long as America accepted the New Order in East Asia, *including the South Seas*. He offered a rationale for the New Order that smacked of *Lebensraum*: Japan needed to solve its over-population problem through free emigration to other East Asian countries. He blamed the China problem on America and Britain for refusing to recognize Manchukuo, which allegedly gave rise to Chiang's hopes of recovering Manchuria. America was denying export of important commodities to Japan and providing positive aid to Japan's enemy, Chiang. Japan had therefore joined a defensive alliance.[76]

1940: JAPAN OPTS FOR WAR • 95

Signing of Tripartite Pact. From left: Japanese Ambassador Saburo Kurusu (leaning forward), Italian Foreign Minister Galeazzo Ciano, and Adolf Hitler. (Heinrich Hoffman, 1939, public domain)

Ambassador Grew lamented in his diary on 2 October that his embassy was losing its ability to find out what the leadership and public were thinking.

> [O]ur reliable and important Japanese channels of information are in general no longer available, partly because the contacts of Japanese with American and British Embassies are likely to bring trouble from the police and partly because most of our Japanese friends appear to have given up all hope of improving relations with the United States. (We know that several of our erstwhile Japanese friends, including women, are on a black list and are being carefully watched, and close friends who used to see us constantly are now afraid to be seen with Americans at all.)[77]

Konoye, on 4 October, said at a press conference, "I believe it is better for the United States if it tries to understand Japan's intention and actively participate in the building of the world's new order. If the United States deliberately misunderstands the true intentions of Japan, Germany, and Italy… and continues its provocative acts, there won't be any other options left to us but to go to war."[78]

No threat of military violence against the government compelled Konoye to say this.

From the inside, the Axis doubtless looked like a successful and expanding enterprise. Hungary by 22 October had committed to signing the pact. In early November, Germany sought Japan's agreement to bring in Romania and Yugoslavia. A week later, Ribbentrop and Matsuoka agreed to include Bulgaria, as well.[79] Matsuoka in mid-October was pursuing an alliance with Thailand but intended to be very careful not to provoke the United States and Britain.[80]

The United States in October issued an evacuation order for all citizens in the Greater East Asian Co-Prosperity Sphere territories. As noted above, Britain that month reopened the Burma Road in support of American policy.[81]

America Starts Helping China Militarily

From mid-1940, Roosevelt's bid for a third term in an election campaign in which both the Democratic and Republican parties promised to keep the country out of war, led the President to avoid any policy moves that might suggest otherwise. This included expansion of support for any allies. Thus, until Roosevelt's victory in November, America really did act like she was not going to intervene. Fortunately, the Germans were stymied in their aspirations to cross the English Channel, the Japanese were stalled in China, and a lull occurred in the war.[82]

On 18 October, Chiang told the U.S. ambassador that he needed combat aircraft piloted by American volunteers to prevent a military collapse. The following month, he sent the major general commanding the Operations Division of the Chinese Air Force to Washington, accompanied by Claire Chennault. After retiring in 1937 on disability, Chennault had gone to China, where he became a technical adviser and accepted the rank of colonel. He had devised a plan for employing a small group of fighter planes to take on the Japanese, based on tactics that exploited the relative strengths and weaknesses of American and Japanese combat aircraft. The Chinese wanted 500 planes in 1941, and the crews to man them. They sought trainer aircraft, materiel to construct 14 airfields, spare parts, and a year's supply of ordnance. They offered $30 million ($640 million in today's currency) for enough equipment for 30 infantry divisions.

Washington extended a $100 million ($2.2 billion in today's currency) credit on 1 December, which marked the beginning of military assistance. America still could not provide gear for ground forces and offered to start with the aircraft. Roosevelt authorized a deal on 19 December and ordered State, War, Navy, and Treasury to make it happen.

Even then, though, American and British demand for aircraft delayed actual delivery until 1942. One hundred P40s were to be available.

Chennault also proposed deploying B-17s with volunteer crews to China to bomb Japan. This idea gained real interest, but neither bombers nor crews were available. Still, Chennault planted the seed for American operations later in the war.[83]

China, Pearl Harbor, and the South

The Emperor was looking for ways to stanch the flow of resources of blood, money, and material in China, not through victory, but by going over to a less costly defensive posture.

Tokyo in mid-November had high hopes that secret negotiations with Chiang Kai-shek that had been taking place via Hong Kong would produce a deal that would end the bloody morass. Chiang appeared to be delaying concluding a treaty because of internal political problems, but he had been open to overtures from Matsuoka. By the end of the month, though, the initiative appeared to have collapsed, Japan signed a treaty with the Wang puppet government in Nanking, and the Emperor was asking uncomfortable questions about what policy should be pursued if the war proved to be prolonged.

Kido told the Emperor on 29 November that the conflict would indeed be prolonged because Japan's power was nearly spent and insufficient to completely defeat Chiang. He advocated a policy of seizing a few more strategic points and rebuilding Japan's war-making strength. The aggressive faction must be kept under control because if they got their way, they would not win and they would prevent rebuilding. "It is indeed alarming thinking of the future of the country," he concluded.

The Emperor on 2 December received Army Chief of Staff General Hajime Sugiyama, who earlier had commanded the Northern Army in China and was not part of the Kwantung clique, and asked him whether it would be possible to strike a decisive blow against Chiang. Sugiyama was a man of commanding air who attracted the respect and approval of his juniors. The general replied that it would be difficult. His Majesty then asked whether it would not be wise to shorten the front in keeping with Japan's financial and material resources. Sugiyama argued that would hand Chiang a propaganda victory but reluctantly agreed to study the question of financial and material resources. The Navy Minister, oddly, favored holding the existing front because he hoped there would soon be important changes in Chunking.[84]

Tokyo had recognized the Nanjing puppet government on 30 November. That same day, the U.S. Government announced the $100 million ($2.2 billion in today's currency) loan to Free China and the transfer of 50 military aircraft.[85]

The Emperor on the third discussed the Soviet Union with Kido. Kido judged that Russia would be the only nation in Europe left unexhausted by the war there and was quite haughty. Japan would be sandwiched between "two powers"—the other evidently the United States. Nevertheless, these powers would become relaxed and ultimately corrupt. If Japan cultivated a spirit of modesty and fortified itself with stern resolution, it could win the "crowning glory."[86]

In the waning days of 1940, Admiral Yamamoto told Fukudome, "I want to have [Rear Admiral Takijiro] Onishi study [a] Pearl Harbor attack plan as a tentative step. After studying the result of his report, the problem may be included in the fleet training program, and I want to keep it top secret by that time."[87] Onishi was a "big shot" in naval aviation.

According to Fukudome, the IJN's annual operations plan—always based on the decisive battle in friendly waters—heretofore had included no option for attacking Hawaii at the beginning of a war because "the staff did not have confidence in the success of the attack," though it was viewed as a possibility later in a war. The major problems were that American reconnaissance was likely to detect an attacking fleet, that even an equal exchange of ship losses would hurt the IJN more than the enemy, and the difficulty of refueling in rough north Pacific waters.[88]

IJN and IJA planners in late 1940 engaged in frequent discussions about the settlement of the southern problem. The IJN insisted that they adopt the assumption that America and Britain were inseparable, and that Britain would respond militarily at once to an invasion of the East Indies—with America joining at some point. The IJA reluctantly agreed. This meant that for the advance to succeed, Japan had to capture the Philippines. It was during this planning period that the concept emerged that, "to be prepared for a long war, its main objective was to establish an invincible position from both a political and military standpoint." Therefore, objectives had to include for resource reasons Java, Sumatra, Borneo, Malaya, and the Celebes; military bases at Singapore, Manila, Hong Kong, Guam, and Wake; and Burma to cut off Chiang and protect the right flank.[89]

After dispatching officers to tour the southern area, the IJA in December ordered three divisions in China to begin training for tropical warfare. It established a center, the Formosa Army Research Department, to gather information on tropical warfare in Southeast Asia.[90]

The IJN, meanwhile, anticipating a region-wide war, on 15 November issued an order for the preparation of expeditionary fleets. By the end of August 1941, these new formations were to exist because of this order: Sixth Fleet, Eleventh Air Fleet, Third Fleet, First Air Fleet, Fifth Fleet, and the Southern Expeditionary Fleet.[91]

The U.S. Embassy in Tokyo reported that senior Japanese Navy officers as of December 1940 were thought to be urging moderation and trying to maneuver Admiral Yonai back into the premiership. They were unusually hospitable and outgoing toward American naval personnel, and they turned out in numbers for a luncheon of the America–Japan Society. Yet they used a formulation that did not appear to strike the U.S. Embassy as being particularly ominous: It was still possible, they said, *to avoid war with America*. If the British were to permit the U.S. Navy to station vessels at Singapore, Japan might have to strike in self-defense!

Ambassador Grew mused,

> This conservative attitude on the part of the Japanese Navy as distinguished from the general extremist attitude of the Army may be ascribed in part to the Navy's broader vision and better comprehension of world affairs. Whether the Navy is also guided by lack of confidence in its power and readiness for war, or whether it desires merely to postpone war until the completion of the battleships now under construction, is a matter for pure speculation.

Japanese cooperation with Germany was blossoming under the Triple Alliance, the embassy noted. The two countries had established mixed commissions, German economic and police experts had arrived in Tokyo, and a Japanese naval and military mission had left for Berlin.[92]

Yet Grew could see where events appeared to be headed. On 14 December, he wrote to President Roosevelt about the situation in Japan. "It therefore appears that sooner or later, unless we are prepared ... to withdraw bag and baggage from the entire sphere of 'Greater East Asia including the South Seas' (which God forbid), we are bound eventually to come to a head-to-head clash with Japan."[93]

What Can We Surmise Japan Took into Account in 1940?

We can assume with high confidence that the Japanese mission in Washington during 1940 had access to accurate information about the United States' expanding naval and other military potential. Documentary evidence proves that, in part because of the public debate surrounding the election contest during 1940, German diplomats and attachés were able to track with accuracy America's industrial retooling, military reorganization and expansion, and even strategic thinking.[94] Japanese officials would have had access to the same information.

Still, as a land power, not that the Japanese would have viewed this as very important, the United States probably appeared feeble. The U.S. Army owned only 66 medium tanks as late as June 1940, and ramping up tank production took two years. Ordnance received a $200 million appropriation in August 1939, mostly for tank production, but only 1,467 medium tanks of all types rolled off the assembly lines through 1941. By July 1941, the Army still was to possess only enough tanks to equip two armored divisions at a time when all branches—plus the British—were demanding scarce production resources to meet their needs.[95]

CHAPTER 6

1940: Germany Dismisses America—Until It Beats France

Mussolini on 5 January 1940 sent Hitler a long letter offering his view of the war and the world, observing that they had communicated little in the preceding four months. Mussolini expressed his conviction that Britain and France could never force Germany, supported by Italy, to capitulate, but he likewise suggested that Hitler was gambling many great achievements in a war with no certainty of bringing the two Allies to their knees. He warned Hitler, "The United States would never allow a complete defeat of the democracies." End the war, he urged, and let the democratic empires collapse from their internal contradictions. Still, he was accelerating his own military buildup. Italy could not and would not commit itself to a long war, and its intervention must occur at the most propitious and decisive moment.[1]

The U.S. military attaché shared Mussolini's views to some degree regarding Italy's ability to conduct a long war, though he badly underestimated the ability of a rapid war to crush a well-prepared enemy, as Germany would prove in France. He reported in April,

> While the Italian military doctrine may still be theoretically based on "Totalitarian war of rapid solution," against a minor, not well prepared enemy, it is believed that the military leaders of Italy well know that such a doctrine is not possible against a major, well prepared enemy, and that Italy cannot successfully engage in a major war at the present time unless she is assured of a supply of essential raw materials from outside sources, in sufficient amounts to sustain a war of long duration. However ... the possibility is apparently fully realized of Italy's being drawn into the war, by the extension of the war to areas affecting her vital interests. Italy is therefore bending every effort, within the means available to her, to be prepared for any future eventuality.[2]

A long war would mean that the enemy would want all the intelligence on the Axis partners that he could get.

First Allied Steps to Winning the Intelligence War

At Bletchley Park in the UK, codebreakers on 17 January read the first wartime messages sent through Germany's military-grade Enigma code machines. Analysts were processing messages within 24 hours of receipt after 3 April.

Polish cryptographers had worked out how the Enigma machine worked and managed through a laborious process to read some coded German messages in the 1930s. A French spy, meanwhile, had provided manuals for the Enigma system and some of the monthly code settings. The British, French, and Polish cryptographers had been cooperating throughout the 1930s when war broke out. Indeed, the Poles had built replicas of the Enigma and just taken steps to provide one each to France and the UK. The Polish cryptographers slipped out of their homeland via Romania as the Germans occupied it and made their way to France.

British codebreaker Alan Turing, meanwhile, had invented an electro-mechanical device that could work out the settings the Germans were using on any given day, and by August a much-improved working version was installed at Bletchley Park.

The Royal Navy, through good luck, acquired three of the Enigma internal disks used only by the German Navy from a crewman rescued after his captain scuttled the U-boat *U-33* in the Firth of Clyde. The submarine had suffered damage from a destroyer's depth charges during a mine-laying mission. A fourth disk fell into British hands in August. The Navy used a more complex system of eight possible disks, rather than the five used by the German Army and Luftwaffe. However, the codebreakers needed some actual unencrypted enemy messages or codebooks to work out the proper settings. In late April, a British warship off Norway boarded a small German vessel and seized encryption documents. This led to the decryption of a week's worth of traffic.

In May, the Wehrmacht made changes to a practice that had been leaving their messages vulnerable to decryption. The Allies were blind again. Ah, but human ingenuity triumphed. A young codebreaker put himself mentally in the shoes of a German communicator setting up his Enigma wheels for the day. He reasoned out the likely actions, assuming a desire for simplicity. His insight led the Air Force analysts to break the Luftwaffe code by 22 May. This lasted through the war with only a few interruptions.[3]

Breaking the naval Enigma code, however, was not a one-time task and required repeated captures of small German vessels and U-boats at sea with care taken to prevent the tossing of codebooks and devices into the water. Remarkably, the Royal Navy, eventually assisted by the U.S. Navy, accomplished the task often enough to make the decrypts operationally useful. The Germans compounded their problem by ultimately dismissing the possibility that the enemy had cracked their codes on several occasions after they witnessed surprising Allied successes at sea.[4]

Meanwhile the Germans, as of May 1940, had broken the Royal Navy's codes. For a brief period, they enjoyed information dominance. On 5 June, acting on intercepts, the battle cruisers *Gneisenau* and *Scharnhorst* attacked and sank the aircraft carrier HMS *Glorious*, and two escort destroyers, off the coast of Norway. Tragically, British codebreakers had alerted the Admiralty that German warships were active in the area, but no alert reached the carrier.[5]

Germany and Italy Shrug Roosevelt Off

President Roosevelt, perhaps lulled by the "phony war" on the Western Front into thinking peace remained possible, in February sent Under Secretary of State Sumner Welles to European capitals to explore any hope of reaching a peace deal, a venture that Hitler, probably with cause, dismissed as nothing but an attempt to buy time for the Allies.[6]

Welles found Italian Foreign Minister Ciano willing to graciously accept his naive assertions that the United States and Italy were the two great neutral parties striving for world peace. Ciano did not sound all that neutral. He badmouthed Ribbentrop as being even more demanding than Hitler and complained that Germany had signed its non-aggression pact with the Soviets without even informing Italy ahead of time. But he conceded that Italy had known of the looming invasion of Poland but had no opportunity to prevent it. He defended Germany's *Anschluss* of Austria as having the support of most Austrians. He proclaimed Italy's fierce support for Finland in her war against Russia. Ciano offered no views regarding American policy.[7] Ciano, in his diary entry on the visit, said little other than that Welles was a true gentleman.[8]

During a meeting on 26 February in Mussolini's large office lit only by a reading lamp, the Duce told Welles that he wished for Italian–American relations to be warm and friendly, but that he had come to doubt that he would ever meet President Roosevelt. The United States should recognize Italy's conquest of Ethiopia instead of the President criticizing it. Mussolini reminded Welles that Italy was not technically neutral because of her relationship with Germany. He supported most of Germany's demands in Central Europe, said the Allies were greatly underestimating Germany's military strength, and offered that if a real war broke out, it would be a long time before any peace negotiations would be possible. Mussolini, too, avoided any discussion of his views of the United States.[9] After the meeting, Mussolini told Ciano that agreement with the Americans was impossible because they viewed everything superficially, whereas Italians considered them fundamentally.[10]

Welles' stop in Germany revealed how utterly irrelevant to German calculations the United States was. Welles arrived in Berlin on 1 March, where an icy Ribbentrop received him. He berated Welles for the poor state of German–American relations and asserted that no German policies impinged on U.S. interests in Europe or the Western hemisphere. The minister's two-hour monologue justified every German act since 1933 and lashed the perfidies of England. Ribbentrop had been to the United States, and all Germany wanted was the same respect of her core interests in Central Europe that the Americans valued so highly in the Monroe Doctrine. The only other party with any voice in the matter was Soviet Russia, and the two parties had reached a complete and satisfactory delimitation of interests. Regarding the present situation, Ribbentrop could see no resolution other than German military victory.[11]

Welles met with Hitler the next day. The Führer presented his own historical discourse and asserted that Germany had to be free of all constraints created for strategic reasons at Versailles (including the very existence of Czechoslovakia and the corridor that had separated Germany from Danzig). At no point did he refer to the substance of German–American relations. Welles did get a taste of the real Hitler when he said, "I believe that German might is such as to ensure the triumph of Germany, but, if not, we will all go down together whether that be for better or worse."[12] Hitler dismissed Welles' mission: "The only thing to say," he wrote Mussolini, "is that he could bring nothing new to the assessment of the situation."[13]

Hitler in his conversation alluded to evidence uncovered in Polish records about America urging that Poland fight. Ribbentrop told Mussolini and Ciano a few days later that the documents proved the "guilt" of the United States for convincing Poland to fight. Mussolini was unimpressed—"we already knew" that France, England, and the United States opposed the authoritarian regimes. Ribbentrop retorted that the cables also showed the strong influence American ambassadors had exerted on British policy, and that they revealed a Jewish-plutocratic clique whose influence reached all the way to Roosevelt through Secretary of the Treasury Henry Morgenthau and oil magnate John Rockefeller. Mussolini opined that Roosevelt had sent Welles to Europe for domestic reasons—popular opinion was against war, and there was nothing he could do to change that. Ribbentrop agreed with the assessment.[14]

Welles met with Hermann Göring on 3 March, and the German gave him the by now familiar party line. At one point, however, he broke in to say that he could not understand why the American people could feel that their vital interests were affected by war in Europe. Indeed, Göring said later that at the time of the visit, German leaders still believed that the United States wanted to stay out of the war, despite the discovery of the documents in Warsaw that suggested Roosevelt was preparing for conflict. Welles reminded Göring that it was only six months after Woodrow Wilson had been elected on a promise to stay out of the European war that the American people had changed its view and overwhelmingly supported intervention.[15]

Although Welles' trip had shown that America was a peripheral concern in Berlin, Ribbentrop in a conversation with Mussolini on 10 March revealed that Hitler was thinking in at least general terms about preventing American entry into the war. Hitler had written to Mussolini that a strong Japan was good for Germany and Italy because it could pressure Britain in the Far East and act as a counterbalance to the United States. Ribbentrop said this was because Washington had not joined the Great War until it received a written commitment from Japan that it would not act against American interests in the Far East and Pacific. If the United States had felt this was necessary from a Japan that had been an ally, the need would be all the greater under current circumstances. Ribbentrop urged Mussolini to send instructions to the Italian embassies in Tokyo and Moscow to encourage them to reach an accommodation as Germany had. "The greater Japan's freedom with respect to Russia, the better it can function as a means of pressure against England and America," he commented.

Mussolini, despite his private warning to Hitler in January about American intervention to prevent a defeat of the democracies, replied that an opinion poll published by the *New York Daily News* showed that 90 percent of Americans wanted to stay neutral and had no desire to be pulled into a war every 20 years to protect England's power in Europe. America's interest would be to stay out of the war—a belief Ribbentrop said he shared. Mussolini claimed the Americans doubted that the Allies would win and did not want to ride a losing horse.

Ribbentrop said that the German army would soon smash the English and French armies and encouraged Mussolini to mount demonstrations even before then to make it easier for Germany.[16]

According to statements by Keitel, Göring, and Fritz Todt, as of March 1940, Hitler privately said that Germany could not sustain a long war, and that it must achieve a great military victory by the end of the year. Among his concerns was America's potential, presumably economic, to strengthen the Western Allies.[17]

By mid-April, Mussolini was becoming anxious to join the war. He presented a strategic appraisal to senior advisers on 6 April. Ciano recorded in his diary, "It is a balanced document which reaches the twofold conclusion that Italy can neither execute a volte face nor remain neutral until the end of the conflict without losing its rank as a Great Power. Therefore, war at Germany's side, for our own purposes and when conditions are favorable; military action: defensive on all fronts and offensive towards Djibouti; aero-naval offensive on a large scale."[18]

At 0200 on 9 April, Mackenson, German ambassador in Rome, requested an urgent meeting with Ciano and arrived at 0630 pale and tired. He relayed that Hitler had decided to occupy Denmark and Norway, and actions were under way. Ciano replied, according to his diary, that, "the reaction of the neutrals, especially the Americans, will be violent." When the two men informed Mussolini, however, he said, "I whole-heartedly approve this action of Hitler's. It is a move which may have incalculable results and it is thus that wars are won. The democracies have been beaten quickly."[19]

The American ambassador, William Phillips, delivered a message from Roosevelt to Mussolini on 1 May. Ciano recorded in his diary,

> It is a warning not to enter the war. Couched in courteous language, it is nonetheless a sharp admonition: If the conflict were to spread, some other states, who intend to remain neutral, would immediately be obliged to reconsider their position. Naturally, Mussolini took it badly. At the moment, he did not say much to the Ambassador, except to reaffirm Italy's right to an outlet to an ocean. Then he wrote an answer to Roosevelt in his own hand. It was cold and hostile and concluded that if the Monroe Doctrine applies for America, the same must also apply for Europe.[20]

America also was briefly on Hitler's mind. He wrote to Mussolini that he intended to be victorious in the West with all possible speed. "The masked American threats of intervention are urging him toward an early victory," Ciano wrote in his diary.[21]

Hitler wrote to Mussolini on 9 May that Germany had obtained information that Britain had demanded that the Netherlands accept British troops and that he had decided to order an attack in the West the following morning to "secure the neutrality of Belgium and Holland through military means."[22]

War in Earnest

The war in the West in the spring of 1940 taught German officers that they could fight and win even when outnumbered so long as they had an aggressive philosophy, good plans, first-rate commanders, some mobility, adequate troops, and air cover. The most senior general officers were surprised by their decisive victory against the Western Allies because they thought the British and French were too strong, and some opposed Hitler's intention to go on the offensive in the West. Following a plan crafted by Lieutenant General Gerd von Rundstedt's chief of staff at Army Group B, Major General Erich von Manstein, Rundstedt's army group, formed the *Schwerpunkt* (point of concentration, a key German concept on offense and defense), striking by surprise with three panzer corps through the heavily forested but thinly defended Ardennes. Army Group A advanced into the Low Countries to pin down the British and French mobile forces that analysis and intelligence reporting indicated would advance from France to meet the army group's attack, thus allowing Rundstedt to cut them off. Army Group C was to pin the rest of the French army along the frontier south of the Ardennes.[23]

Manstein's vision was breathtaking in its audacity and, as a successful plan to overwhelm with a few decisive strokes a numerically and in some ways technologically superior enemy in an entire theater of operations, was never equaled by the Western Allies or Soviets. The original operational scheme had aimed merely at gaining control over the length of the Channel coast to support U-boat warfare against Britain. Manstein had aimed far higher and had conceived of a plan to take France out of the war.[24] Rundstedt called it a reverse Schlieffen Plan because the left wing wheeled northward rather than the right wing southward, as the Germans had tried in the Great War. "My Army Group A was to advance across the Meuse [Maas] as far as the Channel, then wheel against the enemy forces stationed in Belgium and annihilate them!"[25]

The German offensive crashed westward on 10 May. That night, the RAF dropped its first bombs on mainland Germany, ending the "phony war." The War Cabinet authorized air attacks east of the Rhine on 15 May. But the RAF viewed its heavy bombers as too slow and poorly armed to survive German fighters, and its crews flying high and at night could rarely find their targets. Air defense commands in Germany were skeptical that once anticipated raids against major cities and industrial sites would occur.[26]

Ciano recorded in his diary on 10 May, "[Ambassador] Phillips said that the event will have a profound effect on America. He made no predictions, but it would not surprise me at all if America broke relations with Germany immediately, although postponing the decision to enter into the war herself. The question of the United States is a very serious one and one which may easily be judged erroneously."[27]

On 15 May, Ciano wrote, "Roosevelt sends a message to the Duce. The tone is completely different. It is no longer, as previously, a hidden threat, but rather sorrowful and conciliatory. He speaks of the Gospel of Christ, but these are arguments that make little impression on Mussolini's mind, especially today when he believes that victory is already within his grasp."[28]

Phillips on 27 May delivered Ciano another message from Roosevelt after Mussolini refused to receive him.

> Briefly, Roosevelt offers himself as mediator between ourselves and the Allies. He makes himself personally responsible for execution, after the war, of any possible agreements concluded. I reply to Phillips that Roosevelt is on the wrong track. This will not persuade Mussolini from carrying out his intentions. In the last analysis, it is not a matter of this or that claim; Mussolini wants to go to war.[29]

Mussolini established the Commando Supremo on 29 May. Ciano recorded, "I have rarely seen Mussolini so happy. He has realized his fondest dream: He has become the military leader of a country at war."[30]

With German success looking ever more certain, Mussolini wrote Hitler on 30 May that he intended to enter the war on 5 June. Mussolini had over the preceding months told Hitler that public opinion was swinging behind engagement, in part because of the Allied blockade of Italian trade, and now, he said, the people were "impatient" for war against common enemies beside the German people. The navy and air force were at full war strength, and he had about 70 divisions in good condition. Mussolini would take command over all forces.[31] Hitler requested a slight delay, in part so the military commands could consult, and Italy finally declared war against Britain and France on the 10th.[32]

"New demarche from Roosevelt," Ciano recorded on 31 May,

> a more vigorous one, this time. After pointing to the United States' traditional interest in the Mediterranean, he affirms that Italy's entrance into the war will bring about an increase in American arms production and will "double the aid to the Allies in arms and materials." I inform [Phillips] that ... this new demarche of Roosevelt's will suffer the fate of his other attempts; it will make no impression at all on the Duce.[33]

With the ink on a declaration of war barely dry, Ciano met with the King. "He now accepts, but no more than accepts, the idea of war. He believes that Great Britain and France have, in truth, suffered tremendous hard blows, but he is right in attributing great importance to the possible intervention of America."[34]

*

As foreshadowed, this work will show that the Germans went to war against America without having undertaken the most basic strategic assessment, but let it be said: On the day Army Chief of Staff General George Marshall and Chief of Naval Operations Admiral Harold Stark openly told Roosevelt that war with the

Axis Powers was almost inevitable, they were in a similarly lamentable situation regarding their strategic assessment of a war with Germany.

The day that France capitulated, the three men met to discuss a draft document entitled "Basis for Immediate Decisions Concerning the National Defense." The draft mainly focused on possible moves to defend the Western hemisphere, but the men agreed that if the Germans gained control of the French fleet (the French scuttled their fleet), a major portion of the ships in Hawaii would move to the Atlantic, at least for a while. The service chiefs urged a cutoff of war material to Britain that was needed at home, imposing on manufacturers a six- or seven-day work week of two or three shifts, and adoption of a draft.

Roosevelt had his own opinions, and the military men redrafted the document and resubmitted it on 27 June. The document recommended the country adopt a defensive posture; provide nonbelligerent help to Britain, the Commonwealth, and China; expand cooperation in the hemisphere and occupy any areas threatened by Axis control; pass a draft act and accelerate industrial mobilization and manpower training to support it; *prepare concrete plans for an "almost inevitable conflict" with Germany, Japan, and Italy*; and deepen cooperation with the enemies of those countries.[35]

*

Shortly after the capitulation of France, Hitler apparently was skeptical that he would be able to attack the British Isles directly, though planning for such an operation was just beginning, and his mind turned to his next conquest. Hitler met with the chiefs of the army, navy, and air force to discuss plans for the invasion of Britain—Operation *Sea Lion*—on 21 July 1940. A second "summit" occurred ten days later, but Göring did not appear, and Raeder left early. Keitel, Jodl, and army Chief of Staff Halder were also present. After another spirited discussion of the possibilities and difficulties of *Sea Lion*, Raeder departed. Hitler then turned to his senior army generals and revealed a plan that he admitted was not yet fully formulated: He intended to attack and defeat the Soviet Union in early 1941 in a rapid campaign. He sketched out the broad lines of attack and allocation of German forces.[36]

The decision surprised some senior generals because Hitler had signed a non-aggression pact—so far respected by Stalin—and had foresworn any repetition of the Great War's struggle on two fronts. Great Britain, of course, fought on. Hitler initially wished to strike that autumn but was persuaded that the Russian winter would spell disaster for any invasion.[37]

Göring told Nürnberg Tribunal interrogators that he first learned of Hitler's plan to launch a "preemptive" attack on the Soviet Union in late November after Molotov visited Berlin on the 12th and 13th. According to Göring, Molotov had told Hitler Moscow wanted a free hand to occupy Finland and advance on the Dardanelles. There were reports of a large Soviet ground and air buildup in Poland, and Hitler decided that Stalin intended to flank Germany to the north and south and attack while German forces were engaged in the West, such as an invasion of Britain.

Göring said that Hitler asked his views, and after asking for several hours to consider, he told Hitler he opposed an attack:

> The way I looked at it, should Russia again go to war with Finland and expand to the south, it would get into conflict with England, because it was headed for the Dardanelles. I also called the fact to his attention that we already were at war with one of the great world powers, namely, the British Empire, and that without a doubt America, another great world power, would enter the conflict and that it would not be wise to start a conflict with Russia, the third major world power, because that would go beyond our powers. I had no doubts that we would destroy the Russian Army relatively fast. I even held the conviction that this could be done more quickly than the Fuehrer himself believed, but I asked him how he ever expected to get peace with this huge space on his hands. I also told him that the security of this huge space and the security of the extended lines of communication against attacks which were sure to develop from the inside of Asia would take an enormous power to hold, which also was beyond our means. To this was added the fact that my Luftwaffe, which at this time was engaged in successful attack upon England, would have been stopped in the middle of that attack in order to be committed for the new venture. The Fuehrer thanked me for giving him my reasons and for acting as the agent of the Devil as he put it, but he held the danger was so singular that he decided to go ahead as planned, and he got me to help him as always.[38]

Asked more broadly about Hitler's thinking about the United States, the transcript continues:

> I have always told the Führer, and even in front of a witness, that it was my belief that if England would be drawn into a war with Germany, sooner or later America would come to her assistance-unless things were going very well for England right from the beginning.
> Q. But the Führer did not agree?
> A. No. Strangely enough, the Führer held the opinion that America would not enter the war under any condition. He said that America had had such a bad experience in 1918 that America would not participate in a second European conflict unless America itself was touched. He also overestimated considerably the influence of the so-called American isolationists.
> Q. Was that opinion based upon advice and information which he received or merely an offhand opinion, so to speak?
> A. The first part—I mean the part about the bad experience—was based upon a conversation he once had with Lloyd George. This talk on the whole produced in him a completely false opinion of the English and American attitudes. As far as the American isolationists are concerned, I do not know exactly, but I assume that he received his information in the normal manner.[39]

(Göring's statements to the interrogators may be self-serving regarding war crimes in so far as he claimed that he recommended against attacking the USSR, but perhaps he did. On the other hand, he admitted to grossly overestimating Germany's ability to win a quick, decisive victory, which is not in the least self-serving.)

The French collapse appears to have caused German leaders—excluding Hitler—to reappraise America's likely course of action, perhaps recalling warnings from the German Embassy that intervention would occur if the democracies faced utter defeat. Ciano reported to Mussolini that he had met on 19 June with Ribbentrop, who told him that Hitler would offer France a ceasefire to dissuade the government headed by Marshal Pétain from going into exile and waging a long "holy war" against Germany. Hitler hoped Britain would accept a peace that left its empire intact. The two discussed claims to territory and colonies of the defeated countries. Finally, Ribbentrop turned to America. If the war against England lasted very long, the United States probably would intervene, judged Ribbentrop. This could happen soon. He acknowledged the industrial and economic might of the United States but believed that it could not affect events quickly enough to save Britain from an unavoidable catastrophe. He claimed Germany had a few cards to play against Roosevelt, including an incriminating document that would soon be publicized.[40]

America: A Call for Arms

In the States, the rapid French collapse stunned leaders and population alike. Even isolationists could imagine German bombers reducing American cities as they had Rotterdam. All of a sudden, average people wanted vast air defenses. Congress sensed the shift in public opinion, was ready to open its pockets for the national defense, and started asking the military: What do you want? All you have to do is ask.[41]

Congress in May and June approved unheard of spending on military equipment, factories to make the equipment, and manpower. Roosevelt on 16 May asked Congress to increase the ceiling for aircraft building capacity to 50,000; 36,500 for the Air Corps and 13,500 for the navy—doubling the existing capability. The number was so large that it would allow large transfers to the British. Churchill, the new prime minister, had just cabled Roosevelt that the Luftwaffe had a "marked preponderance" in the air (the UK actually had somewhat more fighters, but its intelligence estimates of German strength were highly inflated). Britain, he said, needed every P-40 fighter America could supply.[42]

Marshall got the money to expand the regular army from 227,000 men to 500,000 by 1 July 1941, one million by January 1942, and two million by 1 July 1942. By 26 June, the War Department had $3 billion ($212.4 billion today) to build a world-class army. The navy in June received funding to expand the fleet by 11 percent and add 10,000 airplanes. Roosevelt on 27 June declared a national emergency, and in July Congress approved funds to create a "two-ocean" navy—a 70-percent increase in the fleet.[43] The number of men, the amount of equipment, and the dollar amounts would just keep expanding as the months passed as the military grappled with what it was actually going to need, having never done that before for a coming war.

In June 1940, Roosevelt accepted an initiative from leading scientists and established the National Defense Research Committee (NDRC), which became the Office of Scientific Research and Development (OSRD). This organization coordinated R&D among the services, industry, and academics. Its achievements included the predecessor of the Manhattan atomic bomb project until 1943, radar, sonar, proximity fuses, the Norden bombsight, rocket-propelled weapons, improved bombs, amphibious vehicles, and other weapon systems. Its work, for example, resulted by 1941 and 1942 in the fielding of radar gear small enough to fit on destroyers, submarines, and aircraft, which made the Allies much more lethal during the anti-U-boat battle of the Atlantic.[44]

*

Hitler conceded to the Italian ambassador at the western command post on or about 1 July that if England fought on, it would be because it expected help from America. The British had also not abandoned hope of swinging Russia over to their side.[45]

Following France's capitulation on 22 June, according to Warlimont, Hitler was unhappy that the United States was arming "short of war," but he believed that he would be able to end the war before the United States could get involved. He had succeeded in every military venture thus far, England posed no threat to his hold on the Continent, and he expected that his planned attack on the Soviet Union would go just as well.[46]

Hitler on 21 July ordered OKW to seriously consider the Russia and America questions, according to the official German history of the war.[47] OKW chief Keitel told interrogators after the war that Britain's decision to fight on convinced the High Command that American entry into the war had become probable.[48]

(Warlimont's and Keitel's recollections recorded in the FMS series are consistent with Ribbentrop saying for the first time that American entry into the war was probable if Britain fought on. They also jibed with Hitler's belief that he could still avoid American intervention and that America's mobilization would not be complete until 1942, which implies he expected to be finished by then. The recollections reflect no self-evident attempt to curry favor with the West or to rescue either general from prosecution for war crimes.)

Mussolini shared OKW's view and on 20 August wrote Hitler:

> Unless there is a sudden change, which is always possible in a country of hysterics such as American politicians are, the possibility of American intervention must be viewed henceforth as a probability—especially if, as seems likely—Roosevelt is re-elected. He will not be able to contribute men, but he will provide huge material assistance, above all in aircraft. This is already happening, so it will not be enough to prevent Great Britain's defeat.[49]

Hitler responded, "I fundamentally believe that close cooperation with Japan is the best that one can do, despite all doubts, to keep America out of [our] affairs or to rob its entry into the war of any effectiveness."[50]

Ciano noted in his diary on 4 September, "Cession of 50 American destroyers to Great Britain. In Berlin, there is great excitement and indignation."[51]

Indeed, navy chief Grand Admiral Raeder met with Hitler on 6 September and noted that one of the topics foremost in Hitler's mind was "the problem of the USA." On 14 September, however, Hitler asserted in a meeting that America's rearmament would not be effective until 1945.[52]

On 19 September, Mussolini told Ribbentrop,

> Regarding America, one must be aware that the United States practically already stands on England's side. The Duce did not expect it to send armies to fight in Europe, but the sale of 50 destroyers and the constant assistance to Great Britain proved that America was already against Germany and Italy. That should not cause any worry. What the United Sates can do, it has already done.[53]

Ribbentrop flew to Rome on 19 September to inform Ciano that Germany and Japan would sign a military alliance in Berlin in a few days. He told Ciano that the stroke would have a double edge, against Russia and against America. The threat of the Japanese fleet would keep the latter from making any move. "I express a different opinion: The anti-Russian guarantees are alright; the anti-American note which will induce Washington to increase her economic commitments to Britain is not so good."[54]

Ciano had another conversation with Ribbentrop on 22 September.

> A panoramic survey. Ribbentrop mentions the possibility of the Axis' taking the initiative in breaking off diplomatic relations with the United States. Mussolini would agree. I would not. For the present because I believe that we must at all costs avoid a conflict with America, also because I believe that we would be doing Roosevelt a great service since it would be convenient for him to appear at election time in the role of one who has been attacked. In any case, the decision is not one which must be made immediately, and I hope that I shall be able to win out.[55]

Indeed, Roosevelt was running for re-election for an unprecedented third term. Ciano had asked Ambassador Phillips what Wilkes's nomination meant, and whether America was ready to enter the war. He replied, "On the question of foreign policy, Democrats and Republicans almost agree. We are not thinking about taking part in the conflict at the present time. We are arming on a very large scale and will help Britain with every available means. However, a new development could cause our intervention."[56]

Ciano participated in the signing of the military pact on 27 September. He recorded,

> It takes place more or less in the same way as the Pact of Steel was signed. But the atmosphere is colder. Even the crowd in the street is a small crowd, composed largely of school children—demonstrates methodically and without conviction. Japan is far away. Aid from there is problematical. Only one thing is certain: that the war is destined to be prolonged. The Germans do not like that; they have become accustomed to believing that the conflict would end with the summer. War in the winter is hard.[57]

Hitler, in a meeting with Mussolini in Brenner on 4 October, did not share the OWK's and Mussolini's view on the odds that America would go to war. He reiterated that the British had two hopes—American intervention and Russian help—but argued both would not pan out. Regarding America, one should not assume that intervention was probable, Hitler asserted, especially in light of the Tripartite Pact that had isolated the United States further. The Führer had spoken, and the circle of sycophants around him appeared to have stopped discussing for months thereafter American entry into the war and the implications thereof. As for Russia, said Hitler,

European events had not turned out as Moscow expected, and it could make no move because Germany had shifted its military strength eastward and had 180 infantry and 24 panzer divisions fully ready.[58]

Later in October, Hitler reassured listeners during a meeting in Florence that American military preparations could not be completed before 1942. This, of course, was an accurate forecast. But Hitler was certain that because of his escalating air attacks against Britain and because the U-boats were sinking 800,000 to a million tons of shipping per month, England could not hold out much longer.[59]

Hitler and Ribbentrop met with Molotov in Berlin on 12 November and told him, "England is beaten, and it is only a question of time before she will admit her defeat." She was hoping for help from America, but "the entry of the United States into the war is of no consequence at all for Germany. Germany and Italy will never again allow an Anglo-Saxon to land on the European Continent."

Hitler said America could not "endanger the freedom" of other states until 1970 or 1980 and had no business in Europe, Africa, or Asia. Molotov broke in to agree with that.[60]

Admiral Raeder sent Hitler a strongly worded memo on 14 November arguing that Italian bungling in Greece and North Africa was strengthening the British strategic position in the Mediterranean and that Germany should intervene there as its first priority. Indeed, he wrote, in light of America's growing material assistance to Britain, Germany should put off Operation *Barbarossa* until the overthrow of Britain. Hitler did not agree.[61]

There is little evidence that Germany paid much attention to the election campaign in America. Göring told interrogators that when the Germans read Republican candidate Wendell Wilkie's speeches shortly before election day on 5 November, they realized the outcome would be the same as far as Germany was concerned. The Germans, he said, interpreted Roosevelt's promises to stay out of the European war as nothing but a sop to antiwar sentiment and not as a basic change in policy. Thereafter, he claimed, the Germans attributed little importance to American isolationists.[62] (Once again, Göring appears to have no ulterior motive in this statement.)

Three days after winning the race, Roosevelt publicly announced a plan under which half of American war production would go to the British. His service chiefs were to have other views, but Roosevelt's strong support for the UK's war effort was on the record.[63]

Roosevelt on 29 December delivered a fireside chat by radio that came to be known as the Arsenal of Democracy speech. He told the American people that the only way to stay out of the war was to provide all the military assistance that Britain, the Commonwealth, and China needed to fight the Axis and ensure that they could never pose an unchallenged threat to the Western hemisphere. He promised Britain far more material support in the future.[64]

*

Hitler on 17 December sent guidance to OKW on Operation *Barbarossa*, the invasion of the USSR. He laid out the three lines of advance, set the main effort as the advance north of the Pripet marshes, and ordered that motorized and tank divisions advance without waiting for the infantry divisions as they had done in France. The same message sketched Operation *Marita* to take naval control of the Baltic.

Finally, Hitler stipulated that all continental issues must be wrapped up by the end of 1941, because as of 1942, the United States would be in a position to intervene in the war.[65]

German Considerations in 1940

The German civilian and military leadership should have been able to make some fairly accurate projections of American industrial and military capabilities. Documentary evidence proves that, in part because of the public debate surrounding the election contest during 1940, German diplomats and attachés were able to track with accuracy America's industrial retooling, military reorganization and expansion, and even strategic thinking. They knew the general outlines of modernization plans, except for some decisive technological programs.[66]

With hindsight, we can identify key war-winning factors that the Germans did not take into account:

- German leaders grossly underestimated American war production. As we shall see, Hitler and Mussolini in June 1941 laughed off as "childish" data circulated by the U.S. ambassador in Berlin on planned aircraft and tank output (that were short of actual production). They appear to have dismissed the data available to them out of a presumption that the numbers were lies, and that even if they were true, they would not matter before the war ended.
- Like the Japanese, the Germans did not anticipate that thanks to British success cracking Germany's Enigma code system (and American conquest of Japan's diplomatic codes that provided the reports from Japan's embassy in Berlin), the Americans and British would be reading most of their communications and have nearly comprehensive knowledge of their diplomatic, military, and economic affairs that were communicated electronically.
- As mentioned in the preceding chapter, although aware that America, and presumably Britain, were building heavy, long-range bombers, the Germans' preparations to deal with Allied air power and strategic bombing were badly inadequate, and they abandoned development of a strategic bombing capability of their own.
- They failed to realize they could not defeat the Soviet Union.

CHAPTER 7

Early 1941: Axis Resolution of the America Problem

When summarized in two simple sentences, the Axis leaders' thinking about America as 1941 kicked off almost sounds like a Bond villain at work. Japan was already planning operations that would, leaders recognized, probably lead to war with America, but all would be well because Japan would have the resources to hold an impregnable position. Germany, meanwhile, was preparing to invade the USSR, in part on the dubious assumption that knocking it off would end any threat of America joining the war to help Britain, which would surely see continued resistance as futile.

Japan: On the War Path

The year was but new begun, and senior Japanese officials were thinking openly about the United States as a combatant enemy, and about pursuing Japanese interests to the south that would in fact provoke directly war against America. Matsuoka at the sendoff luncheon for Kichisaburo Nomura, the new ambassador to the United States, on 18 January "practically threatened the United States with war," Grew recorded in his diary. On the 27th, Grew wrote, "There is a lot of talk around town to the effect that the Japanese, in case of a break with the United States, are planning to go all out in a surprise mass attack on Pearl Harbor. Of course, I informed our Government."[1]

Matsuoka on 1 February told Kido that he was going to visit Germany to hear from Hitler personally about Germany's "military operations toward Britain and the United States." He would also visit Soviet Russia. Matsuoka added that he hoped to establish peace in China by April so that Japan could devote its "whole energy" to solution of the "southern problem."[2]

Supposedly, sometime between 27 January and 10 February, Yamamoto sent an unofficial letter to Rear Admiral Takijiro Onishi, commanding Eleventh Air Fleet, outlining his plan to attack Pearl Harbor and asking Onishi to study the feasibility. The primary source for this information, Minoru Genda, provided three different dates in accounts he gave at different times. Onishi consulted a brilliant young airman, Genda, who told him that such an operation was difficult but not impossible. Genda had observed the air war in Europe, travelled across America—and visited Hawaii! Onishi handed the job to an eccentric captain, Kameto Korushima, who over several days crafted a detailed plan.[3]

However, Vice Admiral Fukudome, who worked directly with the fleet admiral, recalled that Yamamoto invited Onishi aboard his flagship in early January 1941 and discussed the matter with him directly; he did not believe a letter was involved.[4]

Either way, concrete formulation of an attack plan was underway early in the new year.

The IJA, meanwhile, was pressing ahead with plans for the southern advance, but because the IJN would carry most of the burden, the army staff at IGHQ thought the navy staff should take the lead. On 10 February, an army colonel shared with the navy staff the army's concept as a "personal" study. The navy staff immediately responded that the use of force in the southern area would cause war with the United States.

A week later, the Navy Section at General Staff Headquarters presented the Army Section with its position in writing. The IJN concluded that Anglo-American military action was definite, and because the southern operation would provoke America to enter the war, preparations begun the previous year for that scenario should be expedited. The navy said its plans for the use of force against Britain and the Netherlands East Indies were already complete and assumed that British-American ties were inseparable, whereas the IJA was still making plans trying to find a way to avoid American involvement. The Army Section began to grasp just how complicated the problem was.

The IJN made its position clear during interstaff discussions in March. It was not contemplating use of force at a "favorable opportunity," as suggested at the liaison conference the preceding year. Use of force in the southern area would lead to war with the United States. Japan should resort to the use of force in the south only if America increased its military pressure on Japan *or imposed an all-out embargo.*[5]

The British were well aware of the direction in Japanese policy, if not the details. Planners shared the Japanese view that a southern advance would lead to conflict with Great Britain, specifically in Malaya and possibly Thailand. British intelligence in February determined that senior officials at the Japanese Embassy in London "think there is very little likelihood of war being averted. It would be Japan's big opportunity, a Crusade, and a way out of the China trouble." British intelligence knew the Japanese Embassy was tracking reports of British reinforcements being sent to the Far East, "but there is a tendency not to treat this very seriously and to take an optimistic view of the wide dispersal of British resources.... There is also a tendency to discount the possibility of any serious American intervention."[6]

The SIS, however, had no intelligence sources in Tokyo. "C," the chief of SIS, indicated to the Foreign Office on 15 February 1941, "At the present time we are not employing any British agents in Japan and do not intend to do so under present conditions."[7] Japan was in the midst of a "spy fever," and the Japanese had arrested several British subjects the preceding August for alleged espionage activities.[8]

Despite war talk about America, China was still the center of attention in Tokyo. Army Chief of Staff Sugiyama returned to the Emperor on 18 January and told him that if the IJA were to evacuate Hankow to shorten the front, it would convey the message to foreign powers that Chiang had dealt Japan a defeat. He promised the Emperor that the army would do its best to establish a more favorable situation by the autumn. His Majesty repeated that Japan could not finance such an extended front in China. In a separate visit, the War Minister promised that the army would reduce the occupation force in China from 700,000 to 650,000 to reduce expenses.[9]

America Starts Getting Its Strategy Sorted and Fuels the China Fire

After months of indecisive discussion between the U.S. Army and Navy over war priorities, President Roosevelt convened a meeting on 16 January attended by Secretary of War Stimson, Secretary of the Navy Frank Knox, General George Marshall, Admiral Harold Stark, and Secretary of State Cordell Hull. He suggested that chances were one in five that Japan and Germany would attack America simultaneously. Roosevelt incorrectly believed that Hitler wanted to involve America in the war as soon as possible. What should the country's military priorities be?

The war council agreed on an overarching direction: American forces would stand on the defensive in the Pacific, and there would be no naval reinforcement of the Philippines. The U.S. Navy should be prepared to convoy ships to Britain and sustain the supply of material. The U.S. Army should not be committed to any aggressive action until it was fully prepared to conduct it.[10]

These discussions prepared the American agenda for the first informal talks with Britain on coordination of war strategy, which occurred on 29 January. These meetings became known as the American British Conversations (ABC). The first gathering agreed on a Germany-first strategy and early elimination of Italy from the war. The Royal Air Force and Air Corps would mount a sustained strategic bombing offensive against German military power and seize air superiority. The U.S. Navy would bear sole responsibility for defense of the Pacific, which would include attacks on the Japanese to hurt their economic potential and draw naval strength away from British defenses along the "Malay Barrier," the string of islands from the Kra Isthmus (the narrowest part of the Malay peninsula) to Timor. Once Germany capitulated, the Allies would shift resources to Asia and defeat Japan.[11]

Roosevelt in January lifted a trade embargo imposed on the USSR when it had invaded Finland.[12]

Congress on 11 March passed the first Lend-Lease Act, designed principally to allow Britain—which had depleted its American assets through cash-and-carry purchases of war goods—to continue receiving American help. Congress on the 27th authorized Britain $7 billion ($120 billion today) in credits.[13]

Roosevelt laid out a plan in March to increase airplane production to 30,000 per year, with 12,000 to go to the Army Air Forces; 6,000 to the U.S. Navy, and 12,000 to the UK. Oddly, his own army had no plans to expand to 12,000 aircraft.[14]

*

It is not clear from Japanese accounts whether Tokyo knew that Washington was beginning a program to multiply its problems in China.

Lauchlin Curry, a Roosevelt envoy, visited Chungking on 10 February to relay that America would soon provide an additional $45 million of military equipment.[15] China qualified for the new Lend-Lease program in March. In principle, that opened the door to a flow of goods from America's rapidly expanding war industry. In practice, China would be a secondary priority and was physically too isolated to benefit much.

Recruitment of pilots to join the American Volunteer Group (AVG) in China commenced in April, though that program was not part of Lend-Lease. Chennault was listed as "supervisor." The first pilots departed for East Asia on a Dutch vessel escorted through the Japanese mandates by American warships, despite the neutrality laws. The first 100 P-40s by then were headed for Rangoon. Training commenced at the end of July at a British Royal Air Force base near Toungoo, Burma.[16]

Chief of Staff General George Marshall on 3 July authorized establishment of the American Military Mission to China (AMMISCA). It would coordinate Lend-Lease acquisitions and form the basis for broader cooperation if war came. The first personnel flew to Chungking on 13 September.[17]

Germany: Invading Russia Will Defeat Britain

On the far side of the planet, Hitler had—since the "summits" with his senior military men in July 1940—conceived a global war plan that seemed to neatly deal with all his enemies: Britain, Stalin, and even America. The Führer gathered key staff officers from the army, Luftwaffe, and navy at the Berghof on 8 and 9 January. After discussing developments in North Africa and Albania, and with Ribbentrop at his side, Hitler turned to Russia. Hitler explained that he had so far pursued the principle of "always destroying the most important enemy position in order to take a step forward." It was time to destroy Russia. The English must then either give in, or he could pursue the war against Great Britain under more propitious circumstances. A Russian collapse "would also enable Japan to turn against the USA with all its strength." That would then prevent America from entering the war against the Axis.[18]

As miscalculations go, Hitler's epic error and Japan's decision to fight America to end the war in China are eerily similar in the essence of the conceptual failure. Expanding one's problem set to fix a single problem must be an incredibly seductive train of thought given how frequently countries pursue that approach. President Harry Truman's decision in October 1950 to allow McArthur to cross the 38th parallel in Korea to "stabilize" the peninsula—despite Chinese warnings of intervention—is just one American example.

Raeder's version of Hitler's talk was that Hitler said,

> Germany must make herself so strong on the Continent that we can handle a further war against England (and America).... If the USA and Russia should enter the war against Germany, the situation would become very complicated. Hence any possibility for such a threat to develop must be eliminated at the very beginning. If the Russian threat were removed, we could wage war on Britain indefinitely. If Russia collapsed, Japan would be greatly relieved; this in turn would mean increased danger to the USA.[19]

Mussolini visited Hitler at the Berghof on 19–20 January. Hitler again reassured him, "I don't see any great danger coming from America, even if she should enter the war."[20]

Publicly, in a speech on 30 January, Hitler said,

> It is obvious to everyone who has respect for the truth that the German nation has no quarrel with the American people. Germany has never claimed any interests on the American continent. If states of the continent enter the European conflict, the situation will quickly alter. Then Europe will defend itself. Let there be no mistake—whoever believes that he can help Britain must realize one thing above all: Every ship, with or without convoy, that comes within range of our torpedo tubes, will be torpedoed.[21]

In early January, the U.S. commercial attaché in Berlin learned from a contact a fairly detailed account of Hitler's plan to invade the USSR and forwarded it to Washington. The attaché continued to meet the source in movie theaters and gather information on planning at the General Staff.[22]

Ribbentrop in February urged Ambassador Baron Hiroshi Oshima that Japan should enter the war against Britain soon. According to a Foreign Ministry memorandum, at a conference in Fuschl on the 13th, the foreign minister told Oshima that Germany had already won the war against England. An invasion would come when conditions were right, particularly regarding the weather. It was in Japan's own interest to strike because it would destroy Britain's position in the Far East, threaten India, and give Japan a free hand to resolve matters that could only be resolved by war. A surprise intervention would also keep America out of the war. She would hesitate to risk her fleet west of Hawaii, particularly in such circumstances. Indeed, if Japan generally respected American interests,

Roosevelt would be unable to make a case for war. Germany had already helped Japan's interests by eliminating France as a factor in Indochina and badly weakening Britain.[23]

OKW on 5 March issued "Basic Order No. 24 Regarding Collaboration with Japan," which provides insight into the German military's thinking about the United States. The order stated:

> The Führer has issued the following order regarding collaboration with Japan:
>
> 1. It must be the *aim* of the collaboration based on the Three Power Pact to induce Japan as soon as possible *to take active measures in the Far East*. Strong British forces will thereby be tied down, and the center of gravity of the interests of the United States of America will be diverted to the Pacific.
>
>   The sooner it intervenes, the greater will be the prospects of success for Japan in view of the still undeveloped preparedness for war on the part of its adversaries. The "Barbarossa" operation will create particularly favorable political and military prerequisites for this. [Marginal note "slightly exaggerated."]
>
> 2. *To prepare the way* for the collaboration it is essential to strengthen the *Japanese military potential* with all means available.
>
>   For this purpose, the High Commands of the branches of the Armed Forces will comply in a comprehensive and generous manner with Japanese desires for information regarding German war and combat experience and for assistance in military economics and in technical matters. Reciprocity is desirable but this factor should not stand in the way of negotiations. Priority should naturally be given to those Japanese requests which would have the most immediate application in waging war.
>
>   In special cases the Führer reserves the decisions to himself.
>
> 3. The harmonizing of the operational plans of the two parties is the responsibility of the Navy High Command.
>   This will be subject to the following guiding principles:
>   a. The common aim of the conduct of war is to be stressed as forcing England to the ground quickly and thereby keeping the United States out of the war. Beyond this, Germany has no political, military, or economic interests the Far East which would give occasion for any reservations with regard to Japanese intentions.
>   b. The great successes achieved by Germany in mercantile warfare make it appear particularly suitable to employ strong Japanese forces for the same purpose. In this connection every opportunity to support German mercantile warfare must be exploited.
>   c. The raw material situation of the pact powers demands that Japan should acquire possession of those territories which it needs for the continuation of the war, especially if the United States intervenes. Rubber shipments must be carried out even after the entry of Japan into the war, since they are of vital importance to Germany.
>   d. The seizure of Singapore as the key British position in the Far East would mean a decisive success for the entire conduct of war of the Three Powers. In addition, attacks on other systems of bases of British naval power-extending to those of American naval power only if the entry of the United States into the war cannot be prevented-will result in weakening the enemy's system of power in that region and also, just like the attack on sea communications, in tying down substantial forces of all kinds (Australia).
>
> A date for the beginning of operational discussions cannot yet be fixed.

> 4. In the *military commissions* to be formed in accordance with the *Three Power Pact*, only such questions are to be dealt with as equally concern the *three* participating powers. These will include primarily the problems of *economic warfare*.
>   The working out of the details is the responsibility of the "Main Commission" with the cooperation of the Armed Forces High Command.
>
> 5. The Japanese must not be given any intimation of the Barbarossa operation.
>
> The Chief of the Armed Forces High Command
> Signed in draft: Keitel[24] [All italics in the original.]

Hitler on 30 March held another session with his generals at the imposing new Chancellery to discuss the looming war on the USSR and the need for *Lebensraum* and material resources. At one point, he described what Germany was to accomplish as the same as the conquest of America. The Volga must be Germany's Mississippi, he said. "It will make Europe into an impregnable fortress, the most blockade-proof place on Earth." The United States could then "get lost as far as we are concerned.... Europe—not America—will be the land of unlimited possibilities."[25]

Axis Leaders Talk Face to Face

Aware that Matsuoka would soon visit Berlin, Ambassador Nomura cabled the Navy Minister from Washington in early March:

> The relations of Britain and America are like those of a happy married couple. It is, I believe, quite impossible to beat the one and hope to remain on friendly terms with the other. The present visit of the Foreign Minister to Europe is arousing deep interest in American official circles, and it is as clear as daylight that the visit will provide a fresh incentive to the strengthening of this country's resolution. I fear that the Foreign Minister, influenced perhaps by internal conditions in Japan, may be veering towards the (pro-Axis?) foreign policy which he once outlined in a public speech.... I would like you to let me know confidentially, in outline at least, the purpose of the Foreign Minister's visit to Europe.[26]

Hitler met with a small circle including Speer, the senior OKW leadership, and Bormann. He told them that America's actions had let the cat out of the bag, and that war with America was sure to come sooner or later. Roosevelt and the Jewish financiers could not allow a German victory in Europe because they would incur huge financial losses. He expressed regret that Germany lacked bombers that could attack America.[27] Hitler had finally changed his mind from his order the preceding October to stop assuming America would join the war.

Matsuoka met with Ribbentrop on 27 March. Ribbentrop said Hitler was in the final stages of the war against Great Britain and headed perhaps the strongest military the world had ever seen. The Luftwaffe was superior to both the British and American air forces. Germany's surface fleet was disrupting sea routes between America and England, and in January and February, a mere eight or nine U-boats at any one time had sunk 750,000 tons per month. By April, 80–90 U-boats would be at sea.

England would have given up already if Roosevelt had not given Churchill hope. It was unclear whether Roosevelt intended to enter the war. It would, in any event, be some time before the help could make any difference, and Germany aimed to end the war by then. The Tripartite Pact, of course, had the goal of keeping America out of the war. America must be kept from taking an active part in the war at all costs before its aid could become too effective.

Ribbentrop went on to urge Japan to attack the British at Singapore. The foreign ministers and ambassadors then went to meet Hitler.[28]

As Matsuoka knew, said Hitler, Germany had only begun to build a navy at the beginning of the war. Nevertheless, her surface ships and U-boats working with the Luftwaffe had already cost Britain the loss of tonnage equal to her total losses in the previous global war. The real U-boat war was just beginning. Germany had absolute supremacy in the air and was preparing the final stroke against England.

The Führer asserted that England had already lost the war but lacked the intelligence to admit it. Britain had two hopes. The first was American help. Germany had taken that into account, and help would not take tangible form until 1942. It would bear no relationship to the increasing productive capacity of Germany. Any attempt at American interference in Europe would be beaten back. The Tripartite Pact had the effect of making America hesitant to enter the war, while German successes against Britain served Japanese interests. England was completely engaged on land and sea and in the air.

America had three choices. She could arm herself, she could arm England, or she could wage war on another front. If she helped England, she could not arm herself. (Here we see one of Hitler's greatest miscalculations.) If she abandoned England, he continued, Britain would be destroyed, and America would face the Tripartite Pact alone. In no case could she wage war on another front.

The second hope was Russia. Both Britain and America aspired to bring Russia into the war and change the balance of power in Europe. Germany had signed well-known treaties with Russia and had between 160 and 180 divisions to defend herself.

Conditions for the Axis were the best one could imagine, and although there was yet some risk, it was the lowest in history. England was engaged and America unready. Russia could not threaten Japan with German divisions massed to her west. England had never tolerated a dominant power in Europe, and in Asia she had played Japan, China, and Russia off against one another. America would do the same when it replaced British imperialism with its own.

Matsuoka related that he favored entering the war and seizing Singapore to drive Britain out of the region, but that cautious pro-American and pro-British circles stood in the way, including two princes. He related that the American ambassador had told him that after the Tripartite Pact was signed, everyone he spoke to had been convinced of German victory. The American had said he believed, instead, that Germany had no chance of winning, and that the decision was risky for Japan.[29]

Meeting with Ribbentrop the next day, Matsuoka asked him what Germany's policy would be toward America if Britain were brought to her knees without America entering the war. That, said Ribbentrop, would depend on the attitude of the United States. Britain might try to set up a government there but would probably fail.

Matsuoka responded that if England collapsed, America would not try to sustain the British Empire. It would more or less annex Canada. Would Germany in such circumstances leave America at peace? Ribbentrop replied that Germany did not have the slightest interest in war against the United States. America would have to satisfy itself with the Western hemisphere, while Germany and Italy controlled Europe and Africa, and the Far East would be reserved for Japan. Russia would be carefully watched.

Matsuoka told Ribbentrop that there were circles in Japan that viewed conflict with America with great misgivings because a war would last five or 10 years. He thought America would not risk its fleet, which is why a war would last for many years.[30]

Matsuoka next went to Rome, where he met with Mussolini and the Pope. According to his account, Mussolini told him that America was now Enemy Number 1, and that Russia was only second. That said, the Duce did not want to provoke America. One should, nevertheless, be prepared for all eventualities, the Italian added.

Matsuoka related his conversations in Rome to Hitler on 4 April. He told Hitler that Japan would do everything in her power to avoid war with the United States. Still, if Japan attacked Singapore, America might come out on the side of Great Britain. Matsuoka said he believed he could use diplomacy to keep the United States from joining the war on Britain's side, but the army and navy must prepare for the worst—war with America. They believed that a war would last five years and be fought out as a guerilla war in the Pacific Ocean and South Seas. He asked for Germany to provide the latest technological knowhow for submarines to help Japan wage that war.

Hitler responded that Germany also viewed war with America as undesirable, but that he had already included it in his calculations. Germany viewed America's capabilities as depending on the available tonnage of shipping. Germany's war at sea weakened not only England but America. Germany would wage war with her U-boats and the Luftwaffe, and her greater experience would be more than a match for America. (Schmider observes that at this time, Hitler expected he would have a four-engine bomber available in the foreseeable future, which was wrong.[31]) Then there was the fact that German soldiers were far superior to Americans.

Hitler told Matsuoka that if Japan came into conflict with the United States, Germany would take the necessary steps at once. Americans would be intent on eliminating one of its enemies first, not with the idea of reaching an agreement with the other, but with the intention of eliminating the second thereafter. Therefore, Germany would promptly take part in a Japanese–American conflict.

We can date Hitler's decision to go to war against America to this conversation at the latest, subject to the condition that Japan become embroiled in hostilities first—a position he stuck to until the event occurred. Perhaps the establishment of Lend-Lease only weeks earlier, the most recent hostile American act, had cemented his intentions. Who knows? But he made this fateful decision with no apparent discussion with anyone about what a belligerent America might do to Germany and vice-versa.

Schmider makes a short reference to Hitler's statement but evidently did not consider it a German commitment to Tokyo. He dismisses Hitler's offer as being bound to the single scenario in which Japan attacked Singapore and advanced southward without attacking the Philippines, and America retaliated militarily. Hitler presumably realized he was making a general statement, and, as we shall see, when Ribbentrop was to assure Oshima on 28 November that Germany would join a war against America initiated by Japan, he used almost the exact same words.[32]

Matsuoka said he had long argued at home that if Japan proceeded with its current policies, war with America would be inevitable sooner rather than later. Japan should act with determination even at the risk of war because the day of reckoning might be postponed for generations if Japan established control over the South Seas. He admitted that he was viewed at home as a dangerous man with dangerous ideas.

Matsuoka claimed that American statesmen would not go to war over China or the South Pacific as long as Japan allowed supplies of rubber and tin to flow. They would go to war, however, if Japan entered the war with the intention of aiding in the destruction of the British Empire.

Matsuoka asked Hitler to keep his discussion of Singapore under tight wraps because exposure in Tokyo could harm him politically. He would have to work patiently to steer Prime Minister Konoye and the Emperor in the right direction.[33]

Japan dramatically eased its worries about the Soviet Union in April, when Matsuoka signed a neutrality pact in Moscow during his return trip from Berlin to Tokyo. Premier Konoye publicly portrayed the agreement as complementary to the Tripartite Pact as a step to keep the European war from becoming global.[34] Matsuoka told his secretary that the pact would induce America to cut a deal. He argued that the great "have-not" powers—Japan, Germany, Italy, and the USSR—were now bound in a web of arrangements that would pressure the "have" Americans to give ground. Some Japanese forces in Manchukuo, which the Soviets officially recognized, would now be available for use elsewhere, and Japan's rear would be secure for fighting in the south and east.[35]

News of the pact alarmed Chiang Kai-shek because China was dependent on the USSR for military aid. The Soviets reassured him that their policy would not change.[36]

According to Walter Warlimont, still assigned to OKW, the agreement came as a complete surprise, but the Germans consoled themselves that the pact freed Japan to deal with the British in the Far East.[37] A message from Foreign Ministry State Secretary Ernst Freiherr von Weizsäcker to Ambassador Ott in Tokyo on 16 April appears to confirm Warlimont's recollection:

> Now that Japan and Russia have signed a neutrality pact, matters have turned out slightly different from what had been anticipated. The reaction here to this pact ... follows the philosophical maxim of "what is, is good." And there are reasons for this. Moscow must of course believe that Berlin had from behind the stage sponsored this pact. Also, the way is now more open for a Japanese drive southward.[38]

Yet even as Matsuoka wrapped up his visit in Moscow, word reached Tokyo from Berlin on 16 April that Germany intended to attack the Soviet Union. This caused some consternation as Japan was now under the obligations of a neutrality pact with the Soviets. Germany, however, had little regard for Soviet military might and indicated that it did not expect Japan to join the pending war in the near future, the Foreign Ministry understood from Oshima.[39]

Japanese Planning Advances

Kido's diary entries in March indicate that the IJA informed the Emperor about its plans for the southern advance. In one conversation on 13 March, the Emperor portrayed the army's movements as "one sided," presumably meaning unilateral.[40] Yet he had been fully involved when the southern advance had become national policy in July of the preceding year.

Meanwhile, Rear Admiral Onishi in late April completed his general plan for the attack on Pearl Harbor. Onishi discussed it with chief of the First Bureau Fukudome. He had concluded that the IJN would have to develop new techniques for using air-dropped torpedoes in the shallow waters and would have to ensure the element of surprise. His preliminary estimate was that the plan had a 60-percent chance of success. Fukudome thought the chance to be about 40 percent.[41] Discussions among planners at the Navy General Staff and Combined Fleet commenced in May.[42]

The War Plans Section of the War Ministry, at the request of the General Staff Headquarters, had been studying the state of Japan's national resources in the event that the country initiated hostilities against America, and in the event she avoided war at all costs. Top members of the General Staff received a briefing on the conclusion on 25 March.

The main points were:

1. In the case of war:
   (a) The existence of doubt concerning Japan's national resources in waging a protracted war against the United States and Britain cannot be denied. Our national resources will generally suffice to frustrate enemy advance for about two years, but there is danger of a temporary liquid fuel shortage toward the end of the second year of war; and with the prolongation of the war, the national economic capability to prosecute the war will weaken steadily.

   The above estimate stems from the inevitable stoppage of imports from abroad, and the difficulties involved in expanding our production power in the event of war. While there is hope that steel and light metal production might be steadily raised each year, there is no prospect for making up for the loss of rare metal and non-ferrous metal imports with our inadequate production facilities of such metals. Since the stockpiles of such metals will be exhausted in two years, a dire shortage of these metals will be experienced from about the third year of the war. A shortage of liquid fuel can also be anticipated to develop by the second year of the war, because the existing stockpile will be heavily drained by then, but it will still be too early to substantially benefit from the resources of newly occupied areas. The shipping problem will become increasingly acute, resulting in a serious drop in coal transportation from overseas sources, and a general decrease in the output of our production industries. The mounting shortage of light industrial materials will also add to the aggravating domestic problems.

   (b) To avoid the consequences stated above, in the event of hostilities owing to an unavoidable development of the situation, it is highly essential to complete military operations in the Southern Area with all possible speed, and to strive to the utmost to prevent destroying the facilities necessary for the exploitation of the resources in the Dutch East Indies. The shipping problem will require the most careful consideration for striking a proper balance in allocating the capacity to fill military and economic requirements.

2. In case war is avoided:
   (a) Assuming economic relations with the United States and Britain are not severed, that trade with the Anglo-American colonies in the Far East could be maintained to some extent, and that economic negotiations with the countries of the Southern Area make some progress, our material strength would decline for the next two years, but it would gradually recover in the third year.
   (b) If our economic relations with Britain and the United States are severed, our material strength will decline rapidly, and its recovery will be quite difficult. Above all, the nation's petroleum stockpile will dwindle steadily each year, resulting in the decline of our national power and military capabilities.
   (c) In any case, it will be difficult to achieve a rapid growth in our national power, or to accomplish a full-scale armament expansion program in the next several years.[43]

On 17 April, the Army and Navy sections of the Imperial General Headquarters adopted a joint policy for the Southern Area. Efforts to obtain agreement for resources from the Dutch were to remain peaceful unless in a case of self-defense or *if the nation's existence were to be threatened by a British, American, and Dutch embargo.*[44]

The IJA and IJN agreed that Japan should occupy the southern half of Indochina and leave open the question of any operations against the USSR. Konoye blessed the decision.[45]

*

The Americans were in for more surprises than just Pearl Harbor. In May, the War Department G-2 in Washington assessed regarding Japan:

> On March 27, 1941 the Army and Navy air forces had, on hand, 2,921 first line planes of all types with 50 percent estimated in reserve, at schools, etc. At the same time, production per month was 144 airframes and 345 engines. The total possible production under full war conditions has been estimated at 250 airframes and 550 engines monthly.
>
> The types of planes now appearing in the Japanese Army and Navy air services have greatly improved over those manufactured in Japan up to 1938. Japanese designs seem to be following the latest developments abroad, although their planes do not come up to the very newest in design or performance.[46]

Oh, was the G-2 wrong about Japanese planes!

Spring in the Fatherland

Germany was still thinking about the United States as a noncombatant, and Hitler wanted to keep it that way even after Roosevelt authorized U.S. Navy vessels to fire on German submarines. The German High Command on 5 March issued a directive on cooperation with Japan that stipulated, "The common aim of strategy must be represented as the swift conquest of England in order to keep America out of the war." Hitler repeatedly instructed Grand Admiral Raeder to avoid any actions at sea that would give Roosevelt cause to enter the war.[47]

Grand Admiral Karl Dönitz, who replaced Raeder at the head of the navy, explained after the war that as of 1941, the German navy lacked sufficient submarines to implement a strategy of wolf-pack warfare against Allied convoys carrying supplies from North America to the United Kingdom. The reason was that the navy had not armed for war against the United States or England, plans for which only emerged after the start of hostilities. The first new models of U-boats would not enter service until 1942.[48]

American prosecutors at Nürnberg leveled bogus charges that Hitler at this time was contemplating aggressive naval warfare against the United States. As evidence, they introduced memos indicating that Hitler had been considering what would be required to capture Atlantic islands with a view toward war at a later date, and his instructions that naval armament priorities must be those programs necessary for the conduct of the war against England "and, should the case arise, against America."[49]

German accounts do not address Hitler's reaction specifically to the establishment of Lend-Lease in March that effectively voided the neutrality acts. The OKW war diary—filled with pressing material on the British landing in Greece and preparations for the invasion of the USSR—merely noted on 12 March, "In USA, Assistance Law signed by Roosevelt." There was no discussion recorded. Apparently referring to Roosevelt's speech the evening of 11 March after signing the law, the OKW war diary on 18 March recorded, "Overall judgment about Roosevelt's speech; it is judged a declaration of war."[50] But Hitler did not want war.

Hitler met privately with Ciano on 20 April, and he hinted to the Italian foreign minister, as he had told Matsuoka, that he was beginning to realize America might become a factor in his calculations. He had long said American mobilization would have no impact until 1942, and 1942 was just around the corner. If the war lasted into 1942 and beyond, Hitler conceded, American aid to Britain would increase and would have to be taken very seriously into consideration. Hitler still put faith in the "Japan card" to menace any American action.[51] Yet, there is no indication that Hitler ordered anyone to take America into consideration in concrete terms, such as formulating war plans.

On 21 May, a U-boat sank an American freighter sailing to South Africa after permitting the crew to take to the lifeboats first. This made clear the captain knew the nationality of the vessel. Roosevelt called the act one of piracy.[52]

Phantom Dawn in Japanese–American Relations

The night before the startling news of a looming German-Soviet conflict arrived from Oshima in Berlin (18 April), Nomura cabled for instructions as to how he was to proceed regarding a "Draft Understanding" between the United States and Japan, a peculiar document that had been drawn up by unofficial intermediaries and had won acceptance from the State Department as a basis for discussion. The army attaché in Washington, meanwhile, cabled that America was headed for war but did not want to fight on two fronts, and he urged Tokyo to take advantage of the situation to arrive at an overall solution.[53] Kido discussed the situation with Konoye by phone, though he did not record the details of the conversation in his diary. "Grave problems have arisen in both East and West at the same time," Kido wrote. "Premier Konoye will be faced by crushing difficulty at the helm of the nation."[54]

The morning of 18 April, a cable from Nomura awaited Japanese officials at the Foreign Ministry. The dispatch contained the details of a conversation with Secretary of State Hull and the contents of a plan tentatively called the Proposal for Japanese Understanding. Konoye later recalled that from the Japanese perspective, the key elements of the proposal were to reach agreement on the prevention of the spread of the European war to the Pacific, terminate the China Incident, and promote bilateral economic cooperation. The American proposal also suggested talks on the international views of the two powers, air and naval strength and navigation in the

Pacific, economic activities of the two powers in the Southwest Pacific, and policies of the two powers regarding stability in the Pacific.[55]

The proposal, crafted by American and Japanese diplomatic amateurs, offered Japan some key wins. The terms, as conveyed to the Germans by the Japanese: Japan and America pledged not to enter the European war of their own initiative and would restrict their policies to defense; America would influence Chiang Kai-shek to come to a direct understanding with Japan; normal trade relations would be restored and the countries would cooperate in exploitation of raw materials in the South Pacific; America would recognize the puppet government in Manchukuo, and the sides would guarantee the status quo in the Philippines. The Germans interpreted the alleged package as an American attempt to sideline Japan in the war and split the Tripartite Pact.[56] With Matsuoka gone, many senior officials mistook the document as an official American communication.[57]

Konoye summoned a liaison conference for that evening. According to his account, a consensus emerged that accepting the American proposal would be the quickest way to end the war in China. Setting up the Wang puppet regime had not helped a bit and talks with Chungking were going nowhere. Chiang was entirely dependent on the Americans, so only they had the good offices to reach an agreement. Agreeing with Washington would provide the "best means" to avoid a U.S.–Japan war and prevent the spread of the European war into the Pacific.

Despite the supposed consensus, objections arose. Japan had to remain true to the Tripartite Pact. If a deal relieved the United States of its Pacific concerns and allowed it to concentrate resources against Germany, it would be improper. The Americans wanted to re-establish the old world order, and there had to be a clear expression of the establishment of a New Order.[58]

Kido on the 19th spoke with the Emperor about the United States, Russia, and Germany and then met with Konoye to discuss Nomura's request for instructions. "Our conclusion was that we must lend every effort to keep our faith with the Axis Powers, and at the same time we must realize the establishment of a new order of the Asian Co-Prosperity Sphere, which is our fixed national policy," Kido confided to his diary.

Konoye held another liaison conference the evening of 22 April. Matsuoka had returned from his European trip that day and been extremely annoyed by the American proposal. The IJA, IJN, and Foreign Ministries had also been reviewing the issue.

Some officials thought Washington was seeking a compromise because of the Japanese-Soviet agreement, some thought German successes had convinced the Americans to back down on China, and others saw it as a plot. The Army and Navy staffs jointly concluded that Washington was trying to prevent the move to the south, increase support to Great Britain, weaken the Tripartite Pact, and establish global hegemony by arming. They argued Japan should take advantage of American preoccupations to settle the China Incident, strengthen military preparedness, and secure a voice in establishing the world order. When the liaison conference members discussed the question, Matsuoka argued that Roosevelt was a "big gambler" and was using his resources to keep the wars in China and Europe blazing. Matsuoka characterized the initiative as 70 percent ill-will and 30-percent good will. He emphasized that Japan should keep faith with Germany and demanded two more weeks to consider the matter.[59]

Kido reported the results to the Emperor on the 21st, and Hirohito expressed his satisfaction with the general situation, according to Kido. They discussed a statement by President Roosevelt that the Emperor considered surprisingly frank and which he ascribed to the influence of the Tripartite Pact. Hirohito said that patience was most important at this juncture. A review of Roosevelt's speeches suggests this was a reference to his Jackson Day radio address on 29 March, in which he said that the country faced mounting threats from aggressive dictatorships on all sides which, unless stopped, would destroy America democracy. But he said the time called for courage and more courage, action and more action, and that America would give full support to those fighting the dictatorships.[60]

Matsuoka's interpretation of German and Italian views, which he related to the liaison conference on 3 May after his return to Tokyo, was that they were certain of victory; would not make peace with Great Britain except, perhaps, an unconditional peace; and believed that American entry into the war might prolong it but would not end it. Matsuoka had told Ribbentrop that if the Soviet Union were willing to sign a neutrality pact, he would do so. Ribbentrop replied, "I understand," but Matsuoka had the feeling the Germany did not believe it would happen.[61] Matsuoka tried to win backing for an attack on Singapore but found no takers.

Japan's initial response, after the liaison conference on 3 May, was to instruct Nomura to tell Hull that German and Italian leaders were confident of victory in Europe, that American participation in the European war would only prolong hostilities, and that Japan would do nothing to injure Germany or Italy. Nomura was to propose a treaty of neutrality. Nomura decided the reply would only enrage the Americans and did not deliver it. He carefully sounded Hull out on the possibility of a neutrality pact but found no interest whatsoever.[62]

The Japanese appear to have concluded by late spring that the United States would go to war against Germany, and, as we have seen, the core of the civilian leadership had already agreed to respect Japan's obligations under the Tripartite Pact. Premier Konoye met on 4 May with Kido to exchange opinions "on the development of the world political situation after the participation [entry] of the USA in the European war, and the measures to cope with the situation."[63]

After this conversation, Kido began receiving information from the imperial military *aide de cabinet* and War Minister Tojo concerning the war in Europe, Germany, and the United States. He kept the Emperor abreast of the course of discussions with Washington and the situation between Germany and the Soviet Union.

Matsuoka tried again to get a decision to attack Singapore at the next liaison conference on 8 May and argued that defeating Britain at Singapore would deter America from becoming involved. "Roosevelt is keen to go to war [in Europe]. You see, he is a huge gambler." Deterrence was necessary. "If the United States were to enter this war, the war will be prolonged, and the world civilization will be destroyed."[64]

Matsuoka argued, "America's actions are certainly tantamount to participation in the war....So far, Hitler has put up with it, but he might unexpectedly go to war with the United States." Ribbentrop evidently had told Matsuoka in Berlin that he estimated there was a 70-percent chance the United States would not enter the war, but Matsuoka now judged the probability was closer to 60 percent.[65]

Berlin sent a cable on 11 May that clearly aimed to dissuade the Japanese government from cutting a deal with Washington, but which also reveals German thinking about America. It read in part:

> It is self evident that it is to be hoped that this historic moment will prevent American entry into the war. Whether it is possible to reach this goal, only the American Government can judge with any certainty. Neither Germany nor Italy has undertaken the slightest thing against America that could serve as an opening for war. If America nevertheless through its policies and related actions joins the conflict, then this will occur because of a calculated decision by men, who like in the Great War—whether on grounds of capitalism or distant imperialist goals of the USA—decide the moment has been reached to lead the United States into a new war. Decisive factors in such a case would probably be internal political reasons, the complete failure of the domestic economic policies irresolvably bound to the name of President Roosevelt, as well as overwhelming influence of the Jews, especially their organizations of the press, and so on.[66]

Roosevelt, asserted Berlin, was already waging war without declaring it through a growing number of non-neutral acts, such as protecting a belligerent through naval "patrol activities" and forming convoys. The President might have decided his policies would inevitably lead to hostilities and be trying to gain the upper hand over antiwar elements at home by sidelining Japan (presumably by showing he could avoid a two-front war).[67]

Ribbentrop, Mussolini, and Ciano discussed the seeming Japanese–American game of footsie among many other matters on 13 May in the Palazzo Venezia. Ribbentrop noted that Matsuoka had warned that for domestic reasons, he would have to do some things that would be difficult to understand in Germany. He said he had confidence in his opposite number. Ribbentrop was certain Japan would enter the war on the side of the Axis Powers. Indeed, he thought the purported American initiative suggested Roosevelt was getting worried because of the poor state of rearmament. In the event of trouble, he could accomplish little and needed to keep his back free. Ribbentrop dismissed American rearmament as "the biggest bluff in world history."[68]

In Tokyo, Matsuoka reassured Ambassador Ott on 18 May that he viewed talks with Washington with skepticism and that he still expected America to enter the war. His negotiations aimed at delaying or preventing that eventuality.[69]

Simultaneously, however, Matsuoka reassured Germany that he would not allow the talks to constrain in any way Japan's commitments under the Tripartite Pact. Germany was concerned among other things that the Americans were trying to ensure security for itself and Great Britain in the Pacific while retaining freedom to help the English in the Atlantic, regardless of the absence of a formal declaration of war. Matsuoka related that the Americans appeared to believe that if they entered the European war, Japan would come in on the side of the Axis—an impression he had sought to strengthen. Nevertheless, he personally assumed that rapid American preparations to enter the war would continue. Matsuoka underscored that he would not let the talks bind Japan's hands in the Pacific or reassure them regarding the security of British possessions. At most, he would guarantee the independence of the Philippines.[70]

The Japanese government decided to pursue talks with the United States with the intention of using the time to restore national strength and using the United States as a mediator to end the war in China, which it had seemingly offered to do. Tokyo determined to continue talks only as long as Japan did not have to "lose her independent position in the Greater East Asia Co-Prosperity Sphere." Moreover, the plan to advance into Indochina was "fixed," irrespective of negotiations with the United States.[71]

Meanwhile, Japanese efforts to "peacefully" pressure the Netherlands East Indies into supplying greater amounts of oil, tin, and other resources were making no headway. The liaison conference on 22 May discussed turning to armed force. The IJA said it would first be necessary to obtain bases in (southern) Indochina and Thailand.[72]

While these events transpired, the Axis Powers missed a golden chance to plug an intelligence leak that would provide the Allies with excellent information on leadership discussions. On 28 April, the German chargé in Washington cabled Berlin, "As communicated to me by an absolutely reliable source, the State Department is in possession of the key to the Japanese coding system and is therefore able to decipher information telegrams from Tokyo to Ambassador Nomura regarding Ambassador Oshima's reports from Berlin."[73] What an intelligence coup! The Germans provided the information to the Japanese, and the Foreign Ministry and Nomura exchanged messages, with Nomura confirming on 20 May that the Americans had broken some codes. The Japanese, however, did not change them.[74]

The Axis appeared to have had some ability to intercept American diplomatic traffic. Ciano, for example, in his diary referred to intercepts of American communications out of Moscow in 1941 and that the Military Intelligence Service had obtained the U.S. Embassy cipher in Rome.[75] But Axis intelligence services were woefully ill informed regarding most matters, such as global American military deployments.

Elsewhere, a series of secret staff conferences early in the year involving senior American, British, Chinese, and Dutch officers convinced Japan that the "ABCD" powers were establishing concrete military cooperation aimed against Japan. The Japanese media blared charges of "ABCD encirclement."[76] The actual conversations did not include the Chinese and were referred to as the America–British–Dutch Conversations.[77]

The Reich Ponders America

Ribbentrop met on 4 May with U.S. Ambassador John Cudahy, whom Roosevelt had sent to Brussels in January shortly before the Germans overran Belgium. Ribbentrop told Cudahy that he viewed him as a true representative of the American people, alongside isolationists Senator Burton Wheeler and pilot-hero Charles Lindberg. Cudahy urged Germany to declare clearly that if the United States provided escort for convoys to Britain, German submarines would sink them. This was the only way to turn the American public against the idea.

Ribbentrop offered Cudahy the most extensive analysis available of a possible American role in the war, though it is unclear to what extent he believed what he was saying and how much was intended to persuade. American intervention, he argued, would be against the country's own interests and constitute a great risk. Great Britain had no prospects, and American aid to its air force would not change that. Conditions were bad and would get worse under German bombing and U-boat blockade.

Germany and Italy were much closer to the Mediterranean than America or Britain, and the United States had no chance of establishing a foothold in the region. The American army was in such a state that it could undertake no assaults in the Europe-Africa hemisphere, it lacked sufficient shipping, and any landing would turn into an American Dunkirk. The distance was too far for the navy, which had to defend two oceans. Ideas of attacking Germany from the air were simply fantastic. It could ship planes to England, but Germany would destroy them and was knocking down British aircraft faster than America could supply more.

The German army had no opponents in Europe. Rommel had only a few divisions in North Africa and would show up Wavell. Germany had 240 divisions and enough war material to last 20 or 30 years. The entire European continent was producing war goods, and even the United States could not match it.

Politically, Germany wanted nothing from the United States and had nothing against the American people. America had no reason to go to war.

Any help for England would come too late. If Roosevelt took the country to war, he would be internationally isolated. America would be at war with Germany,

Italy, Japan, and many other countries. This would be insanity. America could not invade Europe, and Germany could not invade America. The American position in the Far East would immediately be affected.

Cudahy, whatever his politics, cautioned that once America entered the war, "she would not let go very soon."

Cudahy was to interview Hitler before he returned to the States, where he argued against his own country's intervention in Europe.[78]

*

Raeder on 25 May raised with Hitler loosening the rules of engagement of the battleship *Bismarck* merchant raiding group that had sailed for the South Atlantic. Hitler, in essence presenting the flip side of the coin he had offered Matsuoka about entering a Japanese–American war, told Raeder that unless Japan's entry into the war could be guaranteed at the same time, he was unwilling to risk war with America just to sink another 100,000 tons of shipping.[79] Again, Japan's making war was a precondition for war with America.

In late May, the German Embassy in Washington fed hopes that America would remain neutral. It interpreted a speech by Roosevelt as indicating that America was withdrawing its forward defensive line from Europe to the line Greenland–Iceland–Azores–Cape Verde Islands. "This cannot be otherwise interpreted than that the idea of an expeditionary corps has been abandoned for good." It was clearly evident that in the case of England's defeat, America would not go to war unless Germany seized the eastern Atlantic islands or Dakar. The embassy downplayed Roosevelt's declaration of a national emergency as merely intended to impress the British.[80]

Hitler had his own dilettante-level thoughts about the Azores during May. He pictured them as bases for non-existent long-range bombers to attack America after he had finished off Britain and Russia. The navy, meanwhile, had been pressuring Hitler to allow it to attack American vessels because the battle of the Atlantic was not going well; an American destroyer dropped depth charges on a U-boat on 10 April, the first act of violence. But Hitler told Raeder that Roosevelt was still undecided, and he did not want to provoke a war declaration.[81]

The OKW war diary indicates that on 7 June, the German navy was fulminating about American behavior at sea. On 9 June, the diary recorded sinking of a steamer in American waters and the loss of a U-boat to coastal defenses.[82] On 20 June, a German U-boat encountered the battleship *Texas* between Newfoundland and Iceland and maneuvered for a torpedo shot, but the battlewagon got away. When Hitler learned of this, on 22 June he forbade any attacks on American warships even in the blockade zone.[83]

*

Ribbentrop met with Ciano on 2 June at Brenner and lied to his face that "rumors" about a near launch of military operations against Russia were unfounded, or at least premature and exaggerated. But Stalin was concentrating forces in an ominous way, and he was so crazy that one could not rule out an attack. Regarding America, Ribbentrop said a recent speech by Roosevelt had indicated America was still not prepared for war, and he "assumed" (echoing Hitler's hectoring the previous November) the United States would not enter the war if the Japanese energetically pursued a pro-Axis policy.[84]

On 6 June, Oshima reported that he had met with Hitler in Berchtesgaden. The Führer had made the final decision to attack the Soviet Union, and he indirectly called for a joint front against Russia. Matsuoka was skeptical that Germany would actually strike soon, a view shared by the War Ministry.[85] Ribbentrop finally made clear to Ciano, only on 15 June in Venice, that Germany would soon attack Russia. He offered no guess as to how long that would last.[86]

The foreign ministers joined Hitler and Mussolini, and the conversation turned to America. Matsuoka had just issued a strong public statement that Japan would adhere to the Tripartite Pact, and the Führer and Duce concurred that as long as Japan remained firm, America would stay out of the war. Ribbentrop claimed that he had heard from circles close to Roosevelt that the President feared a two-front war.

The leaders discussed figures the U.S. ambassador had circulated to the diplomatic corps regarding planned aircraft production: 18,000 in 1942, 30,000 in 1943, and 60,000 in 1944. Hitler and Mussolini dismissed these numbers—and likewise the "childish" claim that American industry would soon turn out 400 tanks per month—as ludicrous given the manpower and aluminum available.[87] The actual output of combat aircraft would be 25,000 in 1942, 53,000 in 1943, and 75,000 in 1944. Medium tank production in 1942 totaled about 13,000, or more than a thousand per month.

So we see that Hitler's denial in December 1940 that one should assume America would enter the war continued to prevail a mere six months before the United States went to war—a near certain guarantee that the rigid chain of command was spending no wasted time on considering the implications of hostilities.

And yet the pot was starting to simmer. Ciano recorded in his diary on 18 June, "Long telephone conversation with Ribbentrop. Two things have happened, one good and one not so good. The first is the conclusion of a Turco-German pact stipulating neutrality.... The second item is the expulsion from Axis countries of all United States' consuls and of all Axis consuls from the United States. This means that we are rapidly approaching a state of open warfare."[88]

Unbeknownst to these Axis leaders, the Royal Navy's capture of documents from the *U-110* on 9 May included not only the Enigma settings but the details of the "Officer" channel in Enigma. The U-boat commander encyphered the most sensitive communications with his personal code, and then the communications officer encrypted that for transmission via Enigma machine. This knowledge opened the door to Bletchley Park to eventually read the most sensitive Enigma messages.

From September 1941, the British were able to read almost all Enigma messages in, at worst, about 50 hours.[89]

Japan: Military Champs at the Bit for First Step South

Japanese IJA insider and military historian Hattori claimed that neither the IJA nor the IJN actively intended to fight a war against America in the spring of 1941, despite Japan having realized that use of force in the Southern Area would almost certainly lead to war, a lack of any progress in getting the Dutch to accept Japan's peaceful terms, the initiation of preparations for the invasion of the Southern Area and for naval warfare against America, and the analysis that even avoiding war would lead to the country's economic and military eclipse.[90] If Hattori's claim is true, this was one of the greatest acts of self-delusion in history.

Whatever the case, retired and active duty IJN officers by that spring were writing articles and giving speeches imminently pointing to war with the United States. Rear Admiral (ret.) Tanetsugu Sosa evinced a powerful optimism about the outcome. There would be a period of fierce naval action, he expected, that would turn into an endurance test in which the fighting spirit of the Japanese people would prove decisive: "As a result of this war, America will be isolated and thrown into an economic depression of the gravest nature with excess production. There will be a sea of unemployment and social unrest in the United States, especially since America is a conglomeration of various races. Herein lies the weakness of the United States." The retired admiral prophesied the link-up of the German, Italian, and Japanese fleets in the Indian Ocean.[91]

The Americans were now central to Japanese thinking about air defense planning. The Cabinet had met in January to consider measures to deal with air raids.[92] Naval aviators in March met with representatives of the press and fielded questions about the possibility of air raids. Yes, some were probably inevitable, the airmen conceded, but no more than a couple of aircraft carriers could approach Japan as long as the IJN stood guard. A few attacks from the Philippines were the only other possibility.[93]

The American consulate in Keijo (Seoul), Chosen (Korea), on 31 May 1941 sent the embassy in Tokyo an article from the semi-official *Keijo Nippo* on a speech delivered by Commander Sugino on the occasion of Navy Day. The commander told 3,000 guests:

> If anybody should ask me when the Japanese–American war will be started, I will answer that it has already been started. Why did America abrogate the Japanese–American commercial treaty two years ago? That is clearly an aspect of war. Going far back to Japan's pathetic withdrawal from the League of Nations at Geneva, Japanese–American war may be said to have been started.... America, which abounds in materials and regards foreign countries as its possessions, would not export materials when the circumstances became a little disturbed.

America now has the largest fleet ever made by mankind, amounting to 3,500,000 tons, and the American naval authorities brag that seven of [its 17 battleships] can deal with Germany and 10 of [them] can deal with Japan.

Advancing 3,000 miles to the Equator, there is a good place for fostering the co-prosperity sphere of East Asia, which, as you know well, abounds in materials. These materials are necessary for us to maintain national power with the eastern countries. But if we try to secure those materials, America directly puts in a side thrust....

Gentlemen, you need not be anxious. If unfortunately, America should raise any trouble, American airplanes that can invade the territories of Japan may not exceed one hundred, and that means nothing to us. Supposing that America arrays large ships in the Pacific, there is not a single Japanese warrior who will be frightened by it. We navy men consider our selves as forlorn hopes of the Empire. If a million forlorn hopes are stationed in the Pacific, there is no fear at all, although large American ships are coming.

At the time of the Japanese–Russian war, somebody asked Admiral Togo, "What should we do if we are defeated?" and he answered smiling, "I do not think of defeat." This is the Japanese spirit, and I know you think the same way.

There is one thing, however, that we should know, and that is that the war will be a protracted war henceforth, not like the neat naval engagement in the Japan Sea where the rivals decided defeat and victory at one stroke. We should be prepared not to dance a second dance of Germany, which, in World War I, was victorious in war and defeated behind the gun. The navy is certain of victory, and you should live courageously in that certainty and think that the present suffering is a preparation for bounding progress.[94]

On 4 June 1941, two figures representing themselves as businessmen appeared at the U.S. consulate in Osaka and spoke with the consul. The questions quickly became political: "Does America intend to continue support of Great Britain and China?," "What will America do if Japan attacks the Netherlands East Indies?," "What will America do if Japan only monopolizes the oil of the Netherlands East Indies?" Subsequent investigation revealed that the men had posed similar questions to the British consulate, and that the British knew one of them to be a former IJA translator.

The discussion ended when the American diplomat asked his visitors what Japan would do if America became involved in a war with Germany. Mr. Yasuo Kobayashi responded with an impassioned statement that Japan's mission was to establish a new order in East Asia, and that nothing could stand in the way of Japan's "holy war."[95]

The civilian and military leaderships were headed to the same destination—war with America—but perhaps mindful of the Emperor's injunction to exercise patience, a gap was developing between the two groups over the speed of the policy. At a liaison meeting on 11 June, Matsuoka, the firebrand, was suddenly urging a degree of caution because attacking Indochina and Thailand, he argued, would bring Great Britain into the war against Japan. Army Chief of Staff General Sugiyama retorted, "If we are strong, I believe the other side will refrain from action." Navy Chief of Staff Nagano added, "We must build bases in French Indochina and Thailand to launch military operations [southward]. We must resolutely attack anyone who tries to stop us." The next day, Matsuoka won a brief respite to try one last time to negotiate to obtain basing rights. In so doing, he managed to insert delaying language into a policy decision that ended with a clause stating that if Britain, the United States, or the Netherlands tried to obstruct Japan, she "would not refuse the risk of war with Britain and the United States."[96] This clause was dropped from the final version on 25 June.[97]

Kido, on 16 June, learned from the imperial aide-de-camp about the pending occupation of French Indochina. At a liaison conference that day, Matsuoka, knowing Washington would react harshly, declared that such an action would be a great break of international faith, and he urged the IJA and IJN to reconsider. Matsuoka injected the big picture into the parochial regional discussion: Germany was going to attack Russia the following week, according to Oshima's information. "This will mean a world war. Soviet Russia and Britain will become allies. The United States will enter the war on the side of Britain."

The implication was unstated but hung in the air: Germany's decision meant that American involvement was inevitable, and with it war for Japan. Turning back to their parochial problems, Konoye and Matsuoka cabled Oshima in Berlin to ask the Germans to intervene with the Vichy French government to convince it to accept Japanese demands regarding Indochina.[98]

As they planned the occupation of southern Indochina, IJN and IJA staffers assumed Britain would not respond militarily. Nobody thought America might impose an embargo, despite earlier IJN analysis pointing to just that.[99]

Germany Invades the USSR

German preparations to invade what they always referred to as "Russia" continued apace, until the Italian invasion of Albania and Mussolini's botched effort to conquer Greece in October caused delay, because Hitler decided he had to bail the Italians out to deny the British a foothold, in recollection of the Great War's Salonika Front where the Allies had defeated the Austro-Hungarian Empire. The British forced Hitler's hand when they landed troops in Greece in March 1941, which led to German intervention, mounted by forces that were to be part of the southern wing of the *Barbarossa* force. The Germans handily overran the Balkans, but *Barbarossa* was delayed for four weeks.[100]

Hitler wrote to Mussolini explaining why he would launch Operation *Barbarossa* the next day, 22 June. Of interest to this work, he expanded on his idea that his solution had globe-spanning implications:

> It is a matter of indifference whether America enters the war or not, because it is already helping our enemy with all the strength it can mobilize. The situation in England is bad; supply of food and raw materials is ever more difficult. The determination to fight rests essentially on hopes. These hopes are founded exclusively on two presuppositions: Russia and America. We have no possibility of excluding America. Driving away Russia lies within our possibilities. The

exclusion of Russia simultaneously means an enormous unburdening of Japan in the Far East and therewith the possibility that the actions of the Americans will be more strongly threatened by Japanese intervention.[101]

Mussolini replied, "Mr. Roosevelt can do us no more harm than he already has, even if he formally declares war. A war declaration would have no purpose beyond boosting the depressed morale of the English, but the effect would be short-lived."[102]

Ciano in his diary claimed that the Germans did not inform Italy of the offensive until 30 minutes after the first troops had crossed the frontier. Nevertheless, on 21 June he recorded that there were many signs that the beginning of operations was imminent: "How long will the war last? The Germans think that within eight weeks all will be finished.... But if this shouldn't happen? If the Soviet army should prove to have greater powers of resistance than the bourgeois countries, what effect would this have on the world's proletariat?"[103]

Hitler's overweening ambition was to capture simultaneously Leningrad in the far north, Moscow in the center, and the Caucasus in the south in one, huge blitz. Moscow lay 560 miles from the German frontier—roughly equal to the greatest distance covered by the Western Allies from the Normandy beaches into the heart of Germany by May 1945—and the outer edges of Ukraine 700 miles. The Army High Command and OKW believed that the Wehrmacht could defeat the Soviet army in between six and eight weeks, which meant that winter would not be a problem.

For all the fury of North Africa, Sicily, Italy, and Western Europe, the war against the Soviet Union was the decisive theater for the Wehrmacht. Germany launched the operation with some 150 divisions, including one cavalry, 19 panzer (three more than the U.S. Army would ever have), and 15 motorized divisions, or most of the 205 divisions then available. Italian setbacks in North Africa at British hands had forced Hitler to divert a panzer division from *Barbarossa* to North Africa, so Mussolini had not only delayed but weakened the offensive. The Soviets began the conflagration with some 110 rifle divisions facing the Germans, plus 50 tank and 25 mechanized divisions available. Although each was smaller than the American equivalent, this represented about twice the number of divisions General Dwight Eisenhower ever commanded on the Western Front.[104] As of June 1942, Germany had 171 divisions deployed on the Eastern Front and only three fighting the Allies in North Africa. In the decisive month of June 1944, Germany had 157 divisions on the Eastern Front, 56 in France, Belgium, and the Netherlands, and 22 in Italy.[105]

Three army groups—South, Center, and North—each had one of Hitler's main objectives—the Caucasus, Moscow, and Leningrad respectively. They were of roughly equal strength except that Army Group Center had two panzer groups while the other army groups had but one each. Hitler had defined no *Schwerpunkt*, or main point of effort. The army groups were to encircle and destroy Soviet forces near the border, while the panzer groups drove deeper into Soviet territory to prevent Stalin from establishing a defensive line.[106]

The German armies surprised the Soviets and drove deep into the USSR, repeatedly surrounding hundreds of thousands of troops at a time. On 3 July, Major General Franz Halder, chief of the Army High Command (OKH), wrote in his diary, that "the objective to shatter the bulk of the Russian Army this side of the Dvina and Dnepr [Rivers] has been accomplished.... It is thus probably no overstatement to say that the Russian campaign has been won in the space of two weeks. East of [these rivers], we would encounter nothing more than partial forces."[107]

Hitler on 14 July was so confident that the Russians were finished that he advised the army that it would soon be free to downsize. He instructed war production to focus on naval vessels and airplanes for the war against the last remaining enemy, Britain, and "against America should the case arise."[108]

In a meeting with Oshima that same day, Hitler said that confrontation with America was "unavoidable." The only way to keep America out was to destroy the USSR. If it came to war, it might as well happen under his leadership.[109]

Elsewhere, Churchill, Roosevelt, and their senior war chiefs met on 9 and 10 August on a warship off Newfoundland, an event termed the Atlantic Conference. The leaders issued the Atlantic Declaration on 14 August, which spelled out the Allies' key postwar aims in eight common principles. Both countries agreed not to seek territorial expansion, to seek the liberalization of international trade, to establish freedom of the seas, and international labor, economic, and welfare standards. Most importantly, both the United States and Great Britain were committed to supporting the restoration of self-government for all countries occupied during the war and allowing all peoples to choose their own form of government.[110]

The British staff engaged in the ABC process proposed greatly expanding the planned air offensive against Germany to include widespread "morale bombing" of civilians. In light of the course of events, it is interesting that the initial American response was that the idea was "odious."[111]

Behind the scenes, Roosevelt in May had told Army Secretary Stimson to ensure that heavy bomber production reached 500 per month, specifically so they could go to the British. That was a higher rate than Germany or Britain ever achieved; at that time, the UK was producing only 41 heavy bombers per month. On 9 July, he ordered Knox to set up a committee with Stimson and Hopkins to produce a confidential plan laying out how America would raise its production capacity so that it would be larger than those of Germany, Japan, and all other potential enemies combined.[112]

Hitler and Mussolini met on 25 August and barely mentioned the Churchill–Roosevelt conclave. "In any event," commented the Duce, "the attitude of the United States is now completely clear." Hitler blamed it on the Jewish clique around Roosevelt.[113]

Japan Decides to Sit Out the Russian Fight …

At least some Japanese military leaders ultimately concluded that Germany's attack on the Soviet Union ended any American willingness to find a solution with Japan. The Army General Staff asserted to Japanese defense attachés in a circular cable on 9 December 1941 that it had concluded that American "sincerity" regarding finding a negotiated solution with Japan had evaporated after the outbreak of the war between Germany and the Soviet Union.[114] Given the decisions that followed soon thereafter, this appears to be an honest portrayal of Japanese perceptions.

As noted above, Japanese leaders had been receiving reports from the embassy in Berlin from mid-April indicating that Germany was going to attack the USSR. Those warnings continued to arrive until *Barbarossa* launched.[115]

Immediately upon learning of the German attack, Konoye told Kido that the Cabinet must accept responsibility for having signed a neutrality pact with the Soviet Union that interfered with Japan's alliance with Germany. Kido urged him to hold off.[116]

Matsuoka, on receiving the news, gained an audience with the Emperor and told him Japan should attack the Russians. He told the alarmed monarch that Japan would probably soon be at war against the USSR, the United States, and Great Britain. Hirohito told Matsuoka to talk to Konoye, who managed to calm everyone's nerves.[117]

The Army and Navy sections of the Imperial General Staff met on 24 June and agreed on the military's stance regarding the German-Soviet war. Japan would act in the spirit of the Tripartite Pact but not enter the war, proceed with its operations in the Southern Area, continue preparations for war against America and Britain, and take no steps vis-a-vis the USSR that would weaken those preparations. Japan would do what it could to keep America out of the European war, but if she became a belligerent, Japan would act in accordance with the Pact, deciding itself on the manner of the use of force.[118]

Matsuoka admitted at a liaison conference on 25 June that he had been surprised by Germany's decision to invade the Soviet Union, which was hardly true. Perhaps spooked by the reality of a world war, civilian and military leaders agreed to drop the policy clause stating Japan was willing to risk war with the United States and Britain as a consequence of the southern advance. But that did not change the fact that the advance would lead to war, and the only way to fix that was to drop the "fixed" southern policy altogether.

... But Lights the Fuse with America

That was the last thing on the minds of Japan's leaders. Following the conference, Konoye, Nagano, and Sugiyama reported to Hirohito to obtain Imperial sanction. They now argued that American behavior in China and the Netherlands East Indies had become so troublesome and threatening to the Empire that Japan needed to act fast to occupy French Indochina. They said, in part:

> Great Britain and the United States have recently strengthened their political, economic, and military coalition against our Empire by maintaining close liaison with Chungking through the southwest area of China. In view of the above situation, we consider it a most necessary step, besides increasing direct pressure on the Chungking regime, to promote the settlement of the Incident by severing the link between the Chungking regime and the Anglo-American camp, which is strengthening China's fighting will, more than ever, by supporting the regime from the rear....
>
> On the other hand, in the Southern Area, the United States and Great Britain, by cooperating secretly with the Dutch East Indies, are assuming every possible attitude of interference and oppression in political, economic, and military fields towards the Empire....
>
> Therefore, for both the settlement of the China Incident and for establishment of a setup that will insure the stability and defense of East Asia, and the existence and defense of Japan, it is considered urgent to take immediate measures to cope with the joint envelopment scheme taken against Japan by Great Britain, the United States, Netherlands, and China....
>
> Accordingly, the Empire should immediately carry out its policy toward French Indochina and Thailand.[119]

The Army and Navy Sections of IGHQ, in fact, had decided on 11 June that the occupation of southern Indochina and Thailand was to proceed. Necessary diplomatic discussions were to commence, and military preparations for the operation were to begin immediately.[120]

The government and the Imperial General Staff agreed that the American attitude would "stiffen" if Japan moved troops into southern Indochina. Hattori asserts that the Japanese civilian and military leaders judged that the United States knew that an overall embargo would compel Japan to move southward more widely. Indeed, the Imperial General Staff's policy stipulated that Japan would use force to occupy the East Indies if confronted with a general embargo. Therefore, if America took this step, it would mean she had decided to fight Japan anyway.[121]

Over the next week, Matsuoka urged the liaison conference to delay the occupation of Indochina for six months because it probably would lead to war with the United States and Britain and to attack the Soviet Union instead. Navy Minister Oikawa said his service was confident about prospects in a war against the United States and Britain but opposed one that drew the Soviets into the enemy's ranks.[122] The IJA insisted that Japan's Indochina policy was now fixed, regardless of negotiations with Washington, and that the advance would extend as far as the Netherlands East Indies. It committed to preparing secretly its forces in Manchuria for war against the Soviet Union in case later developments made an attack seem advisable.[123] Tojo, probably with an eye toward increasing the army's influence with the Emperor, proposed on 29 June that he planned to meet daily with Hirohito at the palace.[124]

By early July, Matsuoka had lost the struggle, and Japan opted to advance southward even implicitly at the risk of war with America. Premier Konoye and the majority of Cabinet members maintained that Japan must do nothing that would endanger its position in China, such as turning the army north against the Soviet Union. The Emperor privately expressed doubt that Japan had the resources to fight both to the north and south. Kido after the war said Japan had not undertaken the preparations that would be necessary to attack the USSR and further realized doing so would involve the IJA in a winter war that it was unprepared to fight.[125] Nevertheless, the IJA repeatedly suggested to the Germans that an attack on the USSR was just a matter of time, once the Germans had broken the Red Army. Hitler believed as late as August that the IJA would intervene.[126] Therefore, the next step should be tightening the grip on Indochina.

Japan Prepares for War Against America

An imperial conference on 2 July adopted a policy framework approving the southern advance, beginning with French Indochina and Thailand, and defining the goals of Japan's talks with the United States. The IJN supported the southern advance and emphasized the need to obtain raw materials. The IJA supported the policy and justified it primarily as a way to sever the lines of support from the United States and Britain to Chiang Kai-shek. The pro-German Matsuoka struck a discordant note, arguing that Japan should attack the Soviet Union and avoid war with the United States unless she entered the European war, in which case Japan should fight America. Matsuoka nevertheless believed that the only way to settle the China Incident now was to resolve the southern problem—which would cut off outside military support to Chiang. President of the Privy Council Hara preferred to attack the Soviet Union and wanted to avoid war with the United States. Nonetheless, as they had in late 1940, all key policymakers made clear they grasped that such a war was a possible or even likely consequence of their decision. And all agreed that Japan would enter the war if the United States joined the European conflict.[127] This was no military diktat.

According to Konoye's notes, the Empire was to continue diplomatic negotiations that were necessary "from the standpoint of self-existence and self-defense in the southern zone." Konoye recorded in his notes, "Japan will make preparations for war against Britain and the United States" (the adopted document added "in the case that diplomatic negotiations break down") and "will not avoid war against Britain and the United States" if the alternative were to abandon expansion to the south. The IJN's records agree with Konoye's account.[128] The clause was back!

Japanese historian Asada cites several sources as saying that the IJN adopted an aggressive posture favoring the southern advance in part to persuade the IJA to drop any idea of attacking the USSR. Another motivation was to keep the flow of resources to the IJN's buildup, which had taken priority over IJA needs once naval mobilization had commenced in late 1940.[129]

As for talks with the United States, their main purpose would be to keep Washington sufficiently engaged that it would not join the European war—which would force Japan's hand.[130] Konoye noted that Tojo opposed continuing diplomatic negotiations with Washington, while the IJN's attitude was "unclear." He sensed that Tojo had already decided for war. "I believe we will not become embroiled in a war immediately on the grounds that the War Minister has received the Imperial order [at the 2 July conference]. [T]he War Minister will take a very cautious attitude."[131]

That Konoye understood that the southern advance was likely to lead to war with the United States is clear from a letter he sent the Foreign Ministry. "Until the settlement of the Northern Question, armed force should not be used against the southern regions, and steps should be taken toward readjustment of diplomatic relations with America. Naval leaders clearly state that to fight America and the Soviets simultaneously offers almost insurmountable difficulties. From this point of view, it is advisable that the invasion of French Indochina should, if possible, be abandoned."[132] Yet he had accepted that very policy a short while before.

The IJA on 5 July created the Twenty-Fifth Army to conduct the occupation of Indochina. It was to be ready to depart Hainan by 24 July. This consisted of the Guards Division and 21st Independent Mixed Brigade. The IJN established the Southern Expeditionary Fleet to support the invasion. The Twenty-fifth Army planned to depart Hainan by 24 July.[133]

Enraged by U.S. diplomatic pressure to withdraw from China and accusations by Hull that the Japanese foreign minister favored Japan entering the war in support of Nazi Germany (which he did), Matsuoka wanted to break off all talks with Washington. Matsuoka offered an expectation of nearly inevitable American belligerency during a liaison conference meeting on 12 July that would echo in later German rationales for declaring war on America: "[T]he American President is trying to lead his country into the war. There is ... one thread of hope, which is that the American people might not follow him.... We probably cannot prevent American entry into the war in the end."[134]

The remarkable takeaway from Japanese policy discussion from September 1940 through July 1941 is that Japanese leaders accepted that their actions could well lead to war against America, but that the United States per se was not the key driver in the sense of a conclusion that "We must fight the United States because ..." Japan's main priorities led only indirectly to conflict: Increasing desperation to conclude the conflict in China, signing the Tripartite Pact, and the lust to secure sources of raw materials—all were in full cry well before an embargo sealed the deal for war.

Swift Signals

On 7 July, the IJN spokesman said,

> The strengthening of naval and air bases by the United States Navy in the Pacific as well as expansion of the United States fleet itself is directed solely against Japan, while no less important is the fact that the Netherlands East Indies, Australia, the Philippines, and New Zealand are attempting to encircle Japan, rallying under the United States banner.... [A]s a sequel to the German-Soviet war, the northern Pacific situation claims our serious attention in connection with the United States announced aid to the Soviet Union.

He raised the specter of American bases on the Soviet east coast that would threaten security even in the Sea of Japan. The China conflict, he added, was not limited to East Asia anymore but was part of a worldwide disturbance, and he urged the population to prepare for a new conflagration sweeping the Pacific.[135]

The Army and Navy sections of the Imperial General Headquarters, on 9 August, formally terminated consideration of a northern advance and focused only on the southern. The "Outline of Operations by the Japanese Army" stipulated that the 16 divisions in Manchuria and Korea were to remain on strict guard toward the Soviets, the China campaign would continue, and "preparations shall be made promptly for war against the United States and Great Britain, which will be started about the end of November, in the southern area."[136]

The German Embassy in Tokyo in mid-July reported that a conviction reigned in the IJN and IJA that Japan's position of power in East Asia could only be established against the Anglo-Saxon powers. These circles believed that German successes were weakening not only the Soviet Union but also the Anglo-Saxons in the Pacific.[137]

Meanwhile, disagreements between Konoye and Matsuoka over policy toward the United States led Konoye to have his administration resign en masse on 16 July rather than hand Matsuoka's faction a case to argue he had been forced out.[138] Two days later, Konoye formed a new Cabinet, the one that would take Japan to the brink of war. He retained War and Navy Ministers Tojo and Oikawa, but replaced Matsuoka with a military man, Admiral Teijiro Toyoda.[139] In assessing this Cabinet, the U.S. War Department G-2 asserted, "Toyoda ... is expected by some observers to seek by degrees a rapprochement to Great Britain and the United States. General Tojo, called the father of modern Japanese army strategy, holds strong views in keeping with the military circles in Japan; he is not regarded, however, as a fire-eater."[140] Oops.

An Imperial General Headquarters (IGHQ) was established at the imperial palace, where all liaison conferences would henceforth take place. Konoye subsequently claimed that the new Cabinet was committed to repairing relations with America and that he was "mortified" that Washington did not grasp this. Yet planning and troop movements for the invasion of Indochina continued, and the State Department made it clear the United States was aware and that that "action would nullify previous conversations."[141]

At the first meeting of the liaison conference of the new Cabinet on 21 July, the chiefs of the Army and Navy Staffs emphasized that the imperial conference of 2 July had set the policy that the new Cabinet had to implement: "The Supreme Command sees the necessity of especially completing the military measures now in progress for French Indochina in exact conformity with prescribed details and by the given date."[142]

Navy Chief of Staff Nagano threw out a new consideration: "As for war with the United States, although there is now a chance of achieving victory, the chance will diminish as time goes by." America, he argued, would draw matters out while she built her defenses and then "try to settle it." If the leadership concluded that war was unavoidable, he wanted those present to understand that as time passed, Japan's position would become more disadvantageous. He added that seizing the Philippine Islands would help the IJN fight a war.

The Army Chief of Staff thought the meeting had gone much more smoothly than in the past because nearly everyone present had been a military man.[143]

Hirohito apparently grasped the meaning of the near total militarization of the main Cabinet positions. "The Emperor is now in a condition of dread anxiety concerning the relations between the USA and this country," Kido recorded on 25 July.

The Vichy complied with Japanese demands on 21 July. The agreement stipulated that French territory and sovereignty would be respected, the new "defensive alliance" would not be used for offensive purposes, and the French forces would offer no resistance to Japanese troops. Japanese and French authorities negotiated the details of military moves on 23–24 July. With completion of an official accord, Twenty-fifth Army received orders to depart Hainan on the 24th. The treaty was formally signed on 29 July.[144]

On the far side of the world, the inevitable path to war between the United States and Japan was apparent to the Axis leadership. Mussolini wrote Hitler on 25 July, "I am convinced that Japan will stay in our camp because of the ever more meaningful assistance that the United States in supplying to Chiang Kai-shek. It will not march against Russia, but it will occupy Indochina, and that will lead to the break with the United States."[145]

Stumbling Across America's Red Line

Japanese leaders completely misread the Americans in making a decision that would fairly directly lead to war. On 28–29 July, 40,000 Japanese troops moved into southern Indochina. Hattori records that the IGHQ and government shared the view that the "stationing" of Japanese forces in southern Indochina would provoke no serious American reaction, such as the freezing of Japanese assets. Japan's ambassador in Washington, Ambassador Nomura, had warned on 23 July that Washington viewed any advance into southern Indochina as the first step toward Singapore and the Netherlands East Indies. Leaders dismissed this waving red flag because, according to Hattori, they had no such intention of taking those steps *immediately*.[146]

Tipped off by intercepted communications, Roosevelt issued the executive order freezing Japan's assets on the 25th, the day after Vichy authorities agreed to the Japanese occupation. This action effectively cut off the supply of oil, though it was not an outright oil embargo. Britain, Canada, the Netherlands East Indies, New Zealand, and the Philippines followed the American lead. Konoye in his memoirs says that the American sanctions brought opposition to any further negotiations with Washington to the surface, as well as calls for Japan to initiate hostilities. The Japanese public revelation of the invasion and the American announcement that it was freezing Japanese assets came simultaneously.[147]

The operation was a huge miscalculation because the Japanese misread the Americans. The asset freeze caught the high command completely by surprise. Hattori recorded bluntly, "Contrary to the expectations of the Imperial General Headquarters and the Government, the stationing of Japanese troops in French Indochina occasioned the freezing of Japanese assets by the United States, Great Britain, and the Netherlands."[148]

Admiral Ugaki considered the decision a great blunder in retrospect. "I am one of those who enforced the decision [to invade southern Indochina] at the council in the imperial presence," he wrote in his diary. "I should blame myself first before I accuse others.... The occupation of French Indochina had more of an effect on the United States and Britain than Japan had anticipated, resulting in the freezing of funds."[149]

Asada asserts that there is "little doubt" that Nagano knew a total American embargo was a real risk, but most of the well-plugged-in officers, such as Fukudome, that he cites say they did not expect the asset freeze and embargo that would lead to war.[150]

That same day, Ambassador Nomura received instructions to inform President Roosevelt of Japan's plans and to assure him that Tokyo hoped to improve relations with Washington. Events moved too quickly for him to comply.[151]

Finance Minister Ogura trooped to the palace on 26 July to inform Hirohito that the Americans had frozen Japan's financial assets, which effectively ended bilateral trade. London abrogated British, Indian, and Burmese trade agreements with Japan, and the Netherlands followed suit.[152]

Seizing Indochina created the loss of oil supplies and imports from outside the yen bloc that the Japanese most feared. Yet the logic of the "fixed" southern advance—to seize guaranteed raw material supplies—meant that such a break was likely to come within the next six months anyway.

The Japanese took note of a range of American actions. On 23 July, Navy Secretary Knox said, "The US Navy is capable of taking resolute action as may be required to carry out US Far Eastern policy." On 26 July, the United States activated its army forces in the Philippines under General Douglas MacArthur. The British, meanwhile, sent reinforcements to Singapore. On 26 August, Roosevelt announced that he was sending a military mission to Chungking.[153]

Hattori characterized the Japanese reaction:

> Trade between Japan and the foreign countries outside the yen bloc was cut off, thus putting Japan's defense at the crossroads of life and death.... Japan completely lost the means of obtaining the liquid fuel which was indispensable to the existence of a modern state.... Thus, it was considered that if things were left to take their course, the Japanese Navy would be entirely disabled in about two years, and important industries based on liquid fuel would be paralyzed in less than a year, thereby causing a complete breakdown in Japan's national life. Indeed, economic [break] caused greater hardship than the application of military force.[154]

Yet, the American side also misread Japan's likely reaction to an asset freeze. Rear Admiral Richmond Turner, chief of the U.S. Navy War Plans Division, had warned during the policy discussions before the decision that an embargo would push Japan to attack the East Indies, Malaya, and Borneo. Neither the State nor War Departments raised similar concerns.[155]

Konoye's allegedly peace-seeking Cabinet sent a list of "proposals" to Washington on the 31st: 1) Japan will not send troops farther south than Indochina but will not withdraw *"until the war was over in China* [italics added]", 2) Japan will guarantee the neutrality of the Philippines, 3) America will withdraw its armaments from the southwest Pacific, 4) America will cooperate in Japan's obtaining resources from the Netherlands East Indies, and 5) America will mediate in talks between Japan and China and recognize Japan's special position in Indochina even after its troops withdraw. The Americans showed no interest in Japan's ideas.[156]

Both Tojo and Army Chief of Staff Sugiyama, supported by Navy Chief of Staff Nagano, believed that despite a pause in German offensive operations in the Soviet Union, Germany was likely to defeat the Soviets quickly. The Foreign Ministry, however, now anticipated a prolonged war. This disagreement both frames the military's world view over the next few months and is the first entry in what was to become a record of analytic excellence within the diplomatic establishment that was to last through the war.[157]

At the same time, internal discussions indicate that Japanese leaders at first did not grasp that the asset freeze amounted to an oil embargo. For several days, they talked about a cutoff as a possibility.

Even as the first domino in the Pacific war was falling, Nagano on 31 July was delivering his opinion on relations with the United States to the Emperor. Japan, he said, should devote every endeavor possible to avoiding war with America. The admiral expressed a deep antipathy to the Tripartite Alliance, which he called a great hindrance to the restoration of American–Japanese friendship. If Japan lost access to oil supplies (which was happening anyway because of Japan's invasion of southern Indochina that he had supported), current stocks would run out in two years of peace and a year and a half of war. In that case, Japan would have to take decisive action. Kido recorded that, according to the Emperor, Nagano said in response to Hirohito's question whether Japan would win a great victory like the naval battle against Russia, that Nagano was not even sure of a victory at all, let alone one like that in the Sea of Japan. The Emperor expressed his anxiety that this would be a desperate and most dangerous war.[158]

Nagano had spent five years in Americas off and on, including as naval attaché 1920–1923. He considered New York City a second home. As one of the IJN's foremost experts on America, his voice presumably carried some weight with Hirohito.[159]

Kido, however, told the Emperor he thought Nagano's analysis was too simple. He doubted that annulling the Tripartite Pact would restore U.S.–Japan friendship, and that Japan still had other means to pursue that goal. Premier Konoye should consider the options, Kido suggested.[160]

Konoye visited Kido on 2 August, as described in Kido's diary:

> He said he was annoyed that there was an observable tendency for the tough elements in the navy to gather strength, a tendency that would be a great hindrance to maintaining harmony between the Supreme Command and the government. If the USA adopted decisive measures such as to cut us off from supplies of oil, we would run out of oil. Under these circumstances, we would be threatened by an acute national crisis, if we made a mistake in our diplomatic movement. Hence the understanding with the War and Navy Ministers concerning our fundamental national policy should be secured as soon as possible, and if a complete agreement were not reached, there would be no way for the government but to resign en bloc. And it would be the army and the navy that assumed charge of the administration of the country.[161]

That day (Japan time), the United States formally embargoed petroleum exports to Japan.

Konoye on the 4th sent a message to Kido saying he had decided to visit the United States to talk to Roosevelt about "pending problems in [the] Pacific." He had so informed the IJA and IJN. One of his arguments to those ministers was, "If, after a direct meeting with the President, an understanding cannot be obtained, the people will know that a Japanese–American war could not be avoided. This would aid in consolidating their determination." The Navy Minister supported the idea, but Tojo responded in writing that the meeting "is not considered a suitable move."

If the Prime Minister pursued the summit, he would have to firmly stick to Japan's national plan.[162]

Kido, having just received several briefings on the condition of the IJN, met with Konoye on 7 August and shared several opinions with him, which he noted in his diary. In essence, he urged that Japan put off the day of confrontation with the United States for a decade while it strengthened its warmaking capacity. Japan faced a very serious situation, he argued. The government had to meet expeditiously with the IJA to decide a national policy. According to the reports he had received, Japan was not strong enough to fight both the United States and Soviet Union simultaneously. The entire difficult situation could be reduced to one simple problem: oil. Reserves would suffice for two years of peacetime activity but only a year and a half of war. If all these things were true, "we had to conclude that our war with the USA would be a hopeless one." The Dutch East Indies and northern Sakhalin Peninsula would be the chief source of oil supplies if Japan remained cut off from American sources.

Kido continued that occupation of Singapore and the Philippine Islands was an essential prerequisite for a successful landing in the Netherlands East Indies. The probable destruction of oilfields in the East Indies would make it difficult to obtain an adequate oil supply within a year and a half. An attack on the East Indies also would provoke the Americans to declare war, and the need to transport oil over long distances under threat of submarine and air attacks would be very dangerous, and the results would fall short of expectations. Any miscalculation of the oil situation would lead to Japan's defeat.

Japan, Kido argued, could not simply do what it wanted because of shortfalls in its national power: "We might be compelled to exercise the same self-restraint that we had after our victory in the Sino-Japanese War in 1895." Japan should resolve to bear through ten years of hard struggle.

Meanwhile, Japan should do everything to restore friendly relations between the United States and Japan while trying to secure needed raw materials. For this purpose, national policy should be penetrating to the south. Japan needed a ten-year plan to build adequate heavy and mechanical industries, oil-refining capacity, and seaborne transportation.[163]

Kido did not appear to grasp that "penetrating to the south," the fixed national policy, was a sufficient provocation alone to lead to war with America.

Kido consulted with Hirohito on 11 August. The Emperor told him that if the proposed Konoye–Roosevelt meeting were flatly rejected, "we must take a firm resolution." Discussion of relations with the United States involving the Emperor, Tojo, Konoye, Kido, and others became a nearly daily event.[164]

The IJN first informed a handful of key IJA officers only in August of the plan to attack Pearl Harbor. The information was top secret. Fully understanding the challenges faced by the IJN, the army staff made no comment.[165] Clearly, no civilians knew anything about it.

Nomura on 28 August delivered a message from Konoye proposing a summit to Roosevelt at the White House, and the President expressed some interest in holding informal talks. He suggested Juneau, Alaska, as a venue.[166] This meeting never occurred because the distance between the fundamental positions of the two countries was obviously too great to allow for an agreement.

Konoye told Ambassador Grew when he first raised the idea of a summit in the spring that he wanted to meet President Roosevelt in person because he could propose terms (i.e., make concessions) that dared not appear in diplomatic communications because his pro-Axis foreign minister would tell the military, and he would be assassinated.[167] This was total bunk: He had no power to make unilateral concessions.

On 16 August, the Navy Section of IGHQ proposed an "Outline Plan for the Execution of the Empire's National Policy" to its IJA counterparts. The plan called for simultaneously pushing war preparations and a diplomatic offensive. If by late October no diplomatic solution emerged, Japan would use force. The IJN position was consistent with the view formulated in the spring that an embargo would be grounds for military action. The IJA wanted a firm decision that diplomatic failure would trigger war before its launched war preparations, which required large-scale mobilization and troop deployments.[168]

Tokyo Picks a Deadline

The liaison conference on 3 September adopted "The Essentials for Carrying Out the Empire's Policies," which established that if negotiations with the United States had not reached a successful conclusion by the last ten days of October, Japan would decide to go to war against the United States, Britain, and the Netherlands. The IJA had vetted the document during August, when, as we have seen, its leaders believed that Germany would quickly defeat the Soviet Union. The IJA does not appear to have conducted an analysis of its prospects in such a war against America. It assumed the IJN would bear the brunt of the conflict and left that judgment up to the admirals.

Nagano reiterated his view that Japan at the present time had a chance to win a war, but that Japan was growing weaker and the United States stronger. He said he expected a war would be a long one. He hoped the enemy fleet would sail to waters near the home islands, where the navy would have "quite good" chances of destroying it in a decisive battle. This would not end the war, but Japan would be able to enjoy the fruits of the victory to wage a long war. If Japan became mired in a long war without a decisive battle, it would face great difficulty as its resources ran out. Then Japan would have to ensure access to new resources and play not to lose. Japan would have to seize the initiative.[169]

For the record, Sadao Asada writes that during this period, Nagano had an "exaggerated fear" that if the IJN opposed the war, the IJA would stage a coup.[170]

As we shall see, however, Tojo was to suggest later that Japan call the whole southern operation off if Nagano lacked confidence that the IJN could win.

A separate paper defined the minimum conditions to deem a diplomatic solution acceptable. Chief among them was, "That the United States and Great Britain shall not obstruct or interfere with the Empire's settlement of the China Incident.... [America must c]lose the Burma Road and cease extending military, political, or economic aid to the Chiang regime."[171]

Nagano was not alone in thinking Japan could win. Combined Fleet Chief of Staff Ugaki recorded in his diary on 22 October, "To beat such guys [the Americans] into fits will be good for our empire."[172] Ugaki was the right-hand man of Commander of the Combined Fleet Yamamoto, who would command the attack on Pearl Harbor. He knew as well as anyone what would unfold in December across the wide Pacific Ocean.

On 5 September, Konoye told Kido that the Emperor that day had posed many questions to him about the plan of operations against the United States. Konoye had disavowed having any jurisdiction over such matters and urged Hirohito to put his questions to the chiefs of the Army and Navy General Staffs.[173] (According to one account, Konoye did try to describe the military strategy, "By occupying the necessary areas to the south ... we should be able to consolidate an invincible position; by taking advantage of conditions in the interim, we can entertain hopes of being able to bring the war to an end."[174]) Konoye told interrogators after the war, "It is almost impossible for us outside the army circles to understand or know the strategy on which they based their plans.... As a matter of fact, the premiers in those days did not know very much about army plans. They were not taken into the confidence of the military.... [A]ny requests for information were generally turned down."[175]

Hirohito met with Konoye and the military staff chiefs that evening. The Emperor asked Sugiyama how long the IJA would need to finish a war with the United States, to which the general replied, "three months." Hirohito retorted that as War Minister, Sugiyama had told him the war in China would require a month. The interior of China is huge, the general explained. "Is the Pacific not even bigger?" asked the Emperor.

The following morning, the Emperor told Kido that he wanted to ask more questions at that day's Council in the Imperial Presence. Kido urged him to let President of the Privy Council Hara ask the questions on his behalf, "as we were going to decide whether we should declare war upon the USA, a war [on] which we would have to stake everything," Kido recorded in his diary. It was important, however, that Hirohito give an imperial warning to the military to make common cause with the government to reach a successful conclusion to talks with the United States.[176]

At the imperial conference on 6 September, Hara asked most of the questions. The answers were: Japan's minimum demands for a diplomatic agreement included that the United States and Britain agree not to obstruct Japan's resolution of the war in China on its own terms, that they would end support to Chiang and close the Burma Road, that they would neither threaten Japanese interests in the Far East nor increase their military strength in the region, and that they would restore normal economic relations with Japan. Tokyo was prepared to pledge not to advance from Indochina in any direction other than China, to withdraw its troops from Indochina once peace was established in the Far East, and to guarantee the neutrality of the Philippine Islands. Japan would respect its obligations under the Tripartite Pact if the United States entered the European war.

At the time of Pearl Harbor, Koichi Kido was Keeper of the Privy Seal, the key interface between the Emperor and the civilian and military leaderships. He is a major source of information on events inside the leadership. (Wikimedia Commons)

From the outset, Japanese leaders viewed the coming war in global terms that completely escaped the Germans. According to Hattori's account, a supporting document prepared for the conference characterized a Japanese–American war as historically inevitable. Japan's war aim was defined as ejecting American, British, and Dutch influence from East Asia and consolidating the "New Order in Greater East Asia." The war would be long, and the conditions for terminating it unclear. Japan could not compel America to surrender, though the public might throw in the towel after seeing overwhelming Japanese successes or the surrender of Britain. Japan could create an impregnable defensive arc in the south and link Europe and Asia through cooperation with Germany to destroy the Anglo-American coalition.

Konoye stated that the prospect of an American-Soviet alliance against Japan would reduce the empire to helplessness. If diplomacy failed, Japan would have to defend herself. Nagano repeated his points from the liaison conference and added that the American military buildup would make her a great threat to Japan by late 1942. He conceded Japan lacked the means to overcome the enemy and break his will to fight, but she could seize impregnable positions and needed resources in the Southwest Pacific through aggressive and dauntless military operations. Still, Nagano thought a durable, though not a temporary, peace would be preferable to war.

Army Chief of Staff Sugiyama echoed Nagano's statement. Foreign Minister Toyoda reviewed the history of discussions with Washington so far and underlined several times that the United States saw no point in talking if Japan continued its use of force.

The head of the planning board reported that stocks of liquid fuels would run out by June or July of 1942, which was much faster than the two years stipulated in the supporting documents, and that the use of military force to obtain new resources would reduce production by half because of demands on shipping and other factors. If the resources to the south could be captured within four months, Japan would be able to acquire petroleum, aluminum ore, nickel, crude rubber, tin, etc. in six months and exploit them fully within two years.

Hara opined that the policy seemed to place war before diplomacy and indirectly asked whether the reverse would not be better. Navy Minister Oikawa replied that diplomacy and war preparation had equal importance.[177]

Admiral Osami Nagano, pictured here in 1934, was Navy Chief of Staff who in 1941 urged a rapid decision to go to war against America. He was also the first senior military man to hint to Hirohito in 1943 that Japan might lose the war. (Military Intelligence Division, NARA)

By way of admonishment, Hirohito quoted to the senior officers the Emperor Meiji's poem, *The Sea of the Four Quarters*:[178] "Since all are brothers in this world, why is there such constant turmoil?"[179] Nagano and Sugiyama understood the implicit imperial criticism and said diplomacy would take precedence. The Emperor nevertheless told Kido privately that to his great disappointment the Supreme Command had not responded to Hara's question as to whether it attached importance to the negotiations with the United States.[180]

Konoye told interrogators after the war that the military's position coming into the meeting had been that if negotiations did not produce results by the middle of October, war would begin. The government achieved a compromise by which if there were no sign of progress, Japan would prepare for war. Asked repeatedly whether the Emperor and senior leadership had discussed a strategy for waging the war, Konoye said there was no consideration of strategy.[181]

No sane participant could possibly have believed that the United States would accept Japan's minimal conditions. Diplomatic talks, discussed at great length in other works, continued up to the time of the attack on Pearl Harbor, but they never came close to striking a bargain and will not be discussed here.

The IJN phased to total war footing on 1 September.[182] Tojo on 10 September reported to Hirohito on the preparations for war against the United States.[183] The IJA started moving ground forces, which had undergone amphibious and jungle warfare training, to embarkation bases on 18 September. The IJA planned to commit only 20 percent of its strength to the southern advance.[184]

So far as one can tell, Japan marched off toward war without any deep consideration of what resources the United States would be able to commit to the conflict. Konoye convened a group of graduate students at the Total War Research Institute on 27 August. The students were Japan's most promising mid-level officials from various government and military organizations. The group had been running scenarios and examining data for the past six weeks. The group told Konoye that their conclusion was that if Japan went to war against America and its allies, it would necessarily lose. Given the starting premise that Japan occupied the Netherlands East Indies to gain natural resources, they anticipated that the American navy would interdict the flow, defeating the whole purpose.

Konoye had the group present its findings to the Cabinet over two days. Tojo complimented the effort but retorted that the future was full of uncertainties, and one could not predict an outcome. He cautioned them not to talk about their conclusions with others.[185]

Within the state apparatus, years of public official comments showed that the IJN was aware of American naval expansion plans in broad terms. The background notes prepared for the 6 September meeting offered a brief snapshot of the U.S. Army's structure and manpower, including the Air Corps. The regular army as of 1 August was reported to have 500,000 men with an additional 300,000 in the National Guard and 50,000 in the reserves. Another 540,000 were being recruited into the army and guard, for a total strength of 1.4 million. The Japanese assessed the ground forces to consist of 11 infantry divisions (two of which were in territories abroad), four armored divisions, and two cavalry divisions, plus 18 National Guard divisions. The Army Air Corps, the Japanese believed, consisted of 17 squadrons on the mainland and five in the territories, with about 3,500 aircraft deployed with combat units. It offered no information on how the army might expand, what its fighting qualities might be, or how its weaponry and equipment compared to Japanese equivalents.[186] As we have seen, the limited available evidence suggests that the military expected American mobilization to occur on a scale and timeline similar to that in World War I.

Admiral Yonai provided interrogators with data on Japan's expectations of American combat and non-combat aircraft production after the war that is consistent with the record of the policy conference (here fleshed out from Hattori). As of December 1941, America had an estimated total of 3,600 first-line planes, including 900 fighters and 100 four-engine bombers. Estimates were that by

December 1942, America would possess 7,100 first-line planes, including 2,660 fighters and 300 bombers, and by December 1943 16,200 first-line planes, including 5,480 fighters and 2,690 bombers. Japan estimated American production of aircraft of all types as 19,300 in December 1941, 47,900 in December 1942, 85,900 in December 1943, and 100,000 in 1944.[187] Note especially the projections for bomber strength by 1943, yet the assessment suggested no implications of that number.

As a snapshot, the assessment was not bad, though it suggests that important Japanese information was out of date because the National Guard and reserves had been federalized into the regular army in August 1940. As of 7 December, the army consisted of more than 1.6 million men and 34 divisions, of which one cavalry, two armored, and 14 infantry divisions were deemed ready for combat, with another cavalry, two armored, and ten infantry divisions due to reach that status by April 1942. Existing selective service legislation, however, already would supply 2.7 million more men over three years, and a well-conceived organization and training plan was already in place—a major advantage over 1917. On the outbreak of war, the War Department produced a plan to create between three and four divisions per month up to a total of 100 by the end of 1943; upon subsequent discussion, 20 of those were to be armored divisions (actual figures by 1945 were 90 infantry and 16 armored divisions). By March 1945, the manpower of the army's ground and air elements was to reach 8.2 million, though the manpower in combat units sent overseas exceeded that in World War I by only about 25 percent.[188]

The Japanese estimated that turning to mass production methods, America would be able to produce five to six times as much shipping tonnage as Japan, and that by 1943, Japanese tonnage would be about half that of the United States and less than 30 percent by 1944.[189]

Japan did have a good intelligence picture of opposing forces across the Pacific area, and planners knew the enemy was vulnerable. The military services and their agents for years had gathered information on ground, air, and naval strength in the region; the location of airfields and fortifications; and terrain and climatic conditions.[190] That said, Japan's intelligence capabilities against America were weak. The IJN's intelligence staff was tiny by comparison with those of Western navies; its naval attachés were under no requirement to submit intelligence reports; and collection inside America before the war had focused on technical matters, such as torpedo and sonar development.[191]

Admiral Ugaki, who as Yamamoto's operations chief would have had access to the intelligence on the enemy, recorded in his diary on 13 November, "Now our Combined Fleet forces are deploying in preparation for war. Everything is advancing in profound secrecy, taking advantage of the poor preparations for war of the United States, England, and Holland."[192]

The Army and Navy General Staffs shared an assessment of likely Allied responses on the brink of war. As summarized by General Douglas MacArthur's postwar report, drawing on interrogations of senior military officers, the analysis was "shrewd":

1. The Allies would attempt to isolate Japan politically and economically. At the same time, they would step up aid to Chiang Kai-shek in order to hold as many of Japan's effective forces immobile on the Continent as possible.
2. The United States and Great Britain would try to delay Japan's penetration of the southern areas by reinforcing their own air and sea power in the Philippines-Singapore areas and by holding these strategic bases as long as possible. The main body of the United States fleet also might, depending upon the trend of the early operations, attempt a trans-Pacific thrust, presenting the possibility of a decisive sea battle. Allied air and sea forces would harass Japanese sea traffic with guerrilla tactics to interfere with lines of communication.
3. When their mobilization was finally completed, the Allies would attempt a large-scale counteroffensive with air, sea, and ground forces, preparatory to a decisive naval battle. The United States would probably launch its counteroffensive from the southern and middle Pacific, where there were good sites for air bases. An offensive mounted across the northern Pacific seemed unlikely because of unfavorable weather conditions. Should an American offensive be launched early in Japan's southern campaign, the chances were that it would be from the Central Pacific.
4. In the event that the United States and Great Britain elected to avoid decisive battle early in the war, they would probably limit themselves for the time being to submarine and air attacks on Japanese supply lines. At the same time, they would endeavor to secure their communication lines with Australia and India with a view to the eventual use of these territories as bases for the start of a counteroffensive.
5. In all likelihood, Great Britain would be forced to employ the bulk of its strength in Europe and would play a minor role in the Pacific operations. However, it could not be predicted with certainty whether the United States would elect to throw its main strength first against Japan or against the Axis Powers in Europe. Japanese strategists, after carefully weighing the possibilities, estimated that first priority would be given to Europe.
6. The United States and Great Britain, already counting Chiang Kai-shek as an ally, would undoubtedly attempt to bring the Soviets into the war.[193]

Hattori suggests that the IJN's focus on fleet action—albeit with recognition that the air arm would have great influence—completely failed to anticipate the island-hopping amphibious campaign that steadily moved the ground-based air umbrella across the Pacific.[194]

Final Doubts

Premier Konoye, having contributed so much to making a war inevitable, was getting cold feet. On 26 September, Konoye hinted to Kido that he was going to resign, saying he lacked the confidence to tide him over the national crisis that was the logical conclusion of the IJA's intention to start an attack against the United States on 15 October.[195]

Tojo had developed doubts about the commitment of Navy Minister Oikawa and met with him on 27 September. "It seems you intend to change the decision of the Imperial Conference [on the deadline for war]. What is your stand?"

"I have no such intention. However, the world situation is changing every moment, and I am afraid of premature embroilment into a world war by Japan."[196]

President of the Privy Council Hara told Kido on 29 September that negotiations with the United States were going to end in complete failure. Japan would have to make its final resolution as to war against America. By 9 October, Konoye had also concluded that prospects were dim for any compromise with Washington. Kido replied that there was little chance of victory in a war against the United States, and Japan should reconsider the decisions of 6 September. He again urged that Japan adopt a ten- or fifteen-year strategy to strengthen itself economically without paying any attention to the economic oppression of the United States. If necessary, Japan could increase its military forces in China to wrap that problem up.[197]

As it happened, the Japanese army in China had just on 18 September launched its first major offensive of 1941, aimed at capturing Changsha. The Chinese outfought them for a second time on the same battleground, despite the Japanese capturing the city twice. Imperial troops finally retreated to their original lines in January 1942. China was not a problem to be wrapped up.[198]

Konoye during a casual conversation asked Admiral Yamamoto what the chances for victory were. Konoye told interrogators that the admiral replied that the fleet would be able to carry on the fight for about a year and a half, and after that he wouldn't think it could. Konoye commented that the army was more optimistic than the navy but never clarified why. So far as Konoye could tell, the military had no plan for achieving victory against the United States.[199]

Vice Admiral Fukudome told interrogators in December 1945 that he had never heard Yamamoto say that the war could be carried on for a year and a half.[200] By 1949, he had completely changed his story. Fukudome told interrogators then,

> Admiral of the Fleet Yamamoto had said that one year was the limit—that the navy could not hold out for one year and a half. I am quite familiar with the feelings of Admiral of the Fleet Yamamoto, because I acted as his chief of staff for a year and a half. However, I do not clearly know upon what reasoning he based his figures of one year and one year and a half. [Yamamoto] was most concerned about air operations. He believed that the decisive factor of future operations, whether on land or sea, would lie in air operations; that with its present air armaments, the Japanese Navy could not possibly win a war against the United States. Since he frequently made statements to this effect, I think [Yamamoto's] figures for one year and a half were based upon the air strength of the navy.[201]

Yamamoto on 29 September wrote to Nagano,

> It is obvious that a war between Japan and the United States will become protracted. So long as the war continues to Japan's advantage, the United States will not give up the fight. As a result, our resources will be depleted over the course of several years of fighting, and we shall face enormous difficulties in replacing damaged fleets and ordnance. In the end, we shall not be able to stand up to them. The commanders of the First, Second, Third, and Fourth Fleets are virtually unanimous on this.... A war with so little chance of success should not be fought.[202]

The Imperial Conference on 6 September 1941 set a deadline for war against America. (World War II Daily)

For what it is worth, one Japanese source asserts that on 1 October, Navy Minister Oikawa told Konoye that if he decided to accept all American demands in order to normalize relations, the Navy would back him. Chief of Staff Nagano later that day concurred with Oikawa, according to the source.[203] Konoye failed to mention any such initiative by the IJN in his later interviews and writings.

Konoye recalled to the interrogators that he had urged Tojo to pull Japanese troops out of China (meetings occurred on 4 and 12 October at Konoye's villa), but that the general argued that that would crush the morale of the army and merely postpone an "evil day" of reckoning with America for two or three years. America would increase pressure on Japan across the board, and Japan would be forced to take up arms. Tojo's position was that there would be war whether Japan withdrew or not.[204]

Vice Admiral Ugaki formally presented the Combined Fleet's plan to attack Pearl Harbor to the Navy General Staff in early October. The operations staff rejected the plan as too risky. Yamamoto refused to accept the decision. A second meeting occurred around the 15th, and again the staff rejected the plan. Ugaki warned that Yamamoto would resign if the decision stood, though it was not clear that the admiral had told Ugaki that. The debate escalated to Nagano, who decided to approve the plan.[205]

Nagano's support for the plan was lukewarm. As a young officer in the Russo-Japanese War, he had been a member of a team that refloated Russian warships sunk at Port Arthur, which the Japanese refitted and added to their fleet. He suspected that sinking the American warships at Pearl Harbor would be at best a delay. The enemy would be able to reconstitute its fighting strength in about ten months.[206]

Chief Secretary of the Cabinet Kenji Tomita visited Kido on 12 October. He portrayed Tojo as arguing that there was little room for compromise with Washington, and that a final decision for war should be adopted as quickly as possible. Navy Minister Oikawa wanted to steer away from war as much as possible. Tomita asserted that the IJA was not pressing for war for "its own pleasure," and it was still willing to follow Premier Konoye's arguments if they were convincing enough. The country was at a crossroads, Tomita said, and it had to choose between a full reconciliation with the United States or war. A patched-up compromise that collapsed into a war would be the worst outcome.[207]

Hotta, citing a single source, says that top-level naval officers, including the navy minister and chief and deputy chief of the Naval General Staff, formed a consensus on 6 October that it was "folly to start a war with the United States." They thought the IJN should encourage the IJA to withdraw gradually from China.[208] If so, other knowledgeable sources did not discuss such an event. More broadly, Fukudome after the war said that Yamamoto and Nagano were both strongly against the war and only accepted it as the inevitable turn of events. He also said that Admiral Shigetaro Shimada, who was to replace Oikawa as navy minister in the Tojo Cabinet, hoped against hope that war could be prevented.[209]

On the other hand, citing no source, Nelson says Nagano at a meeting on 7 October responded to Sugiyama's query as to whether the IJN lacked confidence in the war: "Not confident about the war? That is not true. Of course, we have never said victory is assured. I've told the Emperor this, too, but we are saying there is a chance of winning for now."[210] Hattori agrees that Sugiyama and Nagano's views were in full accord.[211]

Hirohito told Kido on 13 October that he, too, had practically no hope for a successful outcome of talks with Washington. He thought he would have to issue an imperial proclamation of war against the United States. Hirohito said he regretted that his previous proclamations underscoring his desire for world peace, including at the time of the signing of the Tripartite Alliance, had been interpreted as challenges to the United States and England. He wanted his real intentions reflected in the war proclamation that Kido and Konoye would draft for him.

Hirohito said that Japan would have to pay greater attention to the situation in Europe. It should use diplomacy to ensure that Germany did not reach a separate peace with England or the Soviet Union and to draw Germany into war against the United States. Japan should cultivate ties to the Vatican to create a channel for a possible armistice one day.[212]

Perhaps inspired by Tomita's assertions, Konoye says in his memoirs that on the 14th, he met with Tojo and urged him to accept the "formality" of pulling Japanese troops out of China and "save ourselves from the crisis of a Japanese–American war." The Premier said, "I find it difficult to agree, no matter what is said, to enter upon a great war, the future of which I cannot at all foresee."

Tojo retorted, "If at this time we yield to the United States, she will take steps that are more and more high-handed, and will probably find no place to stop. The problem of withdrawing troops is one, you say, of forgetting the honor and seizing the fruit. But, to this, I find it difficult to agree from the point of view of maintaining the fighting spirit of the army."[213]

During a Cabinet meeting that day, debate over the issue continued. Tojo said the IJA was deploying troops for large-scale operations, and that if the government was confident that America would accept Japan's minimum demands, then war preparations should cease. Toyoda conceded that a solution would require Japanese withdrawal from China and French Indochina. Tojo again rejected the idea. All the gains in China would be for naught. Tojo said there would be a domino effect on security in Manchukuo and Korea.[214] Konoye told interrogators after the war that he already viewed a war as unwinnable.[215]

A widely spread anecdote relates that during this conversation, Tojo said that there were times when one had to have the courage to do courageous things, like stepping off the veranda of Kiyomizu Temple with one's eyes closed. If true, was this Tojo playing the gambler? Or was this Tojo expressing the essence of the British Special Air Service motto, "Who Dares Wins?"

Tojo visited Kido on 15 October and flatly told him that if Konoye did not change his thinking, the Cabinet would have to fall. The Premier later that day told Kido he could not remain in office because the breach between him and Tojo was growing wider every day. He and his Cabinet resigned en bloc the following day. After considering and rejecting several possible premiers, Kido proposed that Tojo take on the responsibility.[216] And so Tojo on the 17th received Hirohito's mandate to become prime minister.

Hattori recorded, "The Imperial command was unexpectedly given to Hideki Tojo, on 17 October, to form the Cabinet.... The reason for this recommendation [by Kido] was that, in this critical situation, the prime minister must be able to administer the national government to meet the situation, and to have complete control over the army. It had nothing to do with the war advocation of War Minister Tojo."[217]

By that day, the war in China had cost Japan 180,000 dead and 323,700 men wounded.[218] This was the problem with riding the tiger. Getting off and pulling out of China would have made clear that all that death and suffering had been the product of bad decisions.

The Tojo Cabinet formed on 18 October 1941 and took Japan to war. From left, front: Navy Minister Shigetaro Shimada; Minister of State Teiichi Suzuki; Prime, Interior, and War Minister Hideki Tojo; Foreign Minister Shigenori Togo.

According to a single Japanese source, after meeting Kido, Tojo met Sugiyama and complained that the navy minister would not say he lacked confidence in going to war, but he talked as if he did. If the navy did not want war, "we must think of some other way."[219] Given Tojo's willingness shortly after this purported conversation to become prime minister and launch a war, if he really had second thoughts, they dispersed quickly.

Chief of Staff of the Combined Fleet Ugaki began writing his diary on 16 October. In his preface, he expressed certainty that war was coming and identified the causes as the China Incident, Japan's accession to the Tripartite Pact, the occupation of northern Indochina, and the occupation of southern Indochina. He noted that he had supported the last decision and offered that he should blame himself before anyone else. "This war will be the greatest on record and a matter of vital importance the welfare of our empire."[220]

Despite intercepting Japanese diplomatic cables, the Americans had no clue how far the Japanese had gone toward a decision for war against America. Yet, as mentioned earlier, Ambassador Grew had the right "feel" for the coming crash. Grew from September to November warned of Japan "risking national hara-kiri" to become impervious to economic embargos abroad rather than yield to foreign pressure. He sought to dash any misconceptions in Washington about Japan's capacity to rush headlong into a suicidal struggle against the United States and argued that a do-or-die effort was not only possible, but probable. Yet, he conceded, Japanese sanity could not be measured by American standards. He warned that Japanese preparations were more than saber rattling and that armed conflict might come with dangerous and dramatic suddenness.²²¹

On the Far Side of the Planet

Berlin did not grasp that Tokyo was gearing up to attack the United States but wanted to keep that very threat alive to constrain Roosevelt's actions against Germany. It appeared to be slightly worried that the Japanese would cut a deal that would ease the danger.

Ribbentrop on 12 September ordered Ambassador Brigadier General Eugen Ott in Tokyo to deliver an oral message to Foreign Minister Toyoda. Roosevelt had just given a speech in which he said that he had issued the U.S. Navy orders to fire on hostile warcraft. Ribbentrop said that Roosevelt showed increasing signs that German victories against the Soviets had hurt him badly, and that he was trying to create conditions in which the American public—which fully understood how hopeless a war against Germany would be—would accept an incident at sea as ground for war with Germany. He was trying to cast Germany as the aggressor when any thinking man could see that Germany was reacting to American provocations with all restraint. Roosevelt knew he did not have the weapons to fight a two-front war, which is why he was trying so hard to negotiate Japan into non-involvement. Germany would continue to respond with restraint to the latest provocation, but German warships would naturally defend themselves against American attacks. Ribbentrop urged Japan not to take any steps in its negotiations that would help Roosevelt rally public support for war.²²²

Toyoda responded that were the United States to attack Germany, Japan would without doubt come in beside its Axis allies. It would, however, decide on the timing and actions within its own government. At this stage, he added, Japan was still trying to keep America out of the war, which was the strategic aim of the Tripartite Pact.²²³

In the Atlantic, meanwhile, Germans and Americans were trading fire. An American destroyer on 4 September pinged a U-boat with sonar for hours, and the German captain fired two torpedoes that missed. The destroyer dropped depth

Admiral Mitsumasa Yonai (left) with Admiral Isoroku Yamamoto (right) photographed in the late 1930s when Yonai was Navy Minister and Yamamoto was Vice Minister. Yonai favored Japanese naval supremacy in Asia but opposed the Tripartite Pact. Yamamoto conceived the victorious attack at Pearl Harbor and the defeated one at Midway. (Wikimedia Commons)

charges that also missed. Roosevelt on 11 September authorized his warships and aircraft to shoot on sight any enemy vessel threatening a U.S.-flagged ship or a ship under American escort. On 17 October, in a night engagement between American, British, and French warships and a U-boat pack, a submarine torpedoed an American destroyer, which limped to port.[224]

*

Ciano in late October traveled to Germany to visit the High Command and go pheasant hunting with Ribbentrop. On the 28th, he recorded in his diary:

> Roosevelt's speech has made a great impression. The Germans are firmly determined not to do anything that might bring about America's entry into the war. At a large luncheon party, Ribbentrop launched into a tirade against Roosevelt. "I have ordered the papers always to print 'Roosevelt the Jew.' I make the prediction that this man will be stoned at the Capitol by his own fellow countrymen." I think that Roosevelt will die of old age, because experience does not give me much faith in Ribbentrop's predictions.[225]

Ciano returned to Rome, where Mussolini told him that he now believed less than ever that the United States would intervene in the war: "It is clear that Roosevelt is barking because he cannot bite." Ciano commented in his diary, "I hope Mussolini is right."[226]

Ciano met with Hitler on 26 October, and the Führer again had little to say about the United States. Reports indicated that the Americans and British viewed the Soviet war as lost already. He had little to offer about his plans for Great Britain, other than to say air bombardment would increase. He did not hide the meaning and mass of American arms deliveries. He said he thought America was interested in grabbing part of the British Empire, not in preventing its collapse.[227]

Mussolini—who a week earlier had said Roosevelt was barking because he could not bite—wrote to Hitler on 6 November, and for the first time the United States was his lead topic. "I am convinced it will enter the war, and at a later time will send an expeditionary corps to Egypt." This time, his guess was not wildly wrong.

The American Arsenal Turns the Ignition Key

Meanwhile, in America, the Joint Chiefs of Staff were at work responding to a requirement from the Secretary of War for an estimate covering American aid to Great Britain in the event of a German invasion. The study noted that U.S. policy included, "Insure that the British Isles are not compelled to capitulate as the result of enemy action (economic blockade and/or actual invasion)." The study addressed two scenarios: 1) aid that America could supply under existing constraints against sending troops abroad and use of naval forces for offensive operations in water areas contiguous to the British Isles, and 2) "That the United States is an active participant in the war, or at least that popular support of any military measures necessary to prevent the capitulation of the British Isles will remove the restrictions relative to the employment of American expeditionary forces in Europe."

The assessment argued that deployments in the second scenario should precede actual invasion because the Germans would otherwise take military action to impede transportation and in order to allow proper coordination with the British. Were such authorization granted immediately, planners recommended dispatching in October 1941 three armored and one infantry divisions, four antiaircraft regiments, and one antitank battalion. Another two armored and three infantry divisions, seven antiaircraft regiments, and two antitank battalions would follow in January 1942. In April, two more armored and four infantry divisions, eight antiaircraft regiments, and four antitank battalions would follow. No air units would be available until April without stripping forces committed to U.S. military priorities, and that month America would send two medium bomber and three pursuit interceptor groups.[228]

America and Britain informally accepted a Soviet request for 1,800 planes on 1 October. The United States approved the Soviet Union for Lend-Lease on 1 November.[229]

*

Looking back over the year 1941 in the USA, the war industrial mobilization system in April began to push for curtailment of civilian production to make room for an anticipated surge in armaments and munitions output. The country could no longer supply both guns and butter. The Office of Production Management (OPM) confronted critical shortages in materials, such as steel, equipment, and machine tools. The combined demand that month from the army, navy, Maritime Commission, and the British far exceeded defense industry's capacity, which would have to increase fivefold. In May, OPM ordered the first conversions from civilian to military production. The organization was business friendly, however, and wanted the transition to be gradual. Shortly thereafter, Roosevelt created the Office of Price Administration and Civilian Supply (OPACS), run by New Dealers who wanted to convert as quickly as possible. With overlapping jurisdictions, they feuded constantly over the pace of "curtailment," which referred to the reduction of resources for civilian production.

In July, OPACS announced a curtailment of 50 percent over 12 months to the auto and consumer refrigerator and laundry equipment industries, which after appeal was reduced to 43.3 percent. OPACS was ready to expand the cuts to other producers when Roosevelt, on 28 August, issued an executive order creating the Supply Priorities and Allocation Board (SPAB), a high-level policy group—including Vice President Henry Wallace and Roosevelt's indispensable man Harry Hopkins—to oversee OPM and OPACS. Donald Nelson became the Executive Director. He was an "all outer" with no patience for the informal military–industry alliances that formed to resist change. Hopkins, the Vice President, and two other board members were also all-outers and formed a majority. Nelson will reappear at a key moment below.[230]

SPAB's greatest achievement was to extract from the military clear projected requirements for equipment and munitions, which the military had never provided before. The Victory Program, completed just before Pearl Harbor, outlined the output needed to defeat the Axis Powers. The program's projections were excessive; it anticipated army strength of 8.7 million men, which was close to the actual 8.2 million. But it incorporated activation of 215 combat divisions (89 were activated), 61 armored division (16 were activated), 19 airborne divisions (five were activated), and 10 mountain divisions (one was activated).[231] The Victory Program anticipated ground forces receiving the largest amount of money, closely followed by air, and then a still respectable share for the navy.[232]

When the program became public, Germany's military attaché in Washington reassured Berlin that the plan appeared to make clear that America could not make a major contribution on the battlefield until autumn 1943. It would also require huge quantities of rubber that could only come from the southern area.[233] America actually was to establish a consortium including Firestone, B.F. Goodrich, Goodyear, Standard Oil, and the United States Rubber Company that produced synthetic GR-S (Government Rubber-Styrene), on a commercial scale.[234]

Donald M. Nelson, as chairman of War Production Board (WPB), played a key role in America's industrial mobilization. (Library of Congress)

At its entry into the global war, America lagged behind Germany and Britain in developing key technologies such as radar (as did Japan). Britain had a fully functional radar-controlled fighter defense net. The German navy was the first in the world to equip all cruisers and battleships in the late 1930s with *Seetakt* surface radars. In December 1941, it introduced the FuMG 39T(C) radar that was to control a complex flak and fighter air defense until the end of the war. The U.S. Navy by Pearl Harbor had just outfitted its carriers and six battleships with a first-generation radar system. The U.S. Army had 350 SCR-268 short-range radars to control antiaircraft guns and searchlights. The Army Air Corps was just receiving its first SCR-270 (mobile) and 271 (fixed) radars that could detect an airplane at 130 miles. None of this equipment could be carried by an airplane or small warship.

It seems counterintuitive in terms of common biases regarding national characteristics, but America (and Britain even earlier) evolved a centralized structure to drive technological innovation, whereas Germany and Japan left that largely to scientific experts and defense industry, in part because of interservice rivalries.[235]

CHAPTER 8

Late 1941: War!

Tojo's war cabinet took power on 18 October 1941. Tojo retained his role as war minister and took on duties as interior minister. None of his predecessors had ever arrogated so many powerful positions to himself. The military leadership promoted him to full general, though he was a month short of the required service time. Tojo named Shigenori Togo, a career diplomat, as his foreign minister. Togo had served as ambassador in Berlin and Moscow and was married to a German.[1]

The new navy minister was Admiral Shigetaro Shimada, who had served as Chief of Staff of the Second Fleet (1929), Chief of Staff of the Third Fleet (1930), Vice-Chief of the Naval General Staff (1935), Commander of the Second Fleet (1937), commander of the Kure Naval Station (1938), commander of the China Fleet (1939), and commander of the Yokosuka Naval Station (1941). The career officer had until now assiduously avoided politics.[2]

Hirohito offered one last chance for the government to talk itself out of war. The Emperor expressed his desire that the new Cabinet devote deep consideration to national policy without feeling bound by the decisions made on 6 September.[3]

Tojo obeyed the Emperor's wish, and the government during late October reconsidered the broad range of national policies. The liaison conference members were to conduct an estimate of prospects for war in the initial phase and in a protracted war lasting several years, an estimate of enemy military intentions, an estimate of shipping required at the outbreak of the war and over the next three years, an estimate of budget requirements, and an estimate of the effects of abandoning plans for war against America and its allies. This led to frustration in the IJN. Nagano at a liaison conference on the 23 October burst out, "The navy is consuming 400 tons of oil an hour. The situation is urgent. We want it decided one way or the other quickly."[4]

Remarkably, senior leaders discussed Japan's war potential seriously for the first time at liaison conferences between 24 and 30 October, when one occurred every day. They found that they lacked solid statistics on many questions. For example, using assumptions about shipbuilding capacity somewhat arbitrarily asserted by Navy Minister Shimada, the director of the planning board calculated that by 1943, the rise in shipping capacity would be less than half that needed to meet all requirements.[5]

Although it is unclear whether these were the numbers considered, data that Admiral Yonai provided to interrogators after the war indicated that the IJN in 1941 expected to lose between 800,000 and 1.1 million tons of shipping in the first year of war, and 700,000 to 800,000 tons annually during the next two years. Replacement tonnage would be 300,000, 500,000, and 600,000 during those respective years. At the end of the third year, Japan would have available 5.25 million tons, against an army and navy requirement of 2.2 million and civilian requirement of 2.85 million tons—just over 5 million tons combined.[6]

Teiichi Suzuki, chairman of the Cabinet Planning Board, said after the war that his organization in 1940 had compared Japanese and American industrial and resource capabilities, but that he did not share the information because he saw clearly that the decision for war was already set, and he thought it was the IJN's job—not his—to stop the war because it would have to fight it. America produced 500 times as much petroleum as Japan, 12 times as much pig iron, nine times as much steel ingot and copper, and seven times as much aluminum. Average industrial output was 74 times that of Japan.[7]

The IJN was skeptical that enough steel would be available over the next five years to keep pace with American fleet expansion plans. The IJA told the liaison conference on 27 October that it had stockpiled sufficient arms to last through 1943 at current budget levels. "We do not know what will happen after 1944," Tojo conceded.[8]

Given that even the Japanese lacked reliable statistics, let us consider the estimates of her future enemies as proxies.

A War Department G-2 economic estimate of Japan published in May 1941 admitted that detailed data often were lacking because Japan's 1937 official secrets act had classified such facts. Nevertheless, a key overall judgment was,

> Even though raw materials were available, Japanese industry has not yet reached the stage where the country would be self-sustaining in the manufacture of all necessary supplies for a serious war.... Japanese machinery production is not 10 percent of that produced by the United States.... The best that Japan could claim in the field of machinery is that she is 80 percent self sufficient.

More than half of Japan's machinery imports came from America. G-2 again: "The essential fact remains that Japan lacks essential raw materials to support either her manufacturing trade or a major war effort." This was a bad call; even if Japan proved unable to support *winning* a major war, she could certainly support waging one. The G-2 estimate included the resources available in the Japanese Empire, Manchukuo, and occupied territory in China, but not the resources to the south.

The report added,

> Japan's commercial fleet as of September 1940 consisted of 4,204 ships of 20 tons or more, including 1,202 of 1,000 tons or more. The China Incident has caused great demands on the available tonnage, so much so, in fact, that at the present time there is an acute shortage of ships for the long hauls from the Indies and the Americas. The naval building program has cut down the available building slips and iron and steel which might be used for commercial ship building.[9]

Japan was well positioned to wage a war of two- or three-years duration, according to London's appraisal. The British Ministry of Economic Warfare assessed in September 1941 that Japan in the preceding four years had been able to wage a war in China and maintain an army in Manchukuo, continue its export trade, and expand industrial and raw material production. Despite the war, of its 22 divisions in China, not more than five had been actively engaged in operations at any one time. The Japanese Empire was self-sufficient in food production for two to three years assuming sufficient labor was made available. Production on the home islands and Manchukuo alone would sustain the Japanese population in reasonably well-fed condition. Agriculture was, however, heavily dependent on fertilizer, including nitrogen, phosphate, and potash.

Japan was also heavily dependent on imported oil—for 6 million of the 7 million tons it would need annually on a full war basis. Synthetic production amounted to only 340,000 tons in 1941, although Tokyo planned to expand capacity to 1.6 million tons by 1943 and 4 million tons by 1945. The Japanese steel industry had relied on imported raw materials, iron ore, pig iron, and scrap to produce about 8 million tons of steel per year. Production of iron ore had doubled from 1936 to 1939, and it appeared that Japan would have sufficient raw materials from the home islands, Manchukuo, and Korea to supply their blast furnaces even if imported supplies were cut off. Huge new ovens in Manchukuo assured adequate supplies of coke, and Japan had sufficient stocks and production of manganese to last several years. Japan had two or more years of stocks plus production of key commodities, including copper, aluminum, cobalt, mercury, and chrome. Nickel supplies were sharply constrained at three months' worth, but the sources were nearby: New Caledonia and especially the Netherlands East Indies.

The army and merchant marine included some 2 million men. Japan could probably mobilize 1.5 million more with little difficulty and another half million without serious difficulty, the British concluded.[10]

*

Tojo at the conference on 30 October proposed three options: 1) Avoid war, if possible, and suffer severe austerity; 2) decide on immediate war; and 3) complete military preparations while negotiating with America. In a private conversation, Sugiyama favored the second option, whereas Tojo favored the third. He told Sugiyama that he did not believe the Emperor, who was anxious about the prospects for war, would approve an immediate war decision.[11] He clearly respected the Emperor and did not threaten a coup to get his way, nor, it appears, did Sugiyama.

Navy Secretary Shimada that day wrote in his diary,

> Under the present circumstances, no matter how hard I try to avoid war, it is impossible.... If the navy opposed the war at this late stage, there would be a real danger of a domestic clash, and in that case we'll lose everything.... We [have] no choice but to agree in order to avoid the worst situation of the army and the navy fighting with each other.[12]

At the liaison conference on 1 November, which lasted 17 hours, the military wore down the civilians who wanted to postpone a decision to go to war. Nagano argued vigorously that now was the time for war:

> If the enemy plans a short war, it is exactly what we want and I am fully confident of repelling him and gaining victory. However, this victory will not be a final victory; there is a strong possibility that the war will be a protracted one. In the event of a protracted war, we should establish the foundation for a long war in the first and second years. During this time, there is a chance for victory. After the third year, the victory will depend on the maintenance and increase of naval strength, material, and spiritual national fighting strength, and changes in the world situation. Therefore, the outcome is difficult to predict.[13]

Eventually, the group reached unanimity that if diplomacy failed to provide an acceptable deal by 30 November, Japan would go to war on 1 December.[14] There is no hint in the record that fear of a coup played any role in the outcome.

Fukudome said after the war that it was only at this time that the Navy Section formally informed the Army Section at IGHQ about the Pearl Harbor attack, though as Hattori recorded, working-level discussions had begun in August. When he presented the plan to IJA operations chief Lieutenant General Shinichi Tanaka, the general had no comments because there was no IJA role, beyond saying that he had not imagined that such an operation was possible, but if it were, it would be wonderful. He wished the IJN success. Somewhat more surprisingly, the IJN only informed Tojo about the same time.[15]

At the request of the Emperor, an imperial conference, which this time included former premiers of Japan, met on 5 November to discuss the formal decision to go to war against the United States, Great Britain, and the Netherlands. General Suzuki of the planning board worried about fighting an extended war against those enemies while the war continued in China, but the prospects for victory in the early months was so great that war was better than waiting around for the enemy to increase the pressure. According to Toland, Sugiyama acknowledged that the war would probably be protracted but that Japan could establish a strategically impregnable position and frustrate the enemy, but this statement does not appear in Hattori's detailed record of the back-and-forth discussion.[16]

Tojo argued that Japan was placed in a position where resort to arms against the United States could not be avoided. According to Tojo's testimony after the war, no one present at the meetings believed Japan should accept American terms. Even Admiral Yonai said Japan could not afford to become "poorer by inches" in terms of its national power, according to Kido's diary.

Some participants expressed "negative and dissuading opinions" about going to war, Tojo later admitted, but they ceded the decision to the government. Former Premier Hiranuma, for example, remarked that he agreed that Japan was equal to a prolonged war with the United States in spiritual strength but doubted its ability in material power, according to Kido's diary. Admiral Okada expressed doubt about maintaining the supply of materials. Others worried about keeping up public support. Konoye expressed concern about resorting to "a hasty war."

Former Premier Reijiro Wakatsuki, Kido recorded, argued, "The war should be fought to the last, even if there was no chance to win, if it was a defensive one for our national existence and independence. But we should avoid the war if we intend to realize our ideals such as the Asiatic Co-Prosperity Sphere or the stabilizing power in Asia, because such a war would be very dangerous."[17]

In the end, there was no formal dissent. The policy was set.[18]

Navy Minister Shimada confirmed to interrogators after the surrender that he actively supported the decision to go to war. After the imperial conference, he consulted extensively with Navy Chief of Staff Nagano on the means of executing the attack on Pearl Harbor. He approved the plan of the Naval General Staff that Washington be given no more than one hour's warning of hostilities.[19]

The IGHQ Navy Section on 5 November ordered the Combined Fleet to make operational preparations for war against America, Britain, and the Netherlands and directed the fleet to advance ships to the assembly points. The Army Section activated the Southern Army and South Seas Detachment on 6 November and ordered them to prepare for invasion of the southern strategic area, including American-administered Guam. Separately, the Commander-in-Chief of the China Expeditionary Force issued orders for the attack on Hong Kong.[20]

The Navy General Staff gathered all fleet commanders in Tokyo sometime between 5 and 7 November, according to Fukudome, and revealed the entire operational plan. Officers were instructed to keep it most secret and to issue only verbal orders. Yamamoto held three separate meetings. At one attended by Fukudome, he discussed what date to start the war. Yamamoto wanted to attack on a Sunday, but the first Sunday of December was too soon given the preparations remaining. He suggested 7/8 December, and Nagano agreed.[21]

In order to ensure the fastest possible resumption of oil production in the East Indies, the IJA decided to use paratroopers for the first time to try to capture the facilities intact. Drilling equipment and personnel stood ready in Japan to rush to the area.[22]

*

From 3 November on, Japanese officials made clear to the German mission in Tokyo that hostilities with America were imminent, as was a large operation to the south, including the Philippines. Ott provided final confirmation 18 November. Ott urged Ribbentrop to seek some trade-offs from Japan before declaring war against America.[23]

Seeing as how Hitler had told Matsuoka that Germany would enter the war if Japan got into one, one might have expected a flurry of last-minute thinking about the military consequences for Germany and furious efforts to gather more intelligence while a German mission existed in Washington. None of this occurred.

Nomura received a cable in Washington on 19 November telling him that if the Japanese short-wave broadcast included the words, "East wind, rain," it would indicate that Japan had decided on war. He was then to destroy his codes.[24]

On 21 November, the IGHQ Navy Section ordered the Hawaii attack force commanded by Admiral Tadaichi Nagumo to advance to the rendezvous point.[25]

Ott cabled Berlin from Tokyo on 23 November that all signs were that Japan was going to move south to occupy Thailand and the Dutch oilfields on Borneo. The Japanese wanted to know if Germany would make common cause if Japan started a war. On the 28th, Ribbentrop told Oshima that Hitler was determined that if Japan went to war against America, Germany would join the war immediately.[26]

On 26 November, the Hawaii attack force sailed for waters northwest of Hawaii.[27]

The government and senior statesmen met on 29 November at the Imperial Palace. After dining with the Emperor, they offered their views informally in a study room. Hirohito opened the conversation by remarking, "The situation has become grave, has it not?" Most said that it would be better to maintain the current situation than to commence hostilities. Others supported going to war. Tojo expressed the government's determination to fight.[28]

According to Tojo, his Cabinet met on 29 November to consider ways of ending the war if it were to develop unfavorably. He told the Cabinet, "We have investigated a plan to negotiate peace at the proper time through the mediation of the Soviet Union or Vatican, but we have not yet secured a definite plan in which we are confident. So, will any member please suggest one?" Apparently, no one did.[29] Staff-level discussions in support of the liaison conferences had been under way since 15 November and come up with nothing better than to become so self-sufficient and invulnerable as to sap America's will to fight, optimally helped along by Britain's surrender and Chiang's capitulation.[30]

Admiral Ugaki recorded what he thought of America in his diary on 29 November. The United States had not accepted a single demand of the Japanese Empire in the negotiations. "How they insult us! ... The only way for us is to make short work of the United States."[31]

What Tojo had wanted for more than a year, he got. The decision, finally and irrevocably taken on 1 December at a Council in the Imperial Presence, was for war, with hostilities to commence in early December. The Emperor told Kido that he had given Tojo approval on the basis of the "affirmative answers" from the navy minister and chief of the Navy General Staff regarding "the success of the war." The military was to complete final preparations, while the diplomats engaged in a last endeavor to reach a settlement.[32] Expecting as much, the Army General Staff had already ordered all attachés abroad on 9 November to collect information on "the extent of the determination of America and Britain to make war on Japan."[33]

Emperor Hirohito after the war cast the decision taken that day in terms of having to *cancel* the attack on Pearl Harbor, rather than choosing to go to war, which smacks

PACIFIC THEATER 1941–1945

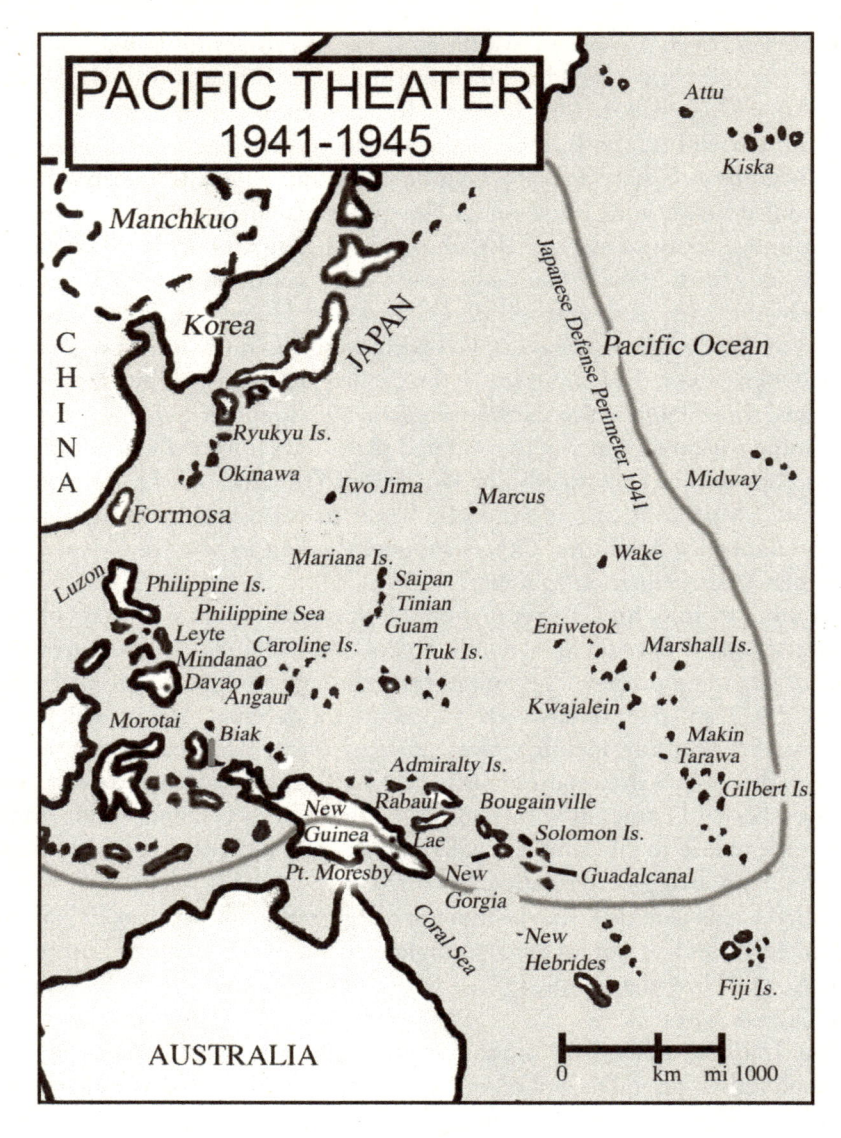

of self-justification. But, as we have seen, his formulation reflected the truth. He told a small group of aides in 1946 that if he had tried to stop the attack, "there would have been a coup d'état" in which he likely would have been assassinated. Even then, he said, "a very violent war" would have broken out. "[T]he oil embargo cornered Japan," he reasoned. "If, at that time, I [had] suppressed opinions in favor of the war, public opinion would certainly have surged, with people asking questions about why Japan should surrender so easily when it had a highly efficient army and navy, well trained over the years." He moreover claimed that he was constrained by the

Meiji Constitution. "It was unavoidable for me as a constitutional monarch under the constitutional polity to do anything but give approval to the Tojo Cabinet on the decision to start the war."[34]

Tojo at his war crimes trial in 1947 agreed with Hirohito's depiction of the political balance of power. "The Emperor had no free choice in the governmental structure setting up the Cabinet and the Supreme Command. He was not in a position to reject the recommendations and advice of the Cabinet and the High Command." The Emperor could indirectly express "hopes and wishes" that were subject to examination by the Cabinet and Supreme Command, but the "recommendations and suggestions, after this careful examination, had to be approved by the Emperor and never to be rejected."[35]

Having received orders to initiate war on 8 December Japan time, Ugaki on 2 December transmitted a message to the fleet: "Climb Mt. Niitaka 1280." This meant, "X-Day has been fixed at 0000 of 8 December."[36]

Ciano recorded in his diary on 3 December:

> Sensational move by Japan. The Ambassador asks for an audience with the Duce and reads him a long statement on the progress of the negotiations with America, concluding with the assertion that they have reached a dead end. Then, invoking the appropriate clause in the Tripartite Fact, he asks that Italy declare war on America immediately after the outbreak of hostilities and proposes the signature of an agreement not to conclude a separate peace. The interpreter translating this request was trembling like a leaf. The Duce gave fullest assurances, reserving the right to confer with Berlin before giving a reply. The Duce was pleased with the communication and said: "We are now on the brink of the inter-continental war which I predicted as early as September 1939." What does this new event mean? In any case, it means that Roosevelt has succeeded in his maneuver. Since he could not enter into the war immediately and directly, he has entered it indirectly by letting himself be attacked by Japan. Furthermore, this event also means that every prospect of peace is becoming further and further removed, and that it is now easy-much too easy-to predict a long war. Who will be able to hold out longest? It is on this basis that the problem must be considered. Berlin's answer will be somewhat delayed, because Hitler has gone to the southern front to see General Kleist, whose armies continue to give way under the pressure of an unexpected Soviet offensive.[37]

The next day, Ciano recorded, "Berlin's reaction to the Japanese move is extremely cautious. Perhaps they will accept because they cannot get out of it, but the idea of provoking America's intervention pleases the Germans less and less. Mussolini, on the other hand, is pleased about it."[38]

Ambassador Ott reported to Berlin on 5 December that the Japanese government was wrestling with how to begin the unavoidable war against America. A declaration of war seemed necessary, but should it be issued simultaneously or after the fact?[39]

On the eve of hostilities, the Japanese defense attaché in Washington sent the Army General Staff an appraisal of American strategy in a war that combined the glaringly obvious with the bizarre—and certainly made no contribution to well-informed decision-making in Tokyo. America would cooperate with the Australians, British,

Dutch, Chinese, and Russians to blockade Japan by destroying her communications and launching air raids. She would devote all her resources to building warships, planes, and bombers to gain absolute supremacy in these arms. Then she would await the right moment to strike a decisive blow against Japan, which would not come before the end of 1942. America would seek bases in Australia, India, China, the South Pacific, and Siberia. Paratroop attacks from the Philippines and Guam could not be discounted. The navy would seek through skillful maneuver to draw the Japanese fleet into an early test of main strength.[40]

Admiral Ugaki enumerated in his diary on 7 December, Japan time, the reasons he thought it was the right time for war. His view focused mainly on the factors driving the timing, rather than the strategic consideration of ending the war in China that had gripped the senior-most leadership. Still, his logic illustrates why war did not seem like a suicidal gamble to a well-informed military man:

1. War preparations were well advanced, though one could never be perfectly prepared.
2. The Army, typically obsessed with the Soviet Union, had "awakened to the importance of the southern areas," if only temporarily.
3. The Tripartite Alliance and occupation of French Indochina had clearly identified America and Britain as the enemies, and if Japan were to fight them, it had "better start while the war situation in Europe is developing favorably for Germany and Italy."
4. Japan had come to realize it could not establish the Greater East Asia Co-Prosperity Sphere without destroying the United States and Britain first. "And our nation is quite tired of the [China] Incident and they want something else at present."
5. The occupation of Indochina had had a bigger effect on the United States and Britain than Japan had expected and provoked the freezing of funds. Unable to buy oil, Japan had to fight for petroleum to remain independent.
6. American war preparations were progressing, and it was time to strike. "If it is delayed two or three years, the material balance between Japan and the United States will become beyond comparison."
7. The Japanese estimated that the Russians, albeit tenacious, would not ally with the United States and Britain this winter.
8. Strong elements of the Navy had insisted that if the war were not begun by December, it should be put off for some time.
9. Research tended to show that if Japan conquered the resource-rich areas to the south, it could fight on indefinitely. "Those in authority" had become convinced of this.
10. The United States had been too rigid diplomatically, so that not even "dove-like" persons wanted to continue negotiations.
11. "The national policy was in accord with strategy, and the latter was stronger than the former." This appears to mean that military strategy drove all other policy.
12. "[I]f this chance had been missed, it would be difficult for us to stand up again."[41]

At sea, the Hawaii task force received a last intelligence report from IGHQ. As of 6 December, nine battleships, three light cruisers, three seaplane tenders, and 17 destroyers were anchored in Pearl Harbor. Four light cruisers and three destroyers were docked. All aircraft carriers and heavy cruisers were operating elsewhere. Other than the last item, all counts were erroneous.[42]

Putting the "World" into the World War

Although Admiral Ugaki was in command of operations in the Southwest Pacific, his flagship received all message traffic related to the Pearl Harbor operation. The Japanese were reading or listening to American communications and knew that the enemy did not expect an attack. They were able to follow battle orders during the raid. During the strike, Ugaki received Japanese pilot reports of their successes against individual targets. It was one occasion when the Japanese enjoyed substantial transparency of the enemy's activities through intercepts, an advantage their foes would enjoy for most of the war.[43]

The Navy General Staff considered the odds of the attack on Pearl Harbor succeeding as fifty-fifty, according to Fukudome, an assessment he shared. It was a "calculated risk." The task force was to take no unnecessary risks, and if there was any doubt, if anything went wrong during the cross-Pacific voyage, the Operations Section intended to call the task force home.[44]

As is widely known, Japanese plans to break diplomatic relations shortly before the attack ran afoul of delays in decoding the message from Tokyo, so by the time Nomura delivered it, Japan had already staged a "sneak attack." The language of the message was not a classic declaration of war in any case.[45]

*

Commander Mitsuo Fuchida, who coordinated the entire attack plan and commanded the first wave, was a veteran of the China war with 3,000 hours in the air.[46] He recalled:

> Under my direct command were 49 level bombers. About 1,500 feet to my right and slightly below me were 40 torpedo planes. The same distance to my left, but about 600 feet above me, were 51 dive bombers, and flying cover for the formation there were 43 fighters....
>
> I had a difficult decision to make. Problem was, I didn't know whether the Americans had caught on or not.... Playing a hunch, I had made up my mind that we could make a surprise attack, and therefore ordered deployment for "Surprise" by raising my signal pistol outside the canopy and firing one "black dragon."
>
> 0749 hours—The sky cleared as we moved in on the target, and Pearl Harbor was plainly visible from the northeast valley of the island. I studied our objective through binoculars. They were there, alright—two, four, eight [battleships].
>
> "Notify whole squadron to plunge into attack!" I ordered the radioman, who began typing the key. The order was in plain code, "*to, to, to*." ["charge!"]
>
> 0755 hours—The first bombs fell on Hickam. The dive-bombers ... divided into three groups and attacked Hickam Field, Ford Island, and Wheeler Field. In a very short time, huge billows of black smoke were rising from these bases.
>
> 0757 hours—Lieutenant Commander [Shigeharu] Murata and his torpedo planes attacked the battleships in the harbor. I saw waterspouts rising alongside the battleships, followed by more and more waterspouts.
>
> My high-level bomber group kept east of Oahu.... I continued to watch the sky over the harbor, and none but Japanese planes were in the air, and there were no indications of air combat.... I ordered the following message sent to the fleet: "I have succeeded in making a surprise attack. Request you relay this report to Tokyo."

0600 hours: In single-file formation, the fighter planes strafed the airfields.

Now it was time to launch our level-bombing attacks.... As my group made its bomb run, enemy anti-aircraft fire suddenly came to life. Dark gray bursts blossomed here and there until the sky was clouded with shattering near misses.... I was startled by the rapidity of the counterattack, which came less than five minutes after the first bomb had fallen.

Suddenly, the plane bounced as if struck by a huge club.

"The fuselage is holed to port," reported the radioman behind me, "and a steering control wire is damaged."

I asked hurriedly if the plane was under control, and the pilot assured me that it was....

0805 hours: The level bombers began to drop their bombs on the battleships.

Suddenly, a colossal explosion occurred in battleship row. A huge column of dark red smoke rose to 1,000 feet.... The attack was in full swing, and smoke from fires and explosions filled most of the sky over Pearl Harbor....

0840 hours: The attack of the second wave was ordered, and they swept in....

As I observed the damage in the three hours that my planes were in the area, the effectiveness of the torpedoes seemed remarkable, and I was struck by the shortsightedness of the USN in being so generally unprepared.[47]

Nagano and other senior officers, including Fukudome, received the report of the successful attack before 0500 hours. They went wild with joy and remarked on the good luck of the task force.[48]

The attack sank or badly damaged 18 ships, destroyed 188 planes and damaged 159 more, and killed 2,403 Americans. But, of course, most of the ships would be repaired and return to battle, and none of the American carriers had been in port.[49]

Zero pilot Sakai participated in the first air attack on Clark Field, Luzon, Philippines. The Japanese had developed flying techniques to stretch the Zero's range

A Japanese view of the attack on Pearl Harbor. (rarehistoricalphotos.com)

far beyond specs to allow fighters to fly the 900-mile round trip from Formosa, with sufficient fuel for combat at the target. Fog delayed the attack by five hours, and pilots left Formosa worried that the Americans, forewarned by Pearl Harbor, would have their defenses at peak readiness. Sakai recorded in his memoir:

> At 1330 we flashed in from the South China Sea and headed for Clark Field. The sight which met us was unbelievable. Instead of encountering a swarm of American fighters diving at us in attack, we looked down and saw some 60 American bombers and fighters neatly parked along the airfield runways. They squatted there like sitting ducks; the Americans made no attempt to disperse the planes and increase their safety on the ground. We failed utterly to comprehend the enemy's attitude....
>
> At 1345, the 27 bombers with their Zero escorts approached from the north and moved directly into their bombing runs. The attack was perfect. Long strings of bombs tumbled from the bays and dropped toward the targets the bombardiers had studied in detail for so long. Their accuracy was phenomenal—it was, in fact, the most accurate bombing I ever witnessed by our own planes throughout the war. The entire air base seemed to be rising into the air with explosions.[50]

While strafing the airfield, Sakai and his wingmen encountered five P-40 fighters, one of which he shot down.

Koichi Kido walked to his office the morning of 8 December, which was Pearl Harbor Day in Japan. He recorded in his diary:

> I was climbing up the Akasaka slope. I saw the rising sun above a building over there. I thought it was symbolic of the destiny of this country that now had entered the war with the USA and England, the two greatest powers in the world. I closed my eyes and prayed for the victory of our navy planes making an attack upon Pearl Harbor by that time.
>
> At 0730, I met with the Premier, the chief of the general staff, and the chief of the navy general staff. I heard from them the great news of our successful attack on Hawaii. I saw the Emperor at 1140 and talked until 1200. I was very impressed by the self-possessed attitude of the Emperor on this day. The imperial proclamation of war was issued.[51]

The Imperial edict declaring war made clear that China was the root cause of hostilities. It read:

> The Emperor of Japan, upon the Throne of a line of Emperors unbroken for ages eternal, blessed with Divine Grace hereby presents to you loyal and courageous subjects:
>
> I do hereby declare war upon America and England. Officers and men of our Imperial Army and Navy, exert your utmost and go forth into battle. Officials and authorities of Our Government, attend to your duties honestly and conscientiously. Each and every subject, do your part diligently, and with the entire nation in one accord putting forth the whole strength of the Empire, make certain that no blunders are made in achieving the objectives of this war.
>
> It has been primarily the glorious and traditional policy of the Imperial Family to contribute to the peace of the world by consolidating and maintaining stability in East Asia. This policy I have faithfully pursued. The constant gist of diplomatic relations of the Empire with the powers of the world has been based upon mutual sharing of prosperity and the promotion of sincere and friendly contacts. But, now, unfortunately we have begun hostilities with America and England. It is indeed an unavoidable happening. But it was not my wish that China, not understanding the true motive of the Empire, should indiscriminately take up arms, disturbing

the peace of East Asia, and finally forcing the Empire to retaliate with military force. Over four years have passed since then. Fortunately, the National Government has been newly set up. The Empire of Japan has taken up a friendly attitude of good neighborliness with this government and has cooperated with it; but the remaining regime in Chungking, dependent upon support from America and England, has forced brother against brother to harbor ill will against each other from opposite sides of the fence. Hiding under the fair name of peace, America and England are aiding the remaining regime, prolonging the disorder in East Asia, and making rampant their inordinate desire of controlling the Orient. Furthermore, they have inveigled the other powers into strengthening their military preparations around Japan and have taken a challenging attitude toward us. They further placed every obstacle in the way of peaceful commercial endeavors of the Empire, and finally, boldly cut off economic relations, which seriously threatened the very existence of our country. I have strived through the Government to restore conditions back to normal while there was yet peace. I have had patience for a long time, but not having the spirit of mutual concession, they have needlessly delayed the solution to the situation. During this time, they have, instead, greatly increased the economic and military threat, striving to force us into submission. The course of affairs has progressed thus far. The years of effort that the Empire has spent in endeavoring to establish stability in East Asia have come to naught, and the Empire faces a dire crisis due to the trend of incidents up to this point. For self-preservation, there is nothing left to do but to spring up in arms and smash all obstacles before us.

By the Divine Spirits of Our Imperial Ancestors Above, I have faith and trust in the loyalty and courage of my subjects, to enlarge upon the great work which the Imperial Ancestors have left us, and immediately weed out the roots of disaster, firmly establishing everlasting peace in East Asia and preserving the glory of the Empire.

Imperial Name   Imperial Seal   Dec. 8, 1941[52]

The Navy Department of IGHQ released this communiqué at 1300 Tokyo time, 8 December:

1. At daybreak of the eighth, the Imperial Navy dared a desperate, grand air attack against the American fleet and military strength in the Hawaii area.
2. At daybreak of the eighth, the Imperial Navy sank the English gunboat *Petoreru*, and the American gunboat *Wake* surrendered.
3. At daybreak of the eighth, the Imperial Navy very successfully bombed Singapore.
4. Early in the morning of the eighth, the Imperial Navy bombed the enemy military installations at Davao, Wake, and Guam.[53]

The Imperial General Headquarters and the government decided at a liaison conference on 10 December to call the war just declared, including the China Incident, the "Greater East Asia War."[54]

Ugaki recorded in his diary on 10 December that according to a radio report, there was talk in Washington about court martialing the navy and air defense commanders responsible for protecting Pearl Harbor. It would be a mistake to treat subordinates so, he thought, because the fault lay in pursuing a confrontational policy toward Japan without preparing militarily to back it up.

He noted the declarations of war among Germany, Italy, and the United States. "Now it has really turned out to be the Second World War. Everything connected with future operations and leadership of the New World Order rests upon the shoulders of our empire."[55]

Japanese submarines on 10 December twice fired torpedoes at the aircraft carrier USS *Enterprise* 200 miles northeast of Oahu and narrowly missed both times. American luck and effective antisubmarine responses denied the IJN a second major triumph at Hawaii.[56]

On 13 December, Ugaki noted his expectation that the war would be a long one. "[W]hen the war becomes protracted, can our leaders and authorities lead our nation for as long as five or ten years, maintaining the people's morale and overcoming every difficulty?"

On the 16th, he added, "[A] blow to Hawaii must have stung them to the quick. But we must bear in mind, on reflection, that they have an enormous predominant air strength—planes and carriers—and we cannot forecast the game they will play to avenge this mishap. Of this future threat we cannot be too careful."[57]

*

The British Secret Intelligence Service in February 1942 provided OSS with a report gathered the fourth week of December obtained the "very reliable indirect means" describing Japan's war aims as communicated to a military attaché abroad:

(i) Japan will in no case link the war in the Far East with the war in Europe. The issue of the war in Europe is of no direct interest to Japan, but it is to Japan's advantage that all the Great Powers in Europe are weakened.

(ii) The Japanese objectives are to occupy Singapore and the whole Malay Peninsula; the Philippine Islands, Borneo, Sumatra, Java, New Guinea and the whole archipelago; and to compel Great Britain and the USA to recognize the above area and also China as the Japanese sphere of interest.

(iii) The Japanese General Staff are convinced that this can be accomplished in six months, because:
  (a) Japan has ample forces available for the tasks in view. If necessary, further divisions can be brought from Japan.
  (b) The Ministry of [the Navy] consider that the American fleet has been so far crippled in the attack on Pearl Harbor that it can no longer effectively interfere with Japanese operations.
  (c) A strong Fifth Column exists in all the territory to be occupied.

(iv) After having occupied the territory as in paragraph (ii) above, Japan will propose peace negotiations with Great Britain and the USA and will invite these Powers to recognize the new status quo.

(v) If Great Britain and the USA accept, Japan will declare herself neutral for the remainder of the European war.

(vi) If Great Britain and the USA do not accept, Japan will threaten to attack India.[58]

Even asked by American interrogators after the war how Japan at this time thought a peace would emerge that granted it the territories it planned to conquer, Keeper of the Privy Seal Kido explained, "The plan was to seek a termination of the war at an opportune moment and that opportune moment would be at a time when the armed forces of the countries would come to a point where the fighting would be fixed [stalemate], but unfortunately for Japan, such a time never came because of the strong pressure by the United States Armed Forces."[59]

Admiral Ugaki, in his capacity as operations chief of the Combined Fleet, was already pondering American counterstrokes. On 25 December, he wrote in his diary,

> We have to investigate and study the organization, routes, and time of US task forces' assaults (including air raids), including the means of destroying them all. It is most certain that, after the organization of the new forces, the United States will come against us for retaliation. If we could destroy them completely, for the time being they will be baffled in attempting anything. This must be done by all means.
>
> Tokyo should be protected from air raids; this is the most important thing to be borne in mind.[60]

Germany: The Rashest of Acts

In Germany, Berlin and other German cities in 1941 were enduring nighttime bombing raids by the RAF, but the state of the strategic air war probably looked reasonably manageable, all things considered. The RAF medium and heavy bomber force was expanding toward a year-end goal of 569 aircraft, and 100-plus bomber raids had struck Cologne, Bremen, and Hamburg in May. Yet, the RAF was dropping about half its bombs on decoy sites when aiming for industrial targets. In fact, the German government decided not to dispute British claims of damage inflicted to ensure secrecy. Improving integration of search lights, flak, and an increasing number of night fighters, meanwhile, raised to the cost of the raids to an average by late 1941 of 10 percent of the bombers dispatched. The night of 7 November, 169 aircraft attacked Berlin and lost 13 percent. That same night, 55 aircraft struck Mannheim and 43 the Ruhr, suffering losses of 13 and 21 percent respectively. Bomber Command decided to cease deep-penetration attacks and stick to targets closer to the coasts. It still lost 141 more bombers through the end of the year. Berlin was to remain free of large-scale air raids for 14 months.[61]

The British by September 1941 received information from a long-time "absolutely reliable" source with access to the German General Staff indicating that the German offensive in the east was exhausting itself, and that the High Command would have to order a halt and adopt a defensive line until spring 1942. The front was to stabilize by 1 November along the line Murmansk Railway–Kalinin–Moscow–Voronezh–River Don–Sea of Azov. The source reported that the Germans hoped there would be a revolution in the USSR over the winter, but they realized that if this did not occur, Germany would not be able to terminate the war in 1942. Schemes to invade Britain had been abandoned, and Germany planned to wage an air war against the British population in 1942.[62]

The Germans did, in fact, stop the advance on 31 October to reorganize and resupply, but attacked again on 15 November.

It was becoming clear that Germany was not going to defeat the USSR in a single stroke as Hitler had expected. As the British source reported, the army in the east was being worn down to a shadow of its starting strength. Hitler's armaments chief Fritz Todt and another solidly loyal industrialist told Hitler on 29 November that Germany could not produce enough armaments to win the war militarily and painted America and Britain's industrial potential in apocalyptic terms. Germany had to end the war through political means. "How then shall I end the war," asked Hitler. He received no real answer.[63]

Germany's fortunes on the Eastern Front quite suddenly suffered a horrendous reverse. On 5 December, the first Soviet counteroffensive of the war blasted out of the ice and snow along a 500-mile front, primarily against Army Group Center, which would soon be reeling back from the outskirts of Moscow.
Meanwhile, near-hostilities simmered in the Atlantic. Hitler on 8 November railed,

> If today new threats particularly from America are directed against Germany, that, too, has received my timely attention. Already more than a year ago, I declared: Regardless of what ship carries war materials, that is, materials for killing men, it will be torpedoed. If now the American President Roosevelt ... now believes he can intimidate us by his order to shoot, then there is only one answer I can give this gentleman. President Roosevelt has ordered his ships to shoot the moment they sight German ships. And I have ordered German ships not to shoot when they sight American vessels but to defend themselves as soon as attacked.[64]

Goebbels recorded in his diary that Hitler was "extraordinarily happy" with the news of Pearl Harbor. Though he does not quote Hitler as saying it, after they had spoken, Goebbels recorded that the Americans would no longer be able to continue full-scale deliveries to the UK, which he may have picked up from his Führer.[65] Walter Warlimont, still a staff officer at OKW, recalled that Hitler and senior commanders received word of the attack "with an ecstasy of rejoicing." Warlimont had visited the United States to assess the capabilities of its defense industries. "The few [of us] who, even at this moment, felt they could see further, became even lonelier." The OKW's situation report for 7 December cited brief wire service reports of the operations unfolding across the Pacific, but from the next day included fairly detailed information from the Japanese Embassy and IGHQ announcements. The OKW chronicles contain the outline of the Japanese war plan as of 5 November, indicating that Tokyo had shared this information.

Japan's entry into the war provoked no instructions from Hitler to the OKW staff for action, however. Nobody had really thought about what Germany should do if America entered the war. Hitler and his entourage, including Generals Wilhelm Keitel, the OKW chief of staff, and Alfred Jodl, the operations chief, boarded a special train to Berlin.[66] There, Oshima waited to request that Germany expeditiously declare war on America.[67]

Ciano recorded in his diary on 8 December,

> A night telephone call from Ribbentrop; he is overjoyed about the Japanese attack on America. He is so happy about it that I am happy with him, though I am not too sure about the final advantages of what has happened. One thing is now certain: that America will enter the conflict, and that the conflict will be so long that she will be able to realize all her potential

force. This morning I told this to the King who had been pleased about the event. He ended by admitting that in the "long run" I may be right. Mussolini was happy too. For a long time, he has favored a definite clarification of relations between America and the Axis.[68]

Hitler on the 9th lifted his restrictions on U-boat attacks against American warships. It would take weeks for boats to reach their positions off the American east coast.[69]

As the Emperor had urged, Japan obtained the signatures of Germany and Italy on a no-single-peace treaty on 10 December. The day seemed particularly cheerful in Tokyo in light of news of the successful Japanese attack against the British warships *Prince of Wales* and *Repulse* off the Malay Peninsula.[70]

Hitler had promised Matsuoka that Germany would declare war, a promise he had reiterated through Ribbentrop and Oshima only a few days earlier. It was one promise he kept. In addition, to all appearances, Hitler seized on making war against America in part to distract attention from the failure of his ambitions to defeat the Soviet Union in 1941. Hitler in June 1942 referred during a dinner conversation to "Japan's entry into the war [that] burst upon us in a critical moment of the eastern struggle."[71]

Hitler declares war against America on 11 December 1941. Sitting at the front bench on the left of image are, right to left, Foreign Minister Joachim von Ribbentrop, Grand Admiral Erich Raeder, Field Marshal Walter von Brauchitsch, Field Marshal Wilhelm Keitel, *Reichsminister* Dr. Wilhelmm Frick, and Josef Goebbels. Armaments chief Franz Todt is seated at the right end of the second bench behind the aforementioned. (Bundesarchiv)

On 11 December, Hitler stepped into the lights at the Reichstag and declared war on the United States. Italy was following suit. Unlike the Japanese declaration of war, which established a strategic explanation for the conflict, Hitler's speech consisted of insults against Roosevelt and the charge that it was the American President who really wanted the conflict. Germany's formal declaration offered,

> Although Germany for her part has always strictly observed the rules of international law in her dealings with the United States throughout the present war, the Government of the United States has finally proceeded to overt acts of war against Germany. It has, therefore, virtually created a state of war. The Reich Government therefore breaks off all diplomatic relations with the United States and declares that under these circumstances brought about by President Roosevelt, Germany too considers herself to be at war with the United States, as from today.[72]

For what little it mattered, Ciano recorded in his diary on 11 December, "[Mussolini] is occupied with thoughts of war against America." Ribbentrop contacted Ciano to request that Italy join Germany in an appeal to all members of the Axis to declare war against the United States.[73]

Jodl called Warlimont from Berlin. "You have heard that the Führer has just declared war on America?"

"Yes, and we couldn't be more surprised," answered Warlimont.

Jodl continued, "The staff must now examine where the United States is most likely to employ the bulk of her forces initially, the Far East or Europe. We cannot take further decisions until that has been clarified."

"Agreed; this examination is obviously necessary, but so far we have never even considered a war against the United States and so have no data on which to base this examination; we can hardly undertake the job just like that."

"See what you can do."[74]

OKW on 14 December issued an optimistic strategic assessment, saying the Japanese attack had robbed the Western Allies of the strategic initiative in 1942. The Western Allies would probably pursue a "Germany first" strategy and would stage a full-scale invasion attempt in 1943. The key in 1942 was to capture the Caucasus oilfields, which would starve the Soviets of oil and position Germany to hit the British in the Middle East and capture the Persian oilfields.[75] Warlimont most likely became privy in January to the intelligence on the results of the Arcadia Conference and from then knew for certain that the Allies planned to move first against Germany.

Reichsmarschall Hermann Göring claimed to interrogators after the war,

> I was astonished when Germany declared war on the United States.... [W]e were not bound under our treaty with Japan to come to its aid since Japan had been the aggressor. Hitler said that we were in effect at war already, with ships having been sunk or fired on, and that he must soothe the Japanese. It was unnecessary for us to accept the responsibility of striking the first blow.... I believe Hitler was convinced that as a result of the Japanese attack, the main brunt of the United States' force would be brought to bear on the Far East and would not constitute such a danger for Germany.[76]

Göring added, "We were convinced there was no chance to avoid war." (FMS note: It is possible that Göring was trying to shift onto Hitler full responsibility for declaring war, but Hitler *was* the one who did it, and Göring was correct that Germany was not bound by treaty to do so. Göring's description of Hitler's rationale is consistent with the message the German army attaché in Washington had been sending back regarding a likely American focus on the Pacific, as well as with Hitler's well-documented comments on the U-boat war. Ribbentrop's testimony at Nürnberg offered a similar explanation for Hitler's thinking.[77])

At this time, according to Göring, the German leadership took seriously Roosevelt's public promises that the United States would build "a bridge of ships" across the Atlantic and send a constant stream of planes. Still, Göring, at least, thought American claims regarding shipbuilding rates were exaggerated, and people around him assumed that the Liberty ships must be shoddily constructed and joked about them as "floating coffins."[78]

For the moment, however, from the Axis perspective, the great American naval power confronted a two-ocean war with less than a one-ocean navy.[79]

Hitler's personal aide Linge told Soviet interrogators that discussion at Hitler's lunch table the day he declared war revolved around America's fighting abilities. Halder, chief of OKH, who had fought Americans in the Great War, was scornful.

Hitler thought America would face shipping constraints, though Japan had a more realistic view. U.S. industry far outproduced rivals in aircraft carriers and other warships, as well as merchantmen. This is the USS *Hornet* under construction on 3 March 1941 at Newport News Shipbuilding. (Wikimedia Commons)

American officers could not compare to Prussians. They were businessmen in uniform who feared for their lives and had a long way to go in the art of war.

Several days later, the Soviet report continued,

> Hitler appeared [in Linge's quarters]. He occasionally dropped in on Linge to listen to popular music on his radio. Hitler received the latest reports from the fronts, then sat down at the desk and asked for his spectacles. It was reported that German submarines had sunk American ships. "Do you see how good this open war against America is for us? Now we can really strike." He pointed out that America was tied down in the Pacific theater. This led one to hope that German submarines could even more effectively disturb the provisioning of Britain from America. Hitler leaned right back and poured out his contempt for the Americans. He said that an American car had never won an international tournament; that American aircraft looked fine, but their motors were worthless. This was proof for him that the much-lauded industries of America were terribly overrated. They didn't really have to perform well, only in an average way, and benefited from lots of discounting.[80]

Hitler at this time had no concept for how to defeat the United States. He hoped that knocking off the USSR in 1942, combined with Japan achieving at least a stalemate in the Pacific, would take care of the America problem.[81]

Military attaché Boetticher met with Hitler and Ribbentrop at the command center in Russia in May 1942 after returning to Germany following the closure of the embassy in Washington. In an account he wrote in 1947, he said Hitler delivered a monologue asserting it would take America years to mass-produce tanks and relating various American offenses against him. Boetticher recorded that he had no opportunity to respond, and that Hitler seemed unaware of his report on mass production of four-engine bombers. He told State Department interviewers, however, that he warned Hitler about the United States' military and industrial potential. Hitler declared that such production was "impossible."[82] (Boetticher did report to Berlin on America's rapidly expanding output of four-engine bombers and projected output of 500 per month by June 1943.[83] He made clear in his FMS account that he was well disposed toward the U.S. Army from his time working with the War Department. He already had friends in the West. In talking to State, he may have meant that he had warned Hitler about bomber output through his reports from Washington.)

Indeed, Hitler had not bothered to mobilize the German economy fully for the war he had started, despite the fact that his conquests had gained access to all strategically important raw materials except oil and rubber, and that he controlled the industries of France and the Low Countries. U.S. Strategic Bombing Survey interrogations after the war indicated that the German leadership still expected to quickly win a short war. The survey attributed the push to increase in war production in 1942, when Albert Speer became armaments chief, to the shock of the defeat before Moscow, not American entry into the war. Even that increase was the result of increased efficiency, not expanded mobilization. Indeed, for most of the war, German industry operated on a single-shift basis, few women entered the work force, and the workweek was shorter than in Great Britain.[84] Tooze, however, notes that the participation of German women in the workforce in 1939 already exceeded the levels reached by Britain and America during mobilization.[85]

Hitler was optimistic. He told Reich's Leader of the SS Heinrich Himmler on 18 January, "The Japanese are occupying all the islands, one after the other. They will get hold of Australia, too. The white race will disappear from those regions."[86] Hitler wrote a long turn-of-the-year message to Mussolini that focused on the Eastern Front and barely acknowledged the dramatic expansion of the war facing the Reich and Italy. Japan's attack was epoch-making and could not be overestimated, Hitler wrote. What could America and Britain accomplish? The Anglo-Saxons and Soviet remnants confronted the unified might of the Axis powers. His faith in ultimate victory had never been stronger. Hong Kong had fallen, the Philippines and Singapore would soon. "I do not believe in the possibility of a long resistance." Churchill, he blustered, would soon have to be saved from his own people.[87]

The Western Allies Forge a Common Front and Material Victory

Churchill and Roosevelt, joined by their military chieftains and senior officials, met in Washington from 22 December to 14 January in the Arcadia Conference, where they laid the foundations for their alliance, including pooling resources under unified commands, starting with the Southwestern Pacific Theater under British General Archibald Wavell. Wavell was to control all air, sea, and ground forces in the theater. The command included the armed forces of Australia and the Netherlands, as well.

Securing the air and sea links between Hawaii and Australia was essential. A Japanese attempt to capture New Caledonia was expected; it was a key link and a source of nickel the Japanese needed.

The new Combined Chiefs of Staff agreed on an astonishing array of other issues. Defeating Germany was to be the priority over Japan, and the Allies were to employ the minimum necessary force in theaters other than the European. America was to send heavy bombers to Britain as units. American troops were to relieve the British in Northern Ireland and Iceland. The Allies were to wear Germany down

President Franklin D. Roosevelt and Prime Minister Winston Churchill in Quebec, Canada, on 12 September 1944. Roosevelt moved with foresight to launch the military and industrial mobilization that produced the Arsenal of Democracy. (NARA)

using air bombardment, blockade, subversive activities, and propaganda while preparing for offensive operations. They were to fill the gaps in an unbreakable ring around Germany. Whatever support could be afforded was to continue for Russia.

Offensive operations against the European continent might be possible in 1943. They discussed conducting joint landings in French Northwest Africa. The Americans proposed basing bombers in China but said the effort should await conditions in which a force of at least 50 planes could operate. The participants approved a plan to increase assistance to China from British bases in Burma and India, which were opened for American use, including organizing and maintaining a volunteer air group. The plan, however, assumed continued access to the Burma Road into China.

Indeed, all the discussions were based on the premise that the Allies would successfully defend Singapore, Burma, the East Indies, and the Philippines. The staffs did consider scenarios in which Singapore and the Philippines fell, but not Burma.[88]

On 1 January, Churchill, Roosevelt, and Soviet and Chinese representatives signed the Declaration of the United Nations. That same day, Executive Director of the Supply Priorities and Allocations Board Donald Nelson supplied to Harry Hopkins for Roosevelt a statement for him to use on America's war production plans. The British had been pushing hard to win larger increases in war output than the American side had previewed at the start of the conference:

> We plan to build—*this year*—fifty thousand completely equipped airplanes; we plan to build and equip—this year—forty thousand tanks; we plan to build one hundred and twelve major combat ships and six hundred minor naval craft; we plan to build at least seven million tons of merchant shipping, we plan to supply the complete equipment and armament for a ground–army force of a size comparable to that which was raised in the World War, and at the same time furnish large quantities of similar equipment for the fighting forces of our Allies.
>
> In stepping up our present monthly production rates to meet the 1942 quotas, we shall reach, by the end of the year, rates that will assure enormously larger annual production for the future. Thus, our annual rate of plane production by the end of 1942 will approximate 80 thousand per year, and our annual tank production rate will be about 60 thousand.[89]

The Japanese initially had an intelligence net that provided some strategically useful information on the Allies: Naval attachés in Latin America. They gathered much of the information from American publications such as *The New York Times*, no longer delivered to addresses in Japan. They reported on convoys to the UK; the transit of warships, including battleships and aircraft carriers, from the Atlantic to the Pacific through the Panama Canal; and a debate in early 1942 over whether the U.S. Navy should transfer escort vessels from the Pacific to the Atlantic to stop heavy losses to German U-boats.

A Japanese spy—"Sutton," a disgruntled U.S. Army officer—obtained the outlines of the Arcadia decisions, which Japan shared with the Germans, including the emphasis on "Germany first" and a holding action in the Pacific. This insight was to feature in Japanese policy discussions in 1942.[90]

American industry produced more bombers than the rest of the world combined during the war. The B-17 heavy bomber (Flying Fortress) entered service before the war. Here, fuselage frameworks for the B-17F bomber are under construction at the Boeing plant in Seattle. (Library of Congress)

CHAPTER 9

Early 1942: The Era of Axis Optimism

The Sun Sure is Rising

Admiral Ugaki wrote in his diary on New Year's Day 1942:

> It has been only 25 days since the war started, yet operations have been progressing smoothly and we have enough reason to hope for completion of the first stage of the war by the end of March. Then what will come next?
> Shall we be dragged into war with the Soviet Union owing to a rash and thoughtless act by the army? Or will the United States and United Kingdom recover their strength sufficiently to fight a great decisive battle in the Pacific? Anyway, the future is filled with brightness. The course of events during this year will determine the fate of the war, and we must work hard, exerting every effort. The main thing is to win, and we surely will win.[1]

Keep in mind that all Japanese military activity at this time revolved around winning the war in China. The Japanese Cabinet in early January 1942 concluded that further efforts to negotiate a peace with Chiang Kai-shek would be futile. With the outbreak of the war in Greater East Asia, Chungking had thrown her lot "irretrievably" with the United States and Britain and appeared prepared to fight it out against Japan. Hereafter, Japan would exert all possible military and political pressure to topple Chiang. The report on the Cabinet meeting read in part, "[W]e feel that we should first establish ourselves securely from a military standpoint within the bounds of Greater East Asia, so that we shall be able to withstand any and all outside pressure during a long and drawn-out world war. At the same time, we must establish access to materials with which to maintain these military bases." Once Japan was firmly entrenched in an unassailable position, Chiang would "automatically fall from power."[2]

In early April, IGHQ informed General Hata, Commander-in-Chief of the China Expeditionary Army, of its intention to launch a giant offensive against the Chungking area, at the proper time, and asked the general to study a plan. The instructions conveyed,

> From around spring of 1943, offensive operations will be launched against the Chungking area with one army with a nucleus of about ten divisions, opening the offensive from the southern

part of Shanxi, and a force with a nucleus of about six divisions from the I'Chang [Yichang, in western Hebei] area. Both will first destroy enemy forces in their immediate areas.... [T]he area army and the force will resume the offensive and capture Chungking and Chang-tu [Chengdu] and occupy strategic areas in Sichuan Province.... The operation will be designated Operations No. 5. [Auxiliary units for the area army, including river crossing, most logistic support, and materiel were to come from the homeland, Manchuria, and the southern area.][3]

But Chiang now had a whole lot of leverage with the Allies, in view of the fact that his armies were tying down 600,000 Japanese troops. In January, he told Washington he wanted a $500 million loan, and despite misgivings that much of the money would be skimmed off, Congress approved the loan on 3 February.[4]

There is no indication that Japanese leaders reckoned with the possibility that having attacked America to cover a strategic advance to the south aimed at ending the war in China, the Nationalist enemy was probably going to have the resources, thanks to America, to fight back even harder.

A Growing Appetite

The Japanese war plan against the Western Allies was built on a traditional one, which foresaw the army smashing the Allies in the Philippines and Malaya while awaiting the decisive naval battle in the western Pacific. In addition, amphibious Japanese forces were to seize resource-rich areas to the south while others pushed rapidly southeastward across the Pacific to establish a defensive perimeter running Burma–Malaya–Netherlands East Indies–northwest New Guinea and the Mandates–Home Islands–Kurils. The Pearl Harbor attack that Yamamoto began considering in spring 1940 was to destroy the battleships and carriers and greatly delay any decisive battle. The army committed half its air strength but only 11 divisions to the effort. By late March, Japanese forces had accomplished nearly all these objectives, and American resistance in the Philippines ended in May.[5]

Indeed, Allied resistance was collapsing so rapidly that by January 1942, the Japanese leadership was debating whether to expand beyond the originally conceived national defense zone. Barging ahead would retain the initiative. On the other hand, it would aggravate an already highly stretched logistical capability. The IJN favored pushing on to deny the Americans forward bases. Admiral Ugaki drafted an operational plan in mid-January that called for the capture of Midway, Johnston, and Palmyra Islands in June; redeployment of airpower to those islands, and then an invasion of Hawaii, which would possibly force the American fleet into a decisive battle. He argued that what would hurt America the most would be the loss of Hawaii and the fleet.[6]

Japanese subs were large enough to carry float planes, and aircraft overflew Pearl Harbor the nights of 19 December, 4 January, and 24 February. They saw that the Americans were working round the clock to refloat their sunken warships.[7] On 11 January, a submarine torpedoed the carrier USS *Saratoga* 500 miles west of Oahu.

The carrier limped to Pearl Harbor and onward for permanent repairs and upgrades to antiaircraft defenses. But she was out of action when the Pacific Fleet struck back at the empire.[8]

The IJN in February wound up on the receiving end for the first time. On the 1st, aircraft from the USS *Enterprise* struck Kwajalein, Taroa, and Wotja. The raids killed the commanding admiral of the Marshall Islands, as well as the Sixth Submarine Fleet commander. Separate attacks elsewhere in the Gilberts by the USS *Yorktown* sputtered out because of foul weather.[9]

On 24 February, a USS *Enterprise* task force raided Wake Island. Ugaki this time took note in his diary but was not impressed. Nevertheless, he conceded, "Though they have a certain flair for strategy—having a task force each in the north and the south, maintaining cooperation between the two—there is nothing much to praise in their actual actions. Only their bold practice of bombarding directly at close range or launching planes should be called quite daring."[10]

On 27 February, Japanese planes killed their first American aircraft carrier, albeit an old one relegated to ferry use, the USS *Langley*. The ship was carrying 32 P-40 fighters and the pilots from Australia to Java. The attackers damaged the vessel so badly that her escorting destroyers had to sink her. Ugaki groused in his diary that she had already been claimed sunk weeks earlier.[11]

*

Initial military operations had succeeded beyond expectations, and Tojo at a liaison conference on 4 February said he would like to consider updating the war policy. Following negotiations between IGHQ and the government, a liaison conference convened on 7 March. The overall appraisal of enemy intentions was that America and Britain would launch counteroffensives against the Axis when their military capabilities allowed. They would give priority to Europe. In Asia, they would base their operations out of Australia and the Indian Ocean area. They would be capable of a large-scale counteroffensive in 1943. Australia was weak in manpower and heavy industry but produced enough food to support a long-term war. Germany would be unable to defeat the Soviets during the year. Chiang, meanwhile, was looking forward to ultimate Allied victory and would fight on unless his outside support disappeared.

The United States would rapidly expand production for total war through 1944, when the expansion of armaments and munitions production would level off because of resource, manpower, and transportation constraints. Because of her dependence on outside sources for manpower, a decline in Britain's fighting power was inevitable. America and Britain combined were capable of rapidly gaining superior fighting forces to carry out a protracted war against Japan. On the whole, their fighting spirit was excellent. They had superior armaments, but their loss of key offensive bases would greatly offset their superiority in armaments. American maritime transportation capacity was inadequate to provide sufficient aid to Britain. The latter was likely to collapse if cut off from her dominions and colonies.

A continuation of the war with no prospect of victory would cause social unrest in America and Britain and lower morale of the public. A British collapse would have a tremendous effect on Americans.[12]

The conclusions for military policy stated:

> The great unexpected gains made by both the Army and the Navy in the early operations have forced the United States and Britain to assume the defensive for the present and have brought about a favorable situation for the defense of our land and the maintenance of our main lines of communications. If this favorable war situation is to be utilized advantageously, it is now necessary to assume a strategic offensive, which is contrary to the earlier planned strategic defensive for the prosecution of a protracted war.
>
> The Army operations, with the exception of some delay in the Philippines, were completed a month ahead of schedule and our casualties were lighter than expected. The Burma operation, which was scheduled to commence after the completion of the Southern Area Operations, has been already launched with strength from the forces committed in the Southern Area Operations made available ahead of schedule.
>
> The Navy operations succeeded in inflicting a heavy blow on the main force of the American and British fleets in the Pacific and in destroying most of the enemy sea forces in the Pacific waters at the opening of the war. In contrast, the loss sustained by our naval forces was far lighter than expected. The balance in naval strength between the enemy and us in the Pacific and Indian Oceans has resulted in a complete reversal from an offensive stand by the enemy to defensive.
>
> Army and Navy air operations have been successful beyond expectation by the destruction of large enemy air strengths with comparatively light losses. Consequently, it is possible to cope with enemy's attempt to rapidly bolster his air power in the Pacific and Indian Oceans.
>
> When the United States and Britain have sufficiently built up their military power, they will be capable of attempting a large-scale offensive utilizing the bases which are still in their hands.[13]

The economic policy conclusion read,

> We have, generally, been able to achieve early success in seizing resources in the areas, as planned, and in cutting off the supply of strategic materials to the United States and Britain. Maritime transportation capacity is being maintained, generally, on the planned level. In the acquisition of materials, especially petroleum, there is every possibility that we shall be successful far beyond our earlier expectations.... In general, our ability to prosecute the war is being strengthened beyond previous estimate, but the food situation will require further consideration.[14]

With this resource base, Japan from 1942 to 1944 was to produce war materials at roughly the same rate as the USSR with a roughly similar raw material reserve, with superior technology. The difference was in emphasis: Japan built mainly to fight an air–sea war, and the Soviets a ground war. Japan received no aid from resource-rich allies, as did the Soviets. Large-scale Soviet aircraft production was possible only because of huge deliveries of bauxite and aluminum under Lend-Lease.

In terms of naval construction, Japan produced roughly the same amount of combat and merchant shipping as the United Kingdom from 1942 to 1945. This included one super battleship (the UK two smaller battleships), 13 aircraft carriers (the UK six), five cruisers (the UK 15), 55 destroyers (the UK 141), and 99 submarines (the UK 111). Japan built 3,392,814 tons of merchant ships (986,159 tons of which were fuel tankers), only 14 percent less total tonnage than the UK.[15]

The IJN wanted to keep the Allies reeling and invade Australia, a key base for an American counteroffensive. The IJA countered that an invasion would require that it pull divisions out of China and Manchuria.[16]

The compromise was to try to sever communications between Australia and America. The new plan could commence without a large infusion of military resources. The next targets were to be Port Moresby in southern New Guinea, New Caledonia, Fiji, and Samoa. The Emperor supplied his sanction on 13 March.[17]

The new stage did not require additional resources but did demand the retention of units that had been expected to be released. The IJA was able to send but a single division back to the homeland and none back to China.[18] John Wood, in *Japanese Military Strategy in the Pacific War*, argues persuasively that this decision led to over-extension that doomed Japan to strategic defeat in the Pacific, primarily by threatening American communications lines to Australia, which provoked an active response with ramped-up resources rather than the defensive battle foreseen under the "Europe first" Allied strategy.[19]

The debate reflected underlying strategic differences between the IJA and IJN that had emerged during IGHQ discussions leading up to the liaison conference. The IJA wanted to stick with the existing plan to defend the current defensive perimeter and wear the enemy down when he came calling in a protracted war. It was an imperfect solution, but Japan had no way to actually defeat America. The IJN wanted to mount operations aimed at Australia, Hawaii, India, and other targets to keep the enemy on the defensive and destroy the enemy fleet in the battles that those operations would inevitably provoke. Ultimately, the IJA accepted the idea of attacking some objectives on the rim of the outer perimeter to forestall their use by the enemy.[20]

Meanwhile, on 1 February, two American carrier task forces staged air strikes in the Marshall Islands, while warships shelled a Japanese airfield. The American side thought the results meager, but the raid caused Admiral Ugaki a great deal of thought about the Americans in his diary:

> They have come after all; they are some guys! ... After experiencing defensive weaknesses ourselves, we cannot laugh at the enemy's confusion at the time of the surprise attack on Pearl Harbor....
>
> The enemy's attempt was most timely because our operations were focused in the southwest Pacific and the defensive strength in the Marshalls was thin. In addition to a fairly big result, they achieved their purpose of diverting our strength. Carriers closed in and heavy cruisers' bombardment was also most daring. It seems we have been somewhat fooled....
>
> The incident was really "a reproach that went to the heart." ... Adventure is one of their characteristics. They took advantage of the situation when we were busy fighting in the south and west and obtained their objective of restraining our southward advance in addition to the actual damage.

They will adopt this kind of method in the future, for it is the easiest for them and most effective. And the most probable move they would make would be an air raid on our capital.[21]

Japanese radio boasted that with the Greater East Asia area already conquered, Japan had all the resources needed to make herself entirely self-sufficient.[22] The American enemy thought about the same: An Office of Naval Intelligence report dated 20 March suggested Japan had already achieved her aims regarding raw materials.

> Six months ago, Japan was begging, cajoling, and threatening in order to purchase vital oil from the Netherlands East Indies; today, Japan occupies (and plans to exploit within six months) oil fields which can supply her with 140 percent of her needs; a year ago, Japan relied on foreign sources for 99 percent of her rubber; now she controls supplies 2,000 percent beyond her needs.
>
> If Japan can exploit the resources of the areas she has recently occupied (Thailand, Indo-China, Malaysia, Netherlands Indies, Borneo, Philippines) and maintain lines of communications, she is on the verge of achieving a degree of self-sufficiency in war materials which rivals (and in some items surpasses) that attained by any other power in history, including the United States.
>
> Economically Japan, plus her Empire and her conquests, is completely self-sufficient in all the vital materials of war, with the possible exemption of iron (80 percent). Only if the war outlasts her stockpiles and she fails to bring home the loot has she lost her gamble; that is a strategic risk which invites Japan's enemies to immediate and obvious action.[23]

Even in China, the Nationalists were beleaguered. The British mission in Chungking reported to London:

> While Chinese have stood up to recent events remarkably well, there is some defeatist talk. And we may have to reckon on increasingly unfavorable features of the situation. These are well known to you and may be summarized as:
> (a) Weariness after five years of war. This is accentuated by fears of inflation and its results.
> (b) Isolation. Absence of road communications and reduction of contact with outer world to a single rather tenuous air line must be increasingly affecting morale.
> (c) Disappointment. After six months of Pacific war, supplies, except air borne, are completely cut off and China for the present more at Japan's mercy than ever before.
> 2. Chinese are also not wholly convinced that the United States and British Empire are determined to carry on the war with Japan to a finish if the war against Germany is won.[24]

Yet, an ominous omen appeared in March. Japan's losses in ships and aircraft exceeded production.[25]

Germany Gloats and Punches Above Its Weight at Sea

Hitler met with Oshima on 3 January and, in the course of the discussion, admitted that he had "no knowledge of how to defeat the US." Meeting with some of his closest loyalists on 15 January, Hitler said, "should this war turn out to be winnable at all, it will only be won by America."[26]

About the same time, however, Hitler ruminated at dinner about the possibility that Great Britain would pull out of the war after losing Singapore to the Japanese, which led him to offer some of his provincial and racist views about the Americans:

> I don't see much future for the Americans. In my view, it's a decayed country. And they have their racial problem, and the problem of social inequalities. Those were what caused the downfall of Rome, and yet Rome was a solid edifice that stood for something. Moreover, the Romans were inspired by great ideas.... As for the Americans, that kind of thing is nonexistent. That's why, in spite of everything, I like an Englishman a thousand times better than an American.
>
> It goes without saying that we have no affinities with the Japanese. They're too foreign to us, by their way of living, by their culture. But my feelings against Americanism are feelings of hatred and deep repugnance. I feel myself more akin to any European country, no matter which. Everything about the behavior of American society reveals that it's half Judaized, and the other half negrified.[27]

For the record, Schmider asserts that any notion that Hitler's racist views of America contributed to his underestimation of his new enemy is "untenable."[28] The theme certainly never arose, for example, in Hitler's conversations with Mussolini about America.

Nazi propaganda chief Josef Goebbels noted in his diary on 24 January with evident satisfaction that Argentina and Chile were leading resistance to an American call at the Rio Conference for all countries in the Americas to break diplomatic ties with the Axis Powers because of the aggression committed against one American state. The reason, Goebbels thought, was that Roosevelt had no victories to show. It apparently did not occur to him to wonder what influence some eventual American victories would have in the Western Hemisphere.[29]

One consequence of Germany's declaration of war was the emergence of an information vacuum. "I am having the question investigated," Goebbels wrote in his diary on 19 February, "as to how we may in the future obtain authentic news from the United States. We have established a number of news bridgeheads in South America. For the present they still function, but of course we don't know how long that will continue."[30] That same month, understanding on the part of senior American civilian and military leaders regarding Germany was expanding, as the British began to share the fruits of their Enigma codebreaking program against Germany.

Ciano recorded in his diary on 18 February, "What seemed fantastic in the past, today appears possible. Japanese victories are wearing down British resistance hour by hour and perhaps preparing a more rapid and favorable conclusion than is now possible to foresee. Actually, the Anglo-Saxon situation has never seemed as desperate, even to me, as it does now. But I believe that they will hold."[31]

On the 24th, Ciano wrote, "Roosevelt's speech: Calm, restrained, but determined. His words are certainly not those of a man who thinks he must seek an early peace. However, this strange interpretation is spreading even in Italy and many honestly believe it."[32]

*

German U-boats claimed a rising toll on transatlantic convoys and ships in American home waters in 1942. The lethality of the fleet exceeded all expectations in Germany

Albert Speer giving a speech in 1943. Speer rationalized German war production and boosted output. (Bundesarchiv)

until May of 1943, and German planners were able to counter the Allies' evolving tactics—increasing dispersal, use of destroyers and air cover—with increasing numbers of submarines.[33] U-boats off the American east coast and in the Caribbean sank 526 vessels, totaling 2,832,000 tons of American, British, and neutral shipping.[34] Dönitz in 1965 claimed that his vessels could have sent a million tons more to the bottom of American waters had Raeder not ordered the most capable part of the fleet into the Mediterranean Sea.[35] If true, his commanding admiral's bad decisions only offset Admiral Ernest King's refusal to provide vessels and aircraft for convoys during the mass sinking event. King had become Chief of Naval Operations and Commander-in-Chief of the United States Fleet in December, and he was determined to keep every resource he could in the Pacific to fight Japan.[36]

The U-boats prospered in 1942 in part because the undersea force adopted a new four-wheel Enigma machine that the British could not decrypt. Called Shark, the code robbed the Royal Navy of its inside information on U-boat movements. This problem ultimately encouraged Britain and America to create what became the world's best SIGINT partnership. The Americans wanted to know why they weren't getting Enigma intelligence on submarines, and the British conceded they could not crack Shark. By the end of the year, deals were to be reached that placed American cryptographers at Bletchley Park, and the American armed services launched technical development programs to create high-speed "bombes," the code-cracking machines at Bletchley Park.[37]

Elsewhere, Germany's armaments chief Todt died in a plane explosion on 7 February, but the competent Nazi loyalists included a similarly talented replacement: Albert Speer.[38] The big picture for weapons production already conformed to the demands established by the war itself. Two of Germany's four top production priorities in 1942 were in fact directed to the air and sea war: flak guns, U-boats, Tiger tanks, and locomotives.[39]

Hitler was in an upbeat mood when he discussed the naval war with Japanese Ambassador Oshima on 24 March 1942:

> I had planned to build six battleships, four aircraft carriers, and a fleet to support them between 1940 and 1944. I am sorry to say, however, that is not working out that way.
>
> Anyway, I am certainly glad you Japanese have been able to win such great victories with your excellent navy. You know, if I had had the Japanese fleet instead of the Italian fleet in the Mediterranean, the situation there would already have been stabilized. All we have been able to do so far has been with submarines, with which we are obtaining fine results. I, myself, have

been surprised at the successes we have met with along the American coast lately. The United States kept up her tall talk and left her coasts unguarded. Now I daresay she is quite surprised. I imagine that the Japanese submarines are active along the West Coast of the United States, and that the United States will not find it possible to defend her shores from now on.[40]

In fact, the IJN never engaged in antimaritime submarine warfare against the west coast (discussed at greater length below). Although the IJN aspired to sever shipping between America and Australia, that was not the central concern like Germany's need to cut off Britain. Moreover, the IJN had plenty of other tasks to worry about, unlike the German navy.

Several days later, Hitler again praised the well-planned Japanese actions and congratulated Oshima on the undreamed rapidity with which the Japanese had captured Singapore. Japan, by entering the war, had brought it to "a decisive stage." Then he unrolled a map and discussed his grand strategy. His troops had suffered in the Soviet winter, true, but, he added, "I have every confidence that as soon as good weather returns, we can crush the Soviet forces completely." Lieutenant General Erwin Rommel was in Africa with three mechanized divisions, and if the Italians could meet their promises for supplying him (the Führer was skeptical), Rommel could reach the Suez Canal. The British, he thought, were planning a landing on the Channel coast, but if they tried, he was ready for them.[41]

Despite Hitler's optimism, Oshima on 6 April signaled a sense of foreboding to Tokyo reflecting America's entry into a European war whose outcome was by no means certain:

> Even though it is granted that Japanese military operations in the Orient have dealt Britain and America a severe blow, this is offset by the restraining power that American participation in the war exercises in Europe, and the general situation cannot be said to have resulted to the advantage of Germany and Italy. Everything now depends on how the German-Russian war develops....
>
> Summing all this up, beyond any doubt, the prowess of the Soviet forces must not be regarded with levity but, on the other hand, the Germans, although they will encounter difficulty of supplying the rear and from difficulties of terrain in strategic areas as is to be expected, will probably be more than a match for them.[42]

The British Secret Intelligence Service, citing a reliable Scandinavian source with good contacts in Berlin, reported in February:

(I) The real cause of the gloom that prevails in Germany today is the anxiety of the people regarding the government's policies. Although people cannot conceive that Germany could possibly be beaten—and they realize full well that defeat means the end of Germany as it is today—there is a wave of pessimism throughout the country.

(II) Reactions to Japan's entry into the war have been varied. Certain sections of the community are pleased. Others are perturbed at the fact that the United States are now a direct enemy of Germany and realize that all their hopes of a compromise peace with the Western powers have been finally dashed. They feel that Europe will become poorer and more hungry as time goes on, whereas the United States, with her inexhaustible resources, will become ever stronger.

> (III) The importance of the serious reverses suffered by the German Army in Russia are not underrated. These reverses have come as a great shock to the German people, who have always been led to believe that the German Army is invincible.[43]

In May, the SIS reported that according to a good German source, Himmler in December had feared a strong adverse public reaction to the reverses on the Eastern Front and planned a large purge, but by mid-March he had concluded the public reaction was not as bad as he had feared.

The same SIS report said that a most secret source had provided a readout of a meeting of Japanese military attachés in Berlin in April. Attachés learned that the Japanese High Command was willing to cooperate more closely with the Axis over exchanging intelligence but was not disposed toward closer coordination of military operations.[44]

An indication of the information vacuum about American intentions, Hitler on 10 April at the OKW morning meeting mentioned foreign press reports that the Americans and British were planning a "big surprise." He thought that might be a landing or a new bombing offensive. Two days later, the meeting discussed a French report indicating that the Americans and British were building a trans-African road from Cameroon to the Sudan that would enable them to move military supplies to British forces in Egypt on a larger scale than the Germans had imagined. Feckless discussion addressed whether there was any way the Germans could interdict the supplies. On 1 May, OKW "learned" that American troops had occupied Venezuela's capital and oilfields. The amount of nonsense that reached Hitler and the military command is astounding.[45]

Hitler reiterated his views of America on 26 April when he told the Germans,

> A clique of Jews who went to the United States dragged that country into war against all its interests only for Jewish-Capitalist reasons. President Roosevelt, owing to his lack of ability, seeks advice from a Brain Trust whose leading men are all Jews. Just as in 1917, the United States was dragged step by step into war by her Judaized President and his Jewish entourage—a war without any reason, against a nation who had never harmed the United States, against a people from whom the United States could never gain anything.[46]

The German and Italian leaders met in Salzburg on 29–30 April. Hitler explained that his offensive in 1942 would aim for the Caucasus oilfields. Apparently in passing, Mussolini was told, "America is a big bluff." Ciano thought that it was the Germans who were bluffing about America, and that when they thought about it, it sent shivers down their spines.[47]

The first American troops had begun arriving in Northern Ireland, but Goebbels, for one, was not impressed. "The American soldiers who landed in Ireland," he wrote in his diary on 23 May, "gave interviews to the big news agencies. These are of a strange and disarming naiveté. One might wish that the Yankees could sometime come in contact with tried and proven front-line soldiers. Their illusions about the European war would surely disappear very quickly."[48]

High Water Mark in the East

The Japanese Navy General Staff on 5 April approved the first operation in stage two of the war to expand the defensive perimeter: The conquest of Midway Island and the western Aleutian Islands. The decision on Midway came after Admiral Yamamoto suggested he would resign if the staff turned the plan down. The IJN requested that the IJA supply a regiment for the Midway invasion, and although the IJA had qualms about the operation, it decided that the war had gone well so far in part because of effective interservice cooperation, and it agreed.[49]

But the first big action against a target on the rim of the outer perimeter was in the Indian Ocean, where on 5–9 April, a carrier task force commanded by Admiral Nagumo attacked the British on Ceylon. Yamamoto had issued the orders for a surprise attack on 9 March. Among other vessels, the Japanese sank the aircraft carrier *Hermes* and two heavy cruisers and shot down some 40 RAF aircraft. Land-based bombers simultaneously struck vessels in Calcutta.[50]

With the help of the codebreakers, the weak British Eastern Fleet avoided engagement, but land-based Blenheim bombers attacked the Japanese carriers from the rear on 9 April. One carrier possessed an experimental radar, which failed to detect the attackers. The British bombs struck close, but Zeroes arrived and destroyed half the force.[51]

The Doolittle Raid

Lieutenant Colonel James Doolittle on 18 April led an audacious air attack on Japan that incorporated 16 stripped-down B-25 Mitchell bombers manned by crews specially trained to launch from the deck of the USS *Hornet* off the Japanese coast. As planned, they bombed targets around Tokyo and proceeded westward to recover in China. All bombers but one that landed in Vladivostok crashed, but most of the airmen survived and returned to service.

"An enemy task force attacked our homeland!" Admiral Ugaki exclaimed in his diary.[52] Tojo's aircraft, returning from an inspection visit, had to dodge one of the American B-25s.[53]

The Foreign Ministry in Tokyo reported on that day, "On the eighteenth, at 2430, enemy planes carried out an air attack on [Tokyo]; however, they were driven off by the fierce defensive fire of our spotters. There were nine enemy planes. Our losses are slight."[54] A circular followed, the intercepted communication cited here verbatim: "A number of enemy planes attacked in Kanto district (Tokyo). (Bombs were dropped in five places).... [Apparently from an aircraft carrier along the coast?], a small force came attacking from all directions. Although the attack was made chiefly with incendiary bombs, the damage was slight since many of the incendiary bombs did not explode."[55] As the day wore on, more details emerged. B-25s from "three" aircraft carriers (there were only two) had attacked near Tokyo, Yokohama, Yokosuka, Kobe, and Niigata. Those aircraft not destroyed had escaped to China.[56]

Ugaki noted in his diary,

> If the enemy carried out attacks from such a long distance, which is about the same as an expected one-way attack, we shall have to revise our countermeasures fundamentally, studying their type planes. In any case, this is one up to the enemy today.... In view of this recent success, undoubtedly the enemy will repeat this kind of operation while attempting raids from China. Therefore, we must take steps to watch far to the east and, at the same time, always keep a sharp lookout to the threat from the west.[57]

Expanding the defense perimeter in East Asia was Japan's historical national security solution. So naturally, thoughts like Ugaki's led planners to favor expanding the perimeter beyond range of air attacks. This changed the entire concept of the ground war in China and strengthened the case for the Midway and Aleutian operations already approved in the Pacific. Midway was to become a base to ease holding carrier task forces at bay.

Captain Toshikazu Ohmae, serving at the Bureau of Military Affairs, told American interrogators after the war that although the Doolittle raid caused little damage, it "caused considerable discussion and confirmed the need for eastward expansion to acquire bases to protect the home islands, the mainland." His interrogators recorded, "Captain Ohmae is probably the most intelligent and well informed Japanese Naval Officer that has been interrogated by this section."[58]

Hattori said that the thought of repeated B-25 raids, with the aircraft recovering in China, was a trigger for a two-prong ground offensive by the China Expeditionary Army to seize potential landing sites, the first launched on 15 May using four divisions and one brigade to capture airbases in Zhejiang and Jiangxi provinces. The second prong struck on 31 May on a two-division front. The operation ended successfully on 1 July.[59]

Admiral Matome Ugaki served as Yamamoto's operations chief and commanded sea and air battle formations throughout the war. He left a diary that survived his futile kamikaze flight at the time Japan surrendered. (Wikimedia Commons)

This was to be only the first time that American bombers triggered large Japanese ground operations in China, the war that all the conquering across the Pacific and southeast Asia was supposed to end. Japanese worries about American air attacks from China were to become a fixture of the way they thought about America, for good reason.

Days after the raid, pilot Sakai received a letter from his cousin in Tokyo, delivered by submarine: "The bombing of Tokyo and several other cities has brought about a tremendous change in the attitude of our people toward the war. Now things are different; the bombs have dropped here on our homes. It does not seem anymore that there is such a great difference between the battle front and the home front." Sakai wrote that the raid unnerved almost every pilot. "The knowledge that the enemy was strong enough to smash our homeland, even in what might be a punitive raid, was cause for serious apprehension of future and heavier attacks.[60]

*

In Italy, Ciano took note of the raid and offered a prophetic assessment: "The Americans have bombed Tokyo and the other Japanese cities. It is the first offensive action since the beginning of the war. I do not think they will be able to do much for the time being; they are still very much behind in their preparations; but as time goes on, they will make their weight felt more and more, especially in the air."[61]

Mussolini and Ciano on 28 April headed to Salzburg to meet Hitler and other German leaders. Ciano thought Hitler looked tired and had developed a few white hairs. Discussions naturally focused on the Eastern Front:

> America is a big bluff. This slogan is repeated by everyone, great and small, in the rooms and anterooms. It is disturbing to think what the Americans will be able to do and, I think, will do, and the Germans are closing their eyes to it. This does not prevent the most intelligent and honest people from realizing what America can do and feeling a chill run down their spines.[62]

*

The Operations Bureau of the Japanese Naval General Staff on 23 April informed the Third Section, responsible for armament, that it wanted all construction of battleships to end after the completion of a third super battleship, and that of planned heavy cruisers as well. All resources should be directed toward construction of aircraft carriers and submarines. The bureau also harped on about inadequate production of naval aircraft.[63]

The Navy General Staff held planning meetings and conducted tabletop exercises for the operation against Midway from 29 April through 4 May. The planners spun the scenario out to the point of an invasion of Hawaii. The exercise suggested such an invasion would not succeed without considerable planning and training.[64]

Roosevelt on 6 May sent a memorandum to Harry Hopkins and the Joint Chiefs that mandated an extremely offensive defense in the Pacific:

> The whole of the Pacific area calls, at the present time, fundamentally for a holding operation....
>   Defense of all essential points in the Pacific Theater is the primary objective. This defense calls for offense in two areas—attacks upon the Japanese lines of communication and the bombing of Japan proper from the east and west.

The objective of this defense strengthened by offensive actions is to destroy or damage as many Japanese naval vessels, merchant ships, and airplanes as possible. In this regard, it is essential to maintain destruction or damage of a much larger number of Japanese ships and planes each month than they can replace. In other words, combat against Japanese ships and planes must be sought out in order to hasten the attrition of Japanese arms.[65]

The Battle of the Coral Sea

The battle of the Coral Sea, fought 4–8 May 1942, was the first action in which aircraft carriers engaged each other, as well as the first in which neither side's ships sighted or fired directly upon the other. The Japanese had organized a major amphibious operation to capture Port Moresby, New Guinea, and Tulagi in the southern Solomon Islands, to implement the expanded defense perimeter. Allied codebreakers discerned first the outlines and then details of the operation and reported that the Japanese planned to send a carrier strike force into the Coral Sea. This gave Nimitz the foreknowledge to arrange his countermeasures. The Japanese expected to run into American carriers based purely on logic.[66]

The IGHQ had already decided to capture Port Moresby in late January and issued operational orders on 2 February, so the March liaison conference had merely ratified this objective. Two fleet carriers and one light carrier constituted the punch of the covering naval force. Japanese elements captured Tulagi on 3 May. Admiral Ugaki recorded in his diary on the 3rd, "We succeeded in landing on Tulagi today, but we are in considerable doubt about the voyage and landing of the Port Moresby Invasion Force."[67]

The U.S. Naval History and Heritage Command summed up the battle:

> The Battle of the Coral Sea, fought in the waters southwest of the Solomon Islands and eastward from New Guinea, was the first of the Pacific War's six fights between opposing aircraft carrier forces. Though the Japanese could rightly claim a tactical victory on "points," it was an operational and strategic defeat for them, the first major check on the great offensive they had begun five months earlier at Pearl Harbor. The diversion of Japanese resources represented by the Coral Sea battle would also have immense consequences a month later, at the Battle of Midway.[68]

The Coral Sea action resulted from a Japanese amphibious operation intended to capture Port Moresby, located on New Guinea's southeastern coast. A Japanese airbase there would threaten northeastern Australia and support plans for further expansion into the South Pacific, possibly helping to drive Australia out of the war and certainly enhancing the strategic defenses of Japan's newly enlarged oceanic empire.

The Japanese operation included two seaborne invasion forces, a minor one targeting Tulagi, in the Southern Solomons, and the main one aimed at Port Moresby. These would be supported by land-based airpower from bases to the north and by two naval forces containing a small aircraft carrier, several cruisers, seaplane tenders, and gunboats. More distant cover would be provided by the big aircraft carriers *Shokaku* and *Zuikaku* with their escorting cruisers and destroyers. The U.S. Navy, tipped off to the enemy plans by superior communications intelligence, countered with two of its own carriers, plus cruisers (including two from the Australian Navy), destroyers, submarines, land-based bombers, and patrol seaplanes.

Preliminary operations on 3–6 May 1942 and two days of active carrier combat on 7–8 May cost the United States one aircraft carrier, a destroyer, and one of its very valuable fleet oilers, plus damage to the second carrier. However, the Japanese were forced to cancel their Port Moresby seaborne invasion. In the fighting, they lost a light carrier (*Shoho*), a destroyer, and some smaller ships. *Shokaku* received serious bomb damage and *Zuikaku*'s air group was badly depleted. Most importantly, those two carriers were eliminated from the upcoming Midway operation, contributing by their absence to that terrible Japanese defeat.[69]

Ugaki on 7 May noted in his diary, "A dream of great success has been shattered. There is an opponent in war, so one cannot progress as one wishes.... [W]e suggested to the chief of staff of Fourth Fleet that they put off the invasion of Port Moresby." Fourth Fleet cancelled the operation after the heavy damage inflicted to its carriers on 8 May. After further consideration at the Combined Fleet, because only one carrier was available and there were insufficient fast transports for the IJA, the operation was put on ice until July.[70]

The Japanese believed that they had sunk both American carriers, although the *Yorktown* suffered only serious damage and underwent repair in time to participate in the battle of Midway the following month.[71] Regarding Allied claims about the battle, according to a German message, Tokyo portrayed the outcome as a "victory that nips at the bud the last offensive effort of England and the United States and the destruction of the *Saratoga* and *Yorktown* destroys every enemy hope for aerial attack on Japan." Admiral Sankichi Takasashi declared, "The Coral Sea victory is the most important after Hawaii.... [T]he enemy's navy may be characterized as not merely incompetent but idiotic."[72] The IJN crowed that it had decoyed the U.S. and British fleets into the northern part of the Coral Sea by small aircraft carriers. The IJN's spokesman said the battle revealed "the faulty strategy and tactical technique of the enemy command."[73] The Emperor issued a rescript to the Chief of the Combined Fleet that read, "We deeply appreciate that the air units of the Combined Fleet, fighting bravely and gallantly in the Coral Sea, crushed an American-British fleet."[74]

Pilot Sakai's unit transferred to Lae on the eastern coast of New Guinea to support the Japanese effort to capture Port Moresby and anchor the outer defense perimeter. Here, though, the Allies were not going to retreat again. Sakai could sense a shift:

> Only 180 miles away from the Allies bastion of Port Moresby, we began our new assignments by flying escort almost daily for our bombers, which flew from Rabaul to hammer the enemy installations in the critical Moresby area. No longer was the war entirely one-sided. As often

as we lashed out at Moresby, Allied fighters and bombers came to attack Lae. The valor of the Allied pilots and willingness to fight surprised us all.... [R]egardless of the odds, their fighters were always screaming in to attack. It is important to point out that their fighter planes were clearly inferior in performance to our own Zeros. Furthermore, almost all our pilots were skilled air veterans.[75]

Still, many developments looked promising. The Americans at Corregidor had just capitulated. On 8 May, the IJA completed occupation of the Burma Road. "What is the Chungking government going to do?" Ugaki asked his diary.[76]

Japanese ideas, at least among government spokesmen, about the boundaries of the Greater East Asia Co-Prosperity Sphere ballooned in May: All of continental Asia to the Persian Gulf and the Caspian Sea, the northern tip of Australia, the Pacific islands short of Hawaii, and possibly Alaska.[77]

Anticipating Axis Military Supremacy and Allied Peace Feelers

In Italy, Ciano mused,

> It is still not clear how things went in the Coral Sea. The Anglo-American communiqués, though admitting certain unspecified losses, are proclaiming victory. On the other hand, the Nipponese are doing the same, and it is well-known that the statements of the Japanese General Staff involve the honor of the Emperor himself. Therefore, they should not lie, although lies in wartime, like the lies that involve a woman's honor, are permissible.[78]

Ciano on 21 May met with a group of Italians repatriated from the United States. He wrote in his diary,

> They all agree on the following points: 1) Today America is not in a position to do very much in the military field. 2) America's industrial preparation is formidable and within a few months production will have risen to incalculable proportions. 3) The war is not popular, but all are determined to fight, even if they have to fight for twenty years to finish it. 4) Sentiment toward Italy is not all that hostile.[79]

Of parenthetical interest, Italian leaders were aware of the Germans' behavior in the USSR. Ciano recorded on 27 May,

> On his return from Russia, Sorrentino gives an account of his impressions and voices his opinions on the future. The first are ugly and the second not reassuring. German brutality, carried out to a point of continuous criminality, is so vividly and objectively revealed in his account that it is sometimes hard to believe that it's true. Massacres of entire populations, rape, murder of children—these are all part of the order of the day. Opposed to this is the Russians' grim determination to fight to the finish and their certainty of victory.[80]

Ambassador Oshima in Berlin on 5 June 1942 sent Tokyo a military assessment of the European war that concluded, "While it is still a little early to prognosticate, I believe that Japan, Germany, and Italy will be able to lay the basis for absolute military supremacy within the current year."[81] Nevertheless, on 6 June he followed what appears to be a sobering appraisal of the United States in which he outlined his view of American strategy and military capabilities.

> On 7 December everyone realized that war was near and preparations were being made. However, the attack on Pearl Harbor was a surprise. That is clear from the Roberts report.... The slogan of both the Democratic and Republican parties is now "Fight and Win," and all are expecting a long, hard war. Admiral Stark stated that the war is hard enough this year and when next year comes, what will happen is anybody's guess....
>
> Roosevelt and Churchill apparently decided between themselves that Germany was the primary enemy. However, now, with things happening as they are in the Pacific, the United States will probably content herself with activity against submarines in the Atlantic. All this talk about establishment of a "second front" in Europe may be called mere gossip. As a matter of fact, the United States is in no position to help England and the Soviet Union with anything much except materials....
>
> The establishment of an army of 3 million and an army air arm of a million, together with a two-ocean navy, have been set as the objective, and work is now progressing in that direction. Everything is assuming the tempo of total war, and the mobilization of labor is gradually getting underway. It is being reported that the output estimated by the President is being exceeded. Shipbuilding is proceeding fairly well, but every day the number of vessels sent to the bottom by submarines is amounting to a high number. The losses are greater at present than Anglo-American capacity for production....
>
> Everyone seems to believe that through superior airplanes the United States can rain terror on her enemies and, through the construction of many submarines, obliterate Japanese supply lines. The lower house [of Congress] has already approved $900 million for the construction of 200,000 tons of submarines.[82]

Hitler in June viewed the Western Allies as divided, but he mistook debate for division. Great Britain and the United States indeed had been arguing since the previous December over whether to stage an invasion of the Continent—the American military's view—or to invade French North Africa—the view held by Churchill and the British military. Churchill and his military chieftains flew to the United States on 17 June; the Joint Chiefs of Staff disagreed over a landing in France but were united in opposing an Operation *Torch* landing in North Africa.[83] Hitler judged,

> That the negotiations between Churchill and Roosevelt continued for eight days must not be attributed ... solely to the fact that Rommel has decisively shattered Britain's position in the Mediterranean. When two people are in general agreement, decisions are taken swiftly. My own conversations with the Duce have never lasted more than an hour and a half, the rest of the time being devoted to ceremonies of various kinds. The only time that our conversations lasted for nearly two days was when things were going badly in Albania, and I had to try to restore the Duce's morale. It is easy, therefore, by comparison to imagine how enormous their difficulties must appear to the Allies. Apart from that, to harness to a common purpose a coalition composed of Great Britain, the United States, Russia, and China demands little short of a miracle.[84]

By July, Hitler told Halder that the Americans and British would soon be brought to "the point of discussing peace terms."[85]

Back in the USA

Ironically, Rommel's defeat in June of the British Eighth Army in Libya ultimately united the West. Roosevelt wanted to get American ground forces into action against Hitler before the end of 1942, in part because he had promised Stalin the Allies would open a second front, and he overruled objections by the American chiefs of staff. The Allies in July settled on conducting an invasion of North Africa—Operation *Torch*.[86]

Moreover, after the Axis captured Tobruk on 21 June, Roosevelt dispatched the first of a series of emergence convoys to Egypt carrying 400 modern American M4 Sherman medium tanks with 75mm guns and self-propelled artillery pieces. In the first two weeks of September, 300 tanks reached Eighth Army.[87] The British had already received and put into action by then hundreds of American M3 medium tanks, a stopgap model that placed a 75mm gun in a side sponson because American industry was still unable to cast a turret large enough.

By the summer of 1942, defense production czar Nelson had realized that industrial capacity could not expand nearly fast enough to meet Roosevelt's targets. In August, he reported to Roosevelt that actual airplane output for 1942 was likely to be 48,000, rather than the announced 60,000. Unless drastic action ensued, 1943 production would fall well short of a planned 125,000. Roosevelt ordered Army Chief of Staff

Before the war, Hitler and Mussolini laughed off the data shared by the U.S. ambassador on tank production. Here, workers in the huge Chrysler tank arsenal near Detroit put together M3 medium tanks. The M3 proved the master of all German tanks on the battlefield when the British first used them in Egypt. (Library of Congress)

General George Marshall and Hap Arnold to calculate how many aircraft would be necessary to establish air dominance. Meanwhile, in October, he lowered his target for 1943 to 107,000 aircraft, including 82,000 combat types. Marshall saw that would require a reallocation of resources from the ground forces and tried to talk Roosevelt out of the idea. The President was firm. Aircraft production was the top priority. Production by the end of 1942 reached 85,423 airplanes, of which 54,094 were combat types.

As a consequence of Roosevelt's shift of resources to aircraft production, reduced future capacity for ground force equipment led to cutting the planned size of the U.S. Army by half, to 100 divisions. That proved to be enough. The value of defense production going to air, navy, merchant marine, and their supporting equipment and munitions, was already 70 percent of the total. By October 1943, the share reached 75 percent.[88]

Germany: The Receiving End of Strategic Air Power

Instead of the peace feelers Hitler expected, the Allies dished out punches to the face.

German perceptions of the Western Allies and their military capabilities, despite Rommel's trouncing of British ground forces, were just beginning to take into account a rapidly expanding strategic air war, a theme that henceforth would prey increasingly on Axis sensibilities. British Bomber Command had restarted its program of strategic bombing of Germany after it became clear in September 1940 that the Germans had given up on daylight attacks against the British Isles following the Battle of Britain. But its approach was relatively ineffective "area bombing" aimed at Berlin and other cities to undermine civilian morale—the very approach the Germans had just proved was a bust against the United Kingdom.[89] The fighting in the Middle East, however, forced London to divert bombers to that theater, high losses had persuaded the British to abandon daylight bombing, and the campaign against Germany degraded into little more than raids.

The Germans had experienced attack by Allied Entente bombers starting in 1915. These raids occurred mostly at night, and the Germans had responded by organizing what became a centralized flak force under the Air Service. Sound detectors were able to identify approaching bombers at a distance or in bad weather. Searchlights arrived at key industrial and transportation facilities to allow aimed fire up to 11,000 feet—later improved lights reached 19,500 feet—rather than ammunition-consuming blind barrage fire. The defenses were lethal enough that bomber pilots started turning the engines off to avoid detection and coasting through their bombing runs. In 1916, the warning system, flak, and fighters became part of a new homeland defense command. In 1917, the Germans produced the first generation of the famed 88mm high-velocity antiaircraft gun. Flak downed 322 Ententes in 1916 and 467 in 1917.

The ground force cooperated with the fighters detailed to air defense. For example, they would fire short rounds in the direction of the enemy aircraft that friendly pilots could see by the explosions.

The bombing raids of the day, however, were mosquitos compared to World War II. Allied aircrews conducted 353 missions and dropped 7,117 bombs.[90]

During the 1930s, German air defense had expanded the flak force at a pace even exceeding aircraft production and with an eye toward the threat of modern, technologically advanced bombers. The Luftwaffe had followed the B-17 development program from 1937. Conveniently enough, development had commenced in 1933 of a 105mm antiaircraft gun with a higher muzzle velocity than the 88mm and a ceiling of 31,000 feet, which would prove to be about the B-17's operational ceiling with a bomb load. Production began in 1938.

On the other hand, the Luftwaffe failed to pursue promising test results of infrared and radar tracking systems and in 1939 killed the radar development program. The Germans went to war with eight Freya radars along the northern coast of Germany. These could detect approaching aircraft at up to 80 miles but provided no information on altitude.[91]

With the British switch to night bombing, the Germans again pushed radar development, striving for a device accurate enough for laying flak. In December 1941, the Luftwaffe introduced the FuMG 39T(C), which could direct flak. This generation of technology remained the standard equipment for the rest of the war, though it received modest improvements along the way.[92] The Allies, of course, were vigorously improving their radar technology.

In February 1942, Air Chief Marshal Arthur T. "Bomber" Harris took charge of Bomber Command. He had just returned from Washington, where he had been a member of the RAF liaison team. Harris was determined to restore the strategic bombing campaign to effectiveness by depriving German industry of workers by leveling cities, and he believed in repeated saturation attacks on key targets. He had a new and improved technological solution, the GEE system that allowed crews to navigate accurately to their target areas (but not point targets), to help achieve his goals. The first modern heavy bombers, the Lancasters, were reaching the line units. His first truly successful attack, on the port of Lübeck, unfolded only a month later on 28 March. Two hundred and thirty-four bombers destroyed the old city center, damaged some arms factories, and killed or wounded more than 1,000 civilians. Hitler labeled the new strategy "terror attacks" and struck back at British cathedral cities, including Bath and York.[93]

The night of 30 May, 1,046 British bombers struck Cologne. Dropping explosive and incendiary bombs, the British killed 469 people, injured 5,027, and drove 45,000 from their homes. At the OKW meeting after the attack, Hitler learned that Churchill had announced that more than a thousand planes had participated, and on 3 June he exploded in anger when the Luftwaffe claimed only 70–80 planes had penetrated the defenses. Maybe the British exaggerated the number, but certainly not by ten times, he snarled. Hitler added that the enemy probably intended the air war to be a "second front." Göring quickly became an unwelcome visitor to the Führer headquarters.[94] Hitler continued to pump money into flak—24 percent of the Wehrmacht's weapons budget and 31 percent of its ammunition budget in the first half of 1942—though flak guns were playing a large role in the ground war in Russia and Africa as well as air defense.[95]

The British area bombing, however, failed to undermine worker morale, and the Germans quickly relocated factories to secure underground locations. By mid-1943, area bombing caused almost no damage to war industry.[96] Interrogations of knowledgeable German officials and the British Strategic Bombing Survey concluded that area bombing into 1944 hardly reduced war production at all. The USSBS gave it somewhat more credit, estimating a decline of 9 percent in overall production in 1943 and 17 percent in 1944; a simultaneous shift in Germany from civilian to war production, however, ameliorated any damage to total munitions output.[97]

The Army High Command's situation report on 31 May recorded another new element in the war raging in North Africa: "American medium tanks are very combat-capable. The enemy is richly equipped with tanks." By June, Army High Command started referring to "English-American" troops and material equipment.[98] Almost 200 M3 Grant medium tanks had gone into battle with the British in May, and though an ugly kludge that mounted a 75mm gun in a side sponson, the model outranged all German tanks on the battlefield.

The German Foreign Ministry on 8 June imposed a ban on travel by foreign diplomats in view of "the air raids expected from now on."[99] Oshima reported on the 19th that "Britain and America have no other means of supporting Russia than by bombing, and it is predicted that from this week on these bombings will reach very large proportions."[100] Yet he also noted the report from North Africa regarding M3 tanks: "American-made tanks have recently improved considerably but are still unable to match the German weapons."[101] On this last point, he had been falsely informed.

Upon the fall of Tobruk on 21 June, Hitler, according to Warlimont, wanted Rommel to press ahead with the aim of destroying the British army in Egypt. If the Axis missed this opportunity, said Hitler, a concentration of British and American forces would reverse the gains. Though non-specific, this is a rare occasion on which Hitler imagined the Americans arriving in North Africa.

He was more worried about a surprise Allied landing in the West, for which he said the Wehrmacht was completely unprepared. One would have to reckon with parachute and glider landings, followed by seaborne troops. He insisted on 25 June that three panzer divisions, the 7th Airmobile Division, the SS Division Das Reich, and the 23d Infantry Division—to be converted to a panzer division—move to the

West. Four days later, he summoned Speer to talk about accelerating construction of shore defenses. He said they had to reckon with large Anglo-American landings.

As for the air raids, on 28 June, the Luftwaffe reported to Hitler that American bombers had struck Romania, violating Turkish neutrality. Thirteen B-24 heavy bombers belonging to what was known as the Halverson Project (HALPRO) after its commanding officer, Colonel Harry Halverson, had struck the Ploesti oilfields on the 21st, having flown 4,000 miles to Egypt via Khartoum in great secrecy. The aircraft recovered to Iraq through Turkish airspace (four had to land there and were interned). The raid proved heavy bombers could penetrate enemy skies and conduct strategic bombing against key economic targets. Hitler canceled the planned withdrawal of German flak units from the country.[102]

Six hundred thirty RAF bombers attacked Düsseldorf on 31 July, the largest raid since Cologne, and set the city center ablaze. But British losses again were high and had been rising over several months, hitting 6 percent in August. One reason was the doubling in the number of night fighters and improved vectoring from ground controllers. Despite the number of burned German cities so far, the air defenses were at least dishing out as much punishment as the enemy could barely tolerate. Goebbels perceived the bombing intensity to be declining as the summer passed, as well as the damage caused.[103]

The American Eighth Air Force in the United Kingdom on 17 August sent a dozen B-17s on a pinpoint daylight raid on France. There was far more to come.[104] The U.S. Strategic Bombing Survey conceded, "Although the Eighth Air Force began operations 17 August 1942, with the bombing of marshaling yards at Rouen and Sotteville in northern France, no operations during 1942 or the first half of 1943 had significant effect. The force was small and its range limited. Much time in this period was devoted to training and testing the force under combat conditions."[105] Indeed, most American combat aircraft were slated to redeploy from the UK to support the coming landings and advance eastward in northwest Africa.

Göring at this time reputedly dismissed as minor the damage caused by American bombers and told Hitler that there was no need for big increases in daylight fighters for defense.[106]

On 19 August, the American 31st Fighter Group participated in its first major operation as part of the RAF air cover for the Anglo-Canadian landing at Dieppe on the French coast, intended to test operations against a defended shore. The German after-action report that went to the High Command said it was possible that American pilots had been involved, but not American ground forces. This was wrong—a small detachment took part in the raid.[107]

*

The Germans had not integrated economic considerations into war planning below a general level of discussion, according to Minister of Armament and Munitions

Albert Speer, which probably resulted in them under-appreciating the use of such planning against them through strategic bombing. Speer told interrogators that in the case of the attack on Russia, for example, obtaining oil was a consideration. An interrogation report recorded, "The formulation of such economic considerations was the responsibility of the *Wirtschaftsamt* [Economic Bureau], OKW." According to Speer, the broad economic factors involved were generally known and discussed, but no detailed analyses were called for or prepared for high-level planning. Economic warfare specialists were not prominent on the military staffs, and no civilian experts were employed or consulted. To remedy this defect, Speer in 1942 created an informal *Heirat für Wirtschaftskriegführung* (Council for Conducting Economic Warfare), for which he selected industrialists and some power experts. The discussion soon showed that the Luftwaffe "stood no chance in attacks on economic objectives in England...."[108]

This shortcoming is ironic given that Hitler's main argument for needing *Lebensraum* was to acquire economic and natural resources. He had told the generals in November 1939, "Today we are fighting for oil fields, rubber, the treasures of the earth."[109]

Speer told interrogators days after the war in Europe ended,

> In 1942, we undertook a study of the possibilities of economic warfare through aerial attack. Unfortunately, the results of these studies were never put into action. While making these studies, we discovered to our terror that it would be possible in the case of Germany to paralyze our industry to such an extent in comparatively short time, that a continuation of the war would become impossible for us. The first attacks of the RAF had no bad effects on the industry. The attacks were mostly aimed against cities, and nearby industrial installations remained untouched.[110]

According to Warlimont, by August information gleaned about the growth and deployment of the U.S. Army was reaching the Wehrmacht operations staff, which included it in daily status reports, but it came from human agents, who lacked any real access. There was no information regarding when American troops might enter battle—they were assumed to be unready—or where, other than somewhere in the European-African theater.[111]

The Battle of Midway

Admiral Ugaki, after the final table-top exercises, wrote in his diary on 28 May, "I firmly believe that God will bless the Combined Fleet. We will go on a major mission to the East in high spirits and inflict heavy damage upon the enemy." The next day, the main body of the Combined Fleet sortied.[112] In fact, one of the exercises resulted in the U.S. Navy ambushing the attackers and sinking three carriers. Ugaki had intervened to reduce the number of direct hits, and two of the carriers were resurrected to fight another day.[113]

On 31 May, Ugaki noted:

> A radio interception indicates that enemy planes and submarines in the Aleutian Islands, Hawaiian Islands, and the mid-Pacific are at a very unusual rate. Exchanges of urgent messages are at a very unusual rate. Certain indications make me suspect that they are taking countermeasures against our suspected movement rather than engaging in operations based on their own initiative.
>
> A sonar could have detected our sortie from Bungo Strait. May they not have suspected a movement of our northern force [sailing toward the Aleutian Islands] through radio intelligence or a report by a Russian vessel? The worst possibility is that they might discover our transport force leaving Saipan on the 28th. Judging from its course and strength, they could suspect that the force was heading toward the Midway district.... Be that as it may, for the time being there is no need to change our plan.[114]

On 1 June, Ugaki wrote, "We believe the enemy are preparing to meet us, after having strongly suspected our movement."[115] So, the fleet command had reason to suspect that the Americans knew they were coming. There would be no surprise. And, on 4 June, the invasion force approaching from the south reported that it had been sighted by an American plane. The plan had anticipated the discovery 24 hours later, which hopefully would draw attention away from the northwest, where the carrier strike group slipped toward the island. Ugaki recorded that this made him nervous.[116]

The Naval History and Heritage Command provides this synopsis of the battle of Midway, 4–7 June 1942:

> U.S. Pacific Fleet Commander Adm. Chester Nimitz placed full trust in his intelligence team following its accurate predictions of Japanese actions at the Battle of the Coral Sea the month prior. The leaders of this team were Cmdr. Joseph Rochefort—the Officer in Charge of Station Hypo, a communications center in the basement of Pearl Harbor headquarters packed with cryptologists, linguists, translators and all-source intelligence analysts—and Cmdr. Edwin Layton, the Pacific Fleet Director of Intelligence (N2). Also on Layton's staff was Lt. Jasper Holmes, who devised a plan to pass false information announcing Midway was having trouble distilling water as a ruse to confirm a vital information gap. The belief that the Japanese were referring to Midway as "AF" was confirmed when a subsequent Japanese transmission relayed, "AF is short on water."
>
> At this time, radio intelligence was intercepting about 60 percent of Japanese fleet communications and translating about 40 percent of that. Analysts chose the right pieces of the puzzle. The Japanese changed their code at midnight on 25 May, just too late to prevent disaster. The Japanese did not collect intelligence until they interrogated and then executed several downed pilots in the midst of the battle, which revealed the US fleet's movements up to that point and the names of the American carriers.[117]
>
> When pressed for specifics on Japanese intentions at Midway, Layton declared to Nimitz the attack would occur on the morning of 4 June from the northwest on a bearing of 325 degrees, 175 miles from Midway at 0600. Nimitz directed his Task Force commanders to employ their limited forces to inflict maximum damage on the Japanese fleet based upon this intelligence estimate and delegated specific battle plans to them. At dawn on 4 June, US scout planes located the Japanese fleet, after which Nimitz remarked to his N2, "Well you were only five miles, five degrees and five minutes off!"

Initial air strikes by Midway-based Navy, Marine Corps, and US Army Air Force planes against Japanese ships were unsuccessful but at great cost but significantly disrupted Japanese decision-making and operations. Torpedo planes were the first carrier-based aircraft to make runs at four Japanese carriers. Despite their devotion to mission, none of their weapons impacted a Japanese ship. However, they likely diverted Japanese defenses just in time for dozens of US carrier-based dive-bombers to arrive when the Japanese carriers were most vulnerable while refueling and rearming their planes. Within the span of several minutes, American bombs tore into four Japanese carriers and all were eventually sunk, along with more than 300 aircraft and three thousand sailors and aviators. By comparison, the US only lost one aircraft carrier, *Yorktown*, and several hundred sailors and aviators.[118]

The situation report from Admiral Nagumo that reached Tokyo on 5 June stated:

> Began attack on Midway at ___ hours. Shot down ___ US planes. ___. Between ___ and eight hours were attacked by over 100 enemy planes of which over 50 were shot down, but remainder scored ___ bomb and torpedo hits. *Akagi*, *Kaga*, and *Soryu* put out of action. Ordered ___ to cover the six transports and withdraw. Shifted flag to *Nagara*. Attacked enemy striking force with other [undoubtedly refers to *Hiryu*] group and obtained three hits on ___. At 1430 enemy made dive-bombing attack on *Hiryu* group and forced it to withdraw from action. This group was attacked again at 1600 by high-level bombers. After withdrawing to [northwest?] ___attacked two *Hornet* class carriers of which one was damaged.
> *Hiryu* damaged ___ but believe will be able to proceed and after landing planes she will retire to west with escort of two destroyers. *Soryu* sunk. *Kaga* also sunk. *Akagi* heavily damaged and unable to take on planes or make any way. Have two destroyers standing by her.[119]

The Japanese reluctantly torpedoed *Akagi* shortly before dawn on 6 June and the abandoned *Hiryu* sank during day.[120] The Navy General Staff ordered Third Carrier Division, part of the Aleutian force, back to Japanese waters with the carriers *Ryuko* and *Hosho*. *Zuikako* and *Shokaku* would proceed to Truk after completing repairs in Japan. The staff believed the latter two would still constitute a formidable striking force.[121]

Ugaki ruminated in his diary:

> The enemy had only two carriers in operational condition and contact with them had been entirely lost since they were seen east of Tulagi for a while on 15 May, after having come down from Hawaii for the Coral Sea battle. Although they were estimated to have returned to Hawaii, we never expected them, even including another one and two converted carriers [there were no converted carriers], to ambush our forces near Midway Island....[122]
> Even though we lost four powerful carriers, we still have eight carriers, including those scheduled to be completed before long, so that we need not be discouraged at all. As we can still hope to make good use of them in the future....[123]
> Thus the distressing day of 5 June came to an end. Don't let another day like this come to us during the course of this war! Let this day be the only one of the greatest failure of my life![124]

The Japanese claimed to have destroyed one aircraft carrier each of the *Enterprise* and *Hornet* classes and to have lost but one carrier and another one damaged.[125] Many Japanese officers after the war cited Midway as the point at which they began to think Japan would lose the war.

Captain Toshikazu Ohmae, who joined the staff of the Southeast Area Fleet the month of the battle, told American interrogators after the war that at this time he still believed Japan could win the war. Nevertheless, the battle had huge implications: "At Midway, although we lost some of our carriers, a large percentage of the pilots were recovered. As there were no carriers for these pilots, the air groups were reorganized and sent to Rabaul where these groups sustained very heavy losses. At the time of the Marshalls Campaign there were no qualified air groups for our carriers, and we could not commit the fleet without carriers."[126]

Rear Admiral Toshitane Takata told interrogators,

> After the Midway Campaign, as you know, the First Air Fleet was very heavily damaged and we had to reorganize the Third Fleet. (Indeed, Admiral Ugaki noted in his diary on 10 June, "The most imperative problem at present is how to rehabilitate the hard-hit carrier-borne air force [of First Air Fleet]."[127]) I had the mission to reorganize the Third Fleet.... 30 percent of the pilots were killed and 40 percent were injured.... 30 percent of the pilots came back to Japan to convalesce, and 40 percent were shifted to the Third Fleet, at Kyushu, to go into further training.... The Third Fleet was organized on 15 July and they figured two months were needed for their next operation; but before they had enough time to reorganize, the Guadalcanal picture came up and they were forced to send these pilots prematurely to Rabaul.[128]

Admiral Soemu Toyoda concurred in his interrogations. "I think what might be termed the turning point was the Battle of Midway. Our losses there had a very serious effect upon us, together with the fact that we used very much fuel at that time, more than we had expected would be necessary; and the effect of that was felt right through afterwards."[129]

On-and-off-again Navy Minister Mitsumasa Yonai commented to interrogators,

> I would pick either Midway or our retreat from Guadalcanal as the turning point, after which I was certain there was no chance for success.... I pick [sic] Midway principally from the naval standpoint because of the heavy fleet losses suffered there. Guadalcanal, on the other hand, I pick [sic] from a more general point. When we had to retreat, taking the whole situation [sic], I felt that there was no further chance of success.[130]

Keeper of the Privy Seal Kido told interrogators that he had not viewed the situation as all that bad after Midway because America's new equipment and weapons had not yet made their appearance. He cited Guadalcanal as the point where the war plan started going off the rails.[131]

Takata and Toyoda indicated that as a direct result of this battle, it was decided to place increased emphasis on the carriers, a theory that had long been held by the younger Japanese naval officers, and that because of this action the older officers were forced to change their way of thinking. But it was too late. "I think that the failure of the Midway Campaign was the beginning of total failure," he concluded. "They should have stopped to think of defense, to consolidate."[132]

Vice Admiral Fukudome recalled in December 1945, "The effect of the Midway Battle was to greatly restrict the area in which [a decisive] fleet engagement could be carried out. The damage we suffered there was so great that the result was concealed from our own public. It is only now that the truth is coming out, and I believe it is giving rise to a considerable problem because of the previous concealment."[133]

The IJN only informed the Army Section of the IGHQ of the disastrous results at the bureau level and higher and at the planning staff.[134]

Admiral Seiichi Ito, Vice Chief of the Naval General Staff, delivered a message to Yamamoto and Ugaki after the Combined Fleet returned to port. The Emperor was not too concerned about the defeat; such things were to be expected in war. They were to keep up their morale and try again.[135]

Yamamoto on 22 June struck Ugaki as "brooding over something and losing spirit." Ugaki did not feel close enough to his Commander-in-Chief to ask why.[136]

Perhaps Ugaki now had the time to consider the wider war, because on 25 June, he wrote in his diary, "In the European theater, Germany is involved in many weak points, but fortunately the situation is favorable in Kharkov, Sebastopol, and North Africa, which may cover these points. I anxiously hope so."[137]

The tide in the Pacific was turning, and the Japanese command acknowledged that de facto. IGHQ on 29 June ordered forces in the Southern Area to shift from offensive operations to "holding and maintaining stability in the strategic regions of the Southern Area." Perhaps responding to the instructions, Ugaki ordered his staff on 30 June "to make a study of defense in general."[138]

At the same time as the battle of Midway, the Northern Force, consisting mainly of Fifth Fleet, invaded Attu and Kiska in the Aleutian Islands stretching southwestward from Alaska. The forces involved barely achieved readiness before departing, the battle of Midway diverted some of the naval covering force, and IGHQ scratched a planned landing on Adak. Yet the operation unfolded smoothly on 8 June, without any enemy interference.[139]

The battleships *Ise* and *Hyuga* were equipped with the very first shipborne radars. None of the ships at Midway had radars to provide early warning of air attack or to direct fighters.[140]

CHAPTER 10

Late 1942: The Shock of Reality

The Axis powers were to suffer setbacks against all their major enemies except China in late 1942. The first occurred for Germany in July, when the heretofore highly lethal U-boat battle off the American coast went sour. Under pressure from Churchill and General Marshall—the army was losing ships and valuable resources intended for the buildup in the UK—Roosevelt finally ordered King to implement convoys, properly escorted, in the waters off the east coast and the Caribbean. Losses to U-boats immediately plummeted.[1]

Berlin Requests More Japanese Heat on Moscow

The British SIS reported on 21 July 1942 from a reliable and very delicate source:

> On July 6th the German Foreign Office represented strongly to the Japanese Ambassador, Oshima, that if Japan cannot declare war on the USSR she should at least adopt more aggressive attitude towards her because Germany is at present making a maximum effort to—
> 1. occupy Caucasus and advance thence through Iran to Iranian [Persian] Gulf;
> 2. occupy and reach Red Sea by Autumn, 1942.
>
> A more aggressive attitude of Japan towards the USSR would assist Germany in the realization of these plans.
> Up to July 6th Japan had not agreed to this and Japan still considers it very difficult to coordinate her military interests with those of other Axis powers. The Military Attaché said, "It is not in Japan's interest for Germany to be able to terminate war quickly."[2]

Halder, OKH chief, confirmed to interrogators after the war that in early 1942, Hitler, while planning his spring offensive, was so certain that the USSR had just spent its last gasp in the winter offensive, that he raised the Persian Gulf as a military objective.[3]

Now there was optimism! Germany's claimed objectives were wildly beyond her means, while the Japanese attaché was concerned Germany might win too quickly.

Japan on 27 July refused the German suggestion that it attack the Soviet Union. Tokyo explained to Ambassador Oshima, "Japan's immediate objective is to carry through to completion its war with America and England. In order to do this, it is necessary to strengthen our offensive against America and England, establish a solid organization in the south, and tighten our grip on China.... At this time, it is necessary to maintain peace in the north insofar as possible."[4] The message handed to the Germans made this point forthrightly.[5]

When Oshima passed the message to Ribbentrop, the German replied,

> Your Excellency has yourself seen the eastern front and knows how things look there at first hand. [Oshima had just returned from a tour.] And, indeed, the war everywhere is progressing more swiftly and favorably than Germany had expected it to. In war, though, we never know what unexpected ups and downs will occur. But if things keep going as at present, by this winter we Axis nations will have won next to a victory. Now, what the three Axis nations must do is take advantage of this situation to the fullest and make our liaison and joint strategy more and more intimate.[6]

Ribbentrop urged the Japanese submarines in the western Indian Ocean to cooperate in the coming battle for Egypt, and to strive to join hands with the Germans in the struggle for the Caucasus and the Near East.[7]

Admiral Ugaki, pondering the German offensive toward the Caucasus, wrote in his diary on 11 July, "If and when the situation in the Near and Middle East turns favorable, we shall have to advance westward in response, too. Attempts to reduce enemy strength and raid enemy sea traffic in the western Indian Ocean, which Italy craves, can be done by submarine, but it involves much risk to employ surface vessels in those attempts. I think we should capture Ceylon, first."[8]

As it happened, Tokyo was engaged in political efforts to prepare the path for a westward advance. The Combined Fleet staff conducted studies of potential Indian Ocean operations in mid-July and crafted a draft plan.[9] Tojo on 27 July gave a speech on the war in which he promised to help India gain full independence from Britain and called on the Muslim territories of the Middle East to seize the opportunity available to them to establish free countries.[10]

All the Axis Powers were pinning great hopes on the looming battle for Egypt. Rommel had attacked in June and driven the British back to El Alamein by July. Mussolini was already planning to visit Egypt, the Japanese Embassy in Rome reported. Oshima was more skeptical about Egypt and judged that the side that was better able to supply itself would overcome the stalemate. Meanwhile, he viewed the opening of a second front in Europe as "practically impossible" for now and entirely dependent on American support to Britain.[11]

Panzer Army Africa on 4 July ran into British defenses at El Alamein that, this time, were to hold firm. The panzer army again reported to the Army High Command that it had encountered American-made tanks. In a status report filed on 21 July, Rommel asked that the Army High Command supply 36 88mm guns, 10 100mm guns, and 100 50mm antitank guns to deal with the M3 Grants.[12] Clearly, the standard 37mm antitank gun was ineffective against the American tanks.

In Germany physicists in summer 1942 briefed an audience including Albert Speer and military armaments chief General Friedrich Fromm on the possibility of providing limitless energy and devastating weapons by tapping the power of the atom. All present were impressed. Under questioning from Fromm, Werner Heisenberg and his colleagues conceded such a weapon would require two or three years to develop and a huge investment. The prospect appeared simply too long term given Germany's pressing military needs of the moment. Indeed, the possibility was irrelevant.[13]

In Japan, Admiral Ugaki was paying attention to the war in Europe and wrote in his diary on 25 July, "The Germans have entered Rostov and are near Stalingrad. The activities of these friendly nations are more welcome than ever before."[14]

On 30 July, Ugaki noted dismal news, originating in a leak published by the *Chicago Tribune* that had eventually reached Japan. "The United States is said to have known all about our strength disposition in the middle of April. They must have succeeded in decoding, which was the cause of our defeat at Midway." The IJN made major changes to its code on 1 August.[15] This change, however, may have been part of a wider increase in security, and it is unclear whether the IJN was convinced its code had been broken.[16]

On New Guinea, fierce air battles raged from April to August. Pilot Sakai recalled,

> The days seemed to blur into one another. Life became an endless repetition of fighter sweeps, of escorting our bombers over Moresby, of racing for fighters on the ground to scramble against the incoming enemy raiders. The Allies seemed to have an inexhaustible supply of aircraft. A week never went by without the enemy suffering losses, and yet the planes came, by twos or threes and by the dozens.[17]

Despite America's Germany-first policy, in 1942, nearly half of army personnel, including air force, went to the Pacific theater. In August, for example, just over half (198 versus 193) the four-engine bombers deployed westward rather than toward Germany.[18] The war material Roosevelt directed to the Pacific was about to hit the Japanese hard.

Guadalcanal: Japan's Best Test the Rest, and Fail

The battle of Guadalcanal in the Solomon Islands represented several key developments in shaping the evolution of Japanese leadership thinking about America: The United States went on the offensive, Japan committed some of its best army divisions to the fight, the navy lost another three aircraft carriers, and—although the final pullout would occur in 1943—by late 1942 it was clear that the Japanese would not win.

The American operation coincided with Japanese amphibious landings on eastern New Guinea aimed at capturing Port Moresby the hard way: over land.[19]

A Marine Corps history captures the landing on Guadalcanal:

> At 0641 on 7 August, [Rear Admiral Richmond] Turner [commander of the amphibious operation] signaled his ships to "land the landing force." Just 28 minutes before, the heavy cruiser *Quincy* (CA-39) had begun shelling the landing beaches at Guadalcanal. The sun came

up that fateful Friday at 0650, and the first landing craft carrying assault troops of the 5th Marines touched down at 0909 on Red Beach. To the men's surprise (and relief), no Japanese appeared to resist the landing. Hunt immediately moved his assault troops off the beach and into the surrounding jungle, waded the steep-banked Ilu River, and headed for the enemy airfield. The following 1st Marines were able to cross the Ilu on a bridge the engineers had hastily thrown up with an amphibian tractor bracing its middle. The silence was eerie and the absence of opposition was worrisome to many riflemen. The Japanese troops, most of whom were Korean laborers, had fled to the west, spooked by a week's B-17 bombardment, the pre-assault naval gunfire, and the sight of the ships offshore....

[The night of 8 August,] a cruiser-destroyer force of the Imperial Japanese Navy reacted to the American invasion with a stinging response. Admiral Turner had positioned three cruiser-destroyer groups to bar the Tulagi-Guadalcanal approaches. At the Battle of Savo, the Japanese demonstrated their superiority in night fighting at this stage of the war, shattering two of Turner's covering forces without loss to themselves. Four heavy cruisers went to the bottom—three American, one Australian—and another lost her bow. As the sun came up over what soon would be called "Ironbottom Sound," Marines watched grimly as Higgins boats swarmed out to rescue survivors. Approximately 1,300 sailors died that night and another 700 suffered wounds or were badly burned. Japanese casualties numbered less than 200 men.[20]

Ugaki recorded in his diary on 7 August,

> The enemy employed a huge force, intending to capture the area once and for all. That we failed to discover it until attacked deserves censure as extremely careless. A warning had been issued two days before. Anyway, we were attacked unprepared. Unless we destroy them promptly, they will attempt to recapture Rabaul, not to speak of frustrating our Moresby operation. Our operations in that area will become extremely unfavorable. We should, therefore, make every effort to drive the enemy down first, even by putting off the Indian Ocean Operation [which the Japanese did].[21]

The IJA was even less prepared. The IGHQ Navy Section had never informed the Army Section that the IJN was constructing an airfield on Guadalcanal and had a small force there to protect 2,700 construction workers.[22]

Vice Admiral Gunichi Mikawa, commanding Eighth Fleet, decided to strike back immediately and ordered all his light warships—five heavy cruisers, two light cruisers, and one destroyer—to race from Rabaul to Guadalcanal. Moreover, most staff officers at IGHQ never expected the Americans to launch an offensive as early as August 1942. The initial IGHQ appraisal concluded that the amphibious assault was probably no more than a reconnaissance operation, and that even if it were a real invasion, Japanese forces could easily recapture the island. Indeed, the existence of the airfield, from which the Americans could threaten Rabaul, meant that a counterattack was needed post-haste.[23]

Japanese readers were treated to a dramatic eyewitness account of the naval engagement in the 15-mile-wide Tulagi Straits off the Solomon Islands on 8 August. The fleet, in only 36 minutes beginning at 2340 hours, claimed the sinking of seven large cruisers, one smaller cruiser, and six destroyers and the disabling of two more destroyers. A correspondent on board the flagship described how the Japanese ships passed two American destroyers without being noticed, deployed in battle formation, and then opened fire with torpedoes and guns under the light of flares dropped by aircraft.[24]

The Foreign Ministry saw the battle as an opportunity to counter American diplomatic efforts in Latin America to bring more countries into the war against the Axis. Foreign Minister Shigenori Togo cabled the embassy in Chile, "In the recent Solomon Islands sea battle, the remaining British and American naval forces in the southwest Pacific have almost been cleared out, and we have consolidated the advantageous battle positions."[25] Togo in a circular message argued that Japanese success or failure in the Pacific would strongly influence the willingness of Latin American countries to supply the United States with war materials at a time when shipping losses to Axis submarines were raising doubts about the abilities of the U.S. Navy.[26]

The Marine Corps history describes the initial Japanese Army response:

> Imperial General Headquarters in Tokyo had ordered Lieutenant General Haruyoshi Hyakutake's Seventeenth Army to attack the Marine perimeter. For his assault force, Hyakutake chose the 35th Infantry Brigade (Reinforced), commanded by Major General Kiyotake Kawaguchi. At the time, Kawaguchi's main force was in the Palaus. Hyakutake selected a crack infantry regiment—the 28th—commanded by Colonel Kiyono Ichiki to land first. Alerted for its mission while it was at Guam, the Ichiki Detachment assault echelon, one battalion of 900 men, was transported to the Solomons on the only shipping available, six destroyers. As a result, the troops carried just small amounts of ordnance and supplies. A follow-on echelon of 1,200 of Ichiki's troops was to join the assault battalion on Guadalcanal....
>
> Too full of his mission to wait for the rest of his regiment and sure that he faced only a few thousand men overall, Ichiki marched from Taivu to the Marines' lines.... At 0130 on 21 August, Ichiki's troops stormed the Marines' lines in a screaming, frenzied display of the "spiritual strength" which they had been assured would sweep aside their American enemy. As the Japanese charged across the sand bar astride the Ilu's mouth, [the] Marines cut them down. After a mortar preparation, the Japanese tried again to storm past the sand bar. A section of 37mm guns sprayed the enemy force with deadly canister. Lieutenant Colonel Lenard B. Cresswell's 1st Battalion, 1st Marines moved upstream on the Ilu at daybreak, waded across the sluggish, 50-foot-wide stream, and moved on the flank of the Japanese. Wildcats from VMF-223 strafed the beleaguered enemy force. Five light tanks blasted the retreating Japanese. By 1700, as the sun was setting, the battle ended.... Colonel Ichiki, disgraced in his own mind by his defeat, burned his regimental colors and shot himself. Close to 800 of his men joined him in death.[27]

It is a delicious irony that Ichiki had commanded the unit that started the China Incident at Marco Polo Bridge in 1937.[28] His action launched Japan on the unwinnable war in China, which led her to go to war against America, which brought the U.S. Marines to Guadalcanal.

The landings got the IJA's attention in China. The China Expeditionary Army had been planning a five-month campaign to capture Chungking and assembled 16 divisions for the push. The fighting in the Solomons forced cancellation of the operation because IGHQ indicated it would need to move divisions earmarked for the offensive from Southeast Asia (Java, Burma, and Hong Kong) to the Solomons instead as reinforcements, along with large amounts of war material.[29]

Admiral Fukudome, chief of the Navy General Staff Operations Branch, sent Ugaki a letter that arrived on 14 August, in which he expressed concern that the IJN would face fuel shortages. He expressed his hope that the view that capital ships were now worthless [presumably a view at Combined Fleet] "should not be advocated too soon, when nobody knew what would happen in the future, and as it also would affect morale." He conceded that the operational use of submarines in a real war had proved less successful than in fleet maneuvers and argued that they should mainly engage in traffic-raiding warfare as Germany was doing.[30]

Admiral Yamamoto viewed the situation in the Solomons as grave and decided to attack the Americans with most of the strength of the Combined Fleet. On 23 August, the Second and Third Fleets advanced to the waters 200 to 400 nautical miles northwest of the Solomons. Yamamoto decided that he had to destroy the American carriers before transports could land U.S. Army reinforcements on Guadalcanal.

Third Fleet carrier planes on 24 August attacked enemy carriers and damaged the *Enterprise* badly. The light carrier *Ryujo*, attached to Second Fleet, however, came under repeated enemy attacks and sank. The outcome was short of the need, and Yamamoto decided the destroyers would have to transport the IJA troops at night. This meant they again would arrive without heavy weapons and with little ammunition. The first run occurred on 28 August.[31]

By the end of August, IGHQ realized it had completely misread the situation on Guadalcanal. It ordered a halt to offensive operations toward Moresby, though an attack to capture an airfield would continue, and ordered Southern Area forces to focus on Guadalcanal. Once that was straightened out, operations were to resume on New Guinea.[32] IGHQ also had to scale back dramatically its planned offensive on Chungking in spring 1943 and acknowledged that it might be unable to move at all, given the resource drain at Guadalcanal.[33]

Let us emphasize that once again, the war against America that was necessary to win the war in China was undercutting the war in China, in this case sparing the Chinese from a major offensive to capture the capital.

As If That Weren't Bad Enough

In Berlin, Oshima told Ribbentrop in early September:

> England and the United States have rich resources and vast production capacity, whereby they are planning to protract this war. It is up to the Axis to thwart that plan and to conclude the struggle in as short a time as possible. Nevertheless, if the war does turn out to be a long one, we must be sure that our production does not fall below theirs.
>
> The way the war is going now, I do not believe it is possible to make a decisive stroke any time soon.... I think we must aim, by all means, to win by 1944.[34]

Japanese forces were committed across a huge expanse of geography, with only a small portion devoted to the American theater. The U.S. Military Intelligence Service as of September 1942 estimated the IJA's order of battle to consist of (non-divisional units not related here unless they made up the entire force):

    Japan: 16 divisions, 477,500 men
    Sakalin: 1 division, 25,000
    Korea: 2 divisions, 50,000
    Manchuria: 33 divisions, 641,000
    North China (including inner Mongolia): 7 divisions, 270,000
    Central China: 11 divisions, 357,000
    South China: 2 divisions, 60,000
    Formosa: 1 depot division, 5,000
    Hainan: 3 brigades, 20,000
    Philippines: 2 divisions, 50,000
    French Indochina: 2 divisions, 50,000
    Burma: 5 divisions, 130,000
    Malaya: 2 divisions, 52,500
    Sumatra: 1 division, 25,000
    Borneo: 1 division, 25,000
    Celebes: 1 division, 25,000
    Banda Sea: 1 division, 25,000
    New Guinea/Solomon Islands: 3 divisions, 77,500
    Java: 2 divisions, 50,000
    Army Air Corps: 175,000

    Total Strength: 2,665,000[35]

Foreign Minister Togo resigned on 1 September after the Foreign Ministry's powers were reduced as part of the creation of a Greater East Asia Ministry to handle all political, economic, and cultural affairs. The change was consistent with the fact that the IJA and IJN were exercising authority over Manchukuo, the Philippines, Netherlands East Indies, and the conquered southern territories in general. Japanese ambassadors in Manchuria, China, French Indochina, and Thailand became officials of the new ministry.[36]

With Pearl Harbor not even a year behind them, the Japanese by September were beginning to feel the effects of American air strikes against Canton, Nanking, and other targets in China, which were becoming "severe." The IJA estimated that American air strength in China amounted to 63 fighters and 23 bombers.[37] The Americans over the summer had replaced the famed Flying Tigers volunteer group that supported Chiang Kai-shek's Nationalist forces with a regular military outfit, the Tenth Air Force. Its 11th Bombardment Squadron (Medium) had arrived equipped with B-25 Mitchell bombers.[38]

The effects of American submarine warfare were even more alarming. An IJN circular transmitted on 30 October reported, "During October, our losses from enemy submarines amounted to 103,000 tons of shipping sunk and 70,000 tons damaged. This is ___ [undecipherable] for Japan. The Emperor, as well as the Chief of Naval General Staff, felt this keenly, particularly when it is realized that since the outbreak of the naval war, over 670,000 tons have been sunk and over 1,000,000 tons damaged."[39]

Asked by American interrogators when he thought the overall war plan was going awry, Keeper of the Privy Seal Kido said it was at the time that U.S. forces became increasingly successful at sinking Japanese shipping. Kido explained that had Japan been able to employ all the natural resources in the conquered areas, it could have fought on much longer. But insufficiency in shipping meant these anticipated developments did not take place.[40]

Commenting in his diary on operations at Guadalcanal, Admiral Ugaki wrote on 12 September, "They bring planes as fast as we shoot them down. It is a real problem."[41] Most of pilot Sakai's comrades died in the air over Guadalcanal while he lay in a hospital recovering from wounds and surgery to his eyes incurred during his first air battle over Guadalcanal. One of the survivors—a highly ranked ace himself—told Sakai later, "There were just too many enemy planes, just too many."[42]

The first significant counterattack by IJA reinforcements brought to Guadalcanal by destroyers of the "Tokyo Express" (even Ugaki adopted the name) and landing craft hit the Marine defenses on the 13th and collapsed with heavy casualties. Ugaki visited the Seventeenth Army headquarters the morning of 14 September and found that the army command was in shock and seemed "at a loss about what to do."

Ugaki considered the causes of the Japanese failure:

> We underestimated the enemy determination to launch their first offensive, staking the President's honor for the intermediate fall election campaign and pouring in fighting strength despite repeated losses, as well as their thorough preparedness in defense and countermeasures. On the other hand, we overestimated our strength deployed in the first-stage operation and sought success in a surprise attack at one stroke with lightly equipped troops of the same (or less) strength as the enemy.[43]

The IJN took a major step forward in the technological war when it introduced the Type H-6 airborne surveillance radar, which could fit in flying boats and medium-sized attack planes. This could detect air (group at 60 miles, single at 40 miles) and probably surface targets. It did not see widespread deployment until 1944. The IJN deployed land-based radars to islands across the Pacific to protect its airbases, but these were unsophisticated and, while able to detect aircraft at 60 miles, could not provide accurate information on altitude or speed. The first ground- and ship-based air detection radar to see wide use, the Type 11, was not to become operational until March 1943, when the IJN decided to equip all ships with radar when possible. Unlike Germany, Japan was to field a wide variety of increasing capable radars during the war.[44]

The Combined Fleet and Seventeenth Army agreed to move the 2d Infantry Division, which had been earmarked for New Guinea, to Guadalcanal and launch another attack in mid-October. Realizing just how bad things were, IGHQ transferred to Seventeenth Army the 38th Infantry Division from the East Indies, and troops from the Kwantung Army, Chinese Expeditionary Army, the Southern Army, and Japan.[45]

War in the Desert: The Arsenal Starts to Arrive

For the Italians, the war in Libya and Egypt was paramount, and by September, Field Marshal Erwin Rommel's drive into Egypt was stalled at El Alamein. Ciano recorded in his diary growing concerns that the offensive would never get moving again because of fuel shortages and catalogued the continual sinking of supply ships by the Allies. On 8 September, an ominous report reached Rome that indicated American war production was starting to influence the battlefield: Rommel was facing a "great increase in the quantity and quality of Anglo-American equipment."[46]

Ciano appears to have concluded that the war was lost just before a series of Axis military disasters made the war's turning point fairly obvious. On 22 September, he recorded,

> By the summer of 1943, the Allies will have a definite air superiority. [Marquis Blanzo Lanza] D'Aieta [Ciano's *chef de cabinet*] tells me about a very confidential talk he had with [Otto Christian Archibald von] Bismarck [a senior German envoy in Italy], who says that now he is sure that Germany will be defeated and will fight to the "bitter end." Italy will find a way out. The policy of moderation which I have always pursued toward Britain and America will help a good deal. It is because of this policy that Ribbentrop in particular, and the Germans in general, hate me.[47]

His entries from 27 to 30 September are bleak:

> I see the Duce after a long absence.... [He] realizes that military events have undermined the morale of the people, especially the résistance at Stalingrad.... I had a visit from Rommel, who says he is going home on leave for six weeks. Mussolini is convinced that he will never come back. He found him upset physically and morally.... From Berlin and Vienna come rather pessimistic reports.... [T]he summer offensive has failed in its objective. Furthermore, the air attacks are terrorizing the German population and often paralyze life in Germany.[48]

Whether or not he believed it, the Duce still put on a happy face. He received the Japanese ambassador on 30 September. "You have heard all these rumors about a so-called second front," the Duce told him, "but it is out of the question this year. Some say it will come next spring, but various reasons lead me to think that it will be impossible then, too. Italy's fight against England, the United States, and Russia may continue for several years to come, but in these several years we will win, I assure you." Mussolini urged Japan to attack Australia, India, and the

Soviet Union. It needed to wrap up the China Incident now that supplies to Chiang were cut off.

Nevertheless, the ambassador warned Tokyo, "Lately, the Axis seems relatively at a standstill.... [W]e must realize that Italy is the weakest spoke in the Axis wheel and England and the United States are not a bit lax in trying to extricate this spoke."[49]

The Americans Join the Ground War Against Hitler

Although gaps exist in the record, a review of the OKW war diary suggests that at no point during 1942 did a meaningful discussion of American activities occur, other than the war at sea. The diary noted on 9 June the landing of American troops and materials in Central Africa, which probably was when they realized the U.S. Army Air Force had established an airbase in Monrovia, Liberia, as part of the air bridge to the Middle East. The British and Lend-Lease deliveries had been using landing strips in British colonies in West Africa on their way to Sudan and then Egypt since 1940.[50]

Only a month before the Anglo-American landings in North Africa, Hitler—citing new agent reports—was worried that the Allies were going to land in France. On 5 October, he ordered several divisions to the area and wanted five coastal divisions organized. Commander-in-Chief West was to put coastal units on alert when the weather was good. Warlimont wrote that a short time after this, the Wehrmacht planning staff, probably unaware or dismissive of Hitler's "agent reports," thought that French Northwest Africa was the likely goal of any Allied landing.[51]

High Command interest in Africa, however, was focused on Egypt and Libya, where British probing attacks at El Alamein the night of 5 October presaged the all-out offensive on 23 October by Eighth Army under the command of Lieutenant General Bernard Montgomery. Prisoners taken during the probes reported having seen no American troops, which was relayed to the Army High Command, so the Germans were at least asking the question.[52]

Montgomery deployed almost 1,000 tanks in his offensive, at least half of which were American built and armed with a 75mm main gun. Rommel had 123 Mark III and Mark IV medium tanks with inferior main guns.[53] This was the first avalanche of American war products to hit the Axis.

The landings in Northwest Africa on 8 November—Operation *Torch*—came as a strategic surprise to the German High Command. OKW, Keitel told his interrogators after the war, expected the United States to turn first to establishing bases on Atlantic islands and the West Africa coast for reasons of both broader war fighting and postwar ambitions. After the landings, according to Keitel, there was no doubt that the Americans would participate in British operations against Italy and probably southern France. Although aware that American divisions were arriving in the UK in growing numbers, OKW judged that several factors argued against the involvement of large American forces on the Continent. These included the success of the U-boat war (until May 1943), the incomplete readiness of the air force for action, and the demands of the war in the Pacific.[54] (FMS note: Boetticher in Washington had been claiming that Washington had a substantial postwar imperialist agenda. Hitler had claimed publicly that Roosevelt intended to "take possession of or gain control over the islands in the Atlantic."[55] (Keitel's admission of suffering strategic surprise serves no self-evident selfish personal agenda.)

On 15 October, a discussion took place at Hitler's headquarters about reports in ever-increasing numbers that Anglo-American landings in West Africa were imminent. Hitler rejected a proposal to permit the French to send reinforcements from Metropolitan France out of concern for Italian sensibilities. Warlimont's recollection was that Hitler or Jodl introduced the subject, which was based on a study that was vague and included a wide range of French possessions as possible targets, such as Dakar. Hitler on 22 October told Mussolini that he expected Allied landings in the West or Norway.

There were voices in OKW who by the beginning of November argued that French North Africa was the most likely place for an Allied amphibious operation, but they had few concrete indications to support their suspicions, and even these officers looked to early 1943 as the likely time for an Allied operation. The Germans had obtained indications from "obscure sources and round-about channels" that troops and ships were concentrating in western England. The types of equipment spotted suggested that this was an amphibious landing force. Similar, but even more vague, information was available concerning North American ports. American agents were reported to be increasingly active in French North Africa, but close monitoring of the Vichy French revealed no grounds for concern. Field Marshal Albert Kesselring, Commander-in-Chief South, claimed after the war that he, for one, had expected landings in North Africa. For Kesselring, however, it was almost academic, because in his view Montgomery's defeat of Rommel had already sealed North Africa's fate, leaving him no better prospects than tying the Allies down there for as long as possible.

Field Marshal Albert Kesselring was a Luftwaffe officer who wound up commanding mostly ground forces at the theater level in North Africa and Italy, and for a brief while at war's end in Germany. Although convicted of war crimes, he contributed excellent reports to the Foreign Military Studies series. (Bundesarchiv)

OKW paid little heed to these indications, but it forwarded warnings of imminent Allied action to Field Marshal Gerd von Rundstedt, Commander-in-Chief West, and to the army command in Norway.[56] (FMS note: There is strong agreement among the knowledgeable contributing authors to the FMS series that the landings came as a surprise, even if it was what some had feared. A selfish ulterior motive for lying about this matter is not obvious.)

As so often, the Italians had been ahead of the Germans in sussing out the future. Ciano told his diary on 9 October,

> Long Talk with General [Cesare] Arne, the Chief of [the Military Intelligence Service]. He is definitely pessimistic. All information and conclusions point to the fact that the Anglo-Saxons are preparing to land in North Africa from where they intend to strike at the Axis. Geographically and logically, Italy must be their first objective. How long will we be able to resist a serious, heavy, and methodical offensive action from the air and sea?[57]

A German general in Rome on 10 October reported to OKW that Commando Supremo was formulating contingency plans in case the Allies landed in Northwest Africa. The Italians thought the Axis should be prepared to overrun the rest of France and conduct landings in Tunisia, protected by the fleet. Mussolini had ordered that three divisions move to Tripoli by early 1943 to be ready to advance into Tunisia. The German naval attaché, however, reported the same day that the Italian navy judged such Allied landings as unlikely.[58]

Commando Supremo on 25 October, against the backdrop of the British offensive just unleashed at El Alamein, requested that OKW take a position on its view that Allied landings at Dakar were likely and possible in Morocco. Attacks on Algeria and Tunisia were unlikely, the Italians argued. OKW's stance was that defense of the colonies was a French responsibility, and that Vichy had a strong incentive to hold onto them. OKW's priorities were to support Panzer Army Africa adequately and strengthen coastal defenses in the West. Regarding the latter, Operation *Anton*—the occupation of southern France—was ready on the shelf. The French were likely to fight only as long as there was hope of success, and the defection of the French army to the Allies had to be prevented.[59]

Operation *Torch* consisted of three task forces and was the largest amphibious operation ever attempted. Western Task Force sailed from the United States to land the 3rd and 9th Infantry divisions, the 2d Armored Division, and supporting elements in Morocco with the aim of capturing Casablanca. Center and Eastern Task Forces sailed from the United Kingdom. The 1st Infantry Division and a combat command of the 1st Armored Division were to land at Oran, Algeria. The eastern operation consisted of the British 11th Infantry Brigade Group, a commando battalion, and a company of American tanks. Its objective was to capture Algiers and then push rapidly eastward into Tunisia.[60]

General Alphonse Juin, who took command of French North Africa in November 1941, was much more resistant to collaborating with the Germans than had been his predecessor, and he secretly ordered French forces in North Africa to prepare to defend against "whomever" attacked. He expected that the Axis was the most likely threat, but he also drew up plans to fight the British.[61]

MEDITERRANEAN LANDINGS 1942-1944

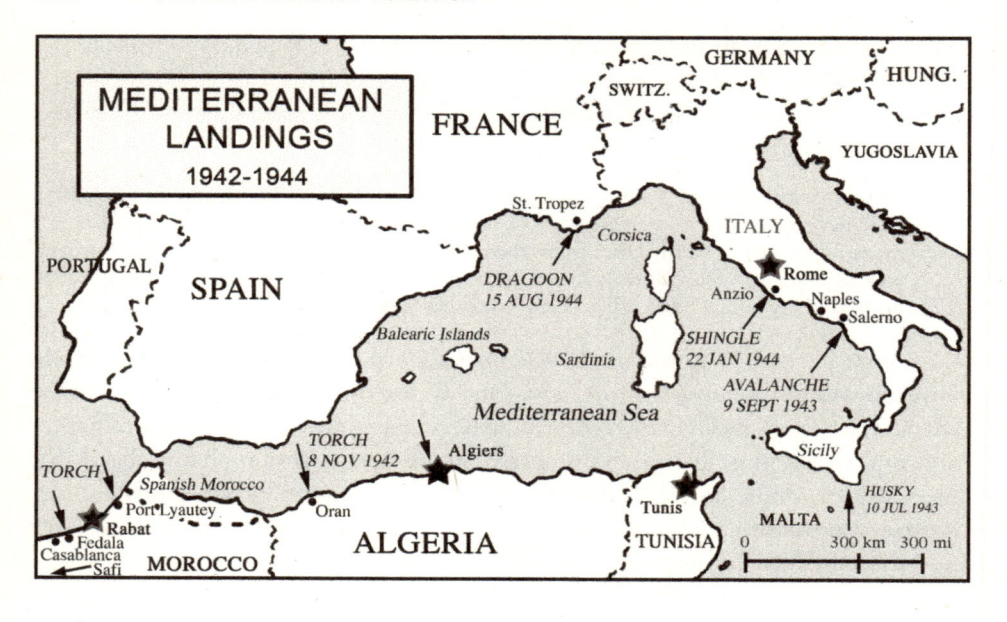

- DRAGOON 15 AUG 1944 — St. Tropez
- SHINGLE 22 JAN 1944 — Anzio
- AVALANCHE 9 SEPT 1943 — Salerno
- HUSKY 10 JUL 1943 — Sicily
- TORCH 8 NOV 1942 — Algiers
- TORCH — Fedala, Casablanca, Safi, Port Lyautey, Rabat (Morocco)

Hitler's public response to the landings was, "Roosevelt attacks North Africa, saying that he must protect it against Germany and against Italy—there is no need to waste a word on these lying phrases of the old cheat. He is without doubt the chief gangster of the whole coterie which opposes us. But the last and decisive word will certainly not be spoken by Mr. Roosevelt—of that he can be convinced."[62]

Ciano met with Hitler, Göring, and Ribbentrop in Munich beginning 9 November, the day after the landings. He recorded, "Hitler is neither nervous nor anxious, but he does not underrate the American action and wants to oppose it with every means. Göring does not hesitate to say that the occupation of North Africa is the first point in favor of the Allies since the beginning of the war." The next day, Hitler decided to send reinforcements to Tunisia.[63]

French resistance in Algeria ended after a perfunctory resistance on 10 March, but the Vichy army in Morocco put up a stiff fight for 74 hours and denied the American invaders their key objective of Casablanca. Although this work focuses on Axis views of America, the Moroccan operation was not a gleaming success even to its commanders. Lieutenant General George Patton told observers from Washington that had the landings in Morocco been opposed by Germans, "we never would have gotten ashore."[64] Major General Ernest Harmon, who commanded the 2d Armored Division, wrote to a friend in December, "Really, I wonder how we will do against real opposition. I am greatly worried."[65]

Germany discerned the end of effective resistance at Oran and Algiers. At 0700 hours on 11 November, Operation *Anton* began, and units of German First Army and Army Group Felber, commanded by Hans-Gustav Felber, crossed the demarcation

TUNISIAN BATTLEFIELDS

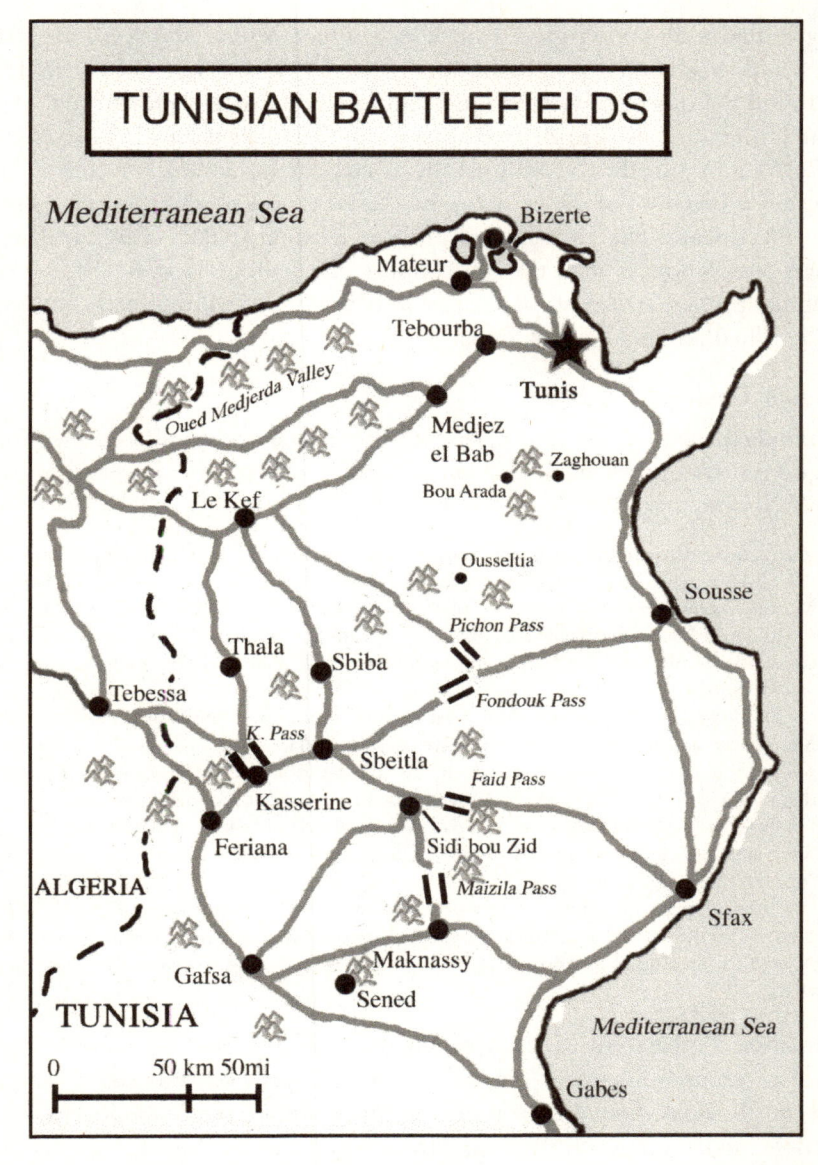

line into unoccupied France, encountering no resistance. The SS Corps occupied Toulon on 27 November. Two Italian divisions landed on Corsica, and the Italian Fourth Army marched into the French Riviera. The French did not resist, and Pétain initially remained in office in Vichy.[66]

German combat aircraft and a handful of troops began landing at an airfield near Tunis on 9 November, the first of 15,500 reinforcements—including 130 tanks—that arrived by the end of the month. Nine thousand Italian troops also moved in, most having shifted west from Tripoli. British forces, meanwhile, advanced from Algiers by land and short seaborne and airborne hops. The OKW war diary recorded the first ground fighting against American soldiers on 17 November, with ten of them captured. Thanks in part to the Axis incursion, the Allies persuaded the French in North Africa to join their cause formally as combatants on 13 November. On 17 November, a battalion of the German 5th Airborne Regiment encountered French holding forces and the British spearhead at Medjez el Bab, Tunisia. The bold German commander bluffed the Allied forces into pulling back. By 10 December, a combination of German resistance and horrifically wet weather had combined to stop the Allied advance toward Tunis.[67]

Operation Torch *Alarms Japan*

The landings in North Africa triggered an immediate appraisal from the Japanese Foreign Ministry of the global situation, the main points of which were summarized in a MAGIC report:

> The German drive in Russia has lost its impetus. Stalingrad still stands; Germany has not reached the Grozny oilfields, and victory cannot be expected, "at least this year," in the Leningrad–Moscow sector. "Thus Germany has failed in her objective for this year in the Soviet [Union]."
> The British recently attacked Rommel in Egypt and the Germans "are hard pressed." Germany is doubtless endeavoring to keep Rommel supplied and to move troops from the eastern front to North Africa.
> Britain and the United States have been active in Africa. The British have completely occupied Madagascar, and this is important when we consider India.... The landings of US troops on the west African coast is something "to which attention must be paid." Both nations are proclaiming that they will drive the Axis out of Africa and use that continent as an offensive base....
> Early in October, Stalin was dissatisfied because of the lack of assistance from the Allies. Since then, however, the Germans have not done so well. The Red Army has not been routed, "nor does it appear that this will happen soon, if ever."
> "The outbreak of the war in greater East Asia and the participation of the United States therein not only made a compromise peace [between Germany and Britain] impossible, but, strange to say, caused the British as well as the German camp to entertain greater hopes of victory."[68]

The Japanese Embassy in Madrid, meanwhile, had reported on 5 November the views of a "certain influential German," who said that the German war machine was stalled on all fronts, there was great poverty and suffering inside the Reich, and that the people might turn against the war. There was dissension between Germany and Italy over the war in North Africa, and the United States and Britain were trying to pull Italy away from the Axis. If events were allowed to drift further, "it may mean the end of the Axis." Germany could not conquer Russia without the help of the Japanese Army.[69]

The Japanese Embassy in Rome reported that the landing of American troops "startled everyone" in Italy. "Naturally the Italian people are greatly alarmed over the North African situation.... During this conversation, [Foreign Minister] Ciano spoke feebly, as if crestfallen. As he was leaving, he spoke a word of congratulations, saying that the announcement of the Japanese victory in the Solomons was certainly gratifying."[70] Ciano had recovered his composure by the 15th and told the Japanese ambassador that the American landings were a "flash in the pan." Axis troops would fight hard and establish a base for counterattack in Tunisia. "Although the highest quarters in Italy regard the North African situation as extremely serious," said the foreign minister, "they do not consider the whole war situation to be alarming yet."[71] Ciano himself recorded that he had reassured the ambassador "within the limits of the possibilities."[72]

"Serious," indeed. Ciano's diary records: "Collapse of the front in Libya." (5 November) "The withdrawal in Libya is assuming more and more the nature of a rout." (6 November)

The Japanese saw potentially dire consequences from the North African landings because of their impact on global opinion and on their cooperation with Vichy France. Foreign Minister Masayuki Tani was to prove to be an extremely sharp strategic thinker. Tani had served in the Japanese embassies both in Berlin and Washington early in his career. A Japanese newspaper article in 1931 portrayed him as resourceful and tactful. IJA officers judged him to be a man with a clear head and above average intelligence, though some criticized him for his skill in making himself pleasing to whomever he met. Though prematurely bald, Tani conveyed a sense of a military man when speaking with IJA officers.[73] Tani on 11 November transmitted a circular that read:

> The occupation of North Africa by the United States forces, if successful, may ultimately sway the final decision of all neutral nations and have a decisive effect on the whole world picture.
>
> As for the Japanese Empire, it is greatly concerned not only with respect to the battle of East Asia but with respect to many other things, such as the tremendous effect it will have upon the [Japanese puppet] Nanking Government. In other words, we are alert in every possible way, ever watching the course of events. The stand France now takes will play a tremendous role in the immediate future.
>
> [To Embassy Vichy:] Will you immediately go to [Prime Minister Pierre] Laval and with this in mind ask him what France intends to do; ask him whether or not he intends to stick to the Axis through thick and thin.[74]

Indeed, Japanese diplomats in Latin America reported with dismay that the American landings had propelled American momentum and were strengthening anti-Axis forces. Foreign Minister Tani cabled Buenos Aires, "This battle in North Africa—the way it is going—gives us no joy. Washington and London are sure to proclaim this attack as the second front and blatantly to declare that it is proceeding favorably for them." He expected this to be persuasive in Latin America.

On 11 November, Tani cabled Berlin, "We here are taking a very serious view of the US Army's landing in Northwest Africa." He demanded information on the reactions of Italy, Spain, and Portugal. The Foreign Ministry ordered missions worldwide to emphasize that despite its attempts to resist Japan's "absolutely indomitable strategy," the United States cannot "get its teeth into the Pacific." Moreover, the landings in Africa were political cover for the fact that the Allies were unable to open a second front in Europe.[75]

Admiral Ugaki recorded in his diary in late September that he viewed the course of the war in Europe with foreboding. The battle in Stalingrad was going poorly for the Germans, and the Allies had established air and sea dominance in the Mediterranean Sea. "It is now time for the Axis powers to get through this hard time, making the utmost effort."[76]

Japan Tries to Fight Back

Ugaki on 8 October participated in a meeting with the navy and army inspection teams. He recorded that the IJA fully appreciated the pressing situation in the Pacific. It planned to transfer five or six divisions plus 25 battalions of engineers to the theater.

The Combined Fleet and IJA were busily working on an operational plan to reestablish control over Guadalcanal. Ugaki recorded on 9 October,

> Whatever happens, we must succeed in the coming operation of recapturing Guadalcanal at any cost. In fact, we're now pursuing the second plan to meet the worst situation envisaged in the operational plan drawn up immediately after the surprise attack on 7 August. If even this fails, what other plan can we make? It would mean that the Combined Fleet would become incapable of doing anything. If so, the commander in chief's stand and my responsibility would face many difficulties. I am trying to be well prepared for that from now on.[77]

The Japanese fleet in late October for days had been searching for the American carriers Ugaki surmised were close to the Solomons based on spotting the battleship *Washington*, which he had learned was a tell that carriers were close. All month, the two hostile fleets had grappled with cruisers, destroyers, and submarines, trading losses to no operational advantage—but achieving Roosevelt's goal of attriting the Japanese fleet. On the 26th, Japanese planes reported spotting three carriers (there were only two) and the covering force launched attack planes. During the battle of Santa Cruz, the Japanese, with three carriers engaged, sank the *Hornet* and damaged the *Enterprise*, but the carriers *Shokaku* and *Zuiho* were damaged too badly to handle aircraft, and the former sufficiently badly to be sidelined for nine months. The Japanese lost about 100 aircraft, along with many of their remaining skilled pilots.

The Japanese mistakenly thought they had sunk three carriers and viewed the battle as a victory. Ugaki nevertheless commented in his diary, "The enemy builds and christens second and third generations of carriers, as many as we destroy."

On Guadalcanal, the Seventeenth Army's "general offensive" by the 2d Infantry Division to recapture Henderson airfield from the Americans broke down on 26 October after four days of heavy losses.[78]

Roosevelt was so concerned that on 24 October, he directly ordered his service chiefs to ensure that enough resources reached Guadalcanal to hold the island, even if that delayed meeting commitments in the European Theater of Operations (ETO). As of that month, America already had more army and navy aircraft in the South Pacific and Australia than it had in the UK, Africa, and the Middle East. This was its largest air campaign launched to that point.[79]

On 29 October, Ugaki recorded that an Army General Staff officer visited him and explained that an area army would be established for the South Pacific region, including Port Moresby, and consist of seven divisions. The Emperor that day sent the Combined Fleet a rescript commending its action in the South Pacific. In presenting the rescript, he referred to Guadalcanal as the "place of bitter struggles" and expressed hope it would soon be recaptured. The IJA, however, shelved any new offensive there until 1943.[80]

The Japanese Reassess Their Grand Strategic Situation

In Tokyo, liaison conferences on 3, 4, and 7 November reexamined previous estimates. Obviously, the American counteroffensive had already begun earlier than expected. The assumption that America would give priority to the war in Europe looked shaky. The first discussion of the American air threat to Japan occurred. Repeated air attacks were likely in 1943 from aircraft carriers and China. The Americans were creating a supply line through Tibet to support bombers in China. Little change in the European war seemed likely.

The adopted document concluded,

> In view of the above situation, if Japan establishes a self-sustaining and invincible political and strategic setup in one or two years by overcoming all difficulties, meets the future successive Anglo-American counteroffensives against Japan by taking as many positive enemy subjugation measures as possible in collaboration with Germany and Italy, and destroys the enemy fighting strength at any time or place, she will eventually be able to deprive America and Great Britain of their fighting spirit and achieve her war objectives.[81]

That was a lot of ifs.

As of early November, the two divisions on Guadalcanal had an effective combat strength of only about four battalions. These included 17,000–18,000 exhausted men backed by only 46 artillery pieces, 12 of them antiaircraft guns. Men were starving, and malaria was widespread. Supplies arriving on the island amounted to between a fifth and a third of requirements. Japanese troops on eastern New Guinea, meanwhile, were retreating under Allied pressure. The three IJN carrier divisions suffered attrition every day and had only a few carrier bombers, 55 to 70 fighters, and 55 to 70 land-attack planes.[82]

Tani on 14 November transmitted a circular assessing the United States, an analysis about which the MAGIC translators observed, "The report is noteworthy for its objectivity and for the shrewdness of most of the inferences and conclusions drawn."[83]

> Latest Report on Developments in the United States
> 1. Policy for Conduct of the War
> The United States apparently entertains the view that this year will be the decisive turning point of the war. She is stressing the importance of taking the offensive and stressing her cooperation with the British. She is also giving England and Russia more assistance. Furthermore, she is gradually beginning a direct offensive against Japan. Lately, the counterattack of the United States against Japan was stronger than expected and it is growing fiercer over a vast area from Australia to the Aleutians. In the Solomons, both sides are now locked in mortal combat. We do not believe that there is any change in the fixed policy of the United States to take the general offensive in a couple of years, i.e., as soon as she is completely prepared.
>
> It would seem that she still stresses Europe primarily but, judging from the distribution of her soldiers and her conduct of the war, she also considers the Pacific scene as very important. On the one hand, she is stationing more and more troops and material in Australia, making this the main jumping-off place for her attack on us. She is also tying up closer with [the Chinese Nationalists]. On the other hand, beyond doubt, she is trying to use the Soviet [Union] to close the back door of the Japanese Empire. The United States now heads the United Nations command in the Southwest Pacific, and the Pacific War Council is being directed by Washington. The American Government, realizing the necessity of satisfying public opinion, has taken political measures and is now in a strong enough position to be able to wage effective warfare in the Pacific. The height of her attack in this area may be expected by the spring of the year after next.
>
> 2. Military Production and Distribution
> The complete changeover from civilian to military production was completed in June. At the end of September, [Chairman of the War Production Board Daniel] Nelson stated that military production had increased three-fold since the beginning of the war but has not yet reached its goal. Furthermore, Roosevelt, after inspecting important plants in 24 states early in October, stated that they were achieving 94 percent of their capacity and that he was satisfied.
>
> On the other hand, it would appear that the supplies of materials and labor are out of step....
>
> The United States is concentrating on its program for building ships and planes. Consequently, she is getting excellent results along those lines. She will probably produce a gross tonnage of 4 million gross tons of ships this year. In the first half-year she completed 230 craft and during July, August, and September, 243. It would seem that the construction of a two-ocean fleet is proceeding smoothly. What is more, the monthly output of airplanes is now 5,000.
>
> The Government has recently lowered the draft age from 20 to 18 years. Four million recruits are expected by the end of this year and nine million by the end of next year.
>
> Laborers in war industries are expected to be increased by 13 million....
>
> In this connection, England and other nations, seeing how the United States is expanding its war effort and sending troops everywhere, are greatly worried over consequent reductions in supplies from the United States. Nevertheless, she is keeping 40 nations supplied. According to Government figures, for 18 months, up to August, the United States let her allies have $5.1 billion [$65 billion today] worth of material....
>
> Summing all this up, in spite of the fact that the English and Americans are both making increasing personal sacrifices, they both firmly believe that they will win in the end, and their morale runs high. Without having become a totalitarian, Roosevelt has a position just as firm as Churchill's. The two men are working together and have welded their two nations and are now leading the combined war effort.

3. General Conditions

The daily war expense amounts to $150 million or more. Prices are about 20 percent higher, and this year's inflation gap is estimated at $10.7 billion. The Government, however, is trying to make this up by taxation and other similar devices.... And, as the people are utterly and absolutely sure that they will win, they are perfectly willing to cough up. So, we cannot hope that the money situation will get out of hand.

The war objective of the Anglo-Saxons is to prevent Germany and Italy from establishing a new order in Europe and to ruin the Japanese Empire's plans for the establishment of a Greater East Asia Co-Prosperity Sphere. The United States also plans to steal a march on England and, taking advantage of her war strain, to seize hegemony over Central and South America and to get virtual control, slowly, slowly, step by step, over Canada, Australia, and India. Washington figures that London has enjoyed this enviable position long enough, and now it is its turn. We can also discern this motive in the recent distribution of arms. Assuredly, the United States is beginning to entertain ambitions of ruling the world.... [84]

Coincidently, Oshima on 14 November sent his own assessment to Tani, drawn from a conference of European-based Japanese diplomatic personnel in Berlin. His analysis, from the viewpoint of sitting in the German capital, focused on Britain and barely mentioned the United States. Oshima emphasized,

The collaboration of the Japanese Empire with its Allies, Germany and Italy, in the prosecution of this war is of world-wide significance. If we win, we must win both in the East and the West, and if we lose it must be the same.... [I]f in a fleeting dream we should imagine it possible to make a separate compromise with the United States and Britain, it would be the end of us.... One essential is that we drive all Anglo-Saxons out of India and the Near and Middle East, establishing contact between Europe and Asia, thus making the exchange of essential materials possible, and thus giving Great Britain a death blow.[85]

Oshima reported that the Red Army had broken through at Stalingrad and "the German Army could not hold it in check."[86] A week later, Oshima criticized the Germans for being focused entirely on the European war and missing the global picture.[87]

The Japanese mission in Berne, however, chimed in on 23 November with a more realistic European perspective based on its German and Italian contacts, including in Berlin during the conference. This analysis emphasized the United States, but it shared with Oshima a strong sense that the European and Pacific theaters were intimately related.

Regarding the Allied landings in North Africa. Germany appears to be quite confident that her countermeasures will succeed (Italy is not optimistic) and takes the view that it will be to her advantage to learn at last the true strength of American forces, which have hitherto been an uncertain quality.... Since the US military regards Germany and Italy as its first enemy, and Japan as the second, the main Allied strength is being concentrated in North Africa. Whether or not Europe is invaded ... will depend, of course, on the way the war goes in Africa, and also very largely on the extent to which Japan is able to restrain the United States and England.... The present situation has strengthened Stalin's will to fight.[88]

The Japanese ambassador in Moscow reported after the landings that the Soviets had not previously considered an African campaign to constitute a second front but now seemed "delighted." "Russia's feeling of confidence in England and the United States has grown stronger.... We think that henceforth the relations of Russia and England and America will become intimate once more."[89] The ambassador argued,

> This is the first opportunity US troops have had to prove themselves under German fire.... It seems that many in Japan are taking this North African action to mean that the United States, despairing of victory in the Orient, is trying to divert the minds of the people from that area; but let none be deceived. Once the United States and England have defeated Germany—and this they are determined to do—they intend to turn their full strength to the East. There is no division on this matter.[90]

Admiral Ugaki wrote in his diary on 26 November after receiving a Navy General Staff intelligence report projecting that after seizing North Africa, the Allies would land on the French Mediterranean coast, "Contemplating this and that, I couldn't help but think that the Axis Powers were facing an extreme crisis."[91]

Tani, on 28 November, sent Oshima a remarkably insightful analysis. He suggested that Germany had failed to secure the necessary oil supplies to sustain a long war. Germany might have weakened Russia, but Russia had weakened Germany, too, and she still had plenty of soldiers and munitions plants. That the Germans, with all their might, had failed to take Stalingrad was "an evil omen." The American penetration of North Africa presented the Reich with a new situation, and Germany now had little prospect of securing the Caucasus or the Near East.

> I believe that Germany will put up a stiff fight for Tunis, and I believe that she will probably succeed, but if she doesn't, things will be bad. When we consider this, in connection with the effect it will have on Italy, it gives us pause and makes us think. If worst comes to worst, in order to stabilize the situation in Italy, German troops will have to take over there.[92]

Tani argued that Germany was failing to exploit the production and manpower of Europe to the limit. Germany, he thought, had little room to expand her own production power. "Now what we want," Tani concluded, "is for Germany to get ready for a long war.... [S]he is a long way from ready. She faces a much harder job than she did when the war first began, and she has a much longer road to travel than she thought she did."[93]

The Japanese War Ministry conceded Japan had already lost the initiative in the Pacific, just as Germany had in Europe. In a message to the military attaché in Berlin in November, the ministry said:

> 1. US Strategy. The United States continues to carry the attack to the Japanese, relying chiefly on her air arm, and spurring Chungking on to resist Japan as much as she possibly can. The recent trend is more and more toward an all-out drive against Japan from Australia, the Aleutians, China, and India. The United States hopes that, taking advantage of the war developments in Europe, she can destroy our shipping, seize bases, and bomb our strategic centers, thus breaking into our defense zone.
> 2. Situation in the South Pacific. Fierce fighting is now going on in the Southern Pacific area. We expected an intense struggle from the start and concentrated on that sector. In the first part of August, a portion of our fleet was sent to the Solomons–New Guinea area and is now

resisting the American attack with all its strength. Taking the viciousness of these engagements into consideration, it is obvious that, with both sides going all-out, a turn in the tide must be reached soon. This may well be a decisive battle between Japan and America....

5. Japan's Strategy. In light of the conditions described above, it may be seen that for the present we must be relentless in our efforts, whatever obstacles we may encounter, to consolidate our position, and be ready at any time to smash the United States' plans for action against us. In the present national emergency, it would be unwise to undertake any new operations.[94]

Ugaki wrote in his diary on 4 December that unless the Japanese destroyed American air power in the Solomons area, "we'll be overwhelmed by the enemy air might…. The enemy doesn't care about losing battleships, cruisers, and destroyers and is trying to beat us with overwhelming air power."

The following day, a conference took place on the Combined Fleet flagship *Yamato*, which included the fleet and staff officers from the Army and Navy General Staffs, the Eighth Area Army, and the Eleventh Air Fleet to discuss the situation on Guadalcanal and Buna, New Guinea. The fleet feared that the Allies were close to securing an airfield near Buna that would allow them to pursue air superiority, as they had at Guadalcanal. Indeed, Allied air power had already rendered virtually impossible resupply of Japanese ground troops on Guadalcanal and at Buna by ship, and deliveries by air, submarine, and small boat were wholly inadequate. The Americans, meanwhile, were delivering supplies in a steady stream protected from Japanese air strikes.

The Army General Staff had approved sending the 65th Brigade and a regiment of the 51st Infantry Division to Buna and earmarked the 20th and 41st Infantry divisions as reserves, to depart Pusan, Korea, and Tsingtao (Qingdao) in Shandong Province, China, respectively. Ugaki knew that would not be enough and urged the IJA to prepare three more divisions.[95]

The IJN lost 901 planes in combat in the Solomons from 1 August 1942 to 1 January 1943, plus 680 to non-combat causes. Japanese industry could easily replenish the machines, but many of the IJN's most seasoned pilots were irreplaceable. Moreover, after the *Ryuho* was torpedoed ferrying aircraft to Rabaul in early December, the IJN shifted away from using carriers to haul airplanes to the battle zone. More pilots would have to fly thousands of miles to reach the South Pacific, and non-combat losses were to rise sharply.[96]

The Germans Wear Blinders

The Germans by comparison appeared to have had no clue as to what made Americans tick. A Foreign Ministry circular laying out guidance for the propaganda line to be aimed at the United States specified,

> You should appeal to the healthy instincts of the American people and point out the sinister role of the Jews on every occasion. You should stimulate the latent anti-Semitism in the United States by means of skillful and well-directed propaganda and never allow the subject of the

Jews to lapse. The responsibility of the Jews is to be stressed: They occupy the key positions in American politics and economics. The impression must be created that it is not in their own cause that the American people are making such unparalleled sacrifices. It is for the benefit of the Jews that Roosevelt is pitting his country against the might of the Tripartite Powers.[97]

Ribbentrop met with Oshima on 11 December and told him:

> I most certainly admit that the breakthrough at Stalingrad was a tactical victory for Soviet forces.... [T]he surrounded Germans are in no danger at all. Before long, they will smash the Soviet troops who are already weakening....
>
> The English and American landing in French North Africa was admittedly a success. Rommel's retreat was bad news for us Germans. It was the greatest fizzle we have seen in this war.... The Tunis area is now practically stabilized. Once Rommel goes back to that area things will change.... [W]e hope to keep Rommel supplied, but there is no guarantee that we will completely control the sea lane. What we are most worried about, to tell you the truth, is that North African situation.
>
> We have an advanced line drawn up the west coast of Europe from northern Norway to the Franco-Spanish border. We also have 50 divisions aligned over that area watching and waiting. Well, if Britain and America want to attack, let them come. The drama will end in a second Dieppe. We are ready for them.... We Germans feel safe in assuming that Britain and America are planning a landing expedition in Europe in order to relieve the pressure on Russia and to lengthen our lines of supplies. I could not say that there will be no landing in the Mediterranean area....
>
> [T]he productive power of the Anglo-Saxons [is not] up to what is generally imagined. What they lack most of all, however, is ships. Of course, the United States is going to produce plenty of airplanes from now on, but nevertheless, they will not be able to engage in any large-scale action next year.... Yes, Germany is sure to win, I am certain.[98]

Asked by Oshima if Germany would go over to a defensive war in 1943, Ribbentrop replied that she would wage all-out war. Oshima asked Ribbentrop, "[D]o you Germans still consider the East the focal point of your struggle, do you consider England and America secondary?"

The German replied, "I think that is so, but wait a little while before you ask me again."

Ribbentrop said that America's ability to direct military power toward Europe was "unpleasant," and he congratulated Japan on checking American power in East Asia. He added it would be desirable for Japan to advance to the western Indian Ocean. He conceded the argument that Japan should not dissipate its power by attacking Russia.

Oshima told him Japan would advance on the Indian Ocean once it had cleared up the situation in the south. Lying tens of thousands of kilometers from the homeland, it was no simple matter, "especially since the resistance of the United States in the vicinity of Australia is tenacious. It is vital first of all to destroy the American fleet and get rid of the stalemate there." It was in the interests of all Axis countries that the activities of the American army in Europe be curbed.[99]

German State Secretary for Foreign Affairs Ernst Bohle, who had just been traveling with Hitler, told a Japanese diplomat in Sofia, "I think the Anglo-Saxon action in North Africa will postpone the conclusion of the war. Germany is of the opinion that it would rather be too optimistic to say definitely that the war will be over in 1944."[100]

The Japanese ambassador in Moscow cabled Tokyo on 21 December that Japan's "sudden decision" to wage war against the United States and Britain had "been based on the success of the Germans." Now that the war "is obviously going against the Axis," it would be foolish not to realize that "one of our impelling reasons has failed us" and that the effect on Japan would be serious. The situation in the Solomons and New Guinea was no cause for rejoicing. "Facing this situation, there will surely be some among our people who will be frightened and lose confidence; but we must encourage them by appealing to patriotism and honor and impress upon them that their determination must not be weakened by the setting of Germany's star, because after all we have no alternative but to fight on."[101]

At Bletchley Park, meanwhile, the British on 13 December figured out how to defeat the German naval four-wheel Enigma machine. The Royal Navy immediately informed U.S. Admiral King that submarine transmissions were going to be readable, but no action should risk tipping the Allies' hand to the Germans.[102]

*

By December 1942, the strategic Japanese rationale for occupying Southeast Asia in order to end the conflict in China, which necessitated other actions that led to war with America, was looking like a bad gambit.

Admiral Ugaki recorded in his diary on 8 December, the first anniversary of Pearl Harbor, "In looking back over the past year, I regret that we have not gained what we wished. I pledge myself to accomplish our war aims by good planning and hard fighting in the future.... [W]e must count to our credit the captured territories and the secured resources. But we must anticipate that the next year won't be as easygoing as this."[103]

Also on the anniversary of Pearl Harbor, Army spokesman Colonel Nakaye Yahagi addressed a national rally in Tokyo. He told the audience:

> The method of the [U.S.] strategy is carry on the war by guerrilla warfare tactics, due to the fact that the nation does not wish to agree to peace terms. The method of a protracted war is to hope for an ultimate victory by a war of long duration, by carrying on a guerrilla war, although America tasted decisive defeats at the beginning of the war....
>
> [A] modern protracted war is a succession of many decisive battles in the course of a war development.... In a marathon race, a participant is not required to run with his best effort from the beginning of the race, but in a marathon hurdle race, one must overcome each hurdle from the beginning of the race. In short, a modern protracted war is something like a marathon hurdle race....
>
> Each of these obstacles represents a decisive battle and each determines the fate of victory in the future. Therefore, it is easy to understand that each decisive battle fought in the Guadalcanal area is a great decisive element [that] decides a fate for the future in the protracted war.[104]

IGHQ on 28 December concluded it could not retake Guadalcanal and ordered the Eighth Area Army to instruct Seventeenth Army to strengthen a line based on rearward positions in preparation for evacuation of the island. An imperial conference on 31 December ratified the evacuation. Losses in the ground fighting so far amounted to 13,000 for the IJA and about 3,800 for the IJN. Through November, losses in the Southern Area amounted to about 90,000 IJA and 40,000 IJN, a far higher loss rate than in China.[105]

Japanese resistance at Buna, meanwhile, collapsed on 29 December. The next day, Ugaki met with Rear Admiral Munetaka Sakamaki, former chief of staff of Eleventh Air Army, who told him that the main reason Japan was losing the air war was a sharp decline in aviation skills. New pilots were a third as skilled as their predecessors. Guadalcanal was hopeless. Indeed, Ugaki recorded in his diary that later that day he learned that the IJA, at a liaison conference in Tokyo, had proposed abandoning Guadalcanal.[106]

Foreign Minister Tani transmitted a circular on 29 December entitled "Summary of Conditions in the United States at the End of the First Year of War." It covered much of the same ground as his November missive but added:

> The American people are optimistic and their optimism is based on that of their officials. As they look back over the military actions of the past year, they conclude that, after successive defeats, they are at last winning and can stop Japan. On the other hand, in Europe the Russians are to a certain extent repelling the Germans on all fronts and winning respectable victories. Not only that, but recent American successes in the Solomons and New Guinea, together with the landing in North Africa, have convinced the Americans that they have taken the initiative and that next year, as production mounts to its peak, they can embark on an all-embracing action.
>
> It would be hard for us to believe that America's plans for action during the coming year are, as yet, thoroughly worked out, but nevertheless next year we can expect a stepping up in military activity. Already a certain amount of initiative is being taken, and ere long we can expect some strong drives. To be sure, heretofore America's leadership has been along political lines, but the trend now, I think, is to take the lead both politically and militarily. This will doubtless have a great effect on the course and trend of the conflict.
>
> At first the people favored knocking us out, but now the landing in North Africa has taken place, and they are endeavoring to steal Italy from the Axis camp through both harshness and pleading. We may therefore judge that for the time being America's main attention is focused across the Atlantic. Nevertheless, from the manner in which she stations her troops, it is not difficult to deduce that she is planning gradually to expand the theater of her activities to both oceans, and we are not, by any means, likely to escape her thrust long.[107]

Tani appeared to be a man already convinced the Axis would lose the war. He reiterated his view that America aimed to supplant Great Britain after the war and "play the role of benevolent maintainer of peace." Tani assessed that "what the United States wishes to do is make herself sure of playing a great role in the future. We cannot help feeling that in this war America's importance is growing by leaps and bounds." Tani proposed a grand intellectual framework for analyzing the enemy: "[W]e should pay close attention to America's attitude toward the matter of post-war arrangements and management as a means of guessing her probable conduct during the war."[108]

Even some in the IJA were having doubts. A circular sent to all military attachés on 9 December reported that Japanese forces were continuing operations in the Solomons and New Guinea, but that Allied air superiority gave the enemy a major advantage in delivery of supplies. "The war situation in general does not permit any optimism," concluded the cable.[109] Captured Japanese documents, meanwhile, indicated to the Americans that the Navy General Staff believed the Allies were only waging a holding action in the Solomons and New Guinea and expected offensive operations aimed at the eastern Netherlands East Indies area; it urged acceleration of the construction of defenses there.[110]

An OSS report originally from Japan and from a secret and reliable source in Europe indicated that as of late 1942 the "Japanese military clique" was greatly displeased with the rate of production in the war material industries. The High Command had threatened changes in the management of certain industries and even the punishment of business leaders.

Meanwhile, according to the report, news of the naval battles in the Solomon Islands had conveyed the impression that the Americans had lost all their ships. But the continuation of the fighting and announcement of numerous Japanese casualties had caused uneasiness among the populace. Moreover, it was apparent that closing the Burma Road had not materially reduced the flow of supplies to the Nationalist Chinese.[111]

Indeed, at a meeting in Berlin of Japanese military attachés, reported to OSS by SIS on 15 December, officers learned that there was a desire in Tokyo to come to an understanding with Chiang Kai-shek to finish the war in a way that would produce victory for neither side. The Japanese could not destroy Chiang, but neither could he destroy the Japanese.[112]

An imperial conference convened on 21 December. The participants placed great hope in strengthening the Wang puppet regime and bringing it into the war as part of a revision of the basic China policy. It was to receive greater autonomy of action, such as a free hand governing the provinces and localities and be encouraged to build popular support for the war.[113] (The Wang regime was to declare war against America and Britain on 9 January.[114])

Army Chief of Staff Sugiyama told the conference, "The [IGHQ] considers that in order to be able to direct and concentrate our war efforts for total victory in the Greater East Asia War against the United States and Great Britain, it is absolutely necessary to maintain and cultivate elasticity for the execution of protracted warfare by curtailing as much of our military burden in the China Area as possible."[115]

Privy Council President Hara commented on the new policy, essentially challenging the government and military to explain how they would execute it. So far, Japanese policy had done the opposite of easing tensions with the Chinese. "In recent years, the anti-British movement changed to the anti-Japanese movement and, once changed, the anti-Japanese movement spread throughout China like the overflow of the Yellow River. The Chinese authorities also became more and more pointedly anti-Japanese on the strength of the assistance of Great Britain and America, and as a result the present situation developed."

Tojo replied that he sympathized with Hara's views, and that the point of the new policy was to make a fresh start. Sugiyama said that he was calling the chiefs of staff from the China Expeditionary Army to Tokyo to make clear that their troops were to treat local Chinese authorities in a dignified manner.[116]

Hara's skepticism was to prove well justified.

CHAPTER 11

Early 1943: Months of Foreboding

Tokyo and Rome began to look at 1943 as the year when they might start losing the war, but Hitler looked at it as the year in which he might yet win it. The year began, however, with a grandiose carving up of the planet. The Axis Powers reached a military agreement on 18 January that established 70 degrees east as the boundary between the European and Asian theaters. India and most of the western Indian Ocean were in Japan's sphere.[1]

America and Britain Define Victory

Roosevelt and Churchill met 14–24 January 1943 in Casablanca to decide on strategic war aims. While Soviet Premier Joseph Stalin received an invitation, he was unable to attend because the Red Army was engaged in a major offensive against the German Army at the time. The most notable developments at the Conference were the finalization of Allied strategic plans against the Axis powers in 1943, and the promulgation of the policy of "unconditional surrender." The U.S. State Department historian summarizes the event:

> The Casablanca Conference took place just two months after the Anglo-American landings in French North Africa in November 1942. At this meeting, Roosevelt and Churchill focused on coordinating Allied military strategy against the Axis powers over the course of the coming year. They resolved to concentrate their efforts against Germany in the hopes of drawing German forces away from the eastern front, and to increase shipments of supplies to the Soviet Union. While they would begin concentrating forces in England in preparation for an eventual landing in northern France, they decided that first they would concentrate their efforts in the Mediterranean by launching an invasion of Sicily and the Italian mainland designed to knock Italy out of the war. They also agreed to strengthen their strategic bombing campaign against Germany. Finally, the leaders agreed on a military effort to eject Japan from Papua New Guinea and to open up new supply lines to China through Japanese-occupied Burma.

The leaders adopted a position that would vex Japanese consideration of possible surrender until one key condition emerged from Allied chieftains, as we shall see.

On the final day of the Conference, President Roosevelt announced that he and Churchill had decided that the only way to ensure postwar peace was to adopt a policy of unconditional surrender. The President clearly stated, however, that the policy of unconditional surrender did not entail the destruction of the populations of the Axis powers but rather, "the destruction of the philosophies in those countries which are based on conquest and the subjugation of other people."

.... Roosevelt wanted to avoid the situation that had followed the First World War, when large segments of German society supported the position, so deftly exploited by the Nazi party, that Germany had not been defeated militarily, but rather, had been 'stabbed in the back' by liberals, pacifists, socialists, communists, and Jews. Roosevelt also wished to make it clear that neither the United States nor Great Britain would seek a separate peace with the Axis powers.[2]

Roosevelt had privately told Admiral King on 12 December 1942, that he thought 20–35 percent of the war effort should go to the Pacific, including China and Burma.[3] This sounded like a lot more than offensive defense while the Allies tackled Germany first. Nevertheless, in the first half of 1943, the deployment of combat aircraft that had evenly favored the two theaters the year before shifted clearly toward the war against Germany. By July, 1,341 B-17s and B-24s were arrayed against the Reich, and only 234 against the Empire of Japan. Ah, but the U.S. Navy had 70 percent of its effort aimed at Japan.[4]

Regarding the strategic bombing campaign, the Allied chieftains set the objective as "destruction and dislocation of the Germany military, industrial, and economic system and the undermining of the morale of the German people to the point where their capacity for armed resistance is fatally weakened."[5] Ninety-three percent of the bomb tonnage that was to drop on the Germans during the war had yet to be dropped.[6]

The British and American Combined Chiefs of Staff approved a joint Combined Bomber Offensive plan in May. The parties agreed that the bombing should hit the key parts of the German war economy, with fighter production at the top of the list. During the conceptual phase, the Americans had added ball bearings to the list, heretofore not much considered, because they were necessary in most complex weapon systems. The other priorities were submarine construction and bases, oil, synthetic rubber, and military transportation. The plan specified that reduction of German fighter strength through disruption of production and attrition in combat was a precondition for overall success. The British were privately concerned that the Americans were overly optimistic about hitting targets deep in Germany during daylight without fighter escort.[7]

Bomber Command launched the "battle of the Ruhr" on 5 March with an attack by 362 bombers on Essen, home of Krupp Steel. Over the next five months, the RAF hit every city in the Ruhr industrial basin, including Duisburg, Bochum, Krefeld, Düsseldorf, Dortmund, the Wuppertal, and Geilenkirchen. The bombers returned to each target several times to disrupt repairs. Instead of a planned surge in steel and armaments production, Hitler and Speer faced a steel shortfall. Ammunition production, which had more than doubled in 1942, climbed only

20 percent in 1943. The bombers also bashed manufacture of components, which hurt factories all over the Reich; there was no increase in aircraft output from July 1943 through March 1944 because of the components shortage. The RAF paid a heavy toll in blood and aircraft: 4,000 crew killed or captured, and 640 bombers shot down or crashed.[8]

In Japan, the IGHQ on 4 January designated the Solomons a defense area and eastern New Guinea for renewed offensive operations. It pinned on the latter its hopes for getting the upper hand.[9]

In keeping with the decision of the imperial conference to bring "China" into the war, Wang visited Tokyo, and on 9 January the "National Government" declared war against America and Great Britain.[10]

The Japanese War Department transmitted a circular on 28 January 1943, not long before the final defeat on New Guinea and Guadalcanal and three and a half months before the American attacks on Attu and Kiska in the Aleutian Islands. "The American Army is strengthening defenses along the New Caledonia–Fiji–Samoa–Hawaii line. It is clear that they plan either to concentrate on forcing evacuations from New Guinea and the Solomons or from Attu and Kiska."[11]

Captain Toshikazu Ohmae, staff officer of the Southeast Area Fleet, told interrogators after the war that after the battle of Guadalcanal, he concluded that Japan would not win the war, but neither would it lose.[12] Keeper of the Privy Seal Kido identified the failure at Guadalcanal and Port Moresby as the combat operations that convinced him the war plan was going awry.[13]

Promoted to a warrant officer, pilot Sakai reported to his original unit, the Tainan Fighter Wing, in January. The wing had moved from Formosa and was now based in central Japan. He recalled, "Of the 150 pilots who had left Tainan during the great Japanese sweep across the Pacific, less than 20 were now alive. These veterans formed the core of the new wing, the majority of the members of which were green pilots rushed through training schools."[14]

Tokyo noted in January 1943 that American P-40s attached to Chinese Nationalist forces had become very active and had penetrated cities in occupied areas, though their efforts were focused on Burma.[15]

Japanese intelligence had a fairly accurate picture of America's sea and air expansion in the first half of 1943. It projected quite accurately ship production through 1946 and was close to the mark on numbers of fleet, escort, and antisubmarine "Jeep" aircraft carriers. It anticipated the termination of plans for additional fast battleships.[16]

The U.S. Army codebreakers, meanwhile, in April 1943, cracked their first high-level IJA code, for water transportation, which revealed plans to move troops and equipment and the maritime assets to move them. The new know-how allowed them to decipher a growing number of IJA codes. About the same time, American collection priorities changed to emphasize the Japanese target and deemphasize the German, in line with Anglo-American COMINT agreements.[17]

Elsewhere, German difficulties in the east provoked a debate among the Japanese as to what to do regarding the Soviet Union. Foreign Minister Tani cabled on 12 January 1943,

> Ever since the outbreak of the Greater East Asia war, the Imperial Government has felt that it would be advantageous to Japan, Germany, and Italy in their war efforts if Russia could be taken out of the anti-Axis camp. To this end, Japan has watched for an opportunity to effect German–Russian peace.... [T]he Army, Navy, and Foreign Office have unitedly kept up [a] careful study to the present time. Now as we look at the results of last year's German–Russian fighting, along with the recent resistance on the part of the Russians, we are giving fresh study to the possibilities and terms for peace.[18]

In Berlin, Hitler met with Oshima in early February amidst the national shock of the encirclement of German Sixth Army at Stalingrad. Oshima told him that Japan was now girding for a longer war than it had expected. Hitler was moving Germany in the direction of a total-war footing, mobilizing two million men from industry and agriculture and a million women to replace them. Hitler told him,

> Now I don't want you to think that I am weakening in my conviction that we will win, but the first question we have to face is disposing of the Soviet Union. It is clear that if, in order to destroy the striking power of Russia, you Japanese would take a hand and help us out in the east, it would be very advantageous in getting this job off our hands. But after all, the Japanese officials who understand their national resources better than anybody else must make this decision.

He went on to argue that the expanding U-boat war was going to prove effective against the United States and England.[19]

It was the Japanese, though, who were beginning to suffer the effects of Allied submarine warfare. By March, attacks were seriously disrupting Japanese shipping off North China and the Shantung (Shandong) Peninsula, at the top of the Yellow Sea opposite Korea.[20]

Oshima, meanwhile, pleaded with Tokyo to attack the Soviets. On 26 January, he cabled:

> The German High Command admits that the situation on the eastern front has suddenly become desperate, and, in the interval between now and the time when German lines can be reorganized and the offensive taken, conditions disastrous to the Reich may develop. Nevertheless, in spite of this, the German leaders have a deep determination to fight the war through. They are increasing the strength of the nation with an iron rod. Their dauntless confidence with respect to the war against Russia, as well as the war against England and the United States, is unshaken. They have determined never to compromise with either the Soviet [Union] or England and the United States—never!
>
> ... I now once again plead that you most seriously consider attacking the Soviet Union.... I feel that it is absolutely necessary for the Premier and the Supreme Command in Tokyo to give the Germans an outline of our war plans. I will tell you why. If we do not do so and the war should not again turn in the Axis favor as we hope it will, and if our two nations do not have any more reliance on each other than they now have, then our mutual consternation and misunderstanding will become ever greater.[21]

According to a report collected by OSS in London, Japanese military attachés met in Rome on 28 January and concluded that Italy was already powerless and could be considered *hors de combat*. The Italian people had already given up the war. The Germans, meanwhile, were going onto the strategic defensive on all fronts. Oddly, they believed that America had mobilized too many men, and that this would stress its war production.

If the Axis were to lose Tunisia, they believed it would affect Japan's strategic planning for two reasons. It would underscore Axis military weakness, and it would open the Mediterranean and Suez Canal routes, which would change the naval equation in the Indian Ocean.[22]

Hitler Hopes, But Some Generals See America Tipping Scales

Berlin did not appear to have any grasp of the inexorable growth of American power that the Japanese could see. The Germans had stopped the mainly American advance into Tunisia with hastily assembled forces, and their first big fight with the U.S. Army was a one-sided drubbing. On 14 February 1943, the Axis launched a crushing counterattack against American II Corps that came to be known as the battle of Kasserine. In five days, mainly German forces sent American troops reeling back to the west side of Kasserine Pass and destroyed almost half of the 1st Armored Division's tanks. As American resistance stiffened, the threat posed to the German rear by Montgomery's Eighth Army forced an end to the Axis rampage.[23]

Ribbentrop told Oshima on 19 February, "I know that while our war with Russia drags on, America's prowess is increasing, but she is not doing so well in Tunisia. Moreover, if England and America try a landing expedition [in Europe], I do not believe they can do so on a scale that will tip the balance of European military power. In any case, we are going to fight harder this year with our U-boats."[24]

After the battle of Kasserine, German commanders believed they had delivered the Americans such a sharp reversal that the enemy would be incapable of action any time soon.[25] (FMS note: This seems perfectly plausible and gives no indication of being written to avoid a war crimes charge.) Eisenhower, however, tapped Major General George Patton to take command of II Corps, which would consolidate on the southern end of the Allied line the American divisions heretofore scattered among British and French formations. With the job came promotion to lieutenant general. Patton took charge on 6 March and surprised the Axis with the speed of his action, although the Axis armed forces were unaware that he was the commanding general.

The Axis line in western Tunisia ran in the gaps along the Eastern Dorsal mountains between stretches of impassable ground from Djebel Tebaga near Maknassy to the sea, which eliminated the need to man a long defensive front. Patton's corps included four divisions, but he was to attack with only the 1st Armored and 1st Infantry

Divisions, while the 9th and 34th Infantry Divisions remained in reserve. On 17 March, his infantry advanced and captured Gafsa from the Italians.

Patton saw the opportunity to strike quickly through Gafsa and El Guettar and capture the heights beyond before the Germans could respond, but his new commander, General Sir Harold Alexander, at 18th Army Group, sent him explicit instructions on 19 March to take the heights east of Maknassy instead. From there, he was to stage an armored raid on the German airbase at Mezzouna. He was not to send large forces beyond the line Gafsa–Maknassy–Faid–Fondouk. Patton, not for the last time, ignored those instructions and ordered Major General Orlando Ward to be ready to roll his 1st Armored Division all the way to the sea.[26] He also told Major General Terry de la Mesa Allen to push through El Guettar with his 1st Infantry Division.

On 21 March, the 1st Armored Division advanced through rain and mud to Maknassy with the pass lying just beyond and reached it late the next day after the Italians pulled out. On 23 March, Colonel Rudolf Lang, 10th Panzer Division, and a hastily assembled force of two panzergrenadier battalions, Italian soldiers on site, and critically an 88mm flak battalion, got to the pass first and from 23 March stuffed the 1st Armored Division's vigorous attempts to break through.[27]

At El Guettar, however, the 10th Panzer Division attacked the 1st Infantry Division dug in on high ground, and the assault shattered—more than half the panzers knocked out—against the might of an artillery-rich American infantry division backed by tank destroyers. News of the Americans' defeat of a first-rate panzer division did not reach OKW, because Commander-in-Chief South Kesselring on 24 March told Fifth Panzer Army commanding general Hans-Jürgen von Arnim to stop sending reports directly to OKW and route them through him. Arnim simply shared these instructions with OKW, which tartly told Kesselring that he was not to interfere with reports going to the High Command. But, as far as Hitler knew, an American attack at El Guettar had been stopped.[28] The 10th Panzer Division's thrust had been costly, but it had stopped Patton from penetrating the last Axis line of defense protecting the communication routes from northern Tunisia to the Mareth Line.

In sum, from the Axis leadership perspective, German and Italian forces had defeated the first American offensive.

Some German generals at the army command level, however, were thinking about the long-term menace posed by America's entry into the war. The first generals captured in North Africa had arrived in November 1942 at the Trent Park prisoner of war facility near London, where British military intelligence expanded a program begun in 1939 to listen in on conversations among the prisoners. The Germans were mostly one- to three-star generals and represented a cross-section of the second layer at the top of the Wehrmacht's command structure. They spoke freely to one another about their views of the course of the war, politics, and their experiences.

One of the first to arrive, Major General Freiherr Wilhelm von Thoma—a panzer division general from the Eastern Front who had been in command of the Afrika Korps when he fell into British hands on 4 November 1942—started a diary that jibed with his oral remarks.[29] Thoma recorded in his diary on 17 January 1943,

> It is, when one considers the war potential of all those in the world against us, only a postponement, no prevention of the outcome. A long war is—measured against the war situation—impossible for little Germany, and since we have already been fighting for several years, it cannot end happily for us. I felt that when America entered the war, and the situation is very similar to when they came in during World War I.[30]

Lieutenant General Hans Cramer, the Afrika Korps commanding general when German resistance in Tunisia collapsed on 12 May, in a similar vein observed during a conversation on 16 May,

> When we older men who have experienced the last war follow this whole business, it makes us think. I can draw such a terrible number of parallels myself that I always say, "It is impossible for this to turn out well." [E]verything has turned out just like last time … but very gradually. If you examine the situation—America is becoming more and more powerful.[31]

Mussolini and Hitler met in April, and the Italian urged the Führer to concentrate more military strength in the Mediterranean and North Africa. Hitler, though, said he would give the Red Army a beating from which it could not recover and then shift his strength back to the West.[32] Ciano had resigned as Foreign Minister on 8 February and disappeared as a valuable inside source on Axis leadership thinking.[33]

After Axis resistance collapsed in Tunisia over three disastrous days, 10–13 May, two Italian-German armies went to the prisoner-of-war stockades. The total loss in manpower, 157,000 Germans and 86,700 Italians, was roughly the same as those taken at Stalingrad.[34]

As we shall see shortly, this coincided almost exactly with the German navy conceding defeat in the battle of the Atlantic.

Japan Again Reassesses After Its Drubbing

Sakai recalled learning in early February of the final Japanese defeat on Guadalcanal:

> Several days after my arrival [at the Tainan Air Wing], [Commander Tadashi] Nakajima wordlessly showed me the report of our withdrawal from Guadalcanal on 7 February 1943, exactly six months after the Americans had landed. The radios blared of strategic withdrawals, tightening our defense lines, but the secret reports revealed a staggering defeat and appalling casualties.
>
> Two full divisions of army troops gone, annihilated by the savagely fighting enemy. The navy had lost the equivalent of an entire peacetime fleet….
>
> What had happened to us? We had stormed through the Pacific with impunity.[35]

The Germans, amusingly enough, were beginning to have doubts about the course of the war in the Pacific. On 5 March, Goebbels wrote in his diary,

> According to American reports, the Japanese suffered a major defeat in the Bismarck Sea. Until now, the Japanese haven't said anything themselves. But the Japanese news reports have not been very dependable recently. The Japanese, too, are not so greatly blessed by the fortunes of war as they were in the first months. We believed they would accomplish much more late this winter than they really did. On the whole, they limited themselves to defending the areas conquered the previous winter.[36]

The IJA in February began transferring combat aircraft from the Manchuria Air Force, heretofore one of its largest, to Rabaul and New Guinea. Units suffered heavy attrition during deployment as their pilots were unused to long flights over water, and their planes had shorter ranges than IJN Zeros. This trickle was to become a flood, and by 1944 the IJA was to be stripping China of aircraft to feed the battle in the Pacific.[37]

Meanwhile, the planned transfer of the 51st Infantry Division via Rabaul to New Guinea came a cropper of American signals intelligence and air power. SIGINT allowed reconnaissance planes to spot the movement from Rabaul. Fifth Air Force bombers on 1–2 March destroyed most of a convoy carrying nearly 7,000 IJA troops to Lae.[38]

The IJN, meanwhile, realized it needed to rethink its defense against the Americans. On 25 March, it adopted a new operations plan. Recognizing that its land defenses of key islands were inadequate, it launched a program to strengthen the forces and fortifications on strategic islands and asked the IJA to provide troops for the first time. The bulk of its carrier strength was to be ready in the Pacific Area to support the strategic points by striking any approaching invasion force. A month earlier, it had reorganized the navy infantry special landing forces into "base units." The 3d Special Base Unit set up on Tarawa, with an element on Makin—the former destined to become one of the toughest fights ever faced by the U.S. Marine Corps. The IJA sent its first battalion to the Marcus Islands in April, while a second destined for the Gilbert Islands had to divert to Bougainville.[39]

The IJN until 1943 had expected that its cadre of pilots would suffer an attrition rate of 20–30 percent, according to Rear Admiral Seizo Katsumata, who commanded several flying corps during the war. It now anticipated a rate of 50 percent. In response, it had to accelerate pilot training, which meant cutting corners and reducing the training time allowed.[40] The decline in pilot training quality was going to incur great costs.

The Americans had a new plan, too. The Joint Chiefs on 28 March separated the Pacific into the Southwest Pacific Area under MacArthur—aimed at reaching China—and the Central Pacific under Nimitz—by November specifically dedicated to capturing the Marshall Islands.[41] Japan was going to face two very different kinds of American warfare.

*

Acting on signals intelligence that provided a precise itinerary, 16 American twin-boom P-38 Lightnings on 18 April intercepted and downed two aircraft bearing the party of Admiral Yamamoto.[42] Yamamoto had decided to visit several forward bases to boost morale. Rear Admiral Ugaki, who was aboard the second plane, subsequently dictated diary entries covering the events to an aide and provides a tip-of-the-spear view of the American enemy:

> [This summary appears in the diary for 18 April 1943.] At 0610 we left Rabaul aboard two medium bombers from the east strip. Six fighters escorted us. The weather was fine with intermittent cumulus.
>
> At 0730, twenty-four enemy P-38s encountered us northwest of Moele Point [Bougainville]. Two enemy planes were shot down but one bomber (commander in chief, ... aboard) was set aflame and shot down in the jungle about six kilometers from the coastline, while another bomber (chief of staff..., aboard) was shot down about 150 meters from the coast near Moele Point. Only the chief of staff and chief paymaster survived and received first aid treatment at the lookout post at Moele Point.[43]
>
> [This elaboration appears in the diary for 18 April 1944.] It got noisy for a while with the handling of machine guns and the wind blowing in.
>
> By the time we lowered altitude to treetop level, air combat had already been in progress between our escorting fighters and the enemy.... [T]he enemy planes bore down mercilessly on the bigger game of the two bombers.... The first plane was staggering southward, just brushing the jungle top with reduced speed, emitting black smoke and flame. It was about 4,000 meters from us.... [T]he plane was no more to be seen, only a pall of black smoke rising to the sky from the jungle.[44]

Admiral Mineichi Koga took command of the Combined Fleet in Truk on 24 April, and he held to the traditional naval view that Yamamoto had left behind. Vice Admiral Shigeru Fukudome, who joined him as chief of staff, replacing Ugaki on 21 May, told interrogators after the war:

> I was a Section Chief at the time that Admiral Koga was Deputy Chief in the Navy General Staff. This was for a period of about one and a half years. Through that association I know that Admiral Koga was conservative and cool, particularly when compared with Yamamoto, who was an extremely colorful officer. However, Admiral Koga settled things in logical manner. From the very beginning, he insisted on the one decisive action, first with ships, and later with shore-based planes. Under the circumstances, this strategy seemed to be the only logical one....
>
> There were those who told him that this point must be defended and that that point must be defended, etc., but it was his conviction that we must concentrate in one big decisive fleet engagement, which the fleet had at least a fifty percent chance of success if such engagement could be made to take place during 1943 ...
>
> He felt that the operations around Guadalcanal and vicinity were against us, and that the American naval forces were bound to push farther and farther north. Just against what point their thrust would be made, of course, could not be guessed; but Koga felt that if he only waited at Truk, that would give him a chance for a decisive engagement against the American fleet when they should proceed north, irrespective of what particular point they might strike ...
>
> But in November, as Bougainville landing operations commenced, he was forced to send his air strength to Rabaul. As it turned out, practically all of them were lost at Rabaul and Bougainville. Consequently, the Fleet air strength was almost completely lost, and although

the Gilbert fight appeared to be the last chance for a decisive fight, the fact that the fleet's air strength had been so badly depleted enabled us to send only very small air support to Tarawa and Makin. The almost complete loss of carrier planes was a mortal blow to the fleet since it would require six months for replacement, ... In the interim, any fighting with carrier force was rendered impossible.[45]

Mamoru Shigemitsu became Japan's new foreign minister in April. He was a long-time China hand who had worked closely with Tojo on China policy. His selection as foreign minister appeared related to Japan's "new China policy," a scheme to grant greater autonomy in the hopes of winning hearts and minds, which had been announced in January in conjunction with the Nanking puppet government's declaration of war against the United States and Britain.[46]

Shigemitsu immediately demonstrated a global strategic sense of the war to match Tani's. On 28 April he sent a message to Oshima on behalf of the Foreign Office and the Japanese High Command expressing deep concern over Hitler's plans to launch a renewed offensive in the Soviet Union. The Japanese clearly believed that Germany was underestimating the Anglo-American threat. In a way, their message to Hitler mirrored his request that Japan attack the Soviet Union. The message read in part:

> The Imperial Japanese Government, seeing the results of this year's drive, fears, and very much fears, that Germany may dissipate her military strength and that in the meantime America and England will be left free to strengthen their striking power and finally to launch a great offensive.
>
> We do not know the full extent of Germany's military power nor have we any detailed information on the exact conditions in Europe, and the Imperial Government is not in a position to pass a flawless judgment. Nevertheless, the Imperial Government is of the opinion that the offensive power of the Axis should be used in a combination to destroy the military strength of the Americans and British. Therefore, it is our view that Germany should, if she so desires, adopt a temporary [defensive] strategy against the Soviet [Union], but that in any event she should destroy the American and British forces in Tunisia and Gibraltar, thwart any thrust against Europe which the Americans and British may make from North African bases, and, while destroying enemy shipping on the sea, assure the military [superiority] of the Axis in Europe.
>
> As far as our Empire, this year we will continue as before our drive in the South Pacific in the face of the British and American counterattacks. In Burma and wherever else may be necessary, we will smash Anglo-Saxon offensives and, at the same time, destroy as much enemy shipping as possible.[47]

Shigemitsu met with the German ambassador in Tokyo on 5 May and told him:

> The Imperial Government does not intend to criticize your decisions, but it so happens that we Japanese are in the same boat with you Germans. Spiritually, too, we are supposed to be, or ought to be, as one. Therefore, it is only right that I should express our military and political opinions to you frankly. We ought to join hands and fight this war to victory shoulder to shoulder. It is absolutely necessary for us to correlate our action much more thoroughly than we have been doing.
>
> Well now, to tell you the truth, we Japanese are very much afraid of that drive you Germans are planning against the Soviet [Union]. You may use up all your expendables in men and material and repeat the same mistake you have already made twice. Then where will you be for men? Where will you be for supplies?
>
> After all, our real enemies are England and the United States, and it is they whom we Japanese intend to fight. The logical thing for you Germans to do would be to fall in line with us.[48]

The German ambassador replied, "I agree with you. We Germans traditionally tend to limit our view to the European continent. You Japanese, on the other hand, take a much broader outlook on the world situation."[49]

Oshima tried to deliver the Japanese message to Ribbentrop, but the foreign minister claimed to be busy with the "post-Tunis situation." Oshima replied to Tokyo that German leaders had repeatedly explained that a successful campaign in the east was a prerequisite for the battle against the Anglo-Saxons. Germany's prospects for going over to the defensive along a 2,000-kilometer front, moreover, were slim. "If that line were to collapse, the whole thing might be over with so far as Germany is concerned."[50] When Oshima finally got to Ribbentrop in June, the conversation went much as Oshima had anticipated, or at least Oshima so reported it.

The Japanese Embassy in Rome, meanwhile, reported that the Italian government feared that the Germans were about to start another offensive on the Eastern Front that would leave Italy without sufficient strength to withstand an Allied invasion. The Italians asked the Japanese to join them in urging Hitler to give more attention to the Mediterranean area. The Italian undersecretary of foreign affairs told the ambassador, "The enemy's air bombardment of all Italy is being carried out with extreme violence.... Although the morale of our people is very high, the outlook will become increasingly grim if we cannot ward off the enemy air attacks." The ambassador wanted to evacuate Japanese nationals from Rome to Vienna.[51]

Japan was becoming worried about the prospects of that kind of aerial devastation to itself at American hands. In January, Tokyo had queried the military attachés in Rome and Berlin, "In the experience of our army it has proved difficult to shoot down the 4-engined heavy American bombers, the B-17 and the B-24, because of their great defensive strength. Please investigate the methods of the German and Italian air forces in shooting down these planes, finding out about strategy, guns, ammunition, etc. Send us the results immediately."

Japan fielded its first flak fire control radar in August, the Type 41, which could detect a group of planes at 30 miles and a single plane at a dozen.[52]

A Japanese press dispatch said, "In view of the priority given to the European theaters of war, the United States does not have sufficient forces in the Far East to launch a strictly military offensive and has apparently decided to limit action to air raids against populated centers in Japan in order to burn our cities and massacre our population." The launching point was expected to be the Aleutian Islands, where the Americans landed on Attu on 12 May.[53]

Perhaps unbeknownst to the Japanese, the U.S. Navy only in May 1943 regained the carrier launch capacity it had fielded in December 1941. It had lost four fleet carriers between May and October 1942. The first *Essex*-class carrier had joined the fleet in December, and three more arrived by May.[54] Carriers, it was to turn out, also posed a threat to the homeland's skies.

*

Rear Admiral Toshitane Tonaka recalled in November 1945 that it was in April or May, after he became a staff officer at the Combined Fleet, that he began to believe Japan would lose the war.[55] One of his first experiences would have been the American landings on Japanese-occupied Attu. The IJN's plan called for a counterinvasion attack by Combined Fleet forces. Submarines engaged the enemy with some success but with the loss of four of seven subs, while Fifth Fleet destroyers opted not to engage the superior enemy force. Koga on 17 May ordered the fleet to gather in Tokyo Bay and departed Truk with the Second Carrier Division, Third Battleship Division, and cruisers and destroyers, and he reached Tokyo Bay. But the Japanese on Attu were clearly near the end, IGHQ decided to withdraw the unit on Kiska on 19 May, and Koga abandoned the operation. The last Japanese evacuated Kiska on 29 July.[56]

In the previous month, the Germans complained to Tokyo about the amount of Lend-Lease material being shipped across the Pacific to the Soviet Union. The IJN was intercepting vessels headed for Siberia, but all shipments were now on Soviet-registered ships, and because of the neutrality pact, Japan could do little to stop them.[57]

The Anglo-American and Soviet successes against Germany and Italy began to influence developments in Japan's backyard. The Japanese Embassy in Saigon cabled Tokyo on 27 April,

> In Indochina they feed the people on the vain hope that the invasion of North Africa by the American and English armies and the Soviet offensive on the eastern front will succeed. Within the Anglo-American party, the Gaullists are becoming very active. This is especially the case among the main body of Army and Navy men who gather together at the Saigon Broadcasting Station and keep up some kind of contacts with London.... The growing strength of the resistance against a policy of cooperation with Japan on the part of the upper strata in French Indochina is a reflection of the vain hopes that they have regarding the stalemate in the war situation in Europe and the Southwest Pacific and also with regard to the landing operations on the mainland of Europe which they are expecting.[58]

With the imminent collapse of Axis resistance in Tunisia, Japanese Foreign Minister Shigemitsu on 8 May polled Japanese diplomats in Europe on the implications. Replies from Italy, Turkey, Portugal, Switzerland, and Hungary generally agreed that the fall of Tunisia had come with unexpected suddenness; an Allied invasion of Sicily, Sardinia, and Italy could be expected; and it was doubtful the Allies would attempt landings elsewhere in Europe.[59] (This was more accurate than the German assessment!)

The Japanese Embassy in Finland offered the most sobering assessment: "Japan is now in the process of building up a Greater East Asia and in order to bring this to a successful completion, Japan may have to make up her mind to fight it out to the end alone."[60]

Shigemitsu told his European missions, "I wish to thank you all for the reports you have sent in since the fall of Tunis concerning military moves, Soviet, American, and British strategy, propaganda, and the consequent reverberations in the various nations. Now, in view of the growing seriousness of the situation, I want you to send me as quickly as possible more reports on those subjects."[61]

Germans Appraise the American Enemy

Though they had been defeated in North Africa, the Germans were not overly impressed with Allied generalship in terms of dash and daring. A German assessment of American commanders in Tunisia noted that the Americans displayed uncertainty and based their battle leadership on careful and methodical plans built on absolute security. They steered away from bold attacks that could have exploited openings that suddenly emerged in the course of events. They held to a plan, even when it was not appropriate to the demands of the moment. They gained success based on overwhelming material superiority.[62]

For the record, the German view of British commanders at about the same time was not much different. After their misadventures in the first eighteen months of combat, British generals had learned to gather all available strength at the point of decision, but they had been unable to free themselves from the methodical approach. Operations from local actions to great battles were meticulously prepared beforehand. British commanders avoided improvised battle leadership with the forces at hand. They never found the courage to send formations with open objectives deep into the Axis rear. (Kesselring plausibly claims in his memoirs that he realized after El Alamein that Montgomery's strategy was that "he played for safety and was correspondingly methodical.") British success was attributed to the Axis inability to logistically sustain German and Italian forces in the field.[63]

Whether citing the Allies' material superiority was merely an excuse for military failure, it was real. German soldiers would refer frequently to this problem through the end of the war.

Goebbels just a month before the collapse in Tunisia had recorded in his diary, "A report on interrogation of American prisoners is really gruesome. These American boys are human material that can in no way stand comparison with our people. One has the impression of dealing with savages."[64] Kesselring commented to interrogators at the end of the war,

> I must admit that the first encounters between German and American troops did not reflect too much credit on the latter. It was an easy matter for our low-level fliers to bring confusion and chaos into the ranks of marching troops, especially at the beginning. It was easy to note quick improvement as time went on, however, and the fighting qualities of the American troops improved noticeably from battle to battle.[65]

(FMS note: Kesselring was convicted of war crimes in 1947, yet, mostly *after his conviction*, produced 35 FMS reports, some among the most detailed and useful in the series.)

Captain Wilhelm Scheidt, who was a member of the historical staff at OKW, observed after the war, "Judging from combat experience in North Africa and his general evaluation of the British and American armies, Hitler considered the British to be the greater danger. This error later proved to be a fatal one, since the Americans showed far more ability for Blitzkrieg than the British."[66]

The Americans also were beginning to make an impression on German views with daylight strategic bombing raids. Goebbels on 8 May confided to his diary, "[Gauleiter Paul] Wegener told me about the day raids on Bremen by American bombers. These were very hard indeed. The Americans drop their bombs with extraordinary precision from an altitude of eight to nine thousand meters. The population has the paralyzing feeling that there really is no protection against such daylight attacks."[67] A few days later, he added, "The day raids by American bombers are creating extraordinary difficulties.... If this condition continues and we find no antidote for these day raids, we shall have to face exceptionally serious consequences, which in the long run will prove unbearable."[68]

Hitler was so disappointed with Göring's performance in the west that by this time, he had sidelined his once favored henchman and taken over making all important decisions regarding the air war.[69] Unable to stop the bombing, Hitler turned to retaliation. The V-1 drone bomb and V-2 ballistic missile promised to deliver terror bombing to British cities. The flak arm of the Luftwaffe provided cover to both programs as the "5th Flak Division" and most of the manpower.[70]

The war at sea was also taking a nasty turn. Grand Admiral Dönitz recalled, "In 1942, our successes exceeded expectations. The falling off in May 1943 was a surprise in its suddenness.... After that, U-boat successes were far behind the expectations originally entertained."[71] German naval intelligence had enjoyed a signals intelligence coup of its own in early 1943 and broken the Anglo-American Naval Cipher 3, used for communications related to convoys. Enigma decrypts tipped the Germans' hand, and the Allies introduced a new code in June.[72]

The Allies in early 1943 had dramatically upped their antisubmarine game. Routine convoying with proper escorts was the leading factor. But they also had a more sophisticated understanding of the threat. The mainstay model VII U-boat could reach only 8 knots submerged but 17 knots on the surface. Fast merchant vessels faced low risk in convoy or alone. Ships able to sail at 14 knots were three times safer than those making 12 knots. Increasing speed from 7 knots to 9 knots offered one-third greater protection. Liberty ships being mass produced by America could achieve 11 knots.

The Allies also figured out that convoys of 60 vessels or larger were safer. The ratio of escorts to U-boats was the key factor in protection, and larger convoys had more escorts.

And more escorts were available. The British were able to send more warships after Operation *Torch*, and America in early 1943 produced 295 destroyer escorts

(UK: corvettes) for its own and Allied use. Allied radar improved vastly during this period, as did depth charges. Better radar allowed aircraft to spot U-boats on the surface and coordinate attacks against them.

American made 4-engine Liberator bombers reached the British in sufficient numbers that only a few hundred miles of sea were beyond the reach of shore-based air patrols. This was the Greenland Air Gap, and it is where Dönitz concentrated his U-boats. But the USS *Bogue*, the first escort carrier, deployed, a firm step toward closing the air gap. U-boat losses totaled 33 from January to April. Now destruction skyrocketed to 41 in May. On 24 May, Dönitz withdrew the wolf packs from the North Atlantic.[73]

Keitel told his interrogators that in the course of 1943, it became apparent that the constraints OKW had assumed would preclude a large American commitment to the Continent—the U-boat successes, an unready air force, and the demands of the Pacific—were no longer valid. Indeed, it now appeared that the Americans would concentrate all but the naval forces essential in the Pacific against Germany. Nevertheless, Keitel said that OKW had *no authoritative information regarding American war plans* throughout the 1942–1944 period.[74] (FMS note: The OKW war diary bears out Keitel's statement that it lacked authoritative information on American war plans. His appraisal of the easing constraints on American power projection are accurate.)

Hitler and Minister of Armament and Munitions Albert Speer responded to the disasters on all fronts in May 1943 by finally launching mobilization for total war. Every man and woman was to register at the labor exchange for assessment as to how they could best contribute to the war effort. All civilian businesses not directly supporting the war were to close. Armament production had already nearly doubled since Speer took charge in February, though the Luftwaffe accounted for half of that gain.[75]

Japan Mulls Allied Grand Strategy

Nearly a half year after the Casablanca Conference, Shigemitsu took note of the announcement of the policy of unconditional surrender. "We cannot escape the impression that the adamant US demand for unconditional surrender by the Axis forestalls the possibility of any peace negotiations." The Americans, who earlier had appeared more suspicious of the Russians than had the British, appeared to be warming to Stalin. The Americans and British, though, appeared to differ about the postwar world. He noted competing proposals from Morgenthau and John Maynard Keynes on the future financial system and a British proposal for regional councils that the Americans perceived to be just a new form of British imperialism. "Their interests will collide when the war is over."[76]

Shigemitsu on 4 June transmitted an analysis of the conflict following Churchill's visit to America for the Washington Conference:

> The purpose of the conference was to decide what strategy to adopt now that the North Africa operations are over. The conference did not result in any change in the plan to place chief emphasis on the European war, i.e. to establish a second front. However, it is thought that, in view of the vehement public opinion in America against Japan, and in order to meet the strong demands of Chungking and to avoid giving Japan time to consolidate her position in East Asia, that the United Nations will undertake a rather heavy offensive in the Pacific area, with India, China, Australia, Hawaii, and Alaska as jumping off points.

Italy, he added, was in a "sad plight," and Germany appeared determined to throw her entire strength and much of her reserves into an offensive in the east. The victories in North Africa were tilting neutral countries toward the Allies, which would be disastrous for the Axis.[77]

The Japanese tried to undermine the American will to fight, but it is doubtful that they held much hope of success. On 1 June, the War Ministry circulated propaganda instructions that said in part, "What we want to do with our propaganda is to create an impression among the Americans that no offensive against Japan can succeed in bringing Japan to her knees, thus discouraging any such offensive." On 7 June, more specific guidance followed:

> Emphasize that an offensive against Japan will merely result in great losses for America—that such an offensive will spill blood but will produce no other results. Impress the fact deeply that losses incurred by the United Nations in such an offensive will not be recovered....
>
> The Japanese air force has superiority in leadership, fighting ability, technical skill, personnel, etc.
>
> If enemy air forces attempt to cross the broad ocean and attack Japan proper and the occupied territories, they will only succeed in strengthening the resolution of the Japanese people....
>
> Ground operations in the Pacific theater are very difficult and costly because of the wild country, difficult terrain, bad weather conditions, etc., and also because of the strength of the Japanese forces.[78]

It is possible that this approach reflected either a genuine belief in the military or in its exaggerated claims to civilian leaders that Japanese forces were causing extremely high casualties to the Americans. A few months later, in September, Foreign Minister Shigemitsu cabled Oshima in Berlin that American casualties in the Pacific were twice as high as Washington had admitted for all theaters of war.[79]

Elsewhere, Major General Kiyotomi Okamoto, head of a liaison delegation from Japan that was visiting Berlin, in late May sent Tokyo a prophetic cable calling attention to Allied strides in military science and technology. He pointed to the impact of radar and sonar, expected more powerful tanks and airplanes, and noted the importance of finding substitutes for scarce materials. Germany and Italy, he said, could compete on a level field with the Allies, but Japan was lagging. "Now [the Allies] are turning the formidable weapon of science against the European Axis, and the time will probably come when we too must come face to face with the monsters of their invention."[80] Asked after the war what the main causes of Japan's defeat were—"lack of airplanes, lack of fuel, etc.?"—Rear Admiral Toshitane Tanaka replied, "1. Insufficiency in scientific or radar research. 2. Lack of mechanical ability, productive ability."[81]

The Allied Side of the Hill

When the Combined Bomber Offensive Plan appeared in June 1943 to implement the Casablanca directive, it dropped submarines from first priority because of the great success combating U-boats at sea. The plan substituted the German aircraft industry. The ball-bearing industry, the supplier of an important component, became a complementary target.[82]

The British and Americans by June finalized a nearly complete integration of their COMINT efforts. A new category of Special Intelligence grouped the various high-grade Axis codes into a tightly controlled compartment available only to senior figures in the respective capitals and field commanders. ULTRA became the joint Anglo-American codeword for high-level COMINT, such as MAGIC and the German Enigma codes.[83]

CHAPTER 12

Late 1943: America Becomes a Rising Priority

The Axis Powers in late 1943 had to reckon with the United States as a rapidly rising line item on their problems list. For Fascist Italy, the Anglo-American alliance executed checkmate. For Nazi Germany, Hitler for the first time had to divert critical resources from the titanic struggle in the east to defend against the Western Allies. For Imperial Japan, it was the dawning realization that the Pacific theater was the main struggle, not the war in China. And for all concerned, the period marked a discernible improvement in American military capabilities and the rapid increase of American-made war materiel on all fronts.

Germany and Italy Lose Another One

"Well, my Führer," said Sonderführer von Neurath, a civilian expert with temporary military-sounding rank who had just returned from Italy, "the Italians say, 'when the war is over'—that's a very frequent expression; at another moment they say, 'You never know what is going to happen.'" Hitler listened intently, as did Keitel, Rommel, and members of the headquarters staff. It was the afternoon of 20 May 1943, and a stenographer tapped quietly away, recording the conversation for posterity. Von Neurath continued,

> The German troops in Sicily have undoubtedly become pretty unpopular. It's easy to see why; the Sicilians consider that we have brought the war to their country and that we've snapped up more or less everything they have. Now we're going to be the reason for the arrival of the English, which, however—and I must emphasize this—the Sicilian peasant would be quite pleased about.... Once they arrive, it's the end of the war.[1]

A week after the Axis collapse in Tunisia, at *Führerhauptquartier*, men were worried that the British were going to invade Sicily. The Americans were an afterthought.

A few moments later, Rommel spoke. "Would it be possible, my Führer, for the Italians to send more troops to Sicily and hold it instead of us?"

"Anything's possible," Hitler replied, "The question is whether they *want* to defend it. What worries me is that it can't be defended."[2]

Commando Supremo did not appear to know for certain where the next Allied invasion would come.[3] Kesselring, however, had a good idea. His headquarters on 30 June signaled OKW that one should expect simultaneous landings on Sicily and Sardinia in the near future. The Americans could field ten and the British eight divisions, he estimated, and their immense shipping capacity would permit the Allies to supply them all.[4]

Even as the Germans put the finishing touches on the planned offensive against the Soviet-fortified Kursk salient on the Eastern Front, Kesselring arrived at Hitler's headquarters in late June to discuss the danger of Anglo-Americans in Italy. Hitler's military adjutant, Otto Günsche, told Soviet interrogators that Hitler reacted calmly to the briefing. He commented that he would rather see such landings in Italy than in France.[5]

The Axis powers had never before had to defend against an amphibious invasion. The war in North Africa had been one among colonial powers already in place, into which Hitler had injected a relatively modest German force. Only the French had confronted Operation *Torch*. This, the first major test for the Axis in the West, was to take place, in the Allies' eyes, on the periphery of Europe. For the Axis, North Africa had been the periphery. Now, the enemy was attacking the Italian homeland. The upcoming battle was to pit the German panzers against an Allied amphibious invasion for the first time.

The Allies in January had decided to follow up the victory in North Africa by invading Sicily in the hope of driving Italy out of the war, which would force the Germans to occupy Italy and pick up Italian military commitments in the Balkans. President Roosevelt also wanted to keep American troops active in the European war during the remainder of 1943 to placate Stalin. The plan for Operation *Husky* ultimately called for two corps to land under British Eighth Army on the southeastern corner of the island. U.S. Seventh Army's II Corps, under Lieutenant General Omar Bradley, controlled the 1st and 45th Infantry Divisions and would assault beaches somewhat farther west around Gela. Patton, who commanded Seventh Army, retained personal control over the 3d Infantry Division, which would land on the left at Licata. British XIII Corps would hit the beach at Cape Passero–Augusta. The landings on 10 July 1943 constituted the largest amphibious assault of the war and put seven divisions ashore.

Once on land, Montgomery's Eighth Army was to push up the east coast to capture the main objective, Messina. Seventh Army was to advance on its left, its mission being to protect Montgomery's flank. Patton had no more specific objective.[6]

Counterattacks by the Hermann Göring Panzer Division and Italian Livorno Division backed by tanks failed to crush the American beachhead, in part because

Axis Dispositions 10 July 1943

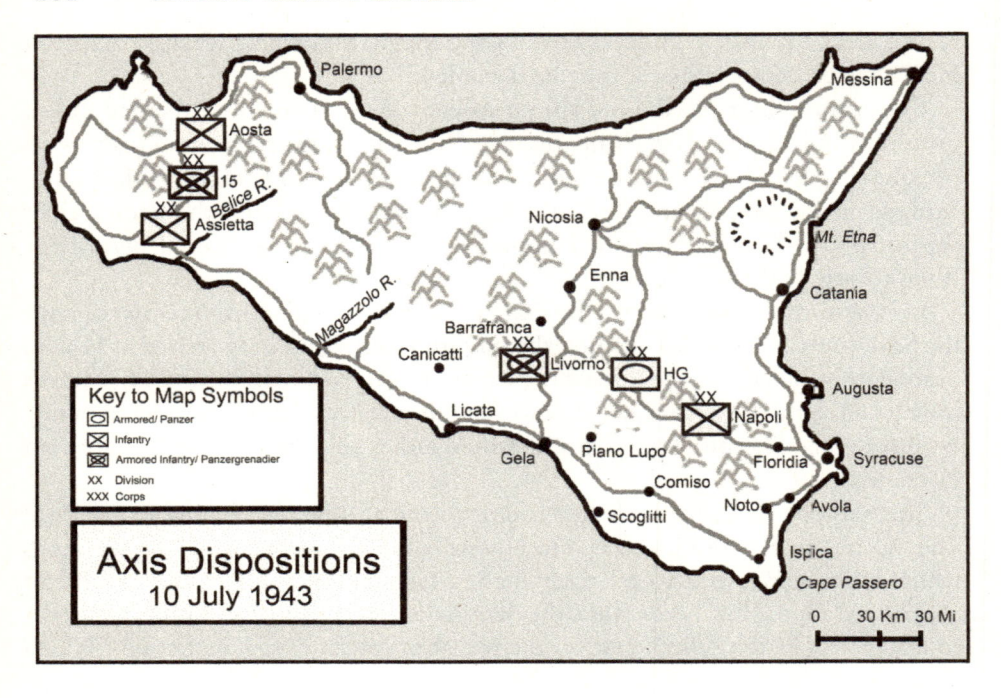

of fierce supporting naval gunfire. The Germans did not draw the appropriate lesson from this experience and were to try again at Salerno to destroy a beachhead with armored counterattacks. Axis forces began a preplanned, slow withdrawal toward the northeastern corner of the island.

Ambassador Oshima reported on 14 July comments from a German official on the Allied landings:

> This invasion was covered as never before by an air umbrella, and there was perfect coordination between land, sea, and air forces.... It is noteworthy that the British forces are far superior to those of the United States.... Conceivably the day has not been lost in Sicily, but it would probably be a little too optimistic to say that. The enemy has already landed too much heavy artillery for there to be much hope.[7]

Ribbentrop forwarded information to Oshima on 12 July that conceded that, viewed objectively, Italy and Germany might be unable to eject the Anglo-Americans from Sicily.[8] The combined Axis setbacks on the Eastern and Mediterranean fronts in Europe dismayed observers in Japan. The Portuguese Embassy in Tokyo reported, "Developments in the war in Europe have discouraged Japan to such an extent that a spokesman for the navy ministry has proclaimed that this country is unalterably determined to continue the war even if she is left absolutely alone."[9] This echoed the view from some diplomats after the North Africa landings that Japan might wind up the last Axis power standing.

Japanese ambassador Shinrokuro Hidaka in Rome on 24 July reported to Tokyo that the Allies possessed "absolute supremacy in the air and on the sea" at Sicily, and despite a stubborn Axis defense of the northeast corner of the island, the island's fall was "just a matter of time." He observed that a recent aerial bombing of Rome had been a

> [t]errible shock to the general public, the government, and prominent Italian leaders.... If the much-awaited air support from Germany does not materialize, it is a foregone conclusion that, after the surrender of Sicily, Italy herself will be invaded.... [W]e must therefore conclude that the situation is very seriously deteriorating and that the enemy have gained a dominating position.... [I]n view of developments on the eastern front and other considerations, we must prepare for the worst and plan accordingly.[10]

Hidaka met with Benito Mussolini from 1300 to 1330 on 25 July, precisely the time between two meetings of the Fascist Council that would result in Il Duce's ouster. Mussolini was agitated, his words at times violent and his thoughts disconnected. With no future, though he did not yet seem to grasp that fully, he thrashed over his past views:

> Always our enemies are the Anglo-Americans. Unless we defeat them, this war will never really end.
> From the very beginning I said to the Germans, "Fight England and America!" I tell them now that in order to do this they must, at all costs, return Ukraine to the Soviet Union. I think that if the war between Germany and Russia were to end now, Germany could fight the Anglo-Americans without the Ukraine. Why does Germany have to take territory where no Germans live? My God! She has been able to do practically nothing since she took those areas.... I don't see why Germany can't use sense and retire to the 1939 line....
> I knew from the very beginning that nobody could strike Russia and get away with it. She is too vast. Everybody now remembers with amusement how at first Hitler boasted, "I will defeat Russia in ten weeks."
> I told Göring that it was asinine to fight a war in which you advanced 500 kilometers and then retreated 500 kilometers. I asked what the sense was in that. Last October several times I said the same thing to Hitler himself.
> Well, don't fool yourself, the Germans themselves are worn to a frazzle.... We Italians, you see, always know when we have had enough, but those Germans don't. They go and go and go and think that, if it is necessary, there will still be time to find a way out....
> As far as Italy is concerned, time has about run out.... Enemy bombers have played hell with our industry. Our synthetic petroleum plant at Livorno was bombed, and it will take three or four months to get it back in shape....
> The next time I see Hitler, I am going to say to him clearly and categorically that he must give up the fight against Russia. You Japanese please do the same thing. Maybe we can both drag Hitler away from that obsession. If we ever hope to win this war, we will have to.[11]

Ultra revealed that Hitler took Mussolini's ouster badly. "They are going to kill him, those Italians! This pack of traitors!"

According to MAGIC, Shigemitsu told the German ambassador in Tokyo, "Well, it looks as though Italy is about done for. I feel keenly that now it is up to us Japanese and Germans to stick closer together. We ought to work hand in hand in the prosecution of the war from now on." The Portuguese minister in Tokyo cabled Lisbon that a real undercurrent of pessimism had taken root in response to war developments in Europe. The Finish minister reported that Mussolini's fall had given the Japanese their "first real scare." In Berlin, the Germans conceded that the Soviets had again seized the initiative, but they were executing a mobile defense, and the Soviets would eventually wear themselves out.[12]

Fast American-made decoding machines, four-wheeled "bombes," arrived in Bletchley Park in August. The Allies now had the horsepower to crack anything the Germans did with the four-wheel Enigma.[13] The SIGINT war was won, and the Axis had no clue.

Germany: Hell From the Heavens

Germany's flak defenses were expanding rapidly on Hitler's orders in the vain hope of protecting the Reich from a deluge of bombs. On 13 January 1943, 659 heavy and 558 light batteries were in action inside the borders of the Reich and the approaches from Great Britain. By mid-June, there were 1,089 heavy and 738 light batteries. In 1943, German industry manufactured 4,416 88mm, 1,220 105mm, 282 single-barrel 128mm, and eight double-barrel 128mm guns, the last of which were for massive flak towers guarding Berlin. The number of searchlight batteries increased from 174 in 1942 to 350 in 1943. After the U.S. Fifteenth Air Force in North Africa and later Italy went into action against targets in Southern Europe, Germany had to divert flak assets to their defense, as well. But 58 percent of heavy batteries and 78 percent of searchlight batteries were still committed to defending the Reich from Anglo-American bombers in the UK.[14]

The first day of Bomber Harris's Operation *Gomorrah* aimed at Hamburg, 24 July, was a hideously momentous occasion in Germany that echoed on the far side of the planet. A series of RAF nighttime raids through 2 August destroyed the urban center of Hamburg. The RAF for the first time employed chaff, codenamed Window, to blind German radars, and of the 792 bombers that participated in first raid, only 12 were lost. Window consisted of 12-inch aluminum foil strips that reflected radar signals.

The U.S. Bombing Survey reported,

> On three nights in late July and early August 1943, [the RAF] struck Hamburg in perhaps the most devastating single city attack of the war—about one-third of the houses of the city were destroyed and German estimates show 60,000 to 100,000 people killed. No subsequent city raid shook Germany as did that on Hamburg; documents show that German officials were thoroughly alarmed and there is some indication from interrogation of high officials that Hitler himself thought that further attacks of similar weight might force Germany out of the war.[15]

As noted, the attack marked the first use of Window to confuse German radars. Churchill had first approved its use on 15 July. The British had developed the countermeasure in 1941 but held off on using it until the danger that the Germans would return the favor didn't matter because British radar could now see through Window. The strips confused night fighters and caused searchlights to swing wildly looking for targets. The Germans were able to design an update to the flak control radars to distinguish between Window and aircraft—as well as frequency hopping to defeat jamming—and deploy it by the end of 1943.[16]

The still diminutive U.S. Eighth Air Force delivered a warning of things to come through its participation in *Gomorrah*. The American role was to conduct precision daylight attacks by 323 B-17 Flying Fortresses on the Blohm & Voss U-boat yards and the Klockner Aero-Engine Factory. Over a three-day period, flak and fighters knocked out 10 percent of the American bombers.[17]

The Strategic Bombing survey observed:

> The city attacks of the RAF prior to the autumn of 1944, did not substantially affect the course of German war production. German war production as a whole continued to increase. This in itself is not conclusive, but the Survey has made detailed analysis of the course of production and trade in 10 German cities that were attacked during this period and has made more general analyses in others. These show that while production received a moderate setback after a raid, it recovered substantially within a relatively few weeks. As a rule, the industrial plants were located around the perimeter of German cities and characteristically these were relatively undamaged.[18]

Speer told interrogators in May 1945, "The American method was more dangerous because it was an economic war technique while the English were aiming for the centers of cities." He said British bombs were far more destructive, however, and had the Americans used British ordnance, synthetic production of oil would have been stopped in October 1944.[19]

Hermann Göring told interrogators after the war that the U.S. Air Force had been decisive in the outcome of the conflict. "Without the American Air Force, the war would still be going on elsewhere but certainly not on German soil." He dated "the first heavy blow" to American attacks on Italian airfields in 1943.[20]

Still, it is worth noting that the German population feared the RAF more than it did the American bombers:

> The Survey has made extensive studies of the reaction of the German people to the air attack and especially to city raids. These studies were carefully designed to cover a complete cross section of the German people in western and southern Germany and to reflect with a minimum of bias their attitude and behavior during the raids. These studies show that the morale of the German people deteriorated under aerial attack. The night raids were feared far more than daylight raids. The people lost faith in the prospect of victory, in their leaders and in the promises and propaganda to which they were subjected. Most of all, they wanted the war to end. They resorted increasingly to "black radio" listening, to circulation of rumor and fact in opposition to the Regime; and there was some increase in active political dissidence—in 1944 one German in every thousand was arrested for a political offense. If they had been at liberty to vote themselves out of the war, they would have done so well before the final surrender. In a determined police state, however, there is a wide difference between dissatisfaction and expressed opposition. Although examination of official records and those of individual plants

shows that absenteeism increased and productivity diminished somewhat in the late stages of the war, by and large workers continued to work. However dissatisfied they were with the war, the German people lacked either the will or the means to make their dissatisfaction evident.[21]

On 1 August, the German flak batteries Hitler had decided he had to leave at the Ploesti oilfields had a field day shooting down B-24s from U.S. Ninth Air Force in North Africa. A low-level surprise attack went awry, and the Germans downed 41 of the 166 bombers that reached the target, a third of the force. Another 13 failed to make it home.[22]

Moreover, American strategic bombing was not yet troubling German war production overmuch. The Survey reported:

> The German anti-friction bearing industry was heavily concentrated. When the attack began, approximately half the output came from plants in the vicinity of Schweinfurt. An adequate supply of bearings was correctly assumed to be indispensable for German war production.
> In a series of raids beginning on 17 August 1943, about 12,000 tons of bombs were dropped on this target—about one-half of one per cent of the total tonnage delivered in the air war. In an attack on 17 August by 200 B-17s on Schweinfurt, the plants were severely damaged. Records of the industry taken by the Survey (and supplemented and checked by interrogation) show that production of bearings at this center was reduced sharply—September production was 35% of the pre-raid level. In this attack 36 of the 200 attacking planes were lost. In the famous and much-discussed second attack on 14 October 1943, when the plants were again severely damaged, one of the decisive air battles of the war took place. The 228 bombers participating were strongly attacked by German fighters when beyond the range of their fighter escort. Losses to fighters and to flak cost the United States forces 62 planes with another 138 damaged in varying degree, some beyond repair. Repeated losses of this magnitude could not be sustained; deep penetrations without escort, of which this was among the earliest, were suspended and attacks on Schweinfurt were not renewed for four months.
> The Germans made good use of the breathing spell. A czar was appointed with unlimited priority for requisitioning men and materials. Energetic steps were taken to disperse the industry. Restoration was aided by the circumstance—which Survey investigations show to have been fairly common to all such raids—that machines and machine tools were damaged far less severely than factory structures. German equipment was redesigned to substitute other types of bearings wherever possible. And the Germans drew on the substantial stocks that were on hand. Although there were further attacks, production by the autumn of 1944 was back to pre-raid levels....[23]

The Allied strategy, the reader will recall, linked the attempted disruption of ball bearing output to a broad assault on aircraft production. The Survey was somewhat more positive regarding those results.

> The attack on the German aircraft industry—primarily on airframe plants—was opened in the summer of 1943. The German aircraft industry had been well distributed over the Reich with a view to the possibility of air attack. Isolated raids early in 1941 and 1942 had caused some further shift in production to eastern territory but only limited steps had been taken to disperse individual plant units in order to reduce their vulnerability. The industry was found to have had substantial excess capacity. The efficiency of the industry was low. Unlike other armaments, procurement was not under the direction of the Speer Ministry but under the Luftwaffe....

In the 1943 attacks, 5,092 tons were dropped on 14 plants, primarily on airframe plants. The records show that acceptances of the Me-109 [sic, Bf 109], Germany's standard single-engine fighter, dropped from 725 in July to 536 in September and to a low of 357 in December. Acceptances of Focke Wulf 190s dropped from 325 in July to 203 in December. As a result of the attacks, the Germans began a more vigorous program of subdividing and dispersing aircraft plants, and this caused part of the reduction in production. A further but undetermined part was the result of poor weather which cut down acceptance flights; it is probable that some planes produced but not accepted during these months were added to acceptance figures in the months following. The Germans as a result of these attacks decided to place increased emphasis on the production of fighter planes.[24]

O'Brien argues that the Survey underestimated the damage inflicted. The first U.S. Air Force precision bombing attack against the Messerschmidt plant in Regensburg by 21 B-17s that recovered to Tunisia cost nine of the bombers and appeared to illustrate the ineffectiveness of the 1943 campaign. The raid nevertheless destroyed more aircraft than Germany lost at Kursk, and perhaps more than all losses on the Eastern Front in summer 1943. Field Marshal Erhard Milch, in charge of aircraft production from 1941–1944, said the raids prevented a planned doubling of fighter production to 2,000 units per month. German sources also reported that as factories dispersed, quality suffered.[25]

Moreover, strategic bomber output kicked into high gear in both America and the UK in 1943. Between January and September 1943, Britain built 1,272 Lancaster heavy bombers, slightly above target. In the first quarter of 1943, America churned out 1,329 B-17s and B-24s, roughly half the total for all of 1942. The target for the year was 4,456 B-17s and 5,928 B-24s.[26]

But German flak and fighter defenses were causing Eighth Air Force unsustainable losses during daylight raids into Germany. The Americans had chosen not to use Window and instead introduced an active radar jammer for a raid on Bremen on 8 October. Eighth Air Force lost 30 of 110 bombers, and 71 percent suffered flak damage. A return to the Schweinfurt ball bearing plant on 14 October by 291 bombers cost 60 aircraft, or 17 percent of the force. Eighth Air Force stopped such raids through the end of 1943. It authorized blind bombing based on radar in bad weather that cut flak losses by half.[27]

Hitler Concedes the Initiative

Hitler met with Oshima on 29 July. Yes, Germany had gone over to the defensive again, but did not intend that the war would end this way, the Führer reassured the ambassador. The army would reorganize, and ammunition production was rising. He would again take the offensive and prevent an Anglo-American landing on the European continent.[28] In order to wage a long war against the Americans and British, he explained, he had to hold onto the resources in Ukraine. Germany would retire into a fortress while it produced the arms it needed.[29] Regarding Italy, he said, "we won't worry too much about it since our neighbor is all right in peace but weak in war. What an ally! If we had only had you Japanese in the position of Italy, we would surely already have won this fight."[30]

An assessment published by the JCS Joint Staff Planners on 5 August offered an assessment of Axis leadership thinking not all that different from Hitler's words.

> Due primarily to inadequate air power, the Axis now lacks the capability of destroying the Russian armed forces, while at the same time containing and defeating the increasing Anglo-American sea, air, and ground pressure against Western Europe. Outside of Russia, the Axis has no offensive capabilities, other than to invade the Iberian Peninsula. This is considered extremely unlikely.
>
> Although German morale is low, the Axis still retains great defensive power. A defensive strategy, however, means ultimate defeat. Consequently, it is difficult to believe that current Axis strategy still visualizes total victory, as once conceived.[31]

Hitler offered Oshima his view of American war fighting. "The Americans and the British are unpredictable; they do not fight in an outright manner the way we Germans and Japanese do. Their policy is first to get airbases and then, under protection from the air, to creep up on us. Before long, as things now look, they are going to be on the Italian mainland."[32]

Bad news continued to pour into Tokyo from Europe. Italy was practically out of the war, reported Major General Okamoto, who also expected Germany to remain on the defensive for a long time. Admiral Dönitz admitted that the U-boat war was faring poorly. Allied use of sonar and escort carriers had caused so many U-boat losses that the Germans had abandoned wolf-pack tactics and halted attacks on convoys for the time being. Field Marshal Milch said the Luftwaffe had "its back to the wall" and that Allied air raids were doing very great harm to German morale.[33]

Asked by interrogators after the war about the impact of deep-penetration air attacks on German strategy, OKW Chief of Operations Alfred Jodl replied, "It was at that time that I laid down the principle: With such control of the air, any offensive fighting on the Western front or the Italian theater of operations with any hope for success is absolutely impossible."[34]

Not that public opinion mattered in Germany, but the Hamburg bombing and Mussolini's ouster in Italy created a sense of panic in some quarters. The Security Service reported that Nazi Party members were not wearing their badges in public anymore. Crowds no longer responded enthusiastically to speeches on triumphs in arms production. Some industrialists concluded the war was lost, and the first trials and executions for defeatism occurred by the hundreds.[35]

In Japan authorities continued to show great interest in the effects and countermeasures against Allied bombing raids in Germany, and the government warned the populace that air raids could be expected in the near future. The government began construction of simple shelters in homes and parks and along roadways. It gave training to new neighborhood firefighting groups.

The prospects were frightening. One Japanese diplomat who visited Hamburg in August reported, "The damage was tremendous, and the scenes of human misery and desolation resembled those in Tokyo and Yokohama after the great fire and earthquake of 1923. It will take some years after the war is over to recover economically."[36] The diplomat added,

> In a word, Germany's proud second-largest city received a fatal blow and was completely destroyed. This was accomplished despite wonderful aerial defenses, and was brought to pass in a short period of five days by three great air raids that lasted a total of seven hours in which 1,700 planes participated. Industry has ceased and production has been cut to such an extent that our misgivings concerning the war strength of Germany have increased.... I wish to make it plain that I am not exaggerating.[37]

Yet, Oshima found during a tour of devastated areas of Hamburg in September that German claims that morale was higher in bombed areas than elsewhere were true. "The residents, to my great surprise, are returning in large numbers. As a rule, in spite of the large damage suffered, they are imbued with a dauntless spirit."[38]

At the end of 1943, the IJA shifted the resources going into tank and field artillery production to antiaircraft guns.[39]

Axis Reduced

During the planning for Operation *Husky*, the Combined Chiefs of Staff considered draft terms for Italy's unconditional surrender should Italy seek terms after a successful Allied occupation of Sicily. They also considered possible action should Italy collapse and possess no organized government and should Italy devolve into civil war between pro- and anti-fascist forces.[40]

American and British strategic planners during July discussed whether to make an exception to the Casablanca demand for unconditional surrender to give the Italians a way to exit the war. A Combined Chiefs of Staff paper dated 5 August assessed that the Italians might fight with an unprecedented vigor to protect their homeland and observed:

> Our announced unconditional surrender policy might be modified, and conditions offered in exchange for surrender, i.e., a deal might be made with the Italians.
> It is highly likely that such a deal could be arranged with prominent figures on the present political scene. Any such move would, however, undercut all United Nations psychological warfare since Casablanca, and make future psychological warfare activities impossible, since no future policy or statement by us would ever be believed. The abandonment of the unconditional surrender policy would arouse in the German regime the hope that we would also make a deal with them.[41]

The final stage of the Axis withdrawal from Sicily unfolded from 13 August with little Allied interference. XIV Panzer Corps completed its retreat to the final line on the 14th.[42]

While the 29th Panzergrenadier and Hermann Göring divisions held off the enemy on 15 August, the 15th Panzergrenadier Division pulled back to Messina and ferried to the mainland. The commanding general of that division ascribed the ease of the operation to the Allies' passive behavior. The entire Italian XVI Corps with 70,000 men, 300 vehicles, and some 80 guns also escaped by sea. The screening force dropped back slowly, blowing up bridges behind it.[43]

Unable to wring a clear decision out of Hitler, Keitel and Kesselring took it upon themselves to order the final evacuation of Sicily without so much as informing Commando Supremo.[44]

The bulk of the 29th Panzergrenadier and Hermann Göring divisions evacuated on 16 August behind a thin rearguard screen. The last men pulled out that night. The evacuation was completed at 0630 hours on 17 August. The Germans had succeeded in withdrawing 60,000 men—with all their heavy weapons.[45]

A German assessment of American military leadership on Sicily noted an improvement over Tunisia in that the enemy quickly absorbed battle lessons. Still, the American soldier had not matured into a fully developed enemy.[46] One division commanding general recalled,

> The troops realized early on that the enemy very often conducted his movements systematically, and that he only attacked after a heavy artillery preparation when he believed he had broken our resistance. This kept him regularly from exploiting the weakness of our situation and gave me the opportunity to consolidate dangerous situations. The old Africa veterans were familiar with the enemy's style, and we behaved ourselves accordingly.[47]

(FMS note: This appears to be an accurate portrayal of American tactics, reflects no intent to curry favor, and reveals no fear of prosecution for war crimes.)

In September, the Tripartite Alliance became a Bipartite one. On the 3rd, the British Eighth Army landed on the toe of Italy and, as Hitler had foreseen, the Allies were on the Italian mainland. Italy surrendered unconditionally on the 8th, and OKW learned of the event from foreign broadcasts of a statement by Eisenhower. The Chief of the Italian General Staff at first denied the announcement as calumny, but Italian Prime Minister General Pietro Badoglio confirmed the capitulation shortly thereafter. The Germans had prepared well for the possibility of betrayal, and OKW that same day ordered its forces in Italy and France to take control over the defense and disarm the Italians. This rendered unconditional surrender meaningless because the government could not implement the Allied terms. Italian representatives signed a formal ceasefire agreement in Syracuse with Eisenhower, Alexander, and a Soviet representative present.[48]

"As far as the effect of the Italian surrender on the various classes in Germany is concerned," cabled Oshima from Berlin, "actually they feel a sort of relief at being freed.... Italy had not been on an equal footing with Germany for some time but had merely become an economic and military burden for the Reich." Tokyo determined to treat Italy and Italians as enemies.[49]

Operation *Avalanche*—the American Fifth Army (which included British X Corps) landings at Salerno—struck on 9 September. The Salerno assault was the Germans' first experience with Anglo-American amphibious operations (the Italians had borne the brunt on Sicily), and the encounter with Allied naval support for landings was shocking. "At Salerno," Oshima learned in Berlin on 14 September, "the most disagreeable feature for the German forces was the shelling by the fleet. The British and Americans showed great skill in coordinating land, sea, and air operations, but, once the troops landed, their fighting was poor as always."[50]

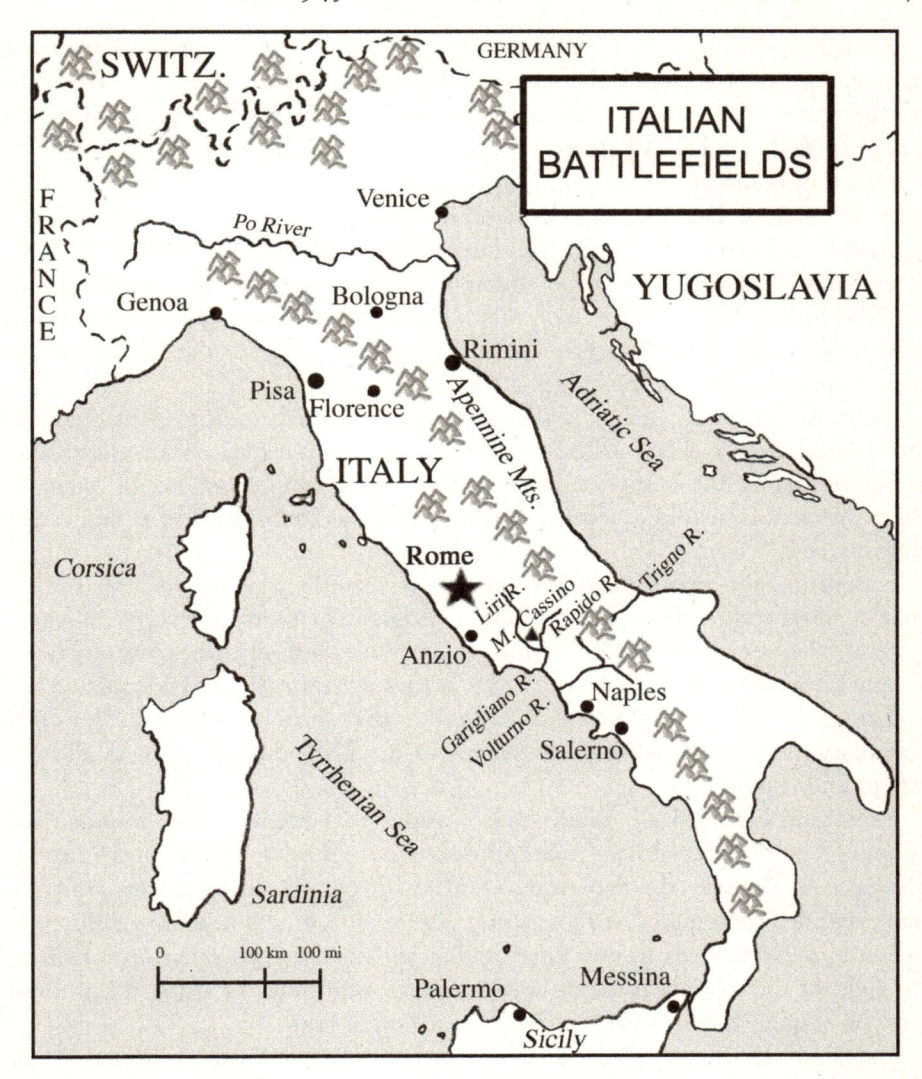

The Italian surrender forced the German High Command to shift from a strategy of trying to hold Italy to one of delaying defense up the peninsula. German commanders viewed the invasion of Italy as a training ground for fighting the inevitable Allied landings on the west European coast.[51]

Kesselring tried to drive U.S. Fifth Army into the sea with furious counterattacks by several panzer and panzergrenadier divisions and very nearly succeeded. The OKW war diary recorded that heavy naval gunfire at Salerno had played a crucial role in stopping XIV and LXXVI Panzer Corps attacks on the beachhead, so Hitler and other senior commanders were informed of this Allied weapon that they could not hope to counter. The Allies also had established air superiority. On 16 September, Kesselring ordered a slow fighting withdrawal to the Volturno River line, which he intended to hold until 15 October. Behind that, his engineers were preparing more fortified belts across the isthmus. A major factor in deciding to fight long and hard was to deny Allied bombers bases from which they could hit the Reich, the very issue simultaneously confronting the Japanese in China.

From this point on, Italy was the one theater in which the Germans accurately anticipated nearly every Allied move—the Germans expected an amphibious operation against the west coast in 1944, for example, and the choice of Anzio was merely a tactical surprise. German resistance remained effective and cohesive until the very end.[52]

Kesselring, the mastermind behind all the planning, explained after the war that he never regarded his forces in Italy as overmatched until the very end when a general collapse occurred in the German armed forces and Allied air power destroyed supply lines. Other than fuel, which was always tight, he received adequate troops and supplies, some directly from defense industries in northern Italy. (The OKW war diary confirms Kesselring's statement in the FMS that he received adequate troops and supplies.)

Kesselring expected all Allied attacks would be backed by "an abundance of supplies," but he was almost philosophical about Allied material superiority and viewed it as the way the Americans went about compensating for an army that had expanded too rapidly and frequently displayed rigidity and predictability in its operations. He referred in one interrogation to "the apparent attempt to facilitate the fight of the soldiers and reduce losses to the minimum by using continuously enormous quantities of weapons and material of all kinds."[53]

Italy's mountainous terrain gave the defenders a tremendous advantage and prevented the Allies from applying the full force of their material superiority for much of the campaign. As the official U.S. Army history put it, "The American mechanized forces for the most part fought the terrain rather than the enemy.... [T]he artillery, tank destroyers, and tanks were often a liability rather than an asset."[54]

*

Oshima met with Foreign Ministry Under Secretary Gustav von Steengracht on 17 September. He had just been with Hitler, he said, and the Führer "was absolutely flourishing and completely confident about the whole war situation." The German told him that Germany had fought at Salerno only to inflict maximum damage, had no intention of waging a long struggle to hold Rome, and would pull its forces back to the north—an accurate statement of policy at the time, but one that was soon overtaken by a decision to wage a delaying battle all the way up the boot. Germany was disarming the Italian military and already at work to set up a new government under Mussolini, who had arrived in Germany after being freed from Italian detention by a daring German commando raid ordered by Hitler.

But some degree of private realism appeared to creeping in. Steengracht, in addressing the Eastern Front, told Oshima (starting with an inaccuracy):

> German strategy on the eastern front this year has been to fight on the defensive without employing her reserve, and since Soviet losses have been incomparably greater than those of Germany, I think that in the main Germany has achieved her aim. However, we must expect that the German forces will continue to retreat, and I earnestly hope that you will not imagine that we have become demoralized.
>
> Regardless of whether the Russians have the strength to undertake a winter offensive, I am confident that they will not be able to penetrate beyond the line that Germany considers her last line of defense. However, I don't mean to say that we have built another "West Wall" on the eastern front.
>
> There has been talk that, if we lose the Ukraine, Russia's war potential will be strengthened. However, we have seen to it that Russia will not get an ounce of bread out of the Ukraine, and we have wrecked the mines and other facilities in such a way that they cannot be used for at least a year or two.[55]

Admiral Dönitz in mid-September told Oshima that the German Navy had resumed attacks against convoys from the United States using new tactics to pick off escort vessels first. He said the Führer had approved doubling the production of submarines, and that Germany was in a technological race against the Allies on direction-finding equipment, torpedoes, and guns that the Third Reich would win. Already, German submarines were spotting Allied patrol aircraft much more quickly and evading air attacks.[56]

According to a reliable OSS source, Hitler met in September with senior Nazi Party leaders at Berchtesgaden to discuss to what extent German morale could be trusted and whether the Nazis would have the backing of the people under further prolonged warfare, in the face of continuous setbacks. The Allied bombing was central to the discussions. The source said the conference indicated that the Nazis were well aware of the real choices facing the German people and they were determined not to give up without a bitter last-ditch fight. The conference decided to "give the German people all the brutal facts and to paint the future awaiting them in the darkest colors. To those elements in favor of an early peace and surrender instead of further useless destruction of German cities and sacrifices, the prospects of unrelenting terror from within and bitter revenge by the oppressed peoples from without were held out. Together with this picture of a Carthaginian peace at the hands of the Allies, the idea was carefully fostered that continuation of the war would soon lead to some sort of stalemate and that the Allied powers, discouraged by long, dragged-out, costly, and inconclusive warfare, would finally call it quits by means of a compromise peace.[57]

Oshima met with Hitler at his headquarters in East Prussia in early October and found him "in excellent form both mentally and physically." Hitler was uncertain about what the Americans and British would do next. "At the moment we cannot judge accurately just how the Allies are going to act from now on, but they have two courses: Either they will go north in Italy, or they will try to land in the Balkans. I am inclined to believe they will take the latter course."[58]

The Allied operations in Italy were affecting the war on the Eastern Front, Hitler continued:

> I had intended that the German Army should take the initiative in several places this summer and wear out the enemy. However, because of the Italian catastrophe, I had to send a total of 24 divisions to the Mediterranean area, which required me to take first-line soldiers from the eastern front and also other troops who could have been sent to the east. Also, I now have to look out for the future and keep powerful forces in reserve.[59]

Hitler conceded the initiative had shifted to the enemy:

> Since the collapse of Italy, what I have been most anxious to do is take the offensive in both the south and the east, but it has become clear that this is impossible because of a lack of planes, parts, and ammunition. Therefore, I have finally had to adopt a defensive strategy, although this is the very first time since the war began that we Germans have had to do so.[60]

Hitler talked about new divisions he was organizing that he would have available in the east by next spring: "We are going to have difficulties in getting out of our present straits. Meanwhile, I think it is the best policy to slap the Americans and British forces as soon as we get a chance, and then to turn again on the Soviet [Union]. I want you to know that I am not worried at all about the way the war is going."[61]

Ribbentrop told Oshima that Germany had pulled a dozen divisions off the Eastern Front because of the situation in the Mediterranean area. Oshima pointed out that Germany could not hope to achieve its war aims in the east and urged Ribbentrop to make a peace deal with the Russians and then turn on the Americans and British. For once, Ribbentrop said he would think about it.[62]

OKW on 3 November 1943 issued *Weisung* (Instruction) 51, which declared, "The danger in the east remains, but an even greater shows itself in the west: the Anglo-Saxon landing!" Indeed, OKW expected the decisive battle of the war to take place on the Western Front. There was plenty of room on the Eastern Front to deal with setbacks, but a successful cracking of the defenses in the West, OKW worried, would quickly lead to unforeseeable consequences. It would weaken forces in the West no longer and would significantly build them up, instead.[63]

To defend the Reich from Anglo-American bombers, the Luftwaffe slashed the number of combat aircraft on the Eastern and Mediterranean fronts during the last four months of the year. By December, 70 percent of its fighters were in the west or the Reich. The loss of experienced fighter pilots in late 1943 resulted in a crisis like that experienced by Japan. Pilots received half the training hours of their British and American counterparts and often were shot down before they earned much experience. By February 1944, Göring worried that he would not be able to man the aircraft that industry was churning out in growing numbers. Inexperienced pilots crashed frequently in bad weather.[64]

In Italy, where Kesselring had been responsible for the war in the south while Army Group B in France managed the north, Kesselring, on 21 November, took charge of the entire Italian theater. He simultaneously filled the roles of Commander-in-Chief Southwest and Commanding General, Army Group C. He would thus fight the Americans all the way up the peninsula.[65]

Kesselring after the war conceded that Allied air attacks complicated supply over the rail network, but the OKW war diary indicates that by early December 1943, Allied air superiority was affecting decision-making for even minor offensive operations. Kesselring proposed on 1 December that he stage a limited objective counterattack to close a breakthrough of a position in the British sector. Any larger attack would be costly and entail many losses because of enemy air power, he assessed. Hitler approved the operation, but only if bad weather kept the enemy from the skies. Kesselring at least still had some bombers and a few fighters; on 3 December, 63 fighter-bombers attacked an enemy tank and truck concentration, and 88 planes bombed Bari port.[66]

Oshima met with Ribbentrop again, on 25 November, to discuss the war. Oshima asked Ribbentrop's views on Anglo-American intentions. The German judged that American troops still were not well enough trained for European operations, which was why the Allied offensive in Italy was lagging. There no longer appeared to be any danger of an Allied landing in the Balkans. All signs pointed to an attempt to establish a second front, probably in Belgium or the English Channel coast. Oshima, having just toured the Atlantic coast defenses (and passed along his report to the Allies thanks to MAGIC), opined that the Anglo-Americans were unlikely to cross the Straits of Dover into the teeth of the defenses. "I am inclined to think that the enemy would prefer to establish a bridgehead in Normandy or on the Brittany Peninsula."

"Yes, that is certainly one possibility," Ribbentrop responded. The Soviet Union was exhausted, he opined, and Germany would fight on to permanently cripple it. "As for our fight against the Anglo-Saxons, while it is true that we have no effective means for dealing directly with America, once Anglo-American forces land on the continent of Europe, we will certainly fix them up properly."[67]

Kesselring reported to OKW on 4 December that the Allies had halted preparations for offensive action along his entire front, other than the battle raging at Cassino.

He was right. He had fought the Allies to a standstill. His nine divisions were pinning down 20 of the enemy's. He offered this appraisal:

> The enemy's superiority in artillery and ammunition is growing. With the means available, nothing can be done about enemy air superiority....
>
> The enemy gathers all of his strength in a narrow area. He wants to "fight cheaply." He has held to his old methodical methods. He must be countered in mobile, fuel-consuming defense, based on defensive strongpoints with no exposure to the rear and unassailable fronts.[68]
>
> Our construction has proved itself, but it must become better.[69]

When the operations staff presented Kesselring's report to Hitler, it judged that no large Allied landings on the "deep coast" were likely any time soon. Boy, was that wrong!

Jodl said after the war that OKW viewed American ground combat performance in North Africa and Italy as "very cautious," which he attributed to the U.S. Army still gaining experience and fighting under British command, which fought systematically and with less daring than the Germans. He conceded that with greater experience, American operations were to become more flexible with broader aims. (FMS note: This seems like a fair observation.)[70]

In probably November the Japanese Army General Staff's Russia Division produced an analysis that concluded the tide was turning against the Germans on the Eastern Front, according to a British SIS report.

> The real underlying cause for the change in the relative strength between Russia and Germany was not the air menace or the Mediterranean situation, but was mainly due to the heavy losses incurred by Germany in the winter of 1942–43, the withdrawal of Germany's allies, and the great increase in numbers, material, and quality which took place within the Russian army.... The Russian forces in the Kursk and Orel attacks were underestimated by the Germans and the German preparation for elastic defense was surprisingly deficient, especially in prepared positions in the rear of operations. This compelled mobile reserves to be deployed haphazardly. It is not likely that the Germans will be able to halt their withdrawal on the middle and lower Dniepr.[71]

Left unsaid was the fact that the Red Army had achieved a major boost in mobility thanks to the arrival of hundreds of thousands of American trucks and half-tracks.[72]

Also in November, Bomber Harris launched a campaign to wipe Berlin from the map, which removed the pressure from the Ruhr basin and allowed that area to recover. The German capital was to remain the focus of RAF attacks until April 1944. The Germans ringed the city with Flak, and night fighters picked off Lancasters on their way to and from Berlin. By March 1944, the defenders had shot down 1,047 bombers and damaged 1,682.[73]

In Italy, Fifteenth Air Force activated in November with 939 large bombers under its command.[74] The Reich now faced a two-front strategic bombing war.

Japan Realizes the War Against America Should Be Top Fight

In late 1943, the Imperial General Staff, the IJA, and even the IJN were just beginning to realize that the Pacific theater was the most critical for Japan and the outcome of the war, not the festering conflict in China.[75] By then, the Imperial General Headquarters was routinely transferring from China first-line divisions to shore up Japanese forces in the Pacific and southeast area. It expanded brigades in China into ersatz divisions lacking mobility to hold occupied areas, while the remaining first- and second-line divisions engaged in limited offensive operations.[76] Rear Admiral Toshitane Takata told interrogators that "higher forces" in Tokyo decided to deploy 300 army planes from China to the area southeast of Truk and to combine army and navy forces there.[77] The Inspector General for Military Education instructed the army schools to switch the curricula from tactics, training, and education for war against the Soviet Union to countering American operations. The schools protested that they had no instructors or material related to American tactics.[78]

The IJA began withdrawing artillery from Manchuria to supply divisions in the Philippines, Iwo Jima, Okinawa, and Japan. American submarine and air attacks sent many of the guns to the bottom of the sea. Okinawa, for example, received only a quarter of the artillery pieces sent its way.[79]

American and Australian forces conducted amphibious assaults on several small islands in the central Solomons. Military historian Hattori observed later, "Prior to the capture of Munda, the enemy occupied Rendova Island. He did this to support the capture of Munda by installing heavy guns on this island facing Munda. The enemy employed these tactics several times. In effecting the landing on Leyte, he first landed on Suluan, and before landing on Okinawa, he landed on the Keramas. However, we failed each time to estimate the enemy's favorite tactics." Landings on New Georgia commenced on 5 July. The IJA and IJN struck back with 170 planes, but army losses were so high it ceased operations. The Allies had also launched a simultaneous offensive on New Guinea on 30 June.[80]

Faced with the looming loss of the central Solomons, IGHQ from mid-July worked desperately to shore up a line in the northern Solomons and the Bismarck Islands. In mid-September, it ordered the 17th Infantry Division to move from the China Expeditionary Army to the northern Solomons.[81]

Japanese intelligence produced on 8 August a report that outlined the capabilities of the B-29 bomber. It anticipated the aircraft would appear on the battlefield sometime after autumn.[82]

The IJA and IJN at IGHQ on 15 September adopted a drastic change in war strategy, which heretofore had emphasized offensive operations. The Allied counter-offensive had struck faster and stronger than anticipated, Italy had dropped out of the war, and previous notions of Axis cooperation no longer made sense. There was a recognition that global events had changed dramatically. The new IGHQ policy had three key elements:

1. To take a long step backward in the Southeast Area, a theater of tremendous war of attrition where a series of desperate struggles had continued ever since the withdrawal from Guadalcanal.
2. To erect an undefeatable strategic position by establishing the so-called absolute national defense sphere.
3. To build up rapidly, in the meantime, the effectiveness of our armed forces, with special emphasis on air power, in order to complete preparations for coping with the mounting Anglo-American counteroffensive on our own initiative.[83]

The IGHQ's estimate of the enemy situation concluded that the Allied offensive would "reach its climax" between the second half of 1943 and late spring of 1944, or, at the latest, by early summer 1944. The enemy would press its offensive in the Southeast Area and from the northeast and step-up air attacks against key occupied areas. The Nationalist Chinese would continue to resist, and Allied air forces in China would strengthen gradually. The Soviets would stay out of the war, but one had to guard against the Americans using airbases in Siberia.

IGHQ estimated Allied front-line strength at approximately 2,500 aircraft and 23 divisions, with a total strength including reserves of 6,000 aircraft and 70–80 divisions. Despite putting emphasis on the European war, American shipbuilding would provide sufficient capacity to support front-line strengths of approximately 4,000 aircraft and 35 divisions by the end of 1943, 5,300 aircraft and 43 divisions by the middle of 1944, and 7,000 aircraft and 60 divisions by the end of 1944.

The main body of the U.S. Pacific Fleet was operating in the waters from Hawaii to the Southeast area with a nucleus of approximately six aircraft carriers, 15 battleships, and 15 cruisers. Another ten converted carriers were escorting convoys. The Americans were expected to field 12 new carriers by the end of 1943, 16 by mid-1944, and 18 by the end of 1944. Those estimates might prove too low.

A mainly British fleet estimated to consist of one carrier and two converted carriers, four battleships, and ten cruisers was operating in the western Indian Ocean. With Italy out of the war, the British could reinforce with up to four or five carriers, several converted carriers, two or three battleships, and ten-odd cruisers.

Approximately 80 American submarines were operating out of Hawaii, Dutch Harbor, Brisbane, and Perth. Ten-odd British submarines were based in the Ceylon area.

In the next year, the enemy would attack from the east and west. He would try to occupy Rabaul and aim offensives toward the Philippines and Mandate Islands (the Marianas, Carolines, Marshall Islands and the Palau group). The enemy would attempt to disrupt sea communications and bomb the homeland and occupied areas. The probability of large-scale operations against islands in the central Pacific was low because of the enemy's carrier strength, but the chance of invasions of the Gilberts and Wake in concert with the offensive against Rabaul by the end of the year was not slight. The enemy would make efforts to capture Burma.[84]

The IJA and IJN would cooperate to execute the operational plan:

- Bolster defenses in the central and southern Pacific, with the strength necessary to conduct counterattacks to be disposed along the line extending from the Banda Sea to the Caroline Islands in order to inflict crippling blows on the enemy and, if possible, frustrate the enemy invasion through initiative attacks.
- In the Southwest Area, defend areas already under control at all costs. Any enemy invading Burma, the Andaman Islands, the Nicobar Islands, or Sumatra will be destroyed.
- In China, efforts will be made to stabilize and retain generally the area under occupation to crush the enemy's will to fight through intensification of pressure.
- Defense of the homeland, oilfields in the Southwest Area, and sea communications routes will be strengthened.
- Efforts will be made on all fronts to conduct raiding operations deep into the enemy rear.[85]

The Japanese badly underestimated Allied air strength. The U.S. Navy alone in September had almost 9,000 aircraft, most devoted to the Pacific. Indeed, the navy alone had almost as many planes as the army, and only 4,000 less than the RAF. By the summer of 1944, the navy was to have about the same number of deployed aircraft—5,000—as the Luftwaffe, with a similar small proportion of four-engine aircraft that were the pride of the air force and RAF.[86]

A liaison conference met on 25 September to approve the new policy. An estimate of the world situation said:

> The United States: The American war aim is the complete defeat of Germany and Japan, especially the latter, for the purpose of establishing a global organization centering around the United States. The United States, intending to bring the war to an early conclusion, will generally complete preparations for victory during this year or the next and will attempt to conquer Germany and Japan with full application of her superior material power in cooperation with Britain, and by utilizing the Soviet Union and Chungking regime.
>
> In case the war is stalemated and the United States deems that the complete defeat of Germany and Japan involves serious difficulty, there is a possibility that she might try to end the war when it becomes possible to minimize the power of Germany and Japan and implant American influence in the Allied nations as well as in the vanquished.[87]

Admiral Seiichi Ito, the deputy chief of the Navy General Staff, defined the boundaries of the sphere that must be held at all costs: Kuril Islands, Bonin Islands, inner South Seas, western New Guinea, the Sunda Islands (Borneo, Java, Sulawesi, Sumatra), and Burma. The sphere offered the advantage of fighting on interior lines; included all the resources needed to wage protracted war; prevented "invasion against our homeland"; safeguarded land, sea, and air transportation; and retained political control over the major nations in the Greater East Asia Co-Prosperity Sphere. The objective was to prevent the enemy from capturing new bases and preventing air raids against vital areas.[88]

An imperial conference on 30 September ratified the new policy. One of Nagano's sentences as he spoke on behalf of both the IJA and IJN captured the situation: "Thus, our estimate is that the situation on all fronts has reached a grave state."

Questioned by President of the Privy Council Hara, Tojo said the plan called for expansion of military aircraft over the next year from 17,000–18,000 to 40,000. Hara asked whether the military was confident that the sphere could be held with 40,000 planes. Nagano replied, "We are determined to hold it by all means.... I cannot predict the outcome of our war with any degree of accuracy." The atmosphere suddenly became tense by the navy's expression of pessimism regarding the future outlook of the war, Hattori recorded.

Tojo strongly disagreed with Nagano's sentiments. "Japan must carry on regardless of Germany's fate. Whatever the future development, there can be no change in Japan's determination to prosecute the war to a successful conclusion."[89]

This moment, with the Emperor present, appears to be the one at which the senior-most Japanese leadership confronted the possibility that the American giant they had unleashed was going to crush them, even if Tojo disagreed.

Elsewhere, the German Embassy in Tokyo reported that a confidential military source said that Japan's loss of shipping in September was the highest in the war.[90] This was because American submarines that month had launched the first effective campaign against Japanese oil tankers hauling fuel from the East Indies.[91]

Tokyo also expected that it would soon have a real fight on its hands in Burma. Tojo in June had told the Thai prime minister, "As you know, we would like to make Burma one of the strategic points of the Co-Prosperity Sphere in Central Asia, and it has become a bulwark of defense for us in the India area. With this view, we are building the Thailand–Burma railroad. At present, our armed strength in Burma is quite adequate." A Japanese War Ministry circular on 29 August began, "It appears that the enemy is planning to retake Burma ...." In September, the German minister in Thailand reported that Japanese forces expected an Allied attack from the south and were preparing for the "coming battle" with extensive airfield construction in Burma. Troop reinforcements to Burma, who were landing in Saigon and moving by riverboat and overland, were placing a heavy strain on Thai roads.[92]

The Brief Attempt to Sideline the China War

The IGHQ in October took direct control over operations north of Australia. It transferred the headquarters of Second Army and an infantry division from Manchuria to the area, as well as a division from Japan. Second Army took charge on 1 December, with instructions to prepare counterattacks against the Allies.

The IJN, meanwhile, created the Fourth Expeditionary Fleet to work with the IJA. As it turned out, the need to strengthen defenses in the central Pacific in early 1944 diverted the resources the Japanese would have needed to accomplish much in that area.[93]

Also in October, IGHQ began moving IJA units from Japan, Korea, Manchuria, and China to the central Pacific to be stationed in the Carolines and Marianas under the new policy. The defenses in the Marshall Islands were so weak, however, that some were diverted there. Allied attacks on shipping made movement difficult. In December 1943, the Allies sank 300,000 tons of shipping, which would spike to 460,000 tons in January 1944—the highest level yet.[94]

The Americans landed on Tarawa and Makin in the Gilberts on 20 November. Although the defenders on Tarawa inflicted heavy casualties on the U.S. Marine Corps, IGHQ lost contact with the Makin garrison in 90 minutes and with Tarawa on the 22nd. The garrison on Makin was annihilated on 23 November, and that on Tarawa on the 25th.[95]

A usually reliable source of the Joint Intelligence Collection Agency (JICA), China Burma India, reported in December that senior Japanese commanders gathered in Singapore in early December to discuss strategy in 1944:

> (1) Regarding the war in general, it was realized that developments in the Far East will largely be dependent on the outcome of the decisive battle to be fought on the European continent in 1944. The fighting between the Soviet and German forces on the eastern front are receiving the most serious attention of the Japs, specifically because the Japs are mostly concerned with the attitude of the Soviets after the possible concluding of the European war before the end of 1944.
> (2) In the Pacific, it was said, the Japs would do their utmost to hold the present position against the Americans. They will not expand further the present line they hold in the Southwest Pacific as, in fact, they have no power to take any offensive; but in case the Americans should attack on them, they would dig in to resist strongly.
> (3) As to the war in China, they have decided not to take any large-scale offensive, but would concentrate their effort on the exploitation and absorption of the economic wealth in the occupied areas so as to carry on the war against the United States.[96]

Both the imperial conference in September and the JICA source—who, judging from the discussion at said conference and the October troop redeployments, reported accurately what was said in Singapore—were wrong about the end of large-scale offensive operations in China. Behind the scenes, key planners were already at work undermining the new strategic approach because the very same American enemy was threatening Japan from the west and south. To the west, American bombers would probably soon be able to attack the home islands. To the south, America's decimation of Japan's transport fleet threatened to cut off the flow of raw materials, whether or not the sources remained in Japanese hands.

Colonel Hattori, chief of the Army General Staff Operations Section, had toured the Southeast Asia front in mid-November and concluded that the direst scenario anticipated in the August strategic plan was emerging. American air support for the Chinese was increasing, and shipping losses were staggering. He pressed the General

Staff to launch an operation in China to establish a land link with Southeast Asia. He argued that Japan would be able to halt the American advance in the Pacific, and with the flow of supplies ensured via the mainland, it could launch a counteroffensive in the Pacific in 1946.

Hattori's own account is muddled. Hattori says that the operational plan for the offensive in China, dubbed ICHI-GO, emerged during autumn of 1943, but he also asserts at one point that the idea for an offensive in China arose from a tabletop exercise in December 1943.

The China Expeditionary Army and IGHQ had in late 1943 been looking at the possibility of an offensive to protect transportation through China and in the East China Sea. The Japanese assessed that the U.S. Air Force had about 130 planes operating out of bases in southwestern China, while the Nationalist had some 200 planes at airbases in central and north China. Allied strength was likely to increase to 500 planes by the spring, including heavy American bombers posing a direct threat to the homeland. Japan, meanwhile, was concentrating air assets in the Pacific and sending few newly produced aircraft to China.

Regarding the ground war, IGHQ assessed:

> As a result of the successive setbacks in operations, the Chungking Forces suffered considerable heavy losses. However, in view of the changes in the international situation and the war situation in the Pacific Ocean area, during the past two years, and the possibility of American material and spiritual aid to China, and the possibility of provisions and light arms self-sufficiency, it must be estimated that the Chungking Regime's determination to continue the war would become stronger rather than weaker.

IGHQ estimated that Nationalist forces had about 3 million men, with 250,000 in nine field armies. The China Expeditionary Force as of late 1943 fielded 620,000 men. It had ammunition sufficient for 20 divisions but only eight months of fuel. The diversion of practically all combat aircraft to the Pacific had ended its air superiority. "Thus," recorded Hattori, "the war situation in China became completely unfavorable."

On 25 November, 20 American bombers and fighters flying from Sichuan attacked the Hsinchu naval airfield on Formosa. This foreshadowed raids on the home islands.[97]

The Cairo Conference Defines Allied War Aims Against Japan

Roosevelt, Churchill, and Chiang met in Cairo from 23 to 27 November to agree on a common set of war aims against Japan. Tokyo on 1 December read the final "Declaration of the Three Powers":

> The several military missions have agreed upon future military operations against Japan.
> The three great Allies expressed their resolve to bring unrelenting pressure against their brutal enemies by sea, land, and air. This pressure is already rising.
> It is their purpose that Japan shall be stripped of all the islands in the Pacific which she has seized or occupies since the beginning of the First World War in 1914, and that all the territories that Japan has stolen from the Chinese, such as Manchuria, Formosa, and the Toscaores [*sic*, probably the Pescadores], shall be restored to the Republic of China.

Japan will also be expelled from all other territories which she has taken by violence and greed.

The aforesaid three Great Powers, mindful of the enslavement of the people of Korea, are determined that in due course Korea shall become free and independent.

With these objectives in view, the three Allies, in harmony with those of the United Nations at war with Japan, will continue to persevere in the serious and prolonged operation necessary to procure the unconditional surrender of Japan.[98]

The declaration caused deep concern at IGHQ but reports of a Roosevelt–Churchill–Stalin meeting in Tehran on 1 December worried the Japanese even more. They had no information but good reason to fret, because Stalin secretly committed the USSR to join the war against Japan three months after Germany's collapse.[99]

Meanwhile, the concern in Tokyo about the capabilities of Japanese war production led to action. Tojo in late September announced a sweeping reorganization of war production to meet the American challenge. The Joint Intelligence Collection Agency (JICA), China Burma India, assessed on 2 October, "The suddenness of the moves seemed to be aimed at shocking the Japanese people into a realization of their plight."[100] The OSS reported in October:

> Complete reorganization of the Japanese war effort and the planned all-out expansion of Japan's war potential and industrial resources contain features of highest economic and military significance.
>
> Though reports from Japan and Japanese occupied territories are sparse and open to varying interpretations, these features demonstrate beyond doubt a governmental, military, and economic machinery strained to the utmost and with maritime communications over-extended to such an extent that a general retrenchment of Japanese holding positions in the Central and Southern Pacific island areas may be confidently expected within the coming months.
>
> Some of the salient features of the Japanese reorganization program were made public throughout the Western world some weeks ago. They have been rightly interpreted as signs of the tremendous difficulties that confront the empire and threaten the Japanese nation with the most formidable crisis in its history....
>
> The program consists of 10 points:
> 1. Unification of management and administration pertaining to internal defense....
> 2. Expansion of air power and the devotion of Japan's full strength to the speedy increase of munitions and armament production.
> 3. Enforcement of a program that will insure complete self-sufficiency of Japan and Manchukuo in foodstuffs and similar vital necessities.
> 4. Thorough mobilization of the people....
> 5. Strengthening of the position and means of internal defense.
> 6. Speedier execution of official business and transfer of as much as possible of the business of national government agencies and organs to local government.
> 7. Reduction in government personnel.
> 8. [C]ontinuous operation of all government on a 24-hour day and night basis, and without holidays.
> 9. Rise and further expansion of the tax and national savings system for the purpose of obtaining additional funds and their use with maximum result.
> 10. Simplification of the price and distribution system.[101]

The OSS report assessed that the key change was that the government was asserting control over four large monopolies—Mitsubishi, Mitsui, Sumitomo, and Yasuda—that had heretofore more or less independently run their own operations and those in China devoted to war production. The Mitsubishi and Sumitomo families had agreed to make the government half-owners, which gave the government a decisive voice in war production.

The JICA report, meanwhile, related that the language on internal security revolved around preparing for the impact of future large-scale air bombardment on industry and the civilian population. Government agencies, state-owned industrial facilities, and even the civilian population were to disperse to areas outside the big cities.

Shigemitsu in December cabled Oshima in Berlin that the

> difficulties involved in regimenting business are very real. Major General Okamoto cannot give you an accurate picture on this subject, since the problem is far more serious than it was when he left for Europe last February. Suffice it to say that we have done everything in our power to meet this problem, and that we are now achieving an epoch-making increase in our power of production. We are therefore convinced that, so far as ships and planes are concerned, we can wage successful warfare both this year and next.[102]

The foreign minister was particularly concerned about shipping. "We are haunted by the numbers of ships we have lost."

The Japanese Diet had continued to meet during 1943, and its members discussed the pressing issues of the day, although the influence on policymaking is unclear. The 81st session started on 28 January, and the 82nd on 5 May. The agenda included plans for the decisive fight with Allied forces, change of officials in charge of internal political affairs, suppression of antiwar factions and those harboring radical thoughts, intensifying anti-American and anti-British propaganda, increasing production of war materials, and devising better and more stringent methods for securing raw materials and foodstuffs from all occupied nations.

The 83d (October) and 84th (December) sessions took place while Japan was suffering reversals on all fronts—defeats in Hunan and west Hupeh, China, the Solomon Islands and New Guinea, plus the American landings in the Marshall Islands. At the meeting on 24 December, Tojo reported on a battle on one of the Pacific islands in which all Japanese defenders had been exterminated.

The 84th session continued into January. Diet members noted that the 83d session had called for strengthening the airplane building industry, and the Diet on 15 January had demanded an increase in aircraft production. A question was put to Tojo whether, if Japan could build 9,000 planes per month, it would be possible to conquer China and defeat the Americans and British in the Pacific. Tojo reportedly could not give a satisfactory reply.[103]

The state of Japanese knowledge of the American enemy in late 1943 was poor, at least in the IJN. Commander Chikataka Hakajima became the chief of the Combined Fleet intelligence staff in November, where he remained until the end of the war. Hakajima told interrogators after the war, "My principal duty was to make estimates of American or other Allied forces, to make deductions on their movements or information received from the central information center." His staff consisted of only three officers and six enlisted men, who monitored radio transmissions. The unit received tactical reports (such as air reconnaissance reports of fleet movements, intercepted messages show) from subordinate units and "fragmentary and very general" information from the Navy General Staff. Hakajima received almost no information from the IJA until routine sharing began in April 1945. He relied primarily on American news broadcasts to establish enemy order of battle. "If your broadcasts were false, my estimates were bad."

When asked how accurate his estimates of American intentions had been, he answered, "Sometimes they were good; sometimes bad. I predicted the Okinawa line of campaign as early as November [1944] and predicted the date of the attack ten days in advance.... On the other hand, I missed the time of the Leyte attack. I thought it would be two months later."[104]

The IJN expanded its electronic intelligence system as the war progressed, and analysts were able to infer enemy operational activity from callsigns and traffic patterns. They were able to decipher some information on ship movements but rarely in time for the information to be actionable. They could track slow-moving convoys across the Pacific.[105] But their repeated surprise at invasion fleets showing up at unexpected places reveals the limitations of their collection and analysis.

Bummed and Blind in Berlin

Meanwhile, in Berlin, Goebbels lamented in his diary on 7 November, "The Americans [bombers] are now accompanied by pursuit planes when they attack in daytime. These carry first-class equipment and our own pursuit planes are not equal to them. It is very humiliating to note how the enemy is leading by the nose in air warfare."[106] The fighters were twin-boom P-38 Lightnings from the 55th Fighter Group, first employed as escorts on a mission to Geilenkirchen on 5 November.[107]

A German High Command circular to all military attachés at the end of 1943 tried to portray the year as one of skillful defensive victories, with all disasters—including the breakthrough at Stalingrad, the fall of Tunisia, and the surrender of Italy—as having been the fault of the Italians:

> With Italy's capitulation, the enemy expected the defense of Southern Europe to collapse. Instead, we have constructed a closely-knit defensive front from the east Pyrenees to Rhodes.... On the eastern front, the breaches in our line made by the Russians, without regard for their tremendous losses in blood and materials, were neutralized by the glorious achievements of the German Eastern Army and its command. In northern and western Europe, defense measures against the expected enemy landings have been completed without interference and have been adapted to the enemy's method of attack, which has been observed again and again.
>
> On the home front, the stepping up of bombings has not produced the reaction expected by the enemy but has strengthened the German people's will to win.[108]

Japanese service attachés had met on 21 November, according to a reliable British SIS source, and concluded that Germany could not win the war but could carry on defensive warfare for a long time.[109]

Weisung 51 had accelerated preparations for the expected second front in the West. A massive program of fortifications launched for the winter months, the main constraints being the supply of concrete and the ability to ship it. As of 11 December, OKW had no new information on Allied intentions except newspaper reports gathered by the mission in Tehran, that suggested the invasion had been pushed off, so Germany could count on at least two to three months of peace.[110]

Hitler received a briefing on the U-boat war on 21 December. "The surface tactics of the U-boats are over, and all operations will have to be conducted under water." This would make finding the enemy the biggest challenge. Air reconnaissance would have to do the job, and not enough long-range Ju 290s were available. Hitler agreed that final production work had to accelerate and that the entire output of those aircraft would go to reconnaissance instead of just half.[111]

OKW's operations staff on 24 December issued notice that the movement of forces to the west to strengthen the right flank of Seventh Army (Cotentin Peninsula, aka Normandy), and Fifteenth Army's coastal defenses to the north would commence on 15 January. The army chief of staff replied the next day that Hitler had moved the date forward to 1 January because it would take so much time given the limitations of the transport net. He was to alert Rundstedt to expect the movement of Allied divisions to southern England beginning in February. Fresh arrivals for newly forming divisions were to include a panzer regiment from the panzer school as the cadre for the Panzer Lehr Division and the personnel from the Hermann Göring Panzer Division. With reinforcements already sent, Germany had 1.3 million soldiers in the west. The arrival of eight panzer and panzergrenadier and nine infantry divisions was expected to create a whole new situation.[112]

CHAPTER 13

Early 1944: The End Becomes Visible

By mid-1944, perceptive Japanese grasped that they faced the real possibility of strategic defeat at America's hands and the destruction of the empire. Perceptive Germans would need a few more months, until the Allied breakout from Normandy, to reach the same conclusion about the war on the Western Front regarding the Anglo-American alliance.

Phillips O'Brien estimates that by 1943, Anglo-American air and sea power was destroying a quarter of the Axis war production potential by interrupting supply lines for raw materials, destroying production facilities, and, in the Pacific, sinking troops and weapons on the way to the battlefield. By 1944, only a minority of munitions and equipment was going to go into battle.[1]

Japan Concedes American Military Superiority

Kido on 6 January mulled in his diary the spillover consequences if Germany should suddenly collapse and surrender unconditionally. "What we must consider first is whether or not Japan should immediately maneuver to bring the war to an end.... In such an event, the enemy will naturally intensify their political offensive against us. Consequently, there will be many so-called Bodoglios [who surrendered Italy] in Japan, and this is what we must guard against."

Kido thought Japan could propose to the Allies creating a council of Japan, Russia, China, and the United States to resolve the issues in the Pacific. All Japanese-occupied areas except Manchuria would be neutralized like Switzerland and placed under the authority of the council. Economic policy would be based on freedom, reciprocity, and equal opportunity. The USSR would be the intermediary for such a proposal.

> The above draft may appear to be too soft and concessive. But when one contemplates the trend of world currents and judges from the results of the China Incident and the Russo-German war, the development of aircraft, the power and potentiality of the United States and Russia, and the drastic decrease in our national strength, one cannot but come to the conclusion that during the coming century or so, Japan must concentrate her efforts to build up her inner strength.[2]

The Japanese could see the growing American military superiority. In early January, the War Ministry transmitted a downbeat message to its military attachés:

> With the occupation of the Gilberts, the enemy has broken through one section of our defensive ring. There is a possibility that the Marshalls will be attacked. In any event, the military situation in the South Seas area indicates that sooner or later attacks will be made against Nauru and the Ocean Islands [the meaning here is unclear]. Despite his great losses in the battles of Bougainville, the enemy is continuing the offensive.
>
> The US fleet, notwithstanding the defeats suffered in the Solomons and Gilberts, has about five aircraft carriers in the Pacific (not including two that have been destroyed) and ten or more auxiliary carriers (not including six that have been destroyed). Their strength is increasing at an average of one aircraft carrier and three auxiliary carriers per month....
>
> The number of British submarines in the South Seas has been increased, and everywhere enemy submarine activity is growing more and more vigorous.[3]

The German military attaché cabled Berlin in January that the Japanese on New Guinea had become encircled. The United States had complete air superiority in New Britain and the Japanese could only receive supplies by small ships along the coast on dark nights. Rabaul was almost destroyed by air attacks. The Japanese were hoping to defend it until next June, when they were expecting their aircraft production to be properly underway. Compared with 80,000 tons of new construction, an average of 140,000 tons of Japanese shipping was being sunk per month.[4]

The Swiss mission in Tokyo reported, "Official circles admit the gravity of Japan's war situation. The American success in the South Seas, which they hardly try to conceal, makes a deep impression. Although the contrary is stated in the press, Japan is beginning to doubt a German victory and is preparing to fight alone. The economic situation in Japan is bad. The people are finding it difficult to obtain enough food."[5]

Anxiety about air raids mounted. On 15 January, the IJA command in Tokyo signaled that a prisoner of war reported that B-29 bombers were arriving in the Southwest Pacific Area. It urged collection of all reports on B-29s.[6] An intelligence report conveying more specifications of the B-29 appeared on 31 January, and a more detailed report on 17 May. The Japanese projections for the number of bombers that would arrive in China and when were fairly accurate.[7] Ambassador Oshima was sending Tokyo a steady stream of hair-curling reports on air raids against German cities, a message driven home when the Royal Air Force on 29 January destroyed large parts of the Japanese chancery and ambassador's residence in Berlin.[8] In February, the French chargé in Tokyo reported that the authorities had launched a campaign to move residents out of the big cities in anticipation of air attacks.[9] The Thai ambassador reported that the Japanese were also evacuating foreign diplomatic missions to small towns.[10]

Admiral King at this very time, early February, informed Marshall that he now envisioned bypassing the huge Japanese naval base at Truk and directly seizing the Marianas. B-29s should be available to deploy there as soon as the islands were in American hands.[11]

War Minister Tojo approved the General Staff plan for ICHI-GO aimed at establishing a railroad connection to Southeast Asia and destroying airbases in southeast China that could host bombers able to reach Japan. General Sugiyama obtained the Emperor's approval on 24 January. Tojo considered carving out a route to the south a distraction, something he reiterated when he became Chief of the General Staff in March.[12] The IGHQ order to the China Expeditionary Army issued on the 24th nevertheless included both objectives.[13]

The operations were to unfold during the spring and summer. Most of the experienced divisions had been shifted to the Pacific, so the IJA would have to rely on newly activated forces short on training and equipment.[14]

The General Staff on 19 February transmitted, "We judge that the time of air raids against Japan from China is gradually drawing near." It cited statements by senior American military officers, the establishment of an air corps headquarters in China, construction of large airfields there, and the expected arrival of B-29s.[15] The Japanese military attaché in Berlin was gathering every scrap of information he could on Allied and German radar technology and sending it to Tokyo for the Tama Technical Laboratories, where technicians raced to catch up to the Americans.[16]

Eighth Army at Rabaul assessed on 1 February, "The Allies will be able to attack Rabaul and Kavieng easily with fighter planes based on [Bougainville] and with naval planes." Attacks by long-range P-38s against the Kavieng supply line would cause "great hardship and sacrifice" for Japanese units in the Rabaul area. Eighth Army anticipated that after destroying Japanese air assets over the next three to six months, MacArthur would land three or four divisions on New Britain.[17]

American forces landed on Kwajalein in the Marshall Islands on 31 January 1944. The Combined Fleet was completely surprised. It had assumed that when the Americans hit the Marshalls, they would start in the south, but instead they went north. Once again, the entire garrison died within four days.[18] Moreover, the only aerial reconnaissance of the sea approaches consisted of bombers that lacked radar, according to an interrogation of Commander Goto Matsuura, then a staff officer in the Marshalls. Of passing interest, land radar was adequate to detect incoming American aircraft and vector fighters to intercept, except for the B-25, which was too fast.[19]

The Japanese government admitted the Americans had landed in the Marshall Islands—part of prewar Japan—on 4 February, three days after the landings had begun. The Diet was outraged by the delay in releasing the news.[20]

Vice Admiral Fukudome, Combined Fleet Chief of Staff at that time, recalled to interrogators:

> By the time that your landing around the Marshalls commenced, we were able to estimate fairly well the strategic situation in that region. There was no change in Admiral Koga's fundamental policy which was the need of one decisive engagement, but the new situation forced the following change: namely, a decision to make the Marianas and the Western Carolines the last line of

defense. The fleet air force was practically gone, so it was decided that all possible land-based planes, both in Japan and at the various fronts, should be concentrated in that region for a big air combat, with surface units participating to as great an extent as possible. Admiral Koga was determined to lead our forces in this final engagement himself. In pursuance of this new plan, Admiral Koga came to Tokyo aboard his flagship on 17 February, leaving Truk on the eleventh, for consultation with central authorities, ordering the rest of the fleet to a point west of the Western Carolines....

The decision of primary importance made at that conference was the adoption in principle of Admiral Koga's plan; namely, that we must absolutely hold the line of defense between the Marianas and West Carolines, and that the necessary defensive preparation for that must be completed by June. To that end it was decided to concentrate the whole of the naval strength in that region, also to bring in a new Thirty-First Army composed of three divisions and to build necessary airfields and coastal defense works....

At that time, three decisions had been taken in Tokyo. The first was to increase the air strength. The First Air Fleet was organized and already training. That fleet was brought under Admiral Koga's command and was shortly to be sent to the Marianas. This southward movement began about 20 February and received attacks as soon as it got there. Second, to increase the Army strength in that region, principally by bringing reinforcements from the Chinese fronts. Thus was organized the Thirty-First Army and its headquarters was soon established in the south. Necessary measures were taken for rushing material for construction of various defensive works, airfields, etc. The third decision was that local naval commanders should be appointed, all to operate under the [Commander-in-Chief] Central Pacific Area Fleet, who was Vice-Admiral Nagumo....[21]

Extreme misfortune crippled the Japanese shift of air power to the crisis region. Rear Admiral Marc Mitcher's Fast Carrier Task Force 58 turned up to raid the Marianas after having pounded Truk for two days. Battle-hardened American pilots engaged the surprised and freshly trained Japanese.[22] Hattori records that 83 planes sortied against the carrier strike force and that First Air Fleet lost 94 planes in air combat and on the ground, "an ominous hint of its fate."[23]

The newly organized First Air Fleet began its southward movement on the twentieth [of February] and was expected to arrive on the twenty-second or twenty-third, but owing to bad weather conditions, only a part of it got away on schedule, so that the number which had arrived by the time of the Task Force attack was probably less than 100, including 18 fighters and the rest being medium land-based planes, reconnaissance planes, and bombers. As this attack occurred while our planes were in the course of their movement to the south, and were not expecting an attack, they were not able to put up a good fight, although they were considered to be crack units. Of this newly trained fleet, approximately one half of that number was lost, and since this took place when we were just commencing to strengthen our defenses there, the loss was a considerable blow....[24]

Fukudome described the theater commander's assessment that the war would be lost if the Marianas and Western Carolines fell to the Americans.[25]

Admiral Koga proceeded to Palau [and] announced his decision to hold that line until death. You will recall that the decision of the Imperial General Headquarters was that it must absolutely be held; and Admiral Koga's feeling was that should that line be lost, there would be no further chance for Japan. To that end, he chose two bases from which he would guide our operations. If the next strike should come north, he would command from Saipan. If the strike should be directed southward, he would command from Davao. Whichever the direction, he was determined to make his last stand and consequently to die at either Saipan or Davao in defending this line. One reason for choosing land bases from which to guide the operations was that there was a decision to change from a decisive naval engagement to an engagement in which land-based air forces would constitute the main strength, but with the fleet units cooperating as fully as possible.[26]

The realization of defeat was to settle in at the senior military command level at roughly the same time in Japan and Germany. The Americans were to land on Saipan, the keystone of the Marianas, in June at nearly the same time that the Allies landed in France. They would secure Saipan in July. As we shall see, the breakout from Normandy in July convinced OKW Chief of Staff Jodl that the war in the west was lost.

Japan's aircraft and pilot losses in combat were only the tip of the iceberg. The far-flung defense perimeter often required pilots to fly their aircraft over open ocean to forward bases thousands of miles distant. The IJN could deliver aircraft by carrier, but after losses at Midway in 1942, it needed to keep carriers ready for battle. It thereafter delivered only half of its aircraft by ship; the rest had to fly. In 1944, the IJN lost 3,635 planes during operations and 6,675 to non-combat causes.

The IJA faced the same problem from the very establishment of the defense perimeter. Two officers involved in the matter told interrogators that IJA pilots suffered an attrition rate of 50 percent when flying from Japan to Formosa to the Philippines to the southern bases. Most of the best mechanics were deployed forward and got trapped there. Lieutenant General Torashiro Kawabe took charge of the IJA Bureau of Aeronautics in August 1944 amidst the large redeployment of IJA aircraft to the Philippines in expectation of an American invasion. He told interrogators that the poor maintenance airfields along the route resulted in only 10 percent of aircraft reaching their destination in combat-ready condition, if they arrived at all. Many simply disappeared during the long journey.

The reasons ran deeper than long flights. Japan was struggling to train new pilots, who got fewer training hours because of fuel shortages due to Allied attacks. Many pilots set off with no instruction in long-distance flying. Fuel shortages also reduced test runs for new engines, meaning fewer problems showed themselves before deployment. Transportation problems left forward airfields short of spare parts and mechanics.[27]

The bright spot was that aircraft production had soared since 1943. The number of planes built in 1942–1943 had met the targets set by the IJA and IJN; neither Germany nor America had met its targets. The IJN's aircraft fleet had doubled from April 1943 to April 1944.[28]

*

Presumably in response to a German query in light of expected Allied landings in Europe, the Japanese War Ministry in February sent to Berlin an analysis of American use of airpower in amphibious landings that offers a feel for the Japanese views of American effectiveness:

> About 20 days before the landing, the air attacks grow more severe, and they attempt to smash our air power and mobile sea power. Airfields in the vicinity of the place where they intend to land are the principal targets.
>
> During the first period (10 to 15 days), air attacks are carried out every day, principally by fighters, with about 100 planes a day participating. First, they try to destroy our fighter planes. Attacks at sea, aimed at the destruction of shipping, are carried out principally by bombers.
>
> The landing and advance are aimed chiefly at airfields or territory suitable for the establishment of airfields. They establish air supremacy and try to cut off our supply lines in the rear and to isolate our ground units.
>
> They are very fast at setting up airfields. With machinery and material at hand, they can set up an airfield on level ground for partial use in approximately 10 days....
>
> Other operations are as follows:
> 1. Cutting off the rear: They place great emphasis on this. They hamper our sea transport with precision torpedo bombings in conjunction with submarine attack.
> 2. Hampering of railway transport.
> 3. Bombing: Formerly the enemy concentrated on [low-level?] bombing, but recently the tendency has been toward medium-altitude precision bombing.[29]

The Japanese General Staff, in turn, asked military attachés in Germany and Italy to obtain German information on how they had conducted the dogged defense of Cassino and the enemy's methods of attack.[30]

In March, the interrogation of a downed American Air Corps colonel provided insight into American strategy that the Vice Chief of the General Staff forwarded to all principal army headquarters:

> The basic enemy strategy against Japan is threefold—the isolation of Japan from her outer zone of resources and the mainland, the bombing of the central part of Japan, and the securing of contact with China. In line with this, he says that their next aim is, first of all, the recapture of the Philippines....
>
> As for the conduct of military operations and advances in the [word missing] area, their offensive is guided by our points of weakness. With the aim of reaching the aforementioned objectives quickly, they will avoid direct capture of our strong positions and will merely try to render them powerless to carry out their functions.
>
> As for the air attacks against the Japanese mainland, the general aim is to launch them from Attu, from China, and particularly from the Philippines. Air attacks by carrier-based units have the disadvantage that they are not continuous.
>
> The air forces will have as their tasks, first, the destruction of our air forces and, second, the breaking of our supply lines, especially the complete destruction of our shipping.[31]

The German naval attaché in Tokyo reported in early March that he was hearing "expressions coming directly or indirectly from Japanese naval officers" to the effect that:

> As is constantly becoming clearer, the war can no longer be brought to a favorable conclusion by military means alone, with the present distribution of forces on the Axis side. The attempt must therefore be made with all available means to bring about an improvement in the political situation.

The state of affairs in the southwest Pacific is so difficult that, in the face of decisive battles to come, Japan cannot afford to leave strong forces in Manchukuo.[32]

On 15 February, Tokyo told IJA shipping authorities, "There is really no excuse for the damage inflicted on three of our ships in the waters around the Philippines by enemy submarines, especially when shipping is so scarce. Recently, enemy submarines have swarmed in the waters around the Philippines, and especially at this time the danger is so great that we are negotiating with the Navy to have sailings more thoroughly convoyed by Army and Navy planes."[33] Four days later, after submarines sank five tankers, Tokyo lamented that "losses sustained by our tankers since the beginning of the year have almost doubled.... [T]he majority of tankers returning to Japan are being lost."[34]

In the midst of this, as briefly mentioned above, American carrier planes battered Truk on 17–18 February. Although most warships had departed, the Americans sank 200,000 tons of commercial shipping.[35] The Americans destroyed all but six of the 270 planes based there (including 135 reserve aircraft), 70–80 of which had been operational. Air attacks on transports near Truk killed 1,100 men of the 52d Division.[36]

The Diet was shocked again by news of huge ship and plane losses. The Japanese press widely claimed that the Truk disaster constituted an immediate potential danger to the Japanese mainland, and that the war was entering its momentous stage. The Thai ambassador reported, "So far as I know, this is the first time that the Japanese have admitted just how serious the situation is." Tojo's government appeared to be near crisis.[37]

On 29 February, the Americans conducted a surprise landing on Los Negros in the Admiralty Islands. The airfield there served as a support field for flights between Rabaul and eastern New Guinea, and 1st Cavalry Division troops captured that on the first day. Once again, communications with the garrison were severed, though some resistance continued until about 25 March. The loss of the Admiralty Islands resulted in the collapse of the outer defenses of the absolute national defense sphere and isolated Rabaul.[38]

Because of the looming offensive in China, instead of pulling more divisions from that theater, the Japanese command reinforced the army in China with divisions from Japan and Manchuria.[39]

*

Despite the mess in the Pacific, the IJA on 6 March 1944 launched one of its planned attacks along the defensive perimeter, aimed at Imphal in India. Troops broke through the Burma–India border on 23 March. The Southern Army had conceived the operation in August 1943 to sever the expanding Allied effort to support Chiang by air from Eastern India, but IGHQ shelved it in November because of the growing crisis on Guadalcanal. War games in Rangoon in June 1943, however, concluded that in view of increasing Allied penetrations into Burma, the army needed to neutralize Imphal. Preliminary operations started in October, and the initial attack in March promised great success.[40]

Also in March, the Japanese combined all sea, ground, and air forces in the Central Pacific under the authority of the Commander-in-Chief Combined Fleet. On 5 March, Combined Fleet Headquarters issued orders for the fleet to gather its remaining strength to meet the enemy in the Carolines and Marianas—dubbed Operation Z. Vice Admiral Ugaki found the order awaiting him when he took command of the First Battleship Division near Singapore after convalescing from the air crash on Bougainville.[41]

Koga on the 8th transmitted All Hands Bulletin No. 1 that offered a frank assessment of American gains before the inevitable exhortation:

> It goes without saying that all ships and units have, for the two years and two months of this political war, fought bravely and dealt the enemy many heavy blows.
> However, the enemy has massed his forces and is gradually increasing the power of his attacks against areas vital to us. The situation is indeed grave.
> The Combined Fleet, strengthened by these crack forces, is prepared to close its ranks to meet this situation, catch the enemy unawares, and annihilate him.[42]

In far-off Madrid the Japanese minister was upset by public admissions of defeats and increased pessimism he was hearing from Tokyo over his shortwave radio. He cabled Tokyo to urge that the propaganda reflect more resolute confidence.

Foreign Minister Shigemitsu sent a reply in early March:

> As you well know, the Japanese Empire faces a most grave military situation. Ever since the China Incident, we have had altogether too much reporting based on nothing more than wishful thinking. As a result, our people have been over-optimistic, which is a serious thing in view of the present dire circumstances.
> Last fall, we began reporting on the war and the international situation in a manner designed to keep the people thoroughly informed as to the facts and to make them more firm in their attitude. The Foreign Office has taken the initiative in this trend.
> I am aware that the new policy is being reflected in our foreign broadcasts.[43]

The German military attaché in Tokyo reported on 20 March a long discussion with General Seizo Arisue, Intelligence Chief of the Army General Staff:

> The principal long-running objective of the Anglo-Saxons is the separation of Japan from plentiful raw materials in the south.... cutting her off by concentric attacks from Luzon and the west. Japan is still limited to strictly defensive operations....
> The Japanese defense received [a] heavy blow with the loss of the Marshalls, especially in torpedo planes.... The Marianas, which are near to the mother country and which are easier to defend by reason of more favorable natural conditions, are now being actively defended by army troops. Between Japan and the southern areas there are at least 35 United States submarines in constant operation. The task of command and troops is complicated by the serious tonnage losses resulting from inadequate Japanese defenses....
> [Regarding American methods:] Heavy air support with artillery and rocket fire from warships or landing craft has accompanied the landings.... Fog protection is often given to landing craft and also to beachheads, particularly those occupied by parachutists. Planes drop fog

cans to spot [targets] of ship artillery.... Abundant technical equipment and excellent training of [engineers] has resulted in surprisingly rapid and smooth USA landings. The landed troops have a formidable fighting power including light tanks, numerous mine and flame throwers. When needed, rapid [resupply] is received by air.

The work of American units is astonishing in combat, terrain coverage, and construction. They often found their way into the Japanese flank. USA mine throwers [mortars?] provide very disturbing concentrated fire. On the other hand, the Anglo-Saxons are very sensitive to surprise raids and night attacks. The most important lessons learned from the recent USA landings: 1) The torpedo plane is the most effective weapon against transports and warships, and 2) Maximum effort must be made to throw back the first landing operations. Counterattacks are very difficult once the beachhead has been established in depth.[44]

Admiral Koga died in an air accident while flying to Davao on 31 March. He had left Nagumo in command of the Marshalls and West Carolines. Koga's operations chief Fukudome summarized, "Admiral Koga took over just when the offensive stage was coming to a close and before preparations were made for the defensive stage and, hence, it was a very difficult period. He was waiting very anxiously for completion of the defensive preparations which was scheduled for June."[45]

Fukudome was on a plane accompanying Koga's, which ran out of fuel and crashed near Cebu, the Philippines. Fishermen working with guerrillas pulled him from the water, badly injured. The IJA learned of the crash from other survivors, and three battalions began a brutal search of hill villages looking for Fukudome. The guerillas agreed to hand him back in exchange for an end to the brutality. The guerillas kept his document satchel, which included Koga's battle plans. These found their way to American intelligence by submarine.[46]

*

The Vichy ambassador in Tokyo observed on 5 April:

> I gather from all sides that the Japanese have abandoned their hopes for an extended prolongation of the European conflict, in which the rest of the world would exhaust itself, and that they now expect that Germany will not win a decisive victory. The Japanese General Staff is said to have come to that conclusion as early as June 1943.
>
> The present Japanese strategy proceeds on the theory that Japan will be left alone to face a reinforced drive by the Allies. The latter will have at their disposal all the resources of American war production—which the Japanese admit they underestimated. (I have recently been informed that, for Japan, the two big surprises of the war were a) the astonishing patriotism of the Russian soldier and b) the great resources of the United States.)[47]

Ugaki, now commanding the Second Mobile Force, including his battleship and three other divisions, recorded glumly in his diary on 18 April:

> Today last year, the war situation didn't seem as bad as it does now! Last year, we had to evacuate our forces from Guadalcanal, yet we could place the rest of the Solomons under our control, and we were convinced of holding the south of Lae and [nearby] Salamaua for a considerable period.
>
> As these days passed, however, the enemy's counteroffensive grew more and more furious. When I look back and think of our lost territories and the losses so far sustained, I can't be surprised at the quick change that has taken place in the last months. The enemy has also

been building themselves up, and the chief of Naval Operations said on the fifteenth that the personnel and materials of the US Navy had reached their peak for the first time since the outbreak of the war, and the Japanese navy would be made to realize it in the next few months. This morning, 10 and 20 large-type planes raided Saipan and Meleyon [Wileai], respectively. Brisk activities of long-range planes are a sign of impending operations of brisk task forces and invasion forces. [The Americans indeed planned to land on Saipan on 15 June.]

Time is running out for a once-[and-]for-all showdown. Even if we can inflict a certain amount of damage on the enemy by staking everything we have, our own strength will be a good deal exhausted. We must calculate how soon he can replenish his strength against our capacity to recover, but we must bear in mind "nothing ventured, nothing gained." Moreover, our doing nothing will only make the enemy swell-headed.

However, it seems to me that we are well absorbed in improving the fighting strength of individual ships only and have no room for studying how to improve the fighting ability of the fleet as a unit. It makes me shudder to wonder if we could successfully carry out the decisive battle, staking the fate of the empire in this way.[48]

On 24 April, Ugaki added—after Japanese reconnaissance spotted multi-carrier task forces in multiple directions—"The enemy's present strength is like a raging fire, so irresistible that a small amount of water can hardly put it out."[49]

Apparently, the Naval General Staff agreed. On 25 April, the Vice Chief of Staff of the Navy cabled Admiral Soemu Toyoda, the newly appointed Commander-in-Chief of the Combined Fleet,

Until the formation of the First Mobile Fleet [comprising the main striking force of the IJN] about the middle of May, we cannot hope to carry out operations that would control the situation. Moreover, as a result of throwing in our land-based air strength against the enemy's gradual advance, and as well dissipating it through non-combatant losses due to inadequacies of base equipment, unfamiliarity with bases, insufficient training, etc., it is very likely that by the time the First Mobile Fleet is formed, there will be no land-based air power to cooperate with it. Accordingly, it is the plan for the present to avoid to the utmost a battle in which our equipment would be wasted by using a small number of seasoned forces. This, of course, barring the possibility of a surprise attack.[50]

The Intelligence Bureau of the Naval General Staff on 9 May provided its estimate of American main forces directed against Japan as of 1 June, excluding ground forces:

1. Naval vessels (including those under repair, with their number undetermined): Battleships: new type, eight; old type, eight. Carriers: regular type, ten; converted carriers, approximately ten; auxiliary, approximately 20. Super cruiser: one. Heavy and light cruisers: 25. *Omaha* class: some. Destroyers: 200. Submarines: 95.
2. First-line planes: army and navy combined, approximately 8,000. Regular and converted carrier-borne planes: 1,200.[51]

On 21 March, Tokyo had informed all principal ground and air headquarters that the IJA and IJN had agreed on an "epochal endeavor" to protect convoys through greater concentration of ships and use of aircraft.[52] By summer, however, lack of escort vessels was to be the main constraint on oil convoys bound for Japan, not the admittedly insufficient tanker capacity, and fuel shortages in the home islands were becoming critical.[53]

The Japanese, at least, were still able to produce oil. A message from Singapore indicated that the Japanese expected to produce in 1944 nearly 20 percent more crude oil and 55 percent more aviation fuel in the Netherlands East Indies than American analysts had reckoned.[54]

Toyoda told his interrogators,

> I took over the Combined Fleet in May [1944]. At that time, we had access to the oil in Borneo and Sumatra. We were able to obtain supplies directly from the south; so while the stock of oil was almost sufficient for purposes of a fleet, the difficulty was in tankers. I had asked for and obtained approximately 80,000 tons of tankers for fleet use, but we began to suffer damages through submarine operations; and by the time of the Saipan operation, the greatest hindrance to the drafting of the operation plans was the fact that we did not have sufficient tankers to support it.[55]

Indeed, the vice navy minister and vice chief of the Naval General Staff cabled on 7 June that shipping losses to submarines alone had totaled 210,000 tons, to their "deepest concern."[56]

The losses were not only ships. In April and May, submarines exploiting SIGINT sank a series of Japanese reinforcement convoys to Palau and New Guinea. The attack on one convoy killed 3,900 men, and though ships rescued 6,800 others, they arrived without their equipment.[57]

Having gone to war against America in hopes of ending the war in China, Japan now escalated the war in China to offset America's sea power that was crippling raw material shipments from Southeast Asia, and to deny the enemy's growing ability to bomb Japanese targets across the region from bases in China. Oh, the irony.

The Twelfth Army launched the first operations aimed at clearing the Beijing–Wuhan railroad, crossing the Yellow River on 17 April. Other armies swung into action in early May. Troops were often able to conduct operations only at night because of enemy air superiority.[58]

ICHI-GO was the largest operation in Japanese military history, encompassing 500,000 men, 100,000 horses, 15,000 vehicles, and 1,500 artillery pieces across a 1,000-mile front. Tojo learned that the initial operation did not include destruction of any enemy airfields and sent a general off to berate the field headquarters. By the time the offensive ended in February 1945, it had established a rail link to Southeast Asia and captured American airfields at Hengyang (Henan Province), Guilin (Guangxi Province), Liuzhou (Guangxi), Nanning (Guangxi), Suichuan (Jiangxi Province), and Nan-hsiung (Guangson Province). (For those interested, Hattori provides a detailed description of the offensive.) However, American air operations so badly damaged the rail corridor that the Japanese could not use it, and long-range B-29s replaced medium-range B-25s and flew out of airfields securely located deeper in China.[59]

German Problems in the Air, and More!

The deployment of the first P-51 Mustangs to Britain in December 1943 and rapid increase in numbers in early 1944 decisively transformed the air war facing Germany. Fighters could now escort bombers deep into the Reich to hit the top-priority target: the German aircraft industry. Paradoxically, two things occurred simultaneously. As with the campaign against ball bearing plants, bombing reduced aircraft output only temporarily. But the new commander of Eighth Air Force, James Doolittle, changed the rules of engagement for escort fighters—rather than protect the bombers, seek out combat with German fighters. The new approach resulted in huge, unsustainable losses among German pilots. The Strategic Bombing Survey noted,

> The claimed losses in January were 1,115 German fighters, in February 1,118 and in March 1,217. The losses in planes were accompanied by losses in experienced pilots and disorganization and loss of the combat strength of squadrons and groups. By the spring of 1944 opposition of the Luftwaffe had ceased to be effective.[60]

Doolittle's raid had sucked the IJA deeper into the China quagmire and led in part to the IJN's disastrous operation at Midway; now he was bringing ruin to the Luftwaffe.

Asked what the main reasons were for the failure of the Luftwaffe against Allied forces, Göring told interrogators, "I most firmly believe the reason was the success of the American Air Force in putting out a long-range escort fighter airplane, which enabled bombers to penetrate deep into Reich territory and still have a constant and strong fighter cover. Without this escort, the air offensive would have never succeeded. Nobody thought such a long-range fighter escort was possible."[61]

Luftwaffe officers interrogated by the Bombing Survey reported that until fighter cover appeared with American bombers, German fighter units attacked following directions radioed by squadron commanders. The advent of fighter cover posed a problem the Germans never solved. They planned to meet the Americans with two large groups of fighters, one to engage the escorts, and the other to attack the bombers. They were never able to muster enough planes for that to work.[62]

At the same time that Germany was running out of pilots, its production of aircraft surged. Measured by airframes, production doubled from February to July 1944. A big reason was that a 72-hour workweek came into force across the engine and airframe industries, and the workforce had expanded by a half million in preceding months. SS chief Heinrich Himmler added tens of thousands of concentration camp inmates to the workforce.[63]

On 1 March, German munitions policy made aircraft production the nation's top priority. Just airframes and engines accounted for an average of 40 percent of industrial output (48.3 percent peak in July). As of March, Germany employed 2 million workers in aircraft production—nearly the same as in America (per capita output was lower mainly because of the bombing). Total munitions production was about 20 percent less than airplanes as a share of the total. Roughly 10 percent of weapon and munitions production was for flak, almost all of which was used against the Anglo-Americans in the west. Panzer production hit its peak in 1944 of 8 percent of output.[64]

Germany, like Japan, was scrambling to train new pilots under time pressure and facing fuel shortages. Aircraft output jumped, but crashes destroyed about 25 percent of them before they reached the battlefield.[65]

The strategic bombing campaign by 1944 was forcing Germany to devote huge amounts of concrete and tens of thousands of workers to building bunkers for Hitler's headquarters, submarine bases, factories, and flak towers. Hitler supposedly was terrified of being killed by bombs. In the second half of 1943, more concrete had gone to these projects than to building fortifications on the French coast or Eastern Front.[66]

At the *Führerhauptquartier*, Hitler was still the optimist. The Luftwaffe had badly bloodied two large RAF attacks on Berlin in January that had caused little damage. It had successfully modified its radar to defeat American jamming. The flak force was just reaching its peak wartime strength. Germany's homeland air defenses consolidated in January in *Luftflotte Reich*, responsible for the Reich, Denmark, and Hungary. In February, the Luftewaffe and navy finally combined their radar programs to accelerate development of a new generation of technology.[67]

Hitler told Ambassador Oshima on 23 January that there was no political solution in the east: "I know that the only way to paralyze Russia is by force of arms." He was looking over his shoulder toward the coast, however. The mere threat of Allied landings was helping the Soviets by pinning down reserves in France. "Even though it means losing a great deal of territory in the east, we can run no risks in the west. That will continue to be the principle upon which we conduct our war on the eastern front.... I think the Red Army's drive has been blunted, and I am confident that we will run into no military crisis in the east."

Hitler expected an invasion in the west soon. "How vast is the seacoast! It would be utterly impossible for me to prevent some sort of landing somewhere or other. But all they can do is establish a bridgehead. I will stop, absolutely, any real second front."

Hitler commented on the campaign in Italy, "At first I decided to defend a line in the northern Apennines. But the Anglo-American strategy was so utterly foolish that I got a chance to hold a line in southern Italy, a line which we originally formed with the idea of holding only temporarily."

Only on the submarine war was Hitler downbeat. He hoped that by summer Germany would have countermeasures against Allied "plane detectors" and could resume the U-boat war.[68] Germany had slashed construction of the Type VII and IX in the closing months of 1943 because they had proved so vulnerable, and naval construction lagged as development on the new Type XXI proceeded.[69] The Germans in mid-January also abandoned using surface vessels as blockade-runners to Japan.[70]

A vice admiral told the Japanese military attaché, "Hitler is in excellent health and supremely confident; his belief in certain victory is beyond all imagination. Hitler points to the example of Frederick the Great, who after seven years of hardship finally achieved victory."[71]

Oshima reassured Tokyo that Germany and her enemies were at "equipoise," and imponderables would tip the balance. Hitler, he argued, "is no mean strategist," the Germans were superior at blitzkrieg, and the German people were dauntless, and when "we consider all those things, we may well conceive that Germany will win."[72]

Anzio: Germans Contain the Out-flanking Attempt

On 22 January, American VI Corps conducted landings at Anzio that faced virtually no resistance at the shore, a seemingly auspicious start to Operation *Shingle*. The corps included the American 3d and British 1st Infantry divisions, the American Ranger Force of three battalions, a British special service brigade with two commando battalions, an American parachute infantry regiment, and an additional parachute battalion. A week before the landings, Fifth Army commander Lieutenant General Mark Clark promised the corps commander, Major General John Lucas, elements of the 45th Infantry and 1st Armored divisions, with more to come if needed.[73]

The operation aimed to end the stalemate the Germans had imposed on the Allies along its winter position. Fifteenth Army Group's Operation Instruction No. 32, issued 2 January 1944, clearly specified, "Fifth Army will prepare an amphibious operation ... with the object of cutting the enemy lines of communication and threatening the rear of German XIV [Panzer] Corps."[74] Lucas, however, viewed his job as establishing and defending a beachhead at Anzio. He judged his initial assault force to be too weak to risk penetrating the Alban Hills that dominated the landing site from a dozen miles inland, although by doing so he could have cut the main highway—and supply route—from Rome to the Gustav Line as Fifth Army had been instructed to do.[75] Lucas's decision decided the terms under which the battle at Anzio was be fought.

Although, as reported above, OKW did not expect an end-around at this time, the German command had anticipated such a landing as this in late 1943 and had issued requirements to commanders in France, the Balkans, and the replacement army in Germany to have formations ready to go to Italy should the need arise. Detailed deployment plans were in place. Construction had also begun on the Gothic Line across the top of the boot before the Po Valley in case an Allied landing rendered lines in central Italy untenable.[76]

For what it is worth, Kesselring thought Lucas had sufficient strength to execute the mission to sever his supply lines and squandered the opportunity.[77] Far from abandoning the Gustav Line, the Germans moved reinforcements toward Anzio at incredible speed and showed every sign of being determined to throw the invaders back into the sea. The Hermann Göring Panzer Division's lead elements arrived within a day. The 29th Panzergrenadier Regiment and 4th Airborne Division concentrated opposite the British, and the 1st Airborne and 26th Panzer divisions were on the way from the Adriatic side of Italy.

Hitler took pleasure during morning briefings in March describing the achingly slow forward movement of American and British forces in Italy. Even the force that had landed behind German lines at Anzio was stymied. His military adjutant Günsche told Soviet interrogators that at this time, Hitler first fastened onto reports of German ambassadors in neutral countries such as Portugal, Spain, Sweden, and Turkey claiming that there was growing anti-Soviet feelings in leading circles in Britain and America. This, Hitler asserted, could lead to a rupture that would end the war in Germany's favor.[78]

*

German military commanders had learned a great deal about Allied amphibious operations in North Africa and Italy, and these lessons spawned a major debate over how to deploy forces in the West to respond to the anticipated landings in France.

The Allies had a fairly clear picture of the argument thanks to intercepted radio messages. For example, the Japanese military attaché in Vichy, who had spoken with Field Marshal Gerd von Rundstedt's chief of staff, reported on 28 February:

> As of last December, the Germans were not planning to hold on tenaciously to the coastal defense lines at every point; their strategy was rather to rely on large-scale attacks to destroy the enemy <u>after he had landed</u>. However, as a result of studying the problem, and because of recommendations which have been made by Rommel, the Germans have now decided that the coastal lines must be held at all cost and that the enemy must not be permitted to set foot on the continent.
>
> The changes in defense plans are the result of German experience at Sicily, Salerno, and Nettuno [Anzio]. In Rommel's opinion, it was bad strategy to allow the enemy to land because 1) after the British and American forces had obtained a bridgehead, the Germans did not quickly move into action against them, and 2) with superiority in the air, the enemy makes it a rule to pound the rear of the defending forces, and that makes impossible a defense in which small units hold the front lines and a large reserve in the rear is used for counterattacks.[79]

Japan Tries to Build a Fortress Asia

A new Southern Army (labeled in MAGIC intercepts "the South Area General Army") became active on 15 April to control operations from Burma to the Philippines. The new commander, General Count Hisaichi Terauchi, wanted to launch counterattacks in Burma, defend the area north of Australia, and prepare the Philippines for "decisive battle." He conceived of a "square fortress" based on Burma, the area north of Australia, the Philippines, and Palembang (on Sumatra) and Halmahera Island in the East Indies. This was to be a kill box, and all enemy forces entering therein were to be annihilated. The army's headquarters moved to Manila.[80]

Terauchi's first general order began, "Cooperating with the Navy, I shall stabilize and secure the strategic regions in the southern area.... [W]e will reinforce our military preparations immediately and prepare for a decisive battle."

Ground and air reinforcements, the latter from Manchuria, poured into the area. A mixed brigade formed on Palau, which to this point had had no organized ground force. Brigades in the Philippines expanded into divisions. On 2 May, the Southern Army assessed that the Allies would focus on the Pacific area and mount only harassing operations in the Indian Ocean. They probably would make an all-out attempt to capture the Philippines sometime after June. Surprise attacks mounted from Australia were possible against Flores Island, Java, and Sumatra.[81]

The Japanese, however, could sense the American strategy imperiling their plans. After Allied landings in April at Hollandia and Aitape, New Guinea, the Second Area Army, responsible for the defense of New Guinea and the eastern Netherlands East Indies, cabled the Imperial General Staff,

> In the present situation at Hollandia and Aitape [word missing] needs no useless words. Bases in this area would permit the enemy to plan jumps to the South Carolines, Philippines, and other areas. In view of the present military preparations in the so-called "four-cornered fortress area," to allow the enemy and especially their aircraft complete freedom of movement, with Hollandia as their base, is certainly no way to plan for the strengthening of the military position of the Imperial Japanese Army. Moreover, if we do not now shatter and block the enemy's arrogant conduct and make this a turning point that will influence the whole military situation, it is clear that henceforth the Imperial Japanese Army's operations will become increasingly difficult.

Southern Army saw the Philippines as the Americans' next campaign.[82]

The attack toward Imphal, meanwhile, had petered out into stalemate by the end of April. The IJA plan had foreseen victory in three weeks, but Allied counterattacks had already put one of the three divisions in the operation onto the defensive. Artillery ammunition was almost exhausted, and Japanese fighting power was down 40 percent and rapidly dwindling.[83]

The IJN on 9 May estimated that,

> Commencing with the Marshall Islands operations, the plan of the US Navy is to force battles for strategic points as a basic policy and to try to bring us into a decisive action. [This is mirror-imaging the IJN's continuing obsession with a decisive battle.] Judging the future by past performance, it is considered likely that the enemy will open large-scale operations accompanied by invasion forces in the principal theaters of war sometime between the last of May and the first part of July.[84]

The IJN estimated that the Allies had a million tons of shipping available in the Central Pacific area and another 800,000 tons in the southwestern area.[85]

Ugaki's Mobile Force rendezvoused with most of the Combined Fleet's remaining strength, including two carrier divisions, at the Tawi Tawi (an island near Mindanao) advanced base on 14 and 15 May. The Combined Fleet's orders anticipated an all-out battle near Palau in the West Carolines.[86]

Ugaki recorded in his diary the estimate of the strategic situation he offered to the officers of the battleship *Musashi* during an inspection. The Allies would expand submarine warfare, advance westward along the coast of New Guinea, and attempt to recapture the Philippines, with the ultimate goals of reaching China as a base to invade Japan and cutting Japan off from the "southwest resources area." On the way, the enemy would attack Palau, Yap, and Saipan. "No longer would our self-existence or self-defense be possible, and beyond that it would mean the end of the empire. We're now being pressed against a wall, and we can't fall back anymore. Unless the main enemy force is destroyed by any means, our future will be doomed."[87]

For Ugaki, the end was visible.

Shipping losses had been so heavy that surface deliveries of supplies to Rabaul and other outposts had ended, and a growing list of garrisons was going to half rations. The Commander-in-Chief of Fourth Fleet on 27 May marked the 39th anniversary of the battle of Tsushima with a message that began, "All forces on Ponape [Pohnpei, in today's Micronesia] and eastward have undergone a severe air offensive for several consecutive days and have faced many hardships and privations. You have bravely stood up to same and achieved magnificent results in repulsing the enemy." He closed by exhorting that "certain victory is in our grasp if we fight for it."[88]

CHAPTER 14

Late 1944: Strategic Defeat

Other than Hitler's fantastical and senseless gamble in the Ardennes offensive, the Axis leaders in late 1944 helplessly watched an oncoming avalanche of American-made (and British and Soviet) military equipment and materiel employed by men who had mastered the art of war. The Germans were on the receiving end of Blitzkrieg in the west and east. The Japanese found the ultimate futility of the Bushido warrior code in suicidal and pointless attacks. But nowhere in the record does one see these leaders asking themselves, "How would our fate look had we not enraged the giant?"

June 1944: Fatal Setbacks in Europe and Asia

On 5 June, a shakedown mission of 84 new B-29s of India-based Twentieth Bomber Command struck Bangkok. The Japanese observers did not recognize the planes for what they were.[1]

The Japanese did recognize that the enemy was taking full advantage of the fact that time was on his side. Southern Army in Manila issued an estimate of enemy intentions on 18 June that observed, "[I]n view of the general situation, the enemy makes fairly cautious plans and thorough preparations." Thus, no landings in the Philippines were likely before September.[2]

The Imperial General Staff evidently had its first inkling of doom. On 30 June, it reported the Americans had 400,000 troops in California and tasked all military attachés in Europe to gather information on any American offensive in the Pacific area, "especially the invasion of the Japanese Empire itself."[3]

A certain awe had emerged at the sheer firepower of the American way of war. An IJA staff message in July warned,

> The maximum use of the firepower of one battleship would be approximately equaled by the combined firepower of five divisions (using the largest caliber shells) or by approximately 40 regiments of light bombers (1,250 planes).... The full force of an Anglo-American fleet of one battleship, three cruisers, and six destroyers would undoubtedly require, to equal it, a powerful army composed of six or seven divisions with full direct artillery support. This concentration of naval firepower is more than we can handle.[4]

A report from Saipan on 16 June stated,

> The enemy who have landed are under close protection from ships in nearby waters, and so as soon as the night-attack units advance, the enemy illuminates the general area by using large-type flares all through the night.... Shells used by enemy naval vessels in their bombardment are mainly those with supersensitive fuses, and the destructive power is great; they use shrapnel at times. Coordination in firing between [ships] and land troops is so accurate and swift that the night-attack unit receives enemy naval fire as soon as the distance from the enemy gets to be some scores of meters.... The enemy has a tremendous number of tanks.... Our preparations against tanks are very weak.[5]

D-Day: The Allies Storm Fortress Europe

An OSS appraisal of a speech delivered by Goebbels in Salzburg on 16 March concluded,

> Again, the invasion of the Continent is to be the turning point. Once the Anglo-Saxons are defeated here, then the danger for Germany is over, and like Athens, Sparta, and Rome of old, the Germans will turn back the invader—so he says.... The whole tone of Goebbels' speech is evidence of the tremendous strain which is being placed on the German war machine. The fact that he has now to call upon the people to emulate Sparta, Athens, and Frederick the Great, indicates that he does not have much left in the way of positive and encouraging propaganda. The numerical and material superiority of Germany's enemies is tacitly, if not actually, admitted in this speech.[6]

Hitler in April decided that the Allied landings would take place at Normandy and Brittany, and his intuition told him that the enemy would try to capture Cherbourg and Brest. Indeed, General of the Artillery Walter Warlimont, Jodl's deputy at OKW, described Hitler's decision as being "for no apparent reason," though Hitler once referred to increasingly detailed information on Allied concentrations in southern England. On 6 May, OKW declared that the Cotentin Peninsula would be the enemy's primary objective, and it ordered that the 2d Fallschirmjäger (Airborne) and 243d Infantry divisions reinforce the sector, and instructed that all troops there be dug in.[7]

Oshima met with Hitler on 27 May and asked him about the looming second front. Hitler expected the Allies to launch diversionary operations in Norway, Denmark, and southwestern France; establish beachheads in Normandy and Brittany; and then launch an all-out second front across the Straits of Dover.[8]

Hitler, according to Warlimont, believed even before D-Day that Allied materiel superiority would lead to German defeat in the West if the landings

General of the Artillery Walter Warlimont held a key position as the High Command's deputy operations officer. Although convicted of war crimes, he produced many of the most reliable and useful Foreign Military Studies reports. (Bundesarchiv)

succeeded. "If we don't throw the invaders back," he told his generals at an afternoon briefing as he gazed out a window, "we can't win a static war in the long run because the materials our enemies can bring in will exceed what we can send to that front."[9]

The D-Day story of Operation *Overlord* is well known and need not be repeated at any length. Preceded by airborne drops and a massive naval and air bombardment, the main Allied invasion force landed on the coast of Normandy in the early hours of 6 June 1944. British I and XXX corps stormed Gold, Juno, and Sword beaches, while U.S. VII Corps landed at Utah and V Corps at Omaha beaches. It was one of the most decisive days of the entire war.

Hitler's military adjutant Günsche told Soviet interrogators that when Keitel and Jodl came to inform the Führer of the Allied assault, Hitler told them, "I am glad that the Anglo-Americans have decided to land in France, and exactly where they were expected. Now we know where we are. We will see how things go from now on."

While they were speaking, Göring arrived. Hitler was animated and shouted, "Göring, have you heard already? This morning the Anglo-Americans have finally landed in France, and right at the place where we expected them! We shall throw them out again!"

According to Günsche, however, within days Hitler's attention again turned primarily to the east, where numerous signs indicated the Soviets were about to launch a major offensive against Army Group Center. That offensive, Operation *Bagration*, began on 23 June, and the German center caved in.[10]

Admiral Ugaki wrote in his diary on 7 June, "Eisenhower announced that the Allied force landed on the north coast of France. Now the second front in Europe has commenced. In spite of German boasting of the completeness of her defense, we cannot but conclude, hearing this announcement, that the Allied forces have made favorable progress. If Germany can't cope with this crisis, the Axis powers both in the East and West will be doomed."[11]

In Tokyo, on 7 June, Foreign Minister Shigemitsu met with Ambassador Heinrich Stahmer, who had replaced Ott in January 1943, to discuss the war situation. He congratulated Germany for "stopping the Anglo-Americans' progress." Stahmer demurred and said the war had reached "an extremely grave stage."

Shigemitsu told the German, "The Americans will probably open a drive against us Japanese, paralleling the second front in Europe. Their landings on western New Guinea and particularly on Biak, in my opinion, are the prelude to such a drive."[12]

The Americans did conduct a similar massive amphibious operation on 15 June, but the objective was Saipan.

From Normandy, Rommel, commanding Army Group B, on 11 June reported that his only option was to establish a continuous front to hem in the Anglo-American bridgehead. The enemy's operations were unfolding more slowly than expected, but the mass of forces arriving was higher than expected. He wanted to replace panzer divisions in the line with infantry divisions. Hitler, though, was to insist the next day on launching more armored counterattacks.

Field Marshal Rundstedt, Commander-in-Chief West, informed OKW that several factors were massively interfering with German operations, including enemy control of the air, naval bombardment, the material wherewithal of enemy forces, and the effective use of paratroopers and glider-landing troops.[13] Note that the issue of material superiority was already front and center long before any generals had cause to explain away their defeats. Five days into the invasion, it is unlikely that anyone was anticipating the worst.

Hitler finally agreed to replace panzer formations in the line with infantry divisions on 16 June after various counterattacks had produced meager results.[14] The war in Normandy was to grind on in bloody fury for another month to the point that some Allied commanders worried that a World War I-like stalemate was emerging.

Field Marshals Erwin Rommel, Commanding Army Group B, left, and Gerd von Rundstedt, Commander-in-Chief West, in January 1944. Rommel crushed the U.S. Army in the first German–American battle at Kasserine. Rundstedt was sacked after telling the High Command in July that the only military option was to make peace. (Wikimedia Commons)

Saipan: The Decisive Naval Battle

Thanks to reconnaissance aircraft, the Combined Fleet knew by 12 June that American task forces including 15 carriers were operating east of the Marianas. The Americans had bombed Saipan heavily and struck Rota, Guam, and Tinian by air or naval bombardment as well. But reconnaissance had failed to spot an invasion fleet, and up to 12 June, the Combined Fleet was uncertain whether landings were in the offing. It had just dispatched a force under Ugaki's command on a repeatedly postponed operation to land army reinforcements at Biak and entice the American fleet into a decisive battle, if possible. It was now clear that the American fleet was otherwise engaged.[15]

At 1600, the Central Pacific Area Fleet on Saipan reported that American minesweepers were clearing lanes off Saipan. Ugaki realized this meant a landing was coming and called off his own operation. The Combined Fleet reached the same conclusion. Shortly thereafter, he received orders to that effect and the Combined Fleet instruction to prepare for Operation *A*—the decisive battle, set for 19 June.[16]

The Combined Fleet signaled all components of A Force at 0800 on the 15th, "The rise and fall of the empire depends on this one battle."[17] Operation *A-GO* was under way.

From the American perspective, conquest of the Marianas would penetrate the inner perimeter of Japan's defenses and provide bases for B-29 long-range bombers to hit the home islands. The key Mariana islands for military purposes were Saipan, Tinian, Rota, and Guam. Saipan hosted two airfields—only one operational—a naval fueling station, and a seaplane base, and nearby Tinian two airfields.

On 15 June, LSTs belonging to the U.S. Fifth Fleet's Northern Attack Force and bearing the Northern Troops and Landing Force massed some 6,000 yards off the western side of Saipan. Operation *Forager* was under way. The Japanese First Air Fleet reported at 0440, "About 15 large-type transports and 15 medium and small ones are sighted off the West Coast of Saipan. Four carriers and other surface craft ... are in sight off the west, too."[18]

Lieutenant General Yoshitsugu Saito, commanding general of the Northern Marianas Army Group, had available to defend the island the 43d Division (reinforced), the 47th Mixed Brigade, an infantry battalion, a tank regiment, an antiaircraft regiment, and two regiments of engineers. Total IJA strength was approximately 22,700 men, supported by some 7,000 naval personnel.[19]

Elements of the Marine V Amphibious Corps were to pry those troops off the island. Lieutenant Russell Gugeler, who gathered oral history of the action from Army amphibian crews using the techniques of Lieutenant Colonel S. L. A. Marshall, summed up Operation *Forager*:

> Briefly, the plan called for the landing of two Marine divisions [2d and 4th], attached units, and necessary supplies within a few hours. This plan was dependent upon the amphibious vehicles and their capability of movement on land and in the water. Prior to the landing the naval and air bombardment would neutralize defensive positions in the landing area. This fire would lift as the amphibious tanks and troop-laden tractors neared the shore and the shock action of a large number of these vehicles should extend the neutralization long enough to allow the first waves to push inland several hundred yards to the initial objective [with the infantry still mounted in LVTs]. This would provide a beachhead sufficiently large for the assault battalions to deploy on the ground and organize for the continuation of the attack. Subsequent waves would debark from the tractors at the beach and mop up resistance that was by-passed by the first waves. This plan to by-pass the beach defenses would also afford defiladed areas inland where troops could debark with greater safety. [The 27th Infantry Division was in Expeditionary Troops reserve and prepared to land on Saipan, Tinian, or Guam; in the event, it was to enter the Saipan beachhead once it was secured.][20]

Only hours after the Saipan landings, Japan faced a two-front war against America. The long-dreaded first B-29 raid on Japan occurred on 16 June, the first bombing of the home islands since the Doolittle raid. Launching from China, the Twentieth Bomber Command attacked the Yawata Iron Manufacturing Works and two secondary targets with 47 B-29s and claimed "good to excellent" results. The command reported one bomber shot down and four missing; the Japanese claimed to have

SAIPAN LANDING
15 June 1944

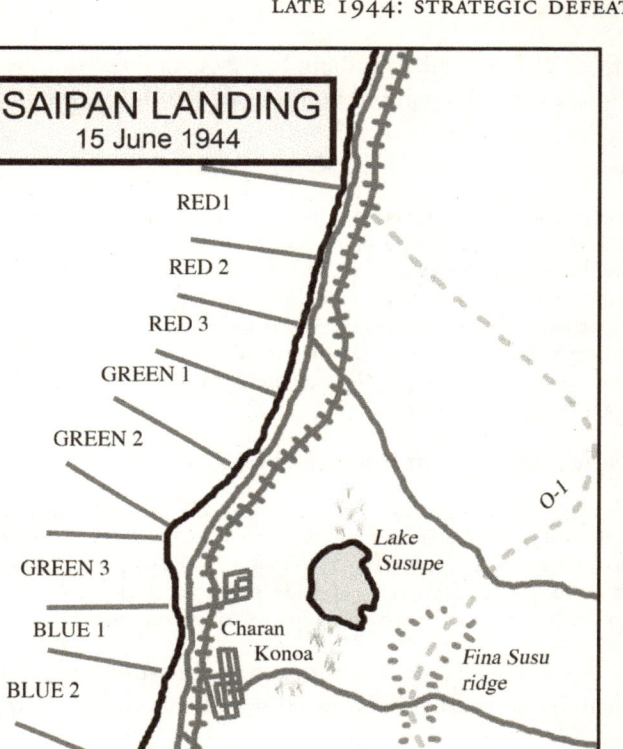

RED 1
RED 2
RED 3
GREEN 1
GREEN 2
GREEN 3
BLUE 1
BLUE 2
YELLOW 1
YELLOW 2
YELLOW 3

Lake Susupe
Charan Konoa
Fina Susu ridge
O-1
Agingan Point

0   1000 yds/m

downed seven. More than 415 people were killed or wounded, and 430 houses destroyed. Three buildings at a glass works in Tobata were destroyed, but only a few windows broken at the iron works.[21] Japan had entered the world of explosions and firebombs, civilian victims, and exaggerated battle-damage assessments.

A Japanese circular reported, "About 0200, 20 American B-29s and B-24s flew over from China and dropped medium and light bombs and incendiaries on Yawata, Kokura, Tobata, and Moji in northern Kyushu." The IJN reported that the damage was "trifling."[22] The Strategic Bombing Survey concurred that because of the small number of planes and the reduced bomb loads the B-29s could carry, the results of the early raids on Japan were not significant.[23]

Pilot Sakai, however, said of the Kyushu raid,

> War came to Japan in June 1944. The effect on our population was unmistakable. On 15 June the people of Japan were shocked to hear that 20 bombers, tremendous giants of the air that dwarfed the powerful B-17, had flown an incredible distance from China to attack a city in northern Kyushu. The raid did little damage, and 20 planes were hardly enough to cause national excitement. But in the homes and the stores, in the factories and on the streets, everywhere in Japan, the people talked about the raid and discussed the fact that our fighters had failed to stop the bombers. They all asked the same question. Who was next? And how many bombers would come?[24]

The Foreign Ministry told its missions abroad,

> We regard the attack as having been aimed primarily at gathering reconnaissance data. It was also a political gesture connected with the second front and the coming American election. It is clear that the enemy sought to slaughter innocent women and children and to upset the people in this country. Our authorities had made ample preparations, however, and the population remained calm; the enemy have merely succeeded in increasing the hatred against themselves.[25]

Whether or not this was true, it was precisely the same reaction that many foreign observers had reported about the reactions of the German population to Allied bombing.

Steaming toward the Americans, Ugaki recorded news of the raid at 0200 16 June. "This is a new tactic. Everywhere there is decisive battle." On Saipan, the Central Pacific Fleet shore component and Base Force burned their codebooks.[26]

The Battle of the Philippine Sea: A Japanese View

Japanese reconnaissance on 16 June identified four American carrier groups with 17 carriers, more than eight battleships, more than 30 cruisers, and more than 55 destroyers. The Japanese had divided among the Mobile Force's A Force, B Force, and Vanguard Force three carrier divisions with but four large and four light carriers (430 carrier aircraft supported by 19 flying boats); five battleships, including the two largest in the world (*Yamato* and *Musashi*); three heavy cruisers; and 28 destroyers. Land-based aircraft were to be almost irrelevant in the coming battle.[27]

The long-anticipated decisive battle, called by the Americans the battle of the Philippine Sea, went horribly wrong for the Japanese fleet in practically every way. A big reason was that the American codebreakers knew every move the Japanese were going to make as soon as orders hit the airwaves. What the SIGINT missed, submarines monitoring the Mobile Force reported by radio.[28]

Ugaki recorded the events daily in his diary, or in outline on days when intensive operations left him no time. Convinced by diversionary air attacks that the Americans planned to invade Palau, the Combined Fleet had made no contingency plans for a battle near Saipan. The belated move to the battle area allowed the enemy to land three divisions and push troops close to the operational airfield on the island before the Japanese fleet challenged him—too late to have any hope of defeating the invasion.

Japanese reconnaissance planes the morning of 19 June spotted three American task forces: one with four to five large carriers, four battleships, and ten others; the second with one large carrier and two small ones, one battleship, and five others; and the third with three large carriers, five battleships, and ten others. "I thought they were just enough and in some respects too much for [our plan], yet felt that our success would be sure," wrote Ugaki.

The First Carrier Division, A Force, launched 53 dive-bombers, 27 torpedo bombers, and 48 Zero fighters in the predawn darkness against Task Force 58. Many of the Zeros were the newest Type 52, redesigned to handle the American F-6F Hellcat and F-4U Corsair, which had dominated the older model. The Japanese planes came under fire from their own Vanguard Force, which downed two aircraft. American fighters intercepted the Japanese aircraft 20 miles from the target, and 97 of the 128 planes launched did not return. According to Ugaki, some of these aircraft had suicide missions on which he placed great hope. Pilots claimed to have hit four carriers, but in fact only one suffered some damage from a near miss. The wave of attack planes launched by the Second Carrier Division could not find the enemy.[29]

By 1000, Japanese reconnaissance had identified four American task forces, which pilots reported included ten large and 13 small carriers, 12 battleships, and 13 cruisers. The more immediate threat turned out to be submarines. *Albacore* torpedoed the light carrier *Taiho* at 0910, and *Cavalla* the carrier *Shokaku* at 1215; both sank within hours. Their aircraft were ordered to recover to the Second Carrier Division and *Zuikaku*, while the Second Division's aircraft flew to Guam. The latter group arrived during an American air raid, and 49 of 50 of them were lost to dogfights. The Vanguard Force lost nine of its ten seaplanes, and 20 more aircraft were destroyed at Rota.[30]

Ugaki wrote in his diary, "Since this morning we had been waiting for a chance to become an attack force, but we now have to admit that, to say nothing of chasing an enemy, not only did we fail to inflict damage on an enemy, but we sustained heavy damage. Is it that heaven still doesn't side with us?"[31]

The Americans dubbed the air battle the Great Marianas Turkey Shoot. Only 25 Japanese carrier planes survived the battle.[32]

On 22 June, Ugaki recorded, "The result of the decisive battle on which we staked so much was miserable. Not only was our loss great, but we could not save Saipan from peril.... It will be extremely difficult to recover from this disaster and rise again." Indeed, the light carrier *Hiyo* had gone to the bottom when American planes found her as the Japanese withdrew on the 20th, and two other carriers had suffered damage.[33]

Ugaki ruminated on the lessons of the defeat on 23 June. The main cause, he judged, was the miscalculation that the Americans planned to attack Palau instead of the Marianas, the failure of reconnaissance to spot the invasion fleet until the day of the landings, the belated order to the fleet to engage, and the failure to prevent the invasion force from establishing a beachhead. The Americans were simply too capable and well-equipped.

> Unless we destroy enemy invasion forces before they have dug in, it is very hard to destroy them on account of their manpower, equipment, and mechanical power. It's preposterous to think that we can let them dig in a little, making it hard for him to pull himself out again, [so that] we can destroy his reinforcements as they come. I once advocated such an idea, though didn't try it, but it's absolutely no good....
>
> [H]e is no mean adversary. His striking range isn't limited to 200 miles; he attacks from 300 miles away as seen this evening. Their shadowing and reconnaissance, whether day or night, are skillful and their reports are very accurate. They seem to be quite confident in taking off and landing planes and operational flights at night. Battleships are used in a ring formation while a CV [carrier] group is situated in its rear. So when our planes dove into the battleship group first and didn't realize the existence of the CVs, it was too late. Fighters were placed 50 to 60 miles outside of the battleship group, and after passing that line, almost no resistance was met....
>
> Simultaneous attacks of strafing by fighters and a small number of torpedo planes also seemed to be planned. Many kinds of bombs were used, too. Those who came to attack the Main Body were said to have dove sharply. The skill of torpedo planes was poor but the timing of the attack was good.... The enemy task force displaying its 32 knots is surely a tough customer.[34]

On Saipan, Allied intelligence netted the scribe for Yamamoto and Nagumo, who was to provide a wealth of inside information on the IJN, and a nearly intact code machine. The roughly simultaneous capture of Biak produced codebooks galore.[35] Japan had few important military secrets left.

The IJN in June lost 789 aircraft in combat, the highest monthly total of the war. It lost 449 more planes to non-combat causes. Most of the pilots—a third of whom were experienced—who engaged in the battle died.[36]

While the war was going sideways for Japan at Saipan, the Allies in eastern India smashed the Japanese line at Imphal on 22 June. With his north wing collapsing, the Fifteenth Army commander the next day proposed retreating to the India–Burma border.[37]

Tojo's last known view of the war's progress emerged in a meeting with Stahmer on 28 June. The United States had committed 35 percent of its ground forces and 41 percent of its air forces to the Far East, Tojo assessed. The Allies' main goals were to push out of Burma and India to China, build airfields in China, and advance across the Pacific to cut Japan off from the South Seas and to capture the Philippines. Japan's main objective in China had shifted from defending occupied territory to denying the U.S. Army territory for airfields.

In the Pacific, Japan would fight to hold its outer defensive line from the Carolines to the Marianas, including Saipan. Tojo continued, "In order to do so, however, we will have to have absolute control of the sea and air, and the truth is we may not be able to achieve that control." In its Pacific attacks,

> the enemy have merely been scratching at the outer wall of our defenses; any possibility of a frontal attack on the Japanese mainland lies in the remote future. Meanwhile, our ground and naval forces in the Pacific are whittling away at the enemy, and we are strengthening the defenses of the Japanese mainland, Formosa, the Philippines, and all our occupied areas. Our real opportunity to crush the enemy will come when they try to attack our main line of defense. There, at last, the inequalities in naval and air strength between ourselves and the enemy will no longer be a factor.[38]

Tojo said Japan had adequate manpower reserves and claimed that aircraft and ship production was increasing, though he conceded that because of high losses, shipping was a major bottleneck. "The ultimate strength of Japan lies in her national structure. The Japanese people are firmly united by the spiritual concept of one people and one family grouped around the Imperial household, and they will literally fight to the very end."[39]

After the Great Marianas Turkey Shoot, Captain Toshikazu Ohmae, told interrogators after the war, he concluded that Japan had little chance to win the war.[40] Ugaki thought so, too. "Neither the Third nor Fourth CV divisions will be ready until the end of July, while as to the First and Second CV divisions, no definite plan can be made. It doesn't seem likely that we'll be able to get through the present crisis under such circumstances," he wrote on 27 June. "Nothing is more deplorable. At what point do those in Tokyo expect to get a chance to win from now on?"[41]

The loss of the Marianas meant that the last line of defense in the central Pacific had been breached. Fukudome—who took command of the newly established Second Air Fleet the day the Americans invaded Saipan—recalled,

> I personally agreed with [Koga], not merely because I was under his orders, that the defense of this line was absolutely indispensable. Fighting to the last man might have been possible, but I felt certain that if this line once were broken, there would be no subsequent recovery of our defensive power. The original Japanese plan must have been to fight to the very last and [that is how it turned out]. But my personal feeling all through was that if that line should be broken, there would be no further chance of success. The loss of the Marianas Islands was, therefore, a heavy spiritual blow to me. I had neither a plan for nor confidence in recovery of those islands. Though the loss of the Marianas was a spiritual blow to me, this does not mean that there was any decrease in my will to fight, for I had been determined from the beginning to fight until dead. It did mean, however, that after that loss I could see no chance for our success.[42]

The Emperor on 6 July expressed his gratitude to the defenders on Saipan for their fighting spirit in language that tacitly acknowledged the battle was lost. On Saipan, Vice Admiral Nagumo and Lieutenant General Saito committed suicide on 6 July to encourage the remaining 3,000 troops in their last-ditch attack the next day. With that, resistance ended.[43]

Meanwhile, the IGHQ suspended the offensive at Imphal on 4 July as yet another failure.[44]

Tojo Quits

Until these developments, commitment to the struggle in the Japanese leadership had been unshaken. By April 1944, however, President of the Privy Council Kido had concluded that Japan could not win the war with Tojo at the helm, and he began to plot Tojo's ouster. At an informal meeting in the home of former Premier Hiranuma on 17 July, it was decided that Tojo's Cabinet was to be replaced so Japan could build "a powerful national cabinet that will surge forward unswervingly." Tojo tried to salvage his position by bringing men of stature into the Cabinet, including former premiers Abe and Yonai, but his efforts foundered. In the waning hours of his term, Tojo accepted a proposal from Kido to separate the positions of war minister and army chief of staff, and General Yoshijiro Umezu, commanding the Kwantung Army, became the new chief of staff.

The Cabinet fell secretly on the 18th, the day IGHQ finally announced publicly that Saipan had fallen. Southern Army Headquarters alerted its subordinate units and concluded, "It is natural that the general resignation will not alter the policies of prosecution of the war at all."[45]

The 20th of July shook the war leaderships at both ends of the Axis. In Tokyo, Tojo's government publicly announced its resignation.[46] At the Führer's headquarters in East Prussia, disgruntled German officers detonated a bomb that nearly killed Hitler.

Keeper of the Privy Seal Kido explained Tojo's resignation:

> The Japanese people in general had placed much expectation on Saipan. They had thought Saipan was heavily fortified and heavily defended, but this proved otherwise, and the consequences greatly shocked the Japanese people. In order to meet that situation, General Tojo ... took upon himself another office—that of Chief of the Army General Staff; and by assuming greater powers, he incited a great deal of opposition against him, which was already growing in Japan and intensified from day to day to a policy of "Down with Tojo." War production at that time was not making any headway, and the people's life was becoming more difficult.
>
> As a consequence, the Tojo government, in order to meet the situation and obtain results, intensified the various controls on the economic life of the people. This, in itself, was another point which drew strong criticism from the people.... These developments culminated in the fall of the Tojo Cabinet in July 1944.[47]

The Swiss minister in Tokyo reported the day the government resigned, "The capture of Saipan is creating a big sensation, and there are signs of demoralization.... For a long time, the Japanese had underestimated their enemies. Now they comprehend more clearly the seriousness of the war and are preparing for the worst."[48]

A Swedish diplomat returning from seven years of service in Tokyo told an OSS officer in Ankara that the fall of Saipan had convinced all ordinary Japanese that the war was lost. But people were so subservient to the government that there would be no internal turmoil. He characterized Tojo as the most hated man in Tokyo as of September, blamed by average Japanese for the China Incident and war with the Allies.⁴⁹

General Kuniaki Koiso, who had been Governor General in Korea, became premier. According to Kido's diary, senior statesmen who proposed his selection viewed him as a pious man having ability and courage. The venerable Admiral Yonai returned as navy minister, while Shigemitsu retained his job as foreign minister and took on the responsibilities of Minister of Greater East Asia. Sugiyama, the man who had expected the Pacific war to be over in three months, returned as war minister.⁵⁰ The new government created the Supreme Council for the Direction of the War, which was to oversee military and industrial affairs, in response to the wish of the Emperor.⁵¹

Lord Keeper of the Privy Seal Kido told interrogators after the war that after the fall of Saipan,

General Kuniaki Koiso became prime minister after the Tojo Cabinet fell following the loss of Saipan in July 1944. Koiso dissolved his government on 5 April 1945 because of the American landings on Okinawa and friction with the military leadership. (Wikimedia Commons)

> It was my opinion [then] that it was advisable to discontinue the war.... First, the fall of Saipan meant the intensification of American air attacks upon the Japanese Home Islands. Secondly, the failure of the navy, upon which our Japanese people had placed a great deal of reliance; and the failure at that time had a very strong influence on our feelings in regard to the war.⁵²

Asked whether there were others who wanted to reconsider further prosecution of the war, Kido replied, "Generally speaking, the so-called Liberals of Japan, congregated at the clubs and quite a large number of the House of Peers and the House of Representatives and most of the so-called Elder Statesmen were of the opinion that something should be done.... It was merely an expression of views and opinions, and nothing was done about it."⁵³

The interrogator asked whether, if the Emperor had issued an Imperial Rescript at this time, the army would have obeyed it. Kido replied, "There was the danger of a coup if the Emperor had prescribed a peace before the fall of Germany."⁵⁴

What is the sound of one hand clapping? There is no indication the Emperor considered such a step.

Konoye told interrogators that after the fall of Saipan,

> Efforts were made to terminate the war, but the army and navy, particularly the army, put up strenuous efforts to forestall such action and were resolved to fight through to the end.... Just as finally the end of the war was brought about by the Emperor, so at that time efforts were

made to persuade the Emperor, particularly through Kido, who was close to the Emperor, to get him to put an end to the war.... The man who put forth the most earnest efforts is probably the present foreign minister [Shigeru Yoshida].[55]

Within the IJA, however, the analysis was bleak. Hattori recorded,

> Since Japan had summoned all her mental and physical strength for the anticipated decisive battle in the Marianas, from the time of the imperial conference in September of the previous year, the effect of its failure was profound. The defeat in the battle of the Marianas naturally cast a dark shadow on the future direction of the war. As a result of the defeat, our air and naval strength, which was the main combat strength for the war against the United States, had virtually collapsed. It was expected that our national fighting strength would decline further, that the Soviet Union might change her former neutral attitude in view of the tragic fate of Germany, and that continued cooperation among the Asiatic countries in the war would become difficult. Signs of unrest in the Japanese people began to appear, though not openly, because of uncertainty about the future of the war. Vigorous activities against the war began to be undertaken by Prince Konoye, senior statesmen close to the Throne, and members of the Imperial household. Criticisms against the war began to be raised loudly by people other than war leaders.[56]

Amidst the political turmoil, another domino fell. Ugaki recorded in his diary that on 21 July, an urgent telegram arrived from Guam reporting that 64 transports, four battleships, two cruisers, and 40 minesweepers were approaching early in the morning and were lowering boats. "Another from the chief of staff, Thirty-First Army, said that they were all prepared to meet an invasion force, expecting to perish." Indeed, on 25 July, the army launched a last-ditch suicide attack, and organized resistance was to end on 12 August. "Now," Ugaki lamented, "important points are falling into enemy hands one after the other and capable commanders are perishing along with their staffs and men."[57] Cataloguing a brutal struggle in which the Japanese were overwhelmed by naval gunfire, tanks, and superior fire from the enemy infantry, Hattori recorded the annihilation of yet another Japanese garrison: "On 10 August, contact outside [Guam] was lost. On the eleventh, the commander of the army died in action, and systematic resistance by the Japanese Army on the island of Guam was brought to an end." The Americans wiped out the troops on nearby Tinian, as well, with the last-ditch assault on 3 August the final gasp of organized resistance.[58]

The Naval General Staff transmitted a cable stating that the next American offensive would aim at the Philippines and occur soon. Wrong again. The next operation was to be landings at Peleliu and Morotai on 15 September.[59]

The Greater East Asia Ministry on 23 July sent a message to its representatives that explained, "The recent shake-up in the cabinet resulted from the present very serious war situation. It is hoped that by such decisive action, the feelings of the people will be stirred up, and the war will be prosecuted with maximum effort. The present state of affairs is indeed very serious. We must realize that we are waging a holy war."[60]

The Vichy ambassador in Tokyo reported,

> The Japanese public gave a cool reception to the formation of the Koiso Cabinet. It considers the men composing the cabinet to be too old to carry on a rigorous war and wonders whether these [people]—Munitions Minister [Ginjiro] Fujiwara, for example, is 75 years old—are not turning toward compromise formulas.... The question arises [as to] whether they will be able to increase industrial production and provide what the army and navy demand.[61]

Koiso, who took office on 22 July, appeared to consider changing the war policy, according to Kido, but the Cabinet "was determined to pursue the policy of all-out continuation of the war."[62] Koiso nevertheless offered the Japanese public no false hopes and told them that the gravity of the situation was without parallel in Japanese history.[63] His new Information Minister Taketora Ogata, the OSS reported, also issued a statement declaring that from then on, the Japanese people must know the complete truth, even if it was unfavorable. Ogata had been president of the *Asahi* newspaper, according to the OSS source. The source also echoed Kido's suggestion that Koiso wanted to pursue peace but said the army insisted on fighting to the bitter end.[64]

True to the promise of truth telling, *Asahi Shinbun* in August published a plethora of bleak news: the shift of farmers to war production had left agriculture to old men, women, and children, and production and productivity were falling; morale of inducted factory workers was poor; people should take air raid warnings seriously. An editorial asked, "Are Our Leaders Leading?" criticized Japanese for blindly following leaders and said Tojo's constant sermons had failed to boost war production. There was a dire airplane shortage; a report from the South Seas said that Japanese soldiers were being attacked by Allied aircraft at will, and another from the Central Pacific said Japanese planes were outnumbered 15:1.[65]

After the military refused his request to play a role at IGHQ, Koiso renamed the liaison conferences the Supreme Council for the Direction of the War with no change in functions.[66] IGHQ on 27 July provided Koiso with a proposal for a new war directive in light of the loss of the Marianas. The IJA had drafted it, and the IJN posed no objections. Hattori provides only a summary, including the following language:

> As a result of losing part of the Marianas, a gap has been formed in the absolute national defense sphere in the Central Pacific Area. Moreover, owing to the decisive naval and air battles fought between Japanese and United States forces in the said sector, the Japanese Navy, which constituted the main fighting force against the United States, expended its fighting strength.... Japan must recognize the cold fact that she is faced with a critical situation under which a single false step in her war planning would incapacitate her even from upholding her national polity [the Imperial Throne]....
>
> Since the United States succeeded in taking the initiative in the war, she is concentrating her total efforts to intensify her all-out political and military offensives. Therefore, it is presumed that the political and military situation will be further aggravated about summer or autumn of this year, thereby leading to the termination of the war.
>
> [In light of projected aircraft, aluminum, and ship production, and homeward transport of fuel] the foregoing amounts are barely enough to meet the minimum requirements for waging

war during the remainder of the current year on the greatly reduced battle front, but it is totally insufficient to meet the needs for, and after, the next year....

[Whether Japan commits all resources to one final battle or avoids major fights in a protracted defense], she must continue the war, singlehandedly, by overcoming all difficulties. Although it might gradually become impossible for Japan to carry out organized warfare, she must fight bravely to defend her homeland at all costs and must bide her time until the enemy loses his will to fight.[67]

The "new" policy ultimately presented to the Emperor for his sanction on 19 August dispensed with the harsh dose of reality. The plan was to destroy American forces in the Central Pacific in decisive battle, hold key islands (the Philippines) to protect transportation routes for resources from the Southern Area, defeat enemy efforts in Burma, frustrate American efforts to bomb Japan from China, and to overpower the enemy forces in China trying to sever transportation links to the south. Koiso concluded, "In short, this plan is aimed at strengthening the conviction of sure victory."[58]

Indeed, American sea and air power was starving the war economy. Only 50 percent of the bountiful oil in the Dutch East Indies shipped to Japan in 1944 arrived. American submarines alone in late 1944 sent so much bauxite to the bottom that Japan in late 1944 produced only half the aluminum it could have with adequate supplies. With the Marianas in hand, U.S. carrier task forces in October entered the South China Sea—heretofore relatively safe for Japanese transports—and targeted commercial shipping along the Chinese coast and around Formosa. TF-38, under Halsey's command, included ten large and eight light carriers. These transport sinkings coincided with Japanese reserves of aviation fuel running low after high burn in the Marianas fighting.[69]

Koiso's domestic program, reported to the Diet on 7 September, aimed to establish a "sure-victory home front," boost aircraft and food production, mobilize more manpower, strengthen homeland defense, defend cities against air attack, and mobilize scientific skills.[70]

IGHQ, for its part, on 24 July issued orders for the next decisive battle, Operation *SHO* (SHO-GO [Victory]). It would occur later in the year around Formosa, the homeland, and in the Philippines. The plan included four variants based on the location of the battle.[71]

At the same time, IGHQ ordered significant changes in the way Japanese forces were to combat the American way of war. Commanders were to horde aircraft until they could attack the invasion convoy en masse. It ordered new airbases constructed to permit the rapid shifting of air units to the point of threat.

Regarding landing operations, heretofore the Japanese had constructed their first line of defense at the beach. The Americans in every case had smashed the defenses and landed successfully. Hattori recorded,

> Commanders at all levels began to doubt the efficiency of our fighting methods. At the time of the fighting on Saipan, in view of its garrison strength, number of guns, and installation positions, it was believed possible to effect a successful defense even against a superior enemy.

However, once the enemy commenced the attack, the bulk of our strength was lost in a very short time and vital key points fell to the enemy. This caused the tendency among all the men and officers to lose faith in the island defense.[72]

The new method involved creating several lines. The first at the beach was to maximize casualties through firepower, including cannons. The main line of resistance was disposed in depth behind the beach line. Next came a reserve line of resistance, then the artillery and antiaircraft positions. The final defense position was for use in "unavoidable circumstances."

The third innovation was suicide attack tactics. Major Katsushige Takada, on his own initiative, had led four planes in a suicide crash dive and sunk an enemy warship during fighting at Biak Island in late May. IGHQ considered establishing a new unit for suicide pilots, but a group within the High Command objected that the "Imperial spirit" did not allow for using humans as bullets, with their death inevitable. So the headquarters ordered field forces to organize informally "temporary" groups manned by volunteers. Nevertheless, the military designed special attack weapons for army and navy use, including *Kaiten* (human torpedoes), *Maruhachi* (explosive ram boats, IJA), and *Shinyo* (explosive ram boats, IJN).[73]

The IJN had also learned many of the same lessons the Anglo-Americans had in the battle in the Atlantic and innovated. Faster vessels reduced the risk of loss to submarines, so smaller, speedier ships were converted to oil tankers. Tanker construction became the top priority. The IJN organized larger convoys with more escorts and with air cover. These changes helped somewhat, but submarines were soon to be joined by air power in the campaign to annihilate Japanese cargo shipping.[74]

With shipping losses surging, the IJN in December 1943 had established the 901st Air Flotilla to provide an air arm to protect shipping lanes from American subs. Captain S. Kamide, its first commanding officer, told interrogators that its initial complement was 48 land-based two-engine bombers and 32 four-engine flying boats. The force grew alongside the American threat. At maximum strength in January 1945, it fielded 80 Nakajima E8N reconnaissance sea planes, 30 Nakajima B59 torpedo bombers, 30 Zeros, 20 Mitsubishi G4M medium bombers, and eight Kawanishi H8K flying boats. An escort fleet provided escort carriers with additional planes. Their only special equipment consisted of radar and magnetic detection devices (MADs). The unit estimated that it destroyed a paltry 20 submarines during its entire existence, most of which Kamide attributed to MAD aircraft.[75]

Lieutenant Commander T. Okamoto, a naval aviator who served as a staff officer at the First Escort Fleet Aviation Squadron and Grand Escort Fleet Headquarters, explained the big picture to interrogators. In addition to the 901st Air Flotilla based on Formosa, Manila, and in Indochina, with 200 planes, the 903d, with 120 planes, was based in Japan, as was the 951st with the same number of planes. The 936th operated out of Singapore and Indochina with 120 planes. A third of the planes had radar and a third MAD. A few aircraft had both.[76]

Rear Admiral Mitsuharo Matsuyama commanded Japanese convoy escorts to protect merchantmen and tankers from the depredations of American submarines. (Military Intelligence Division, NARA)

The MAD could detect a submerged target at between 150 and 250 meters (450–600 feet), according to Okamoto. Aircraft flew 30 to 150 feet above the surface depending on their skill. It was considered reliable enough to warrant dispatching a surface vessel to the point of contact. The IJN credited MAD location with the destruction of 11 subs from August 1944 to July 1945.

IJN Lieutenant JG Y. Okuno from December 1944 served with a convoy protection unit based on Formosa charged with protecting vessels along the Chinese and Indochinese coasts. He gave interrogators a picture of the capabilities the IJN had developed, presumably with no knowledge of similar Allied technological and tactical developments in the Atlantic. His squadron, spread among several bases in the area of operations, had planes equipped with radar and others with magnetic detectors. Radar planes would search the sea lanes, and if one detected a submarine, a MAD platform would attempt to establish an exact location of the submerged sub and a vector of travel. His seaplane carried a MAD, which was so heavy that all weapons and armor had to be removed. After establishing contact, it would drop a lighted buoy and then bomb the spot. IJN Zeros provided fighter cover. Radio connections to the convoy flagship were limited; voice was possible within five miles, and otherwise they had to use the Morse key.[77]

Rear Admiral Mitsuharo Matsuyama commanded naval convoy escort groups in late 1942 between the Netherlands East Indies and the home islands, and in 1944 convoy escorts to Singapore, Saipan, and within the Philippines. He told interrogators that there was a Grand Escort Fleet Headquarters in Tokyo and eight regional headquarters, which oversaw the escort groups. When a sub attacked a convoy, the escort vessels would drop copious number of depth charges. Aircraft sightings of subs were considered accurate within ten miles, and radio direction finding less so. Aircraft with magnetic detectors accompanied the convoy, sometimes as many as four or five. Matsuharo, at least, came to view air attack after 1943 as a much greater threat to convoys than the subs.[78]

The U.S. Navy lost 52 submarines in the Pacific. Japan lost 128.[79]

In terms of aircraft, the Japanese knew well that the Zero—which had been the best fighter in the skies during the glory days—was now outmatched by the carrier-based Grumman F6F Hellcat, which had wreaked havoc in the Marianas. New models of the twin-boom P-38 Lightning were appearing with new engines and more deadly performance. Army pilots in Burma reported encountering the P-51 Mustang, which severely outclassed the *Hayabusa* (Oscars) they were flying. The military rushed development of two replacement aircraft, and pilot Sakai flew both models as a test pilot starting in September.

The first was the *Shiden* (Lightning) designed to outfight the Hellcat. It lacked the range of the Zero, but it was fast, maneuverable, gave the pilot armor protection, and mounted four 20mm cannons. It was difficult to fly, however, especially for unseasoned pilots.

The second was the *Raiden* (Thunder), designed to take on the B-29. It, too, had armor and four 20mm cannons and could reach the extraordinary speed of 400 miles per hour.

Production of both was slow, and bombing attacks were soon to throw the aircraft industry into chaos.[80]

Germany: Collapse of the Western Front

By early July, OKW Deputy Operations Chief Warlimont told interrogators shortly after the war, "We knew that large reserves could be shifted from the United States and that you were able to build up your supplies rapidly. Thus, we were prepared to expect a strong attempt of your forces to break through to the interior of France."[81]

The Germans by now knew they faced a competent enemy in Normandy. Army Group B's intelligence section reported on 10 July,

> The enemy begins attacks with a systematic and mathematically exact destruction of the defenders through artillery barrages and carpet bombing. When [such] attacks fail, they are broken off, only to be launched again with more troops and material.... In the defense, the English infantry have proven especially tenacious. The American infantry is not so tough, but it will fight tenaciously as long as it has sufficient fire support.... Cooperation among ground, air, and naval forces is good.[82]

General of the Infantry Günther Blumentritt, chief of staff of Commander-in-Chief West, told interviewers after the war,

> Although most of the German High Command viewed the British as more dangerous, which resulted in the concentration of more troops and good panzer divisions near Caen, there was a decided shift in opinion as the battles in Normandy progressed. Panzer Lehr Division was actually shifted to the American front, and there is no doubt that other divisions would have been shifted to oppose the Americans had they not been tied down by continued British pressure and an overall lack of reserves. We recognized all along that Montgomery was more methodical than most American leaders, and we admired the quick, deft stroke that cut the Cherbourg peninsula and the speedy regrouping of American forces following the fall of Cherbourg itself. In addition, Pétain told von Rundstedt on several occasions to watch out for the Americans, since they had learned so much of their armored warfare and mobile-mindedness from the Germans.[83]

ETO Battlefields

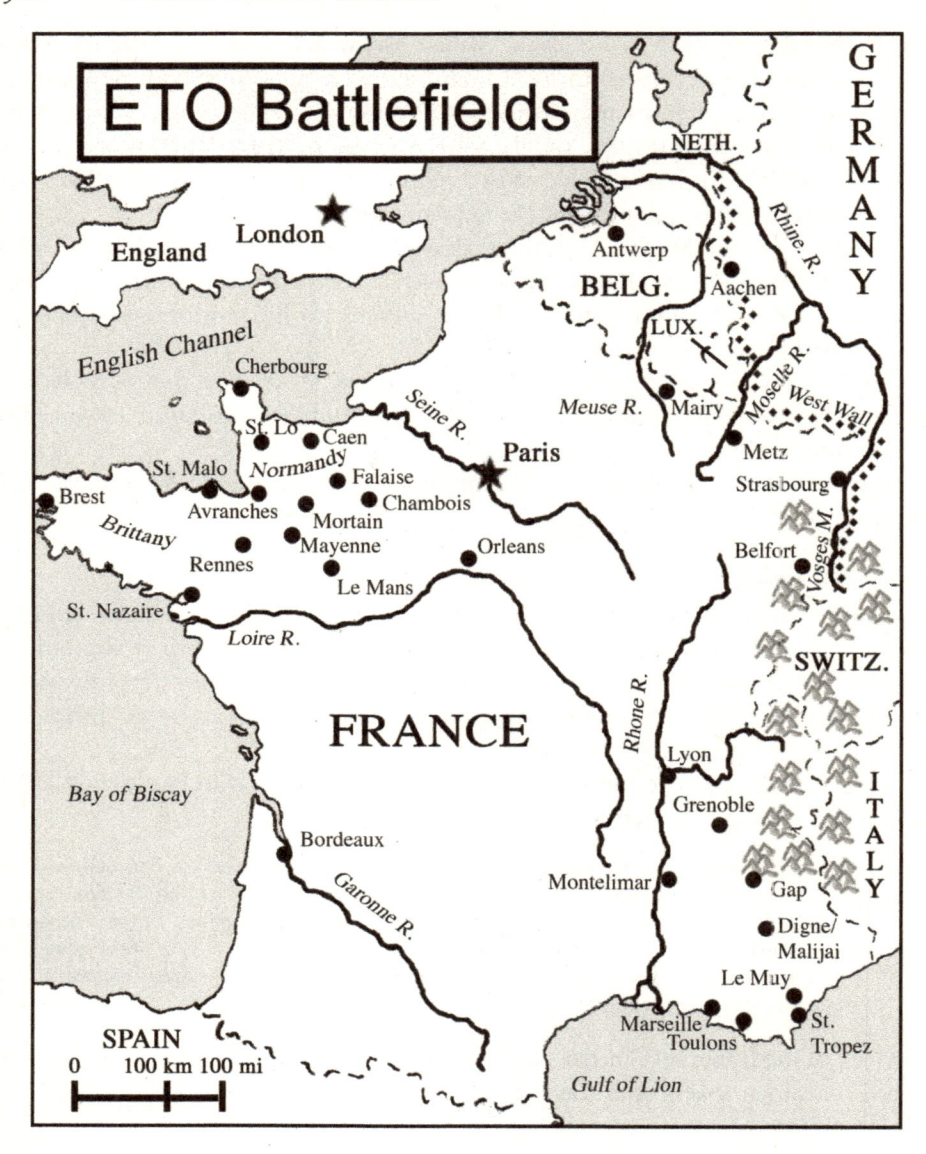

Jodl separately offered a similar assessment to an interrogator. "We had a feeling that the English fought harder than the Americans at first.... We thought they were more dangerous, especially as they employed veteran divisions from Italy plus elements of their Eighth Army. This impression remained unchanged until the Americans carried out their very flexible attack on Cherbourg."[84]

The U.S. First Army on 18 June cut the Cotentin Peninsula and isolated the port of Cherbourg. The OKW war diary indicates that Rundstedt worried that this operation could evolve into an outright breakout and scrambled to build a blocking line. Hitler on 26 June ordered the shift of the Panzer Lehr and 2d Panzer Divisions from the British sector to "destroy" the Americans.[85] (The records suggest that Blumentritt and Jodl were completely forthright in their statements collected by FMS.)

Although not framed as a view about the Americans per se, the crushing power of Allied naval gunfire was shaping German decisions. By 28 June, when Hitler consulted Rundstedt and Rommel, their conclusions were that they had no chance of cutting the beachhead into two, and that a planned counterattack east of the Orne River could not occur so long as naval support was available to the defenders. Rundstedt on 1 July proposed withdrawing the entire German line beyond the range of naval guns. This was what the Japanese were deducing at the same time based on their experience at Saipan—get the heck out of range!

The OKW operations staff viewed Rundstedt's proposal as the final abdication of any intention to destroy the beachhead. That goal could hardly be achieved with a third of the strength of the enemy's. The staff concluded on 1 July that the Wehrmacht could not sustain the attrition in manpower and materiel it was suffering for much longer and endorsed Rundstedt's suggestion. There were two options: try until the last opportunity to win in Normandy and then withdraw to the shortest possible defense line, the West Wall, or commit everything to decisive battle with all the risks that entailed.[86]

Rundstedt told the High Command that the German infantry divisions in Normandy would not be able to stand up before the mass of materiel pouring into the beachhead. Indeed, Rundstedt was sacked on 2 July, effective the next day, after a conversation with OWK chief of staff Field Marshal Keitel during which he reiterated that with the means available to the Allies, German forces would not be able to withstand their attacks. When Keitel asked what Rundstedt recommended, he replied, "You should make an end to the whole war," according to his chief of staff, who listened to the entire conversation.[87] Field Marshal Günther von Kluge became the new Commander-in-Chief West.

Rommel also saw what was coming and begged for more resources. On 15 July he wrote to Rundstedt:

> The situation on the front in Normandy becomes more difficult every day and is nearing a crisis.
>
> Our own losses in the hard fighting, the incredibly strong material resources of the enemy, above all in artillery and tanks, and the unchallenged enemy control of the air, mean that the battle strength of the divisions quickly sinks. Replacements from the homeland come only in spurts....
>
> Under these conditions it must be reckoned that the enemy in the foreseeable future will manage to break through the thin front, especially that of Seventh Army, and strike into the vast interior of France.... [T]here are no mobile reserves to stop a breakthrough of Seventh Army's front.[88]

Allied air superiority arguably delivered a telling blow on 17 July, when a Royal Air Force fighter-bomber machine gunned Rommel's car and seriously wounded the field marshal. Kluge added commanding general, Army Group B, to his portfolio.[89]

On the 18th, Kluge told the High Command that the Normandy fighting had all the hallmarks of a large-scale war of attrition. German losses since D-Day, which were not being made good, amounted to some 2,360 officers and 100,000 men. By 24 July, Kluge counted the loss of nearly 400 more officers and 10,000 non-commissioned officers and men. Only 10,078 replacements had arrived since D-Day.[90]

The catastrophic situation in the east largely accounts for the shortfall in infantry replacements. The Soviets on 22 June launched Operation *Bagration*, attacking Army Group Center with 146 rifle and 43 tank formations. They advanced without pause, and in July expanded the offensive to the front of Army Groups North and A. The Soviets destroyed Army Group Center and 25 German divisions. The High Command was rushing every available resource to the east, where Field Marshal Walter Model had taken command of the army group remnants and was well on his way to reestablishing a front.[91]

The Eastern Front also drew away all panzer replacements. As of 29 July, Army Group B had lost 393 panzers—the equivalent of roughly three panzer divisions—including 12 38(t), 224 Mark IV, 131 Mark V, and 23 Tiger tanks, plus 60 assault guns and 132 armored half-tracks.[92] The Germans, interestingly enough, had not included the French tanks equipping two independent battalions that had been virtually wiped out in the early phase of the Normandy invasion. "[T]hese losses could not now be made good," noted Inspector of Panzer Troops Heinz Guderian in his memoirs, "since after 22 June the whole eastern front threatened to collapse, and all available replacements had to go there instead of to the previously favored western front."[93]

Bagration was the first Soviet operation in which tactical airpower was a major factor, destroying ground targets and preventing movement. One reason for this was that almost all of Germany's fighters were in the west battling the Americans and British.[94]

Officer prisoners of war arriving from Normandy at the Trent Park facility near London also were troubled by the Allies' overwhelming materiel superiority. They talked about how they had watched helplessly as the enemy war machine crushed their units. Most thought the war was lost.[95]

Kluge on 18 July reported the fighting had the characteristics of a "battle of material" and "wear and tear." He marveled that the Americans had lost 1,704 tanks and 293 aircraft. German losses since D-Day amounted to about 100,000 men, including 2,360 officers. Unlike the enemy, his losses were not being replaced.[96] Kluge was badly misinformed on American tank losses, but his figure conveys what the German impression of American numerical superiority was. As of the end of

June, U.S. First Army had only 765 medium tanks, less than half of which were actually with the separate tank battalions fighting in the hedgerows. By the time of Operation *Cobra*, American tank strength was approaching 2,000, many in as yet uncommitted armored divisions.[97]

On 20 July, just five days before the launch of the American breakout from Normandy, a bomb exploded in Hitler's bunker, placed there by a group of army conspirators, including senior general officers. Hitler was wounded by the blast but lived. Hitler's military adjutant Günsche, who with Keitel helped Hitler back to his bunker immediately after the blast, told Russian interrogators that Hitler said, "What luck! I am alive. That is the hand of Providence."[98]

The event set a metaphorical bomb off in the German officer corps, for Hitler was not only the sole political leader that German military commanders had served for more than a decade, he was the commander of the field armies, too. A message circulated to troops in the west on the 21st read: "A small circle of deposed officers has undertaken an assassination attempt against our Führer. The Führer lives! He spoke this night to the German people and his soldiers.... For us soldiers in the West, there is only one slogan: To hold firm on the front against the enemy with unshaken determination and unconditional loyalty to the Führer. Long live the Führer! Long live Germany!"[99]

After the assassination attempt, Hitler's trust in his Wehrmacht commanders, never strong at the best of times, turned into outright paranoia and even hatred.[100] The situation must have seemed menacingly familiar to Kluge, who had risen to command Army Group Center in 1941 as the result of Hitler's sweeping purge of general officers whom he deemed disloyal. Combat generals would fight with one eye looking over their shoulder, seeking any sign that the Gestapo had uncovered a hint, true or false, that they had been involved in the conspiracy.

Nevertheless, Kluge had fully realized the perilous state of his front, and on 21 July, he finally forwarded Rommel's assessment to Hitler and added: "My Führer! I have been here about fourteen days and after conversations with the most important commanders on this hot front, particularly those from the SS, have come to the conviction that the field marshal regrettably sees things correctly." He went on to underscore most of Rommel's points. "Despite heated efforts," he concluded, "the moment is near when the overloaded front will break. And if the enemy gets into open country, orderly control will hardly be possible in light of the insufficient mobility of our troops."[101]

One result of the assassination attack was that Hitler on 21 July named Guderian as his new army chief of staff. Guderian was no friend of Kluge's and immediately suggested that Hitler replace him because he had lacked a "lucky touch" commanding large armored formations. Hitler responded, according to Guderian, "And furthermore, he had foreknowledge of the assassination attempt."[102]

Oshima on 23 July met with Ribbentrop, who offered a remarkable admission:

> Both Chancellor Hitler and I are fully aware that Germany now has a desperate fight on her hands. As a method of getting out of this crisis, some thought is being given to the possibility that peace might be established between England and Germany or Germany and some other country, but for either Chancellor Hitler or me to undertake such a thing under present circumstances would, in reality, be the same as carrying on negotiations for surrender.

Oshima offered an assessment of Germany's plight:

> On the Western Front, the Anglo-Americans have been forced to use more troops than they had expected and the progress of the campaign has been slow. Nevertheless, the enemy has undeniably succeeded in establishing a strong base in northern France. To that extent, it must be recognized that the Germans' strategy of first routing the invading army in the west and then turning to the east has failed. The offensive of the Russian Army in the east is making exceptionally rapid progress and its pressure is increasing daily. Therefore, while there has been no change in Germany's basic strategy of waging a decisive battle on the western front, at present it is urgently necessary to stabilize the eastern front, a task to which every effort is being devoted.[103]

In the air war, meanwhile, American fighter escorts were decimating the Luftwaffe fighter force, leaving flak as the key component of the air defense. Super-batteries (*Grosskampfbatterien*) became the Reich-wide standard flak deployment, allowing one radar to mass the fires of several batteries. A new converter allowed a single radar to control up to 32 batteries and permitted a radar station to take over from another being jammed. Eighth Air Force analysts termed this the most intelligent step the enemy had taken in a long time. Despite having started to drop chaff, German flak was becoming more lethal.[104]

The Cobra Strikes

General Bernard Montgomery, by his own account, formulated the scheme for the Allied escape from the clinging hell of Normandy well before D-Day. The British and Canadians were to draw German armored reserves to the eastern wing around Caen, which would allow Lieutenant General Omar Bradley and his First Army to shove forward at the western wing. The strategy focused on breaking free and posited relatively modest objectives for the movement phase, "a wide sweep to the Seine about Paris," according to Montgomery.[105]

Bradley's battle plan to break out of the Normandy stalemate carried the appropriate name Operation *Cobra*. Major General J. Lawton Collins's VII Corps was to make the main effort in the American center immediately west of St. Lô, with the 83d and 9th Infantry divisions on the left, the 30th Infantry Division in the center, and the 29th Infantry Division on the right to protect the flank. Once a penetration had been achieved, the motorized 1st Infantry Division, with Combat Command B from the 3d Armored Division attached, was to exploit four miles southward to Marigny, then turn west ten miles to the coast to cut off the German left wing. The remainder of the 3d Armored Division, with a 1st Infantry

Division rifle battalion attached, was to secure the southern escape routes. The 2d Armored Division, with the motorized 22d Infantry attached, was to drive through the gap and establish more blocking positions. XIX and V Corps were to launch smaller attacks to pin the Germans in place along their fronts east of VII Corps, while VIII Corps pushed southward down the coast to the west to destroy the German left wing after delaying just long enough for VII Corps to cut off the enemy's retreat.[106]

Kluge accurately anticipated that the main Allied thrust, when it came, would occur in the American sector aimed at taking the area from the Orne River south to Avranches.[107] But, Montgomery's Operation *Goodwood* around Caen, initiated on 18 July, had drawn off most of the German armored strength to face the

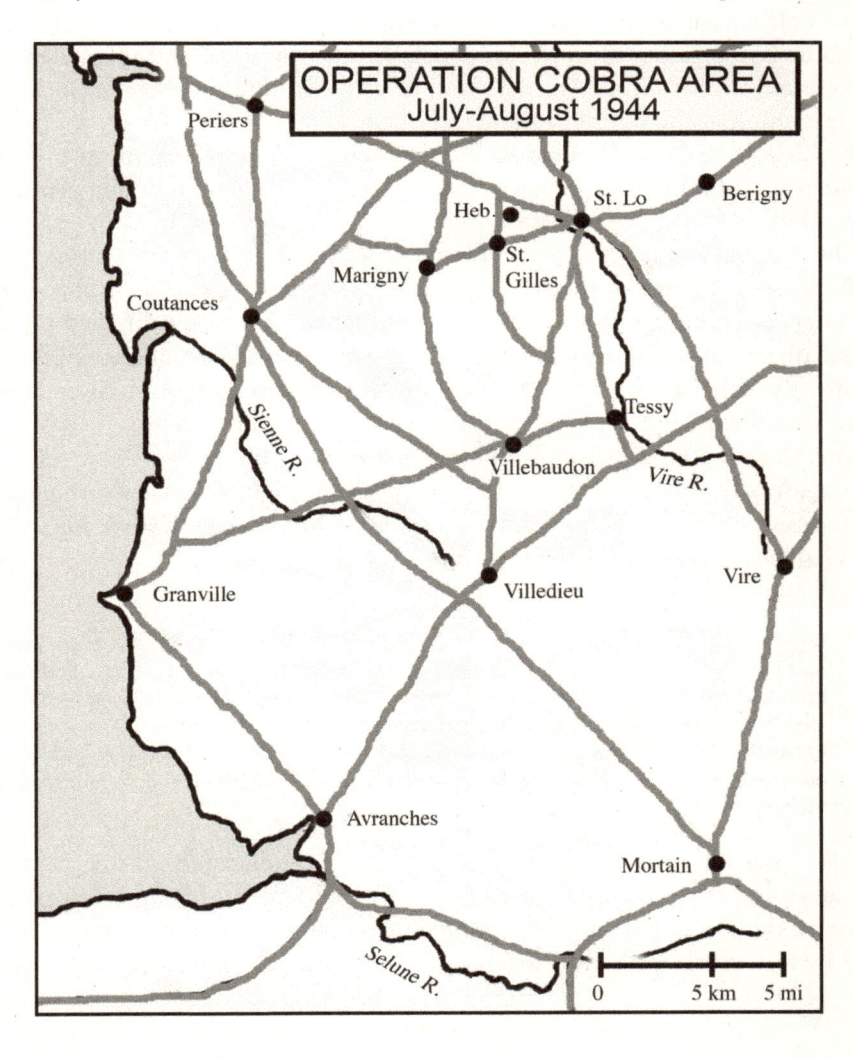

Commonwealth troops, leaving only a much-weakened Panzer Lehr Division facing VII Corps and the 2d SS Panzer and 17th SS Panzergrenadier divisions opposite VIII Corps.

Mobile operations by those two panzer divisions had consumed fuel during mid-July faster than it could be replaced, mainly because of aggressive disruption of rail lines by Allied fighter-bombers. Only six army trains per day were able to get from the German border even to Paris.[108]

The main attack of the Allied breakout began on 25 July, immediately west of St. Lô. Lieutenant General George Patton, who was appointed Bradley's deputy at the head of First Army and was responsible for the right wing of the operation, assumed oversight of VIII Corps operations on 27 July. The VII Corps had already torn a hole ten miles wide and ten miles deep in the German Seventh Army's front. Asked by interrogators when he had concluded the war was lost, Jodl replied, "The war was already lost in the West at the time of the breakthrough at Avranches and the beginning of the war of movement in France."[109]

By his fourth day of combat in Western Europe, Patton had an open door to the interior of France. On 1 August, he and Third Army were officially placed into active duty and began swiftly streaming through the gap into Brittany.

On 3 August, Bradley ordered Patton to leave the minimum necessary force in Brittany and to throw the weight of Third Army east toward Le Mans, behind the German Seventh Army. Conditions were perfect: Seventh Army had prepared no security measures in its rear areas, which were covered by understrength guard troops: the 9th Panzer and 708th Infantry divisions supposed to cover Seventh Army's southern wing were still en route.

The Germans received only scattered reports of Third Army's activities until 10 August, when they first realized that a powerful enemy force was turning north behind Seventh Army. Montgomery's troops were simultaneously smashing through the German front to link up with Patton.

Jodl commented,

> [Our] picture [of the Americans] changed completely at Avranches, where we encountered an operation that was first class, courageous, and with long-range strategic aims.... From a small breakthrough, the Americans executed an operation that resembled our German methods more than those of the English or French. This American planning and execution were a surprise for us. After these operations were repeated, we had the impression that American leadership was more alert, purposeful, and farsighted than that of the British, who clung to more customary methods.[110]

(FMS comment: As noted in the foreword, Jodl's handlers judged that he did his best as a soldier to answer questions, despite facing war crimes charges. It is possible, however, that he would have told British interrogators the opposite, but if you try to construct that hypothetical statement, it would probably not look convincing.)

Allied Advance As of September 1944

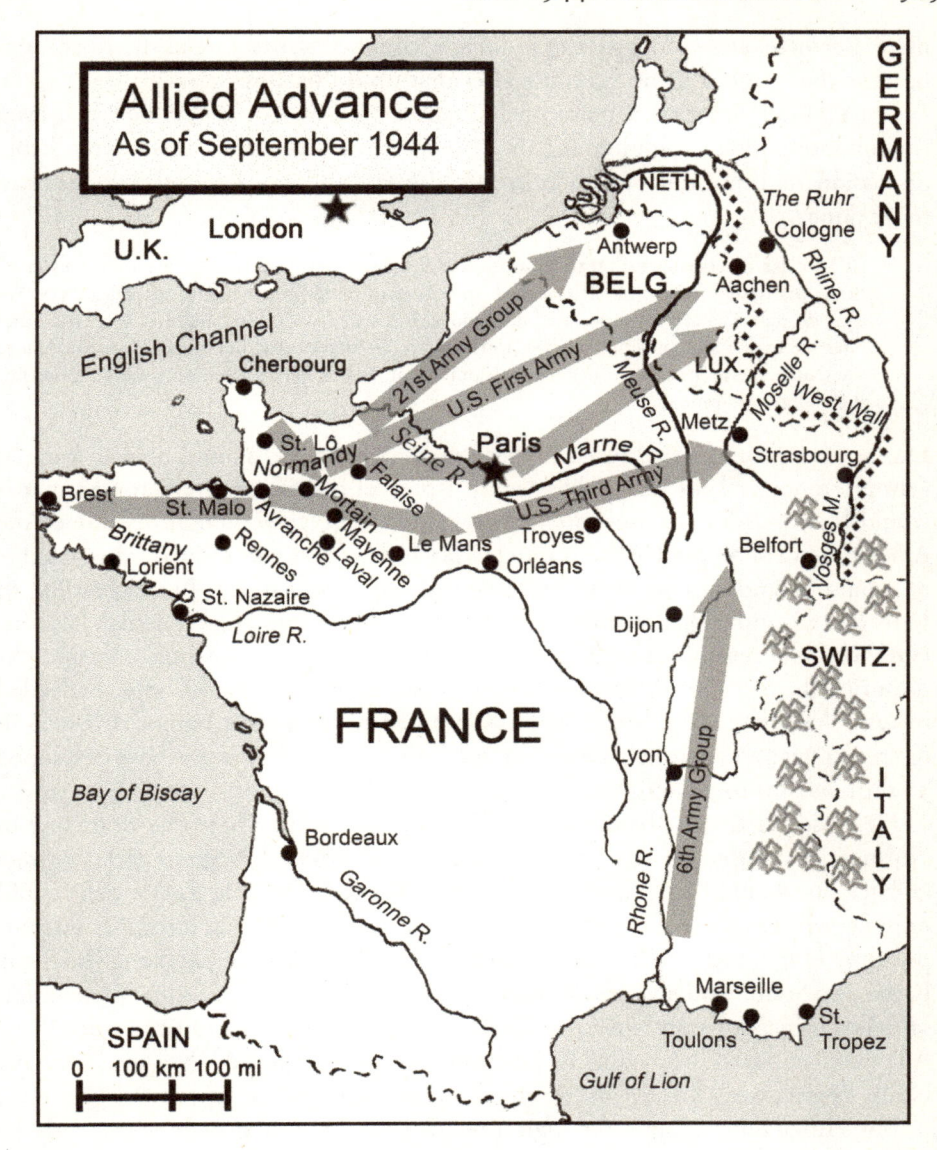

Hitler Sort of Concedes Defeat in the West

Hitler met with Jodl on 31 July to discuss the grand strategic situation. Hitler said he was most worried that day about the situation in the east, where Army Groups North and Center had been mauled, and Soviet troops were nearing the East Prussian frontier. The Führer nevertheless was confident that his countermeasures would stabilize the situation. In Italy, the war was tying down enemy forces that could be used elsewhere, and Germany had to hope it could cling to a line in the Apennines because there would be no stopping after that until the Alps.

Then Hitler dropped a bombshell: France, he said, could not be held, even though losing it would undermine the U-boat war. Hitler's analysis was remarkably dispassionate, if not unclouded, as he was already thinking clearly about what had to be done:[111]

> [It is] clear that an operation in France—and I believe we must be fully aware of this at all times—is totally impossible in so-called open field of battle under today's circumstances. We can't do that. We can move some of our troops, but only in a limited manner. With the other ones we can't move, not because we don't possess air superiority, but because we can't move the troops themselves: the units are not suitable for mobile battle—neither their weapons nor their other equipment.[112]

During the spring debate over whether the panzer reserves should be held back in central France or kept close to the coast, Rommel had perceptively argued that it would be impossible to move the panzers forward quickly enough because of the Allies' control of the air. He had wanted to place as many divisions forward as possible to repulse a landing and to deal with any airborne operations. But, according to Jodl's diary, Rommel had asserted something far more dire and fundamental: "Mobile battle with panzer units is a thing of the past." Movement was possible only at night or during the day with 150 meters between vehicles. The Führer, however, had sided in early April with Rundstedt, who had wanted to hold most panzer divisions in reserve to stage an open-field counterattack.[113] Now Hitler appears to have developed a synthesis of those two opinions.

He reasoned that he barely had had enough strength to hold the short line in Normandy, and that the small fraction of divisions mobile enough to withdraw to a fallback line would be far short of the manpower needed to hold it. Germany could only fight in France if it could reestablish control of the air, but since that was not possible, Hitler and Jodl considered and dismissed trying to stand along the Seine River. The Somme offered possibilities for a delaying line because some preparation of field fortifications was already underway along the river. That might work if the Allies concentrated their effort in the north for a drive toward the Ruhr industrial basin. Eisenhower's broad-front strategy would crush this notion.

But Hitler fully grasped the logical conclusion. "A proper defense can only be established where we have either the West Wall or at least ground conditions to permit this—and that would be the Vosges [Mountains]. There we can organize resistance."

The West Wall, known to the Allies as the Siegfried Line, ran nearly 400 miles from north of Aachen along the German frontier to the Swiss border. The Germans had neglected the defenses after 1940, and Hitler on 23 July, in another sign of strategic realism, had authorized renovating the defenses.

"[Y]ou can see that a breakthrough ... can happen quickly!" Hitler issued his orders. First, OKW, working with the navy, was to identify which ports the Allies would need the most—the only evident bottleneck to a seemingly unlimited supply of reinforcements—and then those ports were to be held. "[W]e should be able to hold the harbor for six, eight, or ten weeks—and those six, eight, or ten weeks will mean a lot in the months of August, September, and October." Hitler's grasp of the supply problems the Allies would face was unerring and better than that of most commanders on the opposing side, who failed, for example, to make capturing and opening the port of Antwerp a top priority.

The second point was to get combat units out safely to the east. "[N]ow we have to demand from [Commander-in-Chief West] that units which are not intended for fixed positions be made mobile—temporarily mobile—and that he report all of this." Hitler also sketched out his plan to withdraw Army Group G from southern France, orders he was to issue in only six more weeks.

Hitler, however, told Jodl that he was not to share the big picture with the army group commanders. Moreover, Hitler was aware that the Allies had excellent intelligence on his intentions, which he blamed on the coup plotters at his headquarters and in Paris rather than Ultra, and that Jodl was not to transmit the Führer's desires through the chain of command but rather tell Kluge only what specifics were needed.

Finally, Hitler and Jodl talked about setting up a central staff to control the Western Front because Kluge was too stretched acting as both chief of Army Group B and Commander-in-Chief West. "He's not in Paris at all," said Jodl. "He's leading the army group. They never see him anymore.... They want to have Rundstedt back, because Kluge is hardly accessible to them."[114]

Jodl contacted Blumentritt at Kluge's headquarters and indirectly told him to expect a withdrawal order and to immediately begin planning and preparations, including sending work crews to assist the Todt Organization in constructing a line along the Somme and Marne rivers.[115]

Given the desperate situation on both fronts, Hitler accepted a proposal by Speer that all war production, including aircraft, be consolidated under his Munitions Ministry. The reorganization occurred on 1 August. Goebbels took charge of mobilizing the home front, and Himmler took command of the reserve army. Speer expressed confidence that qualitative superiority in missiles (the V-2 ballistic missile), aircraft (the jet-powered Me 262 was to reach the first units shortly), production of the new type XXI U-boat (not combat ready until April 1945), and "total war" would overcome the crisis.[116]

The *Cobra* breakout led to serial disasters for the Germans. Patton on 13 August nearly cut off all of Seventh and Fifth Panzer armies, and, ordered to stop advancing to avoid accidental friendly fire, waited for Montgomery to close the Falaise Pocket on 19 August. That delay enabled more formations than Hitler had any right to expect to break out to the northeast. OKW reckoned that perhaps half the troops inside the pocket were able to slip away, most, however, without any heavy equipment. Of the two army, four corps, and thirteen divisional staffs in the pocket, only one corps and two or three divisional staffs were destroyed; the rest were ready for immediate commitment.

The next blow fell when the American-French 6th Army Group invaded southern France on 15 August. Ten days later, American and French divisions from the Normandy force liberated Paris. Montgomery's 21st Army Group liberated Brussels on 3 September, and took Antwerp the following day (although the Germans would block sea access through the Scheldt Estuary for nearly two more months). On 4 September, Supreme Headquarters Allied Expeditionary Force (SHAEF) alerted army commanders, "Enemy resistance on the entire front shows signs of collapse."[117]

The OKW war diary leaves little question that the Germans completely failed to understand Eisenhower's strategic imperative (nor, to be fair, did Montgomery or Bradley for about a month, despite his clear instructions). On 29 August, for example, Eisenhower issued a letter of instruction to Montgomery, Bradley, and other senior officers in which he stated in a concise, one-sentence paragraph (italics added): "It is my intention to complete the destruction of the enemy forces in the West, *and then* to strike directly into the heart of the enemy homeland." He ordered his commanders to act swiftly and relentlessly and to accept risks in order to "close with the German wherever met." On 4 September, Eisenhower underscored, "My intention continues to be the destruction of enemy forces, and this will be the primary task of all elements of the Allied Expeditionary Force."[118] Ike wanted to keep the German army west of the Rhine so he could annihilate it before crossing the river. The OKW in mid-September found his approach inexplicable in the context of German military thinking. Why did the enemy not concentrate his strength at a single point and create a breakthrough?[119] (That is what Montgomery wanted to do, but that is a different story.)

The Miracle in the West

By the beginning of September, German casualties in the West since D-Day had amounted to more than 450,000 men killed, wounded, or captured. Losses in equipment totaled a staggering 1,300 tanks, 500 assault guns, 20,000 other vehicles, and 1,500 pieces of artillery.[120]

Hitler scraped together everything he could to reinforce the Western Front, and for the heretofore great military power, the pickings were slim. Having already stripped the 15th Panzergrenadier Division from Italy, he ordered the 3d Panzergrenadier Division to move north of the Alps, too, and the 105th and 106th Panzer brigades to deploy from their training areas in Germany. Three infantry divisions then in training were to become available on 1 September, and two more skeleton divisions were to be transferred soon. The Führer sent individual static "fortress" infantry battalions, separate infantry march battalions that moved replacements to frontline units, and machine-gun battalions to man the West Wall. To these formations he added 416 field pieces. In all the Third Reich, he had as replacements only 144 Mark IV and 20 Mark V panzers and some 100 assault guns.[121]

Field Marshal Walter Model, who had become Commander-in-Chief West in mid-August after Kluge committed suicide, on 29 August took stock of what he thought he had rescued from the Normandy disaster. From 11 SS and army panzer divisions, each with between five and ten tanks and individual artillery batteries, he thought he could with available replacements build eleven regiment-size *Kampfgruppen* (combined arms battle groups). Eleven remnant infantry divisions, if reinforced with personnel from five fought-out divisions in the Reich, might give him the equivalent of four divisions, albeit lacking key equipment.[122]

In the face of the grim developments in the west, Hitler on 4 September ordered Major General Kurt Student, chief of the *Fallschirmjäger* (airborne/paratrooper) force, to take charge of filling the hole in German lines between Antwerp and Maastricht. Unless it was closed, British armored spearheads would have an open run to the Rhine River. Göring that day had revealed, to an astounded Army General Staff, that he had six parachute regiments in training or refitting and could raise two more—plus 10,000 other Luftwaffe personnel—to use as infantry. Student rushed 18,000 parachute troops from various points around the Reich to the front and added whatever motley mix of policemen, sailors, convalescents, and 16-year-olds that he could get his hands on. Vastly outnumbered but fighting over advantageous swampy ground cut by many streams, the patchwork "First Parachute Army" slowed the British advance to a crawl.[123]

Also on 4 September, Hitler reinstated the old Prussian warhorse Rundstedt as Commander-in-Chief West and ordered Model to command Army Group B full time. Rundstedt submitted an appraisal on 7 September. The enemy had 54 divisions available. The British had 25–27 divisions. The U.S. 12th Army Group had 15–18 divisions and about 1,000 tanks, plus five divisions in Brittany. He had about 100 battle-ready tanks and 135,000 men (the equivalent of about 13 divisions) in his entire command and was moving what he had to the Aachen area.[124]

As noted, Hitler had worked furiously during the collapse in France to put together a scratch force to partially rebuild and man the West Wall. Berlin planned for a seven-week rehabilitation program; the Allies gave the Germans two weeks. On 11 September, command over the West Wall passed from the Replacement Army to Rundstedt and the Field Army.[125]

During September, the Germans managed to throw an estimated 230,000 men into the defense of the West Wall. Of these, some 100,000 formed fresh divisions. Another 50,000 came from fortress battalions, which U.S. First Army termed the "hidden reserve of the German Army."[126]

According to the OKW war diary, the first discussion of a large-scale counteroffensive in the west took place on 6 September. Hitler agreed with the planning staff's assessment that such an undertaking would not be possible before 1 November, and that would depend on being able to extract divisions from the line of battle for rebuilding. Hitler said it would be critical to keep the front as far west as possible.[127]

OKW judged that the West Wall would hold if the Americans failed to break through immediately. It anticipated a concentrated American thrust through the line at Aachen in mid-September. The solidifying defenses and the enemy outrunning his supply lines ensured that no breakthrough occurred. By 25 September, OKW concluded that the immediate crisis had passed.[128]

The planners, meanwhile, began constructing force projections should an offensive be launched against the Allies' wings—the Burgundy forts in the south or Holland in the north. Hitler personally drove the effort, convinced that 70 Anglo-American divisions were too few to hold a 500-mile front, and there had to be holes somewhere which the Wehrmacht could force. The whole idea still hinged on getting panzer divisions off the line for rebuilding.[129]

On 25 September, with the American threat at Aachen dispelled for the moment, Hitler ordered Rundstedt to concentrate on striking back at the British in Holland, where he expected the Allies to shift their main effort for a while. He ordered most of the available panzer units in Army Group B to that sector.[130]

On 27 September, British Ultra codebreakers deciphered a message sent several days earlier directing that all SS formations—beginning with one panzergrenadier and four panzer divisions and three Tiger battalions—be withdrawn for rest and refitting.[131] First Army detected the departure of the 1st, 2d, and 12th SS Panzer divisions, and the 9th and 116th Panzer divisions from its front. The Americans conceded that, "the enemy had been able to stabilize his line."[132] They did not grasp that the panzer units were pulling back to refit for a major offensive. Model had accomplished a "miracle in the West."

Rundstedt's headquarters on 29 September filed its estimate for losses in the west since D-Day, which amounted to 460,900, including some 259,000 taken prisoner.[133] The Luftwaffe had lost much of its early warning radar system and most of the flak in the west, and Allied medium bombers and fighter-bombers could now roam at will throughout the Reich.[134]

As September rolled into October, Hitler settled on a place for his offensive, the "area east of Lüttich" (Belgium)—the Ardennes. The Germans had broken through there in 1940.[135]

There is no indication that Hitler picked the American sector because he still looked down on the American enemy: one surmises he had learned his lesson on that score.

Keitel informed senior commanders in the west of the plan on 10 October. The Allies had told their people to expect a quick victory, he said; he was going to screw their plans with an offensive. Mobile divisions would withdraw to assembly areas in the north and constitute the OKW reserve. Army group commanders were to camouflage these preparations and wage their defensive battles without having to draw on the reserve except in the direst of circumstances.[136] The fight until the offensive would be to protect the assembly areas and participating divisions.

From this point on, the Allied command was as ignorant of German war aims for the next two and a half months as the Germans were of Eisenhower's.

*

Hitler's right-hand general Jodl had decided that the war in the west was lost back in July, and there is evidence that the thought of total defeat was taking root in other parts of the Nazi leadership. Even as Hitler planned his counteroffensive, the OSS began collecting reports in October 1944 that senior German officials were starting to plan for the day the Allies occupied Germany. The most detailed report came out of Switzerland from an informant who had spoken to Martin Bormann, head of the Nazi Party. Himmler was asked to provide plans that he and Bormann had drawn up a year earlier for the establishment of a "German Maquis" guerrilla force, which would have geographic regions in the Alps, Central Germany, and the Silesian mountains. An SS officer was to command each region. Selection of cadre personnel from SS divisions was already allegedly under way.[137]

The OSS station in London on 14 October forwarded a summary of recent British SIS reports. The first, received through a trustworthy channel, indicated that the German Security Service in September had conducted a survey and concluded that 50 to 60 percent of the public would still blindly follow the Nazi Party. Thirty percent were dissatisfied but not dangerous. Only 10 to 20 percent were unreliable and dangerous and were being eliminated.

A second report from a highly placed German official said that Göring in mid-September stated that the battles of Holland and the Rhine would decide the future of Europe. If the Anglo-Americans advanced rapidly, workers and peasants in Western Germany would refuse to implement scorched-earth orders, the Party would split, and the Army would demand an armistice. Western Germany would become part of Western Europe, and the Reich would disintegrate. If the enemy in the west stopped for two or three months, Hitler and Goebbels would be able to implement the scorched earth, and Russia would overrun the entire Reich.[138]

Strategic Bombing Starts to Hurt a Lot

American strategic daylight bombing in June had turned to an industry where its impact would undermine German capabilities on all fronts: oil. Spaatz ordered Eighth and Fifteenth Air Forces, with some support from RAF Bomber Command, to hit synthetic oil plants across the Reich from the UK and Italy, respectively. Air strikes during the month greatly reduced output, even at the cost of many bombers downed or damaged by the heavy flak protecting them. By the end of June, civilian and military leaders realized that the Americans threatened the very foundation of the ability to fight on. Hitler met with Grand Admiral Karl Dönitz, commander of the navy, and Keitel on 9 July, and the latter asked the navy to shift flak to the synthetic oil facilities. Keitel declared that, "at this time, the continuous destruction of these plants constitutes the greatest concern for the [further] conduct of the war." The Luftwaffe had to transfer some guns from Berlin and the Ruhr and strip Eisenach, Weimar, Chemnitz, and Dresden of flak.[139]

The Strategic Bombing Survey concluded:

> With the reduction of German air power, oil became the priority target in the German economy. The bomber force for several months had been adequate for the task. A preliminary attack was launched on 12 May 1944, followed by another on 28 May; the main blow was not struck, however, until after D-Day. In the months before D-Day and for a shorter period immediately following, all available air power based on England was devoted to insuring the success of the invasion. Albert Speer told interrogators, "I have to say that seen from my side of the picture, the American attacks with the effect as of May 1944 brought about the decision of the war, the attacks on the hydrogenation plants were so extensive that our troops on the front could not be supplied with the necessary amount of fuel. Even without the supply from Romania, we would have been in a position to keep the troops supplied with fuel, possibly this material would have been a little scarce. Without the attacks, we could have maintained a constant flow of fuel to the front."[140]
>
> Virtually complete records of the German oil industry were taken by the Survey. In addition, major plants that were subject to attack and their records were studied in detail.[141]

The hydrogenation plants were critical because the Soviets would soon overrun the Romanian oil fields.

> The German oil supply was tight throughout the war and was a controlling factor in military operations. The chief source of supply, and the only source for aviation gasoline, was 13 synthetic plants together with a small production from three additional ones that started operations in 1944. The major sources of products refined from crude oil were the Ploesti oil fields in Romania and the Hungarian fields, which together accounted for about a quarter of the total supply of liquid fuels in 1943. In addition, there was a small but significant Austrian and domestic production. The refineries at Ploesti were attacked, beginning with a daring and costly low-level attack in August 1943. These had only limited effects; deliveries increased until April 1944 when the attacks were resumed. The 1944 attacks, together with mining of the Danube, materially reduced Romanian deliveries. In August 1944, Russian occupation eliminated this source of supply and dependence on the synthetic plants became even greater than before.
>
> Production from the synthetic plants declined steadily and by July 1944 every major plant had been hit. These plants were producing an average of 316,000 tons per month when the attacks began. Their production fell to 107,000 tons in June and 17,000 tons in September. Output of aviation gasoline from synthetic plants dropped from 175,000 tons in April to 30,000 tons in July and 5,000 tons in September. Production recovered somewhat in November and December, but for the rest of the war was but a fraction of pre-attack output.
>
> The Germans viewed the attacks as catastrophic. In a series of letters to Hitler, among documents seized by the Survey, the developing crisis is outlined month by month in detail. On 30 June, Speer wrote: "The enemy has succeeded in increasing our losses of aviation gasoline up to 90 percent by 22 June. Only through speedy recovery of damaged plants has it been possible to regain partly some of the terrible losses." The tone of the letters that followed was similar....[142]

The Germans, naturally, worked frantically to restore output, and the Allies had to bomb the targets almost continuously to keep them off line, even at a high cost in bombers and crews.

> The synthetic oil plants were brought back into partial production and in remarkably short time. But unlike the ball-bearing plants, as soon as they were brought back, they were attacked again. The story of Leuna is illustrative. Leuna was the largest of the synthetic plants and protected by a highly effective smoke screen and the heaviest flak concentration in Europe. Air crews viewed a mission to Leuna as the most dangerous and difficult assignment of the air war. Leuna was hit on 12 May and put out of production. However, investigation of plant records and interrogation of Leuna's officials established that a force of several thousand men had it in partial operation in about 10 days. It was again hit on 28 May but resumed partial production on 3 June and reached 75 percent of capacity in early July. It was hit again on 7 July and again shut down but production started two days later and reached 53 percent of capacity on 19 July. An attack on 20 July shut the plant down again but only for three days; by 27 July, production was back to 35 percent of capacity. Attacks on 28 and 29 July closed the plant and further attacks on 24 August, 11 September, 13 September, 28 September, and 7 October kept it closed down. However, Leuna got started again on 14 October and although production was interrupted by a small raid on 2 November, it reached 28 percent of capacity by 20 November. Although there were six more heavy attacks in November and December (largely ineffective because of adverse weather), production was brought up to 15 percent of capacity in January and was maintained at that level until nearly the end of the war. From the first attack to the end, production at Leuna averaged 9 percent of capacity. There were 22 attacks on Leuna, 20 by the Eighth Air Force and two by the RAF. Due to the urgency of keeping this plant out of production, many of these missions were dispatched in difficult bombing weather. Consequently, the order of bombing accuracy on Leuna was not high as compared with other targets. To win the battle with Leuna, a total of 6,552 bomber sorties were flown against the plant, 18,328 tons of bombs were dropped, and an entire year was required.[143]

Ponder for a moment the massive advantage in material resources that allowed the Allies to direct that scale of destruction against a single industrial facility over a period of months. The number of bomber sorties and tonnage dropped totaled about twice the number of each devoted to the week-long Operation *Gomorrah* that destroyed Hamburg.

Strategic bombing was hurting war industry indirectly, too, by diverting two million workers to clean up and damage repair of the oil and railroad systems. The synthetic fuel industry alone had 150,000 workers so employed. Speer told a group of Nazi Gauleiters in August 1944 that the diversion of labor—only Germans could be trusted—was reducing armament production by 30 percent.[144]

In September 1944, focused strategic bombing of Germany's railroad and inland waterways systems commenced. The Strategic Bombing Survey assessed:

> The attack on transportation was the decisive blow that completely disorganized the German economy. It reduced war production in all categories and made it difficult to move what was produced to the front. The attack also limited the tactical mobility of the German army.
>
> The Survey made a careful examination of the German railway system, beginning as soon as substantial portions were in Allied hands. While certain important records were destroyed or lost during the battle of Germany, enough were located so that together with interrogation of

many German railroad officials, it was possible to construct an accurate picture of the decline and collapse of the system....

Although prior to September 1944, there had been sporadic attacks on the German transportation system, no serious deterioration in its ability to handle traffic was identified by the Survey. The vastly heavier attacks in September and October 1944 on marshaling yards, bridges, lines, and on train movements, produced a serious disruption in traffic over all of western Germany. Freight car loadings, which were approximately 900,000 cars for the Reich as a whole in the week ending 19 August fell to 700,000 cars in the last week of October. There was some recovery in early November, but thereafter they declined erratically to 550,000 cars in the week ending 23 December and to 214,000 cars during the week ending 3 March. Thereafter the disorganization was so great that no useful statistics were kept....

The attack on the waterways paralleled that on the railways; the investigation shows that it was even more successful. On 23 September 1944, the Dortmund-Ems and Mittelland canals were interdicted, stopping all through water traffic between the Ruhr and points on the north coast and in central Germany. By 14 October, traffic on the Rhine had been interdicted by a bomb that detonated a German demolition charge on a bridge at Cologne. Traffic in the Ruhr dropped sharply and all water movement of coal to south Germany ceased.

The effect of this progressive traffic tie-up was found, as might be expected, to have first affected commodities normally shipped in less-than-trainload lots—finished and semi-finished manufactured goods, components, perishable consumer goods and the less bulky raw materials. Cars loaded with these commodities had to be handled through the marshaling yards and after the September and October attacks this became increasingly difficult or impossible. Although output of many industries reached a peak in late summer and declined thereafter, total output of the economy was on the whole well-maintained through November. Beginning in December there was a sharp fall in production in nearly all industries; week by week the decline continued until the end of the war.[145]

For the RAF, Bomber Harris judged that Germany's nighttime air defense crumbled to pieces in September. Losses to flak and night fighters plummeted, in part because the Germans lacked the fuel and pilots to fly more than a handful of the available night fighters. Eighth Air Force also observed a drop-off in the effectiveness of flak in late 1944, in part because of ammunition shortages caused by damage to the chemical industry and transportation systems that moved ammo to the guns.[146]

Adam Tooze summarized Germany's war potential shortfall thusly: "What Germany faced by 1944 was simply the crushing material superiority that German strategists has always feared." Germany that year had produced 34,100 combat aircraft. America, Britain, and the USSR had built 127,300, of which the former manufactured 71,400. Germany had produced 18,300 tanks, and the three Allies 54,100. Similar disparities characterized other measures, such as steel output.[147]

Japan: No Joy on Any Front

Ugaki recorded in his diary on 20 August, "The enemy has established bridgeheads at Toulon and Marseilles in southern France while U.S. forces are advancing on Paris from three directions. The Vichy government has moved elsewhere, and it seems that Paris will fall into enemy hands soon. I think the Germans should put up more resistance. It's regrettable for the Axis powers to see that we're having a bad time both in the west and the east."[148]

Perhaps deceived by Oshima's conversation with Ribbentrop in July that suggested Hitler might consider making peace with one of his enemies, Japanese Foreign Minister Shigemitsu in late August urged the Germans to seek terms with the Soviet Union now that the Russians had reached their prewar borders in order to concentrate its remaining strength against the Anglo-Americans. "It is difficult to know what conditions Russia might require of Germany.... The position of the Japanese Government is that, if we are to achieve victory in our joint war, it is essential for Germany to make peace with Russia, irrespective of the disadvantages involved, and thus bring about a new turn in the war situation."[149] Shigemitsu's fantastical notions mark the end of the long-running, high-quality analysis of the global conflict from the foreign ministry.

Shigemitsu on 30 August informed the Japanese ambassador in Nanking that the Supreme Council for the Direction of the War had decided to make one more bid to reach terms with the Nationalist government in Chungking via the Nanking government. Nanking radioed a message to Chungking in mid-September.[150]

Despite rallying cries from the leadership and media propaganda, some Japanese were beginning to gloomily contemplate their future at American hands. The Portuguese minister in Tokyo reported on 3 September, "The events in [Europe] have only partially been revealed to the people, and an erroneous impression is being given of their importance and consequences. The press also publishes editorials concerning the Pacific, which are absurd and ridiculous. Nevertheless, not only are future air attacks on Japan predicted, but even eventual invasion is now admitted to be probable." The Spanish minister about the same time cabled Madrid, "My previous impression that the Japanese are worried about the gravity of their situation has now been confirmed by the effects of the decline of the German army in Europe ..., the American advance in the Pacific, the loss of 70 percent of merchant shipping, and the relative insufficiency of Japanese resources for a long struggle."[151]

For the first time, Japanese ambassador to the USSR Sato and other diplomats in late August raised in blunt terms the danger that once Germany was finished, the Anglo-Americans would be able to convince Moscow to join the war against Japan. Sato concluded that "the situation plainly demands that we strengthen our determination to continue our dashing fight to the very end, and to pursue a course of action that will not bring shame upon the leading power in Asia."[152]

By early October 1944, Kido, too, was becoming worried over Germany's fate. He told General Shizuichi Tanaka, commander of the Army Staff College, "I think Germany will win, but I am somewhat uncertain. What do you think of the outcome of the war, you as a general?" He told Tanaka that Japan would never lose the war and could fight it to a draw.[153]

The German military attaché in Tokyo met on 21 October with General Kotoku Sato, chief of the Political Division of the War Ministry and member of the Imperial General Headquarters. Sato portrayed the American advances in the Pacific and British operations against Burma as a coordinated strategy of concentric attacks, dominated by the American thrust. Mindanao in the southern Philippines was too far away for operations by the Japanese fleet, which would be directed toward Luzon. Enemy air superiority rendered the defensive battles at Peleliu and Angaur difficult, and the Japanese had written off Morotai. The Japanese could only speculate about British plans for Burma, which would become possible with improved weather in November: "If the German army should fail to hold back the Anglo-Saxon forces, Japan's war prospects, especially in Burma, become much worse."

Sato continued that the Nationalists in China had men but insufficient arms to undertake any major action. Japan's operations there would have no political effect on Chiang, but they might increase air protection of the coastal routes between the southern area and Japan, strongly threatened by (American) airplanes and submarines. For now, the Soviets posed no threat to Manchuria, which was critical to Japan's survival. "A change of Russian attitude is eventually possible in the case of an outcome of the European war unfavorable to Germany."[154]

In China, the Japanese ambassador in Nanking in early October received a reply from the Nationalist government to Tokyo's peace feelers. Chungking would enter peace talks if Japan stopped attacks in China, established at home a system of "direct rule" by the Emperor, and punished those responsible for the China incident. The ambassador's Nanking contacts told him there was no chance of reaching a deal with the Nationalists as long as Japan's war situation in the Pacific continued to deteriorate.[155]

Nevertheless, a campaign to increase war production following the loss of Saipan led to the highest output of equipment during the entire war in the last six months of 1944. The Strategic Bombing Survey observed, "The aircraft and ordnance industries achieved particularly impressive gains in the last quarter of 1944; aircraft reaching its highest peak in October, ordnance in November. This was supported by peak output of metals in September and October." Urban industrial output rose 20 percent from April to October.[156]

This represented a last-gasp surge, however, and rapidly depleted stocks of raw materials. Metals production dropped in November and December. The American blockade of Japan and attacks on transport throughout the Pacific had starved the home islands. Stocks of iron ore in Honshu plummeted from 2.6 million tons in December 1941 to 800,000 tons by June 1944. The monthly average output of finished steel dropped 64 percent from the first to the second half of 1944. Oil imports in the last quarter of 1944 were 67 percent lower than in the same quarter of 1943. Imports of coking coal from China had virtually ceased by year's end, and coal imports from Manchuria were declining rapidly. American mining of harbors was strangling even domestic coal shipments. Bauxite imports had ended entirely by year's end.[157]

The Americans landed on Peleliu and Angaur, the western anchor of the Carolines, on 15 September. The Japanese had moved the 14th Division to the Palau Islands in April, and in light of heavy air strikes, the commander alerted his forces for invasion on the 12th. The 1st Marine Division assaulted Peleliu, while elements of the Army's 81st Infantry Division landed on Angaur. Hattori recorded:

> The enemy approached a point 13 km [8 miles] off the shore southwest of Peleliu aboard about 50 transports. Enemy troops then transferred to about 300 landing craft and approached the beach under cover of fierce bombardment and bombing. The garrison force ... counterattacked and sank more than 60 enemy craft and inflicted heavy losses by attacking enemy troops which had landed with tanks, and thus routed the enemy at 1000. At 1420 hours, the enemy attempted another landing, but the garrison force repulsed him with fierce counterattacks. Because another enemy force landed on the adjacent front, the garrison force again counterattacked and inflicted heavy losses. Subsequently, the enemy finally established a beachhead in that vicinity after being reinforced. The next day, unimaginably fierce fighting continued.[158]

The Japanese did not actually drive any marines into the sea, but they destroyed numerous landing craft and amphibious tractors with artillery, inflicted heavier than expected casualties, and kept much of the landing force pinned to the beach.[159] The landings on Angaur faced less effective resistance.

The Japanese on Peleliu fought on for nearly three months until organized resistance ended on 24 November. The Emperor sent them 10 messages of encouragement during the battle, and Hattori said, "These men displayed the true spirit of the Japanese Army." A Marine Corps history concluded,

> The costs at Peleliu held warnings aplenty for the remaining Allied operations to be conducted across the Pacific to Japan. Even with total local air and naval superiority, with lavish naval gunfire and bombs, with the dreaded napalm weaponry, and with a 4:1 troop superiority, the seizure of Peleliu consumed one American casualty and 1,589 rounds of heavy and light troop ammunition for each single Japanese defender killed or driven from his prepared position. A few months later, the attacks on Iwo Jima and Okinawa would confirm this grim calculus of war against determined Japanese defenders, ably led, in prepared defenses.[160]

It turned out that even overwhelming materiel superiority had its limits at the pointy end of the spear.

Elsewhere, the IJN in early October gained a fairly accurate picture of the American fleet from interrogations of pilots from the *Lexington*, who went down during a raid on the Philippines. From 10 to 18 October, American carrier aircraft, supported by B-29s from China, pounded Japanese targets on Formosa and in the Philippines. The Japanese implemented the air arm's aspects of *SHO-1*, which pitted fighters against the carrier-launched air attacks on Formosa and sent land-based bombers and torpedo bombers to attack task forces in range. On 16 October, IGHQ claimed to have sunk to date ten carriers, two battleships, three cruisers, and one destroyer and to have damaged three carriers, a battleship, four cruisers, and 11 other ships.

Ugaki was skeptical, and he was right. In reality, the Japanese had slightly damaged one carrier and two cruisers, but the announcement triggered victory celebrations in Japan. The Japanese lost 312 aircraft during these engagements, plus many destroyed on the ground.[161] Nevertheless, the illusory destruction of American ships boosted morale and led Koiso to proclaim, "Victory will be ours!"[162]

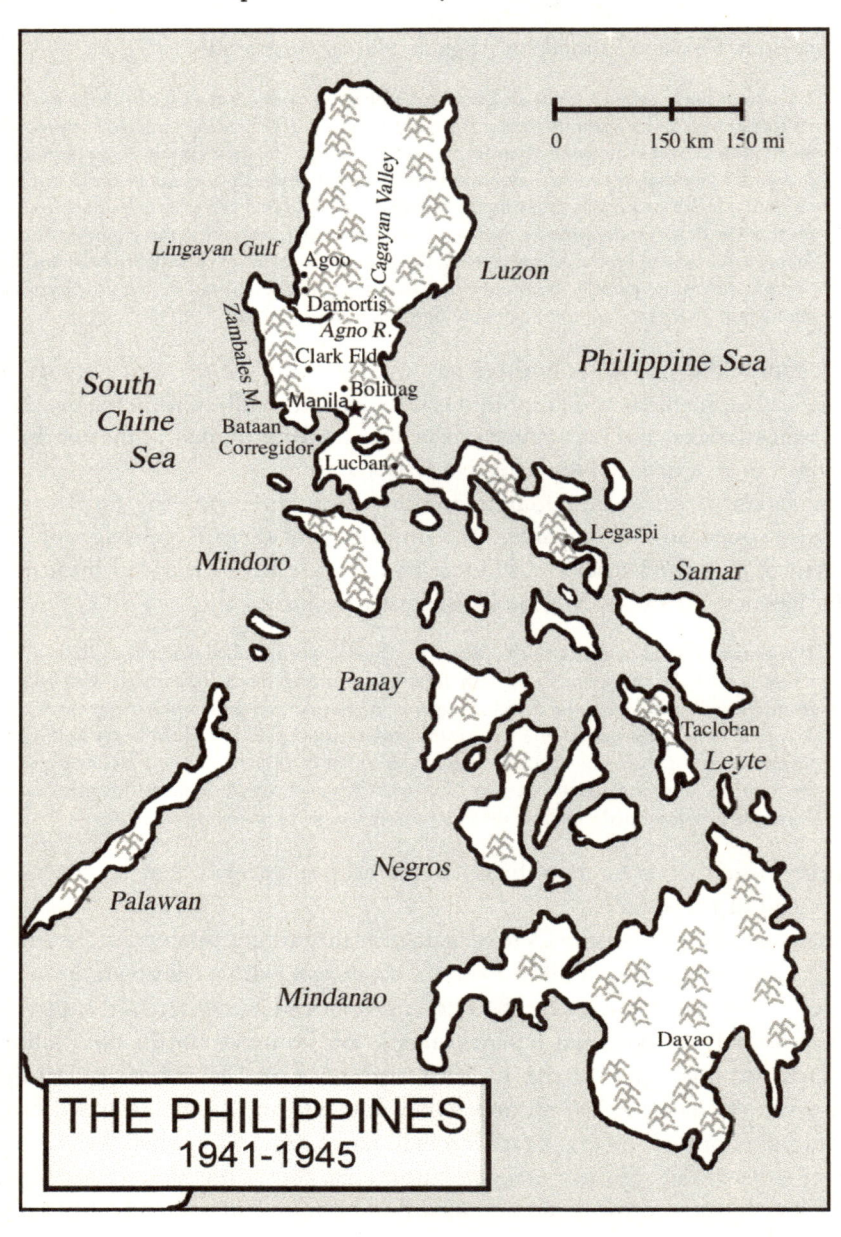

THE PHILIPPINES 1941-1945

Battle of the Philippines

On 17 October, Ugaki recorded in his diary, "No intelligence has been received lately indicating an attempt at large-scale invasion." The next day, reconnaissance reported 18 carriers, battleships, cruisers, and destroyers off Tacloban, on Leyte in the Philippines. "Landing is most likely," Ugaki recorded.[163]

The army and navy chiefs of staff reported to Hirohito on 18 October that an invasion of the Philippines was imminent and requested that he identify the islands as the theater for *SHO-1* and instruct them to attack the American main body in the anticipated decisive battle. Following the report, IGHQ initiated the operation as of 0000 hours on 19 October and ordered air forces to concentrate in the Philippines. Unfortunately, IGHQ was operating on the false assumption that they had sunk most of the American carrier force off Formosa.[164]

The IJN sent more than 1,000 combat aircraft. The 6th Base Air Force fielded 737, joined by 688 more. The IJN's two airbases on the island had 440 aircraft. The IJN was to send another 500 new aircraft, then 600 more two months after the American landings on Leyte. The IJA 4th Air Army, meanwhile, had 200 operational planes on Luzon and received 2,200 more between September and December 1944. The IJA in China had hardly any fighters left.[165]

The Combined Fleet activated *SHO* variant No. 1. The fleet was to enter the area of Tacloban on 25 October. Admiral Takeo Kurita commanded the main body, Second Fleet, consisting of battleships, cruisers, and destroyers, which was to penetrate Leyte Gulf and destroy the invasion fleet. A diversion force, Fifth Fleet, included the Third Carrier Division with four carriers carrying 80 Zeros (28 bomb-equipped) and 36 torpedo bombers. A second diversion force was built around a two-battleship detachment from the Second Battleship Division. The fairly accurate assessment of the American order of battle derived from POWs taken during the Formosa air battles identified 16 carriers, eight or nine battleships, 12–13 cruisers, and 40–45 destroyers.[166]

MacArthur's forces landed on Leyte on 20 October. This time, despite the Allies' information dominance, the Japanese surprised the enemy with a surface attack. The Americans anticipated some Japanese reaction but assumed it would center on aircraft carriers. As the naval battle developed from 23 October, signals intelligence provided the Americans with an at times confusing picture of the Japanese fleet that nevertheless far exceeded the Japanese insight into the Americans.[167]

Vice Admiral Takijiro Onishi arrived in Manila on 20 October to take command of First Air Fleet. The anticipated massive air strikes against the American fleet over the next two days turned out to be feeble. Apparently grasping that fact, he concluded that the only way to attack effectively from the air was to initiate suicide attacks. He ordered the organization of Kamikaze Special Attack units.[168] Kamikaze referred to the Divine Wind that had dispersed Mongol fleets in 1274 and 1281.[169]

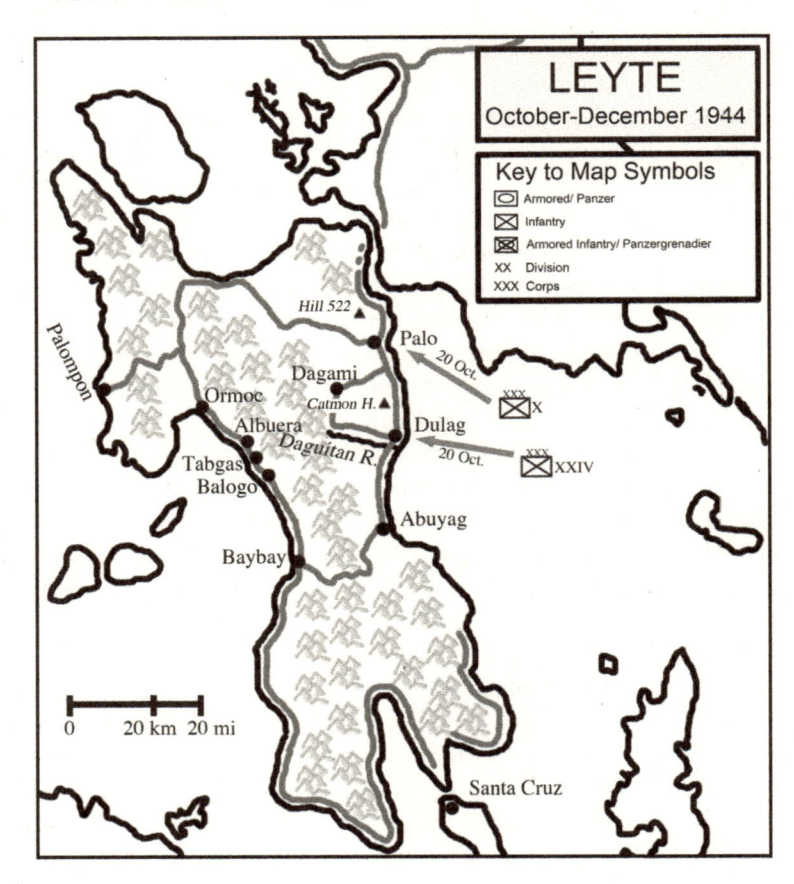

American planners had wanted to capture Leyte, in the heart of the Philippine islands, to obtain an air and logistical base to support planned operations on Luzon, Formosa, and the coast of China. Leyte offered coastal plains suitable for building airfields that would guarantee air supremacy over Luzon. The Leyte invasion would be the largest yet in the Pacific and require the help of ground, air, and naval assets from the Pacific Ocean Area.

Lieutenant General Walter Krueger's Sixth Army, which was to go ashore along Leyte's east coast, consisted of X and XXIV corps and had 174,000 troops available for the initial assault phase. Intelligence reports suggested that the Japanese 16th Division had some 22,000 men on the island, more than half of them combat troops. X Corps was to land on the army's right in the Palo area with the 24th Infantry Division, less one regiment, on its left and the 1st Cavalry Division—fighting as an infantry division with four regiments—on its right. XXIV Corps was to land 15 miles to the south in the Dulag area, with its 7th Infantry Division on its left and 96th Infantry Division on the right.

Japanese combat strength was concentrated in this area. The Japanese battle plan anticipated that the Americans would land on Leyte and Mindanao before Luzon, where the decisive battle was to occur. Lieutenant General Sesaku Suzuki assigned the 100th Division to defend the Davao area on Mindanao and the 16th Division to Leyte Gulf. He had in reserve the 30th and 102d divisions. The latter division would have to move by transports to Leyte to counterattack.[170]

Meanwhile, the battle of the Philippine Sea was another Japanese "decisive battle" disaster. American submarines torpedoed four cruisers on 23 October as the van approached the battle area, two of which sank with two put out of action. The next day, wave after wave of American carrier aircraft bombed and torpedoed the Japanese fleet. In Ugaki's First Battleship Division, two bombs struck the huge *Yamato* and two more *Nagato*, while *Musashi* took 19 torpedoes and 17 bombs and sank. The fight was not entirely one-sided. Japanese land-based bombers damaged the light carrier *Princeton* so badly she had to be sunk by American torpedoes.

Ugaki finally got his wish for a surface battle on 25 October, when his First Battleship Division spotted three carriers (thought to be fleet carriers but only escort carriers), three cruisers, and two destroyers—a surprise to both sides. His division, followed by the majority of the Second Battleship Division, rushed to attack, firing from their forward turrets at 31,000 meters (about 34,000 yards) and closing, despite a smoke screen and squalls, to 22,000 meters. Japanese battleships now possessed ranging radars and used them as the smoke thickened. More units on both sides became engaged, hitting one another with heavy and medium gunfire, and Ugaki at one point witnessed planes leaving the deck of a carrier to strafe his ships. Indeed, American warplanes claimed several victims. Dodging torpedoes complicated tactical maneuver.

In the meantime, a detached force from the Second Division, including two battleships, met disaster. The division lost every vessel but a destroyer to American battleships in the battle of Surigao Strait. The Third and Fourth Carrier divisions conducting a diversionary operation lost four carriers, including *Zuikaku*, *Zuiho*, *Chitose*, and *Chiyoda*.

The Japanese fleet turned for home, harassed by American air attacks that caused further serious damage to *Yamato* and sank a light cruiser. Radio Tokyo announced a great Japanese naval victory had established control over Leyte.[171]

Returning to the kamikazes, the Japanese were just unleashing a weapon that would wreak havoc on American warships for the rest of the war. Now an ensign, pilot Sakai recalled:

> On October 27, 10 days after the first American troops stormed ashore in the Philippines, Imperial Headquarters issued this historic communiqué:
> "The Shikishima Unit of the Kamikaze Special Attack Corps, at 1045 hours on 25 October 1944, succeeded in a surprise attack against the enemy task force, including four aircraft carriers.... Two Special Attack planes plunged together into an enemy carrier, causing great fires

and explosions, and probably sinking the warship. A third plane plunged into another carrier, setting huge fires. A fourth plane plunged into a cruiser, causing a tremendous explosion which sank the vessel immediately afterward."

This was the thunderous beginning of the kamikazes.... As a fighter pilot, I was never inclined to approve of suicide missions, but now there was no denying the tremendous blow which had been struck at the American fleet off the Philippines. Even I had to acknowledge the fact that the suicide dives appeared to be our only means of striking back at the American warships.... The kamikazes gave us tremendous new strength....

This was not suicidal. These men, young and old, were not dying in vain. Every plane which thundered into an American warship was a blow struck for our land. Every bomb carried by a kamikaze into the fuel tanks of a giant carrier means that many more of the enemy killed, that many more planes which would never bomb or strafe our soil....

Again, however, it was a case of too little too late.[172]

On the ground on Leyte, by 30 October, the Japanese Thirty-Fifth Army reported, "The enemy landing strength is much larger than had been expected. Furthermore, the enemy commenced the attack immediately from the beachhead and is already dashing toward the Carigara Plain. On the other hand, our 16th Division has nearly lost its capacity to conduct organized fighting."[173]

By 8 November, Ugaki told his diary, "The land battle on Leyte was also extremely unfavorable to us, and the enemy has established positions almost all over the island." The next day he was appalled to receive a report from the Operations Bureau of the Naval General Staff that the navy expected to have on hand only 418 planes of all types, plus 410 replacements, by the end of the month. "My God! Eight hundred planes! How can we manage with this strength?"[174]

Suicide attacks against the American fleet became the main weapon for the defenders. From November to January 1945, the Fourth Air Army carried out 62 kamikaze attacks with 400 aircraft, while the First Air Fleet launched 106 attacks with 436 aircraft.[175] They were to sink one already damaged escort carrier and damage seven fleet, two light, and 13 escort carriers; five battleships; three heavy and seven light cruisers; and 23 destroyers, plus other ships.[176]

Thirty-Fifth Army on 19 December ordered its remaining troops to withdraw into the mountains in western Leyte and resist in place. Thus, the Japanese effectively ended the battle for the island.[177]

The New Bomber Menace

The Americans had been busily constructing airfields for B-29s in the Marianas. Ugaki recorded that B-29s bombed Truk and that two others, launched from Saipan, scouted Tokyo on 1 November. Pilot Sakai recalled that fighter pilots tried to reach the bombers at some 30,000 feet but failed; this happened again the next day. As if that were not enough, 53 B-29s flying from India on the 5th knocked out the most important docks in Singapore for the next three months.[178]

On 24 November, the Twenty-First Bomber Command launched from Saipan the first raid on Tokyo 1,500 miles distant. One hundred eleven bombers struck the Nakajima Aircraft Works at Musahino, near Tokyo. Bombers heavily damaged Mitsubishi's main engine plant on 13 December and the biggest airframe plant on the 19th. Aircraft production dropped by a third. During the period through 9 March 1945, the B-29s flew 20 major missions, 16 of them against the aircraft industry. Four experimental urban bombings of Tokyo, Kobe, and Nagoya tested the effects of various types of ordnance on Japanese cities.[179]

Japan's weather provided the home islands with some protection. Strong fronts interfered with navigation, and clouds often obscured targets. Even on clear days, high winds at high altitudes played hob with accuracy.[180]

Japanese fighter pilots and flak initially offered stiff resistance. Their effectiveness peaked in January 1945, when more than 5 percent of bombers were lost to enemy action or unexplained causes.[181]

A U.S. Army Air Force analysis of Tokyo's antiaircraft defenses based on photography current as of 11 March 1945 showed that Japan had implemented many of the lessons they had obtained from Germany, although the analysts themselves did not draw that conclusion. They did, however, draw parallels: "This is as many guns as ever protected the German capital of Berlin."

They also called the flak strongpoints "grossbatteries," presumably because they resembled the German practice of having multiple batteries surround a fire control radar. Picking out one example for close examination, the analysts noted, "three of the four grossbatteries in this little defense are radar-controlled." The defense layout around the city also conformed to the basic principles held by U.S. doctrine concerning location relative to target, anticipating a B-29 at 30,000 feet and 300 mph ground speed entering its bombing run and no longer able to take evasive action.

The analysts warned,

> We can't forget missions like the XX Bomber Command B-29 attack on the Singapore Naval Base on 2 March 1945 (see Hq. AAF Intelligence Summary No. 45–8). In opposing this attack, the Japanese defenses were extremely well conducted, engaging formations attacking at altitudes between 19,000 and 25,000 feet with intense and accurate heavy AA fire. Throughout the engagement the flak defenses exhibited a high standard of skill, accuracy, fire discipline and fire direction. It was no small-time flak defense that did this.... If right now the Jap cannot match the German in the quality of his flak, that doesn't necessarily mean that he cannot improve.[182]

Japan's would-be Chinese puppet, Wang Ching Wei, died in Nagoya, Japan, on 13 November.

Two days later, the Japanese fleet underwent a major reorganization. The First Battleship Division was disbanded and Ugaki relieved of command. Sailing aboard *Yamato* back to Japan with a convoy of damaged battleships due for refitting and their escorts, Ugaki on 21 November witnessed the torpedoing of battleship

Kongo by the *Sealion*. *Kongo* sank on the way to port for temporary repairs. *Sealion* also sank a destroyer. That same day, B-29s from China bombed Kyushu, Japan.[183]

Ugaki on 31 December recorded, "We sent off the year of the decisive battle, again having failed to turn the tide of the war. Not only that, we have been further pressed into a corner, and the rise and fall of the empire is now at stake."[184]

Germany's Last Offensive

By early December, Hitler had assembled 28 divisions for his Ardennes offensive, Operation *Wacht Am Rhein* (Watch on the Rhine). This was the largest reserve Germany had been able to accumulate in two years, albeit much weaker numerically than the strike force available when German troops had rolled through the same area in 1940. Factories and repair shops, working furiously, had supplied 1,349 tanks and assault guns in November, and another 950 were delivered in December.[185] Troops below the level of officers and NCOs, however, often were new to battle.

Hitler's plan, delivered to Rundstedt complete to the last detail with "NOT TO BE ALTERED" scrawled across it in the Führer's own handwriting, called for a three-pronged offensive along a 75-mile front between Monschau, Germany, and Echternach, Luxembourg. In the north, the Sixth SS Panzer Army was to strike toward and then cross the River Meuse before heading northwest for Antwerp. In the center, the Fifth Panzer Army was to attack toward Brussels. The German Seventh Army was to reel out a line of infantry divisions to protect the southern flank of the operation. Hitler expected to cut off the Americans in the Aachen area and all the British forces to the north. It just so happened that American troops held the sector through which the Wehrmacht would attack.

Hitler hoped that an epic military disaster would breach Allied solidarity and cause them to seek a negotiated end to the war. He often cited the case of Frederick the Great of Prussia, whose enemies' coalition came apart just when he faced strategic defeat. During planning in October, he declared that the main goal was to destroy Allied forces, not win ground.[186] In this, he sounded surprisingly like Eisenhower.

Launched on 16 December against a thinly held part of the American line, the attack caught the Allies by surprise. In Japan, Vice Admiral Ugaki noted the start of the German offensive in his diary. "I wish them success."[187]

Despite elaborate German safeguards, Allied intelligence picked up many signs of the buildup but, by and large, dismissed the possibility of a German offensive because of a false preconception: Such an attack would be doomed to defeat and therefore irrational to undertake. Hitler was rolling the dice in a bigger game. He hoped that he could drive a wedge deep enough into the Allied camp to induce his enemies to come to terms rather than insist on unconditional surrender.

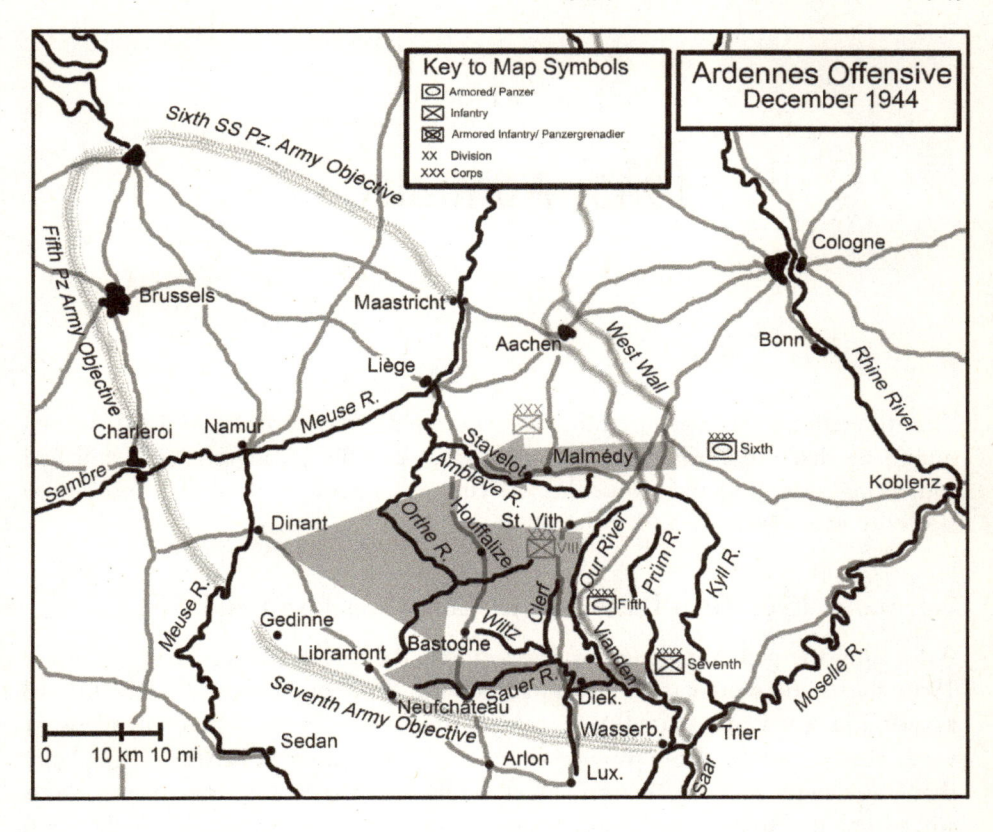

At its greatest penetration, the Bulge extended sixty miles deep and forty miles wide. By the end of the six-week battle, 600,000 American troops had fought 550,000 Germans and beaten them. For the most part, the fighting did not turn on the well-planned movements of large formations. Instead, much of it unfolded at the level of small units and individuals—what generals and commentators at the time described as "fluid."[188]

CHAPTER 15

1945: Annihilation

The difference in leadership thinking between the Axis powers in 1945 turned out to be that the Nazis had nothing to lose, and the Japanese leaders still had something—the Imperial House. Yet the Japanese, having realized that, moved too slowly to avoid being nuked.

Germany: Eyes Turn Back East in Cloud Cuckoo Land

A decision emerged from the *Führerbunker* under the ruins of Berlin during February 1945 that underscored the de-emphasis of the Western Front: 1,675 tanks and assault guns (new or repaired) were sent to the Eastern Front, while only 67 went west. The Führer was more worried about the Soviet threat to Berlin and Hungary than the danger that the Western Allies would leap the Rhine.[1] The panzer assets still available were concentrated opposite Montgomery's command, where the main thrust was expected.

Flak batteries also moved to the east, where they were needed to fight Soviet tanks. The Western Allies had 10,000 bombers and 13,000 fighters, and the remaining guns did what they could to stop them.[2]

"The entire western front had been so weakened after the Ardennes offensive that a defense was no longer possible, only a delaying battle to buy time," recalled Brigadier General Carl Wagener, Army Group B's chief of staff. There were not enough forces at the front, reserves, fuel, or ammunition. The most sensible idea was to pull back across the Rhine, but not only was that notion out of the question at OKW, until February there was a ban in place on even constructing defensive positions on the east bank of the river.[3]

The state of German weakness is impossible to exaggerate. As of 1 February, the Third Reich had less than three and a half months left. This was a vastly different situation from the time Germany capitulated in World War I. Then, its armies still had the means to fight, and the Western Allies expected it to hold the Rhine into 1919. General Erich Ludendorff lost hope in victory and could no longer justify the war, giving rise to the idea of the stab in the back against a still undefeated army.[4] Now, Germany's armies were defeated and in tatters on all fronts. Hitler knew that for him and his regime, surrender offered no prospect of survival.

Ambassador Oshima encountered Ribbentrop at the Foreign Ministry on 3 February, shortly after an extremely heavy bombing of Berlin. The Foreign Minister was just returning from an inspection of the Oder Front. He told Oshima, "In view of the advance of Russian forces toward Berlin, every possible precautionary measure is naturally being taken. However, even if Berlin should become a battlefield, the High Command and the Government would, as a matter of course, remain in Berlin and defend to the last man."

Oshima admitted in a cable the next day that people were depressed, but there were no signs of political unrest or the loss of fighting spirit. "[T]he present Soviet attack shook the entire eastern front and gave rise to a feeling of uncertainty in the country … "[5]

Ribbentrop on 16 February sent a delusional cable to the German missions in Dublin, Lisbon, Madrid, and the Vatican and instructed them to find a way to convey an oral message to "important English and American personalities." The thrust of the message was that Germany was going to have to choose between the East and West, and that if Britain and America were unwilling to make terms, Germany would negotiate with Russia. It was naïve to expect that announced occupation zones would prevent Soviet control over Europe, he argued. The USSR and a communist Germany would be "swallowed up" and America left alone. "The English Crown, the English Conservative Party, and the American governing class should therefore wish that nothing should happen to Adolf Hitler."[6]

*

Following the Yalta Conference, where Churchill, Roosevelt, and Stalin carved up postwar Europe, Ribbentrop told Oshima on 19 February:

> As yet I have not received any reliable information about the Three Powers Conference, but according to our present information and the impressions we have received, the conference was in the main a victory for Stalin. Just as was expected, the three leaders settled their differences on such matters as the Polish problem, and England and the United States accepted in toto the [Soviet-created Polish] Lublin regime. Furthermore, the fact that no reference was made to the Balkans at the conference can only be interpreted as indicating that those countries are to be dealt with according to Russia's interests.
>
> I myself do not find it impossible to understand why the United States is pursuing the policy she is. If she can, with the help of Russia, wreck Europe and then destroy the war potential of Japan, her capitalism will be able to swagger throughout the world. [The next sentence is not clear but refers to England as "allowing Europe to be bolshevized and doing nothing more than increasing her dependence on the United States."][7]

That same day, the nineteenth, Japanese naval attaché Rear Admiral Hideo Kojima and representative on the Tripartite Pact Commission Vice Admiral Katsuo Abe sent an appraisal of Germany's military situation to Tokyo:

> Judging from the views expressed by German authorities, it appears that the German Army is planning in the near future to stake everything on a large scale counterattack in the East, based on the [Prenslau and Cottbus areas].... However, according to the various reports we have been able to obtain, ... the chances of success are poor. If the attack fails, Germany's ability to continue the war will be lost and there will be a danger of complete collapse, except for a certain amount of guerrilla warfare.
>
> Even if the internal situation in this last phase should undermine the German Army's spirit of resistance and the Russians should approach Berlin, Hitler and the government officials would remain in the capital to the end and fight on with determination. It is impossible to say whether the troops and people would follow their example. It is not known whether Hitler plans to commit suicide when he has lost all hope of German recovery.[8]

Oshima on 15 March conveyed a picture of Berlin that revealed how out of touch with reality the German leadership was:

> So far as the date of the German counterattack [on the eastern front] is concerned, it appears that considerable time will be needed for preparation, and there are some who say that they have been led to believe it will take place about the middle of April. Although it is realized that the danger to Berlin will thereby be increased, it is said that Berlin is making preparations to defend itself to the death and that, if the Russian forces cross the Oder and advance on the capital, Germany will take advantage of that situation and attempt to annihilate the Russian Army....
>
> Everyone is unanimously agreed that Germany's operations on the eastern front should take the form of a crushing battle.... Germany is facing unprecedented difficulties because of her general inferiority in aircraft and tanks and because of the campaign inflicted on her transportation system by the continuous air attacks. Although these difficulties are recognized, there is still quite a strong feeling of unwillingness to admit defeat....
>
> As to the western front, it is considered regrettable that a crossing to the east bank of the Rhine should have been permitted, even if only in one sector [at Remagen by U.S. First Army]. While such a crossing is not to be taken lightly, both because of its military and political significance, it is still considered that Germany's most urgent need is to fight a decisive battle on the eastern front. Accordingly, the Germans say that it is inevitable that various sacrifices should have to be made on the western front, but no one is pessimistic because of the war situation there.[9]

Equally disconnected from reality, Ribbentrop approached Oshima in mid-March and asked the assistance of the Japanese military attaché in Stockholm in extending a peace feeler to Stalin, making clear that he had not vetted the idea yet with Hitler. Oshima met Ribbentrop on the 27th, and the foreign minister told him Hitler had told him Germany must "rely on military results to the bitter end." The next day, he told Oshima he had spoken again with Hitler, who remained utterly opposed to the idea. Asked whether Hitler also opposed peace with England and America, Ribbentrop said, "The Chancellor has categorically refused such a thing as a compromise peace with America and England."[10]

*

OKW Chief of Operations Jodl told interrogators after the war,

> I would say in general that in the end the winning of complete air superiority in the whole area of the war has altogether decided the war. I would go so far as to say that our power on land was numerically and, from the point of armament, sufficiently strong, if not to win, at least to hold our own on all fronts, if our own Air Force had kept up on the same level.... In the long run, the most effective thing was after all the strategic bombing against the Zone of the Interior, because there the root and the basis for all armament and war potential was hit and the effect increased from one attack to another. Even if the Luftwaffe had remained strong enough so that we could have temporarily carried on successful operations at the front, it would have done us no good if in the meantime the foundations of our armaments industry were being destroyed, and the transport as well, and the hydrogenation plants.[11]

Jodl's statement, however, does not reflect the fact that his ground forces had already lost the war by the time strategic bombing crippled war production inside the Reich.

The Strategic Bombing Survey attempted to assess the cumulative destruction of Germany's civilian population:

> Official German statistics place total casualties from air attack—including German civilians, foreigners, and members of the armed forces in cities that were being attacked—at 250,253 killed for the period from 1 January 1943 to 31 January 1945, and 305,455 wounded badly enough to require hospitalization, during the period from 1 October 1943 to 31 January 1945. A careful examination of these data, together with checks against the records of individual cities that were attacked, indicates that they are too low. A revised estimate prepared by the Survey (which is also a minimum) places total casualties for the entire period of the war at 305,000 killed and 780,000 wounded. More reliable statistics are available on damage to housing. According to these, 485,000 residential buildings were totally destroyed by air attack and 415,000 were heavily damaged, making a total of 20 percent of all dwelling units in Germany. In some 50 cities that were primary targets of the air attack, the proportion of destroyed or heavily damaged dwelling units is about 40 percent. The result of all these attacks was to render homeless some 7,500,000 German civilians.
>
> The mental reaction of the German people to air attack is significant. Under ruthless Nazi control they showed surprising resistance to the terror and hardships of repeated air attack, to the destruction of their homes and belongings, and to the conditions under which they were reduced to live. Their morale, their belief in ultimate victory or satisfactory compromise, and their confidence in their leaders declined, but they continued to work efficiently as long as the physical means of production remained. The power of a police state over its people cannot be underestimated.[12]

Hitler's aides told Soviet interrogators that Hitler seemed rather uninterested that German cities were being reduced to ruins. Once he said, "You find better cover in ruins and can defend yourself better." On another occasion, he remarked, "After the war I shall build much more beautiful cities than those that have been destroyed. I actually have to be grateful to the Anglo-Americans that they have saved me the work of pulling down parts of towns I wanted to rebuild."[13]

The End

Amidst the collapse, Ribbentrop held a tea party for Japanese diplomats and journalists on 4 April. It was a time for regrets and fantastical thinking. He acknowledged that the Japanese probably thought the decision to attack the USSR had been a mistake, but he said at the time, Germany lacked the air power to invade England and "a quick, decisive war was impossible." There were signs that Stalin, meanwhile, was planning to stab Germany in the back.

As for the current situation, according to MAGIC: "The collapse of the western front makes it useless to consider diplomatic plans at present. If the front is again stabilized, the enemy will probably realize the futility of continuing the war and there will again be room for diplomatic activity.... Germany will try to get out of her present crisis by considerably increasing submarine warfare, and by the use of new fighter planes."[14]

Oshima met Hitler on 12 April and reported the next day,

> Last evening, I had a chance to talk to Chancellor Hitler and he has still not abandoned hope that there will be a turn in the war situation. On the eastern front there are strong indications that the Russian Army will launch a large-scale offensive from the Oder front in the next few days, but we expect to be able to repulse it. The penetration of the Anglo-American armies is extremely deep and it is urgently necessary to stabilize that front, at the very least. Therefore, we will have to counterattack at once. While one cannot prophesy today as to the success of the attack, I think that it will be carried out soon.[15]

Ribbentrop on 13 April informed Oshima that in light of the rapid advance by the Anglo-American armies, Hitler might order the relocation of the government to southern Germany within the course of the day. Oshima replied that he wished to remain in close contact to the very end, regardless of the danger involved. That night at 0100, the Foreign Ministry Protocol Office told him that diplomats remaining in Berlin were requested to evacuate immediately to Badgastein, near Salzburg. When Oshima contacted Ribbentrop, the German said Hitler would consider moving the government and High Command south after developments had been studied a little longer.[16]

Oshima left a ten-man team in Berlin, the head of which reported on 16 April from a regular contact of Oshima:

> The Soviet offensive in the Kuestrin area appears to be not merely a diversionary attack, but the beginning of a real offensive....
> In the West, while the Elbe front has for the moment been stabilized, the situation in Saxony is very bad. The American forces, following the super-highway from Thuringia, are attempting to push ahead to Dresden, and their vanguard has already reached Chemnitz....
> Government agencies for the most part have been moved to South Germany, but Chancellor Hitler himself—together with Göring, Goebbels, Ribbentrop, and Himmler—still remain in Berlin.[17]

Hitler's last references to America came as the Soviets closed on Berlin and were wholly delusional. Hitler misinterpreted Harry Truman's speech upon ascending to the Presidency following Roosevelt's death on 12 April as meaning America would not stand in his way as he continued to battle bolshevism. On 16 April, he said referring to Roosevelt's death, "Now that fate has rid the world of the greatest war criminal of all times, there will come a turning in the tides of war."[18]

Unrelated to Roosevelt's death, the strategic bombing campaign ceased on 16 April for want of targets in Germany. With fighting occurring in Berlin itself, the remaining Japanese destroyed their cryptographic material on 21 April. On 25 April, U.S. First Army linked with Soviet troops at Torgau.[19]

Military adjutant Günsche was present at the daily briefing on 22 April when Hitler, straightening from the situation map, cried in a faltering voice, "Nothing like this has ever happened before! Under these circumstances, I cannot command any more. The war is lost! But if you gentlemen think that I am going to leave Berlin, you are making a very big mistake. I'd rather blow my brains out!" He raised his hand feebly, said, "Thank you, good sirs," and walked out.[20]

Hitler shot himself in the head on 30 April.

On 5 May, Keitel transmitted to "ALL: At 0800B/5/5/45, hostilities ceased against Field Marshal Montgomery's troops. This includes all units of the Army, the Navy, the Air Force, and the SS.... Inform all subordinate troops immediately. Verify receipt of order. Troops remain in position with their weapons. Transport

Lieutenant General Alfred Jodl, Chief of Staff under the Dönitz regime after Hitler's suicide, signs the document of unconditional surrender on 8 May 1945. (NARA)

movements of the Navy at sea are to continue.... Maintain strict obedience and discipline. Further orders follow."[21] Similar orders reached the entire armed forces.

German representatives signed documents of capitulation in the early hours of 7 May. To the world, General of the Army Dwight Eisenhower declared simply, "The mission of this Allied Force was fulfilled at 0241, local time, May 7, 1945."

At midnight on 8 May, the war in Europe was over for everyone.

*

American interrogators asked Keitel on 27 June 1945 whether he thought Japan could defend itself against American heavy bombers. "I don't know," he replied, "but I believe that the defensive power of Japan cannot stand up to this type of bomber warfare.... I judge the situation as much more serious for the Japanese than it was for us."[22]

Japan: Fighting Until Too Late

IGHQ assessed the state of the war in early January and concluded:

1. The enemy will rapidly increase his direct pressure upon the vital areas of Japan, Manchuria, and China and completely isolate our remaining positions in the various parts of the Southern Region and Pacific.
2. Despite our utmost efforts, the period of time during which Japan can carry out organized warfare will end about the middle of 1945. After that, emphasis in our operations and war guidance will inevitably be shifted to guerrilla warfare. Also, the domestic situation, if it follows its present course, will develop various obstacles to war guidance.
3. The period of time during which Japan can count on Germany to continue fighting will end about the middle of 1945....
4. The Soviet Union will surely abrogate the Soviet-Japanese Neutrality Pact, but it is improbable that she will enter the war against Japan or lease bases to the United States before she terminates her war against Germany, which will come about the middle of 1945.[23]

Japan faced the obvious choice of trying to end the war or fighting until the bitter end. And yet, no discussion of that choice occurred in the military or government leadership. The only way to end the war was to surrender unconditionally. Hattori charges that the civilians were slow to grasp just how disastrous the military situation had become.

IGHQ considered only two possibilities: Continue to fight the decisive battle in the Philippines while fortifying Japan, Manchuria, and China in order to prolong the war and wait for the enemy to abandon the fight or abandon the decisive battle and entrench for the sole purpose of extending the war.

The High Command opted for the first plan. Every effort would be made to build up enough air power. Large-scale mobilization would fill new units to make the core defenses impregnable. Vessels would be procured to secure sea transportation and raid the enemy's supply lines. Science would mobilize to develop surprise new attack weapons. The IJA and IJN drafted their first-ever joint operational plan and presented it to the Throne on 20 January.[24]

The Portuguese Minister in Tokyo cabled Lisbon on 30 January, "Despite the seriousness of the situation, the country is not yet prepared, after so many imaginary victories, to recognize the hopelessness of the situation and to begin peace negotiations."[25]

Indeed, on 29 January, the Vice Chief of the Army General Staff had sent military attachés in Europe a gloomy forecast for 1945, including a statement that the Americans "very probably" would attempt a landing on Japan proper about the middle of the year.[26]

The Emperor had asked Kido on 6 January whether it would be wise to consult the elder statesmen about the state of the war and raised it again on the 13th. Kido and Marquis Yasumasa Matsudaira arranged for each of the elder statesmen to meet with Hirohito in a series of one-on-one sessions from 7–26 February. With the exception of Konoye, they all advised that Japan should continue to fight. Tojo had the gall to say that the odds were still even, and one should be neither optimistic nor pessimistic. Konoye said the worst was yet to come and urged that steps be taken to end the war. The Emperor told him that it would be difficult to end the war without some great success against the enemy. Konoye said he doubted that such could be achieved any time soon.[27]

The IJN established its last new fighter wing of the war on 20 January at Matsuyama on Shikoku. Pilot Sakai received orders to join the unit, which gathered many of the IJN's remaining veteran pilots. The unit received the first of the *Shiden* Kawanishi N1K fighters. So many hopes rested on the outfit that pilots were not allowed to apply for kamikaze assignments.[28]

This was also too little too late.

Luzon: Cutting Japan's Supply Jugular

MacArthur intended to invade Luzon right where the Japanese had conducted their main landings in 1941, and for the same reason: The Lingayen Gulf provided direct access to the central plains and Manila. He gave the task to Lieutenant General Walter Krueger and his Sixth Army, supported by the air and naval forces of the Southwest Pacific Area.[29] Once ashore, Sixth Army's I Corps was to protect the beachhead's left flank while XIV Corps drove south to Clark Field and then Manila.[30]

Determined and successful kamikaze attacks met the approaching invasion fleet. Japanese pilots sank an escort carrier and damaged another and the battleships *California* and *New Mexico*, as well as smaller vessels.[31]

IGHQ had ordered its forces on Luzon to wage a delaying battle rather than a decisive one, in part because it had sent divisions to Leyte that it would have used under earlier plans for Luzon.[32] General Tomoyuki Yamashita, the Japanese commanding general, did not intend to defend the central plains–Manila Bay area with his 260,000 troops because American superiority in armor and mobility would have its greatest advantage there. He sought only to pin down MacArthur's forces.

The invasion of Luzon began at 0700 on S-Day, 9 January 1945, with a massive naval bombardment. One hour later, the 40th Infantry Division landed at Lingayen on the right wing near the town of that name, with the 37th,

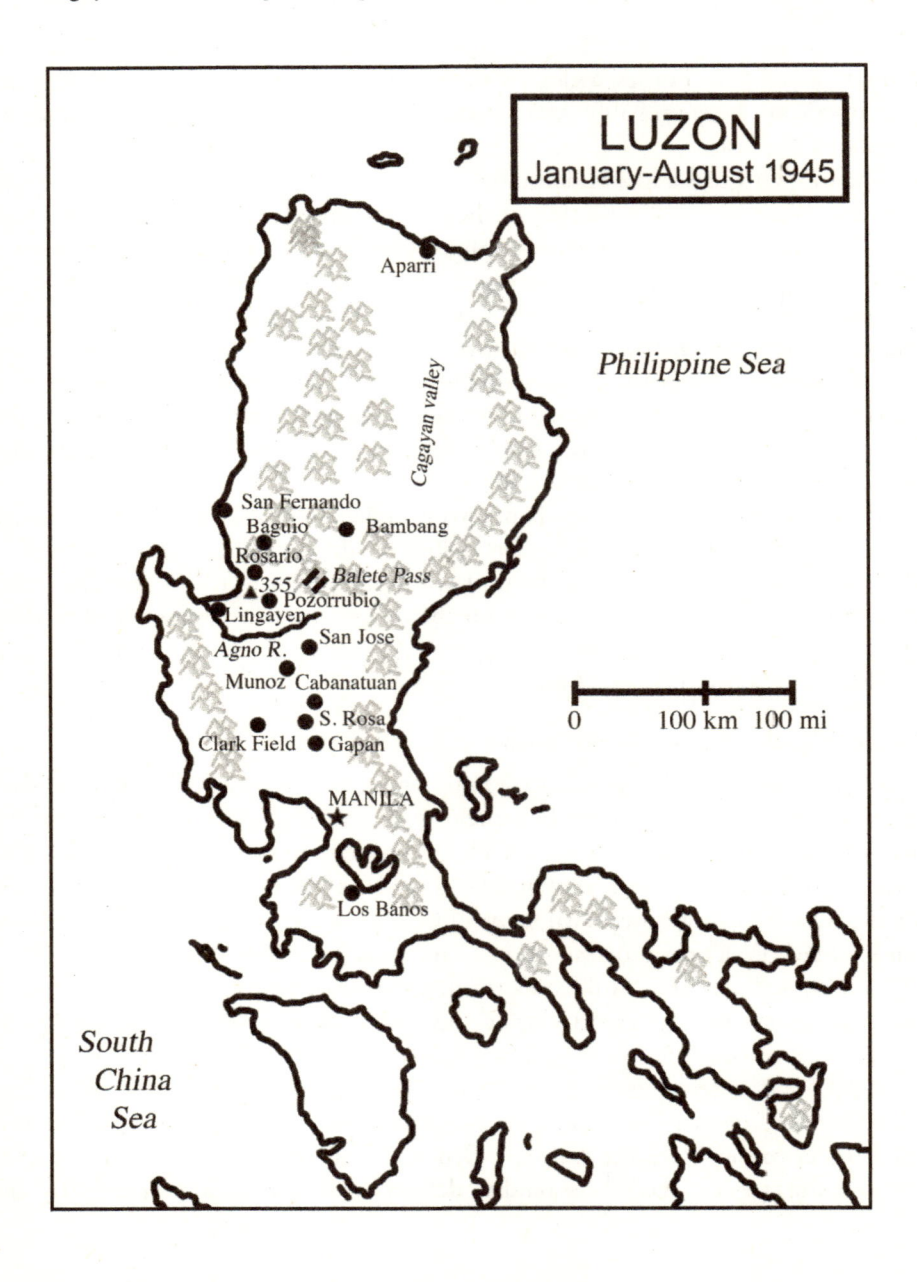

6th, and 43d Infantry divisions strung out to the left.[33] There was no Japanese resistance on shore.

There was little Japanese resistance inland at first, either, and within a few days, Sixth Army had 175,000 men in a 20-mile beachhead. I Corps protected the left flank.[34]

After consolidating its part of the beachhead, XIV Corps on 15 January crossed the Agno River unmolested. On 17 January, MacArthur told Krueger that he wanted XIV Corps to roll south to capture the Clark Field airbase complex with alacrity. Krueger the next day gave XIV Corps the green light. The Americans charged toward Manila, as the Japanese had already largely evacuated the central plain.[35]

The battle for Manila, where the garrison offered the first serious resistance encountered thus far, effectively ended on 24 February, when the 37th Infantry Division fully occupied the old walled city of Intramuros. Strong Japanese forces, primarily naval, disregarded Japanese commander General Tomoyuki Yamashita's plan to hold out in the mountains and fought for possession of the city. Sadly for our purposes, the naval garrison commander did not leave any explanation as to why he defied orders. "The fighting was the toughest yet encountered by our troops," recorded the 129th Infantry Regiment. "It was like Bougainville in reverse, but instead of attacking log and sand pillboxes, we were up against concrete emplacements thoroughly fortified and prepared and strategically emplaced to offer the best fields of fire." The Japanese had constructed pillboxes in the thick-walled concrete structures at nearly every corner, and the GIs advanced from building to building, clearing each one top to bottom. Artillery and antiaircraft guns were often hidden in doorways or behind second-story windows.[36]

The savage fighting in Manila dragged on for another week and left 100,000 civilians dead. Combat operations continued on Luzon until the Japanese surrender, but the Americans had effective control over the Philippine Islands.

The navy minister at the time of the battle of the Philippine Sea, Mitsumasa Yonai, commented to interrogators, "When you took the Philippines, that was the end of our resources, in cutting off the southern supplies."[37]

Convoy interdiction by fleet action and air attacks from Luzon resulted first in efforts to move tankers in small groups rather than large convoys. The Japanese started shipping oil in barrels on regular freighters, and then warships, including several aircraft carriers for which there were no planes. By March, the Japanese had to cancel all southbound convoys, while 70 to 80 percent of northbound traffic was being destroyed. By late March, convoys ceased altogether.[38]

The southern supply area was simultaneously taking a bashing. Ugaki in Japan lamented in his diary on 16 January, "The enemy [U.S. Third Fleet] which attacked the coast of Indochina entered further into the South China Sea and extended its relentless attacks even on Hong Kong, Canton, and Swatow. They completely ignored us." On 26 January, he noted that the British Pacific Fleet had conducted a carrier plane attack against the key oil refineries at Palembang in the Netherlands East Indies. The British struck again with 150 planes on 29 January.[39]

*

Ugaki observed on 3 February that the Soviets had reached a point 15 miles from Berlin. "The prospect is extremely dark. On the 10th, Ugaki was appointed commander of the newly formed Fifth Air Fleet. "I'm now appointed to a very important post, which has the key to determine the fate of the empire, with the pick of the Imperial Navy available at present. I have to break through this crisis with diehard struggles." Two days later, the Emperor received him in a bomb shelter under the imperial garden.[40] The IJN's training arm reorganized into an operational unit, the Tenth Air Fleet.[41]

Meeting in Yalta, Roosevelt, Churchill, and Stalin secretly reached agreement that two or three months after Germany's surrender, the Soviet Union would enter the war against Japan.[42]

OSS acquired a report in mid-February that a recent visitor to Japan had found the Emperor in an extremely nervous condition.[43]

Ugaki recorded the American landings on Iwo Jima on 19 February. "If this island, noted for its fortifications, should fall into enemy hands, the future of our main islands should be feared indeed."[44] IGHQ understood that if the island fell to the enemy, eastern Japan, including Tokyo, would come into range for American fighters escorting the bombers. Plans for elaborate fortifications and interconnecting tunnels were 70 percent complete when the Americans arrived on 19 June.[45]

Hattori recorded:

> At 0600 hours on the 19th, the enemy started landing operations with 130 landing craft under cover of naval bombardment by three battleships, nine cruisers, and 30 destroyers and air cover by planes from five aircraft carriers.... Our garrison unit braved this violent bombardment and bombing and delivered a daring counterattack with artillery fire power and the units at the beach position.... Intercepted enemy wireless on 22 June revealed that the enemy was suffering successive damages and meeting stubborn resistance.... The landing enemy troops were presumed to be the US 4th and 5th Marine divisions.[46]

Off Iwo Jima, a special attack unit (kamikaze) of the Third Air Fleet on 21 February sank the escort carrier *Bismarck Sea* and damaged the carrier *Saratoga* so badly she had to return to the American west coast for repairs. Numerous other vessels suffered damage, as well.[47]

An updated IGHQ assessment on 22 February concluded that the Americans would have occupied the islands surrounding Japan by August or September, while bombing the home islands. They would then commence landings in Japan. There was a chance they would land somewhere on the home islands in June or July.[48]

There is little point in describing how the Japanese planned to fight on their home ground, because that battle never happened. Suffice it to say that IGHQ intended to mobilize 2.4 million men and transfer large quantities of ammunition from the continent. The IJA's mission now was to delay the American advance as long as possible to allow these preparations to continue.[49]

War Clouds to the North

The German military attaché in Tokyo cabled Berlin on 12 January that in the Manchukuo area, the ratio of Soviet to Japanese strength was so unfavorable that Stalin's speech calling Japan an "aggressive nation" had visibly impressed the Japanese General Staff, especially in view of Manchukuo's importance to Japan's war economy.[50] Foreign Minister Shigemitsu by early February was concerned that the USSR would abrogate the neutrality pact. He urged Ambassador Sato in Moscow to sound out Foreign Minister Molotov at their next meeting.[51]

Sato reported on 13 February,

> The communiqué issued at the close of the recent Three Powers [Yalta] Conference is much more forceful than those issued at earlier conferences and gives the impression that complete agreement was reached on all military and political matters discussed.... The text of the communiqué would indicate that the conference was concerned only with Germany and with other European problems. Nevertheless, Russia, who has now agreed to work in such close harmony with the Anglo-Americans, will hardly be able to maintain her present relations with Japan. Indeed, the Soviets may secretly have consented to terminate the Russo-Japanese Neutrality Pact, although they probably intend to continue neutral relations with Japan at least until the expiration of the Pact in April 1946.[52]

Sato got his meeting with Molotov on 22 February. Molotov told him that the Far East had not been on the table at Yalta. "Of course, at the Crimea Conference comments were made, but ... As for continuing the Neutrality Pact, the fact is that we have been so busy lately with other important business that neither I myself nor the government authorities have investigated the matter."[53]

On 5 April, Molotov summoned Sato to tell him the USSR was abrogating the Neutrality Pact, which would take effect on 25 April 1946 upon expiration of its five-year term. Molotov told him, "At the time this treaty was concluded, Russia was not yet at war with Germany, and Japan's war with England and America had not yet begun. After that, Japan began the war with England and America, who are allies of Russia."[54]

Sato followed up on 6 April, reporting that he had failed to mention in his haste that Molotov had told him, "Germany's ally, Japan, has been helping Germany in her war against Russia." He assessed that Russia showed no sign of planning to rush to war, but that if the abrogation was a result of Yalta, "there would be a possibility of serious developments in the future."[55]

Army Vice Chief of Staff Lieutenant General Torashiro Kawabe, appointed five days earlier, on 12 April cabled the military attaché in Berlin, referring to Moscow's abrogation of the Neutrality Pact:

> a. Since the Soviet statement indicates that Russia considers Japan just like an enemy country, we can expect that Russia will subject Japan to increasingly vigorous and open political pressure.
> b. The United States will not necessarily demand immediate participation by Russia in the war against Japan. Russia, however, will carefully gauge the decline of Japan's military strength and at an appropriate stage of the American offensive will probably seize some pretext or other to enter the war against our country.[56]

By May, the Army General Staff was troubled by a growing number of reports that the USSR was shifting troops and equipment from Europe to the Far East. "We must view with alarm the possibility of future military activity against Japan."[57]

The Bombing

Japan's output of aircraft, ordnance, and metals declined further in January 1945 because, concluded the Strategic Bombing Survey, raw material stocks were becoming depleted, strategic bombing was punishing the aircraft industry, and efforts to disperse facilities were interrupting production.[58] Moreover, after the fall of the Marianas, American submarines and air power so thoroughly disrupted transportation that Japanese steel production had dropped by 80 percent by early 1945.[59]

American area bombing of Japanese cities began only in January, when B-29s dropped 152 tons of incendiary (74 percent of the overall mix through war's end), high-explosive, and fragmentation bombs on Nagoya. Ugaki's diary contains an almost daily litany of raids by American bombers and carrier task forces in January and February. In February, 457 tons of bombs struck Tokyo and 174 tons Kobe. The night of 9–10 March, bombers conducted the first low-level incendiary bombing. The Americans found the results so "gratifying" that they added the technique to the repertoire.

Nine thousand three hundred eighty-six tons rained down on Tokyo, Osaka, Nagoya, and Kobe in March. By May, after which the target list expanded dramatically, bombers had struck only six cities. That month, Tokyo absorbed 6,900 tons of bombs. During the last three months of the war, bombers took the war to 60 more Japanese cities because the original cities were totally bombed out. The B-29 strength in the Marianas had grown from 119 on 24 November 1944 to 385 in March, and 1,020 on 14 August. There were hardly enough incendiary bombs to go around; at times, men unloaded newly arrived ordnance from ships and drove it directly to the aircraft hardstands. The U.S. Strategic Bombing Survey reckoned that the bombing rendered 8.3 million of the country's 22 million people homeless and destroyed more than two million buildings.[60]

The capture of Iwo Jima on 1 March and completion of an airstrip one month later provided an emergency landing strip, plus a base to launch bombing raids on northern Japan and provide fighter escorts to missions in the south.[61] Coincidently, American bombing and extensive photo reconnaissance by two B-29s at Okinawa on 1 March convinced Ugaki that the island would be the next American target.[62]

The Survey's report concluded:

> The cities of Japan, like those in Germany, presented a spectacle of enormous destruction. Although the over-all total damage was somewhat greater in Germany than in Japan, the extent of destruction was comparable. Only 160,000 tons of bombs were dropped on Japan's home islands as compared with 1,360,000 tons dropped within Germany's own borders. One hundred and four thousand tons of bombs were dropped on 66 Japanese cities as compared with 542,554 tons of bombs that were dropped on 61 German cities.
>
> As in Germany, the air attacks against Japanese cities were not the cause of the enemy's defeat.... The city raids contributed substantially to [pressure to accept unconditional surrender] by their impact on the social and economic structure of Japan.... Apart from the effects of the air attacks on production, the impact of the raids on the social structure of Japan's cities was calamitous. The attacks spread destruction and privation throughout the islands. Few inhabitants escaped the terror of the raids. Those who were not directly attacked shared the experience of millions of refugees who fled into the country seeking food and shelter. The raids brought home to the people the realization that there was no defense against Allied aircraft; that nothing could prevent the wholesale destruction of every inhabited area in Japan and that further resistance was futile.[63]

The firebombings of Japanese cities, as in Germany, did not undermine the will to fight. Admiral Soemu Toyoda disputed the Survey's conclusion about the effect on the populace and decision-making about surrender.

> The effect on the people's morale was not as great as we had feared. In other words, while people who lost their homes faced extremely difficult times, it did not develop to the point of wanting to give up the war. To be sure, it had an effect on production because it cut off transportation, and in some cases, no doubt, some factory hands stayed away from factories because of the danger of bombing. That affected production to some extent, but affecting the people's will to fight was not as great as we had feared.... [O]utside of bombed areas, especially in the country, people appeared to be almost wholly unconcerned about bombing as was evidenced by their failure to dig air raid shelters, etc.; so that, taking the country as a whole, the effect on morale was very light. I do not believe that the question of air raids came up in the minds of the members [of the leadership conference] as an independent question at all; that is, there was no idea that we must give up the war to avoid even a single additional day of bombing.[64]

The U.S. Strategic Bombing Survey report on Japanese morale—the drafters of which presumably had some incentive to view the impact as significant—acknowledged that war weariness after seven years of conflict and the steady accrual of military reverses had damaged Japanese morale (as foreign embassies had observed above) but argued the bombing had pushed the population to the point where it was unwilling to fight on. The study, which based its judgments on widespread interviews and panels, said Japanese cited the bombing as the main reason that they came to believe they would lose the war. Nevertheless, the report concluded that only a third of the population had personally experienced bombing and—perhaps implicit acknowledgment of

Toyoda's argument—conceded that the differences in attitudes among those had been bombed and those who had not were "small."⁶⁵

MAGIC intercepts catalogued frequent Japanese reports on the bombings with details of the damage caused. For example, the Vice Chief of the Japanese General Staff related that the firebombing of Tokyo the night of 9–10 March destroyed the "greater part" of the wards of Jojo, Honjo, Mukojima, Asakusa, and Shitaya. Foreign Minister Shigemitsu cabled to Oshima:

> Fires were started in many places within the capital, and the number of houses destroyed by fire amount to about 240,000, the number of homeless about 1,050,000. There was damage to the Imperial Bureau of the Imperial Mews of the Department of the Imperial Household [in the Imperial Palace area], the Supreme Court, the Imperial Rule Assistance Association, etc. There was a violent wind that night which made it difficult to bring the fires under control, but officials and citizenry cooperated in a brave struggle and were successful in bringing the fires more or less under control by dawn. There are no particular signs of disturbance among the populace.⁶⁶

Japanese signals intelligence successfully intercepted transmissions associated with the B-29 missions and generally grasped the size and target. In December 1944 and January 1945, when all the raids originated in China, the IJN and IJA met them with hundreds of fighters, concentrated in western Japan because of the B-29s' range limitation. They did not, however, form a joint fighter command. The coastal radar network expanded and provided good coverage. Thirty-seven B-29s went down between December and March.⁶⁷

The Koiso Cabinet underwent reorganization on 10 February. A Formosan government representative in Tokyo indicated that the government had nearly collapsed. "When Premier Koiso expressed his intention of resigning to Kido, the Lord Keeper of the Privy Seal, Kido suggested that there simply be a reorganization of the Cabinet.... Because of problems of the Finance, Foreign, and Munitions Ministries, however, it can be assumed that there will be a second reorganization."⁶⁸

*

The IJA and IJN on 1 March agreed to a joint air operations plan, *TEN-GO*. The IJA committed 1,390 planes, while the IJN planned to use 3,175, including 2,000 special attack planes in Tenth Air Force. The IJN set about training suicide pilots. The IJN was to target task forces, while the IJA gave priority to convoys.⁶⁹

The Vice Chief of the Japanese General Staff issued a circular on 8 March that summarized Japan's overall situation:

> General Summary: To meet the new developments in the war situation, the Empire is making itself firmly prepared for the decisive stage of the war, basing its plan on Japan, Manchukuo, and China. We are making the most thorough preparations and hastening all necessary measures so that we shall be able to muster the national army's total war strength to smash the enemy's attacks and so that, even if the enemy invades the homeland, we shall be able to arouse the whole people to such fanatical zeal as will utterly annihilate the enemy.

Popular Morale and the Political Situation: The development of the Philippine situation to its present phase, together with the situation on Iwo, has had a wide and rather serious effect on the homeland. We must admit that elements of the population have given way to a spirit of unrest. Certain political circles are launching a movement for a new party with national solidarity as its program, but the people evince no great interest in such questions. As a whole, however, the people regard the war as their own and a matter of life and death for them. Confessing that the present critical situation is due to their failure to make efficient use of the total national strength, they are devoting themselves with increasing fervor and self-sacrifice to the war effort.

National Strength and War Strength: Foreseeing ever since last summer the development of the military situation, we have been freeing ourselves from dependence on the resources of the South and have been taking all measures for enabling Japan to wage a modern war with such resources as are available in Japan, Manchukuo, and China.... We are doing everything possible to make sure that, even now when we are cut off from the South, there is no essential diminution in our war strength. However, the transportation crisis caused by the increase in the rate of shipping losses is, even with the contraction of our lines, our most severe difficulty. Hereafter, together with the intensification of our counter-measures against air attacks, we shall plan all necessary counter-measures [to meet the transportation problem].

Manpower Resources and Food Supply: The armed forces, in line with their preparations for repelling any attack on the homeland, are making great efforts for large-scale reinforcement of military strength in Japan proper. At the same time, manpower for other needs is being maintained at the necessary level, and we find it possible to increase the numbers of people used in agriculture and communications.

As for our food supply, a considerable increase in production and greater shipments from Manchukuo and China are matters of vital importance in the conduct of the war, and we are devising measures which will provide for their complete realization.

Effect of Air Raids: The air raids against the homeland are being steadily intensified. Up to the end of February, civilian casualties totaled 4,400 dead and 5,600 wounded. The effect of the air raids is not so great as enemy propaganda claims, but such factors as the loss of Iwo, the neutralization of the Philippines, the activity of enemy [carrier] task forces [attacking Japan], and the advance of enemy air bases will hereafter permit even greater intensification of the air raids. We are planning all necessary counter-measures and, in accordance with the lessons of the European war, we are hastening all steps for the maintenance of production and of land and sea communications. Such as the dispersion and transfer underground of important Greater East Asia installations and equipment.

Conclusion: Henceforth, the war will rage with ever-increasing intensity, particularly about Japan. Throughout the homeland, there are elements which we will have to watch carefully lest they endanger the conduct of the war. Nevertheless, the Army, the Navy, and the Air Force, closely united around the solid core of the Imperial Headquarters, strive forward to the completion of military preparations such as will satisfy the demands of any military situation and insure victory. At this moment, firmly persuaded of inevitable victory, we await in readiness the moment of decision when, we are confident, we shall almost certainly repel the assault and successfully defend the Empire.[70]

IGHQ apparently wanted the public to get the basic message about the strategic situation. The Vichy ambassador in Tokyo cabled his colleague in Peking on 8 March and related that an "unexpected article had appeared in a Japanese paper"—which the intercept analysts commented was probably *Mainichi*. "After having noted that neither the Air Force nor the Navy is in a position to resist the continued advance of the Americans, this periodical states that a landing on Japan is inevitable. This confession of powerlessness, although it is counterbalanced by the assertion that the Army has the power to repulse the invasion, is worth noting, since the newspaper in question is the organ of the military.... [T]he successive reverses on land and sea are interpreted by many as announcing the defeat of the Empire."[71]

On 7 March, German Ambassador Stahmer in Tokyo reported:

> The position of the Koiso Government has for a long time been very shaky, because of profound popular disaffection with the indecision and lack of energy displayed by the leaders of the state, the war situation in the Philippines and Iwo, and internal economic difficulties....
>
> Rumors of an imminent cabinet change have been kindled in political circles by the expressed desire of both Houses that the Diet be reconvened.... It is expected that some eminent Army leader will be asked to form a new government....
>
> It should be emphasized that in Japan there is no close-knit, united leadership, as there is in Germany. Even now, as in the past, the Japanese are governed by heterogeneous political factions, fighting for power among themselves, and striving to make the people serve their own purposes. That struggle for power always exerts an incalculable influence upon dealings among politicians taking part in the formation of a Cabinet, and it is therefore extraordinarily difficult to make forecasts.[72]

Launching his own futile last offensive, Ugaki, given his head by Combined Fleet, sent his air fleet into battle against four carrier groups off the coast of Japan on 18 March. Over the course of five days, his kamikazes damaged several carriers, the *Franklin* so severely she was out for the duration. The action cost him 161 precious aircraft out of 246 engaged, yet he viewed the effort as a success because he (falsely) believed he had sunk five carriers.[73]

The Thai ambassador reported on 29 March, "The private residence of General Tojo, the former Premier, is now strongly guarded by police, as it appears that groups of people threw stones into his house."[74]

Okinawa: Japan's Doorstep

The American landings in the Ryukyus brought the threat to Japan's doorstep. The directive for American forces in the Pacific Ocean Area to capture the Ryukyu Islands, of which Okinawa is the largest, dated to 3 October 1944. MacArthur's forces were first to secure Leyte and Luzon in the Philippines, while Admiral Chester Nimitz's forces occupied Iwo Jima. After the capture of the Ryukyus, which constituted Japan's innermost ring of defenses, the final step was to be the invasion of the Japanese home islands.[75]

Okinawa is some 60 miles long and between 2 and 18 miles wide. The northern two-thirds are mountainous and cloaked in pine forests. The southern third is covered by rolling hills studded with villages and limestone ridges containing many natural caves. It is excellent defensive country, and an estimated 66,000 Japanese troops were thought to be on the island to exploit that terrain. This estimate was low.

Two army and two Marine Corps infantry divisions under Tenth Army, reinforced by amphibian tank and tractor battalions—some 116,000 men in all—made the

OKINAWA
March–July 1945

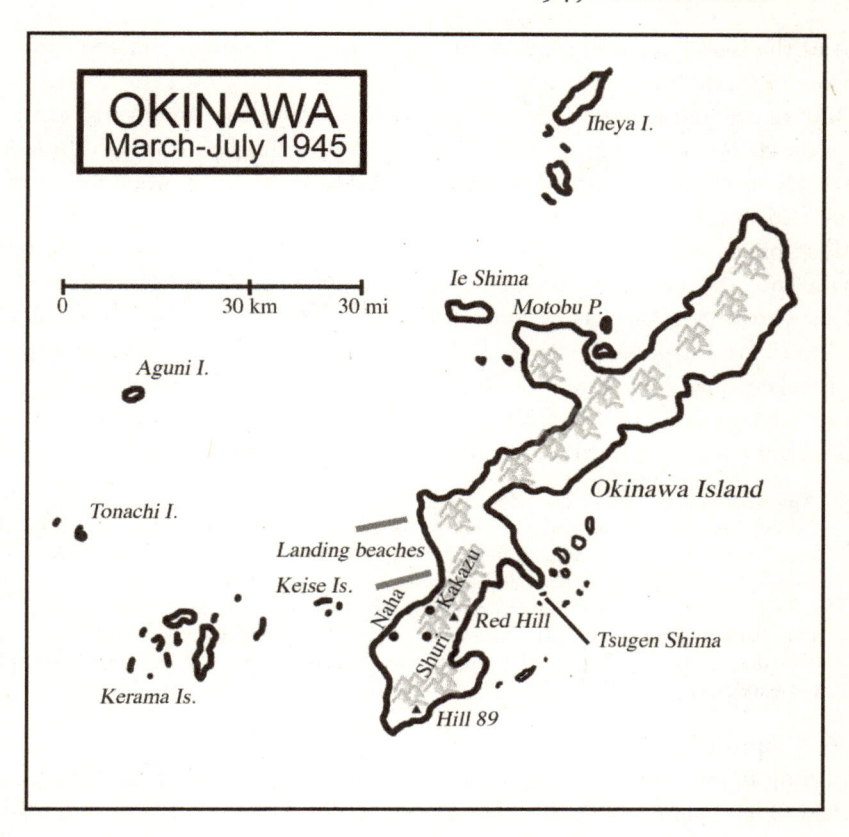

Iheya I.
Ie Shima
Motobu P.
Aguni I.
Okinawa Island
Tonachi I.
Landing beaches
Keise Is.
Naha
Kakazu
Red Hill
Tsugen Shima
Shuri
Kerama Is.
Hill 89

initial landings on 1 April after weeks of preparatory destruction by air and naval assets. The invasion beaches were located on the west coast roughly a third of the way up the island. The III Amphibious Corps landed on the left with its 1st and 6th Marine divisions, and XXIV Corps on the right, the 7th Infantry Division just to the north of the 96th Infantry Division. The vast American force charged ashore amidst an earth-shaking bombardment only to find that there were almost no Japanese troops there to resist them.[76]

Ugaki noted the well-anticipated landings almost in passing. His main concern that day was the difficulty in getting reconnaissance planes through American fighter screens to track enemy fleet movements. Off the very coast of Japan, he was fighting almost blind. His kamikaze planes were taking a steady toll of American warships and lives, but not enough to influence to course of battle at all.[77]

The first signs of serious resistance on land only emerged after the 96th Infantry Division on 2 and 3 April wheeled to advance southward into the rolling hills abreast of the 7th Infantry Division, while the Marines turned to clear the north. The Japanese had concentrated their forces, some 100,000 strong, in the southern third of the island and were waiting in their caves and bunkers for the Americans to come to them.[78]

Despite existing defense plans to fight in the south, the Americans' capture of two airfields on the same day as the landing greatly shocked IGHQ. On 6 April, Thirty-Second Army received orders to suspend its delaying strategy and recapture the airfields, the attack to begin on 8 April.[79]

The Combined Fleet on 6 April delivered final instructions to a newly formed Surface Special Attack (i.e. suicide) Force consisting of *Yamato*, light cruiser *Yahagi*, and six destroyers that was to make a dash to Okinawa and beach *Yamato* in a position to fire at troop transports. Radio intercepts gave the plan away to American codebreakers, and two American submarines spotted and reported on the vessels' departure. Ugaki's Fifth Air Fleet provided fighter cover for the beginning of the sortie. Ugaki recorded in his diary on 7 April,

> [A]n enemy flying boat shadowed the force after our fighters left the scene.... [M]any fighters and bombers thought to be from ... newly discovered American carriers ... headed for *Yama*'s force. From noon, two to three hundred enemy planes repeatedly attacked the force for about two hours. A telegram sent from destroyer *Hatsushimo*, with the First Attack Force commander as the initiator, stated that *Yamato* had been hit by many bombs, *Yahagi* by two torpedoes, with other damage to destroyers. The next telegram from the same destroyer related the alarming news that *Yamato* has been further hit by more torpedoes, with the result that she exploded and sank instantly.[80]

On 6–7 April, the First Air Fleet and 8th Air Division on Formosa also staged supporting attacks and committed 699 planes, including 355 kamikazes. The Japanese claimed to have sunk two battleships, three cruisers, eight destroyers, 21 transports, and 30 other vessels and to have damaged 61 ships.[81]

The IJA called off the ground offensive it had just ordered up on 7 April.[82] That same day, Ugaki recorded the first appearance of B-29s over Japan with P-51 fighter escorts, presumably from Iwo Jima.[83]

Premier Koiso, meanwhile, dissolved his government on 5 April citing 1) the landing on Okinawa, 2) the disasters caused in Japanese cities by American planes, and 3) the internal situation in Japan, which was worsening daily. Japanese broadcasts suggested that an additional reason was Koiso's inability to improve relations with the Imperial Headquarters, the meetings of which he had begun to attend in March.[84]

Explorations of Ending the War

Admiral Kantaro Suzuki, President of the Privy Council, received an Imperial order on 5 April to form a new government and completed the task by the 8th.[85] At a meeting of senior statesmen, former Premier Hiranuma declared, "I am strongly opposed to any advocacy for peace and cessation of hostilities," and therefore, "there is no way out but to fight to the end."[86] The senior statesmen nevertheless agreed to appoint Admiral Suzuki as premier. Kido hinted to him privately that he was to explore finding a way to end the war.[87]

Ugaki observed that Yonai remained the navy minister; another admiral became minister of munitions, transportation, and communications; and a third served as minister without portfolio. "It could be called a Naval Cabinet," he wrote. "The navy, now without ships, is going to fight at the critical time by forming a cabinet with its predecessors. Ha! Ha!"[88]

According to his *chef de cabinet*, Hisatsune Sakomizu, "Mr. Suzuki doubted the possibility of our continuing the war, so right after the Cabinet was formed, he ordered me to study the details of the Japanese fighting power and to advise whether it was sufficient to continue the war. I reached the conclusion at the end of April, rather the beginning of May, that Japan couldn't continue the war."[89]

According to Kido, who had nominated him, Suzuki was his own man "who would come down to rock bottom in considering a fundamental reconsideration of the war policy. The fundamental reconsideration of such a question would require a man of deep sincerity and enormous courage, and there was no other man but Admiral Suzuki because the problem required that he stake his life in pursuing his task."

Admiral Kantaro Suzuki became prime minister on 7 April 1945. Receiving a tacit imperial nod, he set about finding a way to end the war. The atomic bomb attacks opened the door for him to break constitutional practice and hand the decision to Hirohito, who ordered surrender. (Wikimedia Commons)

Suzuki had been a member of the Privy Council since 1941. Asked whether the members of the council at that time shared Matsuoka's optimism about the course of the war in Europe, he replied that he thought the Axis would lose and believed most other members of the council shared that opinion. "I was well known for being opposed to any war against the United States."

Suzuki told interrogators:

> At the time I became Premier, I did not receive any direct order from the Emperor, but I understood clearly from what the Emperor said to me at that time the Emperor was very much concerned over the situation that Japan faced in the war, and he was very concerned over the death of civilians due to bombing, and the general sickness and the great number of civilian casualties, and the great losses in the field of battle. Therefore, I was given to understand that it was the Emperor's desire for me to make every effort to bring the war to a conclusion as quickly as possible. So as Premier, I started out with the purpose of bringing the war to an end as quickly as possible....
>
> I was naturally in a very difficult position because, on the one hand, I had to carry out, to the best of my ability, the mission given me by the Emperor to arrange for a conclusion of the war, whereas if anyone heard of this, I would naturally have been attacked and probably killed

by people opposed to such a policy. So that on the one hand, I had to advocate an increase in the war effort and determination to fight on, whereas through diplomatic channels and any means available, I had to try to negotiate with other countries to stop the war.[90]

Asked what steps Suzuki took to fundamentally reconsider the problem, Kido said, "I am not familiar with what steps he took, but the common-sense view of the situation was not whether something would be done, but how to do it and when to do it." To jump ahead, wheels would begin turning in early June.[91]

The Swiss Minister on 11 April reported:

> Whatever declaration the Government may make [about zealously continuing the war], it can hardly be denied that the Cabinet, with a 78-year-old leader and a Foreign Minister as calm and cold as Togo, will not sacrifice everything to fanaticism like the two preceding cabinets. The retention as Navy Minister of Yonai, who was always considered an amiable and temperate person, is significant. Even more significant, however, is the calling back of Togo, who was shelved as Foreign Minister by General Tojo, who found him to be too soft. The determining reason for the appointment of Togo, who was formerly ambassador to Moscow [1938–1940], is probably the desire to better Japan's relations with the Soviets....
>
> It is impossible to see what the Government can do in the diplomatic field to pull Japan out of the tragic situation into which she is gradually sinking.[92]

The Spanish Minister, some weeks later, reported that Togo was an old acquaintance of his and was "known for his sympathy for Russia and being anti-Nazi in spite of the fact that his wife is German." Translators of the intercept commented that Tokyo Radio had quoted the newspaper *Asahi* as stating that, "Mr. Togo constantly opposed the measures adopted by the Tojo Cabinet." There was no indication, however, that he had opposed the decision to go to war.[93]

*

Misled by vastly inflated claims of ships destroyed by kamikaze attacks, the Naval General Staff on 9 April ordered the Combined Fleet "to shift to a general chase ... overcoming all difficulties." The Combined Fleet issued an operational order declaring that the enemy was in an "unstable condition and the chance of winning now stands fifty-fifty."[94]

Ugaki noted in his diary on 13 April that the British were bombing Formosa. Indeed, Task Force 57, British Carrier Force, with four carriers, conducted strikes on 12–13 April. "They were indeed impertinent," Ugaki commented.[95]

On instructions from Tokyo, Japanese Vice Admiral Abe, representative on the Tripartite Commission, between 15 and 17 April met with Admiral Dönitz, Field Marshal Keitel, and Foreign Minister Ribbentrop seeking a meeting with Hitler to present a proposal that the German fleet sail to the Far East to operate alongside the Japanese Navy. He did not get his meeting, but Hitler replied indirectly that if Germany's situation improved, he would be open to sending submarines to fight with Japan.

On 14 April, the Greater East Asia Ministry transmitted a circular on how officials should respond to Roosevelt's death on 12 April:

> Do not make personal attacks on Roosevelt.
> a. Do not convey the impression that we are exultant over Roosevelt's death.
> b. Avoid observations such as that Roosevelt's death will have an immediate effect on the fighting spirit and war strength of the United States.
> c. Emphasize persistently and in detail the fact of Roosevelt's perseverance in the war, in connection with the various plans before and during the war.
> d. Lay great stress on such things as the mistakes and discords that will now arise in the anti-Axis camp, with even the driving force of Roosevelt has had great difficulty in maintaining cooperation.[96]

Prime Minister Suzuki, meanwhile, publicly expressed sympathy for the American people on the death of Roosevelt.[97]

Ugaki on 22 April recorded that the Combined Fleet issued orders on future air warfare operations. Because strength had fallen so far, air fleets were to launch no major actions against the enemy and to conduct only "air guerrilla warfare." "Now we have come to the stage we have expected to reach for some time."[98] The IJA, which had born the brunt of defending the homeland's airspace ordered its fighters to stop opposing B-29 raids because of fuel and pilot shortages.[99]

Two days later, Ugaki recorded,

> Rough calculations of the loss of aircraft, etc., since 25 March were as follows: 620 missing and 80 destroyed on the ground. The total number of planes under my command at present amount to 620, of which 370 are in operational condition. When we learned that the monthly outputs this month were 600 navy planes and 400 army planes, we couldn't expect to get more replenishment. Even if aircraft are produced, the result will be the same without fuel.[100]

On Okinawa, repeated Japanese counterattacks resulted in bloody failures. The Thirty-Second Army estimated by late April that the enemy had a force five or six times larger than itself, backed by constant sea bombardment. The Japanese "final offensive" on 4 May proved another debacle and consumed much of the available ammunition; henceforth, the Japanese fought only a delaying action. Artillery was limited to 10 shells per gun per day.[101]

On 25 April, Ugaki recorded, "An anti-Axis countries conference is being held in San Francisco today.... It's most mortifying to learn that they plan to discuss how to govern Germany and Japan after the war."[102]

As the inevitable end approached in Germany, Tokyo (presumably inspired by Suzuki) determined that it would report the basic facts honestly to the public and emphasize that the war in the Pacific would intensify. On 5 May, the German naval attaché in Tokyo reported to Dönitz that an influential member of the Japanese Admiralty had said that "since the situation is clearly recognized to be hopeless, large sections of the Japanese armed forces would not regard with disfavor an American request for capitulation even if the terms were hard, provided they were halfway honorable."[103] Admiral Yonai told interrogators that voices in the High Command and high government circles had begun arguing openly for bringing the war to an end.[104]

The Portuguese Minister reported on 6 May,

> Public attention is completely centered on the Okinawa struggle which, according to the Admiral in command of the Japanese Navy, should decide the war in the Pacific. Imperial Headquarters continue to state that 400 [American] ships have been sunk or damaged; and propagandists are using this to draw the conclusion that the fleet is so weakened that it is unable to invade Japan. Nevertheless, fortification of coasts and mountains continues, giving the impression that this country, like Germany, is disposed to prosecute the war to its very end without the least probability of victory. Numerous changes are being made in the Army High Command, and a national guard is being organized to fight as guerrillas against the invaders.[105]

This last comment may have been a reference to the People's Volunteer Corps, which according to Tokyo radio was to include all able-bodied civilians. Its duties were to carry out emergency work on constructing defense installations, decentralizing industry, and improving transport, food and lumber production. Members were also to act as firefighters and, in times of "more acute crisis," as armed units.[106] On 19 May, the Army General Staff weekly intelligence report indicated that central authorities were carrying out a separate conscription law that would convert the organization into a Volunteer Combat Corps and place it under IJA command.[107]

Suzuki told interrogators that the Supreme War Council believed that the Americans would not be content to bomb Japan into submission but would invade the home islands. The military planned to fight a last titanic battle. But even some military men, according to Suzuki, realized that even if the Japanese defeated an invasion, at the cost of massive casualties, Japan would eventually succumb to further attacks from the enemy. Suzuki believed that the military, too, wanted a way out.[108]

When Foreign Minister Togo briefed the Emperor on Germany's surrender, he offered his opinion that it was time to start looking for a way to end the war. Hirohito expressed no strong desire for an early end, but he offered that he hoped it would end soon.[109]

Suzuki's *chef de cabinet* Sakomizu concluded in early May that Japan could not continue the war, as noted above. His conclusion was based on Japan's ability to manufacture airplanes, the amount of factory damage from bombing, ship losses and damage, the food situation, and the sentiment of the people. His reasons were that the public was aware that the army had failed in its promise to defend Okinawa, and they saw that ever fewer fighters rose to challenge the B-29s. There were rumors that American bombers would destroy the crops. Suzuki, unlike Tojo, cared about public opinion, opined Sakomizu. He continued:

> Suzuki decided I was right. He went to the Emperor and came back a short time later. He said to me that we must start some steps toward peace. This was in the middle of May. So we asked [Koki] Hirota [former prime minister] to speak to the Russian ambassador [Joseph] Malik in

private conversation. He did on several occasions, sounding out the Russian attitude toward interceding with America. In the beginning, it looked as we might be successful, but the talks never reached a successful conclusion. In May, Germany collapsed, as you know, and after that the War Minister [Gen. Korechika Anami] asked the Cabinet for a conference in the presence of the Emperor to decide the "fundamental principles of the war"—whether to continue it or not. Of course, we [laughing] had had many rehearsals of that meeting.

The military insisted upon continuing, but I and others had different ideas, although we couldn't actually advocate the stopping of the war because the MPs [military police] were still around. I drafted the memorandum for the conference, and it started with the statement that we should try to "accomplish" the war and keep the Emperor's reign intact and keep the home [national] land. Of course, the military read the word "accomplish" as meaning the war should be continued, but it was followed by the details which I had collected for my report to Mr. Suzuki. The whole thing was presented to the conference in the presence of the Emperor. Those attending were the Prime Minister, the War Minister [Anami], the Navy Minister [Yonai], the Army Chief of Staff [Gen. Yoshijiro Umezu], the Chief of the Navy General Staff [Adm. Soemu Toyoda], and the Foreign Minister [Shigenori Togo]. Each expressed his own opinion, but none expressed his real feelings. But if you read the details of my memorandum, it is clear that the war had to stop. The Emperor himself read the report as well as the others. This was the ninth of June. At that time, the Emperor said nothing.[110]

Hattori's account indicates that Sakomizu's report first went to the Supreme War Direction Council on 6 June. Army Chief of Staff Umezu said the IJA would win the battle of the homeland because it would be able to gather overwhelming force against beachheads unlike on the islands, and the war should go on. Navy Chief of Staff Toyoda took no position on whether the war should continue, laying out the estimate of American intentions and the IJN's plan to respond. Togo pointed to the evidence that war production was going to continue declining. Navy Minister Yonai, who wanted to end the war, remained silent.[111]

The imperial conference actually occurred on 8 June. It covered the same ground as the earlier meeting. The President of the Privy Council added that "It is imperative to continue fighting by any means.... "

Suzuki, however, drove home at the end, "Japan is now faced with a truly critical situation. The hope for our success is desperately slim." The Emperor remained silent and left after Suzuki finished, signaling the end of the conference.[112]

The Diet on 9 June convened in extraordinary session to discuss confronting the decisive battle. Suzuki was concerned that he would have to stake out a hardline position but reluctantly agreed to the session. Demonstrating that the body was not just a rubberstamp, the lower chamber demanded amendments to weaken a wartime emergency measures law (to which the Cabinet reluctantly acceded), and there was an attempt to overthrow the Cabinet. Yonai was disgusted and becoming convinced Suzuki would do nothing to end the war, and he threatened to quit. Kido, however, privately revealed a strategy to do just that, and Yonai decided to stay in the Cabinet to give peace a chance.[113]

The Wartime Emergencies Act gave the government the power to declare war or negotiate and sign peace agreements, heretofore powers reserved to the Emperor under the constitution. Suzuki frankly admitted before the assembly to recent defeats and problems with war production, communications, transportation, and food supplies. He told the deputies that responsibility for directing the war would not rest only with the Imperial Headquarters but be shared with the government. Tacitly acknowledging impending defeat, he told deputies that he hoped to preserve the Emperor system.[114]

*

The Supreme War Direction Council first considered approaching the USSR to mediate peace in mid-May but could not reach a consensus.[115] After the last imperial conference, Kido concluded he had to act to change the "continue to fight" policy. He drafted a memo that underscored Japan's collapsing war-making power and said rapid action was necessary to preserve the existence of the Imperial House. He proposed using an intermediary. Kido secretly vetted the proposal with the Foreign Ministry and Premier's office on 9 June, and then had an audience that afternoon with Hirohito. The Emperor endorsed his initiative.[116]

According to Kido, Suzuki, Togo, and the service ministers agreed that certain steps must be taken to end the war. They decided to request the USSR to mediate a peace. "Several Cabinet sessions were held at the outset, but no agreement could be arrived at. Although the Minister of War felt that there was no choice but to bring the war to an end, the feelings and views within the army, however, were not necessarily so. There were opinions on both sides of the matter."[117] Even the service chiefs of staff eventually conceded that a peace bid stood a better chance while Japan still had significant fighting power and agreed to the proposal on 18 June.[118]

Ugaki, presumably through his excellent navy connections, knew about the plan. Ugaki recorded on 16 June that the government was trying to "seek peace through Soviet Russia," but he was skeptical that "such a trick" would work.[119]

At Kido's suggestion, the Emperor summoned the members of the Supreme War Direction Council on 22 June and told them he wished for them to endeavor to bring about peace. He asked their opinions. Suzuki said the government should endeavor to fulfill His Majesty's wishes. Yonai said he had wanted to make such a proposal earlier, but the idea had not been ripe. Now was the time, and the USSR was the best option. Togo supported Yonai. Umezu said the military had no objections. Anami and Toyoda remained silent. And so the policy changed dramatically, albeit futilely. Sakomizu related:

> The Emperor told them that the conclusion of the document presented in the conference of 9 June seemed to be very paradoxical. He knew the real meaning of the conclusion, he said. "I think it is necessary for us to have a plan to close this war at once as well as one to defend the home islands." [The interrogators noted that Sakomizu explained that the IJA was making much of its plan to defend the home islands.]
>
> As a result of this expression by the Emperor, Suzuki decided to stop the war. After the meeting, when Mr. Suzuki came back, he said to me, "Today the Emperor said what everyone has wanted to say but yet was afraid to say."[120]

The Japanese were receiving peace feelers from the Americans. Captain K. Nishihara, the Japanese Counselor for Naval Affairs in Berne, Switzerland, on 5 June cabled Tokyo that Allen Dulles, the OSS representative in Switzerland, had proposed that a "discussion" between Japan and the United States be held in Switzerland, and that a Japanese admiral be flown there from Tokyo in "absolute secrecy" for that purpose. Nishihara characterized Dulles as a special envoy for Roosevelt who continued to perform that mission under President Harry Truman. He had made the suggestion through a trustworthy third party to a member of Nishihara's staff. Should Japan agree, America would arrange for all flights.[121]

*

The home islands received the last message from the defenders on Okinawa on 19 June.[122] On 23 June, the commanding general of Thirty-Second Army and his chief of staff committed seppuku, and on 25 June, IGHQ announced the end of the Okinawa operation. About 90,000 Japanese soldiers had perished. Kamikaze planes had executed 2,393 attacks during the campaign, sinking or damaging 404 American vessels (36 sunk and 368 damaged).[123]

The IGHQ's plan to protect the home islands, referred to by the Emperor at the meeting where he authorized peace feelers through Moscow, was Operation *Ketsu-Go*, the decisive homeland defense. The section on operations in the initial plan stated, "The Japanese Army will strengthen its combat preparations and establish a strategic organization that will destroy the enemy ... and thus seek ultimate victory in the war." Ugaki recorded that the operation was revealed to senior IJN officers on 26 June at a briefing at the Grand Naval Command Headquarters. "Now at last we have been pressed into the final decisive battle," he mused.[124]

Japan refused to pursue channels other than the Soviet one. On 24 June, the Vice Chief of the Army General Staff rebuked a major general at the Japanese mission in Stockholm, whom the ambassador had reported was putting out peace feelers to the Allies. "As we have said before, Japan is firmly determined to prosecute the Greater East Asia war to the very end."[125]

Captain Nishihara in Berne finally received a reply on 6 July ordering him to make no reply to Dulles.[126]

Konoye, who was not directly involved, told interrogators after the war that the IJA opposed any direct negotiations with America, and the proposal to use Russia as an intermediary was what brought the army on board.[127]

Foreign Minister Togo cabled Ambassador Sato in Moscow on 11 July:

> [G]iving consideration to termination of the war because of the pressing situation which confronts Japan both at home and abroad. Therefore, when you have your interview with Molotov [in accordance with previous instructions] you should not confine yourself to the objective of a rapprochement between Russia and Japan but should also sound him out on the extent to which it is possible to make use of Russia in ending the war.

> We would like to know the views of the Russian Government [on helping end the war] in all haste. Furthermore, the Imperial Court is tremendously interested in this matter....
>
> [Togo added in a cable sent shortly thereafter:] [I]t would appear suitable to make clear to the Russians our general attitude with regard to termination of the war. Therefore, please tell them that: We consider the maintenance of peace in East Asia to be one aspect of world peace. Accordingly, Japan—as a proposal for ending the war and because of her concern for the establishment and maintenance of lasting peace—has absolutely no idea of annexing or holding on to the territories which she occupied during the war.[128]

Some Japanese emissaries noted that Washington appeared to be sending signals that "unconditional surrender" would not require destruction of the Imperial House. Nevertheless, Foreign Minister Togo on 17 July signaled the Japanese Embassy in Moscow,

> [T]he Government is well convinced that our strength still [can deliver] considerable blows to the enemy, but since this does not necessarily enable us to feel an absolutely secure peace of mind, we are maintaining our strength against an enemy who will attack repeatedly. If today America and England were to recognize Japan's honor and existence, they would put an end to the war and save humanity from participation in the war, but if they insist unrelentingly upon unconditional surrender, Japan is unanimous in its resolve to wage a thorough-going war. The Emperor himself has deigned to express his determination.

On 21 July, Togo added, "With regard to unconditional surrender, ... we are unable to consent to it under any circumstances whatever. Even if the war drags on and it becomes clear that it will entail much more bloodshed, if the enemy demands unconditional surrender, the whole country as one man will pit itself against him in accordance with the Imperial will."[129]

The next day, 12 July, Togo sent another desperate message to Sato:

> I have not yet received a wire about your interview with Molotov [which had occurred just before Togo's message above reached the embassy]. Accordingly, although it may smack of attacking without sufficient reconnaissance, we think it would be appropriate to go a step further on this occasion and, before the opening of the Three Powers Conference [in Potsdam], like you to present this matter to Molotov in the following terms:
>
> "His Majesty the Emperor, mindful of the fact that the present war daily brings greater evil and sacrifice upon the peoples of all belligerent powers, desires from his heart that it may be quickly terminated. But so long as England and the United States insist upon unconditional surrender, the Japanese Empire has no alternative but to fight on with all its strength for the honor and the existence of the Motherland. His Majesty is deeply reluctant to have any further blood lost among the people of both sides, and it is his desire for the welfare of humanity to restore peace with all possible speed.
>
> The Emperor's will, as expressed above, arises not only from his benevolence toward his own subjects but from his concern for the welfare of humanity in general. It is the Emperor's private intention to send Prince Konoye to Moscow as Special Envoy with a letter from him containing the statement above."[130]

After reviewing all the preceding messages, Sato tartly replied that he was pessimistic that the initiative would succeed unless Japan were to accept terms "virtually equivalent to unconditional surrender." He also pointed out that Japan had already lost a considerable part of the territory it had occupied. Sato delivered the message to one of Molotov's subordinates on the 13th because the Foreign Minister was too busy to receive him. Molotov departed for Potsdam before issuing any reply.[131]

On 19 July, the Soviets informed Sato that, because the Emperor's message contained no concrete proposals, Moscow would not accept a special envoy.[132]

*

Hattori noted that after Okinawa fell, "Enemy air attacks against the homeland mounted in fury day after day."[133] Ugaki's diary through July presents a daily catalogue of bombings that leveled cities, uncontested naval aircraft attacks on military bases and carriers and battleships sitting like ducks in harbors, and leisurely bombardment of coastal industrial and transportation facilities by American battleships and cruisers free from any Japanese interference. He attributed the absence of interceptors to the lack of fuel (though more generally the military was hoarding aircraft for the final battle), and the frequent absence of antiaircraft fire to ammunition shortages. Yet, in the background, preparations for Operation *Ketsu-Go* continued. Repeated tabletop exercises showed they had a long way to go.

The IJN, for example, was preparing suicide attack boats. Ugaki ordered staff work to estimate the probabilities of success with 5,300 navy and more than 4,000 army kamikaze aircraft.[134] Newly developed, simple-to-use, airborne human bombs included the Oka, dropped from a bomber; the Kikka, a ground-launched rocket airship; and the Tikka, a small, slow, low-flying airplane. The IJA converted bombers into Sakuras carrying three tons of explosives.[135]

In early July, IGHQ conducted a new estimate, despite having almost no intelligence on the enemy. It anticipated the first American landings would occur in the Kyushu and Shikoku areas. It expected that the Americans would have 6,000 land-based aircraft (including 1,500 super-heavy bombers, 1,400 heavy bombers, 1,100 medium bombers, and 2,000 fighters) and 2,600 carrier-based aircraft to support the landings, as well as 424 warships. No more than 60 divisions would be employed. The enemy was judged to possess 26 carriers and 74 special carriers, as well 24 battleships.[136]

The Potsdam Joint Declaration

Sakomizu recalled, "Then on [26 July] came the Potsdam Declaration. Suzuki, Togo, and I talked together, and we felt that this declaration must be accepted as the final terms of peace [surrender], whether we liked it or not. Still, the military side of the government said that the terms of the proclamation were 'too dishonorable.'"[137]

A Foreign Ministry analysis noted that the declaration said, "Japan shall be given an opportunity to end this war" and did not say that Japan had to accept surrender or unconditional surrender. It noted that the document only referred to the "unconditional surrender of the Japanese Armed Forces," instead of the Cairo Declaration's "unconditional surrender of Japan." There were suggestions that punishment would focus on the "militarists" and "war criminals." Togo knew the terms were severe, but about the best Japan could hope for in view of the extremely adverse war situation. Still, it was best to reject the declaration and hope to win slightly better terms in negotiations. The Supreme War Council decided to wait and see what came of the Russian gambit.[138]

Ugaki, certainly, was unprepared to throw in the towel. He thought Japan should demand unconditional surrender of the Allies in retort.[139] He learned on 2 August that he was to be named chief of a new Combined Air Fleet.[140]

Togo on 2 August informed Sato, "It has been decided to send a Special Envoy in accordance with the views of the highest leaders of Government, and along with this we are exerting ourselves to collect the views of all quarters on the matter of concrete terms. (Under the circumstances, there is a disposition to make the Potsdam Three Power Proclamation the basis of our study concerning terms.)"[141]

Sato offered this prophetic reply on 4 August: "[I]f the Government and Military dilly-dally in bringing this resolution to fruition, then all Japan will be reduced to ashes and we will not be able [to avoid] following the road to ruin."[142]

Defeat

Hattori recorded:

> It was sultry, but clear, on the morning of 6 August. At 0709 hours, our radar detected a few enemy planes approaching Hiroshima and an alert was sounded, but the enemy bombers executed a turn over Hiroshima without bombing and soon disappeared. The alert was called off at 0730 hours and people began their work for the day.
>
> At 0800 hours, two B-29s were again sighted. Local radio stations broadcast an alert, but it added that the planes might be a reconnaissance mission. People did not pay much attention and went about their morning activities. The two B-29s came over the city at high altitude. As no bombing was expected, most of the people did not enter air-raid shelters but stood looking up at the bombers. A moment after a parachute was seen dropping from one of the bombers, there was a blinding flash and a terrific explosion in the sky over the heart of the city. It was close to 0815 hours. Instantly, tremendous clouds of smoke and dust rose over the whole city, and Hiroshima was engulfed in horrible darkness. Soon, hundreds of fires were started in the city, and Hiroshima became a flaming inferno.
>
> By evening, the whole city was transformed into smoldering ruins and presented a ghastly scene unparalleled in the history of mankind. Almost all people near the center of the explosion died, and those who somehow managed to survive were groaning in agony and suffering from painful burns. Of the entire population of the city, approximately 78,150 were killed and 51,408 were either injured or missing....
>
> Because communication with Hiroshima was completely destroyed, it was not until the afternoon of the sixth that the first report of the catastrophe reached Tokyo.[143]

August 7 dawned in Japan. Ugaki recorded in his diary:

> A radio broadcast from San Francisco this afternoon said that 17 hours before an atomic bomb had been dropped for the first time in history, on Hiroshima, an army base. Though the result wasn't confirmed due to thick clouds over 30,000 feet high, this bomb was 20,000 times more powerful than the "Grand Slam" bombs of the B-29s and its effect was the equivalent to that of 2,000 kg of TNT. In the experimental explosion made in New Mexico on 16 July, a steel tower on which the bomb was placed evaporated and windowpanes 250 miles away from the spot shook, and men staying six miles away were knocked to the ground.
> According to the above, it is clear that was a uranium atom bomb [it actually used plutonium], and it deserves to be regarded as a real wonder, making the outcome of the war more gloomy.[144]

The news agency Domei called Sakomizu to tell him President Truman had announced that the atomic bomb had been dropped on Hiroshima.

> I called the Prime Minister on the phone and reported the announcement. Everyone in the government and even in the military knew that if the announcement were true, no country could carry on a war. Without the atomic bomb, it would be impossible for any country to defend itself against a nation which had the weapon.
> The chance had come to end the war. It was not necessary to blame the military side, the manufacturing people, or anyone else—just the atomic bomb.... Suzuki tried to find a chance to stop the war, and the atom bomb gave him that chance.
> Suzuki and Togo conferred and reported the news to the Emperor. They also gave their opinion that this was the chance to accept the Potsdam Declaration. Still the War Minister could not make up his mind, publicly, openly.[145]

In Moscow, Molotov had told Ambassador Sato that he would be unavailable to meet with him until 8 August. The meeting occurred at 1700 Moscow time, or midnight Tokyo time. To Sato's great astonishment, he received a declaration of war, effective 9 August.[146]

Ugaki received word on 9 August that a New Delhi broadcast indicated that the Soviets had declared war. He rushed to his headquarters. "Various reports successively received made it clear that the Soviets declared war against us at midnight today, and their warships bombarded Rashin [Korea], while their troops entered northern Korea. Air attacks made [...] Now this country is going to fight against the whole world.... I only hope we do our best in the last battle so that we'll have nothing to regret even if we are destroyed."[147]

That same day, the Americans dropped the second atomic bomb on Nagasaki.

The Supreme War Guidance Council gathered. Kido recalled that the IJA initially tried to minimize the effects of the atomic bomb and said the investigation into the real effects was not yet complete.[148] Yonai, Anami, and Umezu pushed for attaching conditions to acceptance of the Potsdam Declaration, including allowing Japan to disarm at its own pace and no occupation of the homeland. Togo said that if they did so, negotiations would be impossible, and the Allies would invade. Anami and Umezu said the IJA could fight an invasion and if lucky repel it. The meeting ended with agreement in principle on accepting the declaration, but not on adding conditions.[149]

According to attendee Admiral Soemu Toyoda,

> There was no member of that Council who had any fundamental objection to terminating the war, but there was some question raised as to whether or not all the terms of the Potsdam Declaration would be acceptable to Japan. The points upon which considerable discussion took place were three: (1) the question of the Emperor's future position; (2) the question of disposition of war criminals; and (3) the question of Japan's future form of organization. On the first point, namely, the question of the Emperor's position, all the members were united in their view that it should be maintained. On the question of war criminals, the desire was expressed by some of the members that the Japanese government should be permitted to ferret out and try the war criminals; and as regards Japan's "future form of National Organization," the desire was expressed that since the present organization of the country was one based upon the deep convictions of the people we should be permitted to maintain the present form. In other words, determination of the form that it should have in the future should be left to the Japanese people and not, for instance, to a plebiscite organized by Allied authorities.... [A]s there was no agreement, a meeting was called in the presence of the Emperor on the 10th at about 0230 in the morning; and the decision was reached there that, subject to the condition that the Emperor's position should in no way be affected, the term of the Potsdam Declaration would be accepted.[150]

According to Hattori, the meeting of the Supreme War Direction Council and other senior officials in the Imperial Presence began at 2350 on 9 August, following a Cabinet meeting that hashed over the same arguments. Suzuki read a short, proposed response to the Allies: "The Government of Japan accepts the Proclamation of the Three Potsdam Powers, dated twenty-sixth of the previous month, with the understanding that the terms enumerated in the said declaration do not comprise any demand concerning alteration of the status of the Emperor in the national law." The IJA and IJN Chief of Staff Toyota argued for continuing the war. At 0200, Suzuki said that as no decision was emerging, he would submit the issue to Imperial decision. The Emperor met privately with Suzuki.[151]

According to Sakomizu, who was present, although there was no constitutional precedent, because His Majesty was supposed to only respond to government proposals, Suzuki asked the Emperor to make the final decision given the extraordinary circumstances. The Emperor decided to accept the Potsdam Declaration.[152]

Suzuki commented to interrogators, "[W]hen the Emperor took his active role in politics, at the end of the war, it was because the Premier, at his direction, had been able to lead the Government up to the point where it could be left to the Emperor to make the decision; in other words, I had prepared the way."[153]

The Japanese Foreign Ministry on 10 August transmitted a surrender proposal to its missions in Berne and Stockholm to be forwarded to the Allies. The key sentence read, "The Japanese Government are ready to accept the terms enumerated in the Joint Declaration which was issued at Potsdam on July 26, 1945, by the heads of the Governments of the United States, Great Britain, and China, and later subscribed by the Soviet Government, with the understanding that the said Declaration does not comprise any demand which prejudices the prerogatives of His Majesty as sovereign ruler."[154]

Ugaki recorded in his diary on 11 August:

> In the afternoon, the chief of intelligence officer, a look of horror on his face, brought me the most hateful news, which said, "Radio broadcast from San Francisco: Japan applied for acceptance of the Potsdam Declaration on condition that Emperor Hirohito be left as he was; otherwise, unconditional surrender. A few hours later, the Strategical Bombing Force commander at the Marinas announced that atomic bomb attacks would be suspended until Japan replied concerning the Potsdam Declaration."
> My God!...
> After receiving the above news, however, my staff learned through telephone liaisons to the Grand Naval Command Headquarters at Hiyoshi that they had noted comments somewhat confirming the news, which had been considered enemy propaganda. Why wasn't the commander in chief, having the full responsibility, consulted in such an important matter? The above incredible broadcast, while hiding [the decision] from us, gave me a shock....
> We still have enough fighting strength remaining. Furthermore, don't we have large army forces still intact in China and our homeland? It might be the view of some clever fellows to surrender with some strength left, instead of being completely destroyed, if and when we can't avoid defeat anyway. ... Even though it becomes impossible for us to continue organized resistance after expending our strength, we must continue guerrilla warfare under the emperor and never give up the war.[155]

Indeed, the military was initially recalcitrant. The Chief of the General Staff issued an order late on 11 August that said, "[I]n order to preserve the national policy and to defend our Imperial soil, the Imperial Army and Navy shall by no means return the sword to the scabbard, even though this should mean the total annihilation of the armed forces of the entire nation."[156]

Tokyo received the Allied reply via monitored broadcast at approximately 0045 on 12 August. It said that the Emperor's and government's authority would be placed under restriction by the Supreme Commander of the Allied Powers, that the Emperor would be required to ensure the government and IGHQ signed the surrender terms, and that he must issue his command to all Japanese forces to cease fire and disarm. The ultimate form of governance would be up to the Japanese people. Occupation would last until the terms of the Potsdam Declaration were fulfilled.[157]

The military continued to resist accepting the Allied terms in various council and Cabinet meetings over the next several days.[158] On 12 August, the Vice Chief of the General Staff transmitted a circular in which he declared that "the Imperial Army and Navy are resolutely determined to continue their efforts to preserve the national structure ... even if it means their destruction. You are well aware of the fact that as a final move toward the preservation of the national structure, diplomatic negotiations have been opened."[159]

Ugaki's forces continued to conduct kamikaze attacks on 13 August and received operational orders to be ready to implement parts of Operation *Ketsu*. The naval command interpreted American ship movements as signaling possible landings, even though Nimitz had signaled Tokyo from Guam in the clear indicating that because communications through Berne took so long, they could broadcast any messages directly in English on a certain frequency.[160]

Sakai and nine of his comrades, after learning surrender was coming, took off in their fighters after dark without authorization and jumped a B-29, shooting it down. Four cities were bombed that night. The *Raiden* pilots at Atugi revolted and refuse to accept the surrender until troops suppressed the outburst.[161]

Asked how long the war would have continued absent the atomic bomb and Soviet offensive, Kido replied, "As I have said, our decision to seek a way out of this war was made in early June.... It was already our decision.... [Those factors] made the task easier to bring the war to a close by silencing those who would advocate the continuation of the war."[162]

The Emperor formally accepted surrender terms on 14 August, amidst continued American bombing raids. He made the unprecedented decision to summon a meeting of the Supreme War Direction Council himself. The military leaders tearfully begged him to demand further clarification of the Allied terms, but Hirohito told them he trusted the Allies' "considerable good will" toward Japan.[163] Toyoda paraphrased his words:

> Continuation of the war does not promise successful conclusion no matter from what angle the situation is considered. Therefore, I have decided, without suggestions from anyone, to order the conclusion of the war, as I cannot endure the thought of having to kill tens, even hundreds of thousands of my subjects, and moreover to have to be called the disturber of world peace. Moreover, it is extremely difficult for me to have to turn over to the Allied authorities officers and men upon whom I have depended all this time as though they were part of my own body. But I have decided to endure what is unendurable and to accept the terms of the Potsdam Declaration.[164]

Tokyo conveyed the acceptance to the Allies through the embassy in Berne:

> 1. His Majesty the Emperor has issued an Imperial Rescript regarding Japan's acceptance of the provisions of the Potsdam Declaration.
> 2. His Majesty the Emperor is prepared to authorize and ensure the signature by his Government and the Imperial General Headquarters of the necessary terms for carrying out provisions of the Potsdam Declaration. His Majesty is also prepared to issue his commands to all the military, naval, and air authorities of Japan and all the forces under their control to cease active operations, to surrender arms, and to issue such orders as may be required by the Supreme Commander of the Allied forces for the execution of the above-mentioned terms.[165]

Ugaki recorded on 15 August:

> [T]he Grand Naval Command through the Kure Naval Station ordered the suspension of any positive attacks on Okinawa and against Soviet Russia. This seems to be endorsing our surrender. I completely disagreed with the order, as I believe we should fight until the last moment.
> Broadcasts from abroad said that Japan had surrendered unconditionally, and that the Emperor himself would broadcast at noon today. So I made up my mind to ram enemy vessels

at Okinawa, directly leading special attack aircraft, and gave an order to prepare *Suisei* planes at this base immediately.

> At noon, following the national anthem, His Majesty himself made a broadcast. What he said wasn't very clear because of poor radio conditions, but I could guess most of it.... We haven't received the cease-fire order, so there is no room for me to reconsider.... I want to live in the noble spirit of special attack.[166]

Hirohito ended the war with his first personal broadcast ever to the nation at noon on 15 August.

> We, the Emperor, in view of world conditions and the present situation of Japan, hereby announce to you our loyal subjects that in our profound anxiety to bring an end to this state of affairs by some extraordinary measure, we have instructed the Japanese Government to accept the Joint Declaration of the United States, Great Britain, the Soviet Union, and China. In conformity with the precepts handed down by our Imperial ancestors, we have always striven for the welfare of our subjects and for the happiness and welfare of all nations. That is precisely why we declared war against Great Britain and the United States.[167]

Sakai recalled, "Exactly at noon we heard the Emperor personally read the surrender orders to our armed forces, wherever they happened to be. The 2,000 men at Oppama [Airfield] stood rigidly at attention on the field. Most of us had never before heard the Emperor's voice. Many of the men were crying unashamedly."

Sakai raced home to hug his new bride. He had survived the war![168]

Ugaki took to the air in his kamikaze plane with some other diehard pilots and apparently crashed at sea.

Fleet Admiral Chester W. Nimitz, USN, signs the Japanese surrender document aboard the U.S. Navy battleship USS *Missouri* (BB-63) in Tokyo Bay on 2 September 1945. (U.S. Navy)

CHAPTER 16

Taking Stock

Looking at the war from the Axis perspective reveals that the leaders of great powers can embroil themselves in war with an undefeatable enemy for reasons which have little to do directly with their prewar relations with that enemy. As we have seen, for Japan, the attack on Pearl Harbor was a necessary auxiliary operation to the main effort in the southern area intended to secure raw materials for waging war and to cut outside support to the Chinese Nationalists who refused to submit to Tokyo's war machine. Many Americans might be surprised to learn that a Japanese move into southern Indochina lit the fuse to war, and that this outcome completely surprised the Japanese high command. What? In Vietnam? Surely the Japanese had some pressing gripe against America!

In Hitler's case, the offer to go to war against America was an incentive for Japan to go to war first and a seemingly fatalistic assumption that conflict was inevitable because of his wars against Great Britain and the Soviet Union. Again, many Americans might be surprised that Hitler did did not devote considerable strategic discussion with his military leaders before deciding to go to war. For Mussolini, who vacillated on how good an idea taking on America was, it seemed the exciting thing to do at the time.

The Japanese, moreover, achieved their initial war aims in smashing fashion and created the defensive perimeter that they imagined to be impenetrable. The German Army's initial drubbing of American forces in North Africa lent to confidence in the High Command that they faced an inferior enemy. Nobody in the Axis leadership posed the question: What happens when the Americans get better at warfighting, with an avalanche of top-grade equipment to do the job?

Would it really have mattered had they done so? Probably not. Germany and Japan tried mightily to match America's defense production and accomplished some amazing increases in quantity and quality. But it was not enough.

Could the Axis Powers Have Fought a Better War?

Could the Axis high commands have conducted different strategies that might have avoided defeat and annihilation? Again, probably not. Both had huge, failing land wars that consumed most of their ground forces. The Japanese Navy tried a carrier-based strategy that failed because of vessel and pilot losses, and then it returned to the prewar strategy of decisive battle, which also failed. American information-dominance played a key role in both failures and would have in any theoretical alternative strategy.

Japan could have settled for its original defense perimeter, which would have eased logistic problems and avoided the disasters at Midway and Guadalcanal. But the thought of American bombers from China and aircraft carriers bombing the homeland, combined with overconfidence, pushed restraint from their minds. And the Allies would have broken that defensive ring, too. Moreover, the war in China preoccupied the Japanese High Command until mid-1943, by which time perceptive Japanese military leaders already believed Japan was going to lose the war. By then, even stripping the best divisions from China to move to the Pacific was too little, too late.

The eastern campaign preoccupied German leaders until November 1943, and they lacked the attention and resources to do anything in the West other than hunker down in their own hopefully impenetrable defense perimeter. After D-Day, the High Command tried a hold-the-line strategy, and when the Allies broke out, Hitler mounted another hold-the-line strategy along the West Wall. The largest attempt at a mobile offensive strategy in the Ardennes was too little, too late.

Finally, the things the Axis leaders did not know (especially that the Allies were reading most of their secret communications) robbed them of any initiative. The things they knew and did not prepare to beat (especially the Allies' strategic bombing capabilities) ground down their capacity to fight the sea, air, and ground wars.

Two more observations tee up the section below.

First, the German leadership for years expected American isolationists to prevent Roosevelt from entering the war. The Japanese, to their credit, did not put much weight on this factor.

Second, the Japanese and Hitler shared two assumptions as they decided for war. Over the next few years, they expected, the balance between their own nation's power and their enemies' strength would shift toward the other side. The relative military strength of Japan and Germany was the strongest it was ever going to be. Both leaderships concluded that if they struck first, they could win before the United States could mobilize its immense power.

Could History Rhyme?

Mark Twain observed, "History never repeats itself, but it does often rhyme." This was an axiom on the Director of Central Intelligence Red Cell, which pondered, to oversimplify, low-probability, high-impact scenarios embroiling U.S. policy—often using historical analogies. Could a major power start a war with America that it did not really want? Let us consider the case of the People's Republic of China as of 2023–2024. Certain developments in China, the United States, and Ukraine could encourage Chinese leaders to conclude that they face an end to their rapid growth in national power and, in fact, face a future of at best stagnation while America continues to forge ahead. Like the Axis leaders, they could risk using force to achieve their aims on Taiwan or the South China Sea—and bet they could win before America could do anything about it.

Hal Brands and Michael Beckley argue in *Danger Zone: The Coming Conflict with China* that, indeed, Chinese dictator, President, and Communist Party chief Xi Jinping has reached the point where China can disrupt the existing international order but is losing his confidence that time is one his side.[1] Xi has spoken of a grand vision of a (new) world order with China as the most powerful country. He uses phrases that echo Japanese rhetoric: "Asia for Asians" with the Americans pushed out, and "all under heaven being in one family."[2]

Brands and Beckley present the case that following 9/11 and America's wars of choice in Afghanistan and Iraq, Beijing pushed its influence ever more overtly in the vacuum in Asia. America's domestic problems left Washington looking feeble: internal focus on COVID-19, a contested presidential election, and an insurrection at the Capitol. At the first high-level talks between Beijing and the new Biden administration in March 2021, senior representative Yang Jiechi mocked the Americans that "the U.S. does not have the qualification to say it wants to speak to China from a position of strength." The Chinese, the authors assert, were convinced that the era of American hegemony was ending and that of China beginning.

Instead, economic and demographic challenges at home mean that "China is looking at a hard future of stagnation and repression. Its window of opportunity has started to open, but it will not remain open for long.[3]

At the very least, *The Economist* in 2023 chronicled what appears to be the end of China's half-century of furious economic development. China's economy in 1980 produced about 10 percent as much as America's; it is now about three-quarters the size.[4]

The Economist observed, "The signs are that Mr. Xi believes China must prepare for sustained economic and, potentially, military conflict with America. Today, therefore, he emphasizes China's pursuit of national greatness, security, and resilience. He is willing to make material sacrifices to achieve those goals, and to the extent he wants growth, it must be 'high quality.'" The government has kneecapped China's thriving tech companies and bungled fiscal and monetary policy.[5] *The Economist* reckons that the greatest force pulling growth downward is not the oft-cited shrinking and aging of the population but declining growth in labor productivity; once pace-setting, it is likely to slow to a respectable pace for an emerging economy.[6]

China has rapidly expanded and modernized the military since the late 1990s and now has the largest navy on earth. (One notes that, like the Japanese Navy from 1907, the Chinese Navy can have only one possible enemy in mind: America.)

China has also built the world's largest ballistic missile force and is on pace to match the level of the American nuclear arsenal by the 2030s.

However, one key difference to the expansions as compared with those of the Axis powers is that it is affordable relative to the economy, with core defense spending around 1.7 percent of GDP; leaders do not face the pressure that Hitler did to use the military because it will become too expensive to maintain. Moreover, existing expansion plans foresee construction sufficient to keep the numerical edge over America in numbers of ships growing, so China does not face Japan's problem that the U.S. fleet was going to vastly outmatch their own in a few years.[7]

Another key difference is that China would be the manufacturing superpower, not America. China's share of global manufactured goods exports reached a world-leading high of 21 percent in 2021, according to the UN. Its manufacturing growth rate outpaced those of Germany, Japan, South Korea, and America.[8] To be sure, in such a war, technological advantages probably would matter more than production of steel or concrete.

The possibility that isolationist Make America Great Again (MAGA) politicians will retain the ability and intent to block U.S. military assistance to Ukraine might stir Chinese faith in the power of isolationists to prevent U.S. involvement in an invasion of Taiwan or using violence to enforce sovereignty claims to the South China Sea, assuming China avoided attacking U.S. targets directly. Like the attack on Pearl Harbor, keeping the U.S. Navy from intervening in an invasion or sea-grab would be a master stroke. If a MAGA politician wins the presidency in the 2024 national elections, China could well calculate he would stay out of a war, despite his frequent China-bashing.[9] The former president himself in an interview with Meet the Press on 17 September 2023 refused to say whether he would defend Taiwan if he were president. Russian President Vladimir Putin, moreover, almost certainly would back his ally China, and MAGA from the top down has shown it admires Putin and often sides with his policies. As is widely known, the former President in February 2022 called Putin a "genius" and "savvy for invading Ukraine."[10]

*

Still, all in all, the history we have reviewed may be just that: history. Would you like to make a bet?

APPENDIX 1

Timeline

Date	Japan	Germany	Italy
1880s–1890s	Japan modernizes and expands military, adopts policy of forward defense of home islands, defeats China, wins special interests in Korea, occupies Taiwan.		
1910s	IJN selects the United States in 1907 as its notional enemy for budgeting purposes and from 1909 its sole imaginary enemy.		
1920s	1928: Military begins gaining clout in government. Spate of publications appear aimed at convincing the public that the country one day will have to fight the U.S.	1922: Hitler says U.S. entry into World War I decided the outcome, suggests side that wins next war will be the one backed by U.S.	
1930–1935	Japanese annual naval exercises practice "decisive battle" against U.S. fleet.		
1931	"Quick War-Quick Decision" policy emerges as alternative to U.S.-style slow mobilization in World War I. Japan invades Manchuria, which starts long slide to war with U.S.		

Date	Japan	Germany	Italy
1932	Lt. Gen. Hatta portrays U.S. as main enemy, accurately projects number of troops U.S. would send overseas in next war. IJA doctrine focuses only on offense.	Hitler in speech says Europe cannot overcome U.S. production advantages.	
1933	Government cable says one faction favors war with the U.S. immediately because naval balance will worsen after 1936, argues even defeating U.S. fleet would only result in long war.		
1934		Chancellor Hitler in interview says he's been too busy to think about America.	
1935			
1936	Japan quits Washington Naval Limitation Treaty, forms Anti-Comintern Pact with Germany. IJA launches 12-year expansion plan.	German Embassy says nobody in U.S. intends to get involved if new European war breaks out. Anti-Comintern Pact with Japan.	
1937	IJN launches construction program to build 18-inch-gun battleships. Japan invades China south of Great Wall. Aircraft bomb U.S. gunboat *Panay* on Yangtze, "stepping stone to war."	Embassy warns U.S. will support rearmament of Britain and France, will not remain neutral in Far East.	Italy joins Anti-Comintern Pact.
1938	Tokyo declares intention to establish "New Order" in East Asia: China. Forming Axis, tensions with USSR dominate leadership talks—not U.S.	Army chief of staff and finance minister warn Hitler that if war started, U.S. would provide Britain arms on "vast scale," political and propaganda support. Embassy reports Roosevelt preparing public for two-front war, will enter war if democracies face defeat. Hitler tells Mussolini U.S. will not intervene. In speech, dismisses U.S. as racial conglomeration.	Mussolini stops meeting with U.S. officials.

TIMELINE • 391

Date	Japan	Germany	Italy
1939	21 Jan.: PM Hirunama says no choice but to exterminate those who oppose Japan. War crimes prosecutors called this turning point toward Pearl Harbor. U.S. naval attaché reports Japanese believe U.S. will restrict role in Far East to "note writing," evince sense of naval invulnerability vs. U.S. China war costly and dragging on. War in Europe leaves Japan more dependent on U.S. for raw materials.	29 Apr.: FM Ribbentrop tells Hungarian PM U.S. will send arms but no troops if war breaks out. Embassy predicts slow mobilization, strategic defense in Atlantic and Pacific, but again says U.S. will enter war if Allies face defeat. General Staff expects faster U.S. mobilization than in WWI but U.S. will not enter war. Hitler thinks mixed races will prevent U.S. unity. 1 Sep.: Germany attacks Poland. Hitler orders subs not to sink passenger ships to avoid provoking U.S.	Mussolini wants Hitler to wait until 1942 for war. After German attack on Poland, Italian FM Ciano says U.S. entry into war "practically unavoidable."
1940	Jan.: U.S. fleet moves from CA to Hawaii. Feb.: Navy says U.S. hardening attitude, pursuing naval arms race. Tokyo aims to keep U.S. out of war in Europe, per deal with Germany. Jul.: Leadership discusses "southern advance" on NEI and Singapore. IJN says it means war with U.S. eventually. Sep.: Leaders agree to sign Tripartite Pact, make southern advance, peacefully "as far as possible." IJN starts war preparations against U.S. in Nov. Prime Minister Konoye says Japan has enough resources to wage a long war. IJN tells U.S. reps it's still possible to *avoid* war. Yamamoto launches planning for Pearl Harbor.	Hitler tells Göring U.S. will not enter the war under any conditions. He calculates that Japanese threat encourages U.S. neutrality in Europe. 10 May: Germany attacks in West. Ribbentrop expects U.S. entry soon after France falls but says there is time to win before that matters. High Command views entry as probable. Hitler says it can still be avoided. Oct.: Hitler says stop assuming U.S. entry; Germans stop talking about it for months.	Jan.: Mussolini warns Hitler U.S. will not permit complete defeat of the democracies. End the war, he suggests, and democratic empires will collapse on their own. 10 Jun.: Italy declares war on Britain and France.

Date	Japan	Germany	Italy
Early 1941	Mar.: FM Matsuoka says antiwar group fears war with U.S. would last 5–10 years. Army briefs emperor on plan for southern advance. Apr.: General plan for Pearl Harbor completed. Neutrality pact with Russia leaves Japan free for southern advance. Retired senior navy officers publish articles saying war will come soon.	Mar.: Hitler says U.S. can't arm UK and self at same time. No impact on war until 1942. Counts on U-boat war and Luftwaffe. Germany has no interest in war vs. U.S., but Hitler has taken it into his calculations. German experience and soldiers are superior to America's. 4 Apr.: Hitler says Germany would join a U.S.-Japanese war. June: Hitler and Mussolini agree that if Japan remains firm, U.S. will stay out of war. Laughs off as "childish" data circulated by U.S. ambassador on planned aircraft and tank output (that were short of actual production). Hitler tells Mussolini just before attack on USSR that he is indifferent to U.S. entry into war because it is already helping UK with all the resources it can.	Mar.: Mussolini says U.S. now enemy No. 1, Russia No. 2, but don't provoke U.S.
Late 1941	Jul.: Cabinet decides to launch southern advance, even if it leads to war with U.S. Reasons: cut off support to Chiang and obtain raw materials. Japan will prepare for war against the UK and U.S. but will act if that were only option to continue southern advance. Imperial Headquarters (a wartime body) established at Palace. U.S. freezes Japanese financial assets over intervention in Indochina. 3 Sep.: Cabinet decides Japan will go to war if no deal with U.S. by 10 October. 1 Nov: Deadline moved to 30 November. 1 Dec.: Imperial conference issues irrevocable war decision.		

TIMELINE • 393

Date	Japan	Germany	Italy
7/8 December	Japan attacks Pearl Harbor and Philippines.	Hitler overjoyed. Now Germany can hit America hard at sea.	Mussolini thrilled about war with America. Ciano worried, thinks in long run America will turn the tide.
11 December		Germany declares war against America.	
Early 1942	Japan achieves war aims faster and at lower cost than expected. Decides to expand defense perimeter.	U-boat battle of the Atlantic.	
4–7 June 1942	Battle of Midway destroys heart of carrier force and naval air arm. A few conclude Japan will lose war.		
29 June	IGHQ concedes initiative, orders forces in Southern Area outside New Guinea to switch from offensive to holding actions.		
6 July 1942	Americans land on Guadalcanal, completely surprise the Japanese.		
October 1942			Ciano and military intelligence chief expect American landings in northwest Africa. Ciano thinks Italy will be next target and doubts ability to withstand the bashing.

Date	Japan	Germany	Italy
November 1942	Diplomats see Allied landings in Africa as a turning point that threatens Italy's place in Axis and could leave Japan to fight on alone. Leadership reassess strategic situation, realizes American offensive in Pacific has launched earlier than expected. Air attacks on Japan likely in 1943 from China and carriers. If Japan wins all its battles, still possible to achieve unassailable position.	Anglo-American landings in northwest Africa surprise Germans. Hitler and Göring acknowledge American success.	
December 1942–February 1943	Diplomats see America on the offense in east and west, tide turning against Germany, Italy shaky. America to be global power after war. Allied air power already superior. IJA halts offensive operations on Guadalcanal, evacuates forces. IJA: War situation does not permit optimism. Kido sees war plan going off the rails.		Ciano resigns.
May 1943	Diplomats expect invasion of Sicily, Italy. Japan may have to fight on alone after German defeat.	Axis surrenders in Tunisia. Prisoner loss equals Stalingrad.	Axis surrenders in Tunisia.
July 1943			Allies invade Sicily.
September 1943	IJA and IJN radically change war strategy from offense to holding an "absolute national defense sphere." Idea of losing war arises in Emperor's presence.	Germany takes over defense of Italy, moves divisions from eastern front to Mediterranean, and OKW issues *Weisung* 51 that says that main war threat is Allied invasion in west.	Allies invade Italy. Italy surrenders unconditionally. Germany disarms Italians and takes over defense.
October 1943	Japan reorganizes economy to boost war production in face of American output. Changes internal security, industrial and labor dispersal, to deal with expected American bombing.		

TIMELINE • 395

Date	Japan	Germany	Italy
November 1943		OKW declares the Western Front will be more important than the Eastern. Luftwaffe moving most fighters from east and Mediterranean theaters to west.	
December 1943		Japanese service attachés in Europe conclude Germany cannot win but can fight defensively for some time. OKW has no information on Allied plans other than from the the press.	
January 1944	Americans land in Marshalls, part of pre-war Japan.	P-51s escort bombers push deep into Germany, crush Luftwaffe fighter defenses by spring.	
February 1944	Loss of admiralties completes destruction of outer defenses of absolute national defense sphere.		
April 1944	Large 10-month offensive begins in China to deprive Americans of airbases and open land route to Southeast Asia for resources to offset huge shipping losses to U.S. subs and planes.		
May 1944	Adm. Ugaki anticipates doom if main enemy force not destroyed.		
June 1944	Americans invade Saipan. IJN suffers lopsided loss in "decisive battle" in Philippine Sea. Defeat persuades additional IJN officers that Japan will lose. First B-29 raid on Japan from China.	Allies land in Normandy. Hitler believes Allied materiel superiority will carry the day if Germans can't destroy the beachhead. American daylight bombing starts destroying petroleum production, worsening fuel shortages.	

Date	Japan	Germany	Italy
July 1944	Saipan falls. Before dying, Combined Fleet commander Koga says war will be lost if Marianas and Western Carolines fall. Tojo government collapses. Koiso government creates Supreme Council for the Direction of the War. Kido and liberal politicians conclude it would be best to end the war. Draft IGHQ war plan sees intensifying crisis that will lead to termination of war. Must defend homeland even if incapable of organized warfare. Final version foresees another decisive battle and defense of Philippines. Americans invade Guam. Organization of suicide air units begins. War production surges for six months.	C-in-C West Rundstedt tells OKW his troops cannot stand up to the enemy's materiel superiority and suggests ending the war; he is sacked. Assassination attempt wounds Hitler. Americans break out of Normandy in Operation *Cobra*. Jodl decides war in west is lost. Hitler admits he can't hold France and will have to retreat to the West Wall and Vosges Mountains.	
August 1944		U.S. Third Army pushes unopposed toward central France. OKW operations chief Jodl concludes the war in the west is lost. American and French armies land in southern France.	
September 1944	Foreign diplomats in Tokyo report public admissions that an eventual invasion of Japan is likely. Americans invade Carolines.	Hitler's first discussion of big counteroffensive on 6 September. Americans reach West Wall near Aachen. Germans scrape together enough men to hold the line against under-supplied enemy. American bombers start destroying transportation network.	
October–November 1944	Japanese worry that Soviets will join war against them once Germany surrenders. Last-ditch bid to engage Chiang in peace talks; Chiang agrees if Japan ends combat and punishes those responsible. Americans land on Leyte in Philippines on 20 October, crush Japanese fleet in second "decisive battle." Japanese start kamikaze attacks. B-29s from Saipan begin bombings in November.	Static warfare on Western Front; French and Americans reach Rhine in south in November. Forces build for Ardennes offensive. SS leaders start to plan resistance in an occupied Germany.	

TIMELINE

Date	Japan	Germany	Italy
December 1944		Hitler launches Battle of the Bulge. Bombing of transportation causes sharp drop in war production that will continue through end of war.	
January 1945	IGHQ concludes Japan's ability to wage organized warfare will end in mid-1945. Attachés abroad told to expect invasion of Japan by then. Americans invade Luzon 9 January. IGHQ orders delaying battle. Americans start area bombing of cities.	Americans eliminate the Bulge. Most German armor moves to east.	
February 1945	Americans control most of Luzon, planes and ships cut supply lines from Southeast Asia to Japan. Land on Iwo Jima.	German army in west capable only of delaying action.	
March 1945	Japan halts all convoys to Southeast Asia due to horrendous losses. Military paper tells public invasion is inevitable, but IJA will defeat it.	Americans cross Rhine at Remagen.	
April 1945	Americans invade Okinawa. Koiso government falls, replaced by Suzuki. Emperor hints he should find a way to end the war. Suzuki expresses sympathy for Roosevelt's death. Leaders outside military speak openly for end.	Allies quickly overrun western Germany. Hitler commits suicide on 30 April.	
May 1945		Germany capitulates on 7 May.	
June 1945	Okinawa falls. Japanese decide to ask Moscow to broker peace talks with the Allies. Emperor endorses having both plans to end the war and continue it.		

Date	Japan	Germany	Italy
July 1945	Japan conveys request to Soviets. Insist amongst themselves that unconditional surrender is unacceptable. Suzuki and foreign minister privately want to accept terms of Potsdam Declaration on 26 July.		
August 1945	Atomic bomb dropped on Hiroshima 6 August. Soviets declare war 8 August, Nagasaki bombed. Suzuki asks emperor on 9 August to break tradition and make the final decision on surrender. Hirohito rejects military appeals and approves, with understanding that Imperial House will remain. Japan transmits surrender on 10 August.		

APPENDIX 2

Tables

Annual Allied and Axis Naval Construction 1939–1945

USA

	Aircraft Carriers	Battleships	Cruisers	Destroyers	Destroyer Escorts/ Corvettes	Submarines
1939						
1940	1					
1941	1			2		2
1942	18	4	8	82		34
1943	65	2	11	128	298	55
1944	45	2	14	74	194	81
1945	13		14	63	6	31

UK

	Aircraft Carriers	Battleships	Cruisers	Destroyers	Destroyer Escorts/ Corvettes	Submarines
1939			3	22	5	7
1940	2	1	7	27	109	15
1941	2	2	6	39	87	20
1942		2	6	73	71	33
1943	2		7	37	79	39
1944	4		2	31	55	39
1945	4		1	13	7	14

Japan

	Aircraft Carriers	Battleships	Cruisers	Destroyers	Submarines
1939					
1940					
1941	1	1	4		61
1942	6	1	6	10	33
1943	4		3	12	37
1944	5		2	24	39
1945				17	30

Source: John Ellis, *World War II: A Statistical Survey* (Aircraft carriers corrected)

Annual Tonnage of Japanese Tankers Built, Sunk, and Extant, 1941–1945

	Tonnage Built	Tonnage Sunk	Tonnage End of Year
1941			578,000
1942	20,316	9,538	686,000
1943	254,927	169,491	673,000
1944	624,290	754,889	860,000
1945	85,654	351,028	266,948

Source: John Ellis, *World War II: A Statistical Survey*

Allied and Axis GDP (in 1990 dollars, billions)

Country/Year	1938	1939	1940	1941	1942	1943	1944	1945
USA	800	869	943	1,094	1,235	1,399	1,499	1,474
UK	284	287	316	344	353	362	346	331
France	186	199	164	130	116	110	93	101
Italy	141	151	147	144	145	137	117	92
USSR	359	366	417	359	274	305	362	343
Germany	375	411	414	441	444	454	466	322
Japan	169	184	192	196	197	194	189	144

Source: Ralph Zuljan Archive

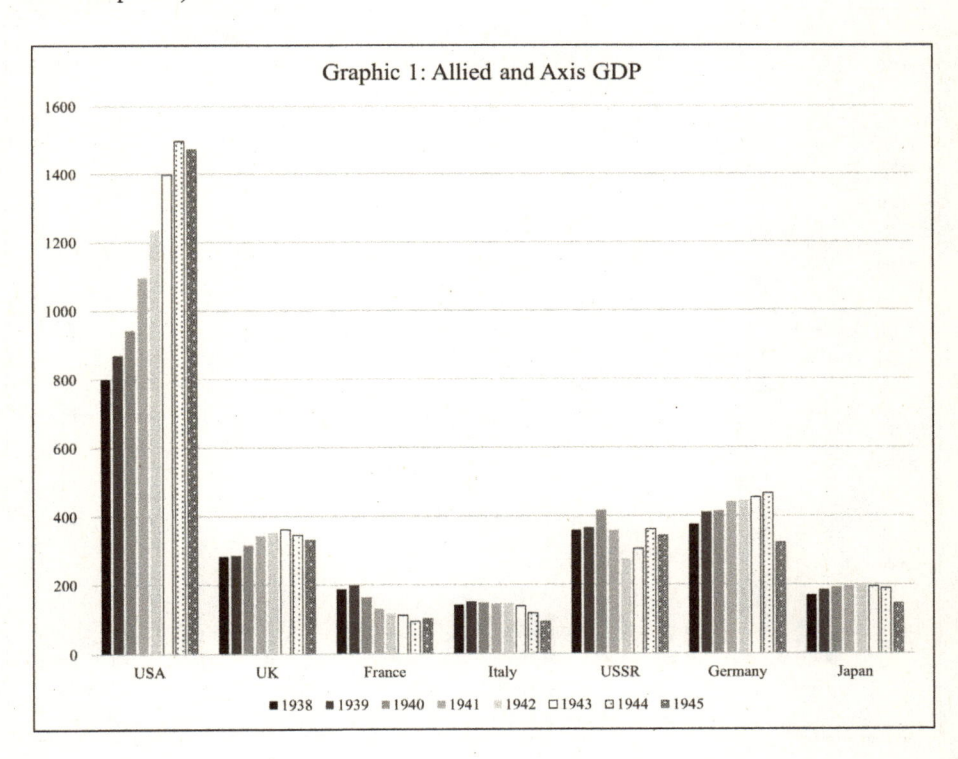

Allied and Axis Military Aircraft Production 1939–1945

Country/Year	1939	1940	1941	1942	1943	1944	1945
USA	5,856	12,804	26,277	47,836	85,898	96,318	49,761
UK	7,940	15,049	20,094	23,672	26,263	26,461	12,070
USSR	10,382	10,565	15,735	25,436	34,845	40,246	20,252
Italy	1,692	2,142	3,503	2,818	528	0	0
Germany	8,295	10,826	11,776	15,556	25,527	39,087	7,544
Japan	4,467	4,768	5,088	8,861	16,693	28,180	8,263

Source: John Ellis, *World War II: A Statistical Survey*

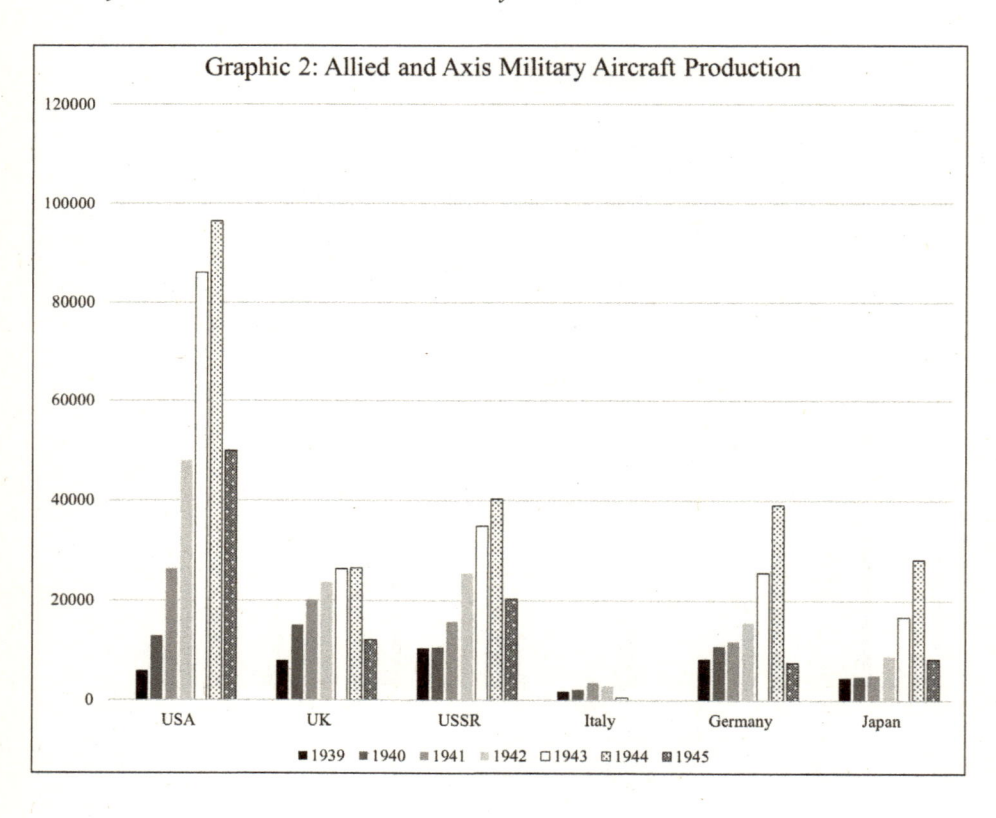

Graphic 2: Allied and Axis Military Aircraft Production

Allied and Axis Fighter Production 1941–1945

Country	1941	1942	1943	1944	1945
USA	4,416	10,769	23,988	38,873	20,742
UK	7,086	9,849	10,727	10,730	5,445
USSR	7,086	9,924	14,590	17,913	9,000
Italy	1,339	1,488	528	0	0
Germany	3,744	5,515	10,898	26,326	5,883
Japan	1,080	2,935	7,147	13,811	5,474

Source: John Ellis, *World War II: A Statistical Survey*

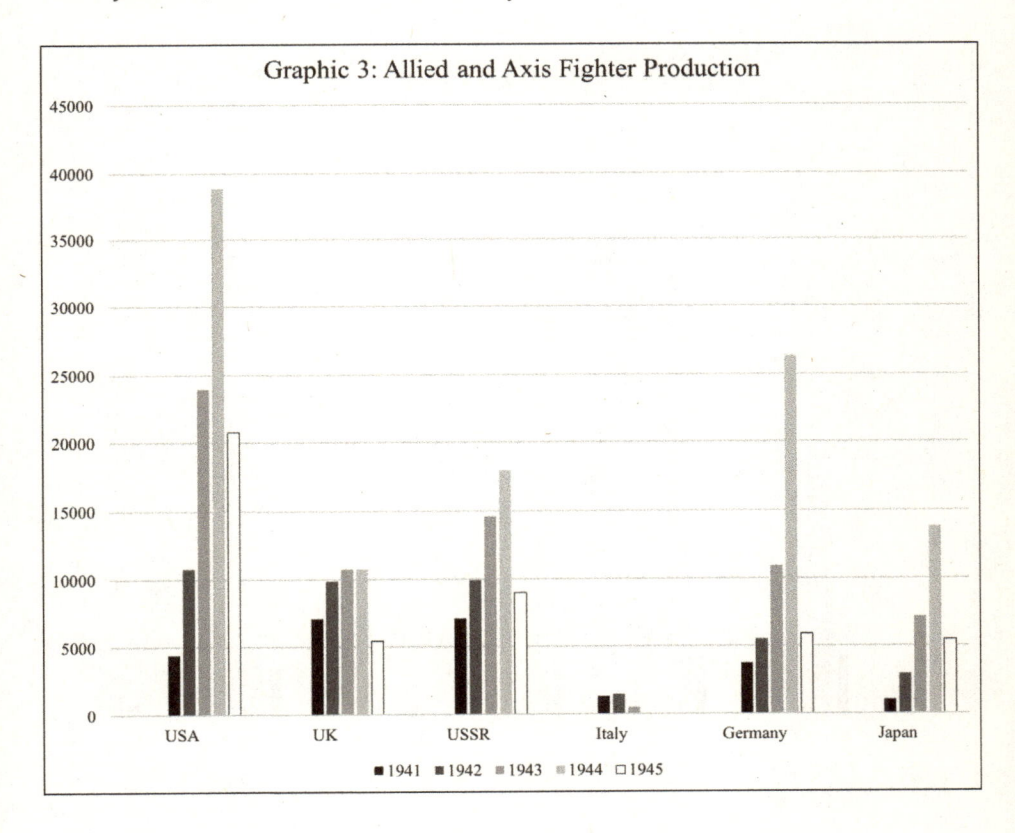

Allied and Axis Bomber Production 1941–1945

Country/Year	1941	1942	1943	1944	1945
USA	4,115	12,627	29,355	35,003	16,087
UK	4,668	6,253	7,728	7,903	2,812
USSR	3,748	3,537	4,074	4,186	2,000
Italy	754	566	103	0	0
Germany	3,373	4,502	4,789	1,982	5,883
Japan	1,080	2,935	7,147	0	0

Source: John Ellis, *World War II: A Statistical Survey*

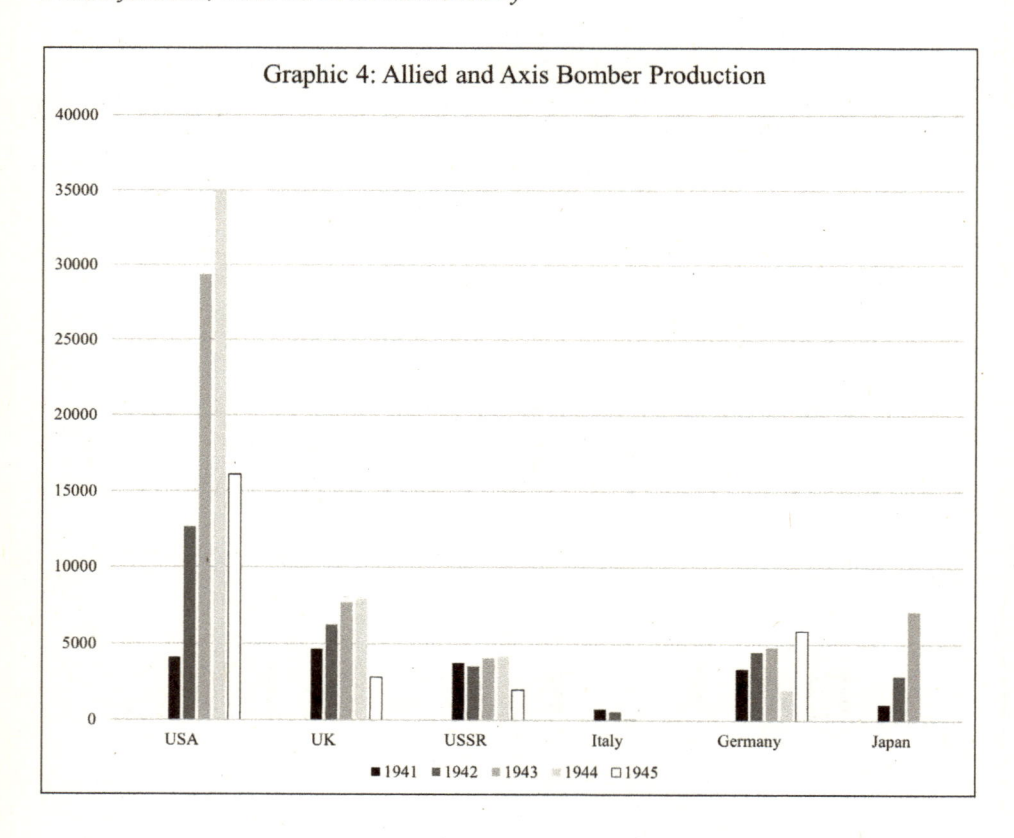

Graphic 4: Allied and Axis Bomber Production

Allied and Axis Tank and SP Gun Production 1940–1945

Country/Year	1940	1941	1942	1943	1944	1945
USA	331	4,052	24,997	29,497	17,565	11,968
UK	1,399	4,841	8,611	7,476	4,600	
USSR	2,794	6,590	24,446	24,089	28,963	15,149
Italy	2,50	595	1,252	336	0	0
Germany	1,643	3,790	6,180	12,063	19,002	3,932
Japan	315	595	557	558	353	137

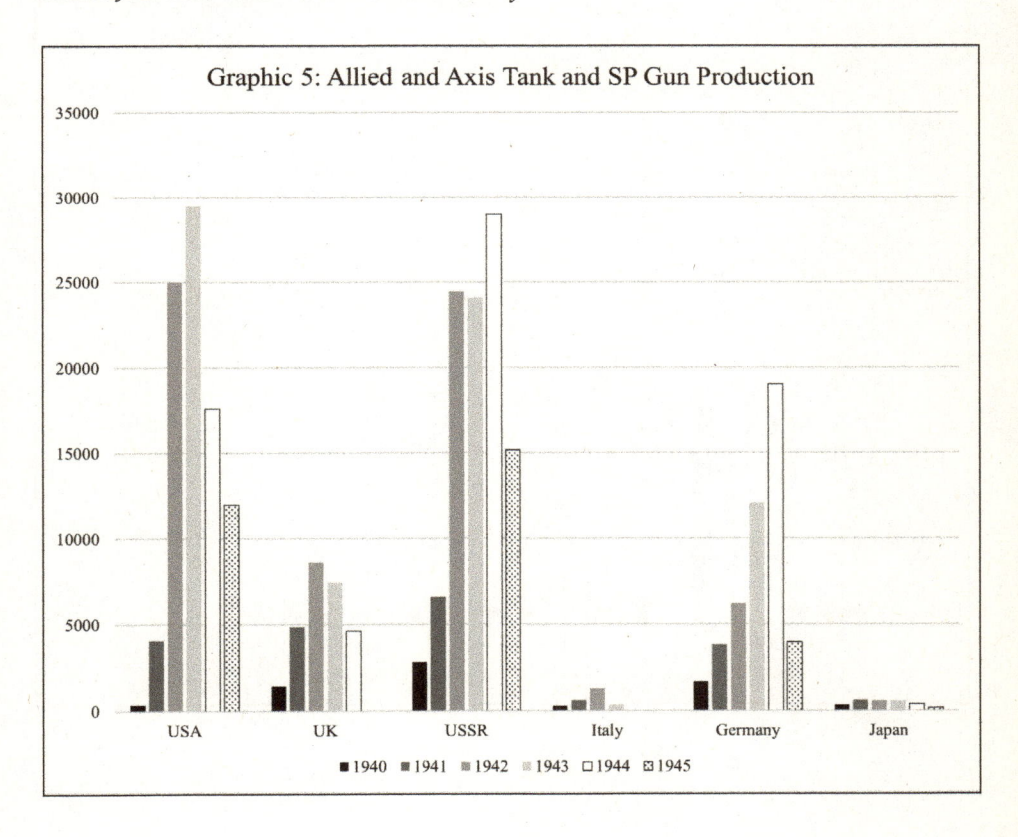

Source: John Ellis, *World War II: A Statistical Survey*

Allied and Axis Merchant Shipping Production 1939–1945 (gross tons)

Country/Year	1939	1940	1941	1942	1943	1944	1945
USA	376,419	528,697	1,031,974	5,479,766	11,448,360	928,8156	5,839,858
UK	629,705	842,910	1,185,894	1,270,714	1,136,804	919,357	393,515
Japan	320,466	293,612	210,373	260,059	769,085	1,699,203	599,563

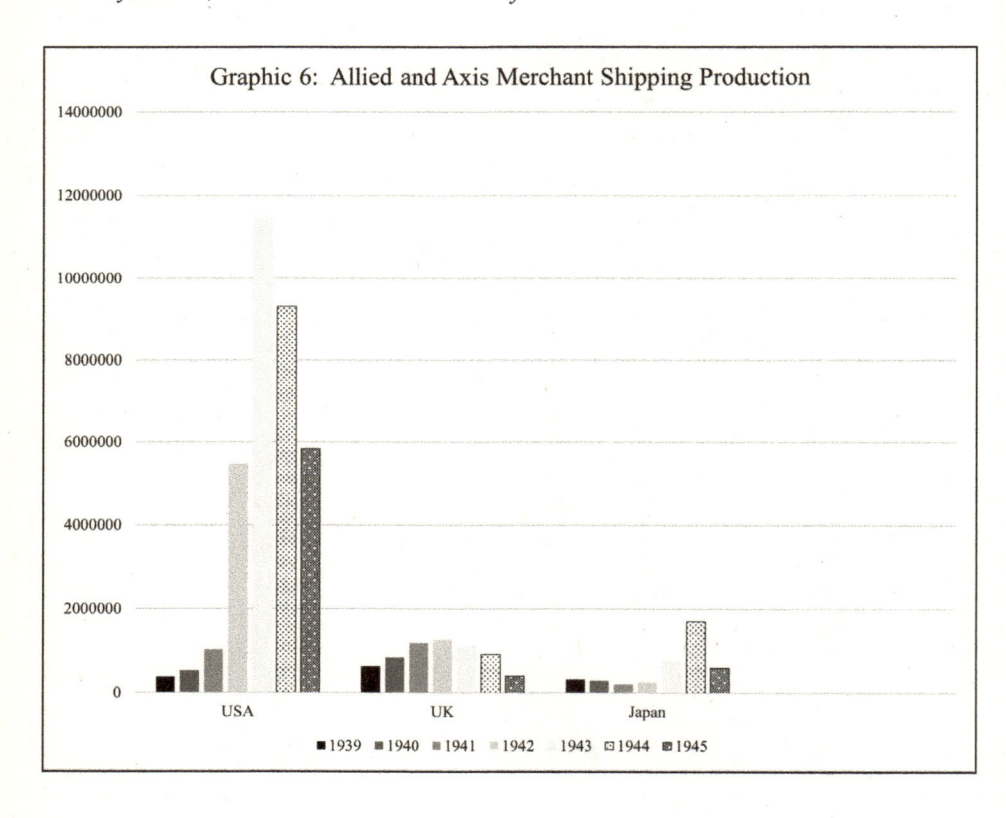

Source: John Ellis, *World War II: A Statistical Survey*

Graphic 6: Allied and Axis Merchant Shipping Production

Endnotes

Preface

1. Russell A. Hart, "Book Review: *Hitler's Fatal Miscalculation: Why Germany Declared War on the United States.* Klaus H. Schmider," *Journal of Military History*, Vol. 86, No. 1, January 2022, 206–7.
2. Klaus H. Schmider, *Hitler's Fatal Miscalculation: Why Germany Declared War on the United States* (Cambridge: Cambridge University, 2021), 2. (Hereafter Schmider.)
3. Schmider, 159.
4. Schmider, 9.
5. "HATTORI, Tekushiro," CIA Information Report ZJJ-84, 18 April 1952, CIA FOIA, www.cia.gov/readingroom/docs/HATTORI%2C%20TAKUSHIRO%20%20%20VOL.%202_0027.pdf as of September 2021.
6. Robert Citino, review of Fighting Patton, Journal of Military History, Vol. 72, No. 2, April 2013, 739–41.

Chapter 1

1. Philip Ziegler, *Between the Wars, 1919–1939* (New York: MacLehose Press, 2016), passim.
2. See Eri Hotta, *Japan 1941: Countdown to Infamy* (New York: Alfred A. Knopf, 2013), 19–20ff, for the case that Japanese leaders were nothing but gamblers. (Hereafter Hotta.)
3. Phillips O'Brien, *How the War Was Won: Air-Sea Power and Allied Victory in World War II* (Cambridge, UK: Cambridge University Press, 2015, passim. (Hereafter O'Brien.)
4. *Generaloberst* Alfred Jodl, "An Interview with Genobst Alfred Jodl: Ardennes Offensive," ETHINT-51, 31 July 1945, National Archives, 9. (Hereafter Jodl, "Ardennes Offensive.")
5. William Hamilton, "Bush Began to Plan War Three Months After 9/11," *The Washington Post*, 17 April 2004, A1.
6. James B. Wood, *Japanese Military Strategy in the Pacific War: Was Defeat Inevitable?* (New York: Rowman & Littlefield Publishers, Inc., 2007), 1–2. (Hereafter Wood.)
7. Liddell Hart, B. H. *History of the Second World War.* New York, NY: G. Putnam's Sons, 1970, 199. (Hereafter Liddell Hart, *History of the Second World War.*)
8. Gordon Prange, *At Dawn We Slept* (New York: Penguin Books, 1981), 3. (Hereafter Prange.)
9. Richard B. Frank, *Tower of Skulls: A History of the Asia-Pacific War, July 1937–May 1942* (New York: W. W. Norton & Company, Inc., 2021), 1–5, 12. (Hereafter Frank.)
10. Jeffrey Record, *Japan's Decision for War in 1941: Some Enduring Lessons* (Carlisle, PA: United States Army Strategic Studies Institute, February 2009, www.strategicstudiesinstitute.army.mil/pdffiles/PUB905.pdf as of November 2010), 1–3. (Hereafter Record.)
11. Record, 6.
12. Grew, *Ten Years in Japan*, 467–70.

13 Wood, 3, 9.
14 *Judgment: International Military Tribunal for the Far East*, Hyperwar, www.ibiblio.org/hyperwar/PTO/IMTFE/index.html as of November 2010, 84ff. (Hereafter *Judgment: International Military Tribunal for the Far East*.)
15 Drea, 163ff.
16 Hiroyuki Agawa, *The Reluctant Admiral: Yamamoto and the Imperial Navy* (New York: Kodansha International, 1979), 158–70. (Hereafter Agawa.)
17 *Judgment: International Military Tribunal for the Far East*, 84ff.
18 Edward J. Drea, *Japan's Imperial Army: Its Rise and Fall, 1853–1945* (Lawrence, KA: The University Press of Kansas, 2009), 52–57. (Hereafter Drea.)
19 Drea, 75.
20 Drea, 77.
21 Drea, 78ff.
22 Drea, 100.
23 Drea, 102–9.
24 Drea, 127–28. Hotta, 95.
25 Wood, 24.
26 "Primary Documents—'21 Demands' Made by Japan to China, 18 January 1915," FirstWorldWar.com, www.firstworldwar.com/source/21demands.htm as of September 2021.
27 John Prados, *Combined Fleet Decoded* (New York: Random House, 1995), 12–13. (Hereafter Prados.) Shigeru Fukudome, "The Hawaii Operation," Dr. David Evans, editor and translator, and Dr. Raymond O'Conner, introduction and commentary, *The Japanese Navy in World War II: In the Words of Former Japanese Naval Officers* (Annapolis, MD: Naval Institute Press, 1986), 8. (Hereafter Fukudome.)
28 Eric Hammel, *How America Saved the World: The Untold Story of U.S. Preparedness Between the Wars* (Minneapolis, MN: Zenith Press, 2009), 21. (Hereafter Hammel.)
29 Takushiro Hattori, *The Complete History of the Greater East Asia War* (Published by Tenkishi Masukagi, 1953, translated by SIA, G-2, Hqs 500th Military Intelligence Service Group, located in Gordon W. Prange Papers, Special Collections, University of Maryland Libraries, Series IV, G-2 Historical Division, box 4), 6. (Hereafter Hattori, Vol. 1.)
30 Drea, 140.
31 Drea, 150–51.
32 *Judgment: International Military Tribunal for the Far East*, 84ff.
33 "Basic Tactical Doctrine," Defense Attaché Tokyo memorandum, 2 March 1932, RG 165, Records of the War Department General and Special Staffs, M1216 Correspondence of the Military Intelligence Division Relating to General Political, Economic, and Military Conditions in Japan, 1918–1941, roll 23.
34 Drea, 146–62.
35 "The Threat of Military Reduction," Military Attaché Tokyo memorandum, 27 March 1931, RG 165, Records of the War Department General and Special Staffs, M1216 Correspondence of the Military Intelligence Division Relating to General Political, Economic, and Military Conditions in Japan, 1918–1941, A2 Cab 52/9, roll 23.
36 "Japan: Political Estimate, August 20, 1941," 10 August 1941, G-2, War Department General Staff, OSS Records, RG 226, Intelligence Reports, Report 163, Entry 16, 190/3/11/4, box 2, 2–3. (Hereafter "Japan: Political Estimate.")
37 "Japan: Political Estimate," 2–3.

38 United States Strategic Bombing Survey, *United States Strategic Bombing Survey (European War) (Pacific War)*, Interrogations of Japanese Officials, Japanese Naval Planning, Nav No. 75, USSBS No. 378, 1 November 1945, www.ibiblio.org/hyperwar/AAF/USSBS/IJO/IJO-75.html. (Hereafter USSBS No. 378.)
39 Ugaki, 22.
40 Rana Mitter, *China's War with Japan, 1937–1945: The Struggle for Survival* (London: Penguin Books, 2013), 25. (Hereafter Mitter.)
41 Hattori, Vol. 1, 8.
42 Koichi Kido diary, located in Gordon W. Prange Papers, Special Collections, University of Maryland Libraries, Series IV, G-2 Historical Division, box 55, (1 of 3), 19 September 1931ff.
43 Hattori, Vol. 1, 9.
44 Hattori, Vol. 1, 11.
45 Joseph C. Grew, *Ten Years in Japan* (New York, Simon & Shuster, 1944), 3–4. (Hereafter Grew, *Ten Years in Japan*.)
46 John Gunther, *Inside Asia: 1942 War Edition* New York: Harper & Brothers, 1942, 53. (Hereafter Gunther.)
47 Grew, *Ten Years in Japan*, 14.
48 Mitter, 25.
49 "Basic Tactical Doctrine," Defense Attaché Tokyo memorandum, 2 March 1932, RG 165, Records of the War Department General and Special Staffs, M1216 Correspondence of the Military Intelligence Division Relating to General Political, Economic, and Military Conditions in Japan, 1918–1941, roll 23.
50 *Judgment: International Military Tribunal for the Far East*, 84ff.
51 Grew, *Ten Years in Japan*, 38–39.
52 Grew, *Ten Years in Japan*, 39.
53 "The National Defense of Japan," Defense Attaché Tokyo memorandum, 28 July 1932, RG 165, Records of the War Department General and Special Staffs, M1216 Correspondence of the Military Intelligence Division Relating to General Political, Economic, and Military Conditions in Japan, 1918–1941, roll 23.
54 Paul A. C. Koistinen, *Planning War, Pursuing Peace: The Political Economy of American Warfare, 1920–1939* (Lawrence, KS: University Press of Kansa, 1998), 1–10. (Hereafter Koistinen, *1920–1939*.)
55 Hammel, 129.
56 Ken Roberts Greenfield, Robert R. Palmer, and Bell I. Wiley, *Army Ground Forces: The Organization of Ground Combat Troops*, CMH Pub 2-1 (Washington, D.C.: Center of Military History, United States Army, 1947), 128–29, 191. (Hereafter *The Organization of Ground Combat Troops*.)
57 Hammel, 126. Koistinen, *1920–1939*, 1.
58 Brian McAllister Linn, *The Echo of Battle: The Army's Way of War* (Cambridge, MA: Harvard University Press, 2007), 106–7.
59 Hammel, 23–24.
60 Hammel, 118.
61 Nobutaka Ike, translator and editor, *Japan's Decision for War: Records of the 1941 Policy Conferences* (Stanford, CA: Stanford University Press, 1967), xix. (Hereafter *Records of the 1941 Policy Conferences*.)
62 Mark Skinner Watson, *Chief of Staff: Prewar Plans and Operations: United States Army in World War II: The War Department* (Washington, D.C.: Office of the Chief of Military History, Department of the Army, 1951), 87.

63 Morton Louis, *The Fall of the Philippines: The United States Army in World War II, The War in the Pacific* (Washington, D.C.: Office of the Chief of Military History, Department of the Army, 1952), 62–63.
64 Prados, 87.
65 Col. Adolf Carlson, "Joint U.S. Army-Navy War Planning On The Eve of The First World War: Its Origins and Its Legacy," 1998, www.strategicstudiesinstitute.army.mil/pubs/download.cfm?q=351 as of July 2018.
66 Stewart Brown, "Japan Stuns World, Withdraws from League," United Press, 24 February 1943.
67 "On the Foreign Policy of Japan vis-à-vis Europe and America Following Withdrawal from the League of Nations," Historical Files Relating to the Cases Tried Before the International Military Tribunal for the Far East, International Prosecution Section Staff Historical Files, RG 331, M1663, roll 23.
68 Ibid.
69 Schmider, 48–49.
70 Grew, *Ten Years in Japan*, 84.
71 Hammel, 29.
72 Prados, 60–63.
73 Wood, 11.
74 *Judgment: International Military Tribunal for the Far East*, 102.
75 "Army Pamphlet on Principles of National Defense," Defense Attaché Tokyo memorandum, 21 November 1934, RG 165, Records of the War Department General and Special Staffs, M1216 Correspondence of the Military Intelligence Division Relating to General Political, Economic, and Military Conditions in Japan, 1918–1941, roll 24. (Hereafter "Army Pamphlet on Principles of National Defense.")
76 "Army Pamphlet on Principles of National Defense."
77 See for example, "An Abstract of 'White Men's Rule Over Colonies in Southeast Asia—Their History and Their Present Political and Economic Position,'" 1 June 1943, OSS Records, RG 226, Intelligence Reports, Report 36032, Entry 16, 190/3/19/4, box 396.
78 See for example, memorandum by Dutch Netherlands East Indies Governor General Jovik on Japanese aims, undated but probably late 1941, OSS Records, RG 226, Intelligence Reports, Report 10717, Entry 16, 190/3/12/2, box 41, annex 1, and "Greater East Asia from a Geographical Viewpoint," 10 April 1942, OSS Records, RG 226, Intelligence Reports, Report 15074, Entry 16, 190/3/12/7, box 74.
79 Office of the United States Chief of Counsel For Prosecution of Axis Criminality, *Nazi Conspiracy and Aggression,* Nuremberg, Germany (1945–1946), Volume 1 (Washington, D.C.: U.S. Government Printing Office, 1946, Library of Congress, www.loc.gov/rr/frd/Military_Law/pdf/NT_Nazi_Vol-I.pdf as of February 2017), 224. (Hereafter *Nazi Conspiracy and Aggression*, Vol. 1)
80 Drea, 182–85. Hattori, Vol. 1, 248–49.
81 Ibid.
82 Schmider, 4–7.
83 Adolf Hitler, *My New Order*, editor Raoul de Roussy de Sales (New York: Reynal & Hitchcock, 1941), 89. (Hereafter Hitler, *My New Order*.)
84 Hitler, *My New Order*, 51–52.
85 Schmider, 29–30.
86 Adolf Hitler, *Mein Kampf*, Kindle English Edition, not dated, locations 2064, 4210, 9184, 9519.

87   Hitler, *My New Order*, 106.
88   Schmider, 25–27.
89   Adam Tooze, *The Wages of Destruction* (London: Penguin Books, 2007), xxiv. (Hereafter Tooze.)
90   James V. Compton, *The Swastika and the Eagle* (Boston: Houghton Mifflin Company, 1967), 7–9. (Hereafter Compton.)
91   Compton, 9–10.
92   Tooze, 38–40.
93   Tooze, 41.
94   Compton, 37.
95   Tooze, 26, 42, 53–54.
96   Tooze, 56–59.
97   Tooze, 126–31.
98   Tooze, 64–66.
99   Tooze, 208. Fritz, 53.
100 Tooze, 211–12.
101 Tooze, 218–30.
102 Tooze, 230–32.
103 Compton, 20–21.
104 Saul Friedländer, *Prelude to Downfall: Hitler and the United States/1939–1941* (New York: Alfred A. Knopf, 1967), 3–5. (Hereafter Friedländer.)
105 "Motorisierung und Mechanisierung im amerikanischem Heer," German military attaché in Washington, D.C., 31 May 1934, T-77, roll 904, frame 5658626, National Archives.
106 Ibid.
107 David Kahn, *Hitler's Spies* (Boston, MA: Da Capo Press, 1978), 76. (Hereafter Kahn.)
108 Records of the German Foreign Ministry, General Foreign Policy Files, USA, 15 June 1936–14 August 1937, German Embassy Washington 714, 4 June 1936, "Growing Worry in the United States About a War in Europe," T120, roll 1324, frame D513976ff, NARA.
109 Records of the German Foreign Ministry, General Foreign Policy Files, USA, 15 June 1936–14 August 1937, German Embassy Washington 1059, 18 August 1936, "Foreign Policy Speech of Roosevelt," T120, roll 1324, frame D513986ff, NARA.
110 Records of the German Foreign Ministry, General Foreign Policy Files, USA, 15 June 1936–14 August 1937, German Embassy Washington 1069, 4 September 1936, T120, roll 1324, frame D513990ff, NARA.
111 Tooze, xxiii.
112 Stephen G. Fritz, *The First Soldier: Hitler as Military Leader* (New Haven: Yale University Press, 2018), 1–3. (Hereafter Fritz.)
113 *Nazi Conspiracy and Aggression*, Vol. I, 179–83.
114 *Nazi Conspiracy and Aggression*, Vol I, 191.
115 *Nazi Conspiracy and Aggression*, Vol. I, 184–87.
116 *Nazi Conspiracy and Aggression*, Vol. I, 190.
117 Hattori, Vol. 1, 12.
118 "Japan: Political Estimate," 4. "Summation of Case Against Hiranuma," Historical Files Relating to the Cases Tried Before the International Military Tribunal for the Far East, International Prosecution Section Staff Historical Files, RG 331, M1663, roll 23, EE-15-16. (Hereafter "Summation of Case Against Hiranuma.")
119 "Summation of Case Against Hiranuma," EE-48.
120 Gunther, 68.

Chapter 2

1. Records of the OSS, Intelligence Reports, "Chronology of Events in Japan and Japanese Occupied Countries Since 1937," April 1945, 127829, RG 226, Entry 16, 190/4/6/3, box 1463. (Hereafter "Chronology of Events in Japan.")
2. "Summation of Case Against Hiranuma," EE-16.
3. Prados, 22.
4. "War Department Budget. Proposed Plans and Projects," defense attaché Tokyo memorandum, 26 June 1936, RG 165, Records of the War Department General and Special Staffs, M1216 Correspondence of the Military Intelligence Division Relating to General Political, Economic, and Military Conditions in Japan, 1918–1941, roll 25.
5. Hattori, Vol. 1, 323.
6. Hattori, Vol. 1, 12.
7. Hotta, 50–51.
8. Gunther, 64–66.
9. Hotta, 36–38.
10. "Japan's Armed Forces and the Constitution," not dated, OSS Records, RG 226, Intelligence Reports, Report 43493, Entry 16, 190/3/21/5, box 502.
11. Mitter, 74.
12. Agawa, 126.
13. Mitter, 46–47, 58–59, 82.
14. Hattori, Vol. 1, 15.
15. Mitter, 79–82; Hotta, 30–31.
16. "Do Bases for a Real Peace Exist Between the United States and Japan? Japan's Peace Terms," Council on Foreign Relations Study Report, 26 November 1941, OSS Records, RG 226, Intelligence Reports, Report 6980, Entry 16, 190/3/12/1, box 30, 8.
17. Hattori, Vol. 1, 15.
18. Hattori, Vol. 1, 15–16.
19. "Summation of Case Against Hiranuma," EE-17. Outline of the Kido diary.
20. Mitter, 96.
21. "Interrogation of Vice Admiral Shigeru Fukudome, IJN" 14 December 1945, translated by the Military Intelligence Section, General Staff, Allied Translator and Interpreter Service, located in Gordon W. Prange Papers, Special Collections, University of Maryland Libraries, Series IV, G-2 Historical Division, box 18.
22. Prados, 41–42.
23. "Chronology of Events in Japan."
24. Mitter, 99.
25. Mitter, 96, 100, 143.
26. Mitter, 121–22, quoting the *North China Herald* of 1 December 1937.
27. Prados, 47–51; Drea, 195.
28. Drea, 193–94.
29. Prados, 47–51.
30. Hattori, Vol. 1, 19–20.
31. Hammel, 30.
32. Merrit, 128–33.
33. Enrik Eberle and Matthias Uhl, ed., *The Hitler Book*. (London: John Murray, 2006), 18–19. The book is a translation of a report prepared for Stalin based on interrogations of prisoners of war. (Hereafter *The Hitler Book*.)

34 Fritz, 52.
35 Records of the German Foreign Ministry, General Foreign Policy Files, USA, 15 June 1936–14 August 1937, German Embassy Washington 489, 6 April 1937, "American Policy in the Far East with Special Consideration of the American Neutrality Act Passage," T120, roll 1324, frame D514001ff, NARA.
36 Records of the German Foreign Ministry, General Foreign Policy Files, USA, 15 June 1936–14 August 1937, German Embassy Washington 528, 26 April 1937, "Return of the 20th Anniversary of the Entry of the United States into the World War and Strengthened English Propaganda," T120, roll 1324, frame D514017ff, NARA.
37 See e.g. records of the German Foreign Ministry, General Foreign Policy Files, USA, 29 September 1937–28 January 1938, German Embassy Washington 1560, 7 December 1937, "American Foreign Policy. Isolation or Activity?" T120, roll 1324, frame D514064ff, NARA.
38 Tooze, 232.
39 Tooze, 235–38.
40 Hossbach notes, document 2261-PS, *Nazi Conspiracy and Aggression*, Vol. I, 376–87.
41 Tooze, 315–17.
42 Tooze, 241.
43 "War Ministry Budget and National Defense Policy," military attaché Rome, 8 June 1937, Records of the War Department General and Special Staffs, RG 165, M1446, Correspondence of the Military Intelligence Division Relating to General Political, Economic, and Military Conditions in Italy, 1918–1941, roll 18.
44 Ibid.
45 Gregory Martin, "German Strategy and Military Assessments of the American Expeditionary Force (AEF), 1917–18," *War in History* Vol. I, No. 2 (July 1994), 160–96, JSTOR copy.
46 Beth Scott, Lt. Col. James Rainey, and Capt. Andrew Hunt, *The Logistics of War* (Maxwell Air Force Base, Alabama: Air Force Logistics Management Agency, 2000), 49. (Hereafter *The Logistics of War*.)
47 *The Logistics of War*, 54–55.
48 U.S. Centennial of Flight Commission, "The U.S. Aircraft Industry During World War I," www.centennialofflight.gov/essay/Aerospace/WWi/Aero5.htm as of February 2012.
49 O'Brien, 28.
50 Schmider, 504ff.
51 O'Brien, 1–6.
52 Prados, 76–79.
53 Marijus Balciunas, "Japan's Purple Machine," 18 March 2004, http://ovid.cs.depaul.edu/Classes/CS233-W04/Papers/PurpleMagic.pdf as of May 2014; Prados, 163–65.
54 Robert Benson, "*A History of U.S. Communications Intelligence during World War II: Policy and Administration*," Center for Cryptologic History, National Security Agency, United States Cryptologic History, Series 4, Vol. 8, 1997, www.nsa.gov/Portals/70/documents/about/cryptologic-heritage/historical-figures-publications/publications/wwii/history_us_comms.pdf as of August 2021, 1–13. (Hereafter Benson.)
55 Benson, 18–21.
56 Benson, 222.
57 United States Strategic Bombing Survey, Interrogation Report 609, 11 December 1946, interrogation of Hisatsune Sakomizu, "Political Activities Leading Up to the Peace," Records of the United States Strategic Bombing Survey, RG 243, M 1654, roll 6, frames 573ff, NARA. (Hereafter Sakomizu.)

Chapter 3

1. Outline of the Kido diary, Historical Files Relating to the Cases Tried Before the International Military Tribunal for the Far East, International Prosecution Section Staff Historical Files, RG 331, M1663, roll 19. (Hereafter "Outline of the Kido diary.")
2. Mitter, 117.
3. Hattori, Vol. 1, 16.
4. "Summation of Case Against Hiranuma," EE-17.
5. Mitter, 147–51.
6. "An Overview of Major Military Campaigns During the Sino-Japanese War, 1937–1945," Edward J. Drea and Hans Van den Ven, chapter 1, *The Battle for China*, Mark Prattie, Edward Drea, and Hans Van de Ven, editors (Stanford, CA: Stanford University Press, 2011), 33. (Hereafter Drea and Van den Ven.)
7. Mitter, 153–54.
8. Drea and Van den Ven, 33.
9. Saburo Sakai with Martin Caiden and Fred Sairo, *Samurai!* (New York: Pocket Books, 1996), 18ff. (Hereafter Sakai.)
10. "Summation of Case Against Hiranuma," EE-24. Agawa, 137.
11. Grew, *Ten Years in Japan*, 244.
12. Gunther, 54, 62.
13. Mitter, 159–61.
14. Hattori, Vol. 1, 21.
15. "Summation of Case Against Hiranuma," EE-17. Drea and Van den Ven, 34. Drea, 205.
16. Mitter, 166, 173, 200.
17. Drea and Van den Ven, 35.
18. Frank, 84.
19. "Summation of Case Against Hiranuma," EE-18. "Chronology of Events in Japan."
20. Mitter, 201ff.
21. United States Strategic Bombing Survey, USSBS No. 373, 9 November 1945, Records of the Office of Strategic Services, XL Intelligence Reports, Report 33308, RG 226, Entry 19A, 190/4/20/4, box 375. (Hereafter USSBS No. 373.)
22. Tooze, 250–53.
23. Fritz, 110.
24. Tooze, 254–55.
25. Friedländer, 24. William L. Shirer, *The Rise and Fall of the Third Reich* (New York: Fawcett Crest, 1962), 498. (Hereafter Shirer.)
26. Records of the German Foreign Ministry, General Foreign Policy Files, USA, 29 September 1937–28 January 1938, German Embassy Washington 36, 28 January 1938, T120, roll 1324, frame D514072ff, NARA.
27. Records of the German Foreign Ministry, General Foreign Policy Files, USA, 1 February–30 December 1938, German Embassy Washington 234, 20 August 1938, T120, roll 1324, frame D514095ff, NARA.
28. Franklin D. Roosevelt, address at Queen's University, 18 August 1938, The American Presidency Project, www.presidency.ucsb.edu/ws/?pid=15525 as of June 2013.
29. Records of the German Foreign Ministry, General Foreign Policy Files, USA, 1 February–30 December 1938, German Embassy Washington 1576, "American Foreign Policy in Relationship to the European Crisis," 12 September 1938, T120, roll 1324, frame D514099ff, NARA.
30. Ibid.

31 Ibid.
32 Ibid.
33 *The Hitler Book*, 35.
34 Tooze, 288–93.
35 United States Department of State, *Foreign relations of the United States diplomatic papers, 1940, General and Europe, Volume II* (U.S. Government Printing Office, 1940, online edition, http://digital.library.wisc.edu/1711.d1/FRUS.FRUS1940vo2 as of April 2011) 12–13. (Hereafter *Diplomatic papers*, 1940, General and Europe.)
36 "War Ministry Budget and National Defense Policy," Military Attaché Rome, 30 April 1938, Records of the War Department General and Special Staffs, RG 165, M1446, Correspondence of the Military Intelligence Division Relating to General Political, Economic, and Military Conditions in Italy, 1918–1941, roll 18.
37 "Verbal der Unterredung zwischen dem Duce, v. Ribbentrop und dem Minister Ciano im Palazzo Venezia," 28 October 1938, Department of Defense, Deptartment of the Army, Office of the Chief of Military History, Ciano Papers: Rose Garden (1938–43), Entry UD288D, 190/017/034/07, box 1, 1–4. (Hereafter Ciano diary, vice Ciano papers. The papers are German translations of Ciano's files, seized after Italy capitulated in 1943.)
38 Friedländer, 8–10.
39 Shirer, 584–85.
40 Hammel, 80.
41 Hammel, 79–80.
42 Hammel, 89–95.

Chapter 4

1   "General Intelligence Summary—Part I Foreign Relations," U.S. Navy Attaché Tokyo, Report No. 184, 24 August 1939, Office of Naval Intelligence, RG 38, 370/15/2/1-4, box 20.
2   Hattori, Vol. 1, 21.
3   Frank, 105.
4   "Summation of Case Against Hiranuma," EE-18–20. Gunther, 53.
5   Gunther, 61.
6   Outline of the Kido diary.
7   "Summation of Case Against Hiranuma," EE-23–24.
8   "War Department Budget. 1939–1940 Army Budget," Defense Attaché Tokyo memorandum, 3 May 1939, RG 165, Records of the War Department General and Special Staffs, M1216 Correspondence of the Military Intelligence Division Relating to General Political, Economic, and Military Conditions in Japan, 1918–1941, roll 25.
9   "Summation of Case Against Hiranuma," EE-21–22.
10 "Japan: Political Estimate," 3, 10.
11 "Naval Policy and Naval Expansion as Enumerated by the Navy Minister in the Diet," U.S. Navy Attaché Tokyo, Report No. 35, 14 February 1939, Office of Naval Intelligence, RG 38, 370/15/2/1-4, box 20.
12 "Examination of Joint Operations by England and America by Captain Yusuke Yoshimi," U.S. Navy Attaché Tokyo, Report No. 29, 15 February 1939, Office of Naval Intelligence, RG 38, 370/15/2/1-4, box 20.
13 Prados, 25–39.
14 "Chronology of Events in Japan."
15 Mitter, 174.
16 Mitter, 176.

17   Drea and Van den Ven, 36.
18   Prados, 17.
19   "Navy—Personnel—Individual Characteristics," U.S. Navy Attaché Tokyo, Report No. 205, 22 September 1939, Office of Naval Intelligence, RG 38, 370/15/2/1-4, box 20. Prados, 37.
20   Edward Jablonski. *Tragic Victories*. New York: Doubleday & Company, 1971, 4. (Hereafter Jablonski, *Tragic Victories*.)
21   Agawa, 13.
22   "Japanese Capital Shipbuilding Program," U.S. Navy Attaché Tokyo, Report No. 231, 11 October 1939, Office of Naval Intelligence, RG 38, 370/15/2/1-4, box 20.
23   "Naval Cadets to be Appointed in 1940," U.S. Navy Attaché Tokyo, Report No. 192, 11 September 1939, Office of Naval Intelligence, RG 38, 370/15/2/1-4, box 20.
24   "Japan's Oil Problem—Diet," U.S. Navy Attaché Tokyo, Report No. 60, 13 March 1939, Office of Naval Intelligence, RG 38, 370/15/2/1-4, box 20.
25   "Summation of Case Against Hiranuma," EE-24–27. "General Intelligence Summary—Part III Finance, Industry, Commerce," U.S. Navy Attaché Tokyo, Report No. 195, 12 September 1939, Office of Naval Intelligence, RG 38, 370/15/2/1-4, box 20.
26   "Summation of Case Against Hiranuma," EE-27.
27   "Japanese Penetration in the Netherlands Indies," American Consulate Batavia, Java, 9 February 1939, Office of Naval Intelligence, RG 38, 370/15/2/1-4, box 16, Consulate Reports—Various.
28   Berlin, 30 January 1939, "Notes from Hitler's Speeches–America," located in Gordon W. Prange Papers, Special Collections, University of Maryland Libraries, Series II, box 4.
29   U.S. Embassy Berlin 603, 24 February 1939, United States Department of State, *Foreign relations of the United States diplomatic papers, 1939, General*, Volume I (Washington, D.C.: U.S. Government Printing Office, 1939, online edition, http://digicoll.library.wisc.edu/cgi-bin/FRUS/FRUS-idx?type=header&id=FRUS.FRUS1940v04 as of September 2014), 23.
30   U.S. Military Attaché Berlin 16,470, 26 (?) February 1939, United States Department of State, *Foreign relations of the United States Diplomatic Papers, 1939, General*, Volume I (Washington, D.C.: U.S. Government Printing Office, 1939, online edition, http://digicoll.library.wisc.edu/cgi-bin/FRUS/FRUS-idx?type=header&id=FRUS.FRUS1940v04 as of September 2014), 24.
31   Ciano diary, 10 March 1939.
32   Friedländer, 11.
33   Ciano diary, 15–19 March 1939.
34   Ciano diary, 15 April 1939; Friedländer, 12–14, 19; Shirer, 630–37.
35   Ibid.
36   Hammel, 115.
37   O'Brien, 47–48.
38   Minutes of meeting, Führer's study, New Reich Chancellery, document L-79, *Nazi Conspiracy and Aggression*, Vol. I, 390–97.
39   Tooze, 302–4.
40   Tooze, 312–13.
41   Tooze, 308–9.
42   "War Department's Budget," Military Attaché Rome, 10 May 1939, Records of the War Department General and Special Staffs, RG 165, M1446, Correspondence of the Military Intelligence Division Relating to General Political, Economic, and Military Conditions in Italy, 1918–1941, roll 18.
43   Ciano diary, 29 April 1939.
44   Friedländer, 22–23.
45   Kahn, 82.

46 Records of the Department of State, Special Interrogation Mission to Germany, 1945–1946 (Poole), RG 59, M679, reel 1, frame 44ff.
47 *Generalfeldmarschall* Wilhelm Keitel, "Beantwortung des Fragebogens fuer Feldmarschall Keitel v. 24.7.45," A-912, 24 July 1945, National Archives, 1ff. (Hereafter "Beantwortung des Fragebogens fuer Feldmarschall Keitel v. 24.7.45.")
48 Records of the Department of State, Special Interrogation Mission to Germany, 1945–1946 (Poole), RG 59, M679, reel 1, frame 44ff.
49 Records of the Department of State, Special Interrogation Mission to Germany, 1945–1946 (Poole), RG 59, M679, reel 1, frame 144ff.
50 GRGC 201, CSDIC (UK), September 1944, WO 208/4364, UK National Archives.
51 Gregory Martin, "German Strategy and Military Assessments of the American Expeditionary Force (AEF), 1917–18," *War in History* Vol. I, No. 2 (July 1994), JSTOR copy, 161–86.
52 Tooze, 318.
53 "Instruktionen des Duce für den Grafen Ciano über die mit Ribbentrop beim nächsten Treffen in Mailand zu behandelnden Fragen," 4 May 1939, Ciano Papers, 15.
54 Ciano Diary, 17 May 1939.
55 "Bericht für den Duce über die Gespräche Ciano-Ribbentrop," 6–7 May 1939, Ciano Papers, 119.
56 Ciano diary, 2.
57 Friedländer, 31–33.
58 "Summation of Case Against Hiranuma," EE-29–31.
59 "Summation of Case Against Hiranuma," EE-31–32. Records of the German Foreign Ministry, T120, roll 101, frame 84587ff, NARA.
60 "Summation of Case Against Hiranuma," EE-32–35. "General Intelligence Summary—Part II Political," U.S. Navy Attaché Tokyo, Report No. 200, 12 September 1939, Office of Naval Intelligence, RG 38, 370/15/2/1-4, box 20.
61 "Summary of All the Evidence Against Hata, Shunroku," 3.
62 "Esmond," January 1941, FO 1093/206, UK National Archives.
63 Records of the German Foreign Ministry, notes shared by Count Magistrati, T120, roll 102, frame 64568ff, NARA.
64 Ciano diary, 9–10 August 1939.
65 Records of the German Foreign Ministry, memorandum 615, 7 August 1939, T120, roll 102, frame 64575ff, NARA.
66 "Unterredungen Salzburg-Berchtesgaden-Bericht," 12 August 1939, Ciano Papers, 40–42.
67 CianodDiary, 11 August 1939.
68 "1. Unterredung mit Hitler in Berchtesgaden," 12 August 1939, Ciano Papers, 47–50.
69 Message from Italian Embassy Berlin to Ciano, 14 August 1939; "Vermerk für S. E. den Botschafter," not dated; "Note über die Unterredung in Schloss Fuschl (Salzburg) von 18. August 1939," not dated; Mussolini letter to Hitler, 21 August 1939; "Erklärande Note über die Italienische Haltung," 21 August 1939; Ciano Papers, 58ff.
70 Ciano diary, 13 August 1939.
71 *General der Artillerie* Walter Warlimont, "German Estimate of United States, Russia, and Dakar," ETHINT-8, 9 August 1945, National Archives, 1. (Hereafter Warlimont, "German Estimate of United States, Russia, and Dakar.")
72 Tooze, 324–25.
73 Mussolini letter to Hitler, 21 August 1939, Ciano Papers, 81.
74 Ciano diary, 22 August 1939.
75 Shirer, 737.

76 "Von S. E. dem Reichsaussenminister an S. E. den deutschen Botschafter in Rom durch Telefon übermittelt mit der Anweidung, ihn mit grösster Eile persönlich S. E. dem Duce auszuhändigen," 25 August 1939, Ciano Papers, 115–17.
77 "Brief der Duce an den Führer, der am 26.8.39, 12 h 10 von S. Exz. dem Grafen Ciano dem kgl. Botschafter in Berlin zur sofortigen Aushändlung an den Führer übermittelt wurde," 26 August 1939, Ciano Papers, 125–26.
78 "Brief des Führers, der am 26.8.39, 15 h 08 von S. Exz. dem Reichsaussenminister telefonisch and S. Exz. Den deutschen Botschafter in Rom zur sofortigen Weitergabe an den Duce durchgegeben wurde," 26 August 1939, Ciano Papers, 127–28.
79 Cianod diary, 25 August 1939.
80 Records of the German Foreign Ministry, letter from Hitler to Mussolini, 26 August 1939, T120, roll 102, frame 64836ff, NARA.
81 Schmider, 166–67.
82 "August 28, 1940: Call Me Meyer," Filminspector.com, http://worldwartwodaily.filminspector.com/2016/08/august-28-1940-call-me-meier.html as of January 2021. The site has the original German text. Edward B. Westermann, *Flak: German Anti-Aircraft Defenses, 1914–1945* (Lawrence, KA: University Press of Kansas, 2001), 5–6. (Hereafter Westermann.)
83 Scitor Corporation, "Technological Innovation During Protracted War: Radar and Atomic Weapons in World War II," prepared for the Director, Net Assessments, Office of the Secretary of Defense, April 2015, www.esd.whs.mil/portals/54/documents/foid/reading%20room/litigation release/litigation%20release%20-%20 technological%20 innovation%20during%20 protracted%20war%20radar%20and%20 atomic%20 weapons%20in%20wwii%20%20 201504.pdf as of February 5–7. This study asserts inaccurately that Japan never fielded a flak control radar. (Hereafter Scitor.)
84 Ciano diary, 3 September 1939.
85 Ciano diary, 15 September 1939.
86 Records of the German Foreign Ministry, Hitler letter to Mussolini, 1 September 1939, T120, roll 102, frame 64737ff, NARA.
87 Records of the German Foreign Ministry. Compton, 13–14.
88 Schmider, 84.
89 Schmider, 82, 151–53.
90 Friedländer, 44–45.
91 Friedländer, 87; Shirer, 869.
92 *Reichsmarschall* Hermann Goering, "German Strategy (1939–1941)," interview with Göring, MS # ETHINT-31, 25 July 1945, National Archives, 2, 5. Hereafter Goering.)
93 Tooze, 328.
94 "Esmond," January 1941, FO 1093/206, UK National Archives.
95 Friedländer, 56–60.
96 Percy E. Schramm, *Kriegstagebuch des OKW, 1940–1941, Teilband I* (Germany: Bechtermünz, 2005), 229E–231E. (Hereafter *Kriegstagebuch des OKW, 1940–1941, Teilband I*.)
97 Fritz, 89.
98 Fritz, 87–93.
99 Westermann, 88.
100 Records of the German Foreign Ministry, German Embassy Rome reports, 12 and 13 October 1939, T120, roll 102, frame 64712ff, and Foreign Ministry Nr. 370 and 450 to Rome, 25 August and 2 September 1939, frame 64744ff, NARA.
101 Records of the German Foreign Ministry, German Embassy Rome Reports, 1 September 1939, T120, roll 102, frame 64850ff and 64739ff, NARA.

102 Italian Embassy Berlin 311, 2 October 1939, Ciano Papers, 271–72.
103 "Summary of All the Evidence Against Hata, Shunroku," 3.
104 "General Intelligence Summary—Part III Finance, Industry, Commerce," U.S. Navy Attaché Tokyo, Report No. 195, 12 September 1939, Office of Naval Intelligence, RG 38, 370/15/2/1-4, box 20.
105 "General Intelligence Summary—Part I Foreign Relations," U.S. Navy Attaché Tokyo, Report No. 184, 24 August 1939, Office of Naval Intelligence, RG 38, 370/15/2/1-4, box 20.
106 Mitter, 211–12.
107 Sakai, 27ff.
108 Sakai, 25–26.
109 Charles F. Romanus and Riley Sunderland, *China-Burma-India Theater: Stilwell's Mission to China* (Washington, D.C.: Center of Military History, 1987, www.history.army.mil/html/books/009/9-1/CMH_Pub_9-1.pdf as of August 2017), 7. (Hereafter *Stilwell's Mission to China*.)

Chapter 5

1 Samuel Eliot Morison, *The Rising Sun in the Pacific: 1931–April 1942* (Annapolis: Naval Institute Press, 1948–2010), 43. (Hereafter Morison.)
2 Interview "Fukudome No. 6," 19 May 1950, Gordon W. Prange Papers, Special Collections, University of Maryland Libraries, Series IV, G-2 Historical Division, box 18.
3 "Fukudome, Shigeru Papers (facsimile)," a draft book by Fukudome translated to English, not dated, Gordon W. Prange Papers, Special Collections, University of Maryland Libraries, Series IV, G-2 Historical Division, box 18, 10ff. (Hereafter Fukudome Papers.)
4 "Notes on Naval Subjects," U.S. Navy Attaché Tokyo, Report No. 34, 29 February 1940, Office of Naval Intelligence, RG 38, 370/15/2/1-4, box 21.
5 "Japanese Naval Views on American-Japanese Relations," U.S. Navy Attaché Tokyo, Report No. 119, 5 August 1940, Office of Naval Intelligence, RG 38, 370/15/2/1-4, box 21.
6 "Japanese Naval Views on American-Japanese Relations," box 21.
7 "Japanese Naval Writer Discusses United States Navy," U.S. Navy Attaché Tokyo, Report No. 21, 15 February 1940, Office of Naval Intelligence, RG 38, 370/15/2/1-4, box 21.
8 "War Department Budget. 1940–1941 Army Budget," Defense Attaché Tokyo memorandum, 16 May 1940, RG 165, Records of the War Department General and Special Staffs, M1216 Correspondence of the Military Intelligence Division Relating to General Political, Economic, and Military Conditions in Japan, 1918–1941, roll 25.
9 "Abe, Nobuyuki," 25 March 1946, Interrogation Reports Submitted to the Executive Committee, International Military Tribunal for the Far East, International Prosecution Section Staff Historical Files, RG 331, M1663, roll 2.
10 Embassy Tokyo telegram, 15 January 1940, United States Department of State, *Foreign Relations of the United States Diplomatic Papers, 1940, The Far East*, Volume IV (Washington, D.C.: U.S. Government Printing Office, 1940), http://digicoll.library.wisc.edu/cgi-bin/FRUS/FRUS-idx?type=header&id=FRUS.FRUS1940v04 as of October 2010), 957–59. (Hereafter *Diplomatic Papers, 1940, The Far East*.)
11 "Notes on Naval Subjects," U.S. Navy Attaché Tokyo, Report No. 25, 15 February 1940, Office of Naval Intelligence, RG 38, 370/15/2/1-4, box 21.
12 "Notes on Naval Subjects," U.S. Navy Attaché Tokyo, Report No. 123, 7 August 1940, Office of Naval Intelligence, RG 38, 370/15/2/1-4, box 21.
13 Interview "Fukudome No. 1," 27 April 1950, Gordon W. Prange Papers, Special Collections, University of Maryland Libraries, Series IV, G-2 Historical Division, box 18. Fukudome Papers, 12.
14 Outline of the Kido diary. "Japan: Political Estimate," 4.

15 *Reports of General Macarthur*, Volume II, Part I, 32, fn 11.
16 "Navy Day Speech in Osaka by Admiral Takahashi," American Consulate Osaka, 28 May 1940, Office of Naval Intelligence, RG 38, 370/15/2/1-4, box 16, Consulate Reports—Various.
17 "General Intelligence Summary—Political," U.S. Navy Attaché Tokyo, Report No. 30, 16 February 1940, Office of Naval Intelligence, RG 38, 370/15/2/1-4, box 21.
18 "Diary of Admiral Kichisaburo Nomura, June–December 1941," reproduced in Goldstein Donald M. Goldstein and Katherine V. Dillon, *The Pacific War Papers: Japanese Documents of World War II* (Washington, D.C.: Potomac Books, Inc., 2004), 139. (Hereafter "Diary of Admiral Kichisaburo Nomura, June–December 1941.")
19 "Press Comment in Chosen Newspapers Concerning the European War and Possible American Participation," American Consulate General Keijo, Chosen, 8 June 1940, Office of Naval Intelligence, RG 38, 370/15/2/1-4, box 16, Consulate Reports—Various.
20 Outline of the Kido diary.
21 Ibid.
22 Grew, *Ten Years in Japan*, 320–21.
23 *Stilwell's Mission to China*, 8.
24 Outline of the Kido diary.
25 *Records of the 1941 Policy Conferences*, xv–xvi. Outline of the Kido diary.
26 United States Strategic Bombing Survey, *United States Strategic Bombing Survey (European War) (Pacific War)*, Interrogations of Japanese Officials, Japanese Naval Planning, Nav No. 76, USSBS No. 379, 17 November 1945, www.ibiblio.org/hyperwar/AAF/USSBS/IJO/IJO-76.html. (Hereafter USSBS No. 379.)
27 *Reports of General Macarthur*, Volume II, Part I, 32, fn 7. "Summary of All the Evidence Against Hata, Shunroku," Historical Files Relating to the Cases Tried Before the International Military Tribunal for the Far East, International Prosecution Section Staff Historical Files, RG 331, M1663, roll 23, 1. (Hereafter "Summary of All the Evidence Against Hata, Shunroku.")
28 Outline of the Kido diary; Embassy Tokyo telegrams, 17–18 July 1940, *Diplomatic Papers, 1940, The Far East*, 964ff; "Summary of All the Evidence Against Hata, Shunroku," 1; "Navy—Personnel—Individual Characteristics," U.S. Navy Attaché Tokyo, Report No. 205, 22 September 1939, Office of Naval Intelligence, RG 38, 370/15/2/1-4, box 20; "Notes on Naval Subjects," U.S. Navy Attaché Tokyo, Report No. 146, 15 September 1940, Office of Naval Intelligence, RG 38, 370/15/2/1-4, box 21.
29 Ernest O. Hauser, "Tojo," *Life*, 30 March 1942, 72. (Hereafter Hauser.)
30 Chen, C. Peter. "Hideki Tojo." World War II Data Base, http://ww2db.com as of November 2010. (Hereafter Chen.)
31 Hauser, 76.
32 Gunther, 62.
33 "Summary Brief re Tojo, Hideki, (General)," 10 April 1946, submitted to General Douglass MacArthur by the International Military Tribunal for the Far East, International Prosecution Section Staff Historical Files, RG 331, M1663, roll 2.
34 Gunther, 62.
35 Hauser, 75.
36 Hauser, 70, 75–76.
37 Gunther, 82–83; Hotta, 60–61; "Summary Brief re Matsuoka, Yosuko," 10 April 1946, submitted to General Douglass MacArthur by the International Military Tribunal for the Far East, International Prosecution Section Staff Historical Files, RG 331, M1663, roll 2.
38 "Summary Brief re Matsuoka, Yosuko," 10 April 1946, submitted to General Douglass MacArthur by the International Military Tribunal for the Far East, International Prosecution Section Staff Historical Files, RG 331, M1663, roll 2.

39 Embassy Tokyo telegram, 21 July 1940, *Diplomatic Papers, 1940, The Far East*, 966–67.
40 Grew, *Ten Years in Japan*, 322–23.
41 Asada, 240–41.
42 Decision taken by a Liaison Conference of the Government and Imperial General Headquarters, 27 July 1940, *Juyo Kokusaku Kettei Bunsho* (File on Important National Policy Decisions), cited in *The Reports of General MacArthur: Japanese Operations in the Southwest Pacific Area, Volume II, Part I*. Washington, D.C.: Center of Military History, facsimile reprint, 1994, www.history.army.mil/books/wwii/MacArthur%20Reports/MacArthur%20V2%20P1/macarthurv2.htm as of May 2012, 31. (Hereafter *Reports of General Macarthur*, Volume II, Part I.)
43 Hattori, Vol. 1, 32ff.
44 Ibid.
45 Hattori, Vol. 1, 38.
46 Outline of the Kido diary.
47 "Notes on Naval Subjects," U.S. Navy Attaché Tokyo, Report No. 131, 5 September 1940, Office of Naval Intelligence, RG 38, 370/15/2/1-4, box 21.
48 Outline of the Kido diary.
49 Hattori, Vol. 1, 39.
50 Ibid.
51 Asada, 239–40.
52 Fukudome, 7.
53 Interview "Fukudome No. 4," 10 May 1950, Gordon W. Prange Papers, Special Collections, University of Maryland Libraries, Series IV, G-2 Historical Division, box 18.
54 "Japanese Potentialities with Respect to Hawaii," memorandum from the G-2 to Chief of Staff, I. B. 165, 17 December 1941, American-British Conversations Correspondence Related to Planning and Combat Operations, 1940–1948, RG 165, Entry 421, 390/37/24/3-390/38/2/3, box 348.
55 Outline of the Kido diary.
56 "Japan: Political Estimate," 13–14.
57 Embassy Tokyo telegram, 5 September 1940, *Diplomatic Papers, 1940, The Far East*, 974–77.
58 Marijus Balciunas, "Japan's Purple Machine," 18 March 2004, http://ovid.cs.depaul.edu/Classes/CS233-W04/Papers/PurpleMagic.pdf as of May 2014. Office of the Chief of Naval Operations, Office of Naval Intelligence, Intercepted Enemy Radio Traffic, 1940–1946, RG 38, Entry A1 344, 38/370/01/2/2, Naval General Staff, box 306, passim.
59 Outline of the Kido diary.
60 Asada, 222.
61 Admiral Matome Ugaki, Donald Goldstein and Katherine Dillon, ed., Masataka Chihaya, trans., *Fading Victory: The Diary of Admiral Matome Ugaki, 1941–1945* (Annapolis, MD: Naval Institute Press, 1991), 5–6. (Hereafter Ugaki.)
62 *Records of the 1941 Policy Conferences*, 4–13; Hattori, Vol. 1, 45ff.
63 Ibid.
64 Ibid.
65 Ibid.
66 Asada, 226.
67 *Reports of General Macarthur*, Volume II, Part I, 32; Drea and Van den Ven, 40; *Stilwell's Mission to China*, 8.
68 Grew, *Ten Years in Japan*, 330–31.
69 Outline of the Kido diary.
70 Hotta, 54.
71 Hattori, Vol. 1, 60.

72 Sakai, 37–38.
73 Outline of the Kido diary.
74 Hattori, Vol. 1, 60.
75 *Nazi Conspiracy and Aggression* Vol. I, 841.
76 Grew, *Ten Years in Japan*, 341.
77 Grew, *Ten Years in Japan*, 339.
78 Hotta, 54.
79 Outline of the Kido diary.
80 Outline of the Kido diary.
81 *Reports of General Macarthur*, Volume II, Part I, 31, fn 7, and 32.
82 Hammel, 200–1.
83 *Stilwell's Mission to China*, 9–13.
84 Outline of the Kido diary. Gunther, 58. "Personalities of Some Leading Military Officials," Defense Attaché Tokyo memorandum, 7 January 1932, RG 165, Records of the War Department General and Special Staffs, M1216 Correspondence of the Military Intelligence Division Relating to General Political, Economic, and Military Conditions in Japan, 1918–1941, roll 23. (Hereafter "Personalities of Some Leading Military Officials.")
85 Mitter, 222.
86 Outline of the Kido diary.
87 Fukudome Papers, 13. Fukudome, 9–10.
88 "Interrogation of Vice Admiral Shigeru Fukudome, IJN" 14 December 1945, translated by the Military Intelligence Section, General Staff, Allied Translator and Interpreter Service, located in Gordon W. Prange Papers, Special Collections, University of Maryland Libraries, Series IV, G-2 Historical Division, box 18, 9–10.
89 Hattori, Vol. 1, 252–59.
90 Toland, 157.
91 Hattori, Vol. 1, 188.
92 Embassy Tokyo telegram, 24 December 1940, *Diplomatic Papers, 1940, The Far East*, 981–84.
93 Grew, *Ten Years in Japan*, 359–61.
94 Friedländer, 82–85.
95 Memorandum from Chief of Ordnance to Gen. Jacob L. Devers, Chief, Army Field Forces, 3 August 1948, NARA, RG 337, Army Field Forces Headquarters, box 9, folder 470.8; *The Organization of Ground Combat Troops*, 56–61, 321–26; Robert Stewart Cameron, *Americanizing the Tank: U.S. Army Administration and Mechanized Development Within the Army, 1917–1943* (dissertation, Temple University, August 1944, UMI Dissertation Services: Ann Arbor, Michigan, 1996), 521–22.

Chapter 6

1 Records of the German Foreign Ministry, Mussolini letter to Hitler, 11 January 1940, T120, roll 102, frame 64888ff, NARA; "Brief des Duce and den Führer vom 5. Januar 1940," 5 January 1940, Ciano Papers, 291.
2 "War Department Budget," Military Attaché Rome, 13 April 1940, Records of the War Department General and Special Staffs, RG 165, M1446, Correspondence of the Military Intelligence Division Relating to General Political, Economic, and Military Conditions in Italy, 1918–1941, roll 18.
3 Hugh Sebag-Montefiori, *Enigma: The Battle for the Code* (London: Weidenfeld and Nicholson), 2004, 34–93. (Hereafter *Enigma*.)
4 *Enigma*, 1–4.
5 *Enigma*, 138–40.

6. Records of the German Foreign Ministry, Hitler letter to Mussolini, 8 March 1940, T120, roll 102, frame 64955ff, NARA. Friedländer, 65.
7. *Diplomatic papers*, 1940, General and Europe, 22ff.
8. Ciano diary, 26 February 1940.
9. *Diplomatic papers*, 1940, General and Europe, 27ff.
10. Ciano Diary, 26 February 1940.
11. *Diplomatic papers*, 1940, General and Europe, 33ff.
12. *Diplomatic papers*, 1940, General and Europe, 43ff. Records of the German Foreign Ministry, memorandum of conversation Hitler–Welles, 4 March 1940, T120, roll 102, frame 64944ff, NARA.
13. Records of the German Foreign Ministry, Hitler letter to Mussolini, 8 March 1940, T120, roll 102, frame 64955ff, NARA.
14. Records of the German Foreign Ministry, memorandum of conversation Ribbentrop–Mussolini–Ciano, 10 March 1940, T120, roll 102, frame 64977ff, NARA.
15. *Diplomatic papers*, 1940, General and Europe, 51ff. Goering, 5.
16. Records of the German Foreign Ministry, memorandum of conversation Ribbentrop–Mussolini, 11 March 1940, T120, roll 102, frame 65007ff, NARA; "Verbal der Unterredung zwischen dem Reichsaussenminister und dem Duce in Beisein des Grafen Ciano und des Botschafters v. Mackensen am 10. März 1940 im Palazzo Venezia, Rom," not dated, Ciano Papers, 319ff.
17. Tooze, 337.
18. Ciano diary, 6 April 1940.
19. Ciano diary, 9 April 1940.
20. Ciano diary, 1 May 1940.
21. Ciano diary, 4 May 1940.
22. Letter from Hitler to Mussolini, 9 May 1940, Ciano Papers, 389.
23. B. H. Liddell Hart, *The German Generals Talk* (New York: Quill, 1979), 108ff. (Hereafter Liddell Hart, *The German Generals Talk*.)
24. Marshal Erich von Manstein, *Lost Victories* (Minneapolis, Minnesota: Zenith Press, 2004), 100ff. (Hereafter Manstein.)
25. *Generalfeldmarschall* Gerd von Rundstedt, "Campaign in the West (1940)," MS # C-053, not dated, National Archives, 2. (Hereafter Rundstedt.)
26. Westermann, 89–91.
27. Ciano diary, 10 May 1940.
28. Ciano diary, 15 May 1940.
29. Ciano diary, 27 May 1940.
30. Ciano diary, 29 May 1940.
31. "Botschaft des Duce an den Führer vom 30. Mai 1940," 30 May 1940, Ciano Papers, 404ff.
32. Letter from Hitler to Mussolini, 31 May 1940, Ciano Papers, 406ff.
33. Ciano diary, 31 May 1940.
34. Ciano diary, 1 June 1940.
35. Hammel, 160–62.
36. *Kriegstagebuch des OKW, 1940–1941, Teilband I*, 199E.
37. Helmut Greiner, "Operation 'Barbarossa,'" MS # C-065i, not dated, National Archives, 1–6. (Hereafter Greiner, "Operation 'Barbarossa.'")
38. "Pretrial Interrogations, I. Hermann Wilhelm Goering," Office of the United States Chief of Counsel For Prosecution of Axis Criminality, *Nazi Conspiracy and Aggression,* Nuremberg, Germany (1945–1946) (Washington, D.C.: U.S. Government Printing Office, 1946), Library of Congress, www.loc.gov/rr/frd/Military_Law/pdf/NT_Nazi-Suppl-B.pdf as of January 2015), Supplement B, 1,110–11. (Hereafter *Nazi Conspiracy and Aggression*, Supplement B.)

39 Ibid, 1114–15.
40 "Vermerk für den Duce," 19 June 1940, Ciano Papers, 414–17.
41 Hammel, 150.
42 O'Brien, 129.
43 Hammel, 165–66, 207, 219.
44 Hammel, 247–48.
45 Message from Italian Embassy Berlin to Ciano, 31 July 1940, Ciano Papers, 421ff.
46 Warlimont, "German Estimate of United States, Russia, and Dakar," 1–2.
47 Tooze, 408.
48 "Beantwortung des Fragebogens fuer Feldmarschall Keitel v. 24.7.45," 3.
49 Letter from Mussolini to Hitler, 24 August 1940, Ciano Papers, 441ff.
50 Letter from Hitler to Mussolini, 17 September 1940, Ciano Papers, 445ff.
51 Ciano diary, 4 September 1940.
52 Shirer, 1009, 1012.
53 "Verbal der Ünterredung des Duce mit Ribbentropim Beisein der Exz. Ciano, Alfieri, und Mackensen," 19 September 1940, Ciano Papers, 450ff.
54 Ciano diary, 14 September 1940.
55 Ciano diary, 22 September 1940.
56 Ciano diary, 3 July 1940.
57 Cianod diary, 27 September 1940.
58 "Besprechung Duce-Führer in Beisein von Ciano-Ribbentrop," 4 October 1940, Ciano Papers, 459ff.
59 "Besprechung Duce-Führer in Beisein von Ciano-Ribbentrop," 28 October 1940, Ciano Papers, 469ff.
60 Shirer, 1054–56.
61 Shirer, 1072–73.
62 Goering, 5.
63 O'Brien, 136.
64 Hammel, 233–35.
65 Percy E. Schramm, *Kriegstagebuch des OKW, 1940–1941, Teilband II*. Germany: Bechtermünz, 2005, 996. Tooze, 409, misquotes this to say, "intervene decisively."
66 Friedländer, 82–85.

Chapter 7

1   Grew, *Ten Years in Japan*, 366, 368.
2   Outline of the Kido diary.
3   Toland, 151; Interviews "Genda No. 1," 21 March 1947, and "Genda No. 4," 24 March 1947, Gordon W. Prange Papers, Special Collections, University of Maryland Libraries, Series IV, G-2 Historical Division, box 19.
4   Interview "Fukudome No. 1," 27 April 1950, Gordon W. Prange Papers, Special Collections, University of Maryland Libraries, Series IV, G-2 Historical Division, box 18; Fukudome Papers, 12.
5   Hattori, Vol. 1, 91–92.
6   "Japanese Plans," C/5853, 14 February 1941, FO 1093/245, UK National Archives.
7   C/5863, 15 February 1941, FO 1093/237, UK National Archives.
8   Tokyo 235, 13 February 1941, and Tokyo 1417, 1 August 1940, FO 1093/237, UK National Archives.
9   Outline of the Kido diary.
10 Hammel, 203–4.

ENDNOTES • 425

11. Hammel, 204, 267, 277; O'Brien, 175–76; Morison, 49.
12. O'Brien, 174.
13. Hammel, 235–37.
14. O'Brien, 176.
15. Mitter, 234.
16. *Stilwell's Mission to China*, 18–19.
17. *Stilwell's Mission to China*, 28, 31.
18. Introduction to the *Kriegstagebuch des OKW, 1940–1941, Teilband I*, 199E–200E.
19. Shirer, 1075–76.
20. Shirer, 1077.
21. Berlin, 30 January 1941, "Notes from Hitler's Speeches–America," located in Gordon W. Prange Papers, Special Collections, University of Maryland Libraries, Series II, box 4.
22. Shirer, 1104–5.
23. Memorandum quoted in *Nazi Conspiracy and Aggression*, Vol I, 843–46.
24. Order quoted in *Nazi Conspiracy and Aggression*, Vol I, 847–49.
25. Fritz, 126.
26. GZ #5175-H-DI, 10 March 1941, Office of the Chief of Naval Operations, Office of Naval Intelligence, Intercepted Enemy Radio Traffic, 1940–1946, RG 38, Entry A1 344, 38/370/01/2/2, Naval General Staff, box 306.
27. Schmider, 107.
28. "Record of the Conversation Between the Reich Foreign Minister and Japanese Foreign Minister Matsuoka in the Presence of Ambassadors Ott and Oshima at Berlin on March 27, 1941," 31 March 1941, U.S. Department of State, *Documents on German Foreign Policy 1918–1945, Series D (1937–1945), Vol. XII, The War Years, February 1–June 22 1941* (Washington, D.C.: U.S. Government Printing Office, 1962), 376ff. (Hereafter *DGFP Series D, XII*.)
29. "Record of the Discussion Between the Führer and Japanese Foreign Minister Matsuoka in the Presence of the Reich Foreign Minister and Ambassadors Ott and Oshima, March 27, 1941," 1 April 1941, *DGFP Series D, XII*, 386ff.
30. "Record of the Conversation Between the Reich Foreign Minister and Japanese Foreign Minister Matsuoka on March 28, 1941," 31 March 1941, *DGFP Series D, XII*, 405ff.
31. Schmider, 522.
32. Schmider, 198–99, 545.
33. "Record of the Conversation Between the Führer and Japanese Foreign Minister Matsuoka in the Presence of the Reich Foreign Minister and Minister of State Meissner at Berlin, April 4, 1941," 4 April 1941, *DGFP Series D, XII*, 453ff.
34. "Japan/Soviet Neutrality Pact," US Navy Attaché Tokyo, Report No. 55, 16 April 1941, Office of Naval Intelligence, RG 38, 370/15/2/1-4, box 22.
35. Hotta, 59.
36. Frank, 167.
37. Warlimont, *Inside Hitler's Headquarters*, 145.
38. Weizsäcker to Ott, 16 April 1941, *DGFP Series D, XII*, 570.
39. Outline of the Kido diary; Schmider, 212. Schmider (173) asserts that this information was not shared within the Japanese leadership and that the case shows the disorganization and ineptitude of the Japanese government. Kido knew, so almost certainly the Emperor did, too.
40. Outline of the Kido diary.
41. Fukudome, 10–11.
42. Interview "Fukudome No. 1," 27 April 1950, Gordon W. Prange Papers, Special Collections, University of Maryland Libraries, Series IV, G-2 Historical Division, box 18.

43 Hattori, Vol. 1, 91–92.
44 Hattori, Vol. 1, 93.
45 Hotta, 128.
46 "Japan: Economic Estimate, May 27, 1941," 27 May 1941, G-2, War Department General Staff, OSS Records, RG 226, Intelligence Reports, Report 162, Entry 16, 190/3/11/4, box 2, 47. (Hereafter "Japan: Economic Estimate.")
47 Walter Warlimont, *Inside Hitler's Headquarters, 1939–45* (Novato, CA: Presidio: 1964), 208. (Hereafter Warlimont, *Inside Hitler's Headquarters*.)
48 *Grossadmiral* Karl Doenitz, "U-Boats Against US–UK Shipping," ETHINT-29, not dated, National Archives, 1. (Hereafter Dönitz, "U-Boats Against US-UK Shipping.")
49 Memoranda quoted in *Nazi Conspiracy and Aggression*, Vol I, 859–60.
50 *Kriegstagebuch des OKW, 1940–1941, Teilband I*, 353, 363.
51 "Unterredung Cianos mit dem Führer," 20 April 1941, Ciano Papers, 553ff.
52 Hammel, 297–98.
53 *Records of the 1941 Policy Conferences*, xx–xxiii.
54 Outline of the Kido diary.
55 Fumimaro Konoye, "Memoirs of Prince Konoye," Exhibit No. 173 in U.S. Congress, *Hearings of The Joint Committee on the Investigation of The Pearl Harbor Attack*, Part 20, 3985–86. (Hereafter "Memoirs of Prince Konoye.")
56 German Embassy Tokyo 675, 4 May 1941, *DGFP Series D, XII*, 711ff.
57 Hotta, 67ff.
58 "Memoirs of Prince Konoye," 3986.
59 "Memoirs of Prince Konoye," 3987. *Records of the 1941 Policy Conferences*, 19–21.
60 Outline of the Kido diary; Jackson Day Dinner Radio Address, 29 March 1941, Franklin D. Roosevelt, Master Speech File, 1898–1945, Franklin D. Roosevelt Presidential Library & Museum, www.fdrlibrary.marist.edu/_resources/images/msf/msf01422 as of August 2018.
61 *Records of the 1941 Policy Conferences*, 20, 25.
62 "Memoirs of Prince Konoye," 3989.
63 Outline of the Kido diary.
64 Hotta, 111.
65 *Records of the 1941 Policy Conferences*, 29.
66 Records of the German Foreign Ministry, Outgoing 367, 11 May 1941, T120, roll 16, frame 24906ff, NARA.
67 Ibid.
68 "Record of the Conversation Between the Reich Foreign Minister and the Duce in the Presence of Count Ciano in the Palazzo Venezia on May 13, 1941," 14 May 1941, *DGFP Series D, XII*, 797ff.
69 German Embassy Tokyo 759, 17 May 1941, *DGFP Series D, XII*, 847ff.
70 Records of the German Foreign Ministry, Germany Embassy Tokyo 677, 5 May 1941, Tokyo 685, 6 May 1941, and Tokyo 714, 9 May 1941, T120, roll 16, frame 24892ff, NARA.
71 MAGIC Diplomatic Summary 609, 25 November 1943, RG 457, MAGIC Far East Summaries March 20, 1942–Aug. 15, 1945, Entry 9006, 190/37/3/1-4, box 8.
72 *Records of the 1941 Policy Conferences*, 36ff.
73 German Embassy Washington 1181, 28 April 1941, *DGFP Series D, XII*, 661.
74 Nelson, 79.
75 Ciano diary, 20 July and 30 September 1941.
76 *Reports of General Macarthur*, Volume II, Part I, 32. Hotta, 146, 153.
77 Hammel, 267–68.

78 "Record of the Conversation Between the Foreign Minister and the Former American Ambassador in Brussels, Mr. Cudahy, in the Presence of Ambassador Dieckhoff and Counselor of Legation Sallet, on May 4, 1941," 5 May 1941, *DGFP Series D, XII*, 704ff; "John Cudahy, Former U.S. Ambassador, Dies in Fall," AP, *St. Petersburg Times*, 7 September 1943, 2.
79 Schmider, 447.
80 German Embassy Washington 1539, 28 May 1941, *DGFP Series D, XII*, 901ff.
81 Shirer, 1149–51.
82 Percy E. Schramm, *Kriegstagebuch des Oberkommando der Wehrmacht (Wehrmachtführungsstab), 1. Januar 1942–31. Dezember 1942, Zweiter Halbband, Band 2* (Bechtermünz, Germany, 2005), 402–93. (Hereafter *Kriegstagebuch des OKW 1. Januar 1942–31. Dezember 1942, Zweiter Halbband, Band 2*.)
83 Hammel, 299. *Kriegstagebuch des OKW, 1. Januar 1942–31. Dezember 1942, Zweiter Halbband, Band 2*, 409.
84 "Vermerk des Grafen Ciano für den Duce," 2 June 1941, Ciano Papers, 564ff.
85 Outline of the Kido diary.
86 "Vermerk des Grafen Ciano für den Duce," 15 June 1941, Ciano Papers, 561ff.
87 "Record of the Conversation Between the Führer and the Duce in the Presence of the Reich Foreign Minister and Count Ciano at the Brenner on June 2, 1941, 3 June 1941, *DGFP Series D, XII*, 940ff.
88 Ciano diary, 18 June 1941.
89 *Enigma*, 151–63, 171–72.
90 Hattori, Vol. 1, 123.
91 "Miscellaneous Notes on Naval Subjects," U.S. Navy Attaché Tokyo, Report No. 48, 24 March 1941, Office of Naval Intelligence, RG 38, 370/15/2/1-4, box 22.
92 "Emergency Measures for Air Defense," U.S. Navy Attaché Tokyo, Report No. 18, 5 February 1941, Office of Naval Intelligence, RG 38, 370/15/2/1-4, box 22.
93 "Japanese Views on the Possibility of Air Raids," U.S. Navy Attaché Tokyo, Report No. 42, 12 March 1941, Office of Naval Intelligence, RG 38, 370/15/2/1-4, box 22.
94 "Speech by Commander Sugino in Keijo on Navy Day, 1941," American Consulate General Keijo, Chosen, 31 May 1941, Office of Naval Intelligence, RG 38, 370/15/2/1-4, box 16, Consulate Reports—Various.
95 Memorandum, American Consulate Osaka to U.S. Embassy Tokyo, 5 June 1941, Office of Naval Intelligence, RG 38, 370/15/2/1-4, box 16, Consulate Reports—Various.
96 *Records of the 1941 Policy Conferences*, 47–53.
97 Hattori, Vol. 1, 128.
98 Outline of the Kido diary. *Records of the 1941 Policy Conferences*, 54.
99 Hattori, Vol. 1, 128.
100 *Generalmajor* Burkhart Müller-Hillebrand, "Der Zusammenhang Zwischen dem deutschen Balkanfeldzug und der Invasion in Russland," MS # C-101, November 1951, National Archives, 4, 12ff. (Hereafter Müller-Hillebrand.)
101 Letter from Hitler to Mussolini, 21 June 1941, Ciano Papers, 567ff.
102 Letter from Mussolini to Hitler, 23 June 1941, Ciano Papers, 573ff.
103 Ciano diary, 3. Ciano diary, 21 June 1941.
104 David M. Glantz, and Jonathan M. House, *When Titans Clashed: How the Red Army Stopped Hitler* (Lawrence, Kansas: University of Kansas Press, 1995), 31. (Hereafter Glantz and House, *When Titans Clashed*); Bevin Alexander, "Barbarossa," MilitaryHistoryOnline.com, www.militaryhistoryonline.com/wwii/articles/barbarossa.aspx, 4 February 2006, as of July 2009; Greiner, "Operation 'Barbarossa,'" 9; Guderian, 125; *Generalmajor* Burkhart Müller-Hillebrand, "Der

105 "World War II Statistics," World War II website, www.world-war-2.info/ as of July 2009.
106 Guderian, 120–21.
107 Glantz and House, *When Titans Clashed*, 58.
108 Shirer, 1117.
109 Schmider, 223.
110 U.S. Department of State, Office of the Historian, "The Atlantic Conference & Charter, 1941," http://history.state.gov/milestones/1937-1945/atlantic-conf as of May 2014.
111 Hammel, 278.
112 O'Brien, 176–78.
113 "Führer Headquarters memorandum," 25 August 1941, Ciano Papers, 599ff.
114 Translation Reports of Intercepted Japanese Army Attaché Messages Aug. 25, 1941–August 1945 (0457-A1-9004), Entry 9004, SRA3645-SRA3652, 190/36/11/7, box 5.
115 Schmider, 213–15.
116 Outline of the Kido diary.
117 "Memoirs of Prince Konoye," 3993.
118 Hattori, Vol. 1, 139.
119 Hattori, Vol. 1, 129–30.
120 Hattori, Vol. 1, 123–24.
121 Hattori, Vol. 1, 130–31.
122 *Records of the 1941 Policy Conferences*, 56ff.
123 "Summation of Case Against Hiranuma," EE-37–38. "Extracts from the notes of Prince Konoye," Historical Files Relating to the Cases Tried Before the International Military Tribunal for the Far East, International Prosecution Section Staff Historical Files, RG 331, M1663, roll 19. (Hereafter "Extracts from the notes of Prince Konoye."); *Records of the 1941 Policy Conferences*, 70ff.
124 Outline of the Kido diary; Hattori, Vol. 1, 142ff.
125 United States Strategic Bombing Survey, USSBS No. 308, 10 November 1945, Records of the Office of Strategic Services, XL Intelligence Reports, Report 28973, RG 226, Entry 19A, 190/4/20/1, box 356. (Hereafter USSBS No. 308.)
126 Schmider, 227–30.
127 *Records of the 1941 Policy Conferences*, 77–90.
128 "Extracts from the notes of Prince Konoye." *Records of the 1941 Policy Conferences*, 78; "Memoirs of Prince Konoye," Appendix III, 4018–19.
129 Asada, 251ff.
130 *Records of the 1941 Policy Conferences*, 79.
131 "Extracts from the notes of Prince Konoye,"
132 "Memoirs of Prince Konoye," 3994.
133 Hattori, Vol. 1, 131–32.
134 *Records of the 1941 Policy Conferences*, 98–103.
135 "Notes on Naval Subjects," U.S. Navy Attaché Tokyo, Report No. 80-41, 29 July 1941, Office of Naval Intelligence, RG 38, 370/15/2/1-4, box 22.
136 Hattori, Vol. 1, 154.
137 Records of the German Foreign Ministry, Germany Embassy Tokyo 677, 5 May 1941, Tokyo 1217, 13 July 1941, and Tokyo 714, 9 May 1941, T120, roll 16, frame 24959ff, NARA.
138 "Memoirs of Prince Konoye," passim. Outline of the Kido diary.
139 "Third Konoye Cabinet," U.S. Navy Attaché Tokyo, Report No. 79-41, 29 July 1941, Office of Naval Intelligence, RG 38, 370/15/2/1-4, box 22.

140 "Japan: Political Estimate," 20–21.
141 "Memoirs of Prince Konoye," 3997ff.
142 Hattori, Vol. 1, 164–65.
143 *Records of the 1941 Policy Conferences*, 106–7.
144 Hattori, Vol. 1, 132.
145 Records of the German Foreign Ministry, T120, roll 102, frame 65284ff, NARA.
146 Hattori, Vol. 1, 166.
147 "Memoirs of Prince Konoye," 3998, 4004. "Summation of Case Against Hiranuma," EE-38. Hotta, 143. Asada, 258.
148 Hattori, Vol. 1, 166.
149 Ugaki, 5, 40.
150 Asada, 253.
151 Hattori, Vol. 1, 132–33.
152 Outline of the Kido diary. *Records of the 1941 Policy Conferences*, 107–108. *Reports of General Macarthur*, Volume II, Part I, 33.
153 Hattori, Vol. 1, 166.
154 Hattori, Vol. 1, 166.
155 Edward S. Miller, *Bankrupting the Enemy: The U.S. Financial Siege of Japan Before Pearl Harbor* (Annapolis, MD: Naval Institute Press, 2007), 174.
156 "Memoirs of Prince Konoye," 3998.
157 *Records of the 1941 Policy Conferences*, 114.
158 Koichi Kido diary, (2 of 3), 31 July 1941 ff.
159 Prados, 103–4.
160 Outline of the Kido diary.
161 Ibid.
162 "Memoirs of Prince Konoye," 3999–4000. Outline of the Kido diary.
163 Outline of the Kido diary; Koichi Kido diary, (2 of 3), 7 August 1941. There are minor differences in the translations.
164 Outline of the Kido diary.
165 Hattori, Vol. 1, 320.
166 *Records of the 1941 Policy Conferences*, 124.
167 "The Failed Attempt to Avert War with Japan, 1941," Association for Diplomatic Studies & Training, 27 November 2013, https://adst.org/2013/11/the-failed-attempts-to-avert-war-with-japan-1941/ as of September 2021.
168 Hattori, Vol. 1, 170–71.
169 *Records of the 1941 Policy Conferences*, 129–33.
170 Asada, 267.
171 Hattori, Vol. 1, 173.
172 Ugaki, 12.
173 Outline of the Kido diary.
174 Nelson, 104, citing the official Japanese post-war history.
175 USSBS No. 373.
176 Outline of the Kido diary; *Records of the 1941 Policy Conferences*, 133–34.
177 *Records of the 1941 Policy Conferences*, 133ff; Hattori, Vol. 1, 176ff.
178 Outline of the Kido diary.
179 "Memoirs of Prince Konoye," 4005.
180 *Records of the 1941 Policy Conferences*, 151, fn 36; Outline of the Kido diary.
181 USSBS No. 373.

182 Hattori, Vol. 1, 188.
183 Outline of the Kido diary.
184 Hattori, Vol. 1, 189.
185 Hotta, 164ff.
186 *Records of the 1941 Policy Conferences*, 163.
187 United States Strategic Bombing Survey, AAF Annex #1, 29 January 1946, Records of the Office of Strategic Services, XL Intelligence Reports, Report 43064, RG 226, Entry 19A, 190/4/20/4, box 429. (Hereafter Yonai data.); Hattori, Vol. 1 cites IGHQ data, 263.
188 *The Organization of Ground Combat Troops*, 51–54, 169, 181, 190.
189 Hattori, Vol. 1, 263.
190 *Reports of General Macarthur*, Volume II, Part I, 21.
191 Prados, 64–72.
192 Ugaki, 29.
193 Statements by Col. Ichiji Sugita, Staff Officer (Intelligence), Imperial General Headquarters, Army Section, and Rear Adm. Tomioka and Col. Hattori, Vol. 1, cited in *Reports of General Macarthur*, Volume II, Part I, 51–52.
194 Hattori, Vol. 1, 280.
195 Outline of the Kido diary.
196 Hattori, Vol. 1, 190.
197 Outline of the Kido diary.
198 Drea and Van den Ven, 41–42.
199 USSBS No. 373.
200 "Interrogation of Vice Admiral Shigeru Fukudome, IJN," 14 December 1945, translated by the Military Intelligence Section, General Staff, Allied Translator and Interpreter Service, located in Gordon W. Prange Papers, Special Collections, University of Maryland Libraries, Series IV, G-2 Historical Division, box 18, 3.
201 "Full Translation of Interrogation of Admiral Fukudome," 13 May 1949, translated by the Military Intelligence Section, General Staff, Allied Translator and Interpreter Service, located in Gordon W. Prange Papers, Special Collections, University of Maryland Libraries, Series IV, G-2 Historical Division, box 18.
202 Nelson, 110, citing *Kozen Kaigi* and the Japanese official post-war history.
203 Hotta, 192–93.
204 USSBS No. 373. Nelson, 112. John Toland, *The Rising Sun: The Decline and Fall of the Japanese Empire, 1936–1945* (New York: The Modern Library, 2003), 109–10. (Hereafter Toland.)
205 Interviews "Fukudome No. 2," 2 May 1950, "Fukudome No. 3," 4 May 1950, and Gordon W. Prange Papers, Special Collections, University of Maryland Libraries, Series IV, G-2 Historical Division, box 18.
206 Prados, 136.
207 Outline of the Kido diary.
208 Hotta, 197.
209 Interview "Fukudome No. 4," 10 May 1950, Gordon W. Prange Papers, Special Collections, University of Maryland Libraries, Series IV, G-2 Historical Division, box 18.
210 Nelson, 113.
211 Hattori, Vol. 1, 191.
212 Outline of the Kido diary.
213 "Memoirs of Prince Konoye," 4009–10.
214 Drea and Van den Ven, 42.
215 USSBS No. 373.

216 Outline of the Kido diary.
217 Hattori, Vol. 1, 195.
218 Hattori, Vol. 1, 194.
219 Hotta, 210, citing Inhaba Masao, Kobayashi Tatsuo, and Shimada Toshiko, Tsunoda Jun, editors, *Taiheiyo Senso e no Michi (Bekkan)*, Asahi Shimbunsha, 1988, 545.
220 Ugaki, 5.
221 Grew, *Ten Years in Japan*, 467–70.
222 Records of the German Foreign Ministry, outgoing 979, 12 September 1941, T120, roll 16, frame 25006ff, NARA.
223 Records of the German Foreign Ministry, Germany Embassy Tokyo 1811, 15 September 1941, and 1850, 20 September 1941, T120, roll 16, frame 25011ff, NARA.
224 Hammel, 302–3.
225 Ciano diary, 28 October 1941.
226 Ciano diary, 31 October 1941.
227 Ciano report to Mussolini, 26 October 1941, Ciano Papers, 603ff.
228 "Disposition of Forces for the Defense of the British Isles," memorandum from the Acting Assistant Chief of Staff, G-2, to the Assistant Chief of Staff, War Plans Division, 7 October 1941, American-British Conversations Correspondence Related to Planning and Combat Operations, 1940–1948, RG 165, Entry 421, 390/37/24/3-390/38/2/3, box 338.
229 Hammel, 238.
230 Paul A. C. Koistinen, *Arsenal of World War II: The Political Economy of American Warfare, 1940–1945* (Lawrence, KS: University Press of Kansa, 2004), 74, 130–35, 181ff. (Hereafter Koistenin, *1940–1945*.)
231 Hammel, 246. Koistenin, *1940–1945*, 187.
232 O'Brien, 49.
233 Schmider, 146.
234 "U.S. Synthetic Rubber Program," American Chemical Society, www.acs.org/content/acs/en/education/whatischemistry/landmarks/syntheticrubber.html as of May 2022.
235 Scitor iii–v, 5, 15, 19; Westermann, 96, 177.

Chapter 8

1 Gunther, 62–63.
2 "Admiral Shimada (Shigetaro)," 9 March 1946, Interrogation Reports Submitted to the Executive Committee, International Military Tribunal for the Far East, International Prosecution Section Staff Historical Files, RG 331, M1663, roll 2; Hattori, Vol. 1, 197.
3 Outline of the Kido diary; Hattori, Vol. 1, 197.
4 *Records of the 1941 Policy Conferences*, 186; Hattori, Vol. 1, 197–98.
5 *Records of the 1941 Policy Conferences*, 188ff; Hattori, Vol. 1, 198.
6 Yonai data.
7 Hotta, 224; Nelson, 128–29, citing *Kozen Kaigi* and the Japanese official post-war history.
8 *Records of the 1941 Policy Conferences*, 191–92.
9 "Japan: Economic Estimate," 1, 35–36, 61, passim.
10 "Japan—Major Industrial and Raw Material Position," Ministry of Economic Warfare, Enemy Resources Department, L/33/3/12, 7 September 1941, Office of Naval Intelligence, RG 38, 370/15/2/1-4, box 16, Consulate Reports—Various; *Records of the 1941 Policy Conferences*, 195ff.
11 Hattori, Vol. 1, 200–1.
12 Cited by Asada, 273.
13 Hattori, Vol. 1, 203.

14 *Records of the 1941 Policy Conferences*, 199ff.
15 Interview "Fukudome No. 4," 10 May 1950, Gordon W. Prange Papers, Special Collections, University of Maryland Libraries, Series IV, G-2 Historical Division, box 18.
16 Toland, 130; Hattori, Vol. 1, 213ff.
17 "Summation of Case Against Hiranuma," EE-39–40; Outline of the Kido diary; Drea, 220.
18 Toland, 131.
19 "Admiral Shimada (Shigetaro)," 9 March 1946, Interrogation Reports Submitted to the Executive Committee, International Military Tribunal for the Far East, International Prosecution Section Staff Historical Files, RG 331, M1663, roll 2.
20 Hattori, Vol. 1, 223; "Imperial General Headquarters Navy Directive No. 1," 5 November 1941, translated by the Military Intelligence Section, General Staff, Allied Translater and Interpreter Service, located in Gordon W. Prange Papers, Special Collections, University of Maryland Libraries, Series IV, G-2 Historical Division, box 6, 2.
21 Interview "Fukudome No. 5," 12 May 1950, Gordon W. Prange Papers, Special Collections, University of Maryland Libraries, Series IV, G-2 Historical Division, box 18.
22 Hattori, Vol. 1, 288.
23 Schmider, 248–54.
24 Shirer, 1158.
25 Hattori, Vol. 1, 223.
26 Shirer, 1159–61.
27 Hattori, Vol. 1, 223.
28 Hattori, Vol. 1, 230–31; Koichi Kido diary, (2 of 3), 29 November 1941.
29 Parrott.
30 Hattori, Vol. 1, 283–86.
31 Ugaki, 31.
32 Translation Reports of Intercepted Japanese Army Attaché Messages Aug. 25, 1941–August 1945 (0457-A1-9004), Entry 9004, SRA3645-SRA3652, 190/36/11/7, box 5; Outline of the Kido diary; Hattori, Vol. 1, 231ff.
33 Translation Reports of Intercepted Japanese Army Attaché Messages Aug. 25, 1941–August 1945 (0457-A1-9004), Entry 9004, SRA15876, 190/36/11/7, box 21.
34 David E. Sanger, "In a Memoir, Hirohito Talks of Pearl Harbor," *The New York Times*, 15 November 1990, www.newyorktimes.com as of December 2010.
35 Lindesay Parrott, "Tojo Makes Plea of 'Self-Defense'," *The New York Times*, 26 December 1947, www.newyorktimes.com as of December 2010. (Hereafter Parrott.)
36 Ugaki, 34.
37 Ciano diary, 3 December 1941.
38 Ciano diary, 4 December 1941.
39 Records of the German Foreign Ministry, Germany Embassy Tokyo 2657, 5 December 1941, T120, roll 16, frame 25043ff, NARA.
40 Translation Reports of Intercepted Japanese Army Attaché Messages Aug. 25, 1941–August 1945 (0457-A1-9004), Entry 9004, SRA18021, 190/36/11/7, box 24.
41 Ugaki, 40–41.
42 Hattori, Vol. 1, 381.
43 Ugaki, passim.
44 Interview "Fukudome No. 6," 19 May 1950, Gordon W. Prange Papers, Special Collections, University of Maryland Libraries, Series IV, G-2 Historical Division, box 18.
45 Hattori, Vol. 1, 236.
46 Toland, 156.

47. Capt. Mitsuo Fuchida, *From Pearl Harbor to Calvary*, "Fuchida Mitsuo, Papers (facsimile)," not dated, Gordon W. Prange Papers, Special Collections, University of Maryland Libraries, Series IV, G-2 Historical Division, box 17.
48. Interview "Fukudome No. 6," 19 May 1950, Gordon W. Prange Papers, Special Collections, University of Maryland Libraries, Series IV, G-2 Historical Division, box 18.
49. Toland, 235.
50. Sakai, 46.
51. Outline of the Kido diary.
52. 3138 ATIS, Enemy Publication No. 6 Hawaii-Malaya Naval, Records of the Office of Strategic Services, XL Intelligence Reports, RG 226, Entry 19A, 190/4/13/4, box 42. (Hereafter ATIS 3138.)
53. ATIS 3138.
54. Hattori, Vol. 1, 4.
55. Ugaki, 51–52.
56. Morison, 217.
57. Ugaki, 54, 56.
58. "Japan and the War in the Far East," undated but per NARA 18 February 1942, OSS Records, RG 226, Intelligence Reports, Report 12026, Entry 16, 190/3/12/3, box 47.
59. USSBS No. 308.
60. Ugaki, 61–62.
61. Westermann, 122–35.
62. C/7645, 25 September 1941, FO 1093/206, UK National Archives.
63. Tooze, 507.
64. Munich, 8 November 1941, *Volkischer Beobachter*, 9 November 1941, "Notes from Hitler's Speeches–America," located in Gordon W. Prange Papers, Special Collections, University of Maryland Libraries, Series II, box 4.
65. Gerhard Weinberg, "Four Days in December: Germany's Path to War With the U.S," History Net, www.historynet.com/four-days-in-december-germanys-path-to-war-with-the-u-s.htm as of December 2020.
66. Warlimont, *Inside Hitler's Headquarters*, 208; *Kriegstagebuch des OKW, 1. Januar 1942–31. Dezember 1942, Zweiter Halbband, Band 2*, 799, 803, 1,240.
67. Records of the German Foreign Ministry, Germany Embassy Tokyo 2690, 5 May 1941, Tokyo 685, 8 December 1941, T120, roll 16, frame 25088ff, NARA.
68. Ciano diary, 8 December 1941.
69. *Kriegstagebuch des OKW, 1. Januar 1942–31. Dezember 1942, Erster Halbband, Band 2*, 143.
70. Outline of the Kido diary.
71. H. R. Trevor-Roper, editor, *Hitler's Table Talk: 1941–1944* (New York: Enigma Books, 2008), 406. (Hereafter *Hitler's Table Talk*.)
72. Shirer, 1173–77.
73. Ciano diary, 11 December 1941.
74. Warlimont, *Inside Hitler's Headquarters*, 208.
75. Tooze, 505. Fritz, 238.
76. Goering, 3–7.
77. Shirer, 1169.
78. Goering, 3–7.
79. Morison, 209.
80. *The Hitler Book*, 79.
81. Fritz, 219.

82 *General der Artillerie* Boetticher, "Eindruecke und Erfahrungen des Militaer-und Luftattaches bei der Deutschen Botschaft in Washington, D.C. 1935–1941," MS # B-484, Historical Division, Headquarters United States Army, Europe, 27 April 1947, National Archives. 10–11. Records of the Department of State, reel 1, to Germany, 1945–1946 (Poole), RG 59, M679, frame 44ff.
83 Schmider, 131.
84 United States Strategic Bombing Survey, *Summary Report (European War)* (Washington, D.C.: USSBS), 30 September 1945, www.ibiblio.org/hyperwar/AAF/USSBS/ETO-Summary.html as of January 2015. (Hereafter USSBS, *European War*.)
85 Tooze, 358.
86 *Hitler's Table Talk*, 116.
87 Letter from Hitler to Mussolini, 29 December 1941, Ciano Papers, 637ff.
88 "Proceedings of the American-British Joint Chiefs of Staff Conferences, Held in Washington, D.C., on Twelve Occasions Between December 24, 1941, and January 14, 1942," JCS File Copy, undated, www.ibiblio.org/hyperwar/Dip/Conf/Arcadia/ARCADIA.PDF as of July 2018.
89 Memorandum, "Statement by the Supply Priorities and Allocations Board," Donald M. Nelson to Harry Hopkins, 1 January 1942, Hopkins Paper, https://history.state.gov/historicaldocuments/frus1941-43/d195 as of July 2018.
90 Toland, 257; Prados, 149, 295–99.

Chapter 9

1 Ugaki, 65.
2 MAGIC Far East Summaries (0457-A1-9001), SRS 732, 1 October 1942, RG 457, Entry 9001, 190/36/13/05->, box 3.
3 Hattori, Vol. 2, Part IV, 160–61.
4 Mitter, 244–45.
5 Wood, 11–14.
6 Ugaki, 75.
7 Prados, 281–82.
8 Morison, 260.
9 Frank, 501.
10 Ugaki, 94.
11 Ugaki, 95. Morison, 359ff.
12 Hattori, Vol. 2, Part III, 103–7.
13 Hattori, Vol. 2, Part III, 108–9.
14 Hattori, Vol. 2, Part III, 109.
15 O'Brien, 14, 63.
16 Hattori, Vol. 2, Part III, 112–13.
17 Hattori, Vol. 2, Part III, 114–18.
18 Hattori, Vol. 2, Part III, 152.
19 Wood, 14–15, 39.
20 Hattori, Vol. 2, Part III, 123.
21 Ugaki, 81–84.
22 "An Analysis of the GEA Policy and Its Political Background," Hawaii Postal Censorship Station Special Report, June 1942, OSS Records, RG 226, Intelligence Reports, Report 19817, Entry 16, 190/3/14/2, box 136, 2. (Hereafter "An Analysis of the GEA Policy and Its Political Background.")
23 Office of Naval Intelligence report 38-42, 20 March 1942, OSS Records, RG 226, Intelligence Reports, Report 13909, Entry 16, 190/3/12/6, box 64.
24 Chungking 784, 28 May 1942, FO 1093/245, UK National Archives.

25 O'Brien, 58.
26 Schmider, 9.
27 *Hitler's Table Talk*, 145.
28 Schmider, 55.
29 Louis P. Lochner, trans. and ed., *The Goebbels Diaries* (New York: Doubleday & Company, Inc.: 1948), 42. (Hereafter *The Goebbels Diaries*.)
30 *The Goebbels Diaries*, 92.
31 Ciano diary, 18 February 1942.
32 Ciano diary, 24 February 1942.
33 Dönitz, "U-Boats Against US-UK Shipping," 1–2.
34 O'Brien, 231.
35 Introduction to the *Kriegstagebuch des OKW, 1940–1941, Teilband I*, 199E.
36 O'Brien, 235–40.
37 *Enigma*, 249–56.
38 Tooze, 509.
39 O'Brien, 21.
40 MAGIC Far East Summaries (0457-A1-9001), SRS 557, 28 March 1942, RG 457, Entry 9001, 190/36/13/05->, box 1.
41 MAGIC Far East Summaries (0457-A1-9001), SRS 559, 31 March 1942, RG 457, Entry 9001, 190/36/13/05->, box 1.
42 MAGIC Far East Summaries (0457-A1-9001), SRS 579, 22 April 1942, RG 457, Entry 9001, 190/36/13/05->, box 1.
43 Records of the OSS, Intelligence Reports, "German Morale at Christmas," 12371 C, 21 February 1942, RG 226, Entry 16, 190/3/12/4, box 53.
44 Records of the OSS, Intelligence Reports, untitled, 16276 S, 18 May 1942, RG 226, Entry 16, 190/3/12/4, box 90.
45 Percy E. Schramm, *Kriegstagebuch des Oberkommando der Wehrmacht (Wehrmachtführungsstab), 1. Januar 1942–31. Dezember 1942, Erster Halbband, Band 2*, (Germany: Bechtermünz, 2005), 319, 325. (Hereafter *Kriegstagebuch des OKW, 1. Januar 1942–31. Dezember 1942, Erster Halbband, Band 2*.)
46 Berlin, 26 April 1941, BBC, "Notes from Hitler's Speeches–America," located in Gordon W. Prange Papers, Special Collections, University of Maryland Libraries, Series II, box 4.
47 Shirer, 1190.
48 *The Goebbels Diaries*, 226.
49 Ugaki, 109–10; Hattori, Vol. 2, Part III, 131.
50 Ugaki, 98, 109–10; Hattori, Vol. 2, Part III, 123–24.
51 Prados, 272–77.
52 Ugaki, 111.
53 Prados, 289.
54 MAGIC Far East Summaries (0457-A1-9001), SRS 579, 22 April 1942, RG 457, Entry 9001, 190/36/13/05->, box 1.
55 MAGIC Far East Summaries (0457-A1-9001), SRS 580, 23 April 1942, RG 457, Entry 9001, 190/36/13/05->, box 1.
56 MAGIC Far East Summaries (0457-A1-9001), SRS 587, 1 May 1942, RG 457, Entry 9001, 190/36/13/05->, box 1.
57 Ugaki, 113–14.
58 United States Strategic Bombing Survey, *United States Strategic Bombing Survey (European War) (Pacific War)*, Interrogations of Japanese Officials, Japanese Naval Planning, Nav No. 43, USSBS

No. 192, 30 October 1945, www.ibiblio.org/hyperwar/AAF/USSBS/IJO/IJO-43.html. (Hereafter USSBS No. 192.)
59 Hattori, Vol. 2, Part III, 135–36.
60 Sakai, 108.
61 Ciano diary, 20 April 1942.
62 Ciano diary, 29 April–1 May 1942.
63 Ugaki, 116.
64 Ugaki, 117–20.
65 O'Brien, 138.
66 Prados, 301–3.
67 Ugaki, 119.
68 "Battle of Coral Sea," Naval History and Heritage Command, www.history.navy.mil/our-collections/photography/wars-and-events/world-war-ii/battle-of-the-coral-sea.html as of September 2017.
69 Ibid.
70 Ugaki, 122, 125.
71 GZ #2121, 11 May 1942, Office of the Chief of Naval Operations, Office of Naval Intelligence, Intercepted Enemy Radio Traffic, 1940–1946, RG 38, Entry A1 344, 38/370/01/2/2, Naval General Staff, box 306.
72 MAGIC Far East Summaries (0457-A1-9001), SRS 597, 11 May 1942, RG 457, Entry 9001, 190/36/13/05->, box 1.
73 MAGIC Far East Summaries (0457-A1-9001), SRS 613, 28 May 1942, RG 457, Entry 9001, 190/36/13/05->, box 1.
74 GZ #1498, 13 May 1942, Office of the Chief of Naval Operations, Office of Naval Intelligence, Intercepted Enemy Radio Traffic, 1940–1946, RG 38, Entry A1 344, 38/370/01/2/2, Naval General Staff, box 306.
75 Sakai, 74–75.
76 Ugaki, 124.
77 "An Analysis of the GEA Policy and Its Political Background," 1–2.
78 Ciano diary, 9 May 1942.
79 Ciano diary, 21 May 1942.
80 Ciano diary, 27 May 1942.
81 MAGIC Far East Summaries (0457-A1-9001), SRS 630, 16 June 1942, RG 457, Entry 9001, 190/36/13/05->, box 1.
82 MAGIC Far East Summaries (0457-A1-9001), SRS 626, 11 June 1942, RG 457, Entry 9001, 190/36/13/05->, box 1.
83 Liddell Hart, *History of the Second World War*, 311.
84 *Hitler's Table Talk*, 406.
85 Shirer, 1195.
86 Liddell Hart, *History of the Second World War*, 311–12.
87 Tooze, 590.
88 O'Brien, 48–54.
89 Edward Jablonski. *Terror from the Sky* (New York: Doubleday & Company, 1971), 150.
90 Westermann, 21–26.
91 Westermann, 68–70, 88, 95–96.
92 Westermann, 96, 177.
93 Jablonski, *Tragic Victories*, 111–13; O'Brien, 74; Westermann, 150; *Kriegstagebuch des OKW, 1. Januar 1942–31. Dezember 1942, Erster Halbband, Band 2*, 163.

94 Jablonski, *Tragic Victories*, 130–31; *Kriegstagebuch des OKW, 1. Januar 1942–31. Dezember 1942, Erster Halbband, Band 2*, 394, 400.
95 Westermann, 139.
96 *Kriegstagebuch des OKW, 1. Januar 1942–31. Dezember 1942, Erster Halbband, Band 2*, 165.
97 O'Brien, 74–75.
98 *Kriegstagebuch des OKW, 1. Januar 1942–31. Dezember 1942, Erster Halbband, Band 2*, 397, 421.
99 MAGIC Far East Summaries (0457-A1-9001), SRS 625, 10 June 1942, RG 457, Entry 9001, 190/36/13/05->, box 1.
100 *Kriegstagebuch des OKW, 1. Januar 1942–31. Dezember 1942, Erster Halbband, Band 2*, 443, fn 1.
101 MAGIC Far East Summaries (0457-A1-9001), SRS 640, 26 June 1942, RG 457, Entry 9001, 190/36/13/05->, box 1.
102 *Kriegstagebuch des OKW, 1. Januar 1942–31. Dezember 1942, Erster Halbband, Band 2*, 449, 456, 458; "Striking Oil: The First American Bombing Raid over Europe in World War II," American Battle Monuments Commission, www.abmc.gov/news-events/news/striking-oil-first-american-bombing-raid-over-europe-world-war-ii#.W1D5Fy2ZPOQ as of July 2018.
103 Westermann, 175.
104 Jablonski, *Tragic Victories*, 151.
105 USSBS, *European War*.
106 Westermann, 180.
107 *Kriegstagebuch des OKW, 1. Januar 1942–31. Dezember 1942, Erster Halbband, Band 2*, 449, 456, 458.
108 "Interrogation of Albert Speer," Combined Intelligence Objectives Subcommittee, Evaluation Report No. 53, 18 June 1945, Records of the Judge Advocate General, RG 153, Entry 135, Dossier Files, 153/270/2/9/04->, box 57 (270/2/10/05).
109 Fritz, 92.
110 Interview No. 11, "Minutes of Meeting with Reichminister," 19 May 1945, RG 243, Records of the U.S. Strategic Bombing Survey, Interrogations, Entry 32, 190/063/007/04, box 1, 1.
111 *Kriegstagebuch des OKW, 1. Januar 1942–31. Dezember 1942, Erster Halbband, Band 2*, 620.
112 Ugaki, 129–30.
113 Prados, 313–14.
114 Ugaki, 131.
115 Ugaki, 135.
116 Ugaki, 137.
117 Prados, 315–20, 328–29.
118 Rear Admiral Paul Becker, USN (Ret), "The Battle of Midway Still Teaches the Value of Intelligence, Decisive Action," *The Sextant*, 2 June 2017, http://usnhistory.navylive.dodlive.mil/2017/06/02/the-battle-of-midway-still-teaches-the-value-of-intelligence-decisive-action/ as of October 2017.
119 #566, 5 June 1942, Office of the Chief of Naval Operations, Office of Naval Intelligence, Intercepted Enemy Radio Traffic, 1940-1946, RG 38, Entry A1 344, 38/370/01/2/2, Naval General Staff, box 306.
120 Ugaki, 152–53.
121 COM 14 070224-T.I., 7 June 1942, and BELL-101030-TI, 10 June 1942, Office of the Chief of Naval Operations, Office of Naval Intelligence, Intercepted Enemy Radio Traffic, 1940–1946, RG 38, Entry A1 344, 38/370/01/2/2, Naval General Staff, box 306.
122 Ugaki, 140.
123 Ugaki, 147.
124 Ugaki, 152.

125 MAGIC Far East Summaries (0457-A1-9001), SRS 626, 11 June 1942, and SRS 629, 15 June 1942, RG 457, Entry 9001, 190/36/13/05->, box 1.
126 USSBS No. 192.
127 Ugaki, 159.
128 United States Strategic Bombing Survey, *United States Strategic Bombing Survey (European War) (Pacific War)*, Interrogations of Japanese Officials, Japanese Naval Planning, Nav No. 31, USSBS No. 129, 25 October 1945, www.ibiblio.org/hyperwar/AAF/USSBS/IJO/IJO-31.html. (Hereafter USSBS No. 129.)
129 USSBS No. 378.
130 USSBS No. 379.
131 USSBS No. 308.
132 Ibid. USSBS No. 268.
133 United States Strategic Bombing Survey (European War) (Pacific War), Interrogations of Japanese Officials, Japanese Naval Planning, Nav No. 115, USSBS No. 503, 9–12 December 1945, www.ibiblio.org/hyperwar/AAF/USSBS/IJO/IJO-115.html. (Hereafter USSBS No. 503.)
134 Hattori, Vol. 2, Part III, 147.
135 Ugaki, 165.
136 Ugaki, 166.
137 Ugaki, 167.
138 Hattori, Vol. 2, Part III, 153; Ugaki, 167.
139 Hattori, Vol. 2, Part III, 139–40, 146.
140 Scitor, 26.

Chapter 10

1 O'Brien, 234, 239–41.
2 OSS Records, RG 226, Intelligence Reports, Report 18994, 21 July 1942, Entry 16, 190/3/13/7, box 121.
3 GRGC 332, CSDIC (UK), 7 August 1945, WO 208/4365, UK National Archives.
4 MAGIC Far East Summaries (0457-A1-9001), SRS 668, 30 July 1942, RG 457, Entry 9001, 190/36/13/05->, box 1.
5 MAGIC Far East Summaries (0457-A1-9001), SRS 673, 4 August 1942, RG 457, Entry 9001, 190/36/13/05->, box 2.
6 MAGIC Far East Summaries (0457-A1-9001), SRS 695, 26 August 1942, RG 457, Entry 9001, 190/36/13/05->, box 2.
7 Ibid.
8 Ugaki, 170.
9 Ugaki, 171.
10 MAGIC Far East Summaries (0457-A1-9001), SRS 673, 4 August 1942, RG 457, Entry 9001, 190/36/13/05->, box 2.
11 MAGIC Far East Summaries (0457-A1-9001), SRS 683, 14 August 1942, RG 457, Entry 9001, 190/36/13/05->, box 2.
12 *Kriegstagebuch des OKW, 1. Januar 1942–31. Dezember 1942, Erster Halbband, Band 2*, 477, 515–16.
13 Tooze, 510.
14 Ugaki, 173.
15 Ugaki, 174.
16 Prados, 343.
17 Sakai, 119.

18 O'Brien, 201, 204.
19 Hattori, Vol. 2, Part IV, 6.
20 Henry I. Shaw, Jr. *First Offensive: The Marine Campaign for Guadalcanal*, Marines in World War II Commemorative Series (Washington, D.C.: Marine Corps Historical Center, 1992), www.ibiblio.org/hyperwar/USMC/USMC-C-Guadalcanal.html as of October 2017. (Hereafter Shaw.)
21 Ugaki, 177.
22 Hattori, Vol. 2, Part IV, 6.
23 Hattori, Vol. 2, Part IV, 7, 9–10.
24 MAGIC Far East Summaries (0457-A1-9001), SRS 699, 30 August 1942, RG 457, Entry 9001, 190/36/13/05->, box 2.
25 MAGIC Far East Summaries (0457-A1-9001), SRS 691, 22 August 1942, RG 457, Entry 9001, 190/36/13/05->, box 2.
26 MAGIC Far East Summaries (0457-A1-9001), SRS 692, 23 August 1942, RG 457, Entry 9001, 190/36/13/05->, box 2.
27 Shaw.
28 Shaw.
29 Drea and Van den Ven, 43; "The Strategic Correlation Between the Sino-Japanese and the Pacific Wars," Tohmatsu Haruo, chapter 18, *The Battle for China*, Mark Prattie, Edward Drea, and Hans Van de Ven, editors (Stanford, CA: Stanford University Press, 2011), 33. (Hereafter Haruo.)
30 Ugaki, 183.
31 Hattori, Vol. 2, Part IV, 8, 13–14.
32 Hattori, Vol. 2, Part IV, 17.
33 Hattori, Vol. 2, Part IV, 161.
34 MAGIC Far East Summaries (0457-A1-9001), SRS 727, 26 September 1942, RG 457, Entry 9001, 190/36/13/05->, box 3.
35 "Order of Battle of the Japanese Army," September 1942, US Military Intelligence Service, OSS Records, RG 226, Intelligence Reports, Report 20997, Entry 16, 190/3/14/4, box 151.
36 MAGIC Far East Summaries (0457-A1-9001), SRS 708, 8 September 1942, RG 457, Entry 9001, 190/36/13/05->, box 3.
37 MAGIC Far East Summaries (0457-A1-9001), SRS 739, 8 October 1942, RG 457, Entry 9001, 190/36/13/05->, box 3.
38 Jablonski, *Tragic Victories*, 47.
39 COM 14-062158-DI, 30 Octber 1942, Office of the Chief of Naval Operations, Office of Naval Intelligence, Intercepted Enemy Radio Traffic, 1940–1946, RG 38, Entry A1 344, 38/370/01/2/2, Naval General Staff, box 307.
40 USSBS No. 308.
41 Ugaki, 210–14.
42 Sakai, 202–4.
43 Ugaki, 210–14.
44 Martin Favorite, "Japanese Radar Equipment in WWII," not dated, www.combinedfleet.com/radar.htm as of February 2021. (Hereafter Favorite.); Scitor, 27.
45 Hattori, Vol. 2, Part IV, 19–20.
46 Ciano diary, 8 September 1942.
47 Ciano diary, 22 September 1942.
48 Ciano diary, 27–30 September 1942.
49 MAGIC Far East Summaries (0457-A1-9001), SRS 735, 4 October 1942, RG 457, Entry 9001, 190/36/13/05->, box 3.

50 *Kriegstagebuch des OKW, 1. Januar 1942–31. Dezember 1942, Erster Halbband, Band 2*, 413. "South Atlantic air ferry route in World War II," IPFS, https://ipfs.io/ipfs/QmXoypizjW3WknFiJnKLwHCnL72vedxjQkDDP1mXWo6uco/wiki/South_Atlantic_air_ferry_route_in_World_War_II.html as of July 2018.

51 Percy E. Schramm, *Kriegstagebuch des Oberkommando der Wehrmacht (Wehrmachtführungsstab), 1. Januar 1942–31. Dezember 1942, Zweiter Halbband, Band 2* (Germany: Bechtermünz, 2005), 794, 797. (Hereafter *Kriegstagebuch des OKW, 1. Januar 1942–31. Dezember 1942, Zweiter Halbband, Band 2*.)

52 Schramm, *1. Januar 1942–31. Dezember 1942, Zweiter Halbband, Band 2.*, 810.

53 Tooze, 590.

54 "Beantwortung des Fragebogens fuer Feldmarschall Keitel v. 24.7.45," 3–4.

55 Kahn, 82.

56 *Generalmajor* Christian Eckhard, "Study of the Situation in the High Command of the Wehrmacht Shortly Before, During and After the Allied Landing in North Africa, 1942," MS # D-066, 1947, National Archives. (Hereafter Eckhard, "Study of the Situation."); *General der Artillerie* Walter Warlimont, "Stellungsnahme zu Berichten Deutscher Offiziere: Zu den Berichten Ueber die Anglo-Amerikanische Landung in Franzoesisch-Nord Afrika im November 1942," MS # C-090, 13 February 1951, National Archives, 5–8. (Hereafter Warlimont, "Zu den Berichten Ueber die Anglo-Amerikanische Landung in Franzoesisch-Nord Afrika im November 1942."); Helmut Greiner, "Notes on the Situation Reports and Discussions at Hitler's Headquarters from 12 August 1942 to 17 March 1943," MS # C-065a, not dated, National Archives, 85. (Hereafter Greiner, "Notes on the Situation Reports and Discussions at Hitler's Headquarters from 12 August 1942 to 17 March 1943."); *Generalfeldmarschall* Albert Kesselring, "The War in the Mediterranean, Part II: The Fighting in Tunisia and Tripolitania," MS # T-3 P1, not dated, National Archives, 1 (Hereafter Kesselring, "The War in the Mediterranean, Part II: The Fighting in Tunisia and Tripolitania."); Albert Kesselring, *The Memoirs of Field-Marshal Kesselring* (St. Paul: MBI Publishing, 2007), 132. (Hereafter Kesselring Memoirs.)

57 Ciano diary, 9 October 1942.

58 *Kriegstagebuch des OKW, 1. Januar 1942–31. Dezember 1942, Zweiter Halbband, Band 2*, 816, fn 2.

59 *Kriegstagebuch des OKW, 1. Januar 1942–31. Dezember 1942, Zweiter Halbband, Band 2*, 859, fn 2.

60 *Algeria-French Morocco*, The U.S. Army Campaigns of World War II Series (Washington, D.C.: Center of Military History, n.d., online reprint of CMH Pub 72-11, www.ibiblio.org/hyperwar/USA/USA-C-Algeria/index.html as of July 2018).

61 Christine Levisse-Touze, *L'Afrique du Nord Dans la Guerre 1939–1945* (Paris: Albin Michel, 1998), 177ff.

62 Berlin, 30 January 1941, "Notes from Hitler's Speeches–America," located in Gordon W. Prange Papers, Special Collections, University of Maryland Libraries, Series II, box 4.

63 Ciano diary, 9–10 November 1942.

64 "Narrative of Observer's Tour with W.T.F., French Morocco," not dated. Included in "Report of Observers: Mediterranean Theater of Operations," Volume 1, 22 December 1942–23 March 1943.

65 Ernest Harmon letter to "Dave," 27 December 1942, records of the Armored Board, Army Ground Forces, classified correspondence, RG 337, NARA.

66 Greiner, "Notes on the Situation Reports and Discussions at Hitler's Headquarters from 12 August 1942 to 17 March 1943," 113–16. *Oberst* Rudolf Lang, "Battles of Kampfgruppe Lang in Tunisia (10. Pz. Div.) December 1942 to 15 April 1943, Part I," MS # D-173, not dated, National Archives. (Hereafter Lang.)

67. "Eisenhower Report on 'Torch'," scanned copy from the Ike Skelton Command and General Staff College Combined Arms Research Digital library, http://cgsc.contentdm.oclc.org/cdm/singleitem/collection/p4013coll8/id/110/rec/3, as of July 2018. (Hereafter "Eisenhower Report on 'Torch'."); Liddell Hart, *History of the Second World War*, 329, 335; Greiner, "Notes on the Situation Reports and Discussions at Hitler's Headquarters from 12 August 1942 to 17 March 1943," 124; *Kriegstagebuch des OKW, 1. Januar 1942–31. Dezember 1942, Zweiter Halbband, Band 2*, 980.
68. MAGIC Far East Summaries (0457-A1-9001), SRS 774, 12 November 1942, RG 457, Entry 9001, 190/36/13/05->, box 4.
69. MAGIC Far East Summaries (0457-A1-9001), SRS 774, 12 November 1942, RG 457, Entry 9001, 190/36/13/05->, box 4.
70. MAGIC Far East Summaries (0457-A1-9001), SRS 780, 18 November 1942, RG 457, Entry 9001, 190/36/13/05->, box 4.
71. MAGIC Far East Summaries (0457-A1-9001), SRS 785, 23 November 1942, RG 457, Entry 9001, 190/36/13/05->, box 4.
72. Ciano diary, 15 November 1942.
73. "Personalities of Some Leading Military Officials," A2 Cab 52/9.
74. MAGIC Far East Summaries (0457-A1-9001), SRS 775, 13 November 1942, RG 457, Entry 9001, 190/36/13/05->, box 4.
75. MAGIC Far East Summaries (0457-A1-9001), SRS 776, 14 November 1942, RG 457, Entry 9001, 190/36/13/05->, box 4.
76. Ugaki, 221.
77. Ugaki, 227–28.
78. Ugaki, 249–51.
79. O'Brien, 378–79.
80. Ugaki, 253–56.
81. Hattori, Vol. 2, Part IV, 43–49.
82. Hattori, Vol. 2, Part IV, 31, 89.
83. MAGIC Far East Summaries (0457-A1-9001), SRS 782, 20 November 1942, RG 457, Entry 9001, 190/36/13/05->, box 4. The actual translation is listed as Tab A to this report but at the National Archives is physically included with SRS783.
84. MAGIC Far East Summaries (0457-A1-9001), SRS 783, 21 November 1942, RG 457, Entry 9001, 190/36/13/05->, box 4.
85. MAGIC Far East Summaries (0457-A1-9001), SRS 786, 24 November 1942, RG 457, Entry 9001, 190/36/13/05->, box 4.
86. MAGIC Far East Summaries (0457-A1-9001), SRS 803, 11 December 1942, RG 457, Entry 9001, 190/36/13/05->, box 4.
87. MAGIC Far East Summaries (0457-A1-9001), SRS 801, 9 December 1942, RG 457, Entry 9001, 190/36/13/05->, box 4.
88. MAGIC Far East Summaries (0457-A1-9001), SRS 789, 27 November 1942, RG 457, Entry 9001, 190/36/13/05->, box 4.
89. MAGIC Far East Summaries (0457-A1-9001), SRS 792, 30 November 1942, RG 457, Entry 9001, 190/36/13/05->, box 4.
90. MAGIC Far East Summaries (0457-A1-9001), SRS 810, 18 December 1942, RG 457, Entry 9001, 190/36/13/05->, box 4.
91. Ugaki, 286.
92. Ibid.

93 MAGIC Far East Summaries (0457-A1-9001), SRS 809, 17 December 1942, RG 457, Entry 9001, 190/36/13/05->, box 4.
94 MAGIC Diplomatic Summary 386, 16 April 1943, RG 457, MAGIC Far East Summaries March 20, 1942–Aug. 15, 1945, Entry 9006, 190/37/3/1-4, box 4.
95 Ugaki, 293, passim.
96 O'Brien, 383–85.
97 MAGIC Diplomatic Summary 546, 23 September 1943, RG 457, MAGIC Far East Summaries March 20, 1942–Aug. 15, 1945, Entry 9006, 190/37/3/1-4, box 7.
98 MAGIC Far East Summaries (0457-A1-9001), SRS 808, 16 December 1942, RG 457, Entry 9001, 190/36/13/05->, box 4.
99 Ibid.
100 MAGIC Far East Summaries (0457-A1-9001), SRS 821, 20 December 1942, RG 457, Entry 9001, 190/36/13/05->, box 4.
101 MAGIC Far East Summaries (0457-A1-9001), SRS 823, 31 December 1942, RG 457, Entry 9001, 190/36/13/05->, box 4.
102 *Enigma*, 263–64.
103 Ugaki, 298–99.
104 Special Release, 9 January 1943, OSS Records, RG 226, Intelligence Reports, Report 26861, Entry 16, 190/3/16/2, box 232.
105 Hattori, Vol. 2, Part IV, 101, 106.
106 Ugaki, 315–18.
107 MAGIC Diplomatic Summary 289, 9 January 1943, RG 457, MAGIC Far East Summaries March 20, 1942–Aug. 15, 1945, Entry 9006, 190/37/3/1-4, box 3.
108 Ibid.
109 MAGIC Diplomatic Summary 328, 17 February 1943, RG 457, MAGIC Far East Summaries March 20, 1942–Aug. 15, 1945, Entry 9006, 190/37/3/1-4, box 3.
110 CINCPAC 220315, 22 March 1943, Office of the Chief of Naval Operations, Office of Naval Intelligence, Intercepted Enemy Radio Traffic, 1940–1946, RG 38, Entry A1 344, 38/370/01/2/2, Naval General Staff, box 307.
111 "Japanese Difficulties," 15 December 1942, Foreign Broadcast Intelligence Service, OSS Records, RG 226, Intelligence Reports, Report 25401, Entry 16, 190/3/16/5, box 252.
112 OSS Records, RG 226, Intelligence Reports, Report 28131, 3 February 1943, Entry 16, 190/3/16/7, box 270.
113 Hattori, Vol. 2, Part IV, 75ff.
114 Hattori, Vol. 2, Part V, 27.
115 Hattori, Vol. 2, Part IV, 82–83.
116 Hattori, Vol. 2, Part IV, 84–85.

Chapter 11

1 Hattori, Vol. 2, Part IV, 115.
2 "The Casablanca Conference, 1943," Office of the Historian, U.S. Department of State, https://history.state.gov/milestones/1937-1945/casablanca, not dated, as of July 2018.
3 O'Brien, 196.
4 O'Brien, 205–7.
5 USSBS, *European War*.
6 Westermann, 185.

7   O'Brien, 276–79.
8   Tooze, 597–98, 602.
9   Hattori, Vol. 2, Part IV, 112.
10 Hattori, Vol. 2, Part IV, 87.
11 MAGIC Diplomatic Summary 550, 27 September 1943, RG 457, MAGIC Far East Summaries March 20, 1942–Aug. 15, 1945, Entry 9006, 190/37/3/1-4, box 7.
12 USSBS No. 192.
13 USSBS No. 308.
14 Sakai, 205.
15 MAGIC Diplomatic Summary 319, 8 February 1943, RG 457, MAGIC Far East Summaries March 20, 1942–Aug. 15, 1945, Entry 9006, 190/37/3/1-4, box 3.
16 Prados, 440–41.
17 Benson, 82–83.
18 MAGIC Diplomatic Summary 295, 15 January 1943, RG 457, MAGIC Far East Summaries March 20, 1942–Aug. 15, 1945, Entry 9006, 190/37/3/1-4, box 3.
19 MAGIC Diplomatic Summary 322 and 323, 11 and 12 February 1943, RG 457, MAGIC Far East Summaries March 20, 1942–Aug. 15, 1945, Entry 9006, 190/37/3/1-4, box 3.
20 MAGIC Diplomatic Summary 378, 8 April 1943, RG 457, MAGIC Far East Summaries March 20, 1942–Aug. 15, 1945, Entry 9006, 190/37/3/1-4, box 4.
21 MAGIC Diplomatic Summary 308, 28 January 1943, RG 457, MAGIC Far East Summaries March 20, 1942–Aug. 15, 1945, Entry 9006, 190/37/3/1-4, box 3.
22 "Meeting of Japanese Military Attachés in Rome," 14 May 1943, OSS Records, RG 226, Intelligence Reports, Report 34477, Entry 16, 190/3/18/7, box 368.
23 *Tunisia* (CMH Pub 72-12) (Washington, D.C.: Center of Military History, not dated), 17.
24 MAGIC Diplomatic Summary 341, 2 March 1943, RG 457, MAGIC Far East Summaries March 20, 1942–Aug. 15, 1945, Entry 9006, 190/37/3/1-4, box 4.
25 *Generalleutnant* Alfred Gause, "Military Operations Against American Troops in Africa," MS # D-145, Historical Division, Headquarters United States Army, Europe, 1946, National Archives. (Hereafter Gause.)
26 Ladislas Farago, *Patton: Ordeal and Triumph* (New York: Ivan Obolensky, Inc., 1963), 249–50. (Hereafter Farago.)
27 Lang.
28 Schramm, *Kriegstagebuch des Oberkommando der Wehrmacht (Wehrmachtführungsstab), 1. Januar 1943–31. Dezember 1943, Erster Halbband, Band 3*, (Germany: Bechtermünz, 2005), 239. (Hereafter *Kriegstagebuch des OKW, 1. Januar 1943–31. Dezember 1943, Erster Halbband, Band 3.*)
29 Sönke Neitzel, editor, *Tapping Hitler's Generals: Transcripts of Secret Conversations 1942–45* (Barnsley, South Yorkshire: Frontline Books, 2013, Kindle edition), location 578. (Hereafter Neitzel, *Tapping Hitler's Generals.*)
30 Ibid, location 683.
31 Ibid, location 1490.
32 MAGIC Diplomatic Summary 391, 21 April 1943, RG 457, MAGIC Far East Summaries March 20, 1942–Aug. 15, 1945, Entry 9006, 190/37/3/1-4, box 4.
33 Ciano diary, 8 February 1943.
34 Warlimont, *Inside Hitler's Headquarters*, 313.
35 Sakai, 206.
36 *The Goebbels Diaries*, 273.
37 O'Brien, 410.
38 Prados, 449–50.

39 Hattori, Vol. 2, Part V, 43–44.
40 Scitor, 11–12.
41 O'Brien, 392–93.
42 USSBS No. 503. Ugaki, 330. Prados, 459–61.
43 Ugaki, 330.
44 Ugaki, 353–54.
45 USSBS No. 503.
46 MAGIC Diplomatic Summary 391, 21 April 1943, RG 457, MAGIC Far East Summaries March 20, 1942–Aug. 15, 1945, Entry 9006, 190/37/3/1-4, box 4.
47 MAGIC Diplomatic Summary 400, 30 April 1943, RG 457, MAGIC Far East Summaries March 20, 1942–Aug. 15, 1945, Entry 9006, 190/37/3/1-4, box 4.
48 MAGIC Diplomatic Summary 414, 14 May 1943, RG 457, MAGIC Far East Summaries March 20, 1942–Aug. 15, 1945, Entry 9006, 190/37/3/1-4, box 5.
49 Ibid.
50 MAGIC Diplomatic Summary 417, 17 May 1943, RG 457, MAGIC Far East Summaries March 20, 1942–Aug. 15, 1945, Entry 9006, 190/37/3/1-4, box 5.
51 MAGIC Diplomatic Summary 448, 17 June 1943, RG 457, MAGIC Far East Summaries March 20, 1942–Aug. 15, 1945, Entry 9006, 190/37/3/1-4, box 5.
52 Favorite.
53 MAGIC Diplomatic Summary 426, 26 May 1943, RG 457, MAGIC Far East Summaries March 20, 1942–Aug. 15, 1945, Entry 9006, 190/37/3/1-4, box 5.
54 O'Brien, 391.
55 USSBS No. 268.
56 Hattori, Vol. 2, Part V, 52, 56.
57 MAGIC Diplomatic Summary 425, 25 May 1943, RG 457, MAGIC Far East Summaries March 20, 1942–Aug. 15, 1945, Entry 9006, 190/37/3/1-4, box 5.
58 MAGIC Diplomatic Summary 431, 31 May 1943, RG 457, MAGIC Far East Summaries March 20, 1942–Aug. 15, 1945, Entry 9006, 190/37/3/1-4, box 5.
59 MAGIC Diplomatic Summary 428, 28 May 1943, RG 457, MAGIC Far East Summaries March 20, 1942–Aug. 15, 1945, Entry 9006, 190/37/3/1-4, box 5.
60 MAGIC Diplomatic Summary 428, 28 May 1943, RG 457, MAGIC Far East Summaries March 20, 1942–Aug. 15, 1945, Entry 9006, 190/37/3/1-4, box 5.
61 MAGIC Diplomatic Summary 421, 21 May 1943, RG 457, MAGIC Far East Summaries March 20, 1942–Aug. 15, 1945, Entry 9006, 190/37/3/1-4, box 5.
62 "Das Wehrpotential und die Wehrmächte Grossbritanniens und der USA," Generalstab des Heeres, Abteilung Fremde Heere West, folder containing data on U.S. Army training, tactics, and equipment, T-78, roll 442, frame 6415820ff, National Archives.
63 "Bewertung der britischen Führung und Truppe nach den Kampferfahrungen in Nordafrika," Generalstab des Heeres, Abteilung Fremde Heere West, folder containing data on U.S. Army training, tactics, and equipment, T-78, roll 442, frame 6415992ff, National Archives. Kesselring Memoirs, 140.
64 *The Goebbels Diaries*, 317.
65 *Generalfeldmarschall* Albert Kesselring, "An Interview with Genfldm Albert Kesselring: General Questions," ETHINT-72, 6 May 1946, National Archives, 7.
66 *Rittmeister* Wilhelm Scheidt, "Hitler's Conduct of the War," ETHINT-20, 12 July 1949, National Archives, 9.
67 *The Goebbels Diaries*, 354.
68 Ibid., 381.

69 Westermann, 200.
70 Westermann, 208.
71 Dönitz, "U-Boats Against US-UK Shipping," 2.
72 *Enigma*, 317.
73 O'Brien, 254–64; Tooze, 593.
74 "Beantwortung des Fragebogens fuer Feldmarschall Keitel v. 24.7.45," 4.
75 Tooze, 593.
76 MAGIC Diplomatic Summary 437, 6 June 1943, RG 457, MAGIC Far East Summaries March 20, 1942–Aug. 15, 1945, Entry 9006, 190/37/3/1-4, box 5.
77 MAGIC Diplomatic Summary 441, 10 June 1943, RG 457, MAGIC Far East Summaries March 20, 1942–Aug. 15, 1945, Entry 9006, 190/37/3/1-4, box 5.
78 MAGIC Diplomatic Summary 461, 30 June 1943, RG 457, MAGIC Far East Summaries March 20, 1942–Aug. 15, 1945, Entry 9006, 190/37/3/1-4, box 5.
79 MAGIC Diplomatic Summary 544, 21 September 1943, RG 457, MAGIC Far East Summaries March 20, 1942–Aug. 15, 1945, Entry 9006, 190/37/3/1-4, box 7.
80 MAGIC Diplomatic Summary 439, 8 June 1943, RG 457, MAGIC Far East Summaries March 20, 1942–Aug. 15, 1945, Entry 9006, 190/37/3/1-4, box 5.
81 USSBS No. 268.
82 USSBS, *European War*.
83 Benson, 105ff, on adoption of ULTRA 112.

Chapter 12

1 Warlimont, *Inside Hitler's Headquarters*, 319–20.
2 Ibid., 326.
3 Commando Supremo, Segnalzioni su Possibilita' Azioni Nemiche, 15 Jan–19 Aug 1943, T821, roll 21, frame 899ff, National Archives; Commando Supremo, Occupazione della Sicilia, 23 June 1943, T821, roll 348, frame 53ff, National Archives.
4 Schramm, *Kriegstagebuch des Oberkommando der Wehrmacht (Wehrmachtführungsstab), 1. Januar 1943–31. Dezember 1943, Zweiter Halbband, Band 3*, (Germany: Bechtermünz, 2005), 752. (Hereafter *Kriegstagebuch des OKW, 1. Januar 1943–31. Dezember 1943, Zweiter Halbband, Band 3*.)
5 *The Hitler Book*, 120.
6 Field Marshal Lord Carver, *The Imperial War Museum Book of The War in Italy 1943–1945* (London: Pan Books, 2002), 4–10. (Hereafter Carver.); *Sicily* (CMH Pub 72-16) (Washington, D.C.: Center of Military History, 1999), 6–9. (Hereafter *Sicily*.)
7 MAGIC Diplomatic Summary 483, 22 July 1943, RG 457, MAGIC Far East Summaries March 20, 1942–Aug. 15, 1945, Entry 9006, 190/37/3/1-4, box 6.
8 MAGIC Diplomatic Summary 480, 19 July 1943, RG 457, MAGIC Far East Summaries March 20, 1942–Aug. 15, 1945, Entry 9006, 190/37/3/1-4, box 6.
9 MAGIC Diplomatic Summary 488, 27 July 1943, RG 457, MAGIC Far East Summaries March 20, 1942–Aug. 15, 1945, Entry 9006, 190/37/3/1-4, box 6.
10 MAGIC Diplomatic Summary 487, 26 July 1943, RG 457, MAGIC Far East Summaries March 20, 1942–Aug. 15, 1945, Entry 9006, 190/37/3/1-4, box 6.
11 MAGIC Diplomatic Summary 492, 31 July 1943, RG 457, MAGIC Far East Summaries March 20, 1942–Aug. 15, 1945, Entry 9006, 190/37/3/1-4, box 6.
12 MAGIC Summaries 488, 489, and 517, 27 and 28 July and 25 August 1943, RG 457, MAGIC Far East Summaries March 20, 1942–Aug. 15, 1945, Entry 9006, 190/37/3/1-4, box 6.

13 *Enigma*, 312–13.
14 Westermann, 215; USSBS, *European War*.
15 USSBS, *European War*.
16 Scitor, 11–12, 17.
17 Westermann, 185.
18 USSBS, *European War*.
19 Interview No. 11, "Reichminister Albert Speer," 31 May 1945, RG 243, Records of the U.S. Strategic Bombing Survey, Interrogations, Entry 32, 190/063/007/04, box 1, 13.
20 "Hermann Goering," Air P/W Interrogation Detachment, A.P.W.I.D. (Ninth Air Force Adv) 65/1945, 1 June 1945, Records of the Judge Advocate General, RG 153, Entry 135, Dossier Files, 153/270/2/9/04->, box 56(270/2/10/05).
21 USSBS, *European War*.
22 Westermann, 221.
23 USSBS, *European War*.
24 Ibid.
25 O'Brien, 76–80, 268.
26 O'Brien, 272–75, 268.
27 Westermann, 221, 229–30.
28 MAGIC Diplomatic Summary 522, 30 August 1943, RG 457, MAGIC Far East Summaries March 20, 1942–Aug. 15, 1945, Entry 9006, 190/37/3/1-4, box 6.
29 MAGIC Diplomatic Summary 501, 9 August 1943, RG 457, MAGIC Far East Summaries March 20, 1942–Aug. 15, 1945, Entry 9006, 190/37/3/1-4, box 6.
30 MAGIC Diplomatic Summary 512, 20 August 1943, RG 457, MAGIC Far East Summaries March 20, 1942–Aug. 15, 1945, Entry 9006, 190/37/3/1-4, box 6.
31 "Strategic Concept for the Defeat of the Axis in Europe," JCS 444, 5 August 1943, American-British Conversations Correspondence Related to Planning and Combat Operations, 1940–1948, RG 165, Entry 421, 390/37/24/3-390/38/2/3, box 338.
32 MAGIC Diplomatic Summary 503, 11 August 1943, RG 457, MAGIC Far East Summaries March 20, 1942–Aug. 15, 1945, Entry 9006, 190/37/3/1-4, box 6.
33 MAGIC Diplomatic Summary 518, 26 August 1943, RG 457, MAGIC Far East Summaries March 20, 1942–Aug. 15, 1945, Entry 9006, 190/37/3/1-4, box 6. MAGIC Diplomatic Summary 551, 28 September 1943, RG 457, MAGIC Far East Summaries March 20, 1942–Aug. 15, 1945, Entry 9006, 190/37/3/1-4, box 7.
34 Interview No. 17, "Colonel General Jodl," 19 May 1945, RG 243, Records of the U.S. Strategic Bombing Survey, Interrogations, Entry 32, 190/063/007/04, box 1, 2.
35 Tooze, 603.
36 MAGIC Summaries 502 and 523, 10 and 31 August 1943, RG 457, MAGIC Far East Summaries March 20, 1942–Aug. 15, 1945, Entry 9006, 190/37/3/1-4, box 6.
37 MAGIC Diplomatic Summary 517, 25 August 1943, RG 457, MAGIC Far East Summaries March 20, 1942–Aug. 15, 1945, Entry 9006, 190/37/3/1-4, box 6.
38 MAGIC Diplomatic Summary 538, 15 September 1943, RG 457, MAGIC Far East Summaries March 20, 1942–Aug. 15, 1945, Entry 9006, 190/37/3/1-4, box 7.
39 O'Brien, 58–59.
40 "Collapse or Unconditional Surrender of Italy," 344-1 (JCS 302), 11 May 1943, American-British Conversations Correspondence Related to Planning and Combat Operations, 1940–1948, RG 165, Entry 421, 390/37/24/3-390/38/2/3, box 346, which includes a British draft of surrender terms and proclamation.

41 "Italy and the Allies," unnumbered Combined Chiefs of Staff paper, 5 August 1943, American-British Conversations Correspondence Related to Planning and Combat Operations, 1940–1948, RG 165, Entry 421, 390/37/24/3-390/38/2/3, box 338.
42 *Kriegstagebuch des OKW, 1. Januar 1943–31. Dezember 1943, Zweiter Halbband, Band 3*, 937ff. Commando Supremo, Operazioni in Sicilia del 1 al 17 Agosto [1943], T821, roll 21, frame 238, National Archives.
43 Commando Supremo, Operazioni in Sicilia del 1 al 17 Agosto [1943], T821, roll 21, frame 239, National Archives; *Oberstleutnant* Eberhard Rodt, "Studie Über den Feldzug in Sizilien bei der 15. Pz. Gren. Div. Mai–August 1943," MS # C-077, not dated, National Archives, 26. (Herafter Roth.)
44 Warlimont, *Inside Hitler's Headquarters*, 379.
45 Commando Supremo, Operazioni in Sicilia del 1 al 17 Agosto [1943], T821, roll 21, frame 240–241, National Archives; *Kriegstagebuch des OKW, 1. Januar 1943–31. Dezember 1943, Zweiter Halbband, Band 3*, 963–64.
46 "Das Wehrpotential und die Wehrmächte Grossbritanniens und der USA," Generalstab des Heeres, Abteilung Fremde Heere West, folder containing data on U.S. Army training, tactics, and equipment, T-78, roll 442, frame 6415820ff, National Archives.
47 Roth, 30.
48 *Kriegstagebuch des OKW, 1. Januar 1943–31. Dezember 1943, Zweiter Halbband, Band 3*, 1076–1078.
49 MAGIC Diplomatic Summary 536, 13 September 1943, RG 457, MAGIC Far East Summaries March 20, 1942–Aug. 15, 1945, Entry 9006, 190/37/3/1-4, box 7.
50 MAGIC Diplomatic Summary 541, 18 September 1943, RG 457, MAGIC Far East Summaries March 20, 1942–Aug. 15, 1945, Entry 9006, 190/37/3/1-4, box 7.
51 *Generalfeldmarshal* Albert Kesselring and *General der Kavalerie* Siegfried Westphal, "Questions Regarding the General Strategy During the Italian Campaign," MS # B-270, November 1950, National Archives. (Hereafter Kesselring and Westphal.)
52 *Kriegstagebuch des OKW, 1. Januar 1943–31. Dezember 1943, Zweiter Halbband, Band 3*, 1093ff. Thomas E. Griess, editor, *The Second World War: Europe and the Mediterranean*, West Point Military History Series (Wayne, N.J.: Avery Publishing Group, Inc., 1984), 234. (Hereafter Griess.); Kesselring and Westphal, 3ff.
53 Kesselring and Westphal, passim and 38 for quotation.
54 Martin Blumenson, *Salerno to Cassino: United States Army in World War II, The Mediterranean Theater of Operations* (Washington, D.C.: Center of Military History, 1993), 159. (Hereafter Blumenson, *Salerno to Cassino*.)
55 MAGIC Diplomatic Summary 545, 22 September 1943, RG 457, MAGIC Far East Summaries March 20, 1942–Aug. 15, 1945, Entry 9006, 190/37/3/1-4, box 7.
56 MAGIC Diplomatic Summary 551, 28 September 1943, RG 457, MAGIC Far East Summaries March 20, 1942–Aug. 15, 1945, Entry 9006, 190/37/3/1-4, box 7.
57 "Secret Conference at Hitler's Berchtesgaden Residence," September 1943, OSS Records, RG 226, Intelligence Reports, Report 46933, Entry 16, 190/3/22/5, box 549.
58 MAGIC Diplomatic Summary 562, 9 October 1943, RG 457, MAGIC Far East Summaries March 20, 1942–Aug. 15, 1945, Entry 9006, 190/37/3/1-4, box 7.
59 Ibid.
60 Ibid.
61 Ibid.
62 MAGIC Diplomatic Summary 560, 7 October 1943, RG 457, MAGIC Far East Summaries March 20, 1942–Aug. 15, 1945, Entry 9006, 190/37/3/1-4, box 7.

63 OKW Kriegsschauplätze im Rahmen der Gesamt-Kriegsführung, January–March 1944, T-77, roll 1430, frame 728ff.
64 O'Brien, 290–95.
65 *Kriegstagebuch des OKW, 1. Januar 1943–31. Dezember 1943, Zweiter Halbband, Band 3*, 1295.
66 *Kriegstagebuch des OKW, 1. Januar 1943–31. Dezember 1943, Zweiter Halbband, Band 3*, 1326, 1332.
67 MAGIC Diplomatic Summary 627, 13 December 1943, RG 457, MAGIC Far East Summaries March 20, 1942–Aug. 15, 1945, Entry 9006, 190/37/3/1-4, box 8.
68 *Kriegstagebuch des OKW, 1. Januar 1943–31. Dezember 1943, Zweiter Halbband, Band 3*, 1337.
69 *Kriegstagebuch des OKW, 1. Januar 1943–31. Dezember 1943, Zweiter Halbband, Band 3*, 1337–38.
70 Jodl, "U.S. Operations; German Defense; Ruhr; Last Days, 1–2."
71 Platinum 83, 9 November 1943, OSS Records, RG 226, Sources and Methods Files, Report 163, Entry 210, 250/64/21/01, box 441, WN 16503, NARA.
72 Tooze, 601.
73 O'Brien, 283–84; Tooze, 602.
74 O'Brien, 285.
75 Wood, 28.
76 Drea and Van den Ven, 43.
77 USSBS No. 268.
78 Drea, 242.
79 O'Brien, 59.
80 Hattori, Vol. 2, Part V, 59–61.
81 Hattori, Vol. 2, Part V, 69.
82 Prados, 441.
83 Hattori, Vol. 3, 1.
84 Hattori, Vol. 3, 2–4.
85 Hattori, Vol. 3, 4–5.
86 O'Brien, 214.
87 Hattori, Vol. 3, 5–6.
88 Hattori, Vol. 3, 13–14.
89 Hattori, Vol. 3, 19–33.
90 Platinum 85, 21 October 1943, OSS Records, RG 226, Sources and Methods Files, Report 163, Entry 210, 250/64/21/01, box 441, WN 16503, NARA.
91 O'Brien, 73.
92 MAGIC Summaries 546 and 573, 23 September and 20 October 1943, RG 457, MAGIC Far East Summaries March 20, 1942–Aug. 15, 1945, Entry 9006, 190/37/3/1-4, box 7.
93 Hattori, Vol. 3, 49–50.
94 Hattori, Vol. 3, 51.
95 Hattori, Vol. 3, 68.
96 "Notes on Japanese Strategy," 11 June 1944, original report dated 12 December 1943, Joint Intelligence Collection Agency, China Burma India, OSS Records, RG 226, Intelligence Reports, Report 59164, Entry 16, 190/3/25/7, box 713.
97 Hattori, Vol. 3, 83ff, 245ff; Takeshi, 395–96.
98 Hattori, Vol. 2, Part V, 108–9.
99 Hattori, Vol. 2, Part V, 109–11.
100 "The Economic Situation in Japan," 2 October 1943, Joint Intelligence Collection Agency, China Burma India, OSS Records, RG 226, Intelligence Reports, Report 47078, Entry 16, 190/3/22/5, box 551.

101 "Japan Reorganization Program," 29 October 1943, OSS Records, RG 226, Intelligence Reports, Report 46937, Entry 16, 190/3/22/5, box 549.
102 MAGIC Diplomatic Summary 623, 9 December 1943, RG 457, MAGIC Far East Summaries March 20, 1942–Aug. 15, 1945, Entry 9006, 190/3/37/7, box 6.
103 "Japanese Diet Meetings in Relation to the Present Operations on the Peiping-Hanko Railway," Office of Naval Operations Intelligence Report 445-44, 8 June 1944, OSS Records, RG 226, Intelligence Reports, Report 81924, Entry 16, 190/3/22/5, box 549.
104 USSBS Interrogation No. 309, copy contained in Office of the Chief of Naval Operations, Office of Naval Intelligence, Intercepted Enemy Radio Traffic, 1940–1946, RG 38, Entry A1 344, 38/370/01/2/2, Naval General Staff, box 306.
105 Prados, 592–94.
106 *The Goebbels Diaries*, 498.
107 The American Air Museum in Britain, "VIII Fighter Command FO-170 Bomber Escort," not dated, www.americanairmuseum.com/mission/1904 as of December 2021.
108 MAGIC Diplomatic Summary 657, 12 January 1944, RG 457, MAGIC Far East Summaries March 20, 1942–Aug. 15, 1945, Entry 9006, 190/37/3/1-4, box 9.
109 London to OSS, IN 7438, 20 December 1943, OSS Records, RG 226, Sources and Methods Files, Report 163, Entry 210, 250/64/21/01, box 442, WN 16633–16641, NARA.
110 *Kriegstagebuch des OKW, 1. Januar 1943–31. Dezember 1943, Zweiter Halbband, Band 3*, 1346–47, 1352–53.
111 *Kriegstagebuch des OKW, 1. Januar 1943–31. Dezember 1943, Zweiter Halbband, Band 3*, 1,376.
112 *Kriegstagebuch des OKW, 1. Januar 1943–31. Dezember 1943, Zweiter Halbband, Band 3*, 1384–86, 1394–95.

Chapter 13

1 O'Brien, 87.
2 Koichi Kido diary, (2 of 3), 6 January 1944.
3 MAGIC Diplomatic Summary 666, 21 January 1944, RG 457, MAGIC Far East Summaries March 20, 1942–Aug. 15, 1945, Entry 9006, 190/37/3/1-4, box 9.
4 Platinum 153, 24 January 1944, OSS Records, RG 226, Sources and Methods Files, Report 163, Entry 210, 250/64/21/01, box 441, WN 16503, NARA.
5 MAGIC Diplomatic Summary 665, 20 January 1944, RG 457, MAGIC Far East Summaries March 20, 1942–Aug. 15, 1945, Entry 9006, 190/37/3/1-4, box 9.
6 SRS-09, 28 February 1944, MAGIC Far East Summaries, Feb. 10, 1944–Oct. 2, 1945 (0457-A1-9001), RG 457, Entry 9001, 190/36/13/04->, box 1.
7 Prados, 441.
8 MAGIC Diplomatic Summary 683, 7 February 1944, RG 457, MAGIC Far East Summaries March 20, 1942–Aug. 15, 1945, Entry 9006, 190/37/3/1-4, box 9.
9 MAGIC Diplomatic Summary 705, 29 February 1944, RG 457, MAGIC Far East Summaries March 20, 1942–Aug. 15, 1945, Entry 9006, 190/37/3/1-4, box 9.
10 MAGIC Diplomatic Summary 701, 25 February 1944, RG 457, MAGIC Far East Summaries March 20, 1942–Aug. 15, 1945, Entry 9006, 190/37/3/1-4, box 9.
11 O'Brien, 396.
12 Takeshi, 398–99.
13 Hattori, Vol. 3, 248, 251.
14 Hattori, Vol. 3, 251.
15 MAGIC Diplomatic Summary 724, 19 March 1944, RG 457, MAGIC Far East Summaries March 20, 1942–Aug. 15, 1945, Entry 9006, 190/37/3/1-4, box 10.

16. MAGIC Diplomatic Summary 766, 30 April 1944, RG 457, MAGIC Far East Summaries March 20, 1942–Aug. 15, 1945, Entry 9006, 190/37/3/1-4, box 10.
17. SRS-06, 20 February 1944, MAGIC Far East Summaries, Feb. 10, 1944–Oct. 2, 1945 (0457-A1-9001), RG 457, Entry 9001, 190/36/13/04->, box 1.
18. Hattori, Vol. 3, 75.
19. United States Strategic Bombing Survey, *United States Strategic Bombing Survey (European War) (Pacific War)*, Interrogations of Japanese Officials, Japanese Naval Planning, Nav No. 30, USSBS No. 123, 20 October 1945, www.ibiblio.org/hyperwar/AAF/USSBS/IJO/IJO-30.html.
20. MAGIC Summaries 698 and 705, 22 and 29 February 1944, RG 457, MAGIC Far East Summaries March 20, 1942–Aug. 15, 1945, Entry 9006, 190/37/3/1-4, box 9.
21. USSBS No. 503.
22. Phillip A. Crowl, *The United States Army in World War II: The Marianas Campaign* (Center of Military History, U.S. Army, Washington, D.C., 1993, https://history.army.mil/html/books/005/5-7-1/CMH_Pub_5-7-1.pdf as of December 2021), 56.
23. Hattori, Vol. 3, 78.
24. USSBS No. 503.
25. Hattori, Vol. 3, 78.
26. USSBS No. 503.
27. O'Brien, 69–72, 83.
28. O'Brien, 404–5.
29. SRS-39, 13 April 1944, MAGIC Far East Summaries, Feb. 10, 1944–Oct. 2, 1945 (0457-A1-9001), RG 457, Entry 9001, 190/36/13/04->, box 1.
30. MAGIC Diplomatic Summary 760, 24 April 1944, RG 457, MAGIC Far East Summaries March 20, 1942–Aug. 15, 1945, Entry 9006, 190/37/3/1-4, box 10.
31. SRS-49, 25 April 1944, MAGIC Far East Summaries, Feb. 10, 1944–Oct. 2, 1945 (0457-A1-9001), RG 457, Entry 9001, 190/36/13/04->, box 1.
32. MAGIC Diplomatic Summary 1072, 2 March 1945, RG 457, MAGIC Far East Summaries March 20, 1942–Aug. 15, 1945, Entry 9006, 190/37/3/1-4, box 14.
33. SRS-12, 1 March 1944, MAGIC Far East Summaries, Feb. 10, 1944–Oct. 2, 1945 (0457-A1-9001), RG 457, Entry 9001, 190/36/13/04->, box 1.
34. SRS-14, 6 March 1944, MAGIC Far East Summaries, Feb. 10, 1944–Oct. 2, 1945 (0457-A1-9001), RG 457, Entry 9001, 190/36/13/04->, box 1.
35. Ugaki, 333.
36. Hattori, Vol. 3, 76.
37. MAGIC Summaries 698 and 705, 22 and 29 February 1944, RG 457, MAGIC Far East Summaries March 20, 1942–Aug. 15, 1945, Entry 9006, 190/37/3/1-4, box 9.
38. Hattori, Vol. 3, 79–80.
39. Haruo, 433–34.
40. Hattori, Vol. 3, 164, 186ff.
41. Ugaki, 336.
42. SRS-91, 19 June 1944, MAGIC Far East Summaries, Feb. 10, 1944–Oct. 2, 1945 (0457-A1-9001), RG 457, Entry 9001, 190/36/13/04->, box 1.
43. MAGIC Diplomatic Summary 715, 10 March 1944, RG 457, MAGIC Far East Summaries March 20, 1942–Aug. 15, 1945, Entry 9006, 190/37/3/1-4, box 10.
44. Platinum 307, 20 March 1944, OSS Records, RG 226, Sources and Methods Files, Report 163, Entry 210, 250/64/21/01, box 442, WN 16507, NARA.
45. USSBS No. 503.
46. Prados, 550–51.

47 MAGIC Diplomatic Summary 757, 21 April 1944, RG 457, MAGIC Far East Summaries March 20, 1942–Aug. 15, 1945, Entry 9006, 190/37/3/1-4, box 10.
48 Ugaki, 361.
49 Ugaki, 363–64.
50 SRS-144, 11 August 1944, MAGIC Far East Summaries, Feb. 10, 1944–Oct. 2, 1945 (0457-A1-9001), RG 457, Entry 9001, 190/36/13/04->, box 2.
51 Ugaki, 369
52 SRS-29, 30 March 1944, MAGIC Far East Summaries, Feb. 10, 1944–Oct. 2, 1945 (0457-A1-9001), RG 457, Entry 9001, 190/36/13/04->, box 1.
53 SRS-97, 25 June 1944, MAGIC Far East Summaries, Feb. 10, 1944–Oct. 2, 1945 (0457-A1-9001), RG 457, Entry 9001, 190/36/13/04->, box 1.
54 SRS-20, 16 March 1944, MAGIC Far East Summaries, Feb. 10, 1944–Oct. 2, 1945 (0457-A1-9001), RG 457, Entry 9001, 190/36/13/04->, box 1.
55 USSBS No. 378.
56 Ugaki, 388.
57 Prados, 553.
58 Hattori, Vol. 3, operations at night 246, 258ff.
59 Hattori, Vol. 3, 248; Takeshi, 392, 399–402.
60 USSBS, *European War*; O'Brien, 320.
61 Interview No. 56, "Reichsmarschal Herman Goering," 6 July 1945, RG 243, Records of the U.S. Strategic Bombing Survey, Interrogations, Entry 32, 190/063/007/04, box 2, 7.
62 Interview No. 36, "Interrogation of Officers of the Luftwaffe," 21 June 1945, RG 243, Records of the U.S. Strategic Bombing Survey, Interrogations, Entry 31, 190/063/007/03, box 1.
63 Tooze, 627, 629–32.
64 O'Brien, 21–22, 26.
65 O'Brien, 69–70.
66 O'Brien, 301.
67 Westermann, 234–37.
68 MAGIC Diplomatic Summary 675, 30 January 1944, RG 457, MAGIC Far East Summaries March 20, 1942–Aug. 15, 1945, Entry 9006, 190/37/3/1-4, box 9.
69 O'Brien, 299.
70 MAGIC Diplomatic Summary 710, 5 March 1944, RG 457, MAGIC Far East Summaries March 20, 1942–Aug. 15, 1945, Entry 9006, 190/37/3/1-4, box 10.
71 MAGIC Diplomatic Summary 694, 18 February 1944, RG 457, MAGIC Far East Summaries March 20, 1942–Aug. 15, 1945, Entry 9006, 190/37/3/1-4, box 9.
72 MAGIC Diplomatic Summary 679, 3 February 1944, RG 457, MAGIC Far East Summaries March 20, 1942–Aug. 15, 1945, Entry 9006, 190/37/3/1-4, box 9.
73 Martin Blumenson, *Anzio: The Gamble That Failed* (New York, NY: Cooper Square Press, 2001), 56. (Hereafter Blumenson, *Anzio: The Gamble That Failed*.)
74 "Operation Instruction No. 32," H.Q. 15 Army Group, 2 January 1944.
75 Griess, 239.
76 History, Fifth Army. "The German Operation at Anzio: A Study of the German Operations at Anzio Beachhead from 22 Jan 44 to 31 May 44," GMDS by a combined British, Canadian, and U.S. staff, not dated. (Hereafter "The German Operation at Anzio."); *Kriegstagebuch des OKW, 1. Januar 1943–31. Dezember 1943, Zweiter Halbband, Band 3*, 1180ff.
77 Kesselring and Westphal, passim.
78 *The Hitler Book*, 141–42.

79 MAGIC Summaries 713 and 716, 8 and 11 March 1944, RG 457, MAGIC Far East Summaries March 20, 1942–Aug. 15, 1945, Entry 9006, 190/37/3/1-4, box 10.
80 Hattori, Vol. 3, 99–100, 125. Robert Ross Smith, *The United States Army in World War II, The War in the Pacific: The Approach to the Philippines* (Washington, D.C.: Center of Military History, United States Army, 1996, https://history.army.mil/html/books/005/5-8-1/cmhPub_5-8-1.pdf as of December 2021), 93.
81 SRS-84, 12 June 1944, MAGIC Far East Summaries, Feb. 10, 1944–Oct. 2, 1945 (0457-A1-9001), RG 457, Entry 9001, 190/36/13/04->, box 1. Hattori, Vol. 3, 103.
82 SRS-89, 17 June 1944, MAGIC Far East Summaries, Feb. 10, 1944–Oct. 2, 1945 (0457-A1-9001), RG 457, Entry 9001, 190/36/13/04->, box 1.
83 Hattori, Vol. 3, 219.
84 SRS-147, 14 August 1944, MAGIC Far East Summaries, Feb. 10, 1944–Oct. 2, 1945 (0457-A1-9001), RG 457, Entry 9001, 190/36/13/04->, box 2.
85 SRS-107, 5 July 1944, MAGIC Far East Summaries, Feb. 10, 1944–Oct. 2, 1945 (0457-A1-9001), RG 457, Entry 9001, 190/36/13/04->, box 2. See Ugaki 368 on the continued focus on a decisive battle, which he found wrong-headed.
86 Ugaki, 370–71.
87 Ugaki, 372.
88 SRS-74, 31 May 1944, MAGIC Far East Summaries, Feb. 10, 1944–Oct. 2, 1945 (0457-A1-9001), RG 457, Entry 9001, 190/36/13/04->, box 1.

Chapter 14

1 SRS-87, 15 June 1944, MAGIC Far East Summaries, Feb. 10, 1944–Oct. 2, 1945 (0457-A1-9001), RG 457, Entry 9001, 190/36/13/04->, box 1.
2 SRS-167, 3 September 1944, MAGIC Far East Summaries, Feb. 10, 1944–Oct. 2, 1945 (0457-A1-9001), RG 457, Entry 9001, 190/36/13/04->, box 2.
3 SRS-107, 5 July 1944, MAGIC Far East Summaries, Feb. 10, 1944–Oct. 2, 1945 (0457-A1-9001), RG 457, Entry 9001, 190/36/13/04->, box 2.
4 SRS-168, 4 September 1944, MAGIC Far East Summaries, Feb. 10, 1944–Oct. 2, 1945 (0457-A1-9001), RG 457, Entry 9001, 190/36/13/04->, box 2.
5 SRS-176, 12 September 1944, MAGIC Far East Summaries, Feb. 10, 1944–Oct. 2, 1945 (0457-A1-9001), RG 457, Entry 9001, 190/36/13/04->, box 2.
6 Records of the OSS, Intelligence Reports, "Goebbels' Recent Speech," A-23272-a, 17 March 1944, 62781, RG 226, Entry 16, 190/3/12/4, box 760.
7 Percy E. Schramm, *Kriegstagebuch des Oberkommando der Wehrmacht (Wehrmachtführungsstab), 1. Januar 1944–22 Mai 1945, Erster Halbband, Band 4* (Germany: Bechtermünz, 2005), 302–3. (Hereafter *Kriegstagebuch des OKW, 1. Januar 1944–22 Mai 1945, Erster Halbband, Band 4*.); Liddell Hart, *The German Generals Talk*, 237; Warlimont, *Inside Hitler's Headquarters*, 409.
8 MAGIC Diplomatic Summary 798, 1 June 1944, RG 457, MAGIC Far East Summaries March 20, 1942–Aug. 15, 1945, Entry 9006, 190/37/3/1-4, box 11.
9 *General der Artillerie* Walter Warlimont, "From Invasion to the Siegfried Line," ETHINT-1, 19–20 July 1945, National Archives, 9. (Hereafter Warlimont, "From Invasion to the Siegfried Line.")
10 *The Hitler Book*, 148–49.
11 Ugaki, 389.
12 MAGIC Diplomatic Summary 812, 15 June 1944, RG 457, MAGIC Far East Summaries March 20, 1942–Aug. 15, 1945, Entry 9006, 190/37/3/1-4, box 11.

13 *Kriegstagebuch des OKW, 1. Januar 1944–22 Mai 1945, Erster Halbband, Band 4*, 314.
14 *Kriegstagebuch des OKW, 1. Januar 1944–22 Mai 1945, Erster Halbband, Band 4*, 316.
15 Ugaki, 393–96.
16 Ugaki, 396–99.
17 Ugaki, 400.
18 Ugaki, 399.
19 Maj. Carl Hoffman, *Saipan: The Beginning of the End, USMC Historical Monograph*, Historical Branch, G-3 Division, Headquarters, U.S. Marine Corps, 1950 (online version at Hyperwar: A Hypertext History of the Second World War, www.ibiblio.org/hyperwar/, as of February 2007), 1–12. (Hereafter Hoffman.)
20 Lt. Col. James Rogers, "Command Control of an Armored Amphibian Battalion" (*The Cavalry Journal*, January–February 1945), 5.
21 MAGIC Diplomatic Summary 818, 21 June 1944, RG 457, MAGIC Far East Summaries March 20, 1942–Aug. 15, 1945, Entry 9006, 190/37/3/1-4, box 11.
22 SRS-91, 19 June 1944, MAGIC Far East Summaries, Feb. 10, 1944–Oct. 2, 1945 (0457-A1-9001), RG 457, Entry 9001, 190/36/13/04->, box 1.
23 U.S. Strategic Bombing Survey, *The Effects of Air Attack on Japanese Urban Economy, Summary Report* (Washington, D.C.: USSBS, March 1947, http://babel.hathitrust.org/cgi/pt?id=mdp.39015022928447;view=1up;seq=1). (Hereafter *The Effects of Air Attack on Japanese Urban Economy, Summary Report.*)
24 Sakai, 214.
25 MAGIC Diplomatic Summary 822, 25 June 1944, RG 457, MAGIC Far East Summaries March 20, 1942–Aug. 15, 1945, Entry 9006, 190/37/3/1-4, box 11.
26 Ugaki, 401–2.
27 Ugaki, 402–3, 408, 412.
28 Prados, 570ff.
29 Ugaki, 400–23, O'Brien, *Many of the Zeros*, 374.
30 Ugaki, 410–11.
31 Ugaki, 411.
32 Hattori, Vol. 3, 157.
33 Ugaki, 416.
34 Ugaki, 419–23.
35 Prados, 578–80.
36 O'Brien, 376.
37 Hattori, Vol. 3, 222–23.
38 MAGIC Diplomatic Summary 838, 11 July 1944, RG 457, MAGIC Far East Summaries March 20, 1942–Aug. 15, 1945, Entry 9006, 190/37/3/1-4, box 12.
39 Ibid.
40 USSBS No. 192.
41 Ugaki, 425.
42 USSBS No. 503; Ugaki, 402.
43 Hattori, Vol. 3, 159; Ugaki, 428–29.
44 Hattori, Vol. 3, 164.
45 "Summation of Case Against Hiranuma," EE-40. "Interrogation," 26 March 1946, Interrogation Reports Submitted to the Executive Committee, International Military Tribunal for the Far East, International Prosecution Section Staff Historical Files, RG 331, M1663, roll 2. SRS-1677, 13 September 1944, MAGIC Far East Summaries, Feb. 10, 1944–Oct. 2, 1945 (0457-A1-9001), RG 457, Entry 9001, 190/36/13/04->, box 2; Ugaki, 432–33. Hattori, Vol. 3, 167.

454 • BETTING AGAINST AMERICA

46 MAGIC Diplomatic Summary 849, 2 July 1944, RG 457, MAGIC Far East Summaries March 20, 1942–Aug. 15, 1945, Entry 9006, 190/37/3/1-4, box 12.
47 USSBS No. 308.
48 MAGIC Diplomatic Summary 853, 26 July 1944, RG 457, MAGIC Far East Summaries March 20, 1942–Aug. 15, 1945, Entry 9006, 190/37/3/1-4, box 12.
49 Records of the OSS, Intelligence Reports, "Civilian Morale in Japan," 107985, 8 December 1944, RG 226, Entry 16, 190/4/1/2, box 1215.
50 MAGIC Diplomatic Summary 851, 24 July 1944, RG 457, MAGIC Far East Summaries March 20, 1942–Aug. 15, 1945, Entry 9006, 190/37/3/1-4, box 12. Hattori, Vol. 3, 179, citing Kido.
51 MAGIC Diplomatic Summary 882, 24 August 1944, RG 457, MAGIC Far East Summaries March 20, 1942–Aug. 15, 1945, Entry 9006, 190/37/3/1-4, box 12.
52 Ibid.
53 Ibid.
54 USSBS No. 308.
55 USSBS No. 373.
56 Hattori, Vol. 3, 164.
57 Ugaki, 434–36.
58 Hattori, Vol. 3, 161–62.
59 Ugaki, 436.
60 MAGIC Diplomatic Summary 854, 27 July 1944, RG 457, MAGIC Far East Summaries March 20, 1942–Aug. 15, 1945, Entry 9006, 190/37/3/1-4, box 12.
61 MAGIC Diplomatic Summary 855, 28 July 1944, RG 457, MAGIC Far East Summaries March 20, 1942–Aug. 15, 1945, Entry 9006, 190/37/3/1-4, box 12.
62 USSBS No. 308.
63 MAGIC Diplomatic Summary 895, 6 September 1944, RG 457, MAGIC Far East Summaries March 20, 1942–Aug. 15, 1945, Entry 9006, 190/37/3/1-4, box 13.
64 "Appointment of New Japanese Minister of Information, and Its Significance," Records of the OSS, Intelligence Reports, 88900, 28 October 1944, RG 226, Entry 16, 190/3/32/3, box 1022.
65 Records of the OSS, Intelligence Reports, "Review of Tokyo Asahi for August, 1944," 117096, undated, RG 226, Entry 16, 190/4/3/5, box 1335.
66 Hattori, Vol. 3, 275.
67 Hattori, Vol. 3, 269ff.
68 Hattori, Vol. 3, 290ff.
69 O'Brien, 73, 418, 434–35.
70 Hattori, Vol. 3, 317.
71 Hattori, Vol. 3, 330–31.
72 Hattori, Vol. 3, 343–45.
73 Ibid.
74 O'Brien, 434–38.
75 United States Strategic Bombing Survey, *United States Strategic Bombing Survey (European War) (Pacific War)*, Interrogations of Japanese Officials, Japanese Naval Planning, Nav No. 74, USSBS No. 371, 12 November 1945, www.ibiblio.org/hyperwar/AAF/USSBS/IJO/IJO-74.html.
76 United States Strategic Bombing Survey, *United States Strategic Bombing Survey (European War) (Pacific War)*, Interrogations of Japanese Officials, Japanese Naval Planning, Nav No. 48, USSBS No. 200, October 1945, www.ibiblio.org/hyperwar/AAF/USSBS/IJO/IJO-48.html.

77 United States Strategic Bombing Survey, *United States Strategic Bombing Survey (European War) (Pacific War)*, Interrogations of Japanese Officials, Japanese Naval Planning, Nav No. 56, USSBS No. 228, 1 November 1945, www.ibiblio.org/hyperwar/AAF/USSBS/IJO/IJO-56.html.html.
78 United States Strategic Bombing Survey, *United States Strategic Bombing Survey (European War) (Pacific War)*, Interrogations of Japanese Officials, Japanese Naval Planning, Nav No. 57, USSBS No. 229, 31 October 1945, www.ibiblio.org/hyperwar/AAF/USSBS/IJO/IJO-57.html.
79 "War in the Pacific: Pacific Offensive," www.nps.gov/parkhistory/online_books/npswapa/extContent/wapa/guides/offensive/sec6.htm as of February 2021.
80 Sakai, 264–66.
81 Warlimont, "From Invasion to the Siegfried Line," 16.
82 Anlagen zum Kriegstagebuch, Oberkommando Heeresgruppe B, Ic, 1 July–31 December 1944, T311, roll 1, frame 7000892ff, National Archives.
83 *General der Infanterie* Günther Blumentritt, "OB West and the Normandy Campaign (Jun–Jul 1944)," ETHINT-73, 8–11 January 1946, National Archives, 1. (Hereafter Blumentritt, "OB West and the Normandy Campaign (Jun–Jul 1944).")
84 *Generaloberst* Alfred Jodl, "U.S. Operations; German Defense; Ruhr; Last Days," ETHINT-52, 2 August 1945, National Archives, 1. (Hereafter Jodl, "U.S. Operations; German Defense; Ruhr; Last Days.")
85 *Kriegstagebuch des OKW, 1. Januar 1944–22 Mai 1945, Erster Halbband, Band 4*, 317–18.
86 *Kriegstagebuch des OKW, 1. Januar 1944–22 Mai 1945, Erster Halbband, Band 4*, 322–23.
87 *Kriegstagebuch des OKW, 1. Januar 1944–22 Mai 1945, Erster Halbband, Band 4*, 324. Blumentritt, "OB West and the Normandy Campaign (Jun–Jul 1944)," 2–3.
88 Heeresgruppe B, Ia, Lagebeurteilungen, Wochenmeldungen, T311, roll 3, frame 7002241ff, National Archives.
89 *Kriegstagebuch des OKW, 1. Januar 1944–22 Mai 1945, Erster Halbband, Band 4*, 325–26.
90 Schramm, "OKW War Diary (1 Apr–18 Dec 44)," MS # B-034, 1947, National Archives, 56–57.
91 Guderian, 267ff.
92 Anlagen zum Kriegstagebuch, Oberkommando Heeresgruppe B, Versorgungs Führung, 1 July–31 July 1944, T311, roll 1, frame 7000828, National Archives.
93 Guderian, 265.
94 O'Brien, 363ff.
95 Neitzel, *Tapping Hitler's Generals*, location 916.
96 *Kriegstagebuch des OKW, 1. Januar 1944–22 Mai 1945, Erster Halbband, Band 4*, 326.
97 Steven Zaloga, *Armored Thunderbolt* (Mechanicsburg, PA: Stackpole Books, 2008), 168.
98 *The Hitler Book*, 157.
99 Anlagen zum Kriegstagebuch, Oberkommando Heeresgruppe B, Ic, 1 July–31 December 1944, T311, roll 1, frame 7000925, National Archives.
100 Heinz Guderian, *Panzer Leader* (New York, NY: Ballantine Books, 1972), 272. (Hereafter Guderian.)
101 Heeresgruppe B, Ia, Lagebeurteilungen, Wochenmeldungen, T311, roll 3, frame 7002243ff, National Archives.
102 Guderian, 272.
103 MAGIC Diplomatic Summary 856, 29 July 1944, RG 457, MAGIC Far East Summaries March 20, 1942–Aug. 15, 1945, Entry 9006, 190/37/3/1-4, box 12.
104 Westermann, 247–49.
105 Bernard Law Montgomery, *The Memoirs of Field Marshal the Viscount Montgomery of Alamein, L.G.* (New York: The World Publishing Company, 1958), 200, 227–28.

106 *Northern France*, CMH Pub 72–30 (Washington, D.C.: U.S. Army Center of Military History, not dated), 7. (Hereafter *Northern France*.); Report of operations, First Army. AAR, VIII Corps.
107 Schramm, "OKW War Diary (1 Apr–18 Dec 44)," MS # B-034, 1947, National Archives, 56.
108 Anlagen zum Kriegstagebuch, Oberkommando Heeresgruppe B, Versorgungs Führung, 1 July–31 July 1944, T311, roll 1, frame 7000805ff, National Archives.
109 *Generaloberst* Alfred Jodl, "An Interview with Genobst Alfred Jodl: Ardennes Offensive," ETHINT-51, 31 July 1945, National Archives, 9. (Hereafter Jodl, "Ardennes Offensive.")
110 Jodl, "U.S. Operations; German Defense; Ruhr; Last Days," 1.
111 Helmut Heiber and David M. Glantz, editors, *Hitler and His Generals: Military Conferences 1942–1945* (New York: Enigma Books, 2004), 444–49. (Hereafter Heiber and Glantz.)
112 Heiber and Glantz, 445.
113 Tagebuch, *Generaloberst* Jodl, 13 April 1944, T-77, roll 1430, frame 893ff. Professor *Major* Percy Schramm, "OKW War Diary (1 Apr–18 Dec 44)," MS # B-034, 1947, National Archives, 6–7. (Hereafter Schramm, "OKW War Diary [1 Apr–18 Dec 44].); *Kriegstagebuch des OKW, 1. Januar 1944–22 Mai 1945, Erster Halbband, Band 4, 1. Januar 1944–22 Mai 1945, Erster Halbband, Band 4*, 209–10.
114 Heiber and Glantz, 445–60.
115 Tagebuch, Generaloberst Jodl, 31 July 1944, T-77, roll 1430, frame 893ff.
116 Tooze, 637–38, passim regarding weapon technology.
117 FWD-13765, "Eisenhower to All Army Commanders: Present condition of the enemy and future missions," 4 September 1944.
118 FWD-13765, "Eisenhower to All Army Commanders: Present condition of the enemy and future missions," 4 September 1944.
119 *Kriegstagebuch des OKW, 1. Januar 1944–22 Mai 1945, Erster Halbband, Band 4, 1. Januar 1944–22 Mai 1945, Erster Halbband, Band 4*, 357; *The Hitler Book*, 386.
120 Dwight D. Eisenhower, *Crusade in Europe* (Garden City, NY: Doubleday and Company, Inc., 1948), 302. *Major* Percy Ernst Schramm, "OKW War Diary (1 Apr–18 Dec 1944)," MS # B-034, not dated, National Archives, 151.
121 Heeresgruppe B, Ia, Führerbefehle, T311, roll 3, frame 7002327ff, National Archives.
122 Heeresgruppe B, Ia, Lagebeurteilungen, Wochenmeldungen, T311, roll 3, frame 7002268, National Archives.
123 Liddell Hart, *History of the Second World War*, 559. Chester Wilmot, *The Struggle for Europe* (Ware, England: Wordsworth Editions Limited, 1997), 479. (Hereafter Wilmot.)
124 *Kriegstagebuch des OKW, 1. Januar 1944–22 Mai 1945, Erster Halbband, Band 4, 1. Januar 1944–22 Mai 1945, Erster Halbband, Band 4*, 369.
125 *Kriegstagebuch des OKW, 1. Januar 1944–22 Mai 1945, Erster Halbband, Band 4, 1. Januar 1944–22 Mai 1945, Erster Halbband, Band 4*, 159–60.
126 *Kriegstagebuch des OKW, 1. Januar 1944–22 Mai 1945, Erster Halbband, Band 4, 1. Januar 1944–22 Mai 1945, Erster Halbband, Band* 4, 377–78. First United States Army, Report of Operations, 1 August 1944–22 February 1945, 57.
127 *Kriegstagebuch des OKW, 1. Januar 1944–22 Mai 1945, Erster Halbband, Band 4, 1. Januar 1944–22 Mai 1945, Erster Halbband, Band 4*, 367.
128 *Kriegstagebuch des OKW, 1. Januar 1944–22 Mai 1945, Erster Halbband, Band 4, 1. Januar 1944–22 Mai 1945, Erster Halbband, Band 4*, 189.
129 *Kriegstagebuch des OKW, 1. Januar 1944–22 Mai 1945, Erster Halbband, Band 4, 1. Januar 1944–22 Mai 1945, Erster Halbband, Band 4*, 431.

130 *Kriegstagebuch des OKW, 1. Januar 1944–22 Mai 1945, Erster Halbband, Band 4, 1. Januar 1944–22 Mai 1945, Erster Halbband, Band 4*, 192–93.
131 Charles B. MacDonald, *The Battle of the Bulge* (London: Guild Publishing, 1984), 62. Hereafter MacDonald, *The Battle of the Bulge*.
132 First United States Army, Report of Operations, 1 August 1944–22 February 1945, 55.
133 *Kriegstagebuch des OKW, 1. Januar 1944–22 Mai 1945, Erster Halbband, Band 4, 1. Januar 1944–22 Mai 1945, Erster Halbband, Band 4*, 376.
134 Westermann, 260.
135 *Kriegstagebuch des OKW, 1. Januar 1944–22 Mai 1945, Erster Halbband, Band 4, 1. Januar 1944–22 Mai 1945, Erster Halbband, Band 4*, 431.
136 *Kriegstagebuch des OKW, 1. Januar 1944–22 Mai 1945, Erster Halbband, Band 4, 1. Januar 1944–22 Mai 1945, Erster Halbband, Band 4*, 407.
137 Records of the OSS, Intelligence Reports, "Preparations for Nazi Resistance," 101937, 28 October 1944, RG 226, Entry 16, 190/3/12/4, box 1157.
138 London to OSS, IN 22834, 14 October 1944, OSS Records, RG 226, Sources and Methods Files, Report 163, Entry 210, 250/64/21/01, box 440, WN 15969–15977, NARA.
139 Westermann, 262–63.
140 Interview No. 11, "Minutes of Meeting with Reichminister," 19 May 1945, RG 243, Records of the U.S. Strategic Bombing Survey, Interrogations, Entry 32, 190/063/007/04, box 3, NARA.
141 USSBS, *European War*.
142 Ibid.
143 Ibid.
144 O'Brien, 75–76.
145 USSBS, *European War*.
146 Westermann, 271–76.
147 Tooze, 639–40.
148 Ugaki, 443.
149 MAGIC Summaries 883 and 888, 25 and 30 August 1944, RG 457, MAGIC Far East Summaries March 20, 1942–Aug. 15, 1945, Entry 9006, 190/37/3/1-4, box 12.
150 MAGIC Diplomatic Summary 944, 25 October 1944, RG 457, MAGIC Far East Summaries March 20, 1942–Aug. 15, 1945, Entry 9006, 190/37/3/1-4, box 13.
151 MAGIC Diplomatic Summary 895, 6 September 1944, RG 457, MAGIC Far East Summaries March 20, 1942–Aug. 15, 1945, Entry 9006, 190/37/3/1-4, box 13.
152 MAGIC Diplomatic Summary 892, 3 September 1944, RG 457, MAGIC Far East Summaries March 20, 1942–Aug. 15, 1945, Entry 9006, 190/37/3/1-4, box 13.
153 "Interrogation," 26 March 1946, Interrogation Reports Submitted to the Executive Committee, International Military Tribunal for the Far East, International Prosecution Section Staff Historical Files, RG 331, M1663, roll 2.
154 Platinum 442, 21 October 1944, OSS Records, RG 226, Sources and Methods Files, Report 163, Entry 210, 250/64/21/01, box 442, WN 16508–16511, NARA.
155 MAGIC Diplomatic Summary 944, 25 October 1944, RG 457, MAGIC Far East Summaries March 20, 1942–Aug. 15, 1945, Entry 9006, 190/37/3/1-4, box 13.
156 *The Effects of Air Attack on Japanese Urban Economy, Summary Report*.
157 Ibid.
158 Hattori, Vol. 3, 358.
159 Brig. Gen. (Ret) Gordon Gayle, *Bloody Beaches: The Marines at Peleliu* (Washington, D.C.: The Marine Corps Historical Center, 1996, www.ibiblio.org/hyperwar/USMC/USMC-C-Peleliu/index.html as of June 2018), 4ff. (Hereafter Gayle.)

160 Hattori, Vol. 3, 359; Gayle, 48.
161 Ugaki, 465–84.
162 Hattori, Vol. 3, 367–68.
163 Ugaki, 478–79.
164 Hattori, Vol. 3, 372–76.
165 O'Brien, 426.
166 Ugaki, 480, 484; Prados, 163–65, 589–600.
167 Prados, 601ff, 629ff.
168 Hattori, Vol. 3, 379–80.
169 Prados, 622.
170 M. Hamlin Cannon, *Leyte: The Return to the Philippines: The United States Army in World War II, The War in the Pacific* (Washington, D.C.: U.S. Army Center of Military History, 1993). 1–4, 22–33; "Seizure of Leyte—Report of the Participation of Task Force Seventy-Nine," memorandum FE25/A16-3(3) from Commander, Task Force 79, to Commander, Seventh Fleet, 18 November 1944; Hattori, Vol. 3, 349–50.
171 Ugaki, 487–500; Prados, 664ff.
172 Sakai, 273–75.
173 Hattori, Vol. 3, 387.
174 Ugaki, 511–13.
175 Hattori, Vol. 3, 404.
176 Prados, 688.
177 Hattori, Vol. 3, 414.
178 Ugaki, 505, 508; Sakai, 275.
179 *The Effects of Air Attack on Japanese Urban Economy, Summary Report*; O'Brien, 80.
180 *The Effects of Air Attack on Japanese Urban Economy, Summary Report*.
181 Ibid.
182 "Tokyo: A Study in Jap Flak Defense." Naval History and Heritage Command website. Reproduces an undated Army Air Force intelligence analysis, spring 1945, www.history.navy.mil/research/library/online-reading-room/title-list-alphabetically/t/tokyo-study-jap-flak-defense.html as of February 2021; Westermann, 157–58.
183 Ugaki, 516–17, 520.
184 Ugaki, 531.
185 Wilmot, 577.
186 Wilmot, 576; *Kriegstagebuch des OKW, 1. Januar 1944–22 Mai 1945, Erster Halbband, Band 4, 1. Januar 1944–22 Mai 1945, Erster Halbband, Band 4*, 435ff.
187 Ugaki, 530.
188 Gerald Astor, *A Blood-Dimmed Tide: The Battle of the Bulge by the Men Who Fought It* (New York: Dell, 1992), v. (Hereafter Astor.)

Chapter 15

1 Wilmot, 663–64.
2 Westermann, 279–80.
3 *Generalmajor* Carl Wagener, "Die Folgen der Ardennen-Offensive," MS # A-964, 4 February 1946, National Archives, 9–10; Third Army G-2 periodic report, 4 February 1945.
4 Fritz, 23–24.
5 MAGIC Diplomatic Summary 1049, 7 February 1945, RG 457, MAGIC Far East Summaries March 20, 1942–Aug. 15, 1945, Entry 9006, 190/37/3/1-4, box 14.

6   MAGIC Diplomatic Summary 1065, 23 February 1945, and 1066, 24 February, RG 457, MAGIC Far East Summaries March 20, 1942–Aug. 15, 1945, Entry 9006, 190/37/3/1-4, box 14.
7   MAGIC Diplomatic Summary 1063, 21 February 1945, RG 457, MAGIC Far East Summaries March 20, 1942–Aug. 15, 1945, Entry 9006, 190/37/3/1-4, box 14.
8   MAGIC Diplomatic Summary 1074, 4 March 1945, RG 457, MAGIC Far East Summaries March 20, 1942–Aug. 15, 1945, Entry 9006, 190/37/3/1-4, box 14.
9   MAGIC Diplomatic Summary 1087, 17 March 1945, RG 457, MAGIC Far East Summaries March 20, 1942–Aug. 15, 1945, Entry 9006, 190/37/3/1-4, box 15.
10 MAGIC Diplomatic Summary 1104, 3 April 1945, RG 457, MAGIC Far East Summaries March 20, 1942–Aug. 15, 1945, Entry 9006, 190/37/3/1-4, box 15.
11 Interview No. 62, "Col. General Alfred Jodl," 7 July 1945, RG 243, Records of the US Strategic Bombing Survey, Interrogations, Entry 32, 190/063/007/04, box 3, 9.
12 USSBS, *European War*.
13 *The Hitler Book*, 184.
14 MAGIC Diplomatic Summary 1118, 17 April 1945, RG 457, MAGIC Far East Summaries March 20, 1942–Aug. 15, 1945, Entry 9006, 190/37/3/1-4, box 16.
15 MAGIC Diplomatic Summary 1117, 16 April 1945, RG 457, MAGIC Far East Summaries March 20, 1942–Aug. 15, 1945, Entry 9006, 190/37/3/1-4, box 16.
16 Ibid.
17 MAGIC Diplomatic Summary 1120, 19 April 1945, RG 457, MAGIC Far East Summaries March 20, 1942–Aug. 15, 1945, Entry 9006, 190/37/3/1-4, box 16.
18 *The Hitler Book*, 204, 219.
19 Griess, 406–7; MAGIC Diplomatic Summary 1124, 23 April 1945, RG 457, MAGIC Far East Summaries March 20, 1942–Aug. 15, 1945, Entry 9006, 190/37/3/1-4, box 16.
20 *The Hitler Book*, 229–30.
21 ULTRA 1433/5/D70/L37, 5 May 1945, RG 38, Office of the Chief of Naval Operations, Entry A1 344, 38/370/01/2/2.
22 Interview No. 55, "Field Marshal Wilhelm Keitel," 27 June 1945, RG 243, Records of the US Strategic Bombing Survey, Interrogations, Entry 32, 190/063/007/04, box 4, 23.
23 Hattori, Vol. 4, 2.
24 Hattori, Vol. 4, 2–4, 28.
25 MAGIC Diplomatic Summary 1049, 7 February 1945, RG 457, MAGIC Far East Summaries March 20, 1942–Aug. 15, 1945, Entry 9006, 190/37/3/1-4, box 14.
26 MAGIC Diplomatic Summary 1101, 31 March 1945, RG 457, MAGIC Far East Summaries March 20, 1942–Aug. 15, 1945, Entry 9006, 190/37/3/1-4, box 15.
27 Hattori, Vol. 4, 250–52.
28 Sakai, 276–79.
29 Robert Ross Smith, *Triumph in the Philippines: The United States Army in World War II, The War in the Pacific* (Washington, D.C.: Office of the Chief of Military History, Department of the Army, 1963), 18–19. (Hereafter Smith, *Triumph in the Philippines*.)
30 *Luzon*, the U.S. Army Campaigns of World War II Series (Washington, D.C.: Center of Military History, n.d., online reprint of CMH Pub 72–28, www.army.mil/cmh-pg/brochures/luzon/72-28.htm as of July 2006). (Hereafter *Luzon*.)
31 Ugaki, 532.
32 Hattori, Vol. 4, 67.
33 *Luzon*, passim.
34 *Luzon*, 9.
35 Smith, *Triumph in the Philippines*, 142; *Luzon*, 9.

36 AAR, 129th Infantry Regiment.
37 USSBS No. 379.
38 Hattori, Vol. 4, 6. Prados, 703.
39 Ugaki, 533–35.
40 Ugaki, 536–37.
41 Hattori, Vol. 4, 46.
42 Hattori, Vol. 4, 20, quoting the U.S. State Department's release of the Yalta Agreement in 1946.
43 Records of the OSS, Intelligence Reports, 115594, 24 February 1945, RG 226, Entry 16, 190/3/12/4, box 1157.
44 Ugaki, 540.
45 Hattori, Vol. 4, 113–15.
46 Hattori, Vol. 4, 115–16.
47 Ugaki, 541–42.
48 Hattori, Vol. 4, 21.
49 Hattori, Vol. 4, 27.
50 MAGIC Diplomatic Summary 1058, 16 February 1945, RG 457, MAGIC Far East Summaries March 20, 1942–Aug. 15, 1945, Entry 9006, 190/37/3/1-4, box 14.
51 MAGIC Diplomatic Summary 1051, 9 February 1945, RG 457, MAGIC Far East Summaries March 20, 1942–Aug. 15, 1945, Entry 9006, 190/37/3/1-4, box 14.
52 MAGIC Diplomatic Summary 1059, 17 February 1945, RG 457, MAGIC Far East Summaries March 20, 1942–Aug. 15, 1945, Entry 9006, 190/37/3/1-4, box 14.
53 MAGIC Diplomatic Summary 1066, 24 February 1945, RG 457, MAGIC Far East Summaries March 20, 1942–Aug. 15, 1945, Entry 9006, 190/37/3/1-4, box 14.
54 MAGIC Diplomatic Summary 1107, 6 April 1945, RG 457, MAGIC Far East Summaries March 20, 1942–Aug. 15, 1945, Entry 9006, 190/37/3/1-4, box 15.
55 MAGIC Diplomatic Summary 1109, 8 April 1945, RG 457, MAGIC Far East Summaries March 20, 1942–Aug. 15, 1945, Entry 9006, 190/37/3/1-4, box 15.
56 MAGIC Diplomatic Summary 1116, 15 April 1945, RG 457, MAGIC Far East Summaries March 20, 1942–Aug. 15, 1945, Entry 9006, 190/37/3/1-4, box 16.
57 MAGIC Diplomatic Summaries 1141 and 1169, 10 May and 7 June 1945, RG 457, MAGIC Far East Summaries March 20, 1942–Aug. 15, 1945, Entry 9006, 190/37/3/1-4, box 16.
58 *The Effects of Air Attack on Japanese Urban Economy, Summary Report.*
59 O'Brien, 441.
60 *The Effects of Air Attack on Japanese Urban Economy, Summary Report.*
61 Ibid.
62 Ugaki, 544–45.
63 *The Effects of Air Attack on Japanese Urban Economy, Summary Report.*
64 USSBS No. 378.
65 *The Effects of Strategic Bombing on Japanese Morale*, Washington DC: USSBS, June 1947, http://babel.hathitrust.org/cgi/pt?id=mdp.39015002274416;view=1up;seq=1.
66 MAGIC Diplomatic Summary 1084, 14 March 1945, RG 457, MAGIC Far East Summaries March 20, 1942–Aug. 15, 1945, Entry 9006, 190/37/3/1-4, box 14.
67 Prados, 704–5.
68 MAGIC Diplomatic Summary 1057, 25 February 1945, RG 457, MAGIC Far East Summaries March 20, 1942–Aug. 15, 1945, Entry 9006, 190/37/3/1-4, box 14.
69 Hattori, Vol. 4, 46.
70 MAGIC Diplomatic Summary 1085, 16 March 1945, RG 457, MAGIC Far East Summaries March 20, 1942–Aug. 15, 1945, Entry 9006, 190/37/3/1-4, box 15.

71. MAGIC Diplomatic Summary 1081, 11 March 1945, RG 457, MAGIC Far East Summaries March 20, 1942–Aug. 15, 1945, Entry 9006, 190/37/3/1-4, box 14.
72. MAGIC Diplomatic Summary 1091, 21 March 1945, RG 457, MAGIC Far East Summaries March 20, 1942–Aug. 15, 1945, Entry 9006, 190/37/3/1-4, box 15.
73. Ugaki, 554–559; Hattori, Vol. 4, 119.
74. MAGIC Diplomatic Summary 1108, 7 April 1945, RG 457, MAGIC Far East Summaries March 20, 1942–Aug. 15, 1945, Entry 9006, 190/37/3/1-4, box 15.
75. Roy E. Appleman, James M. Burns, Russell A. Gugeler, and John Stevens, *Okinawa: The Last Battle: United States Army in World War II, The War in the Pacific* (Washington, D.C.: Center of Military History, United States Army, 1993), 1–4. (Hereafter Appleman, et al.)
76. Field Order 1, Operation *Iceberg*, files the 776th Amphibian Tank Battalion. AAR, 776th Amphibian Tank Battalion.
77. Ugaki, 568–69.
78. Appleman, et al., passim.
79. Hattori, Vol. 4, 123.
80. Ugaki, 567, 573–75; Prados, 710ff8.
81. Hattori, Vol. 4, 123.
82. Hattori, Vol. 4, 124.
83. Ugaki, 576.
84. MAGIC Diplomatic Summary 1114, 13 April 1945, RG 457, MAGIC Far East Summaries March 20, 1942–Aug. 15, 1945, Entry 9006, 190/37/3/1-4, box 15.
85. Ugaki, 572, 577; Hattori, Vol. 4, 256ff.
86. "Summation of Case Against Hiranuma," EE-40.
87. Hattori, Vol. 4, 261.
88. Ugaki, 577.
89. Sakomizu.
90. Records of the Office of Strategic Services, XL Intelligence Reports, Report 43068, RG 226, Entry 19A, 190/4/20/4, box 430. (Hereafter USSBS No. 531.)
91. USSBS No. 308.
92. MAGIC Diplomatic Summaries 1117 and 1118, 16 and 17 April 1945, RG 457, MAGIC Far East Summaries March 20, 1942–Aug. 15, 1945, Entry 9006, 190/37/3/1-4, box 16.
93. MAGIC Diplomatic Summaries 1117 and 1118, 16 and 17 April 1945, RG 457, MAGIC Far East Summaries March 20, 1942–Aug. 15, 1945, Entry 9006, 190/37/3/1-4, box 16.
94. Ugaki, 578.
95. Ugaki, 583.
96. MAGIC Diplomatic Summary 1117, 16 April 1945, RG 457, MAGIC Far East Summaries March 20, 1942–Aug. 15, 1945, Entry 9006, 190/37/3/1-4, box 16.
97. MAGIC Diplomatic Summary 1120, 19 April 1945, RG 457, MAGIC Far East Summaries March 20, 1942–Aug. 15, 1945, Entry 9006, 190/37/3/1-4, box 16.
98. Ugaki, 595.
99. O'Brien, 438.
100. Ugaki, 596.
101. Hattori, Vol. 4, 127.
102. Ugaki, 596.
103. MAGIC Diplomatic Summary 1142, 11 May 1945, RG 457, MAGIC Far East Summaries March 20, 1942–Aug. 15, 1945, Entry 9006, 190/37/3/1-4, box 16. "Japanese Reaction to German Defeat," SRH-075, 21 May 1945, Studies on Cryptology 1817–1977 (0457-A1-9002), Entry 9002, 190/36/9/01, box 24.

104 USSBS No. 379.
105 MAGIC Diplomatic Summary 1143, 12 May 1945, RG 457, MAGIC Far East Summaries March 20, 1942–Aug. 15, 1945, Entry 9006, 190/37/3/1-4, box 16.
106 MAGIC Diplomatic Summary 1145, 14 May 1945, RG 457, MAGIC Far East Summaries March 20, 1942–Aug. 15, 1945, Entry 9006, 190/37/3/1-4, box 16.
107 MAGIC Diplomatic Summary 1153, 22 May 1945, RG 457, MAGIC Far East Summaries March 20, 1942–Aug. 15, 1945, Entry 9006, 190/37/3/1-4, box 16.
108 USSBS No. 531.
109 Hattori, Vol. 4, 270.
110 Sakomizu.
111 Hattori, Vol. 4, 286–99.
112 Hattori, Vol. 4, 300ff.
113 Ugaki, 631; Hattori, Vol. 4, 286, 304ff.
114 "87th Provisional Meeting of the Japanese Diet," Records of the OSS, Intelligence Reports, 139657, 31 July 1945, RG 226, Entry 16, 190/4/9/4, box 1617.
115 Hattori, Vol. 4, 273.
116 Hattori, Vol. 4, 305–7.
117 USSBS No. 308.
118 Hattori, Vol. 4, 308–9.
119 Ugaki, 633.
120 Sakomizu.
121 MAGIC Diplomatic Summary 1171, 9 June 1945, RG 457, MAGIC Far East Summaries March 20, 1942–Aug. 15, 1945, Entry 9006, 190/37/3/1-4, box 17.
122 Ugaki, 637.
123 Hattori, Vol. 4, 131–35.
124 Ugaki, 639; Hattori, Vol. 4, 135ff.
125 MAGIC Diplomatic Summary 1189, 27 June 1945, RG 457, MAGIC Far East Summaries March 20, 1942–Aug. 15, 1945, Entry 9006, 190/37/3/1-4, box 17.
126 MAGIC Diplomatic Summary 1212, 20 July 1945, RG 457, MAGIC Far East Summaries March 20, 1942–Aug. 15, 1945, Entry 9006, 190/37/3/1-4, box 18.
127 USSBS No. 373.
128 MAGIC Diplomatic Summary 1204, 12 July 1945, RG 457, MAGIC Far East Summaries March 20, 1942–Aug. 15, 1945, Entry 9006, 190/37/3/1-4, box 18.
129 "MAGIC Diplomatic Extracts," 17–24 July 1945, Studies on Cryptology 1817–1977 (0457-A1-9002), Entry 9002, 190/36/9/01, box 18.
130 MAGIC Diplomatic Summary 1205, 13 July 1945, RG 457, MAGIC Far East Summaries March 20, 1942–Aug. 15, 1945, Entry 9006, 190/37/3/1-4, box 18.
131 MAGIC Diplomatic Summary 1206, 14 July 1945, RG 457, MAGIC Far East Summaries March 20, 1942–Aug. 15, 1945, Entry 9006, 190/37/3/1-4, box 18.
132 MAGIC Diplomatic Summary 1212, 20 July 1945, RG 457, MAGIC Far East Summaries March 20, 1942–Aug. 15, 1945, Entry 9006, 190/37/3/1-4, box 18.
133 Hattori, Vol. 4, 173.
134 Ugaki, passim.
135 Hattori, Vol. 4, 165.
136 Hattori, Vol. 4, 177.
137 Sakomizu; Hattori, Vol. 4, 262.
138 Hattori, Vol. 4, 316–22.
139 Ugaki, 651–52.

140 Ugaki, 653.
141 MAGIC Diplomatic Summary 2025, 2 August 1945, RG 457, MAGIC Far East Summaries March 20, 1942–Aug. 15, 1945, Entry 9006, 190/37/3/1-4, box 18.
142 MAGIC Diplomatic Summary 1226, 5 August 1945, RG 457, MAGIC Far East Summaries March 20, 1942–Aug. 15, 1945, Entry 9006, 190/37/3/1-4, box 18.
143 Hattori, Vol. 4, 324–25.
144 Ugaki, 655.
145 Sakomizu.
146 Hattori, Vol. 4, 326.
147 Ugaki, 656.
148 USSBS No. 308
149 Hattori, Vol. 4, 330–31.
150 USSBS No. 378.
151 Hattori, Vol. 4, 335ff.
152 Sakomizu.
153 USSBS No. 531.
154 MAGIC Diplomatic Summary 1233, 10 August 1945, RG 457, MAGIC Far East Summaries March 20, 1942–Aug. 15, 1945, Entry 9006, 190/37/3/1-4, box 18.
155 Ugaki, 658–59.
156 USSBS No. 378.
157 Hattori, Vol. 4, 343–44.
158 Hattori, Vol. 4, 346ff.
159 MAGIC Diplomatic Summary 1236, 13 August 1945, RG 457, MAGIC Far East Summaries March 20, 1942–Aug. 15, 1945, Entry 9006, 190/37/3/1-4, box 19.
160 Ugaki, 661–62.
161 Sakai, 295–98.
162 USSBS No. 308.
163 Hattori, Vol. 4, 353–54.
164 USSBS No. 378.
165 MAGIC Diplomatic Summary 1237, 14 August 1945, RG 457, MAGIC Far East Summaries March 20, 1942–Aug. 15, 1945, Entry 9006, 190/37/3/1-4, box 19.
166 Ugaki, 663–64.
167 "Japan's Surrender Manoeuvers," SRH-090, 29 August 1945, Studies on Cryptology 1817–1977 (0457-A1-9002), Entry 9002, 190/36/9/01, box 26.
168 Sakai, 298–99.

Chapter 16

1 Brands, Hal, and Michael Beckley. *Danger Zone: The Coming Conflict with China*. Manhattan, NY: W. W. Norton & Company, 2022, xiv–xv. (Hereafter *Danger Zone*.)
2 *Danger Zone*, Kindle edition, 1–2, 5–6. (Note: The Kindle edition labels page 1 as "xvi," and all subsequent page numbers are too low by one.)
3 *Danger Zone*, 21–25.
4 See, for example, "Is Chinese Power About to Peak?" and "How soon and at what height will China's economy peak?" *The Economist*, 11 May 2023, online version (hereafter "How soon?"); see also "Xi's failing model: Why he won't fix China's economy" *The Economist*, 26 August 2023.
5 "Why China's economy won't be fixed," *The Economist*, 24 August 2023, online version.
6 "How soon?"

7   "China v America: how Xi Jinping plans to narrow the military gap," *The Economist*, 8 May 2023, online version; "largest ballistic missile force": *Danger Zone*, 9.

8   William Bratton, "China's dominance of manufacturing is growing, not shrinking," *Nikkei Asia*, 3 September 2022, https://asia.nikkei.com/Opinion/China-s-dominance-of-manufacturing-is-growing-not-shrinking as of October 2023.

9   "Pence warns against Trump, GOP 'isolationism,'" *The Hill*, 18 September 2023, online version; Tom McTague and Peter Nicholas, "How America First Became America Alone," *The Atlantic*, 20 October 2023, online version; Josh Kraushaar, "The deepening GOP divide on Ukraine," *Axios*, 26 February 2023, online version.

10   Joseph Gideon, "Trump calls Putin 'genius' and 'savvy' for Ukraine invasion," *Politico*, 23 February 2022, online version.

Glossary

Adm.	Admiral
Capt.	Captain
Col.	Colonel
COMINT	Communications Intelligence, AKA SIGINT
CV	Aircraft carrier
ENIGMA	German code machines
ETO	European Theater of Operations
G-2	Intelligence staff
Gen.	General
IGHQ	Imperial General Headquarters
IJA	Imperial Japanese Army
IJN	Imperial Japanese Navy
Lt.	Lieutenant
Lt. Col.	Lieutenant Colonel
Lt. Gen.	Lieutenant General
MAGIC	Codename for intercepted Japanese diplomatic communications
Maj.	Major
Maj. Gen.	Major General
NCO	Non-commissioned officer
OKW	Oberkommando der Wehrmacht, the High Command
Panzer	German tank
Panzergrenadier	German armored infantry
Pvt.	Private
Sgt.	Sergeant
SIGINT	Signals Intelligence, AKA COMINT
SHAEF	Supreme Headquarters Allied Expeditionary Force
Ultra	Anglo-American codename for all shared high-end intercepts

Bibliography

Books and Booklets

Agawa, Hiroyuki. *The Reluctant Admiral: Yamamoto and the Imperial Navy*. New York: Kodansha International, 1979. This is a translation of *Yamamoto Isoroku*, published in Japanese, with abridgements approved by the author.

Appleman, Roy E., James M. Burns, Russell A. Gugeler, and John Stevens. *Okinawa: The Last Battle: United States Army In World War II, The War in the Pacific*. Washington, D.C.: Center of Military History, United States Army, 1993.

Blumenson, Martin. *Anzio: The Gamble That Failed*. New York, NY: Cooper Square Press, 2001.

Brands, Hal and Michael Beckley. *Danger Zone: The Coming Conflict with China*. Manhattan, NY: W. W. Norton & Company, 2022.

British Officers Attached to Japanese and Russian Forces in the Field. *The Russo-Japanese War*: Vol. I. London: His Majesty's Stationary Office, 1908.

Cameron, Robert Stewart. *Americanizing the Tank: U.S. Army Administration and Mechanized Development Within the Army, 1917–1943*. Dissertation, Temple University, August 1944. UMI Dissertation Services: Ann Arbor, Michigan, 1996.

Cannon, M. Hamlin. *Leyte: The Return to the Philippines: The United States Army in World War II, The War in the Pacific*. Washington, D.C.: U.S. Army Center of Military History, 1993.

Compton, James V. *The Swastika and the Eagle*. Boston: Houghton Mifflin Company, 1967.

Carver, Field Marshal Lord. *The Imperial War Museum Book of The War in Italy 1943–1945*. London: Pan Books, 2002.

Drea, Edward J. *Japan's Imperial Army: Its Rise and Fall, 1853–1945*. Lawrence, KA: The University Press of Kansas, 2009.

Eberle, Enrik and Matthias Uhl, ed. *The Hitler Book*. London: John Murray, 2006.

Eisenhower, Dwight D. *Crusade in Europe*. Garden City, NY: Doubleday & Company, Inc., 1948.

Ellis, John. *World War II: A Statistical Survey*. New York: Facts on File, Inc., 1993.

Evans, Dr. David, editor and translator, and Dr. Raymond O'Conner, introduction and commentary. *The Japanese Navy in World War II: In the Words of Former Japanese Naval Officers*. Annapolis, MD: Naval Institute Press, 1986.

Farago, Ladislas. *Patton: Ordeal and Triumph*. New York: Ivan Obolensky, Inc., 1963.

Frank, Richard B. *Tower of Skulls: A History of the Asia-Pacific War, July 1937–May 1942*. New York: W. W. Norton & Company, Inc., 2021.

Friedländer, Saul. *Prelude to Downfall: Hitler and the United States/1939–1941*. New York: Alfred A. Knopf, 1967.

Fritz, Stephen G. *The First Soldier: Hitler as Military Leader*. New Haven: Yale University Press, 2018.

Glantz, David M. and Jonathan M. House. *When Titans Clashed: How the Red Army Stopped Hitler*. Lawrence, Kansas: University of Kansas Press, 1995.

Goldstein, Donald M. and Katherine V. Dillon. *The Pacific War Papers: Japanese Documents of World War II*. Washington, D.C.: Potomac Books, Inc., 2004.

Greenfield, Ken Roberts, Robert R. Palmer, and Bell I. Wiley. *Army Ground Forces: The Organization of Ground Combat Troops*. CMH Pub 2–1. Washington, D.C.: Center of Military History, United States Army, 1947.
Grew, Joseph C. *Ten Years in Japan*. New York, Simon & Shuster, 1944.
Griess, Thomas E., ed. *The Second World War: Europe and the Mediterranean*. West Point Military History Series. Wayne, NJ: Avery Publishing Group, Inc., 1984.
Guderian, Heinz. *Panzer Leader*. New York, NY: Ballantine Books, 1972.
Gunther, John. *Inside Asia: 1942 War Edition*. New York: Harper & Brothers, 1942.
Hammel, Eric. *How America Saved the World: The Untold Story of U.S. Preparedness Between the Wars*. Minneapolis, MN: Zenith Press, 2009.
Heiber, Helmut and David M. Glantz, eds. *Hitler and His Generals: Military Conferences 1942–1945*. New York: Enigma Books, 2004.
Hitler, Adolf. *Mein Kampf*. Kindle English Edition, n.d.
Hitler, Adolf. *My New Order*. Raoul de Roussy de Sales, ed. New York: Reynal & Hitchcock, 1941.
Hotta, Eri. *Japan 1941: Countdown to Infamy*. New York: Alfred A. Knopf, 2013.
Ike, Nobutaka, trans. and ed. *Japan's Decision for War: Records of the 1941 Policy Conferences*. Stanford, CA: Stanford University Press, 1967.
Jablonski, Edward. *Terror from the Sky*. New York: Doubleday & Company, 1971.
Jablonski, Edward. *Tragic Victories*. New York: Doubleday & Company, 1971.
Kahn, David. *Hitler's Spies*. Boston, MA: Da Capo Press, 1978.
Kesselring, Albert. *The Memoirs of Field-Marshal Kesselring*. St. Paul: MBI Publishing, 2007.
Koistinen, Paul A. C. *Arsenal of World War II: The Political Economy of American Warfare, 1940–1945*. Lawrence, KS: University Press of Kansas, 2004.
Koistinen, Paul A. C. *Planning War, Pursuing Peace: The Political Economy of American Warfare, 1920–1939*. Lawrence, KS: University Press of Kansas, 1998.
Konoye, Fumimaro. "Memoirs of Prince Konoye." March 1942. Exhibit No. 173 in U.S. Congress, *Hearings Of The Joint Committee on the Investigation of The Pearl Harbor Attack*, Part 20, 3985–4029.
Levisse-Touze, Christine. *L'Afrique du Nord Dans la Guerre 1939–1945*. Paris: Albin Michel, 1998.
Liddell Hart, B. H. *History of the Second World War*. New York, NY: G. Putnam's Sons, 1970.
Liddell Hart, B. H. *The German Generals Talk*. New York: Quill, 1979.
Linn, Brian McAllister. *The Echo of Battle: The Army's Way of War*. Cambridge, MA: Harvard University Press, 2007.
Lochner, Louis P., trans. and ed. *The Goebbels Diaries*. New York: Doubleday & Company, Inc., 1948.
Louis, Morton. *The Fall of the Philippines: The United States Army in World War II, The War in the Pacific*. Washington, D.C.: Office of the Chief of Military History, Department of the Army, 1952.
MacDonald, Charles B. *The Battle of the Bulge*. London: Guild Publishing, 1984.
Manstein, Field Marshal Erich von. *Lost Victories*. Minneapolis, Minnesota: Zenith Press, 2004.
Miller, Edward S. *Bankrupting the Enemy: The U.S. Financial Siege of Japan Before Pearl Harbor*. Annapolis, MD: Naval Institute Press, 2007.
Mitter, Rana. *China's War with Japan, 1937–1945: The Struggle for Survival*. London: Penguin Books, 2013.
Montgomery, Bernard Law. *The Memoirs of Field Marshall the Viscount Montgomery of Alamein, L.G.* New York: The World Publishing Company, 1958.
Morison, Samuel Eliot. *The Rising Sun in the Pacific: 1931–April 1942*. Annapolis: Naval Institute Press, 1948-2010.
Neitzel, Sönke, ed. *Tapping Hitler's Generals: Transcripts of Secret Conversations 1942–45*. Barnsley, South Yorkshire: Frontline Books, 2013. Kindle edition.
Nelson, Craig. *Pearl Harbor: From Infamy to Greatness*. New York: Scribner, 2016.
Northern France. CMH Pub 72-30. Washington, D.C.: U.S. Army Center of Military History, not dated.

O'Brien, Phillips. *How the War Was Won: Air-Sea Power and Allied Victory in World War II*. Cambridge, UK: Cambridge University Press, 2015.
Prados, John. *Combined Fleet Decoded*. New York: Random House, 1995.
Prange, Gordon. *At Dawn We Slept*. New York: Penguin Books, 1981.
Prattie, Mark, Edward Drea, and Hans Van de Ven, eds. *The Battle for China*. Stanford, CA: Stanford University Press, 2011.
Sakai, Saburo, with Martin Caiden and Fred Sairo. *Samurai!* New York: Pocket Books, 1996.
Schramm, Percy E. *Kriegstagebuch des OKW, 1940–1941, Teilband I*. Germany: Bechtermünz, 2005.
Schramm, Percy E. *Kriegstagebuch des OKW, 1940–1941, Teilband II*. Germany: Bechtermünz, 2005.
Schramm, Percy E. *Kriegstagebuch des Oberkommando der Wehrmacht (Wehrmachtführungsstab), 1. Januar 1942–31. Dezember 1942, Erster Halbband, Band 2*. Germany: Bechtermünz, 2005.
Schramm, Percy E. *Kriegstagebuch des Oberkommando der Wehrmacht (Wehrmachtführungsstab), 1. Januar 1942–31. Dezember 1942, Zweiter Halbband, Band 2*. Germany: Bechtermünz, 2005.
Schramm, Percy E. *Kriegstagebuch des Oberkommando der Wehrmacht (Wehrmachtführungsstab), 1. Januar 1943–31. Dezember 1943, Erster Halbband, Band 3*. Germany: Bechtermünz, 2005.
Schramm, Percy E. *Kriegstagebuch des Oberkommando der Wehrmacht (Wehrmachtführungsstab), 1. Januar 1943–31. Dezember 1943, Zweiter Halbband, Band 3*. Germany: Bechtermünz, 2005.
Schramm, Percy E. *Kriegstagebuch des Oberkommando der Wehrmacht (Wehrmachtführungsstab), 1. Januar 1944–22 Mai 1945, Erster Halbband, Band 4*. Germany: Bechtermünz, 2005.
Scott, Beth, Lt. Col. James Rainey, and Capt. Andrew Hunt. *The Logistics of War*. Maxwell Air Force Base, Alabama: Air Force Logistics Management Agency, 2000.
Sebag-Montefiori, Hugh. *Enigma: The Battle for the Code*. London: Weidenfeld & Nicholson, 2004.
Schmider, Klaus H. *Hitler's Fatal Miscalculation: Why Germany Declared War on the United States*. Cambridge: Cambridge University, 2021.
Shirer, William L. *The Rise and Fall of the Third Reich*. New York: Fawcett Crest, 1962.
Smith, Robert Ross. *Triumph in the Philippines: The United States Army in World War II, The War in the Pacific*. Washington, D.C.: Office of the Chief of Military History, Department of the Army, 1963.
Toland, John. *The Rising Sun: The Decline and Fall of the Japanese Empire, 1936–1945*. New York: The Modern Library, 2003.
Tooze, Adam. *The Wages of Destruction*. London: Penguin Books, 2007.
Trevor-Roper, H. R., ed. *Hitler's Table Talk: 1941–1944*. New York: Enigma Books, 2008.
Ugaki, Admiral Matome, Donald Goldstein and Katherine Dillon, ed., Masataka Chihaya, trans. *Fading Victory: The Diary of Admiral Matome Ugaki, 1941–1945*. Annapolis, MD: Naval Institute Press, 1991.
U.S. Department of State. *Documents on German Foreign Policy 1918–1945, Series D (1937–1945), Vol. XII, The War Years, February 1–June 22 1941*. Washington, D.C.: U.S. Government Printing Office, 1962.
Warlimont, Walter. *Inside Hitler's Headquarters, 1939–45*. Novato, CA: Presidio: 1964.
Watson, Mark Skinner. *Chief of Staff: Prewar Plans and Operations: United States Army in World War II: The War Department*. Washington, D.C.: Office of the Chief of Military History, Department of the Army, 1951.
Westermann, Edward B. *Flak: German Anti-Aircraft Defenses, 1914–1945*. Lawrence, KA: University Press of Kansas, 2001.
Wilmot, Chester. *The Struggle for Europe*. Ware, England: Wordsworth Editions Limited, 1997.
Wood, James B. *Japanese Military Strategy in the Pacific War: Was Defeat Inevitable?* New York: Rowman & Littlefield Publishers, Inc., 2007.
Zaloga, Steven. *Armored Thunderbolt*. Mechanicsburg, PA: Stackpole Books, 2008.
Ziegler, Philip. *Between the Wars, 1919–1939*. New York: MacLehose Press, 2016.

Articles and Internet Resources

Alexander, Bevin. "Barbarossa." MilitaryHistoryOnline.com, www.militaryhistoryonline.com/wwii/articles/barbarossa.aspx, 4 February 2006, as of July 2009.

Algeria-French Morocco. The U.S. Army Campaigns of World War II Series. Washington, D.C.: Center of Military History, n.d. (Online reprint of CMH Pub 72–11, www.ibiblio.org/hyperwar/USA/USA-C-Algeria/index.html as of July 2018.)

The American Air Museum in Britain, "VIII Fighter Command FO-170 Bomber Escort," not dated, www.americanairmuseum.com/mission/1904 as of December 2021.

"August 28, 1940: Call Me Meyer," Filminspector.com, http://worldwartwodaily.filminspector.com/2016/08/august-28-1940-call-me-meier.html as of January 2021.

Balciunas, Marijus. "Japan's Purple Machine," 18 March 2004, http://ovid.cs.depaul.edu/Classes/CS233-W04/Papers/PurpleMagic.pdf as of May 2014.

Becker Rear Admiral Paul, USN (Ret), "The Battle of Midway Still Teaches the Value of Intelligence, Decisive Action," *The Sextant*, 2 June 2017, http://usnhistory.navylive.dodlive.mil/2017/06/02/the-battle-of-midway-still-teaches-the-value-of-intelligence-decisive-action/ as of October 2017.

Benson, Robert, "A History of U.S. Communications Intelligence during World War II: Policy and Administration," Center for Cryptologic History, National Security Agency, United States Cryptologic History, Series 4, Vol. 8, 1997, www.nsa.gov/Portals/70/documents/about/cryptologic-heritage/historical-figures-publications/publications/wwii/history_us_comms.pdf as of August 2021.

Bratton, William, "China's dominance of manufacturing is growing, not shrinking," *Nikkei Asia*, 3 September 2022, (https://asia.nikkei.com/Opinion/China-s-dominance-of-manufacturing-is-growing-not-shrinking as of October 2023.

Brown, Stewart. "Japan Stuns World, Withdraws from League," United Press, 24 February 1943.

Carlson, Col. Adolf. "Joint U.S. Army-Navy War Planning On The Eve of The First World War: Its Origins and Its Legacy," 1998, www.strategicstudiesinstitute.army.mil/pubs/download.cfm?q=351 as of July 2018.

Chen, C. Peter. "Hideki Tojo." World War II Data Base, http://ww2db.com as of November 2010.

"China v America: how Xi Jinping plans to narrow the military gap," *The Economist*, 8 May 2023, online version.

Crowl, Phillip A. "The United States Army in World War II: The Marianas Campaign." Center of Military History, U.S. Army, Washington, D.C., 1993, https://history.army.mil/html/books/005/5–7–1/CMH_Pub_5–7–1.pdf as of December 2021.

"Eisenhower Report on 'Torch'." Scanned copy from the Ike Skelton Command and General Staff College Combined Arms Research Digital library, http://cgsc.contentdm.oclc.org/cdm/singleitem/collection/p4013coll8/id/110/rec/3, as of July 2018.

Favorite, Martin. "Japanese Radar Equipment in WWII," not dated, www.combinedfleet.com/radar.htm as of February 2021.

Gayle, Brig. Gen. (Ret) Gordon. "Bloody Beaches: The Marines at Peleliu." Washington, D.C.: The Marine Corps Historical Center, 1996, www.ibiblio.org/hyperwar/USMC/USMC-C-Peleliu/index.html as of June 2018.

Gideon, Joseph, "Trump calls Putin 'genius' and 'savvy' for Ukraine invasion," *Politico*. 23 February 2022, online version.

Hamilton, William. "Bush Began to Plan War Three Months After 9/11." *The Washington Post*, 17 April 2004, A1.

Hart, Russell A. "Book Review: "Hitler's Fatal Miscalculation: Why Germany Declared War on the United States." Klaus H. Schmider." *Journal of Military History*, Vol. 86, No. 1, January 2022, 206–207.

Hauser, Ernest O. "Tojo." *Life*, 30 March 1942, 69–78.

"HATTORI, Tekushiro," CIA Information Report ZJJ-84, 18 April 1952, CIA FOIA, www.cia.gov/readingroom/docs/HATTORI%2C%20TAKUSHIRO%20%20%20VOL.%202_0027.pdf as of September 2021.

Hoffman, Maj. Carl. "Saipan: The Beginning of the End, USMC Historical Monograph." Historical Branch, G-3 Division, Headquarters, U.S. Marine Corps, 1950 (online version at Hyperwar: A Hypertext History of the Second World War, www.ibiblio.org/hyperwar/, as of February 2007).

"Is Chinese Power About to Peak?" and "How soon and at what height will China's economy peak?" *The Economist*, 11 May 2023, online version.

Judgment: International Military Tribunal for the Far East. Hyperwar, www.ibiblio.org/hyperwar/PTO/IMTFE/index.html as of November 2010.

Kraushaar, Josh, "The deepening GOP divide on Ukraine," *Axios*, 26 February 2023, online version.

Luzon. The U.S. Army Campaigns of World War II Series. Washington, D.C.: Center of Military History, n.d. (Online reprint of CMH Pub 72–28, https://history.army.mil/brochures/luzon/72-28.htm).

Martin, Gregory. "German Strategy and Military Assessments of the American Expeditionary Force (AEF), 1917–18," *War in History* Vol. I No. 2 (July 1994), pp. 160–196, JSTOR copy.

McTague, Tom, and Peter Nicholas, "How America First Became America Alone," *The Atlantic*, 20 October 2020, online version.

Naval History and Heritage Command, "Battle of Coral Sea," www.history.navy.mil/our-col.ections/photography/wars-and-events/world-war-ii/battle-of-the-coral-sea.html as of September 2017.

Office of the United States Chief of Counsel For Prosecution of Axis Criminality. "Nazi Conspiracy and Aggression." Nuremberg, Germany (1945–1946), Volume 1. Washington, D.C.: U.S. Government Printing Office, 1946. Library of Congress, www.loc.gov/rr/frd/Military_Law/pdf/NT_Nazi_Vol-I.pdf as of February 2017.

Parrott, Lindesay. "Tojo Makes Plea of 'Self-Defense'." *The New York Times*, 26 December 1947, www.newyorktimes.com as of December 2010.

"Pence warns against Trump, GOP 'isolationism,'" *The Hill*, 18 September 2023, online version.

"Primary Documents—'21 Demands' Made by Japan to China, 18 January 1915," FirstWorldWar.com, www.firstworldwar.com/source/21demands.htm as of September 2021.

The Reports of General MacArthur: Japanese Operations in the Southwest Pacific Area, Volume II, Part I. Washington, D.C.: Center of Military History, facsimile reprint, 1994, www.history.army.mil/books/wwii/MacArthur%20Reports/MacArthur%20V2%20P1/macarthurv2.htm as of May 2012.

Record, Jeffrey. "Japan's Decision for War in 1941: Some Enduring Lessons." Carlisle, PA: United States Army Strategic Studies Institute, February 2009, www.strategicstudiesinstitute.army.mil/pdffiles/PUB905.pdf as of November 2010.

Rogers, James, Lt. Col. "Command Control of an Armored Amphibian Battalion," *The Cavalry Journal*, January–February 1945.

Romanus, Charles F. and Riley Sunderland. *China-Burma-India Theater: Stilwell's Mission to China*. Washington, D.C.: Center of Military History, 1987, www.history.army.mil/html/books/009/9–1/CMH_Pub_9–1.pdf as of August 2017.

Roosevelt, Franklin D., address at Queen's University, 18 August 1938, The American Presidency Project, www.presidency.ucsb.edu/ws/?pid=15525 as of June 2013.

Roosevelt, Franklin D., Jackson Day Dinner Radio Address, 29 March 1941, Franklin D. Roosevelt, Master Speech File, 1898–1945, Franklin D. Roosevelt Presidential Library & Museum, www.fdrlibrary.marist.edu/_resources/images/msf/msf01422 as of August 2018.

Sanger, David E. "In a Memoir, Hirohito Talks of Pearl Harbor." *The New York Times*, 15 November 1990, www.newyorktimes.com as of December 2010.

Scitor Corporation. "Technological Innovation During Protracted War: Radar and Atomic Weapons in World War II." Prepared for the Director, Net Assessments, Office of the Secretary of Defense, April 2015.

Shaw, Henry I., Jr. *First Offensive: The Marine Campaign for Guadalcanal*. Marines in World War II Commemorative Series, Washington, D.C.: Marine Corps Historical Center, 1992, www.ibiblio.org/hyperwar/USMC/USMC-C-Guadalcanal.html as of October 2017.

Smith, Robert Ross. *The United States Army in World War II, The War in the Pacific: The Approach to the Philippines*. Washington, D.C.: Center of Military History, United States Army, 1996, https://history.army.mil/html/books/005/5-8-1/cmhPub_5-8-1.pdf as of December 2021.

"South Atlantic air ferry route in World War II." IPFS.

"Striking Oil: The First American Bombing Raid over Europe in World War II." American Battle Monuments Commission, www.abmc.gov/news-events/news/striking-oil-first-american-bombing-raid-over-europe-world-war-ii#.W1D5Fy2ZPOQ as of July 2018.

Summary Report (European War). Washington, D.C.: USSBS, 30 September 1945, www.ibiblio.org/hyperwar/AAF/USSBS/ETO-Summary.html as of January 2015.

"The Casablanca Conference, 1943." Office of the Historian, U.S. Department of State, https://history.state.gov/milestones/1937-1945/casablanca, not dated, as of July 2018.

"The Failed Attempt to Avert War with Japan, 1941," Association for Diplomatic Studies & Training, 27 November 2013, https://adst.org/2013/11/the-failed-attempts-to-avert-war-with-japan-1941/ as of September 2021.

"Tokyo: A Study in Jap Flak Defense." Naval History and Heritage Command website. Reproduces an undated Army Air Force intelligence analysis, spring 1945, www.history.navy.mil/research/library/online-reading-room/title-list-alphabetically/t/tokyo-study-jap-flak-defense.html as of February 2021.

United States Department of State. *Foreign relations of the United States diplomatic papers, 1939, General, Volume I*. Washington, D.C.: U.S. Government Printing Office, 1939, online edition, http://digicoll.library.wisc.edu/cgi-bin/FRUS/FRUS-idx?type=header&id=FRUS.FRUS1940v04 as of September 2014.

United States Department of State. *Foreign relations of the United States diplomatic papers, 1940, The Far East*, Volume IV. Washington, D.C.: U.S. Government Printing Office, 1940, online edition, http://digicoll.library.wisc.edu/cgi-bin/FRUS/FRUS-idx?type=header&id=FRUS.FRUS1940v04 as of October 2010.

United States Department of State. *Foreign relations of the United States diplomatic papers, 1940. General and Europe*, Volume II. U.S. Government Printing Office, 1940, online edition, http://digital.library.wisc.edu/1711.dl/FRUS.FRUS1940vo2 as of April 2011.

United States Department of State. *Papers relating to the foreign relations of the United States, Japan: 1931–1941 (in two volumes)*, Volume I. Washington, D.C.: U.S. Government Printing Office, 1943, http://digicoll.library.wisc.edu/cgi-bin/FRUS/FRUS-idx?type=header&id=FRUS.FRUS193141v01 as of February 2017.

United States Department of State. *Papers relating to the foreign relations of the United States, Japan: 1931–1941 (in two volumes)*, Volume II. Washington, D.C.: U.S. Government Printing Office, 1943, http://digicoll.library.wisc.edu/cgi-bin/FRUS/FRUS-idx?type=header&id=FRUS.FRUS193141v02 as of February 2017.

United States Strategic Bombing Survey. *United States Strategic Bombing Survey (European War) (Pacific War)*. Washington, D.C.: USSBS, July 1946, www.ibiblio.org/hyperwar/AAF/USSBS/.

United States Strategic Bombing Survey. *The Effects of Air Attack on Japanese Urban Economy, Summary Report*. Washington, D.C.: USSBS, March 1947, http://babel.hathitrust.org/cgi/pt?id=mdp.39015002274416;view=1up;seq=1.

The Effects of Strategic Bombing on Japanese Morale. Washington, D.C.: USSBS, June 1947, http://babel.hathitrust.org/cgi/pt?id=mdp.39015002274416;view=1up;seq=1.

U.S. Centennial of Flight Commission. "The U.S. Aircraft Industry During World War I," www.centennialofflight.gov/essay/Aerospace/WWi/Aero5.htm as of February 2012.

"U.S. Synthetic Rubber Program," American Chemical Society, www.acs.org/content/acs/en/education/whatischemistry/landmarks/syntheticrubber.html as of May 2022.

U.S. Department of State, Office of the Historian. "The Atlantic Conference & Charter, 1941," http://history.state.gov/milestones/1937–1945/atlantic-conf as of May 2014.

"War in the Pacific: Pacific Offensive," www.nps.gov/parkhistory/online_books/npswapa/extContent/wapa/guides/offensive/sec6.htm as of February 2021.

Weinberg, Gerhard. "Four Days in December: Germany's Path to War With the U.S." History Net, www.historynet.com/four-days-in-december-germanys-path-to-war-with-the-u-s.htm as of December 2020.

"Why China's economy won't be fixed," *The Economist*, 24 August 2023, online version.

"Xi's failing model: Why he won't fix China's economy" *The Economist*, 26 August 2023.

Unpublished Studies

Blumentritt, *General der Infanterie* Günther. "OB West and the Normandy Campaign (Jun–Jul 1944)." ETHINT-73, 8–11 January 1946. National Archives.

Boetticher, *General der Artillerie*. "Eindruecke und Erfahrungen des Militaer-und Luftattaches bei der Deutschen Botschaft in Washington, D.C. 1935–1941." MS # B-484, Historical Division, Headquarters United States Army, Europe, 27 April 1947, National Archives.

Ciano, Count Galeazzo. *Diary*. Records of the Judge Avocate General, RG 153, 270/1/5/07, boxes 14–17, National Archives.

Doenitz, *Grossadmiral* Karl. "U-Boats Against US-UK Shipping." ETHINT-29, not dated. National Archives.

Eckhard, *Generalmajor* Christian. "Study of the Situation in the High Command of the Wehrmacht Shortly Before, During and After the Allied Landing in North Africa, 1942." MS # D-066, National Archives.

Gause, *Generalleutnant* Alfred. "Military Operations Against American Troops in Africa."

Goering, *Reichsmarschall* Hermann. "German Strategy (1939–1941)." This is an interview with Göring. ETHINT-31, 25 July 1945. National Archives.

Greiner, Helmut. "Notes on the Situation Reports and Discussions at Hitler's Headquarters from 12 August 1942 to 17 March 1943." MS # C-065a, not dated, National Archives.

Hattori, Takushiro. *The Complete History of the Greater East Asia War*. Published by Tenkishi Masukagi, 1953, translated by SIA, G-2, Hqs 500th Military Intelligence Service Group, located in Gordon W. Prange Papers, Special Collections, University of Maryland Libraries, Series IV, G-2 Historical Division, Box 4.

Jodl, *Generaloberst* Alfred. "An Interview with Genobst Alfred Jodl: Ardennes Offensive." ETHINT-51, 31 July 1945. National Archives.

Jodl, *Generaloberst* Alfred. "U.S. Operations; German Defense; Ruhr; Last Days." ETHINT-52, 2 August 1945. National Archives.

Keitel, *Generalfeldmarschall* Wilhelm. "Beantwortung des Fragebogens fuer Feldmarschall Keitel v. 24.7.45." A-912, 24 July 1945. National Archives.

Kesselring, *Generalfeldmarschall* Albert. "The War in the Mediterranean, Part II: The Fighting in Tunisia and Tripolitania." MS # T-3 P1, not dated, National Archives.

Kesselring, *Generalfeldmarschall* Albert. "An Interview with Genfldm Albert Kesselring: General Questions." ETHINT-72, 6 May 1946. National Archives.

Kesselring, *Generalfeldmarshall* Albert and *General der Kavalerie* Siegfried Westphal. "Questions Regarding the General Strategy During the Italian Campaign." MS # B-270, November 1950. National Archives.

Lang, *Oberst* Rudolf. "Battles of Kampfgruppe Lang in Tunisia (10. Pz. Div.) December 1942 to 15 April 1943, Part I." MS # D-173, not dated, National Archives.

Müller-Hillebrand, *Generalmajor* Burkhart. "Der Zusammenhang Zwischen dem deutschen Balkanfeldzug und der Invasion in Russland." MS # C-101, November 1951. National Archives.

"Operation 'Barbarossa.'" MS # C-065i, not dated. National Archives.

Rodt, *Oberstleutnant* Eberhard. "Studie Über den Feldzug in Sizilien bei der 15. Pz. Gren. Div. Mai-August 1943." MS # C-077, not dated. National Archives.

Rundstedt, *Generalfeldmarschall* Gerd von. "Campaign in the West (1940)." MS # C-053, not dated. National Archives.

Scheidt, *Rittmeister* Wilhelm. "Hitler's Conduct of the War." ETHINT-20, 12 July 1949. National Archives.

Schramm, Percy. "OKW War Diary (1 Apr-18 Dec 44)." MS # B-034, 1947. National Archives,

Warlimont, *General der Artillerie* Walter. "From Invasion to the Siegfried Line." ETHINT-1, July 1949. National Archives.

Warlimont, *General der Artillerie* Walter. "German Estimate of United States, Russia, and Dakar." ETHINT-8, 9 August 1945. National Archives.

Warlimont, *General der Artillerie* Walter. "Stellungnahme zu Berichten Deutscher Offiziere: Zu den Berichten Ueber die Anglo-Amerikanische Landung in Franzoesisch-Nord Afrika im November 1942." MS # C-090, 13 February 1951, National Archives.

Index

Abe, Vice Admiral Katsuo, 352, 370
Abe, Premier Nobuyuki, 69, 80, 314
Abyssinia (Ethiopia), 1, 39
Admiralty Islands, 293
Afghanistan, 386
Agawa, Hiroyuki, 7, 35
Andaman Islands, 279
air defense
    Germany, 3, 72, 75, 105, 165, 180, 207–10, 256, 264–67, 275–76, 285, 298–99, 326, 334–38, 350
    Italy, 43, 71–72
    Japan, 135, 200, 253, 269, 288, 346–47
air power (*see also* bombing)
    Allied, 44, 113, 180, 208–9, 272, 275, 287, 297, 305, 336ff, 350, 352, 385
    Axis views of Allied airpower, 180, 192, 199–201, 203–4, 207, 218, 224, 237, 245, 265, 272, 275, 292, 298, 305, 310, 330, 353, 360, 377
    Germany, 28, 44, 53–54, 57, 72, 113, 180, 207, 268, 275, 331, 336
    Japan, 15, 44, 48, 60–61, 78, 85, 190, 233, 237, 240, 250–51, 274–75, 277, 280, 282, 284, 290–91, 293, 296, 311–12, 343–44, 346, 356, 364, 368, 371, 377
    United States, 44, 57, 96, 206–7, 222, 233, 237, 243–44, 250, 279, 282, 285, 298, 303, 311, 318–19, 335ff, 362
    USSR, 324
Alaska, places
    Attu, 215, 245, 253–54, 292
    Aleutian Islands, 22, 199–200, 212–13, 215, 234, 236, 245, 253
    Dutch Harbor, 278
    Kiska, 215, 245, 254
Allen, Major General Terry de la Mesa, 248
Albania, 63, 67, 117, 137, 205

Alexander, General Sir Harold, 248, 270
Algeria, 227–28
Algeria, places
    Algiers, 227–28
    Oran, 227
Allied material and materiel superiority
    degree of superiority, 44, 104, 113, 155, 167, 180–81, 304–5, 323–24, 337, 341, 348
    German views of, 51, 55, 74, 113, 180–81, 209, 253, 272, 305–7, 323–24
    Italian views of, 113, 181–82, 224
    Japanese views of, 51, 155, 167, 192, 194, 218, 223, 232, 237, 279, 295–96, 341
American–British–Dutch conversations, 132
American Military Mission to China (AMMISCA), 117, 147
American Volunteer Group (AVG, Flying Tigers), 96, 117, 187, 222, 245
amphibious operations, Allied
    Angaur, 340–41
    Anzio, *Shingle*, 300ff
    Guadalcanal, 214, 218ff
    Guam, 316, 382
    Hollandia, 302
    Iwo Jima, 360
    Kwajalein, 289
    Leyte, 277, 343ff, 366
    Los Negros, 293
    Luzon, 343, 345, 357ff, 366
    Makin and Tarawa, 281
    Mindanao, 345
    Morotai, 316, 340
    Munda, 277
    New Guinea, 302
    Normandy, *Overlord*, 305ff
    North Africa, *Torch*, 205–6, 210, 225ff, 261

Peleliu, 316, 340–41
Saipan, *Forager*, 296–97, 306ff
Salerno, *Avalanche*, 270ff
Sicily, *Husky*, 261ff, 269–70
Okinawa, 277, 363, 366ff, 371, 375, 377
amphibious operations, Japanese
Alaska, 215
French Indochina, 83–84, 143, 145
Midway, 199, 212
Netherlands East Indies, 190ff
New Guinea, 190, 218, 202, 250, 284, 288, 306
Tulagi, 202
Anglo-American cooperation
American British Conversations (ABC), 116, 139
antisubmarine warfare, 109, 110–11, 130, 195–96, 216, 239, 256–57, 268, 273
Arcadia, 186ff
Atlantic Conference, 139
Cairo Conference, 282–83
Casablanca Conference, 243ff
Churchill visit to Washington June 1942, 205
Combined Chiefs of Staff, 186, 244, 269
Intelligence, 56, 113, 179, 195–99, 239, 245, 259, 264
Lend-Lease Act, 117, 123, 126, 164, 192, 225, 254
strategy debates, 205
U.S. war production for Allies, 112, 187, 206–7, 209, 225, 276
war strategy, 56, 116, 139, 163–64, 186ff, 205, 243ff, 282–83
Yalta Conference, 360
Angaur Island, 340–41
Anami, War Minister General Korechika, 373–74, 379
Araki, War Minister General Sadao, 6
Ardennes offensive, *see* Battle of the Bulge
Argentina, 195
Argentina, places
Buenos Aires, 231
Arisue, General Seizo, 294
Arita, Foreign Minister Hachiro, 82
Aritomo, Yamagata, 7
Arne, General Cesare, 227
Arnim, General Hans-Jürgen von, 248

Arnold, Lieutenant General Henry "Hap", 63, 207
Asada, Sadao, 7, 91, 93, 143, 146, 150
atomic bomb
U.S. program, 109
German views of, 2
Japanese views of, 2, 46, 369, 378–79, 381–82
Austria, 41–42, 97
Australia, 87, 92, 119, 144, 156, 173–74, 186, 191, 193, 197, 202–3, 219, 224, 233–36, 238, 258, 277, 380, 301–2
Australian Navy, 203, 219, 236, 280
Axis cooperation
Anti-Comintern Pact, 1, 32, 42, 61, 72
creation of Axis, 32, 42, 50, 55–56, 59–61, 68, 93–96, 99, 111
disagreements, 69, 70, 72, 118, 130, 216–17, 252, 254
Japan, reservations about alliance in, 61, 68–69, 80, 84, 89, 148
Japanese sharing plans to attack America, 170, 181
Military cooperation, 62, 99, 111–12, 118–20, 123–24, 126, 152, 181, 198, 243
no separate peace treaty, 159, 182
sharing information about Allied military, 253, 291–92, 294–95, 347
Tripartite Pact signed, 111
Axis intelligence capabilities
Germany, 30, 132, 165, 195, 198, 211, 226, 256–57, 268, 328
Italy, 131–32, 286
Japan, 132, 155, 171, 174–75, 187, 190, 212–13, 218–19, 245, 284–85, 288, 292, 296, 310–11, 316, 341, 343, 364, 367, 398
Azores, 133

B-29, threat to Japan, 64, 288, 297, 304, 308–10, 341, 346ff, 362, 378–79
Badoglio, Prime Minister General Pietro, 270
Battle of the Bulge, 304, 333–35, 348ff
Beck, General Ludwig, 51
Beckley, Michael, 386
Belgium, 63, 69

Belgium, places
    Brussels, 332
    Lüttich, 334
Biden administration, 386
Bismarck Islands, 277
Bismarck, Otto Christian Archibald von, 224
Blomberg, General Erich von, 42
Blumentritt, General of the Infantry Günther, 321–23, 332, 355
Boetticher, General Friedrich, 66, 185, 226
Bolivia, 1
bombing (*see* air defense)
    Allied technological advances, 208, 257, 264–65, 378–79
    Anglo-American strategy, 116, 139, 186ff, 244
    Germany and occupied areas, attacks on, 105, 180, 207–11, 244–45, 256, 259, 276, 264–69, 285, 288, 298ff, 335ff, 350–51, 353, 355
    Italy, attacks on, 253, 263, 265
    Japan and occupied areas, attacks on, 96, 199–201, 222, 233, 281, 284, 292, 304, 307–9, 341, 347–48, 362ff, 377, 382
    Japanese bombing in China, 60
    Japan's attempts to keep bombers out of range, 200–1, 288, 297, 312
Bohle, State Secretary for Foreign Affairs Ernst, 238–39
Bonin Islands, 78, 279
Bormann, Martin, 120, 335
Borneo, 98, 147, 171, 179, 194, 297
Bougainville, 250–51, 289
Bradley, General Omar, x, 326ff, 332
Brands, Hal, 386
Brauchitsch, Field Marshal Walter von, 74
Bullitt, Ambassador William, 53
Bush, George W., President, 4
Burma, 83, 98, 146, 187, 192, 220, 243, 252, 280, 293, 301, 340
Burma, places
    Rangoon, 117, 293
    Toungoo, 117
Burma Road, 84, 93, 151, 187, 241, 279, 312
Byas, Hugh, 37

Canada, 146
Cape Verde Islands, 133

Carolines, 78, 281, 290, 293, 295, 302
Celebes, 98
Central Pacific Area, 250
Ceylon, 199
Chennault, Major General Claire, 60, 96
Chiang, Kai-Shek, President, 36, 49–50, 83, 96–97, 128, 145, 156, 189, 222, 241, 282, 340
Ciano, Count Galeazzo, ix, 54–55, 62–63, 65, 67–73, 75, 95, 102–6, 108–11, 127, 130–31, 133–34, 138, 163, 173, 181–83, 195, 198, 201, 204, 224, 227–28, 230–31, 249
Chile, 195, 220
China (*see* Japan, war in China)
China, places
    Anhui Province, 49
    Beijing, 297, 386
    Bias Bay, 49
    Canton, 49, 359
    Chang-tu (Chengdu), 190
    Changsha, 76, 157
    Chungking (Chongqing), 39, 49, 76, 97, 117, 128, 147, 189–90, 220, 258, 339–40
    Formosa, 291, 313, 318, 341, 343, 368
    Guilin, 297
    Guangsong Province, 297
    Guangxi Province, 76, 297
    Hainan Island, 143, 145
    Henan Province, 49, 285, 297
    Hengyang, 297
    Hong Kong, 83, 98, 170, 220, 359
    Hsinchu, 282
    Huayuankou, 49
    Hunan Province, 49
    Hupeh, 284
    I'Chang (Yichang), 190
    Jiangsu Province, 49
    Jiangxi Province, 200, 297
    Jiujiang (Kiukiang), 48
    Manchuria (Manchukuo), 141, 144, 222, 283, 292, 340, 356
    Mukden (Shenyang), 1, 6, 8, 13–14
    Nan-hsiung, 297
    Nanning, 297
    Nanking (Nanjing), 39–40, 60, 97, 339–40

Sichuan (Szechuan) Province, 49, 76
Shanghai, 38–39
Shanxi Province, 190
Shantung (Shandong) Province, 237
Shantung (Shandong) Peninsula, 246
Suichuan, 297
Swatow, 359
Taierzhuang, 48
Tianjin, 37
Tibet, 233
Tsingdao (Qingdao), 237
Wuhan (Hankow), 39, 49, 116, 297
Xuzhou (Hsuchow), 48
Zhejiang Province, 200
Chinese army
   Strength and capabilities (*see* Japan, war in China)
   Yellow River flood, 49
Chingwei, Wang, 50, 60, 241, 347
Citino, Robert, x
Clark, Lieutenant General Mark, 300
Collins, Major General J. Lawton, 326
Commando Supremo, Italian high command, 106, 227, 261, 270
Compton, James, vi
conquest, citing America's behavior as model Germany, 102, 120
Coral Sea, battle of, 202ff
Cramer, Lieutenant General Hans, 249
Cresswell, Lieutenant Colonel Lenard, 220
Cudahy, Ambassador John, 132–33
Curry, envoy to China Lauchlin, 117
Czechoslovakia, 41–42, 62–63

D'Aieta, Marquis Blanzo Lanza, 224
Dakar, 227
Daniels, Secretary of the Navy Josephus, 18
Declaration of the United Nations, 187, 383
Denmark, 63, 299
Dieckhoff, Ambassador Hans, 66
Dönitz, Grand Admiral Karl, 74, 124, 196, 256–57, 268, 273, 336, 355, 370–71
Donovan, William, 45
Doolittle, Lieutenant Colonel James, 199, 298, 308
Doolittle raid, 199–201
Dulles, Allen, 375

Eisenhower, General Dwight, x, 270, 306, 330, 356
Egypt, 217, 224–25
Egypt, places
   Cairo, 282, 378
   El Alamein, 44, 217
European Theater of Operations (ETO), 233

Federal Bureau of Investigation (FBI), 45
Fiji, 193
Finland, 254
Flores Islands, 102
France, 63, 300
France, German invasion of, 72, 74–75, 82, 87, 105–7
France, places
   Avranches, 328
   Brest, 305
   Brittany, 275, 305
   Caen, 326
   Cherbourg, 305, 322
   Corsica, 229
   Cotentin peninsula, 305, 322
   Dieppe, 210
   Falaise, 331
   Le Mans, 328
   Marigny, 326
   Marseilles, 338
   Normandy, 275, 286, 305
   Paris, 328, 331
   Sotteville, 210
   Rouen, 210
   St. Lô, 328
   Toulon, 338
   Vichy, 145–46, 231, 301
Franks, Richard, 4
French Indochina, 82–83, 93–94, 136–37, 141–42, 222, 254
French Indochina, places
   Hanoi, 50
   Saigon, 280
French Northwest Africa, 187, 210, 225–26
Friedländer, Saul, vi
Fritsch, General Werner von, 42
Fromm, General Friedrich, 217
Fuchida, Commander Mitsuo, 175ff
Fujiwara, Minister of Munitions Ginjiro, 317

Fukudome, Vice Admiral Shigeru, 78, 80, 89–90, 97ff, 115, 124, 146, 157, 159, 169–70, 175–76, 214–15, 221, 250, 289–91, 295, 313
Fushimi, Chief of Naval General Staff Prince, 89–93

Genda, Minoru, 114–15
German Air Force (Luftwaffe, *see also* air power)
  pilot losses, 275, 298–99
German Army (Heer)
  Afrika Korps, 249
  Ardennes Offensive (*see* Battle of the Bulge)
  Army General Staff, 333
  Army Group A, 105
  Army Group B, 105, 325, 333–34, 350
  Army Group C, 275
  Army Group Center, 138ff, 181, 306, 325
  Army Group Felber, 228–29
  Army Group G, 331
  Army Group North, 138ff
  Army Group South, 138ff
  Fifth Panzer Army, 331, 348
  First Army, 228
  First Parachute Army, 333
  military operations (*see* war plans, Germany; Germany, appraisal of military situation; and listed battles)
  Panzer Army Africa, 217
  Seventh Army, 286, 328, 331, 348
  Sixth SS Panzer Army, 348
German Navy (Kriegsmarine)
  U-boat war, 74, 112, 120–21, 124, 133, 182, 195–97, 216, 226, 246, 249, 256–57, 268, 273, 286, 299
Germany
  appraisal of U.S. intentions and capabilities, 3, 24, 30–31, 40–41, 43, 51–53, 55, 58, 65–67, 70–71, 73–74, 102–3, 108–9, 111–12–114, 117–18, 120ff, 130, 132–34, 162–63, 165, 198–99, 201, 207, 211, 225–26, 228, 238, 247–50, 255–57, 261, 265, 270ff, 273, 275–76, 298, 300, 305–6, 321–322, 328, 333–34, 350–51, 354
  appraisal of war situation, 120ff, 180–84, 186, 194, 196–97, 238–39, 246, 257, 261, 264, 267–68, 275, 285–86, 288, 299, 305–6, 321ff, 330–33, 335, 384
  decision to abandon A-bomb effort, 217–18
  decision to go to war with non-U.S. powers, 41–42, 64, 67–68, 72, 107, 117, 205, 209, 213, 216–17
  decision to go to war with U.S., 2, 51, 166, 173, 178, 182–83, 384
  lack of planning for war with America, 181, 183, 185, 194ff, 225, 384
  pivot, Western Front becomes more important, 260, 274–75, 286, 299
  pivot back, Soviet threat most dire, 324, 350
  realization the war is lost, 286, 291, 335
  surrenders, 356
Germany, places
  Aachen, 334, 348
  Badgastein, 354
  Berghof, 70, 117–18
  Berlin, 3, 27, 29–30, 41, 43, 51–52, 56, 58, 62–64, 66, 68–71, 75, 85, 94, 99, 102–3, 107, 110–13, 118, 120, 123–24, 127, 130–31, 137, 140, 162, 165–66, 171, 173, 180–81, 183, 185, 197–98, 204, 207, 216, 221, 224, 231, 335–36, 241, 246–47, 253, 258, 264, 270–71, 276, 284–85, 288–289, 291, 299, 333, 336–37, 350–52, 354–55, 360–62
  Berchtesgaden, 70, 134, 273
  Bochum, 244
  Bremen, 180, 264
  Brenner (Pass), 111
  Chemnitz, 336, 354
  Cologne, 180, 208–9
  Cottbus, 352
  Dortmund, 244
  Dresden, 336, 354
  Duisburg, 244
  Düsseldorf, 210, 244
  Eisenach, 336
  Essen, 244
  Fuschl, 118
  Geilenkirchen, 244, 285
  Hamburg, 180, 264, 268–69
  Innsbruck, 62
  Krefeld, 244
  Kuestrin, 354

Leuna, 337
Lübeck, 208
Mannheim, 180
Monschau, 348
Munich, 53–55, 228
Potsdam, 376–77
Prenslau, 352
Regensburg, 267
Remagen, 352
Rheydt, 66
Salzburg, 198, 354
Schweinfurt, 266
Torgau, 355
Vienna, 224, 253
Weimar, 336
Wuppertal, 244
Gilbert Islands, 191, 250, 252, 281, 288
Goebbels, Josef, 181, 195, 198–99, 210, 256, 285, 305, 315, 335, 354
Göring, Hermann, x, 41, 103–4, 107–8, 183–84, 209, 227, 256, 263, 265, 275, 298, 306, 333, 354
Government Code and Cypher School (GC&CS), 46
Great Britain (United Kingdom), 64, 146, 150–52, 155–56, 169–70, 179, 191–92
Greece, 69, 112, 127, 137
Greenland, 133
Grew, Joseph, 5, 49, 59, 83, 86, 94–95, 98–99, 114, 122, 150, 161–62
Guadalcanal, battle of, 218ff, 240, 249, 251, 293, 295, 385
Guam, 98, 170, 178, 220, 307ff, 316
Guderian, Inspector of Panzer Troops Heinz, 324–25
Günshe, military aide to Hitler Otto, 261, 301, 306, 325
Gugeler, Lieutenant Russell, 308

Hakajima, Chief Combined Fleet Intelligence Commander Chikataka, 284–85, 289, 343, 370
Hakko Ichiu, 7, 10, 23, 83
Halder, Major General Franz, 74, 107, 139, 205, 216
Halverson, Colonel Harry, 210
Hammel, Eric, x, 37
Hanfstaengl, Ernest, 26

Hara, President of the Privy Council Yoshimichi, 92, 151ff, 157, 241–42, 280
Harbord, General James, 17
Harmon, General Ernest, 227
Harris, Air Chief Marshal Arthur "Bomber", 207, 276
Hata, War Minister Shunroku, 75, 84, 142, 189
Hatta, General Shinji, 16
Hattori, Takushiro, viii–ix, 36–37, 88, 145–46, 156, 159–60, 169, 200, 277, 280–82, 290, 297, 316, 318, 341, 356, 360, 373, 377–78, 380
Heim, General (first name unknown), 66
Heisenberg, Werner, 218
Hidaka, Ambassador Shinrokuro, 263
Himmler, Heinrich, Reich Leader of the SS, 186, 198, 315, 335, 354
Hindenburg, President Paul von, 31
Hiranuma, Prime Minister Kiichiro, 59, 68, 169, 314, 368
Hirohito, Emperor, 81, 82–83, 88–90, 93, 97, 116, 124, 128ff, 140–41, 145, 148–49, 151–54, 159, 166, 171ff, 177–78, 193, 233, 280, 313, 315, 357, 360, 369, 372, 374, 376, 379–80, 382
Hirota, former Prime Minister Koki, 372
Hitler, Adolf
America, views of, 25–27, 29, 44, 62–63, 66, 71, 73–74, 104, 108, 110–12, 114, 117–18, 120, 122ff, 124, 126–27, 134, 181, 184–85, 194–95, 198, 205, 209, 256, 268, 274, 301, 305, 352
accepts that the war is lost, 355
assassination attempt on, 314, 324
Frederick the Great, victory from jaws of defeat, 300, 348
Führer principle, 31–32
concedes Germany cannot hold France, 330ff
concedes Germany has lost the initiative, 267–68, 274
Germany would join a Japanese-American war, 123, 133, 171
declares war, 24
dismisses U.S. production figures, 134, 184, 238
suicide, 352, 355
view of Japan, 55, 195, 250

INDEX

Hollandia Island, 302
Holmes, Jasper, 212
Hong Kong, 186
Hopkins, Harry, 139, 164, 187, 201
Hotta, Eri, viii, 4, 159, 170–71
Hull, Secretary of State Cordell, 82, 116, 127, 129
Hungary, 254, 299, 336
Hyakutake, Lieutenant General Haruyoshi, 220

Iceland, 133, 186
Ichiki, Colonel Kiyono, 220
Imperial General Headquarters (IGHQ), 39, 48–50, 145ff, 150, 173, 178, 181, 189, 191, 193, 202, 215, 219–21, 223, 240–41, 245, 254, 277, 280, 282, 288, 290, 293, 302, 304, 313, 318–19, 341, 343, 356, 360, 365, 368, 375, 377, 382
Imperial Japanese Army (IJA)
    4th Air Army, 343
    6th Base Airforce, 343
    Army General Staff, 7, 11, 23, 140, 171, 173, 233, 237, 281, 294, 314, 357, 362, 372, 375
    belief in victory, 151–52, 154, 233, 342
    casualties in China, 160
    Central China Area Army (CCAA), 39
    China Expeditionary Army, 189, 200, 220, 223, 242, 282, 288
    China Expeditionary Command, 76
    China Expeditionary Force, 170
    decision to abandon Guadalcanal, 240
    deployments for war begin, 154, 160
    distribution of ground forces, 221–22
    doctrine shift late in war, 318–19
    Eighth Area Army, 237, 240, 289
    Fourth Air Army, 346
    India, invasion of, 293ff, 346
    Kwangtung Army, 37, 49, 223, 314
    Manchuria Air Force, 250
    North China Area Army, 48
    Northern Marianas Army Group, 308
    military operations (*see* war plans, Japan; Japan, appraisal of military situation; and listed battles)
    People's Volunteer Corps/Volunteer Combat Corps, 372

    Seventeenth Army, 223–24, 232, 240
    Shanghai Expeditionary Army, 39
    South Seas Detachment, 170
    South Area General Army, 301
    Southern Army, 170, 223, 293, 301, 304
    Square Fortress, 301ff
    Surface Special Attack Force (*see* suicide tactics)
    Tenth Army, 39
    Thirty-First Army, 290, 316, 346
    Thirty-Fifth Army, 346
    Thirty-Second Army, 368, 375
    Twelfth Army, 297
    Twenty-Fifth Army, 143, 145
    war plans (*see* war plans)
Imperial Japanese Navy (IJN)
    6th Base Air Force, 343
    901st Air Flotilla, 319
    903d Air Flotilla, 319
    936th Air Flotilla, 319
    951st Air Flotilla, 319
    antisubmarine warfare, 293, 296–97, 319–20, 359
    belief in victory, 150–52, 159, 192, 213, 233
    China Fleet, 166
    Central Pacific Area Fleet, 290, 307, 309
    Combined Fleet, 78, 80, 89ff, 158, 161, 170, 180, 203, 211, 215, 221, 224, 232, 253, 294, 296, 302, 307ff
    Combined Air Fleet, 378
    decisive battle, hopes for and attempts at, 150, 156, 189–90, 214–15, 251, 289–90, 296, 307ff, 345, 375
    deployments for war begin, 155, 170
    doctrine, 21, 60–61, 78, 80, 150, 201, 214, 221 250–51, 289–90
    Eighth Fleet, 219
    Eleventh Air Fleet, 98, 237
    escort Fleet, 319
    Fifth Air Fleet, 360
    Fifth Fleet, 98, 343
    First Air Fleet, 98, 214, 308, 343, 346, 368
    First Fleet, 60
    First Mobile Fleet (a.k.a. Mobile Force), 296, 302
    Fourth Fleet, 203
    Grand Escort Fleet Headquarters, 320

482 • BETTING AGAINST AMERICA

Guadalcanal/Savo, 219, 221, 232, 237, 240, 251
Hawaii attack force, 171
Indian Ocean, 191–92, 199, 217, 219, 302
informs IJA of plan to attack Pearl Harbor, 149, 169
informs Tojo of plan to attack Pearl Harbor, 169
military operations (*see* war plans, Japan; Japan, appraisal of military situation; and listed battles)
naval construction shifts to aircraft carriers, subs, 201
Naval General Staff, 12, 89, 91, 159, 166, 170, 175, 201, 215, 223, 296–97, 316, 346, 370
Northern Force (Aleutians), 212, 215
Pearl Harbor, attack on, vii–viii, 4, 11, 51, 78, 80, 90, 97–98, 114–15, 124, 149, 151, 158–59, 169–70, 175ff
pilot losses, 203, 213–14, 232, 237, 240, 245, 250, 290–91, 311–12
Port Moresby Invasion Force, 202
request to IJA to provide troops for Pacific islands, 250
Second Fleet, 221
Second Air Fleet, 313
Second Area Army, 302
Shipping losses, 223, 246, 250, 280–81, 284, 288, 293, 297, 303, 313, 318, 340, 359, 362
Sixth Fleet, 98
Sixth Submarine Fleet, 191
Southeast Area Fleet, 214
Southern Expeditionary Fleet, 98, 143
submarines, use of, 197, 221, 237
Tenth Air Fleet, 360
Third Fleet, 98, 214, 221
Third Air Fleet, 360
Tokyo Express, 221
war plans (*see* war plans below)
India, 87, 118, 146, 187, 217, 236, 258, 293
India, places
Calcutta, 199
Imphal, 293, 302, 312–13
Inukai, Prime Minister Tsuyoshi
Iraq, 386

Ireland, places
Dublin, 351
Ishiwari, Kanji, 23
Itagaki, General Seishiro, 49, 59, 61, 75
Italian Army
Fourth Army, 229
military operations
Albania, 63
Greece, 112
North Africa, 112, 227
size and organization, 42, 65
Italy
appraisal of U.S. intentions and capabilities, 2, 54, 58, 75, 111, 163, 173, 198, 201, 227, 247
appraisal of war situation, 73, 75, 195, 224, 231, 247, 253, 263
decision to go to war with U.S., 2, 67, 173, 178, 183, 384
realization that the war is lost, 224, 263, 313
unconditional surrender, 270
Italy, places
Anzio, 272, 300–1
Augusta, 261
Cassino, 275, 292
Florence, 112
Gela, 261
Licata, 261
Livorno, 263
Messina, 261, 269
Milan, 68
Rome, 3, 55, 62–63, 70–72, 75, 104, 111, 122, 132, 163, 195, 217, 224, 227, 230, 243, 247, 253, 263, 273, 300, 305
Salerno, 270–72, 301
Sardinia, 264
Sicily, 254
Ito, Masanori, 79
Ito, Vice Chief Naval General Staff Admiral Seiichi, 215, 279–80
Iwane, General Matsui, 39
Iwo Jima, 277, 360, 362

Japan
abolition of political parties, 80, 90–91
appraisal of U.S. intentions and capabilities, 3, 16–17, 43, 49, 58–60, 78–79, 82, 92ff, 99, 115, 120ff, 135ff, 140–41,

INDEX • 483

  143–44, 149, 154–56, 160, 173–74,
    205, 217, 219, 222–23, 230ff, 233ff,
    236–37, 239–41, 245, 257–58, 277ff,
    282–83, 291–92, 294–96, 302–5,
    312–13, 340, 360, 376–77
  appraisal of war situation, 147, 178–79,
    190–91, 189–94, 197, 203–5, 215, 219,
    221–23, 225, 230ff, 233ff, 236–41, 246,
    252–53, 262–64, 268, 275, 277–85,
    288–89, 291–97, 302, 304, 306, 312,
    316–18, 326, 338–42, 352, 356,
    359–60, 372–74, 384
  anticipating American invasion of home
    islands, 303, 313, 339, 357, 360,
    364–66, 374, 377
  consideration of joining a German-American
    war, 129, 131, 130, 142, 162,
  coups and coup threats, 6–7, 150–51, 172,
    315
  decision-making process, 11–12, 15, 35,
    39, 47, 58–59, 81, 83–84, 142–43, 149,
    151–52, 166ff, 284, 293, 314–15, 357,
    366, 373–74
  decision to go to war with U.S., 2, 39, 78,
    87–92, 95, 114–16, 121–31, 135–37,
    141–46, 148–51, 158–61, 166ff,
    177–78, 369, 384
  decision to expand the defense perimeter,
    192–93, 199ff, 293, 385
  decision to shift from offense to defense in
    southern area, 215, 236–37, 240, 301
  ending the war, consideration of how to,
    159, 171, 179, 279, 287, 315–16, 357,
    369ff, 372–75, 378–79
  estimate of own war potential, 166–68,
    191–93, 284, 365
  forward defense doctrine, 7–9
  Greater East Asia Co-Prosperity Sphere, 131,
    174, 204
  Greater East Asia Ministry, 222
  Greater East Asia War, viii, 178, 241, 246,
    375
  leadership views of America, 10–11, 19–20,
    84ff, 92–95, 171
  miscalculation on southern French
    Indochina, 141ff, 145ff
  pivot to Pacific from China war, 232, 241,
    260, 277, 280–81, 289, 385

  plan to cut off materiel to Nationalists
    through southeast Asia, 83, 87, 141
  realization the war is lost, 213–14, 240,
    253–54, 262, 279–80, 286, 290–92,
    303, 317–18, 356, 372–73, 379–80
  southern advance, goals and plans, 81, 87ff,
    97ff, 114, 124, 131, 136ff, 142, 144–45,
    149, 153, 189–92
  Soviet entry into war, fear of, 340, 361ff, 379
  Supreme Council for the Direction of the
    War, 315, 317, 339, 374, 378–80, 382
  Supreme National Defense Council, 80–81
  surrender, decision to, 380–83
  unified military command, emergence of,
    294, 357, 365
  war cabinets, 144, 160–61,
  war in China, 12–16, 20–21, 35–40, 47–50,
    60–61, 76–77, 88, 97, 116, 144, 147,
    151–52, 157, 159–60, 166, 179, 189,
    193–94, 200, 220–21, 236, 241–42,
    278, 280–82, 284, 288, 293, 297, 340,
    343, 356, 385
Japan, places
  Atugi, 182
  Choshu, 7
  Hiroshima, 378–79
  Hiyoshi, 381
  Keramas Islands, 277
  Kobe, 347, 362
  Kokura, 309
  Kure, 166, 382
  Kyushu, 214, 309, 377
  Matsuyama, 357
  Moji, 309
  Musahino, 347
  Nagasaki, 379
  Nagoya, 347, 362
  Niigata, 200
  Oppama, 383
  Osaka, 80–81, 362
  Shikoku, 377
  Ryukyu Islands, 366ff
  Tainan, 245
  Tobata, 309
  Tokyo, 199, 339–40, 347, 362, 364, 378
  Yawata, 309
  Yokohama, 269
  Yokosuka, 166, 200

Jiang, Baili, 39
Jiechi, Yang, 386
Jinping, Xi, 386
Jodl, General Alfred, x, 70, 107, 183, 116, 306, 323, 328, 330, 332, 353, 355
Johnston Island, 190
Juin, General Alphonse, 227

Kamide, Captain S., 319
Kamikaze Special Attack Corps (*see* suicide tactics)
Kasserine, battle of, 247
Katsumata, Rear Admiral Seizo, 250
Kavieng, 289
Kawabe, Lieutenant General Torashiro, 291, 362
Kawaguchi, Major General Kiyotake, 220
Keitel, Field Marshal Wilhelm, x, 66, 104, 107, 181, 225, 257, 270, 306, 323, 333–34, 336, 355, 370
Kesselring, Field Marshal Albert, 226, 255, 261, 270, 272, 275–76, 300
Keynes, John Maynard, 257
Kido, Koichi, 47, 59, 80, 82–84, 88, 90–94, 97, 114, 124, 128ff, 140, 145, 148–49, 150–52, 157, 159–60, 169ff, 177, 179, 214, 223, 287, 314ff, 339, 357, 364, 370, 373–74, 382
King, Admiral Ernest, 106, 196, 244, 288
Kluge, Field Marshal Günther von, 261, 301, 306, 323ff, 332
Knox, Navy Secretary Frank, 116, 139, 147
Kobayashi, Yasuo, 136
Koga, Admiral Mineichi, 250–51, 289–91, 293, 295
Koiso, Prime Minister General Kuniaki, 315, 317ff, 342, 364, 366, 368
Kojima, Rear Admiral Hideo, 352
Konoye, Prime Minister Fumimaro, viii, 35, 47, 50, 58, 80, 84, 92, 95, 123, 126–28, 140–44, 146–52, 154, 156, 158–59, 169–70, 315–16, 357, 375
Konoye proposal to meet Roosevelt, 148–50
Korea, 118, 160, 281, 379
Korea, places
  Pusan, 237
  Rashin, 379
  Seoul (Keijo), 135
Korushima, Captain Kameto, 115

Krueger, Lieutenant General Walter, 343, 357ff
Kurils, 190, 279
Kurita, Admiral Takeo, 343
Kwajalein, 191, 289

Lang, Colonel Rudolf, 248
Laval, Prime Minister Pierre, 231
Layton, Commander Pacific Fleet Director of Intelligence (N2) Edwin, 212
League of Nations, 9, 16, 19, 27, 37, 85, 135
Liddell Hart, B. H., 4
Lindbergh, Charles, 63
Linge, Heinz, 40, 184–85
Liberia, 225
Liberia, places
  Monrovia, 225
Libya, 224, 231
Libya, places
  Tobruk, 209
  Tripoli, 227
Lochner, Louis, 27
Los Negros Islands, 293
Lucas, Major General John, 300
Ludecke, Kurt, 26
Ludendorff, General Erich, 351
Luxemburg, places
  Echternach, 348

Mackensen, Ambassador Hans Georg von, 71
MacArthur, General Douglas, 118, 146, 156, 250, 343, 357ff, 366
Madagascar, 230
MAGIC, viii, ix, 45–46, 230, 233, 259, 263, 275, 301, 354, 364
Makin, 250, 252
Malay Barrier, 116
Malaya, 98, 147, 190
Malik, Soviet Ambassador to Japan Joseph, 372
Manchukuo (Mancuria), 6, 36, 47, 76, 124, 128, 160, 193, 277, 281, 302, 365
Manchurian (Mukden) Incident, 12–14, 15, 19, 22, 38,
Mandate Islands (Marianas, Carolines, Marshalls, Palau), 78, 190, 278, 362
Manstein, Major General Erich von, 105
Malaya, 179
Malaya, places
  Kra Isthmus, 116

INDEX • 485

Marcus Islands, 250
Marianas, 78, 281, 288–89, 307ff
Marshall, General George C., 106, 116, 207, 288
Marshall Islands, 78, 194, 250, 281, 284, 288, 293, 295, 302
Matsudaira, Marquis Yasumasa, 357
Matsuoka, Foreign Minister Yosuke, 84–86, 90, 92ff, 97, 114, 120ff, 128ff, 136, 140–42, 144, 182, 251
Matsuura, Commander Goto, 289
Matsuyama, Rear Admiral Mitsuharo, 320
May, Karl, 26
Meiji, Emperor, 7–8, 11
Meiling, Song, 38, 60
Meleyon (Wileai), 296
Mexico, 18, 86, 357, 379
Midway, battle of, 44, 199–200, 202–3, 211ff, 385
Midway Island, 190
Mikawa, Vice Admiral Gunichi, 219
Milch, Field Marshall Erhard, 267–68
Military Tribunal for the Far East, 1, 5, 7, 23, 33, 84,
Mitcher, Rear Admiral Marc, 290
Mitter, Rana, 35
Model, Field Marshal Walter, 333
Molotov, Foreign Minister Vyacheslav, 107, 112, 361, 375–77, 379
Montgomery, Field Marshal Bernard, 225–26, 255, 261, 327, 331–32, 355
moral embargo on Japan, U.S., 49
Morotai, 316, 340
Morgenthau, Treasury Secretary Henry, 257
Morocco, 227ff
Morocco, places
    Casablanca, 227
Munda Island, 277
Munich Agreement, 53, 55, 227
Murata, Commander Shigeharu, 175
Mussolini, Benito
    America, views of, 63, 100, 104, 110–11, 122, 163, 173, 182, 217, 224–25, 263
    Japan, view of, 145
    toppled from power, 263

Nagano, Admiral Osami, 136, 141, 145–46, 148, 150–53, 157–59, 166, 169–70, 176, 280

Nagumo, Admiral Tadaichi, 171, 199, 213, 290, 312–13
Nakajima, Commander Tadashi, 249
Nauru, 288
naval aviation (*see* air power)
Nelson, Donald, 164–65, 187, 206–7
Netherlands, 63, 69, 146, 150, 155, 169–70
Netherlands, places
    Antwerp, 331–33
    Maastricht, 333
Netherlands East Indies, 62, 89, 98, 144, 146, 194, 320
Netherlands East Indies, places
    Flores Island, 302
    Halmahera, 301
    Java, 98, 179, 191, 220, 302
    Palembang, 301, 360
    Sulawesi, 279
    Sumatra, 98, 179, 297, 301–2
    Timor, 116
Neurath, Konstantin, Foreign Minister, 41
Neurath, *Sonderführer* (first name unknown), 260
Neutrality Acts, American, 67, 73
New Britain, 288
New Georgia, 277
New Guinea, 179, 193, 202–4, 218, 221, 233, 240, 243, 245, 277, 279, 293, 297, 303
New Guinea, places
    Aitape, 302
    Biak, 306–7
    Buna, 237, 240
    Lae, 204, 295
    Port Moresby, 193, 202, 221
    Salamaua, 295
New Caladonia, 193
New Order in East Asia, 50, 58
New Zealand, 87, 144, 146
Nicobar Islands, 279
Nimitz, Admiral Chester, 212, 250, 366, 382–83
Nishihara, Captain K., 375
Nomura, Admiral Kichisaburo, 39, 82, 114, 120, 127–29, 146, 150, 295
Non-Aggression Pact, German-Soviet, 69, 71, 102, 107
Non-Aggression Pact, Japanese-Soviet, 123–24, 361

North Africa, 226ff, 238, 240, 252, 226, 238, 305
Norway, 101, 104, 226

Oberkommando der Wehrmacht (OKW), German High Command, ix, 66, 70, 110, 113, 119–20, 124, 126–27, 133, 138, 181, 183, 198, 208, 211, 225–27, 230, 248, 256–57, 261, 268, 270–72, 274–76, 286, 291, 300, 305, 307, 321–23, 330–35, 350, 353
O'Brien, Phillips, 44, 267, 286
O'Conner, Dr. Raymond, 4
Office of Strategic Services (OSS), 35, 45, 179, 241, 247, 271, 283–84, 305, 314, 317, 335, 360, 375,
Ogata, Taketora, 317
Ogura, Finance Minister Matasune, 146
Ohmae, Captain Toshikazu, 200, 213, 245, 313
Oikawa, Admiral Koshiro, 84, 141, 144, 153, 156–59
oil embargo (*see* U.S. freezes Japanese assets)
Okada, Keisuke, Prime Minister, 169
Okamoto, Major General Kiyotomi, 258, 268, 284
Okamoto, Lieutenant Commander T., 319
Okawa, Dr. Shumei, 10–11, 13
Okuno, Lieutenant JG Y., 320
Onishi, Vice Admiral Takijiro, 97ff, 114–15, 124, 343
Operation *Cobra* and the race across France, 326ff, 331ff
Oshima, Ambassador Baron Hiroshi, 118, 123, 127, 134, 139, 171, 181, 194ff, 204–5, 209, 216–17, 221, 235–36, 238, 246, 252–53, 258, 261, 267–75, 284, 288, 299–300, 305, 326, 339, 351–52, 354
Oshima, Kosei, 11
Ott, Ambassador Brigadier General Eugen, 131, 173

Pacific Ocean Area (POA), 250, 366
Pact of Steel, 68
Palau, 297, 302–3, 310
Palmyra Island, 190
Pariani, General Alberto, 42, 54, 65
Patton, General George, 227, 247ff, 328ff, 331
Peleliu Island, 316, 340–41

People's Republic of China, 385ff
petroleum and fuel, strategic role
  Germany, 65, 236, 336ff
  Japan, 89–92, 125, 148ff, 153, 166, 170–71, 192, 194, 211, 214, 221, 280, 291, 293, 297, 318, 359, 377
Pershing, General John, 43
Pescadores, 282
Pétain, Marshal Phillipe, 321
Peru, 1
Philippines, 98, 123, 128, 144–46, 179, 186, 190, 192, 194, 222, 277–78, 291–92, 295, 301–4, 313, 320, 341, 356
Philippines, battle of, 343ff
Philippines, places
  Cebu, 295
  Clark Field, 176–77, 357, 359
  Davao, 178, 291, 295, 345
  Dulag, 343
  Lingayan Gulf, 357–58
  Luzon, 340
  Manila, 98, 301, 343, 357, 359
  Mindanao, 340
  Palo, 343
  Tacloban, 343
  Tawi Tawi, 302
Philippine Sea, battles of, 310ff, 345
Phillips, Ambassador William, 105–6
Plan Black, 18
Plan Orange, 3, 57
Poland, German invasion of, 61, 63–64, 67, 69–73
Ponape (Pohnpei) Island, 303
popular support for war
  Germany, 197–98, 265–66, 268–69, 273–74, 353
  Italy, 106, 224, 247
  Japan, 83, 169–70, 241, 294, 314, 363–64
  United States, 52, 109, 204, 234–35, 240
Portsmouth Treaty, 9, 13
Portugal, 231, 254, 301
Portugal, places
  Lisbon, 357
Potsdam Conference and Declaration, 376–78, 381
Prange, Gordon, 4
Putin, Vladimir, 387

Rabaul, 203, 213, 219, 250–51, 278–79, 288–89, 293, 303
racism, as a factor in policy
  Germany, 29, 56
  Japan, 23
Raeder, Admiral Erich, 41, 74, 107, 110, 112, 118, 124, 133, 196
Record, Jaffrey, 4–5
Red Army, Chinese, 1
Rendova Island, 277
Ribbentrop, Foreign Minister Joachim von, 96, 102, 108–11, 118, 120ff, 129–30, 133–34, 163, 171, 181, 183–184, 217, 221, 227, 238, 253, 261, 274–75, 326, 339, 351–54, 370
Rio Conference, 195
Rochefort, Commander Joseph, 212
Rockefeller, John
Romania, 210, 266, 336
Romania, places
  Ploesti, 210, 266, 336
Rommel, Field Marshal Erwin, 196, 205–6, 217, 224, 226, 260, 301, 306–7, 323ff, 330
Roosevelt, Franklin D.
  authorizes shoot on sight of U-boats, 162–63, 181
  Axis views of, 7, 20, 26–7, 29–30, 39–40, 51–52, 63, 71, 86, 92, 102ff, 110–11, 119–21, 126, 129–30, 132–34, 138, 140, 148–50, 162–63, 173, 181, 183, 195, 198, 205, 226, 228, 234, 238, 283, 351, 354, 360, 371, 385
  war leadership, 40, 45, 47, 51, 56–57, 67, 73, 96, 99, 107, 109, 112, 116–17, 126–27, 139, 146–47, 162–64, 181, 186ff, 201–2, 206–7, 216, 218, 233, 243–44, 261, 282–83
Roosevelt, President Theodore, 9
Rota Island, 307ff
Royal Air Force (EAF), 72, 105, 207–10, 244–45, 264–65, 276, 288, 335, 337–38
Royal Army (UK)
  15th Army Group, 300
  18th Army Group, 248
  21st Army Group, 332–33
  Eighth Army, 225, 247, 261ff, 270
  Tunisia, operations, 230

Royal Navy (UK)
  capture of codes and Enigma equipment, 134–35
  Pacific Fleet, 39, 360, 370
Rundstedt, Field Marshal Gerd von, 105, 226, 286, 301, 307, 322ff, 333–34
Russo-Japanese War, 9, 17, 59, 158, 287
Russia (*see* USSR)

Saipan, 290–92, 296, 297, 303, 307ff, 320
Saito, Lieutenant General Yoshitsugu, 308, 313
Sakai, pilot Saburo, 48, 176–77, 201, 203–4, 218, 223, 245, 249, 309, 345–46, 357, 382–83
Sakamaki, Rear Admiral Munetaka, 240
Sakomizu, Hisatsune, 46, 240, 369, 372, 374, 379–80
Samoa, 193
Santa Cruz, battle of, 232
Sato, General Kotoku, 339
Sato, Ambassador to USSR Naotaki, 339, 376–79
Scheidt, Captain Wilhelm, 256
Schmider, Klaus, vi–vii, 24–25, 123, 195
Schramm, Percy, 74
Secret Intelligence Service (SIS/MI-6), British, 46, 69, 74, 116, 198, 216, 241, 276, 286, 335
Sekine, Rear Admiral Gumpei, 89
Shiatori, Foreign Office spokesman Mr. T., 16
Shigemitsu, Foreign Minister Mamoru, 252, 257–58, 263–64, 284, 294, 306, 315, 339
Shimada, Navy Minister Admiral Shigataro, 61, 159, 166, 168, 170
Shirer, William, 63
Siegfried Line (*see* West Wall)
signals intelligence (SIGINT), American prewar, 45–46, 91, 131, 146
signals intelligence, British, before U.S. entry into war, 100–1
Singapore, 89, 98, 123, 129–30, 146–47, 178, 186, 281, 320, 346
Sugino, Commander (first name unknown), 135
Savo, battle of, 219–220
Smith, Truman, 40
Solomon Islands, 202, 218, 220, 240, 245, 284, 288, 293

Song, Meiling, 38, 60
Soong, T. V., Chiang representative, 83, 116
Sorrentino (first name unknown), 204
Sosa, Rear Admiral (ret.) Tanetsugu, 135
Southwest Pacific Area (SWPA), 250
Spaatz, General Carl, 64, 335
Spain, 231, 301
Spain, places
  Guernica, 1
  Madrid, 230, 294, 339, 351
Speer, Armaments Minister Albert, 120, 185, 196, 210–11, 244, 257, 265, 331, 336
Spratley Islands, 61
Stalin, Joseph, xi, 1, 107, 117, 134, 139, 206, 230, 243, 237, 261, 283, 351–52, 354, 360
Stahmer, Ambassador Heinrich, 306, 312, 366
Stark, Admiral Harold, 78, 116
Steengracht, Foreign Ministry Under Secretary Gustav von, 272–73
Stimson, Secretary of War Henry, 116, 139
Student, Major General Kurt, 333
Sudan, 225
Sudan, places
  Khartoum, 210
Sugiyama, General Hajime, 37, 97, 116, 136, 141, 147, 151–53, 159, 161, 168–69, 241, 288, 315
suicide tactics, Japanese, 311, 319, 343–46, 360, 366–67, 375, 377, 381–82
Sunda Islands (Borneo, Java, Sulawesi, Sumatra), 279
Supreme Headquarters Allied Expeditionary Force (SHAEF), 332
Surigao Strait, battle of, 345
Suzuki, Kantaro, Prime Minister, 368ff, 379ff
Suzuki, Lieutenant General Sesaku, 345
Suzuki, Prime Minister Teiichi, 46, 167, 169
Sweden, 301
Sweden, places
  Stockholm, 352
Switzerland, 254, 375
Switzerland, places
  Berne, 235, 375, 382
  Geneva, 27, 85, 135

Taiwan, 386
Takahashi, Admiral Sankichi, 81
Takada, Major Katsushige, 319

Takashi, Admiral Sankichi, 203
Takata, Rear Admiral Toshitane, 213–14, 277
Tanaka, Lieutenant General Shinichi, 339
Tanaka, IGHQ Operations Chief General Shizuichi, 169
Tanaka, Rear Admiral Toshitane, 254, 259
Tani, Foreign Minister Masayuki, 231, 233–34, 236, 240, 246
Tarawa, 250, 252
Taroa Island, 191
technological innovation, 109–10, 165, 208, 215, 223, 257–59, 264–65, 289, 299, 310, 319–21, 331, 345, 378–79
Temmo, Jimmu, Emperor, 7
Tehran Conference, 361
Terauchi, General Count Hisaichi, 301–2
Thailand, 136, 141–42, 171, 222, 280
Thailand, places
  Bangkok, 304
Thoma, Major General Freiherr Wilhelm von, 249
Tinian Island, 307ff, 316
Togo, Foreign Minister Shigenori, 166, 220, 222, 370, 373–76, 378–79
Tonaka, Rear Admiral Toshitane, 254
Todt, Fritz, 104, 181, 196
Togo, Admiral Heihachiro, 9
Tojo, General Hideki, 46, 49, 83–85, 92–94, 141, 143–44, 147–49, 153–54, 156–57, 159–61, 166–68, 171, 191, 199, 217, 242, 252, 280, 283–84, 293, 297, 312–14, 357, 370, 372
Tojo cabinet falls, 314
Toland, John, 169
Tominaga, Major General Kyoji, 94
Tomita, Chief Secretary of the Cabinet Kenji, 159–60
Tooze, Adam, 71, 338
Toyoda, Admiral Soemu, 296–97, 373–74, 380, 382
Toyoda, Foreign Minister Admiral Teijiro, 144, 153, 160, 214, 363
Treaty of Versailles, 1, 28, 32, 103.
Tripartite Pact (*see* Axis, creation of)
Truk, 288, 290, 293, 346
Truman, President Harry, 118, 354, 375
Tulagi, 202

Tunisia, 227ff, 238, 252, 254
Tunisia, battles in, 247ff, 254
Tunisia, places
   Djebel Tebaga, 247
   El Guettar, 248
   Faid, 248
   Fondouk, 248
   Gafsa, 248
   Kasserine, 247
   Maknassy, 247–48
   Medjez el Bab, 230
   Mezzouna, 248
   Tunis, 229–230, 236, 238, 253–54
Turkey, 210, 254, 301
Turkey, places
   Ankara, 314
Turner, Rear Admiral Richmond, 147, 218
Twain, Mark, 385

Ugaki, Admiral Matome, 91, 145, 151, 155, 158, 161, 171, 174ff, 178–80, 189–91, 193–94, 200, 202–3, 211–15, 217–18, 221, 223, 232, 236–37, 239, 250, 293, 295–96, 306–7, 310ff, 316, 338–39, 342–43, 345–48, 359–60, 363, 366–67, 369–71, 375, 377, 379, 381–83
Ukraine, 385
Umezu, General Yoshijiro, 314, 373–74, 379
unconditional surrender, Allied demand for, 243–44, 257, 269, 376–78
United Kingdom, places
   Bletchley Park, 239, 264
   London, xi, 19, 22, 34–35, 56, 73, 115, 146, 194, 207, 231, 235, 247–48, 254, 324, 335
   Northern Ireland, 186, 198
   Trent Park, 248
United States, places
   Adak, 215
   Attu, 215, 245, 292
   Hawaii, 178, 190
   Kiska, 215, 245
   Pearl Harbor, 78, 80
   San Francisco, 15, 371, 379, 381
   Washington, D.C., vii, 5, 10, 16, 22, 30, 32, 35, 40, 46, 51–52, 55–56, 58, 60–63, 65–66, 68, 76, 79, 82–83, 86, 92, 96, 99, 104, 111, 117–18, 120, 126–28, 130–31, 133, 137, 141, 143–44, 146–47, 153, 157, 159, 161, 165, 170–71, 178, 184–86, 190, 208, 226, 228, 231–32, 234–35, 258, 376, 386
U.S. Coast Guard, 45
U.S., views of
   China, 38, 76, 83, 96–97, 117, 187, 190
   Germany, 63
   Japan, 60, 76
   possibility of war, 17–18, 47, 51, 99, 106–7, 112, 116, 147, 161–64
   Soviet Union, 116
U.S. Army Air Force
   Eighth Air Force, 210, 265, 298, 326, 335, 337
   Fifth Air Force, 250
   Fifteenth Air Force, 276, 335
   Halverson Project (HALPRO), 210
   Ninth Air Force, 266
   Tenth Air Force, 222
   Tenth Army, 366ff
   Twentieth (also XX) Bomber Command, 308
   Twenty-First (also XXI) Bomber Command, 347
U.S. Army
   6th Army Group, 332
   12th Army Group, 333
   activated in the Philippines, 147
   Fifth Army, 272ff, 300ff
   First Army, 325ff, 352, 355
   Military Intelligence Division (MID), 45
   mobilization plans, 155, 205, 207
   Seventh Army, 261ff
   Signal Intelligence Service (SIS), 45
   Sixth Army, 343ff, 357ff
   Tenth Army, 166ff
   Third Army, 328ff
U.S. freezes Japanese assets, 146–47
U.S. Joint Chiefs of Staff, 163, 201, 250
U.S. mobilization system, 43–44, 51, 107, 164–65, 205
U.S. Navy
   Atlantic Fleet, 18
   Asiatic Fleet, 18
   deployment to Hawaii, 78, 81

Fifth Fleet, 308
naval supporting gunfire, Axis views of, 107, 272, 304, 316, 323, 360
Office of Naval Intelligence (ONI), 45
OP-20-G (SIGINT), 45–46,
operations against Japan, 191, 193–94
Pacific Fleet, 18, 78, 90, 191, 212, 278,
Panay incident, 39
Station Hypo (SIGINT on IJN), 212
Third Fleet, 359
USSR
aid to China, 38
declares war on Japan, 379
policy toward Japan, 283
Operation *Bagration*, 306, 324
Stalin promises to join war against Japan, 283, 360
USSR, German invasion of (*Barbarossa*), 37, 107–8, 110, 124, 134, 138–40
USSR, places
Grozny, 230
Kharkov, 215
Kursk, 44
Lake Khasan, 49
Leningrad, 138, 230
Moscow, 181, 236, 339, 379
Mount Zozernaya, 49
Port Arthur, 159
Rostov, 218
Sebastopol, 215
Stalingrad, 218, 224, 230, 232, 235–36, 238, 246, 249, 285
Vladivostok, 199

V-1 and V-2 programs, 256, 331
Vatican, 159, 171, 351

Wagener, Brigadier General Carl, 350
Wakatsuki, Premier Reijiro, 170
Wake, 98, 178, 191, 279
Wallace, Vice President Henry, 164
Wang, Jinwei, 97, 128, 252
Washington Naval Limitation Treaty, 32
war budgets
Germany, 50–51
Italy, 54, 65
Japan, 59, 79, 87
United States, 56–57, 87, 99, 109

war plans
China, 38–39, 76
Germany, 51, 66–67, 70, 72, 107, 114, 117–18, 180, 196, 210, 216–17, 227, 249, 264, 267–68, 270, 272, 274, 300, 350, 352–54
Italy, 54, 56, 63, 67, 70, 106, 227, 301, 306–7, 323ff
Japan, 23–24, 48–49, 78, 80, 97ff, 114–15, 124ff, 141ff, 144–45, 150–52, 158, 179–80, 189–93, 201–4, 209–10, 213, 217, 232–33, 245, 250, 254, 277–82, 288–91, 293, 301, 310–13, 317–19, 343ff, 356–58, 361, 365, 370–72, 374–75, 377
United States, 56, 107, 116, 186ff, 250, 261ff, 288, 308, 326ff, 366ff
war production
Germany, 27–29, 41, 44, 50–54, 64, 185, 196, 209, 236, 244–45, 257, 264–267, 287, 298–99, 331, 338, 350
Great Britain, 192–95, 267, 338
Italy, 58
Japan, 34–35, 44, 48–49, 58–59, 61, 192–93, 241, 280, 287, 291, 313, 318, 340–41, 347, 362, 373–74
United States, 17, 40, 44, 51, 109, 161–65, 187, 206–7, 112, 117, 139, 164–65, 187, 206–7, 256–57, 267, 283ff, 288, 338
Ward, Major General Orlando, 248
Warlimont, General Walter, x, 70, 110, 124, 181, 183, 226, 305, 321
Wavell, General Archibald, 132, 186
Wegener, Gauleiter Paul, 256
Welles, Under Secretary of State Sumner, mission of, 102ff
Weizsäcker, Ernst Freiherr von, 124
West Wall, 273, 323, 330, 332–34, 385
Wilkie, Wendell, 112
Wilson, Ambassador Hugh, 56
Wood, James, 5
Wood, John, 193
Woodward, Robert, 4
Wotja Island, 191

Yahagi, Colonel Nakaye, 239
Yalta Conference, 351, 360–61

Yamamoto, Admiral Isoruku, viii, 60–61, 78, 80, 89, 97ff, 114–15, 151, 157–59, 162, 170, 190, 199, 215, 250–51, 312
Yamamoto's prediction for the war, 157, 221
Yamashita, General Tomoyuki, 357
Yap Island, 303
Yat-sen, Sun, 50
Yonai, Admiral Mitsumasa, 59, 84, 162, 169, 214, 314, 359, 370, 372–74, 379

Yoshida, Admiral Zengo, 84, 89
Yoshida, Foreign Minister Shigeru, 316
Yue, General Xue
Yugoslavia
  Croatia, 70
  Dalmatia, 70

Zongren, General Li, 48